Applications of Big Data in Large- and Small-Scale Systems

Sam Goundar
British University Vietnam, Vietnam

Praveen Kumar Rayani
National Institute of Technology, Durgapur, India

A volume in the Advances in Data Mining and
Database Management (ADMDM) Book Series

Published in the United States of America by
IGI Global
Engineering Science Reference (an imprint of IGI Global)
701 E. Chocolate Avenue
Hershey PA, USA 17033
Tel: 717-533-8845
Fax: 717-533-8661
E-mail: cust@igi-global.com
Web site: http://www.igi-global.com

Library of Congress Cataloging-in-Publication Data

Names: Goundar, Sam, 1967- editor. | Rayani, Praveen Kumar, 1989- editor.
Title: Applications of big data in large and small-scale systems / Sam
   Goundar and Praveen Kumar Rayani, editors.
Description: Hershey, PA : Engineering Science Reference, [2021] | Includes
   bibliographical references and index. | Summary: "This book addresses
   the newest innovative and intelligent applications related to utilizing
   the large amounts of big data being generated that is increasingly
   driving decision making and changing the landscape of business
   intelligence, from governments to private organizations, from
   communities to individuals"-- Provided by publisher.
Identifiers: LCCN 2020026763 (print) | LCCN 2020026764 (ebook) | ISBN
   9781799866732 (hardcover) | ISBN 9781799866749 (paperback) | ISBN
   9781799866756 (ebook)
Subjects: LCSH: Big data--Industrial applications. | Data mining. |
   Decision making.
Classification: LCC QA76.9.B45 A668 2021 (print) | LCC QA76.9.B45 (ebook)
   | DDC 005.7--dc23
LC record available at https://lccn.loc.gov/2020026763
LC ebook record available at https://lccn.loc.gov/2020026764

This book is published in the IGI Global book series Advances in Data Mining and Database Management (ADMDM)
(ISSN: 2327-1981; eISSN: 2327-199X)

British Cataloguing in Publication Data
A Cataloguing in Publication record for this book is available from the British Library.

All work contributed to this book is new, previously-unpublished material. The views expressed in this book are those of the
authors, but not necessarily of the publisher.

For electronic access to this publication, please contact: eresources@igi-global.com.

Advances in Data Mining and Database Management (ADMDM) Book Series

David Taniar
Monash University, Australia

ISSN:2327-1981
EISSN:2327-199X

MISSION

With the large amounts of information available to organizations in today's digital world, there is a need for continual research surrounding emerging methods and tools for collecting, analyzing, and storing data.

The **Advances in Data Mining & Database Management (ADMDM)** series aims to bring together research in information retrieval, data analysis, data warehousing, and related areas in order to become an ideal resource for those working and studying in these fields. IT professionals, software engineers, academicians and upper-level students will find titles within the ADMDM book series particularly useful for staying up-to-date on emerging research, theories, and applications in the fields of data mining and database management.

COVERAGE

- Data Analysis
- Data Mining
- Profiling Practices
- Data Quality
- Association Rule Learning
- Database Security
- Web-based information systems
- Text Mining
- Factor Analysis
- Enterprise Systems

IGI Global is currently accepting manuscripts for publication within this series. To submit a proposal for a volume in this series, please contact our Acquisition Editors at Acquisitions@igi-global.com or visit: http://www.igi-global.com/publish/.

Titles in this Series

For a list of additional titles in this series, please visit:
http://www.igi-global.com/book-series/advances-data-mining-database-management/37146

Developing a Keyword Extractor and Document Classifier Emerging Research and Opportunities
Dimple Valayil Paul (Department of Computer Science, Dnyanprassarak Mandal's College and Research Centre, Goa University, Goa, India)
Engineering Science Reference • © 2021 • 229pp • H/C (ISBN: 9781799837725) • US $195.00

Intelligent Analytics With Advanced Multi-Industry Applications
Zhaohao Sun (Papua New Guinea University of Technology, Papua New Guinea)
Engineering Science Reference • © 2021 • 330pp • H/C (ISBN: 9781799849636) • US $225.00

Handbook of Research on Automated Feature Engineering and Advanced Applications in Data Science
Mrutyunjaya Panda (Utkal University, India) and Harekrishna Misra (Institute of Rural Management, Anand, India)
Engineering Science Reference • © 2021 • 392pp • H/C (ISBN: 9781799866596) • US $285.00

Blockchain and AI Technology in the Industrial Internet of Things
Subhendu Kumar Pani (Orissa Engineering College,BPUT, India) Chittaranjan Hota (Birla Institute of Technology and Science, India) Guangzhi Qu (Oakland University, USA) Sian Lun Lau (Sunway University, Malaysia) and Xingcheng Liu (Sun Yat-sen University, China)
Engineering Science Reference • © 2021 • 330pp • H/C (ISBN: 9781799866947) • US $225.00

Challenges and Applications of Data Analytics in Social Perspectives
V. Sathiyamoorthi (Sona College of Technology, India) and Atilla Elci (Hasan Kalyoncu University, Turkey)
Engineering Science Reference • © 2021 • 324pp • H/C (ISBN: 9781799825661) • US $245.00

Multidisciplinary Functions of Blockchain Technology in AI and IoT Applications
Niaz Chowdhury (The Open University, Milton Keynes, UK) and Ganesh Chandra Deka (Ministry of Skill Development and Entrepreneurship, New Delhi, India)
Engineering Science Reference • © 2021 • 255pp • H/C (ISBN: 9781799858768) • US $245.00

Handbook of Research on Engineering, Business, and Healthcare Applications of Data Science and Analytics
Bhushan Patil (Independent Researcher, India) and Manisha Vohra (Independent Researcher, India)
Engineering Science Reference • © 2021 • 583pp • H/C (ISBN: 9781799830535) • US $345.00

Advanced Deep Learning Applications in Big Data Analytics
Hadj Ahmed Bouarara (Tahar Moulay University of Saida, Algeria)
Engineering Science Reference • © 2021 • 351pp • H/C (ISBN: 9781799827917) • US $245.00

701 East Chocolate Avenue, Hershey, PA 17033, USA
Tel: 717-533-8845 x100 • Fax: 717-533-8661
E-Mail: cust@igi-global.com • www.igi-global.com

Table of Contents

Detailed Table of Contents

Chapter 1

    Sam Goundar, The University of the South Pacific, Fiji
    Akashdeep Bhardwaj, University of Petroleum and Energy Studies, India
    Shavindar Singh, The University of the South Pacific, Fiji
    Mandeep Singh, The University of the South Pacific, Fiji
    Gururaj H. L., Vidyavardhaka College of Engineering, India

Big data is emerging, and the latest developments in technology have spawned enormous amounts of data. The traditional databases lack the capabilities to handle this diverse data and thus has led to the employment of new technologies, methods, and tools. This research discusses big data, the available big data analytical tools, the need to use big data analytics with its benefits and challenges. Through a research drawing on survey questionnaires, observation of the business processes, interviews and secondary research methods, the organizations, and companies in a small island state are identified to survey which of them use analytical tools to handle big data and the benefits it proposes to these businesses. Organizations and companies that do not use these tools were also surveyed and reasons were outlined as to why these organizations hesitate to utilize such tools.

Chapter 2

    Archana Purwar, Jaypee Intitute of Information Technology, Noida, India
    Indu Chawla, Jaypee Intitute of Information Technology, Noida, India

Nowadays, big data is available in every field due to the advent of computers and electronic devices and the advancement of technology. However, analysis of this data requires new technology as the earlier designed traditional tools and techniques are not sufficient. There is an urgent need for innovative methods and technologies to resolve issues and challenges. Soft computing approaches have proved successful in handling voluminous data and generating solutions for them. This chapter focuses on basic concepts of big data along with the fundamental of various soft computing approaches that give a basic understanding of three major soft computing paradigms to students. It further gives a combination of these approaches namely hybrid soft computing approaches. Moreover, it also poses different applications dealing with big data where soft computing approaches are being successfully used. Further, it comes out with research challenges faced by the community of researchers.

    Poonam Nandal, Manav Rachna International Institute of Research and Studies, India
    Deepa Bura, Manav Rachna International Institute of Research and Studies, India
    Meeta Singh, Manav Rachna International Institute of Research and Studies, India

In today's world where data is accumulating at an ever-increasing rate, processing of this big data was a necessity rather than a need. This required some tools for processing as well as analysis of the data that could be achieved to obtain some meaningful result or outcome out of it. There are many tools available in market which could be used for processing of big data. But the main focus on this chapter is on Apache Hadoop which could be regarded as an open source software based framework which could be efficiently deployed for processing, storing, analyzing, and to produce meaningful insights from large sets of data. It is always said that if exponential increase of data is processing challenge then Hadoop could be considered as one of the effective solution for processing, managing, analyzing, and storing this big data. Hadoop versions and components are also illustrated in the later section of the paper. This chapter majorly focuses on the technique, methodology, components, and methodologies adopted by Apache Hadoop software framework for big data processing.

    Supriya M. S., Ramaiah University of Applied Sciences, India
    Keerthana Sasidaran, Ramaiah University of Applied Sciences, India

Big data and machine learning currently play an important role in various applications and in research. These approaches are explored in depth in this chapter. The chapter starts with a summary of big data and its implementation in a number of fields, and then deals with the problems that big data presents and the need for other technology to resolve these issues/challenges. Big data can best be used with the aid of the machine learning model, even though they are not directly related. Thus, the paradigms of machine learning that support big data can be combined with big data technology, thus providing insight into a range of big data machine learning approaches and techniques. Although big data cannot rely solely on the few paradigms of machine learning, the underlying problems are addressed. New machine learning algorithms are needed that can explore the full scale of the big data process and enable software engineering firms to come up with better solutions.

    Jayashree K., Rajalakshmi Engineering College, India
    Swaminathan B., Rajalakshmi Engineering College, India

The huge size of data that has been produced by applications that spans from social network to scientific computing is termed big data. Cloud computing as a delivery model for IT services enhances business productivity by reducing cost. It has the intention of achieving solution for managing big data such as high dimensional data sets. Thus, this chapter discusses the background of big data and cloud computing. It also discusses the various application of big data in detail. The various related work, research challenges of big data in cloud computing, and the future direction are addressed in this chapter.

Chapter 6

Sam Goundar, The University of the South Pacific, Fiji
Karpagam Masilamani, The University of the South Pacific, Fiji
Akashdeep Bhardwaj, University of Petroleum and Energy Studies, India
Chandramohan Dhasarathan, Madanapalle Institute of Technology and Science, India

This chapter provides better understanding and use-cases of big data in healthcare. The healthcare industry generates lot of data every day, and without proper analytical tools, it is quite difficult to extract meaningful data. It is essential to understand big data tools since the traditional devices don't maintain this vast data, and big data solves the major issue in handling massive healthcare data. Health data from numerous health records are collected from various sources, and this massive data is put together to form the big data. Conventional database cannot be used in this purpose due to the diversity in data formats, so it is difficult to merge, and so it is quite impossible to process. With the use of big data this problem is solved, and it can process highly variable data from different sources.

Chapter 7

Supriya M. S., Ramaiah University of Applied Sciences, India
Meenaxy Roy, Ramaiah University of Applied Sciences, India

Smart farming may also be called digital farming. The world is changing and digitizing at a quick rate. So all the work from agriculture to the stock market will become more productive and faster. Speed and efficiency play a key role in coping with the rapid pace of life and growing population. Smart agriculture has removed many of the problems faced by farmers during the conventional farming process. Several technologies are useful in this field, which make them work comfortably. Productivity in all areas of this sector can be increased with the aid of new technologies such as IoT and big data. Data can be accessed and analyzed from any part of the world with the help of IoT devices. The chapter offers insight into technology, such as big data and IoT, its applications in smart farming, as well as future innovations and opportunities.

Chapter 8

Nilesh Kumar Sahu, Birla Institute of Technology, India
Manorama Patnaik, Birla Institute of Technology, India
Itu Snigdh, Birla Institute of Technology, India

With an ever-increasing amount of data created, it has become a major challenge for infrastructures and frameworks to process a lot of information inside stipulated time and resources. So as to effectively extract from this information, organizations are required to discover new devices and strategies in particular for large information preparation. Therefore, data analytics has become a key factor for organizations to uncover hidden data and accomplish the upper hand in the market. As of now, tremendous distributions of larger data and information processing make it hard for experts and specialists to discover points they are keen on and track forward-thinking. This chapter puts forth an outline of data analytics, extension, and discoveries just as opportunities emancipated by analysis of data. The chapter also deals with various applications of data analytics which include applying an algorithmic or mechanical procedure to infer bits of knowledge, for instance, going through a few informational collections to search for significant connections between one another.

Chapter 9

The main objective of data visualization is to communicate information clearly and effectively through graphical means. It doesn't mean that data visualization needs to look boring to be functional or extremely sophisticated to look beautiful. To convey ideas effectively, both aesthetic form and functionality need to go hand in hand, providing insights into a rather sparse and complex data set by communicating its key-aspects in a more intuitive way. This chapter analyses the following aspects of data visualisation. First, it describes data visualisation. Second, it describes the importance of data visualisation in business. Third, it describes different types of data visualisation methods used in business and familiarises some tools available for data visualisation. Last, it describes the recent developments in data visualisation and its future research directions.

Chapter 10

The last few years have seen great developments in econometrics for a better understanding of economic phenomena. The range of areas in which econometric models are successfully applied has steadily widened including finance and business management. Econometric analysis is concerned with the quantitative relationships between economic variables and it can provide an important input into the decision-making process. The range of areas in which econometric models are successfully applied has steadily widened including finance and business management. Econometrics has enhanced our understanding of the way the managerial decision works. Econometrics is used in doing quantitative analysis of actual economic phenomena based on theory and observations. An economic model is based on a set of assumptions to simplify the complex economic phenomena. This chapter is an attempt to review the application of econometrics using business data. The main objective of this chapter is to chart the application of this science in various fields of business management.

Chapter 11

For an organization every year, a large amount of information is generated regarding its employees, customers, business partners, suppliers, etc. Volume, which is one of the attributes of big data, is aptly named because of the vast number of data sources and the size of data generated by these sources. Big data solutions should not only focus on the technological aspects, but also on the challenges that may occur during the project lifecycle. The main purpose of this research is to build on the current diverse literature around big data by contributing discussion on factors that influence successful big data projects. The systematic literature review adopted in this study includes relevant research regarding such critical success factors that are validated in previous studies. The study compiled these critical success factors as provided in the literature regarding big data projects. Notable success factors for big data projects were compiled from literature such as case studies, theoretical observations, or experiments.

Chapter 12
Shailesh Pancham Khapre, Amity University, Noida, India
Chandramohan Dhasarathan, Madanapalle Institute of Technology and Science, India
Puviyarasi T., Madanapalle Institute of Technology and Science, India
Sam Goundar, British University Vietnam, Vietnam

In the internet era, incalculable data is generated every day. In the process of data sharing, complex issues such as data privacy and ownership are emerging. Blockchain is a decentralized distributed data storage technology. The introduction of blockchain can eliminate the disadvantages of the centralized data market, but at the same time, distributed data markets have created security and privacy issues. It summarizes the industry status and research progress of the domestic and foreign big data trading markets and refines the nature of the blockchain-based big data sharing and circulation platform. Based on these properties, a blockchain-based data market (BCBDM) framework is proposed, and the security and privacy issues as well as corresponding solutions in this framework are analyzed and discussed. Based on this framework, a data market testing system was implemented, and the feasibility and security of the framework were confirmed.

Chapter 13
Dhivya P., Bannari Amman Institute of Technology, India

Traffic control light frameworks are generally used to control and screen the stream of cars through the intersection of numerous streets. As the quantity of street clients always increments and assets gave are constrained, savvy activity flag controller is an exceptionally real prerequisite. One disadvantage of customary methodologies for movement administration is that they don't consider the distinctive valuations of holding up time lessening of the drivers. This chapter proposed another component for versatile activity control utilizing machine learning. In the proposed framework, the authors are utilizing picture sensor in the LED publication which catches the pictures of streets in every one of the bearings and returns the number of head checks of the vehicles to a machine learning calculation. The machine learning calculation is intended to take in the rush hour gridlock thickness without anyone else with first caught picture and consider reference. In this manner, the proposed activity control framework will be an exceptional technique for self-learning and security improving.

Chapter 14
Laxmi Kumari Pathak, Amity University, Ranchi, India
Pooja Jha, Amity University, Ranchi, India

Chronic kidney disease (CKD) is a disorder in which the kidneys are weakened and become unable to filter blood. It lowers the human ability to remain healthy. The field of biosciences has progressed and produced vast volumes of knowledge from electronic health records. Heart disorders, anemia, bone diseases, elevated potassium, and calcium are the very prevalent complications that arise from kidney failure. Early identification of CKD can improve the quality of life greatly. To achieve this, various machine learning techniques have been introduced so far that use the data in electronic health record (EHR) to predict CKD. This chapter studies various machine learning algorithms like support vector machine, random forest, probabilistic neural network, Apriori, ZeroR, OneR, naive Bayes, J48, IBk (k-nearest neighbor), ensemble method, etc. and compares their accuracy. The study aims in finding the best-suited technique from different methods of machine learning for the early detection of CKD by which medical professionals can interpret model predictions easily.

Chapter 15

Nitika Kapoor, Chandigarh University, India
Parminder Singh, Chandigarh Engineering College, Landran, India

Data mining is the approach which can extract useful information from the data. The prediction analysis is the approach which can predict future possibilities based on the current information. The authors propose a hybrid classifier to carry out the heart disease prediction. The hybrid classifier is combination of random forest and decision tree classifier. Moreover, the heart disease prediction technique has three steps, which are data pre-processing, feature extraction, and classification. In this research, random forest classifier is applied for the feature extraction and decision tree classifier is applied for the generation of prediction results. However, random forest classifier will extract the information and decision tree will generate final classifier result. The authors show the results of proposed model using the Python platform. Moreover, the results are compared with support vector machine (SVM) and k-nearest neighbour classifier (KNN).

Chapter 16

Elangovan Ramanujam, Department of Information Technology, Thiagarajar College of
Engineering, Madurai, India
L. Rasikannan, Department of Computer Science and Engineering, Alagappa Chettiar
Government College of Engineering, India
S. Viswa, Department of Information Technology, Thiagarajar College of Engineering,
Madurai, India
B. Deepan Prashanth, Department of Information Technology, Thiagarajar College of
Engineering, Madurai, India

Machine learning is not a simple technology but an amazing field having more and more to explore. It has a number of real-time applications such as weather forecast, price prediction, gaming, medicine, fraud detection, etc. Machine learning has an increased usage in today's technological world as data is growing in volumes and machine learning is capable of producing mathematical and statistical models that can analyze complex data and generate accurate results. To analyze the scalable performance of the learning algorithms, this chapter utilizes various medical datasets from the UCI Machine Learning repository ranges from smaller to large datasets. The performance of learning algorithms such as naïve Bayes, decision tree, k-nearest neighbor, and stacking ensemble learning method are compared in different evaluation models using metrics such as accuracy, sensitivity, specificity, precision, and f-measure.

Chapter 17

Madhana K., PSG College of Technology, India
Jayashree L. S., PSG College of Technology, India

The medical advancement in recent years is addressing challenges of the dependent people like senior citizens, physically challenged, and cognitively impaired individuals by providing technical aids to promote a healthier society. The radical improvement in the digital world is trying to make their life smoother by creating a smart living environment via ambient assisted living (AAL) rather than hospitalization. In this chapter, an Edge-based AAL-IoT ecosystem is introduced with the prime objective of delivering telehealthcare to elderly and telerehabilitation to disabled individuals. The proposed framework focuses on developing smart home, an intelligent atmosphere for real-time monitoring in regard to meet the needs of independent and isolated individuals. The supporting technologies to leverage the edge computing concept, to enable scalability and reliability are also studied. A case study on proposed architecture for quarantined patient monitoring remotely in the event of epidemic or pandemic diseases is presented.

Chapter 18

   Imran Aslan, Health Management Department, Faculty of Health Sciences, Bingöl University, Turkey

Developments in technology have opened new doors for healthcare to improve the treatment methods and prevent illnesses as a proactive method. Internet of things (IoT) technologies have also improved the self-management of care and provided more useful data and decisions to doctors with data analytics. Unnecessary visits, utilizing better quality resources, and improving allocation and planning are main advantages of IoT in healthcare. Moreover, governments and private institutions have become a part of this new state-of-the-art development for decreasing costs and getting more benefits over the management of services. In this chapter, IoT technologies and applications are explained with some examples. Furthermore, deep learning and artificial intelligence (AI) usage in healthcare and their benefits are stated that artificial neural networks (ANN) can monitor, learn, and predict, and the overall health severity for preventing serious health loss can be estimated and prevented.

Preface

INTRODUCTION

Data, being in the form of text and numbers is no longer the norm. Now, apart from text and numbers, data constitutes video, audio, graphics, tactile data, and sensory data. Gone are the days, when data was only curated by authorised, qualified and conveyors of data/information holding positions in esteemed institutions, organisations and government departments. Today, more data is being created by individual users in a single minute as compare to data created in an entire year 20 year ago. Billions of users through their mobile devices using social media are creating unstructured data in the form of posting their videos on Facebook and YouTube, creating, playing, and downloading music, posting messages and emojis, uploading their personal photos, photos of their pets and other activities that their do, tagging people, and chatting in groups. All these social media activities result in generating large volumes of data, different velocities of data, diverse varieties of data. For example, according to (Ali, September 2020), in one minute, 41,666,667 messages are shared on Whatsapp, 1,388,889 people make video/voice calls, 150,000 messages are shared on Facebook, 500 hours of video are uploaded on YouTube, 2,704 TikTok installed.

Applications of Big Data are many, but the widest and most used applications of Big Data are from the media and the entertainment industry. Facebook, Google, and Amazon are the largest companies in the world now and their founders the richest man today. These companies own social media applications, and the users generate terabytes of data every minute. Data analytics are applied to the Big Data collected and the individual social media users are served advertisements based on these analytics extracted from their online and social media posts and activities. The revenue generated from these activities (in billions) are what is driving these companies to develop and provide more applications, generate more data, collect, analyse, advertise and earn more money. Another common application of Big Data is on customer sentiment analysis. The retail industry due to is competitive nature and fickle customers relies totally on customer sentiment analysis to gauge the satisfaction of its customers. Web crawlers embedded with specialised algorithms scrap all emotions expressed by the customers in the form of emoticons, likes, dislikes as well as keywords used in messages and posts. The retail outlet then responds accordingly.

With individuals and organisations undergoing digital transformations and the industries headed towards the 4th Industrial Revolution (4IR)/Industry 4.0, the creation, collection, and analytics of Big Data are going to grow exponentially. For many organisations, Big Data and Big Data Analytics and the business intelligence they provide are part of their critical standard operating procedures and core business process. Doing otherwise might have an impact on the survival of their business. We are still in the midst of the coronavirus pandemic, and almost all activities have moved online. Due to social distancing mandated by our governments and in order to not expose ourselves to the virus we are working from home, shopping alone, ordering takeaways, streaming movies, and entertaining ourselves online with the myriad of social media apps available. This ongoing explosion in activity is the aggregate output of 4.5 billion internet users today as reported by (Ali, 2020, September 15), and a number that is projected to increase even further in coming years. Big Data and Big Data Applications in Large- and Small-Scale Systems are relevant today and will be for the future as its use will make our work easier and our systems smarter.

BIG DATA

The vast amount of data that organizations and individuals create, exchange, and deal with is termed as 'Big Data'. Big Data is so large that it is not possible for standard computers to store and process Big Data. Specialised databases, analytics software, data mining techniques and powerful computers with superfast processors, memory and huge amount of storage are needed. When does data become Big Data? For data to be considered Big Data, it must satisfy the **5 "Vs"** characteristics as proposed by Big Data Scientists and Industry Experts. These characteristics are known as 1. Volume; 2. Velocity; 3. Variety; 4. Veracity, and 5. Value. These 5 Vs are explained with an example from the huge amount of data collected within the health industry. Hospitals and private clinics collect huge amount of medical data from patients through x-rays, medical tests, blood tests, lab tests, and all other tests that happen within the field of medicine and healthcare. All these data can be mined to check for emerging patterns. For example, the results of patient's tests can be mined against the symptoms to check for not so obvious disease diagnosis, etc. Or the symptoms showed by a patient can be mined against all existing patients to determine what the diagnosis was, the treatment received and its success.

The 5 Vs will be characterized as follows:

1. **Volume**: the amount of data created/generated and collected in terms of volume. For example, the total amount of data collected within a day at a large hospital might be one terabyte (1 TB) on a normal day and 2 TB on a busy day. Data collected from all hospitals in the district might results in five petabytes (5 PB) of data.
2. **Velocity**: denotes the speed in which new data is generated and the movement of data across platforms. It determines the speed at which data analysis should be done. For example, how long does it take for x-ray results to be stored as digital data, the blood tests, lab tests and all other tests needs to be digitised and stored in a specific format to be usable and analysed.
3. **Variety**: simply put is referring to all the different types of data being generated and used. Data can be structured or unstructured. Structured data usually comes in forms of text, numbers and in tables and can be said as organized data. Unstructured data consists of text, images, audio, and video, which needs to be organized for machines to analyze such data. For example, the x-rays as images, the blood sugar level as numbers, and heartbeat as audio.
4. **Veracity**: refers to how dependable data is since it becomes a difficult task to maintain the quality and the reliability of data due to the variety of data available. Simply put, veracity is referring to the unreliability of data. For example, how correct are the blood test results? Have the results been tampered with? Can someone hack and change data?
5. **Value**: refers to the worth of the data. In other words, value is referring to the financial gain a company can obtain if it collects Big Data and employs Big Data analytics. For example, after

collecting and doing Big Data Analytics, the hospital can quickly and accurately diagnose diseases as compared to its competitors, provide better treatment, and reduce cost of disgnosis.

As stated earlier, Big Data cannot be stored and processed by standard computers. So, how do we store and process Big Data? There are now a few frameworks available to deal with how we store and process Big Data. Some of the common frameworks that are freely available are **Hadoop** <https://hadoop.apache.org/> by the Apache Foundation, **Spark** <https://spark.apache.org/> and **Cassandra** <https://cassandra.apache.org/> all community led, free and open source software.

For example, Hadoop uses a distributed file system where large chunks of data are broken down into smaller manageable chunks and distributed among different computer for storage. Apart from that copies of small chunks are also stored on different computers in a distributed way. Therefore, apart from managing data into small chunks, the distributed file system also keeps your data safe with backup copies decentralized. Hadoop uses the Map Reduce technique to breakdown complex tasks into smaller and simple tasks. These smaller and simple tasks are then distributed to different machines for processing. The distributed tasks are completed in a parallel fashion and the results assembled in the end. This parallel processing enables the tasks to be processed easily and at a much faster rate. However, the Map Reduce technique used by Hadoop is good for batch processing of data, not real time processing of data. There are many applications that require real time processing of data, for example Online Transaction Processing (OLTP). For these applications, Spark, which is also an open source, but a cluster computing framework is used. Spark technique overcomes all limitations of Hadoop.

Bano, et al. (2015) defines Big Data as the huge amount of data, which requires innovative technologies and architectures to make it possible to extract worthwhile information from it by capturing and the analysis process. In the corporate domain, Big Data is becoming increasingly imperative. As businesses continue to implement information systems, the amount of data that is created in the routine process is growing at a rapid rate and thus becoming more difficult to handle. Data, as stated earlier is the most valuable asset that will enable the business to mine imperative information leading to significant decisions and business intelligence and thus giving competitive advantages to businesses. With the ever-growing need for information, data is labelled as the most valuable asset to any organization or company. Assuncao, et al. (2015) stated that despite the popularity on analytics and Big Data, putting them into practice is still a complex and time-consuming endeavor. Big Data offers substantial value to organizations willing to adopt it, but at the same time poses a considerable number of challenges for the realization of such added value". Having the infrastructure in place to collect Big Data and then having the resources to comply with 5 Vs characteristics of Big Data is not something that happens overnight.

In the pursuit of collecting Big Data, doing Big Data Analytics, and making money, organisations, namely social media companies have gone rogue in their attempt to get our data and violate our privacy. There have been a number of cases where social media applications like Facebook and web portals like Google have been tracking our activities, locations, and other applications that we use. They continue doing so even when we are not using their applications or are online. Our personal data have become quite valuable to them. Legislations like the GDPR (General Data Protection Regulations) have been introduced within the European Union to prevent organisations from collecting and distributing data outside the European Union. Other jurisdictions have implemented their own data privacy and security laws. However, the way in which Big Data and the results of Big Data analytics are being used are causing some serious concerns amongst academic and researchers. There are claims of Artificial Intelligence being used for Big Data Analytics and the biases introduced into the system. There are allegations of human biases, racial stereotyping, gender bias, and other biases being part of Big Data Analytics. As the results of Big Data Analytics are being used to decide whether you will get a job, get promoted or get fired, success in your home loan application, what jail sentence a criminal may face, which university you will get accepted to, research is needed to overcome these Big Data challenges.

BIG DATA ANALYTICS

There are four major processes of Big Data Analytics:

1. **Prescriptive Analytics:** this type of analysis is of high significance, however, is seldom used. Prescriptive analysis will be better suited to answer definite questions, to find solutions to a given situation. Prescriptive analysis is related to both predictive and descriptive analysis.
2. **Predictive Analytics** is forecasting the future based on past analysis. This consists of certain types of methods that use past and current data to predict future results and these are usually based on statistical techniques.
3. **Diagnostic Analytics** is used when reasons need to be sought for the occurrence of some event.
4. **Descriptive Analysis** is used to uncover patterns and relationships.

Apart from the three major Big Data Analytics tools discussed above, there are many other tools available in the current market. A few of these tools are briefly described below:

- **MongoDB:** is a cross platform object-oriented database program which is free and open source. The development of MongoDB software began in 2007 by the 10gen software company now known as MongoDB. This software is also considered as one of the most popular NoSQL databases.
- **Qlik:** Qlik was previously known as QlikTech and was founded in Sweden in 1993 as a software company in business intelligence. It is a user-friendly tool which allows for instant report generation.
- **RapidMiner:** was developed by Rapid Miner company, and it was previously known as YALE (Yet Another Learning Environment). Rapid Miner is a data science software platform that is used for business and commercial applications supporting machine learning processes.
- **SAP:** is enterprise software with the domain of providing business intelligence solutions and collaborative planning, supported by predictive analysis and machine learning technology. Its key features include data visualization, reporting and analysis, mobile data analytics and interactive role-based dashboards.
- **SAS:** is a collection of software that mines data, makes necessary changes, manages, and retrieves data from different sources whereby statistical analysis is performed on this data. Advanced options are provided to the users as well as graphical user interface for non-technical users.
- **Tableau:** is a software that has capabilities to produce data visualization products with its focus on business intelligence. Tableau Software also has mapping functionality.
- **ArcGIS**: is basically an information system that deals with geographical and spatial data.
- **Clarity**: is an integrated modular management information system for business that enables data entry, analysis, and report generation.
- **Cognos**: is a data analytical tool for business intelligence and performance management.

- **Crystal Reports**: SAP crystal reports is business intelligence software which is suitable for small and medium sized businesses. Some of the features of this software include writing customized reports from multiple data sources, visualizing data in dashboards and scorecards, displaying key performance indicators, and other metrics in relation to project or department performance.
- **DNS Analytics** allows for the collection and analysis of DNS (Domain Name Servers) traffic on a particular computer network, assisting in identifying threats and malware. It allows visual representation of data in form of bar graphs and tables enabling the user to monitor the domains data logs.
- **Google Analytics** is a freemium web analytics service offered by Google that tracks and reports website.
- **Heatmap**: is a graphical representation of data that uses a system of color-coding to represent different values. This is used to track user behaviour on the web, such as identifying the number of clicks or scrolls on a website.
- **Oracle analytics:** has all the core "capabilities and languages on a powerful in-database architecture" which includes data mining algorithms implemented in the database as presented by Big Data Analytics Advanced Analytics in Oracle Database.
- **SQL Server:** is a product of Microsoft, a relational database management system which has the primary function of storing and retrieving data when being requested by other software applications.
- **Webmaster:** reveals the way Google views a website online and if there are any problems with the site, then webmaster uses its tools to fix such problems as presented by Difference between Google Analytics and Google Webmaster Tools.

The following benefits are realised when using Big Data Analytic Tools:

- Use of tools such as tableau gives visual analysis. This will help in easy interpretation of the result which can be easily understood by all stakeholders. It further makes it easier to understand subtle trends with in the datasets with means of visual aids.
- Increases the efficiency in business and enables better decisions to be made for the future growth and direction of the business.
- Using Big Data analytics assists companies to gain competitive advantage and outdo their competitors. Accurately analyzed data can be used by the competitor companies or any new company joining the industry to derive schemes to maintain value and enhance their business processes with inventive ideas.
- Supports the businesses in their objectives for new developments and progression opportunities by consolidating and analyzing industry data. These businesses have sufficient data about the items and administrations, purchasers and providers, customer inclinations evaluated.
- Enhances and improves businesses processes. Stock is easily adjusted by the vendors based on the predictive analysis and models based on the search trends from the web or data from social sites. Predictive analytics empowers users to have more confidence in areas of forecasting
- It provides a clear understanding of the data in the system. It provides a clearly understanding and representation of the available data which allows detailed decision making
- Provides a better insight about users and their actions and provides an easier method of capturing data, which can later be used in marketing plan

- Huge amounts of data are analyzed in a short amount of time, hence its time saving and makes it easier to collaborate, sharing analytics with clear facts and figures included with visual aids
- Real-Term and Long-Term Application usage reporting which allows monitoring of customer usage and helps in troubleshooting internet issues.
- Security attacks and vulnerabilities are identified based on the user traffic and host behavior such as spamming, Denial of Service attacks, Port-Scans
- Better interpretation of data to stakeholders and people who do not have experience with complex datasets to make efficient decisions.

APPLICATIONS OF BIG DATA

Big Data is now being used in almost all industries. Its applications are diverse. For example, it is used widely by the banking and finance industry for risk analysis, to prevent fraud, combat money laundering, making decisions on loan applications, monitor financial market and identify unlawful trading. In addition to that retail traders, big banks, hedge funds use Big Data for trade analytics used in high-frequency trading, pre-trade decision-support analytics, sentiment measurement and predictive analytics. The media and entertainment industry use Big Data to analyse customer behaviour, collect customer data, track customer activities, and serve targeted advertisements and offers to customers. Being able to determine a customer's interests enables target marketing and sales conversion success. For example, when you start a YouTube video, the advertisement that is shown to you at the beginning of the video is what Big Data Analytics has determined to be your recent interest in terms of what your recently searched for. Another example is when you watch live sports and all the statistics that appear on your screen plus prediction for the winning team. Which movie is recommended next for you on Netflix, music on Spotify, video on YouTube, and product on Amazon are all based on Big Data decisions?

The healthcare sector has immensely benefitted from Big Data applications. Patients are now given wearable devices to monitor their vital signs and apps to install on their phones. These wearable devices and apps from millions of users sends huge volumes of data to be analysed. Hospitals can now make their diagnosis decisions based on Big Data Analytics instead of requiring patients to undergo time consuming, tedious, and costly tests in the labs. The contact tracing app that tracks people infected with coronavirus makes use of data collected from an infected patient to warn others of their proximity, track the spread of infections, and decide on lockdowns, isolations, and movement of people. The use of Big Data in education has really improved the quality of education and has had a profound impact on student success. For example, at my university, we look at the number of times a student logs into the Learning Management System, the number of clicks made on the web page and the amount of time spent on the learning page to determine whether the student is actively learning or needs intervention and counselling. Comments on discussion forums can be analysed to understand student's satisfaction in courses and the issues being faced.

Predicting weather patterns and natural disasters are also domains in which Big Data applications can be utilised to keep people safe and provide an early warning system. Predictions of hurricanes, cyclones and floods have become more precise than what it was ten years ago. This is due to the ability of Big Data Analytics to mine the data on weather patterns from the last 50 years to arrive at accurate predictions in terms of when the cyclone will make landfall, the intensity of gale force winds and the amount of rain. Now weather office is able to warn people days in advance of impending hurricanes and floods.

The same is being utilised for climate change effects using models and simulations. Low lying islands and coral atolls are being warned that in the next 50 years the sea level will rise and inundate them. The manufacturing sector is using Big Data and Internet of Things to transform into smart factories and do smart manufacturing. Use of supply chains and management of these supply chains based on data analytics are enabling factories to predict customer demand and manufacture products accordingly. It is providing information on the supply of rare raw materials used for production and warning manufacturers to start looking for alternatives or substitutes to be used in manufacturing while controlling carbon emissions.

The amount of data collected by governments from its citizens, taxpayers, businesses, government departments and everyone else is phenomenal. Thus, the application of Big Data and Big Data Analytics in government cannot be ignored. For the government to be on top of things, and especially those providing e-Government services, e-Citizenship, and promoting open data, Big Data is the way to go. With Big Data Analytics, governments would be able to detect fraud, leaks in the economy, tax payment evasions and tampering, economic forecasts, market predictions, climate change and weather patterns, and the list goes on. With predictive analytics, the government would be aware of the percentage of people retiring (going on social welfare benefit), the number of new people joining the workforce (taxable income) and about every aspect of its income and expenditures. Any unexplained income and expenditures outside the prediction model should be a cause for alarm and investigated. Population growth prediction models based on Big Data will provide government opportunities to plan in advance, identify areas for future housing projects and plan to make available the required infrastructure and utilities to its people.

In today's competitive environment and capricious customers, it is critical for retailers to gauge customer satisfaction and retain customer loyalty. In addition to having a physical store, many retailers sell online as well, while some only sell online. And all sales are now being made without the constraint of geographical barriers or country boundaries. Almost all retailers now have social media presence, and/or website for their customers to interact with. Customers now read reviews of retail outlets before deciding to buy from them. The same is true for the hotels, restaurants, and others in the hospitality industry. All these organisations can collected data from millions of customers, analyse their sentiments and improve their customer service. Millions of transactions that take place at the Point of Sale (POS) of large retail outlets are analysed to determine what is selling and what is not. Inventory gets updated and new stocks ordered automatically. Repeat customers are tracked and target with new offers to entice them into buying new products and buy more. New customers are targeted with personally target advertisements offering deals and discounts. Big Data helps forecast sales, new outlets, demographics, and customer demands.

As people move from rural areas and other countries move and migrate to metropolitan cities for work, it causes congestion for pedestrians and traffic. Most metropolitan city dwellers face the daily delays and spend hours stuck in traffic jams while commuting to and from work. There are some applications like Google Maps and other GPS and navigation systems that assists drivers in avoiding traffic jams, but that is not the solution. The transportation system requires structural changes in terms of identifying bottlenecks, widening roads, understanding peak traffic hours. Governments are now using Big Data and Big Data Analytics to control traffic, identify traffic bottlenecks and offer diversion, plan for new roads and routes. These are all part of the intelligent transport systems equipped with Internet of Things (IoT) sensors sending traffic data with the Smart Cities concept. Big Data helps governments and city planners to understand the trends in population growth and car ownership and plan for new routes and modify existing ones to accommodate self-driving/autonomous cars. Private sector organisations can make use of Big Data in transportation as well. They can use it for revenue management, technological enhancements, logistics and for competitive advantage (by consolidating shipments and optimizing freight movement). Efficient supply chain management, green transportation, and smart manufacturing are concepts are based on Big Data Analytics. Already, we have seen how individuals with the use of applications like Google Map and other GPS systems are planning their routes.

BIG DATA RESEARCH AND PRACTICE

With the COVID-19 pandemic intensifying and the increase in infection rates and deaths, researchers (Ahmed, et al., 2021) propose a framework that uses Big Data and Internet of Things (IoT) to predict the spread and infection rates of the pandemic. In a paper published by them, they "demonstrate a health monitoring framework for the analysis and prediction of COVID-19. Their framework takes advantage of Big Data Analytics and IoT. They perform descriptive, diagnostic, predictive, and prescriptive analysis by applying big data analytics using a novel disease real data set, focusing on different pandemic symptoms.: Their "work's key contribution is integrating Big Data Analytics and IoT to analyze and predict a novel disease". Their "neural network-based model is designed to diagnose and predict the pandemic, which can facilitate medical staff." They "predict the pandemic using neural networks and also compare the results with other machine learning algorithms". They claim, "results reveal that the neural network performs comparatively better with an accuracy rate of 99%". As the scientists, researchers and medical experts panic in regard to how this pandemic is going to be controlled, Big Data Analytics and Internet of Things might be a step in the right direction to find the panacea for all.

According to (Martinez, Viles, & Olaizola, 2021), "data science has employed great research efforts in developing advanced analytics, improving data models and cultivating new algorithms." They add "few methodologies have been proposed on the literature that tackle these types of challenges, some of them date back to the mid-1990, and consequently they are not updated to the current paradigm and the latest developments in big data and machine learning technologies". In addition, fewer methodologies offer a complete guideline across team, project, and data & information management. In their research paper, they "explore the necessity of developing a more holistic approach for carrying out data science projects. They first review methodologies that have been presented on the literature to work on data science projects and classify them according to their focus: project, team, data, and information management. Finally, they propose a conceptual framework containing general characteristics and a methodology for managing data science projects with a holistic point of view should have. They propose that their framework can be ideally used by other big data and data science researchers as a roadmap for the design of new data science methodologies or the updating of existing ones.

Over the last three years, researchers (Bauer, et al., 2021), "have been running a large-scale data processing platform for applying analytics to corporate data at scale on an OpenStack private cloud instance." Their "platform makes a wide variety of corporate data assets, such as sales, marketing, customer information, as well as data from less conventional sources such as weather, news and social media available for analytics purposes to hundreds of globally distributed teams across the company." They "control every layer in the stack from the processing engines down to the hardware and they report their experiences in building and operating such a system." In their paper, they describe their technical choices and also describe how their platform evolved as the actual workloads were created by users on their large-scale data processing platform. Common data governance principles have to be adhered to ensure proper data management across the various datalake components. Data governance covers data management aspects such as data security, availability, consistency, integrity, and compliance, and it helps to balance the requirements of the data owner, i.e., the organization making data available.

Weather forecasting plays a fundamental role in the early warning of weather impacts on various aspects of human livelihood, writes (Ren, et al. 2021). They claim, "for instance, weather forecasting provides decision making support for autonomous vehicles to reduce traffic accidents and congestions, which completely depend on the sensing and predicting of external environmental factors such as rainfall, air visibility and so on. It has been proven that deep learning method can effectively mine the temporal and spatial features from the spatio-temporal data." Meteorological data is a typical big geospatial data. To improve weather forecasting, (Ren, et al. 2021) suggest "deep learning-based weather prediction (DLWP) is expected to be a strong supplement to the conventional method. At present, many researchers have tried to introduce data-driven deep learning into weather forecasting and have achieved some preliminary results." In their paper, they survey the state-of-the-art studies of deep learning-based weather forecasting, in the aspects of the design of neural network (NN) architectures, spatial and temporal scales, as well as the datasets and benchmarks." Then they analyze the advantages and disadvantages of DLWP by comparing it with the conventional NWP and summarize the potential future research topics of DLWP.

According to (Zhang, et al., 2020), "social science concerns issues on individuals, relationships, and the whole society. The complexity of research topics in social science makes it the amalgamation of multiple disciplines, such as economics, political science, and sociology, etc." To solve those issues, computational social science emerges due to the rapid advancements of computation technologies and the profound studies on social science." The authors state that "with the aids of the advanced research techniques, various kinds of data from diverse areas can be acquired nowadays, and they can help us look into social problems with a new eye. As a result, utilizing various data to reveal issues derived from computational social science area has attracted more and more attentions." In their paper, they assert that "to the best of our knowledge, we present a survey on data-driven computational social science for the first time which primarily focuses on reviewing application domains involving human dynamics." The state-of-the-art research on human dynamics is reviewed from three aspects: individuals, relationships, and collectives. "Specifically, the research methodologies used to address research challenges in aforementioned application domains are summarized. In addition, some important open challenges with respect to both emerging research topics and research methods are discussed."

Most of the existing medicine recommendation systems that are mainly based on electronic medical records (EMRs) are significantly assisting doctors to make better clinical decisions benefiting both patients and caregivers (Gong, et al., 2021). The authors mention "even though the growth of EMRs is at a lighting fast speed in the era of big data, content limitations in EMRs restrain the existed recommendation systems to reflect relevant medical facts, such as drug-drug interactions." To address these challenges, (Gong, et al., 2021), focus on recent advances in graph embedding learning techniques and propose a novel framework, called Safe Medicine Recommendation (SMR), in their paper. They propose that, "SMR first constructs a high-quality heterogeneous graph by bridging EMRs (MIMIC-III) and medical knowledge graphs (ICD-9 ontology and DrugBank). Then, SMR jointly embeds diseases, medicines, patients, and their corresponding relations into a shared lower dimensional space. Finally, SMR uses the embeddings to decompose the medicine recommendation into a link prediction process while considering the patient's diagnoses and adverse drug reactions." They conduct extensive experiments on real datasets are conducted to evaluate the effectiveness of proposed framework.

FUTURE TRENDS OF BIG DATA

According to (Botha, 2020), the following future trends might be observed for Big Data:

"Big data becomes wide data: in big data environments, scalable cloud concepts eliminate the limiting local IT infrastructures of companies. A major theme of the year 2020 is "Wide Data." This means that IT is increasingly looking at the fragmented, widely distributed data structures created by inconsistent or incorrectly formatted data and data silos.

Data competence as a service: a combination of data synthesis and data analysis will further develop the effective use of data. It will be essential that users receive assistance in reading, working, analyzing, and communicating the data.

DataOps and Self-Service Analytics: data analytics is already successfully implemented on the business level with modern self-service tools. With DataOps, an agile solution is now available for data management. This means that users are now able to significantly increase the speed and quality of data management by using automated and process-oriented technologies."

As we collect Big Data, the management of Big Data becomes a critical issue, actually a data governance. As more and more companies and enterprises jump on to the big data bandwagon, it is only fair to analyze the risk that comes along with organizations accumulating such progressively large quantities of big data. (Hackernoon, 2019). Data Governance (DG) is the process of managing the availability, usability, integrity, and security of the data in enterprise systems, based on internal data standards and policies that also control data usage. Effective data governance ensures that data is consistent and trustworthy and does not get misused. Not only is there a massive risk that enterprises might misuse big data, either in a weak attempt to make more money or to sell consumer data to suspicious third parties, there is also a considerable chance that with big data, organizations might be tempted to forego the significance of data governance entirely. As the accumulation and use of big data within organizations grow more rampant, experts expect to see a renewed focus on companies' data governance as one of the future trends.

In the future, we might deal more with streaming data and perform Big Data transactions in real time. According to (Colombo & Ferrari, 2019), in recent years, the number of Big Data platforms that provide support to data stream management has grown exponentially. Apache Spark is probably the most popular open-source framework which supports the analysis of continuous streams of data. Apache Storm is another open source distributed real-time computation system which can also be used for real-time analytics and continuous computation. In addition, several commercial solutions exist, such as, for instance, Amazon Kinesis, which is a service for real-time processing of streaming data on the cloud, and IBM Streaming analytics, a platform supporting risk analysis and decision making in real-time. Due to the growing emphasis to real-time analysis of data flows, access control enforcement mechanisms targeting continuous flows of data are strongly required. A few results have been presented in the past years in the field of Data Stream Management Systems (DSMSs). A framework, called FENCE, has been proposed by (Nehme, et al., 2013) which supports continuous access control enforcement. "Data and query security restrictions are modeled as meta-data, denoted security punctuations, which are embedded into the data streams. Different enforcement mechanisms have been proposed, which operate by analyzing security punctuations, such as special physical operators which are integrated within query execution plans with the aim to filter the tuples which can be analyzed."

ABOUT THIS BOOK

With new technologies, such as computer vision, internet of things, mobile computing, e-governance and e-commerce, and wide applications of social media, organizations generate a huge volume of data and at a much faster rate than several years ago. Big data in large-/small-scale systems, characterized by high volume, diversity, and velocity, increasingly drives decision making and is changing the landscape of business intelligence. From governments to private organizations, from communities to individuals, all areas are being affected by this shift. There is a high demand for big data analytics that offer insights for computing efficiency, knowledge discovery, problem solving, and event prediction. To handle this demand and this increase in big data, there needs to be research on innovative and optimized machine learning algorithms in both large- and small-scale systems.

Applications of Big Data in Large- and Small-Scale Systems includes state-of-the-art research findings on the latest development, up-to-date issues, and challenges in the field of big data and presents the latest innovative and intelligent applications related to big data. This book encompasses big data in various multidisciplinary fields from the medical field to agriculture, business research, and smart cities. While highlighting topics including machine learning, cloud computing, data visualization, and more, this book is a valuable reference tool for computer scientists, data scientists and analysts, engineers, practitioners, stakeholders, researchers, academicians, and students interested in the versatile and innovative use of big data in both large-scale and small-scale systems.

The many academic areas covered in this publication include, but are not limited to:

- Big Data
- Big Data Analytics
- Big Data Applications
- Big Data Tools
- Big Data Trends
- Big Data Projects
- Business Intelligence
- Cloud Computing
- Data Visualization
- Econometrics
- Healthcare
- Image Processing
- Internet of Things
- Machine Learning
- Smart Cities
- Smart Farming
- Soft Computing

Industry influencers, academicians, and other prominent stakeholders certainly agree that Big Data has become a big game-changer in most, if not all, types of modern industries over the last few years. As Big Data continues to permeate our day-to-day lives, applications become pervasive.

ORGANIZATION OF THE BOOK

This edited book is organized into eighteen chapters. The chapters have been organised to first introduce the readers to the introductory concepts of Big Data and Big Data Analytics and then look at Big Data Applications. Next. Big Data and its convergence with other technologies and applications are presented. A brief description of each of the chapters is as follows:

Chapter 1: Big Data and Big Data Analytics – A Review of Tools and Their Applications

Big Data is emerging and the latest developments in technology has spawned enormous amount of data. The traditional databases lack the capabilities to handle this diverse data and thus has led to the employment of new technologies, methods, and tools. This research discusses Big Data, the available Big Data analytical tools, the need to use Big Data analytics with its benefits and challenges. Through a research drawing on survey questionnaires, observation of the business processes, interviews and secondary research methods, the organizations, and companies in a Small Island State are identified to survey which of them use analytical tools to handle Big Data and the benefits it proposes to these businesses. Organizations and companies that do not use these tools were also surveyed and reasons were outlined as to why these organizations hesitate to utilize such tools.

Chapter 2: Applications of Big Data in Large and Small Systems – Soft Computing

Nowadays, big data is available in every field due to the advent of computers and electronic devices and the advancement of technology. However, analysis of this data requires new technology as the earlier designed traditional tools and techniques are not sufficient. There is an urgent need for innovative methods and technologies to resolve issues and challenges. Soft computing approaches have proved successful in handling voluminous data and generating solutions for them. This chapter focuses on basic concepts of big data along with the fundamental of various soft computing approaches that give a basic understanding of three major soft computing paradigms to students. It further gives a combination of these approaches namely hybrid soft computing approaches. Moreover, it also poses different applications dealing with big data where soft computing approaches are being successfully used. Further, it comes out with research challenges faced by the community of researchers.

Chapter 3: Emerging Trends of Big Data in Cloud Computing

In today's world where data is accumulating at an ever-increasing rate, processing of this big data was a necessity rather than a need. This required some tools for processing as well as analysis of the data that could be achieved to obtain some meaningful result or outcome out of it. There are many tools available in market which could be used for processing of big data. But the main focus on this paper is on Apache Hadoop which could be regarded as an open-source software-based framework which could be efficiently deployed for processing, storing, analyzing and to produce meaningful insights from large sets of data. It is always said that if exponential increase of data is processing challenge then Hadoop could be considered as one of the effective solutions for processing, managing, analyzing, and storing this big data. Hadoop versions and components are also illustrated in the later section of the paper. This paper majorly focuses on the technique, methodology, components, and methodologies adopted by Apache Hadoop software framework for big data processing. The chapter concludes with summarizing emerging trends of big data in cloud computing and its applications.

Chapter 4: Machine Learning for Big Data

Big data and machine learning currently play an important role in various applications and in research. These approaches are explored in depth in this chapter. The chapter starts with a summary of big data and its implementation in a number of fields, and then deals with the problems that big data presents and the need for other technology to resolve these issues/challenges. Big data can best be used with the aid of the machine learning model, even though they are not directly related. Thus, the paradigms of machine learning that support big data can be combined with big data technology, thus providing insight into a range of Big Data Machine Learning approaches and techniques. Although Big Data cannot rely solely on the few paradigms of machine learning, the underlying problems are addressed. New machine learning algorithms are needed that can explore the full scale of the Big Data process and enable software engineering firms to come up with better solutions.

Chapter 5: Big Data in Cloud Computing

Huge size of data that has been produced by applications that spans from social network to scientific computing is termed big data. Cloud computing as a delivery model for IT services, enhances business productivity by reducing cost. It has the intention of achieving solution for managing big data such as high dimensional data sets. Thus, this chapter discusses the background of big data and cloud computing. It also discusses the various application of big data in detail. The various related work, research challenges of big data in cloud computing and the future direction would be addressed in this chapter.

Chapter 6: Big Data Analytics in Healthcare – A Developing Country Survey

This abstract provides better understanding and use-cases of Big data in healthcare. Healthcare industry generates lot of data every day and without proper analytical tools it is quite difficult to extract meaningful data. It is essential to understand Big data tools since the traditional devices do not maintain this vast data and Big Data solves the major issue in handling massive healthcare data. Health data from numerous health records are collected from various sources and this massive data is put together to form the Big data. Conventional database cannot be used in this purpose due to the diversity in data formats, so it is difficult to merge, and so it is quite impossible to process. With the use of Big data this problem is solved, and it can process highly variable data from different sources.

Chapter 7: Big Data With IoT for Smart Farming

Smart farming may also be called digital farming. The world is changing and digitizing at a quick rate. So, all the work from agriculture to the stock market will become more productive and faster. Speed and efficiency play a key role in coping with the rapid pace of life and growing population. Smart agriculture has removed many of the problems faced by farmers during the conventional farming process. Several technologies are useful in this field, which make them work comfortably. Productivity in all areas of this sector can be increased with the aid of new technologies such as IoT and Big Data. Data can be accessed and analyzed from any part of the world with the help of IoT devices. The chapter offers insight into technology, such as big data and IoT, its applications in smart farming, as well as future innovations and opportunities. The chapter concludes with identifying the benefits of using Big Data with Internet of Things for Smart Farming.

Chapter 8: Data Analytics and Its Applications in Brief

With an ever-increasing number of data created, it has become a major challenge for infrastructures and frameworks to process a lot of information inside stipulated time and resources. So as to effectively extract from this information, organizations require to discover new devices and strategies particular for large information preparation. Therefore, Data Analytics has become a key factor for organizations to uncover hidden data and accomplish upper hands in the market. As of now, tremendous distributions of larger Data and information processing make it hard for experts and specialists to discover points they are keen on and track forward-thinking. This chapter puts forth an outline of Data Analytics, extension, and discoveries just as opportunities emancipated by Analysis of Data. The chapter also deals with various applications of Data Analytics which include applying an algorithmic or mechanical procedure to infer bits of knowledge, for instance, going through a few informational collections to search for significant connections between one another.

Chapter 9: Data Visualisation in Business

The main objective of data visualization is to communicate information clearly and effectively through graphical means. It does not mean that data visualization needs to look boring to be functional or extremely sophisticated to look beautiful. To convey ideas effectively, both aesthetic form and functionality need to go hand in hand, providing insights into a rather sparse and complex data set by communicating its key-aspects in a more intuitive way. This book chapter analyses the following aspects of data visualisation. First, it describes data visualisation. Second, it describes the importance of data visualisation in business. Third, it describes different types of data visualisation methods used in business and familiarises some tools available for data visualisation. Last, it describes the recent developments in data visualisation and its future research directions.

Chapter 10: Application of Econometrics in Business Research – An Analysis Using Business Data

The last few years have seen great developments in econometrics for a better understanding of economic phenomena. The range of areas in which econometric models are successfully applied has steadily widened including finance and business management. Econometric analysis is concerned with the quantitative relationships between economic variables and it can provide an important input into the decision-making process. The range of areas in which econometric models are successfully applied has steadily widened including finance and business management. Econometrics has enhanced our understanding of the way the managerial decision works. Econometrics is used in doing quantitative analysis of actual economic phenomena based on theory and observations. An economic model is based on a set of assumptions to simplify the complex economic phenomena. This chapter is an attempt to review the application of econometrics using business data. The main objective of this chapter is to chart the application of this science in various fields of business management.

Chapter 11: A Review on Critical Success Factors for Big Data Projects

For an organization every year, a large amount of information is generated regarding its employees, customers, business partners, suppliers, etc. Volume, which is one of the attributes of Big Data, is aptly named because of the vast number of data sources and the size of data generated by these sources. Big Data solutions should not only focus on the technological aspects, but also on the challenges that may occur during the project lifecycle. The main purpose of this research is to build on the current diverse literature around Big Data by contributing discussion on factors that influence successful Big Data projects. The systematic literature review adopted in this study includes relevant research regarding such critical success factors that are validated in previous studies. The study compiled these critical success factors as provided in the literature regarding Big Data projects. Notable success factors for Big Data projects were compiled from literature such as case studies, theoretical observations, or experiments.

Chapter 12: Blockchain-Based Data Market (BCBDM) Framework for Security and Privacy – An Analysis: Big Data

In the Internet era, incalculable data is generated every day. In the process of data sharing, complex issues such as data privacy and ownership are emerging. Blockchain is a decentralized distributed data storage technology. The introduction of blockchain can eliminate the disadvantages of the centralized data market, but at the same time, distributed data markets have created security and privacy issues. It summarizes the industry status and research progress of the domestic and foreign big data trading markets and refines the nature of the blockchain-based big data sharing and circulation platform. Based on these properties, a Blockchain-Based Data Market (BCBDM) framework is proposed, and the security and privacy issues as well as corresponding solutions in this framework are analyzed and discussed. Based on this framework, a data market testing system was implemented, and the feasibility and security of the framework were confirmed.

Chapter 13: A Study on Self Regulating Traffic Light Control Using RFID and Machine Learning Algorithm

Traffic control light frameworks are generally used to control and screen the stream of cars through the intersection of numerous streets. As the quantity of street clients always increments and assets gave are constrained, savvy activity flag controller is an exceptionally real prerequisite. One disadvantage of customary methodologies for movement administration is that they do not consider the distinctive valuations of holding up time lessening of the drivers. This chapter proposed another component for versatile activity control utilizing machine learning. In the proposed framework we are utilizing picture sensor in the LED publication which catches the pictures of streets in every one of the bearings returns number of head checks of the vehicles will be sent to a machine learning calculation. The machine learning calculation is intended to take in the rush hour gridlock thickness without anyone else with first caught picture and consider reference. In this manner the proposed activity control framework will be an exceptional technique for self-learning and security improving.

Chapter 14: Application of Machine Learning in Chronic Kidney Disease Risk Prediction Using Electronic Health Records (EHR)

Chronic Kidney Disease (CKD) is a disorder in which the kidneys are weakened and become unable to filter blood. It lowers the human ability to remain healthy. The field of biosciences has progressed and produced vast volumes of knowledge from electronic health records. Heart disorders, anemia, bone diseases, elevated potassium, and calcium are the very prevalent complications that arise from kidney failure. Early identification of CKD can improve the quality of life greatly. To achieve this, various Machine Learning techniques have been introduced so far that use the data in Electronic Health Record (EHR) to predict CKD. This chapter studies various Machine Learning algorithms like Support Vector Machine, Random Forest, Probabilistic Neural Network, Apriori, ZeroR, OneR, Naive Bayes, J48, IBk (k-Nearest Neighbor), Ensemble method, etc. and compares their accuracy. The study aims in finding the best-suited technique from different methods of Machine Learning for the early detection of CKD by which medical professionals can interpret model predictions easily.

Chapter 15: Heart Disease Prediction Using Decision Tree and Random Forest Classification Techniques

The data mining is the approach which can extract useful information from the data. The prediction analysis is the approach which can predict future possibilities based on the current information. We propose a hybrid classifier to carry out the heart disease prediction. The hybrid classifier is combination of random forest and decision tree classifier. Moreover, the heart disease prediction technique has three steps which are data pre-processing, feature extraction and classification. In this research, random forest classifier is applied for the feature extraction and decision tree classifier is applied for the generation of prediction results. However, random forest classifier will extract the information and decision tree will generate final classifier result. We will show the results of proposed model using the Python Platform. Moreover, the results are compared with Support Vector Machine (SVM) and K-Nearest neighbour classifier (KNN).

Chapter 16: Predictive Strength of Ensemble Machine Learning Algorithms for the Diagnosis of Large-Scale Medical Datasets

Machine learning is not a simple technology but an amazing field having more and more to explore. It had a number of real-time applications such as weather forecast, price prediction, gaming, medicine, fraud detection, etc. Machine learning has an increased usage in today's technological world as data is growing in volumes and machine learning is capable of producing mathematical and statistical models that can analyze complex data and generate accurate results. To analyze the scalable performance of the learning algorithms, this chapter utilizes various medical datasets from the UCI Machine Learning repository ranges from smaller to large datasets. The performance of learning algorithms such as Naïve Bayes, Decision Tree, k- Nearest Neighbor, and Stacking ensemble learning method are compared in different evaluation models using metrics such as Accuracy, Sensitivity, Specificity, Precision, and F-Measure.

Chapter 17: Role of Edge Computing to Leverage IoT-Assisted AAL Ecosystem

The medical advancement in recent years is addressing challenges of the dependent people like senior citizens, physically challenged and cognitively impaired individuals by providing technical aids to promote a healthier society. The radical improvement in the digital world is trying to make their life smoother by creating a smart living environment via Ambient Assisted Living (AAL) rather than making them hospitalized. In this chapter, an Edge-based AAL-IoT ecosystem is introduced with the prime objective of delivering tele healthcare to elderly and telerehabilitation to disabled individuals. The proposed framework focuses on developing smart home, an intelligent atmosphere for real-time monitoring in regard to meet the needs of independent and isolated individuals. The supporting technologies to leverage the edge computing concept, to enable scalability and reliability are also studied. A case study on proposed architecture for quarantined patient monitoring remotely in the event of epidemic or pandemic diseases is presented.

Chapter 18: Technologies and Applications of Internet of Things (IoT) in Healthcare

Developments in Technology have opened new doors for healthcare to improve the treatment methods and prevent illnesses as a proactive method. Internet of Things (IoT) technologies have also improved the self-management of care and provided more useful data and decisions to doctors with data analytics. Unnecessary visits, utilizing better quality resources, and improving allocation and planning are main advantages of IoT in healthcare. Moreover, governments and private institutions have become a part of this new state-of-the-art development for decreasing costs and getting more benefits over the management of services. In this chapter, IoT technologies and applications are explained with some examples. Furthermore, deep learning and Artificial Intelligence (AI) usage in healthcare and their benefits are stated that Artificial Neural Networks (ANN) can monitor, learn, and predict and the overall health severity for preventing serious health loss can be estimated and prevented.

ACKNOWLEDGMENT

I would like to especially acknowledge my Fellow Editor (Praveen Kumar) for all the work he did towards this book. His initial involvement in proposing and getting this book off the ground is much appreciated as are his words of encouragement and support. We are proud to present the book on the *Applications of Big Data in Large- and Small-Scale Systems*. We would like to thank all the reviewers that peer reviewed all the chapters in this book. We also would like to thank the admin and editorial support staff of IGI Global Publishers that have ably supported us in getting this issue to press and publication. And finally, we would like to humbly thank all the authors that submitted their chapters to this book. Without your submission, your tireless efforts and contribution, we would not have this book.

For any new book, it takes a lot of time and effort in getting the Editorial Team together. Everyone on the Editorial Team, including the Editor-in-Chief is a volunteer and holds an honorary position. No one is paid. Getting people with expertise and specialist knowledge to volunteer is difficult, especially when they have their full-time jobs. Next was selecting the right people with appropriate skills and specialist expertise in different areas of Big Data, Big Data Analytics, Big Data Applications, and other technologies converging with Big Data.

Every book and publisher have its own chapter acceptance, review, and publishing process. IGI Global uses an online editorial system for chapter submissions. Authors are able to submit their chapters directly through the e-Editorial Discovery system. The Editor-in-Chief then does his own review and selects reviewers based on their area of expertise and the research topic of the article. After one round of peer review by more than three reviewers, a number of revisions and reviews, a chapter and subsequently all the chapters are ready to be typeset and published.

I hope everyone will enjoy reading the chapters in this book and will learn much from it. I hope it will inspire and encourage readers to start their own research on Big, Data, Big Data Analytics, and Big Data Applications. Once again, I congratulate everyone involved in the writing, review, editorial and publication of this book.

Sam Goundar
Editor-in-Chief

REFERENCES

Ahmed, I., Ahmad, M., Jeon, G., & Piccialli, F. (2021). A framework for Pandemic Prediction Using Big Data Analytics. *Big Data Research*, 100190.

Ali, A. (2020, September 15). *Here's what happens every minute on the internet in 2020*. Retrieved February 03, 2021, from https://www.visualcapitalist.com/every-minute-internet-2020/

Assuncao, M., Calheiros, R., Bianchi, S., Netto, M., & Buyya, R. (2015). Big Data computing and clouds: Trends and future directions. *Journal of Parallel and Distributed Computing, 79-80*, 3–15. doi:10.1016/j.jpdc.2014.08.003

Bano, S. (2015). Big Data: An emerging technology towards scalable system. *International Journal of Innovative and Emerging Research in Engineering, 2*(3), 2015.

Bauer, D., Froese, F., Garcés-Erice, L., Giblin, C., Labbi, A., Nagy, Z. A., Pardon, N., Rooney, S., Urbanetz, P., Vetsch, P., & Wespi, A. (2021). Building and Operating a Large-Scale Enterprise Data Analytics Platform. *Big Data Research, 23*, 100181. doi:10.1016/j.bdr.2020.100181

Botha, M. (2020, March 9). *These are the big data trends 2020*. Retrieved February 05, 2021, from https://towardsdatascience.com/these-are-the-big-data-trends-2020-49c4db330ba1

Colombo, P., & Ferrari, E. (2019). Access control technologies for Big Data management systems: Literature review and future trends. *Cybersecurity, 2*(1), 1–13. doi:10.118642400-018-0020-9

Gong, F., Wang, M., Wang, H., Wang, S., & Liu, M. (2021). SMR: Medical knowledge graph embedding for safe medicine recommendation. *Big Data Research, 23*, 100174. doi:10.1016/j.bdr.2020.100174

Hackernoon. (2019). *5 big data trends for the post-pandemic future*. Retrieved February 05, 2021, from https://hackernoon.com/5-big-data-trends-for-the-post-pandemic-future-zmx3ux6

Martinez, I., Viles, E., & Olaizola, I. G. (2021). Data Science Methodologies: Current Challenges and Future Approaches. *Big Data Research*, 100183.

Nehme, R. V., Lim, H. S., & Bertino, E. (2013). Fence: Continuous access control enforcement in dynamic data stream environments. In *Proceedings of the third ACM conference on Data and application security and privacy* (pp. 243-254). 10.1145/2435349.2435383

Ren, X., Li, X., Ren, K., Song, J., Xu, Z., Deng, K., & Wang, X. (2021). Deep Learning-Based Weather Prediction: A Survey. *Big Data Research*, *23*, 100178. doi:10.1016/j.bdr.2020.100178

Zhang, J., Wang, W., Xia, F., Lin, Y. R., & Tong, H. (2020). Data-driven computational social science: A survey. *Big Data Research*, 100145.

Chapter 1
Big Data and Big Data Analytics:
A Review of Tools and its Application

Sam Goundar

iD https://orcid.org/0000-0001-6465-1097

The University of the South Pacific, Fiji

Akashdeep Bhardwaj

iD https://orcid.org/0000-0001-7361-0465

University of Petroleum and Energy Studies, India

Shavindar Singh

The University of the South Pacific, Fiji

Mandeep Singh

The University of the South Pacific, Fiji

Gururaj H. L.

iD https://orcid.org/0000-0003-2514-4812

Vidyavardhaka College of Engineering, India

ABSTRACT

Big data is emerging, and the latest developments in technology have spawned enormous amounts of data. The traditional databases lack the capabilities to handle this diverse data and thus has led to the employment of new technologies, methods, and tools. This research discusses big data, the available big data analytical tools, the need to use big data analytics with its benefits and challenges. Through a research drawing on survey questionnaires, observation of the business processes, interviews and secondary research methods, the organizations, and companies in a small island state are identified to survey which of them use analytical tools to handle big data and the benefits it proposes to these businesses. Organizations and companies that do not use these tools were also surveyed and reasons were outlined as to why these organizations hesitate to utilize such tools.

DOI: 10.4018/978-1-7998-6673-2.ch001

INTRODUCTION

With the ever-growing need for information, data is labelled as the most valuable asset to any organization or company. "Society is becoming increasingly more instrumented and as a result, organizations are producing and storing vast amounts of data" as stated by Assuncao, et al. (2014). This vast amount of data that organizations produce and deal with is termed as 'Big Data'. Bano, et al. (2015) defines Big Data as huge amount of data, which requires innovative technologies and architectures to make it possible to extract worthwhile information from it by capturing and analysis process. In the corporate domain, Big Data is becoming increasingly imperative. As businesses continue to implement information systems, the amount of data that is created in the routine process is growing at a rapid rate and thus becoming more difficult to handle. Data, as stated earlier is the most valuable asset that will enable the business to mine imperative information leading to significant decisions and business intelligence giving competitive advantages to businesses.

Hence, to enable businesses and organizations to mine relative patterns and obtain relevancy and reliability from this significantly huge amount of data, Big Data analytics have a major role to play. Ross, et al. (2014) described Big Data analytics as the process of examining large and varied data sets to uncover hidden patterns, unknown correlations, market trends, customer preferences and other useful information that can help organizations make more-informed business decisions. This research will identify business and organizations in a Small Island State that currently use analytical tools to deal with data in their areas of expertise. Big Data analytics is new to the Small Island State and businesses are still adapting to this new technology. The research will try to include both the companies that do and do not use analytical tools to analyses Big Data with appropriate reasons.

It will further try to ascertain the benefits of using such tools for those companies and organizations that currently employ analytical tools to handle Big Data. On the contrary, the challenges faced by the companies and organizations while using analytical tools will be discussed in this research. Assuncao, et al. (2014) stated that despite the popularity on analytics and Big Data, putting them into practice is still a complex and time-consuming endeavor. Big Data offers substantial value to organizations willing to adopt it, but at the same time poses a considerable number of challenges for the realization of such added value" In the following sections of the paper, a background of Big Data and analytical tools will be outlined.

Following the background will be a brief literature review of some analytical tools. Moving on, the authors present the research questions that we would like to investigate to get insights into the use of Big Data analytical tools in companies and organizations in a Small Island State, which will be established by the discoveries of our research and conclusion. Big Data and Big Data Analytics as depicted in Figure 1 is now being applied through all domains of the business environment.

BACKGROUND

The recent years has seen a substantial escalation in data in various fields. Data is generated in form of text, images, audio, video, social media and so forth. One of the key reasons for this increase in data results from instrumented businesses processes. With such increase in data, the term "Big Data" has been used to describe these enormous datasets. Big Data does not have a rich history as the past only

Figure 1. Big Data and Data Analysis (Moka, et al., 2017)

involved basic data analysis with the use of simple data techniques and traditional databases. As businesses grew, so did the competition.

The business processes evolved and resulted in an ever-increasing need for data and information and thus the year 1943, marked the appearance of the first data-processing machine. This machine was named Colossus, developed by the British to decipher Nazi codes during World War II. According to Rijmenam, et al. (2018) Colossus could search for patterns in intercepted messages at a rate of 5,000 characters per second. The benefit of this device was that it reduced the task from weeks to hours. In the year 1949, a research was conducted on high storage volume objects like photographic data and punch cards as presented in Big Data Timeline - Series of Big Data Evolution (2015).

This also remarked that the term Big Data was first mentioned in 1997 referring to a paper on Visualization published by David Ellsworth and Michael Cox of NASA's Ames Research Centre (Cox & Ellsworth, 1997). They mentioned about the challenges in working with large unstructured data sets with the existing computing system. They also stated that Big Data probably originated in lunch-table conversations at Silicon Graphics Inc. (SGI) in the mid-1990s, in which John Mashey figured prominently (Diebold, 2012). Despite the references to the mid-nineties, the term became widespread as recently as in 2011.

In 2001, Doug Laney defined the dimensions of Big Data in a research paper titled 3D Data Management: Controlling Data Volume, Velocity, and Variety. As the years progressed, the data grew from gigabytes to petabytes to Exabyte to zettabytes and it continues to grow. Until 2015, research has shown that nearly 2.5 quintillion of data is produced every day, with Google being the largest Big Data company that stores 10 billion gigabytes of data while Amazon was the company which has the greatest number of servers.

Big Data is not new in the technological world. However, for the Small Island States' businesses and organizations, they are still adapting to Big Data concepts and its tools. According to our survey, only a few of the major Big Data tools are being utilized. Upon conducting the survey, the findings reveal that few businesses in the Small Island State use Big Data analytic tools such as Tableau, Oracle, SAP (Systems Applications Products), and SAS (Statistical Analysis System), while a few others use MySQL and Excel. With the current rate of data generation and growth, it is highly likely that most businesses in the Small Island State would use Big Data analytics in the near future.

LITERATURE REVIEW

Big Data is being commonly used to accredit the diverse and rapid increase. The term Big Data is often used synonymously with related concept such as Business Intelligence (BI) and data mining (Furht & Villanustre, 2016). Data comes from a variety of sources and although organizations mostly capture transactional data, (Furht & Villanustre, 2016) in their work acclaim that businesses of today obtain additional data at a progressive speed from its operative environment. Data obtained from the web, and in form of test, time, and location together with sensor and social network, are some examples of Big Data.

Although Big Data is an evolving subject in the modern business and technological era, without the appropriate tools and techniques to derive important data, Big Data on its own is meaningless. Gandomi, et al. (2015) stated that Big Data are worthless in a vacuum. Its potential value is unlocked only when leveraged to drive decision-making. Watson, et al. (2014) stated similar sentiments, as collecting and storing Big Data does not create business value. Value is created only when the data is analyzed and acted on.

In addition, Big Data comes with its benefits and challenges. Zicari, et al. (2014) presented the challenges faced with Big Data and categorized them as data challenges, process challenges and management challenges. Data challenges are further discussed under topics such as volume, variety, combining multiple data sets. Velocity, veracity, data quality, data availability, and data discovery are discussed next. Punia et al. (2021) proved that quality and relevance, data comprehensiveness, personally identifiable information, data dogmatism and scalability are discussed last.

Alsghaier (2017) also stated that many companies fail to obtain Big Data analytics because they did not have the required infrastructure for implementation while some other companies do not consider the privacy license by entering unauthorized information. Hence, to analyze and to handle Big Data analytics, there are many available tools and technologies, and more research are being carried out to develop more tools in support.

One of the commonly used technique is Hadoop. Bano, et al. (2015) mentioned Hadoop as a system that is becoming popular for Big Data analytics with an entire ecosystem of tools being developed around it (Herodotos, 2011). Punia et al. (2020) also proposed that Hadoop presents key characteristics when performing parallel and distributed computing, such as data integrity, availability, scalability, exception handling, and failure recovery. Hadoop is a popular choice when you need to filter, sort, or pre-process large amounts of new data in place and distill it to generate denser data that theoretically contains more information as mentioned by Zakir (2015).

The benefits of using such tools are significant for any organization or company. Thi, et al. (2017) in their research indicated that some of the positive factors applicable in Big Data analytics include "offering information search, recommendation system, dynamic pricing and customer service to interact with the community member". Similar sentiments are expressed by Nawsher, et al. (2014) and Bhardwaj et al. (2020) indicating that by harnessing Big Data, businesses gain many advantages, including increased operational efficiency, informed strategic direction, improved customer service, new products, and new customers and markets. With the use of appropriate tools for Big Data analytics, Kumar et al. (2020)

presented that, constructive benefits can be realized by organizations allowing them to confront the challenges with Big Data.

METHODS

Due to time constraints, convenience sampling was used as the major method of obtaining data. Sedgewick (2013) illustrated convenience sampling as a type of non-probability where the sample is taken from a group of people who are easy to reach. A set of questionnaires was distributed to selected individuals from prominent companies and organizations in the Small Island State. These individuals were mostly selected from the Capital City of the Small Island State. Few of these individuals were also interviewed.

The responses were recorded and then analyzed. Altogether, there were twelve (12) respondents whereas nine (9) participants did not respond to our questionnaires. Hence, the findings are based on the responses given by the participants. Furthermore, observations were made about the data handling processes on a few local organizations, in terms of which tools are being used and what benefits do these tools present.

Secondary research through the Internet via ProQuest and Google Scholar was also conducted, studying the current journals, articles, case studies and publications to obtain information on Big Data and Big Data analytical tools. The information gathered from these journal papers were compared with the responses given by the participants of our research. The outcome of this research are validated against the Technology Acceptance Model (TAM).

RESULTS

Big Data

Big Data is the term referring to huge amounts of data. Bagiwa, et al. (2017) indicated that Big Data are high-volume, high-velocity, and/or high-variety information assets that require new forms of processing to enable enhanced decision making, insight discovery and process optimization. Furthermore, Watson, et al. (2014) indicate that this data is commonly referred to as Big Data because of its volume, the velocity with which it arrives, and the variety of forms it takes. The term Big Data does not necessarily mean that the data is big. Instead, it refers to the concept of volume, velocity, and variety. Businesses of the modern era tend to interpret Big Data with the assistance of its analytical tools to uncover new insights and gain competitive advantage over its competitors.

Big Data Concepts

In general, the Big Data concepts comprise of the three V's. These are Volume, Velocity and Variety. Figure 2 illustrates the concept of volume, velocity, and variety and its relationship to the rapid increases in the volume of data from terabytes to zettabytes, structured and unstructured data, as well as batch and stream data processing.

Figure 2. Big Data by the three V's by Bagiwa, et al. (2017)

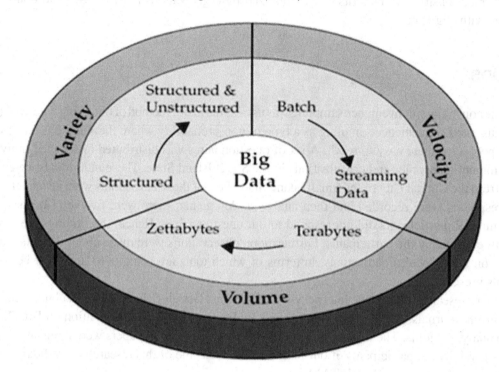

- **Volume** is referred to the huge quantity of data that is generated every single second. This usually is because of the social media data exchanges, innovative business processes, or simply any form of data creation and exchange.
- **Velocity** denotes the speed in which new data is generated and the movement of data across platforms. It refers to the speed at which data analysis should be done.
- **Variety** simply put is referring to all the different types of data being generated and used. Data can be structured or unstructured. Structured data usually comes in forms of tables and can be said as organized data. Unstructured data consists of text, images, audio, and video, which needs to be organized for machines to analyze such data as stated by Gandomi, et al. (2015).

Apart from Volume, Velocity and Variety, the other V's of Big Data concepts include the following:

- **Veracity** refers to how dependable data is since it becomes a difficult task to maintain the quality and the reliability of data due to the variety of data available. Simply put, veracity is referring to the unreliability of data. As stated by Assuncaoa, et al. (2014), Veracity refers to how much the data can be trusted given the reliability of its source.
- **Value** refers to the worth of the data. In other words, value is referring to the financial gain a company can obtain of it employs Big Data analytics.

Major Processes of Big Data Analytics

There are four major processes of Big Data analytics:

- **Prescriptive Analytics:** this type of analysis is of high significance, however, is seldom used. Prescriptive analysis will be better suited to answer definite questions, to find solutions to a given situation. Prescriptive analysis is related to both predictive and descriptive analysis.
- **Predictive Analytics** is forecasting the future based on past analysis. This consists of certain types of methods that use past and current data to predict future results and these are usually based on statistical techniques.
- **Diagnostic Analytics** is used when reasons need to be sought for the occurrence of some event.
- **Descriptive Analysis** is used to uncover patterns and relationships.

Big Data Analytics Tools

There are varieties of tools available in the current market. A few of the eminent tools are briefly described below:

- **Apache Spark**: Apache Spark's "key point of this open source Big Data tool is it fills the gaps of Apache Hadoop concerning data processing" (Verma, 2018). Data processing is done much faster than the traditional disk processing. It facilitates distributed task transmission and scheduling. This software was originally developed at the University of California Apache Spark (2018).
- **Hadoop**: This is one of the most prominent tools used for data analytics, which can process data in large scales. It is 100% open source and be run on a cloud infrastructure as well. It is a collection of open-source software, which solves massive data problems using a network of computers. Hadoop was released in 2006 Apache Hadoop (2018).
- **MongoDB:** is a cross platform object-oriented database program, which is free and open source. The development of MongoDB software began in 2007 by the 10gen software company now known as MongoDB (2018). According to Zakir (2015), this software is also considered as one of the most popular NoSQL databases.
- **Qlik:** Qlik (2018) was previously known as QlikTech and was founded in Sweden in 1993 as a software company in business intelligence. It is a user-friendly tool, which allows for instant report generation.
- **RapidMiner:** was developed by Rapid Miner company, and it was previously known as YALE (Yet another Learning Environment). Rapid Miner is a data science software platform that is used for business and commercial applications supporting machine-learning process as presented by RapidMiner (2018).
- **SAP:** is enterprise software with the domain of providing business intelligence solutions and collaborative planning, supported by predictive analysis and machine learning technology. Its key features include data visualization, reporting and analysis, mobile data analytics and interactive role-based dashboards as stated by SAP Analytics Cloud (2017)
- **SAS:** is a collection of software that mines data, makes necessary changes, manages, and retrieves data from different sources whereby statistical analysis is performed on this data. Advanced options are provided to the users as well as graphical user interface for non-technical users as mentioned by SAS Software (2018).
- **Tableau:** is a software that has capabilities to produce data visualization products with its focus on business intelligence. Tableau Software (2018) also has mapping functionality.

Big Data Analytics Tools in Use

Based on the responses received, the following tools were listed as being used currently by businesses within the capital city of the Small Island State.

- **ArcGIS**: is an information system that deals with geographical and spatial data.
- **Clarity**: is an integrated modular management information system for business that enables data entry, analysis, and report generation.
- **Cognos**: is a data analytical tool for business intelligence and performance management.
- **Crystal Reports**: SAP crystal reports is business intelligence software, which is suitable for small and medium sized businesses. Some of the features of this software include writing customized reports from multiple data sources, visualizing data in dashboards and scorecards, displaying key performance indicators, and other metrics in relation to project or department performance as per SAP Crystal Reports Software (2018).
- **DNS Analytics** allows for the collection and analysis of DNS (Domain Name Servers) traffic on a particular computer network, assisting in identifying threats and malware. It allows visual representation of data in form of bar graphs and tables enabling the user to monitor the domains data logs as per DNS Made Easy (2017).
- **Excel**: Microsoft Excel allows for manipulation of numbers using formulas and functions. This software is used by nearly all businesses in the Small Island State for electronic record keeping.
- **Google Analytics** is a freemium web analytics service offered by Google that tracks and reports website traffic, as described by Google Analytics (2018).
- **Heatmap**: does Heatmap (2018) mention a graphical representation of data that uses a system of color-coding to represent different values as. This is used to track user behavior on the web, such as identifying the number of clicks or scrolls on a website.
- **Oracle analytics:** has the entire core "capabilities and languages on a powerful in-database architecture" which includes data mining algorithms implemented in the database as presented by Big Data Analytics Advanced Analytics in Oracle Database (2013).
- **SAP:** as mentioned in the earlier section, is enterprise software with the domain of providing business intelligence solutions and collaborative planning, supported by predictive analysis and machine learning technology. Its key features include data visualization, reporting and analysis, mobile data analytics and interactive role- based dashboards as presented by SAP Analytics Cloud (2017).
- **SAS:** as mentioned in the earlier section, is a collection of software that mines data, makes necessary changes, manages, and retrieves data from different sources whereby statistical analysis is performed on this data. Advanced options are provided to the users as well as graphical user interface for non-technical users as per SAS Software (2018).
- **SQL Server:** is a product of Microsoft, a relational database management system that has the primary function of storing and retrieving data when being requested by other software applications as presented by Microsoft SQL Server (2018).
- **TABLEAU:** as mentioned in the earlier section, is a software that has capabilities to produce data visualization products with its focus on business intelligence. It also has a mapping functionality as per Tableau Software (2018).

- **Webmaster:** reveals the way Google views a website online and if there are any problems with the site, then webmaster uses its tools to fix such problems as presented by Difference between Google Analytics and Google Webmaster Tools (2018)

Figure 3 shows the percentage of the businesses that use analytical tools in comparison with those that do not. 40% of the businesses that do use the tools comprise of the eight (8) respondents that had given positive responses. Three (3) businesses stated that they do not use such tools since there is no real need, which makes up the 15%, while nine (9) participants did not provide any response, which constitutes to the remaining 45%.

Figure 3. Big Data Analytics Processes – Ross, et al. (2014)

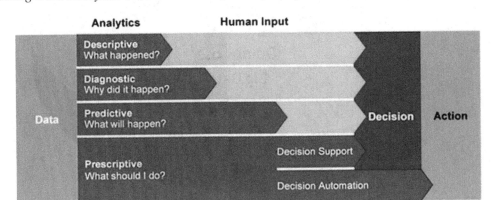

These figures however do not represent the whole business community in the Small Island State. Rather, we tried to reach the twenty (20) prominent companies/ businesses based in the capital city of the Small Island State as most businesses and organizations are based there. Sampling businesses from the capital city of the Small Island State would give us an indicative generalization for the rest of the state.

Figure 4 shows the percentage of the analytical tools used in comparison with each other. From the responses retrieved, it is quite evident that business in Small Island State mostly uses Microsoft SQL, which gives the highest percentage of 21%.

Renowned analytical tools such as SAP, Oracle and Tableau are being utilized by few businesses, which give them an equal percentage on 11% each. Cognos, Crystal, Google Analytics, Heatmap and SAS constitute of 5% each, revealing that they are used by very few businesses.

However, as mentioned earlier, these figures only represent the evidence from the nine (9) participants that have stated they use analytical tools to handle Big Data.

Figure 5 provides an analysis on the percentage of different types of tools used in comparison with other tools by the businesses in the Small Island State.

Data Used for Data Analytics

The business that was surveyed mainly deal with the following kinds of data:

Figure 4. Big Data Tools in Use

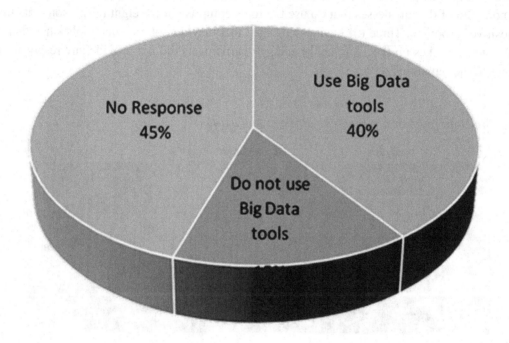

Usage of Big Data Tools

- Sales data
- Customer data
- IT data
- Internal financial data
- Mobile application development
- Operational data
  - Employee records
  - Customer details and history
  - Financial records
  - Managerial data
- Project data
- Employee data
- User data
- Structured: From data warehouses for ERP system, POS, and Analytical systems Unstructured: Legacy systems and transactional data from various systems ISP/IP Operations Team deals with customer circuit data and their IP details.
- Security Team deals with wire-captures of user data for analysis and threat identification.
- DNS data and DNS queries made by customers.
- Spatial data

Figure 5. Comparison of Big Data Tools Used

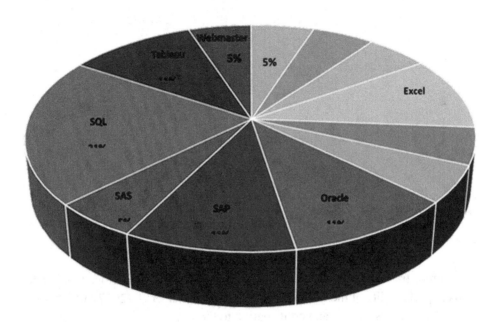

Tools Used

- Statistical data.

As illustrated in Figure 6, based on the responses given by the participants, business in Small Island State (those that were surveyed) mostly deals with customer data and sales data, and hence they use analytical tools to analyze these types of data.

Benefits of Big Data Analytics

With the use of analytical tools, the companies / businesses stated the following benefits:

- Using Big Data tools provides initiative, and it is great for modern day analysis.
- Use of tools such as tableau gives visual analysis. This will help in easy interpretation of the result, which can be easily understood by all stakeholders. It further makes it easier to understand subtle trends with in the datasets with means of visual aids.
- Increases the efficiency in business and enables better decisions to be made for the future growth and direction of the business.
- Using Big Data analytics assists companies to gain competitive advantage and outdo their competitors. The competitor companies or any new company joining the industry to derive schemes to maintain value and enhance their business processes with inventive ideas can use accurately analyzed data.
- Supports the businesses in their objectives for new developments and progression opportunities by consolidating and analyzing industry data. These businesses have sufficient data about the

Figure 6. Data Types Frequently Used in Data Analytics

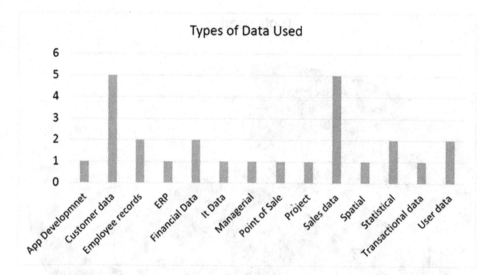

items and administrations, purchasers and providers, customer inclinations that can be evaluated. It also adds to profitability of the business. As stated by Farah, et al. (2017) allows for personalization of customer's needs, wants, and contribution to the profit of the organization.

- Enhances and improves businesses processes. Stock is easily adjusted by the vendors based on the predictive analysis and models based on the search trends from the web or data from social sites. Predictive analytics empowers users to have more confidence in areas of forecasting
- It provides a clear understanding of the data in the system. It provides a clearly understanding and representation of the available data which allows detailed decision making
- Provides a better insight about users and their actions
- Provides an easier method of capturing data, which can later be used in marketing plan
- Huge amounts of data are analyzed in a short amount of time, hence its time saving
- Makes it easier to collaborate, sharing analytics with clear facts and figures included with visual aids
- Real-Term and Long-Term Application usage reporting which allows monitoring of customer usage and helps in troubleshooting internet issues.
- Security attacks and vulnerabilities are identified based on the user traffic and host behavior such as spamming, Denial of Service attacks, Port-Scans
- Allows organizing and displaying data so that it adds meaning to it.
- Better interpretation of data to stakeholders and people who do not have experience with complex datasets to make efficient decisions.

Why Not Big Data Analytics?

The only reason by the participants that do not use analytical tools was that they do not deal with vast amount of data; therefore, according to them there is no real need for the use of such analytical tools.

Challenges of Using Big Data Analytics

The companies / businesses in their response stated the following challenges:

- Some companies state that their employees are still learning to use these analytical tools. There are also technical knowledge gaps whereby end users lack the technical background to consume such analysis and in few cases, the staff lack the necessary skill to use the tools. Most employees are not from an analytics background thus it is a challenge to advocate and get the teams to engage in analytics projects. It becomes a difficult task to keep updated with the tools. Further to this, to upgrade the skill set of the employees, appropriate training must be provided which is both costly and time consuming.
- Require understanding of mathematical logics make it difficult to use. On the same note, understanding of the features of the tools used is also time consuming and a challenge as well.
- With the unceasing rate of data expansion, new technologies are being constantly introduced; hence, companies face difficulty with identifying which technology would get them the best results with the least risks and complications.
- Unavailability of experts. Only few people can understand the complexity of Big Data which springs a talent gap in the field of Big Data
- Accessibility of data. Businesses face challenges in dealing with huge amounts of data every day. Thus, the challenge remains to make data easily accessible and convenient for administrators.
- Synchronization of data. With diverse data, different forms of data need to be structured in such a way that patterns and relevancy can be discovered when analysis is done.
- Unstructured data may lead to false and inaccurate results, which will provide an inaccurate view of the businesses operations and growth.
- Data entry must be done correctly in its correct fields to get accurate result. Even though the tools are efficient in terms of data analyzing, inaccurate or noisy data will give unreliable and inaccurate results.
- Such analysis cannot be carried out on production systems hence data is warehoused which brings about other challenges such as storage and maintaining data quality.
- Security is also a challenge. Due to the nature of such analytical data, security is paramount hence; many resources are dedicated in this area.
- Handling multiple systems. To provide a global picture, data from multiple systems need to be consolidated. Various systems mean different architectures and technologies, bringing all this information to a structured and consolidated form takes a lot of effort.
- Due to the tools being vendor-locked with minimum APIs for extensions, it becomes a challenge to create custom reports or even extract some data features.
- Retaining Long-Term Reports such as 2 years of traffic is a challenge due to storage limitations.
- Efficiently collecting data. Data collection is also a challenge, as there are many forms of data available, which are both structured and unstructured.
- Identifying new tools, which could be used to do the required work.
- Cost of tools. The software needs to be purchased with the required hardware. This is costly for the businesses. They also must be updated with any development or updates in the tools or technology.

DISCUSSION

Based on the literature reviews and the responses given by the participants, 73% (8 out of 11) of the participants have stated that they utilize analytical tools. The most common tool being used is MySQL (Figure 5) and the most common type of data being analyzed is customer data and sales data (Figure 6). Other tools such as Tableau, SAP, SAS, and Oracle are being significantly utilized. Since data is growing inevitably, Small Island States may see plenty other tools being used by local businesses in adaptation to new tools and technologies.

Moreover, the current businesses have stated the benefits they are obtaining from using analytical tools, together with the challenges they face. Analytical tools do provide modern day analysis, enabling businesses to gain competitive advantage and business intelligence, increasing efficiency in their business processes with better data analysis leading to accurate decisions.

On the contrary, since Big Data and analytical tools are slowly gaining acceptance in Small Island States, challenges will be an issue. Businesses have admitted that their employees often lack the skillset to use these tools and are still in the learning process. It becomes difficult to understand the processes, while trying to deal with limitless data each day.

Technology Acceptance Model

Thus, validating our findings against the Technology Acceptance Model, considering the "perceived usefulness" factor, business in Small Island States do accept moving with the technology and their responses indicate that the performance of the business is enhanced by utilizing analytical tools. Technology Acceptance Model is an information systems model whereby users come to accept and use a technology. One of the factors of this model is perceived usefulness, which attains that by using technology, performance will be maximized as proposed by Technology Acceptance Model (Davis, 1989).

The findings reveal that most businesses are using analytical tools, which is an indication that they accept the innovations in technology and are ready for new developments. The list of benefits stated by respondents in their respective responses (Table 1 in the Appendix) is also a clear indication that employment of analytical tools to handle diverse data is certainly maximizing the performance of the business, enhancing, and improving their processes and operations, giving them competitive advantage and business intelligence.

CONCLUSION

Big Data undoubtedly is having a huge impact on the technological and the business world in the modern era. As data is growing, similarly technology is advancing with the introduction of new and latest technologies. Businesses face the challenge to deal with the massive amount of data in their aim to gain completive advantage and business intelligence. With the right tools and technologies, businesses can certainly mine relative patterns in data and uncover hidden insights, which would transform their business processes. It will allow them to improve efficiency and productivity and explore more opportunities.

The objective of this paper was to determine the Big Data concepts and current analytical tools being used. It further aims to identify which of the analytical tools are used locally by businesses in Small Island States, what benefits these tools propose and the challenges faced in using analytical tools.

Businesses in Small Island States are slowly adapting to the technological advancements and are utilizing analytical tools such as Oracle. SAP, SAS and Tableau to name a few. Although these tools are not being used on a large scale, the near future appears to be encouraging, considering the competitive advantage the businesses are aiming to obtain and the ever-increasing growth of data.

FUTURE RESEARCH

With the massive growth of data, soon analytical tools will be common in Small Island States. The researchers could include the processes and technical requirements of such tools.

Our research was confined to a specific number of participants within one geographical area. We do believe that we have included the prominent companies around the Suva area, which according to our understanding deal with diverse and large amounts of data. We have conducted surveys and then compared the results with similar work done by other authors to ascertain our findings. However, we would like to recommend future researchers to expand the scope of their research and to include companies and businesses from different geographical locations. The number of participants can also be widened so that we can get more precise facts when collecting and analyzing data.

REFERENCES

Alsghaier, H. M. A. (2017). The Importance of Big Data Analytics in Business: A Case Study. *American Journal of Software Engineering and Applications*, 111-115.

Apache Hadoop. (2018a, October 21). Retrieved from Wikipedia: https://en.wikipedia.org/wiki/Apache_Hadoop

Apache Spark. (2018b, October 23). Retrieved from Wikipedia: https://en.wikipedia.org/wiki/Apache_Spark

Assuncao, M., Calheiros, R., Bianchi, S., Netto, M., & Buyya, R. (2015). Big Data computing and clouds: Trends and future directions. *Journal of Parallel and Distributed Computing, 79-80*, 3–15. doi:10.1016/j.jpdc.2014.08.003

Bagiwa, L. I. (2017). Big Data: Concepts, Approaches and Challenges. *International Journal of Computer Networks and Communications Security*, 181-187.

Bano, S. (2015). Big Data: An emerging technology towards scalable system. *International Journal of Innovative and Emerging Research in Engineering, 2*(3), 2015.

Bhardwaj, A., Al-Turjman, F., Kumar, M., Stephan, T., & Mostarda, L. (2020). Capturing-the-Invisible (CTI): A Novel Approach for Behavior-based Attacks Recognition in Industrial Control Systems. *IEEE Access: Practical Innovations, Open Solutions, 8*(1), 104956–104966. doi:10.1109/ACCESS.2020.2998983

Big Data Analytics Advanced Analytics in Oracle Database. (2013). *An Oracle White Paper*, 1- 12.

Big Data Timeline-Series of Big Data Evolution. (2015, Aug 26). Retrieved from DeZyre: https://www.dezyre.com/article/big-data-timeline-series-of-big-data-evolution/160

Cox, M., & Ellsworth, D. (1997, August). Managing Big Data for scientific visualization. In ACM siggraph (Vol. 97, pp. 21-38). ACM.

Davis, F. D. (1989). Perceived usefulness, perceived ease of use, and user acceptance of information technology. *Management Information Systems Quarterly, 13*(3), 319–340. doi:10.2307/249008

Diebold, F. X. (2012). On the Origin (s) and Development of the Term. *Big Data.*

Difference between Google Analytics and Google Webmaster Tools. (2018). Retrieved October 25, 2018, from Career Bless: https://www.careerbless.com/web/website/general/topic1.php

Made Easy, D. N. S. (2017, December 13). Retrieved from Ultimate Guide to DNS Analytics: https://social.dnsmadeeasy.com/blog/ultimate-guide-dns-analytics/

Farah, B. (2017). Profitability and Big Data. *Journal of Management Policy and Practice*, 47-52.

Furht, B., & Villanustre, F. (2016). Introduction to Big Data. In *Big Data technologies and applications* (pp. 3–11). Springer. doi:10.1007/978-3-319-44550-2_1

Gandomi, A. M. H., & Haider, M. (2015). Beyond the hype: Big Data concepts, methods, and analytics. *International Journal of Information Management, 35*(2), 137–144. doi:10.1016/j.ijinfomgt.2014.10.007

Google Analytics. (2018, October 21). Retrieved from Wikipedia: https://en.wikipedia.org/wiki/Google_Analytics

Heatmap. (2018). Retrieved from Optimizely: https://www.optimizely.com/optimization- glossary/heatmap/

Herodotou, H. (2011). *Hadoop performance models.* arXiv preprint arXiv:1106.0940.

Kumar, M., Punia, S., Thompson, S., Gopal, D., & Patan, R. (2020). Performance Analysis of Machine Learning Algorithms for Big Data Classification. *International Journal of E-Health and Medical Communications, 12*(4).

Microsoft, S. Q. L. Server. (2018, October 18). Retrieved from Wikipedia: https://en.wikipedia.org/wiki/Microsoft_SQL_Server

Moka, J. A. (2017). *Big Data Analysis.* Retrieved from Data Science Central: https://www.datascience-central.com/profiles/blogs/big-data-analysis

MongoD. B. (2018, October 18). Retrieved from Wikipedia: https://en.wikipedia.org/wiki/MongoDB

Nawsher, K. I. Y. (2014). Big Data: Survey, Technologies, Opportunities, and Challenges. *TheScientificWorldJournal*, 1–18. PMID:25136682

Punia, Kumar, Aggarwal, & Malik. (2020). Object Based Learning Using Multi-Dimensional Games. *Journal of Discrete Mathematical Sciences and Cryptography, 23*(2), 509-524. ” doi:10.1080/09720529.2020.1728904

Punia, S. K., Kumar, M., & Sharma, A. (2021). Intelligent Data Analysis with Classical Machine Learning. In *Intelligent Computing and Applications. Advances in Intelligent Systems and Computing*, (vol. 1172). Springer. doi:10.1007/978-981-15-5566-4_71

Qlik. (2018, August 27). Retrieved from Wikipedia: https://en.wikipedia.org/wiki/Qlik

RapidMiner. (2018, October 5). Retrieved from Wikipedia: https://en.wikipedia.org/wiki/RapidMiner

Rijmenam, M. V. (2018). *A Short History of Big Data*. Retrieved from Dataflow: https://datafloq.com/read/big-data-history/239

Ross, D. (2014, March 18). *Prescriptive Analysis*. Retrieved from duncan3ross: https://duncan3ross.files.wordpress.com/2014/03/gartner2.gif

Analytics CloudS. A. P. (2017). Retrieved from SAP: https://www.sap.com/products/cloud- analytics.html

SAP Crystal Reports Software. (2018). Retrieved from Software Advice: https://www.softwareadvice.com/bi/sapcrystalreports-profile/

SoftwareS. A. S. (2018, September 14). Retrieved from Wikipedia: https://en.wikipedia.org/wiki/SAS_(software)

Sedgwick, P. (2013). Convenience sampling. *BMJ (Clinical Research Ed.)*, *347*, f6304.

Tableau Software. (2018, September 21). Retrieved from Wikipedia: https://en.wikipedia.org/wiki/Tableau_Software

Technology Acceptance Model. (2018, October 8). Retrieved from Wikipedia: https://en.wikipedia.org/wiki/Technology_acceptance_model

Thi, M. L. (2017). Effects of Pros and Cons of Applying Big Data Analytics to Consumers' Responses in an E-Commerce Context. *Sustainability*, 1–19.

Watson, H. J. (2014). Tutorial: Big Data Analytics: Concepts, Technologies, and Applications. *Communications of the Association for Information Systems*, 1247–1268.

Zakir, J. T. S. (2015). Big Data Analytics. *Issues in Information Systems*, 81–90.

Zicari, R. V. (2017). Big Data: Challenges and Opportunities. *Big Data Computing*, 103-128.

APPENDIX

Table 1. The list of benefits stated by respondents in their respective responses

Business	Type of Data	Tools	Benefits	Challenges
Coke	Sales data	TABLEAU, SQL Server, Excel	Initiative and great for modern day analysis. Visual analysis using tableau	Learning to use it. Require understanding of mathematical logics make it difficult to use
Digicel	Customer data, IT data, Internal financial data	SQL, EXCEL, Oracle, SAP, SAS	Big Data means a large chunk of raw data that is collected, stored and analyzed through various means, which can be utilized by organizations to increase their efficiency and take better decisions. Big Data can be in both - structured and unstructured forms. Structured Data is more easily analyzed and organized into the database. Unstructured Data, on the other hand, is much harder to analyze and uses a variety of formats. In addition, traditional data models and processes do not easily interpret it. The use of Big Data is becoming common these days by the companies to outperform their peers. In most industries, existing competitors and new entrants alike will use the strategies resulting from the analyzed data to compete, innovate and capture value. Big Data helps the organizations to create new growth opportunities and entirely new categories of companies that can combine and analyze industry data. These companies have ample information about the products and services, buyers and suppliers, consumer preferences that can be captured and analyzed. It also understands and optimizes business processes. Retailers can easily optimize their stock based on predictive models generated from the social media data, web search trends and weather forecasts.	**Uncertainty of Data Management Landscape:** Because big data is continuously expanding, there are new companies and technologies that are being developed every day. A big challenge for companies is to find out which technology works bests for them without the introduction of new risks and problems. **The Big Data Talent Gap:** While Big Data is a growing field, there are very few experts available in this field. This is because Big data is a complex field and people who understand the complexity and intricate nature of this field are far few and between. Another major challenge in the field is the talent gap that exists in the industry **Getting data into the big data platform:** Data is increasing every single day. This means that companies have to tackle limitless amount of data on a regular basis. The scale and variety of data that is available today can overwhelm any data practitioner and that is why it is important to make data accessibility simple and convenient for brand managers and owners. **Need for synchronization across data sources:** As data sets become more diverse, there is a need to incorporate them into an analytical platform. If this is ignored, it can create gaps and lead to wrong insights and messages. **Getting important insights through the use of Big data analytics:** It is important that companies gain proper insights from big data analytics and it Is important that the correct department has access to this information. A major challenge in the big data analytics is bridging this gap in an effective fashion.
iTvTi	Data that has to do with our mobile application development	*We do not deal with diverse data therefore we don't need analytical tools*		
Link Technologies	Operational data for example employee records, customer details and history, financial records and managerial data	SQL and Crystal Reports	It provides a clear understanding of the data in the system. IT provides a clearly understanding and representation of the available data which allows detailed decision making	Staffs lack skill of the tool. It is challenging to keep the tool updated.
Pace Technologies	The company maintains simple data such as customer/sales records, project data, employee data, etc.	*We do not deal with diverse data therefore we don't need analytical tools*		
Power Marketing	User data.	Google analytics, Webmaster, Heatmap.	Better insight about users and their actions	No, easy to use.
Reddy Group of Companies	Sales data, Customer data	We use Hotel Software named Clarity. We are not using any specific software to do analysis but our hotel software has built in reports and data entry capability	Easier method of capturing data, which can later be used in marketing plan	Yes, Data entry must be done correctly in its correct fields to get accurate

continued on following page

Table 1. Continued

Business	Type of Data	Tools	Benefits	Challenges
Tappoos	Structured From data warehouses for ERP system, POS and Analytical systems Unstructured Legacy systems Transactional data from various systems	Bi Tools like Cognos, MSSQL analytics Oracle Analytics SAP reporting	Number one benefit is such tools make it easier to understand subtle trends with in the datasets with means of visual aids. Analyzing huge amounts of data at a glance Allows better decision making Makes it easier to collaborate - sharing analytics with clear data included with visual aids. Predictive analytics empowers users to have more confidence in areas of forecasting	Technical knowledge gaps End users lack the technical background to consume such analysis Lots of time is take providing trainings Maintaining Data warehouse's Such analysis cannot be carried out on production systems hence data is warehoused which brings about other challenges such as storage and maintaining data quality. Security Due to the nature of such analytical data, security is paramount hence; many resources are dedicated in this area. Handling multiple systems To provide a global picture, data from multiple systems need to be consolidated. Various systems mean different architectures and technologies, bringing all this information to a structured and consolidated form takes a lot of effort.
Telecom Fiji Limited	ISP/IP Operations Team deals with customer circuit data and their IP details. Security Team deals with wire-captures of user data for analysis and threat identification. DNS data and DNS queries made by customers.	Application Usage Reporting Tool Security Analysis and Detection Tool In the process of developing a DNS Analytics tool that would analyze all queries to the DNS server for locally hosted domains.	Real-Term and Long-Term Application usage reporting which allows monitoring of customer usage and helps in troubleshooting internet issues. Security attacks and vulnerabilities are identified based on the user traffic and host behavior such as spamming, DDoS attacks, Port-Scans Once developed, the DNS Analytics tool will give real-time DNS query statistics on the top domain hits and this information can be used for isolating malicious domains.	Due to the tools being vendor-locked with minimum APIs for extensions, it becomes a challenge to create custom reports or even extract some data features. Skillset: Most engineers do not come from an analytics background thus it is a challenge to advocate and get the teams to engage in analytics projects. Retaining Long-Term Reports such as 2 years of traffic is a challenge due to storage limitations.
United Nations Office for the Coordination of Humanitarian Affairs	Spatial data Statistical data.	ArcGIS Tableau	Allows organizing and displaying data so that it adds meaning to it. Better interpretation of data to stakeholders and people who do not have experience with complex datasets to make efficient decisions.	Efficiently collecting data. Preparing raw datasets to feed into the tools for processing. Understanding of the features of the tools used. Identifying new tools, which could be used to do the required work. Cost of tools.
Carpenters Finance	Categorical data Numerical data	None	Easily manipulate our data and present it in different ways or according to user's needs	Communication - Working with another person's code - Duplicate code through the program - Not planning your code - Security threats - Estimating how long a task will take to complete

Chapter 2
Applications of Big Data in Large and Small Systems:
Soft Computing

Archana Purwar

Jaypee Intitute of Information Technology, Noida, India

Indu Chawla

Jaypee Intitute of Information Technology, Noida, India

ABSTRACT

Nowadays, big data is available in every field due to the advent of computers and electronic devices and the advancement of technology. However, analysis of this data requires new technology as the earlier designed traditional tools and techniques are not sufficient. There is an urgent need for innovative methods and technologies to resolve issues and challenges. Soft computing approaches have proved successful in handling voluminous data and generating solutions for them. This chapter focuses on basic concepts of big data along with the fundamental of various soft computing approaches that give a basic understanding of three major soft computing paradigms to students. It further gives a combination of these approaches namely hybrid soft computing approaches. Moreover, it also poses different applications dealing with big data where soft computing approaches are being successfully used. Further, it comes out with research challenges faced by the community of researchers.

1. INTRODUCTION

The term "Big data" has been coined among the biggest trends leading to an upsurge of research, small and large scale systems for various tasks like prediction, classification, commodity detection, association, recommendations and others (Gupta et al., 2020; Zhou et al., 2014) . These systems produce big data by making uses of latest new advancements such as internet of things, web 3.0, wireless sensor networks etc. Big data are not simply enormous arrangements of data but also providing a lot of insights for business professionals, industrialist, academicians and others. Capability in big data requires experimentation and

DOI: 10.4018/978-1-7998-6673-2.ch002

assessment, in the case of growing new models or improving present models. It gives rise to big data analytics. Therefore, big data computing needs intelligent methods to mine indispensible knowledge (outcomes) without losing critical data. These intelligent methods are believed to be trained and obtaining non obvious outputs from hefty volume of data generated from small and large scale systems. Real world data coming from commercial, healthcare, education financial and other industries is often imprecise and uncertain. Hence, soft computing approaches coming under the umbrella of artificial intelligence not only provide solution to handle imprecision and uncertainty problem but also derive the solution in an analogous way as persons can accomplish. The wisdom of human beings is one of the important areas of soft computing approaches for big data analytics. Soft computing (SC) approaches (Sanchez et al., 1997) aspire to develop acceptance for indistinctness, uncertainty as well as partial truth to obtain robust, tractable and cheap solutions for complex big data computing problems. Soft computing consists of mainly three principal components. First is fuzzy logic, second is artificial neural networks, and third one is evolutionary computing. The chief cause of recognition for soft computing methods is collaboration derived from its constituents. The chief characteristic of SC approaches is its built-in ability to form hybrid soft computing systems (Bonissone et al. 1999; Das et al., 2020) in which its components may be either loosely or tightly integrated to design solutions.

This synergism of SC components gives integral thinking and looking through techniques s that permit to join domain related as well as experimental data to design adaptable computational methods and solutions for complicated problems resulting from big data technology. Soft computing as well as hybrid soft computing methods are heavily being used to analyze data in NASA, agricultural, healthcare, e-commerce, track cycling, biomedical, electromagnetic signals and other applications (Cianchetti et al.,2018) .

2. BIG DATA WITH ANALYTICS

Big data is mainly depicted with its volume, variety as well as velocity. Volume means the quantity of data, variety includes structured, unstructured as well as unstructured kind of data and velocity is the rate at which data is being spawned due to advent of newer technologies. To handle big data and analyze this voluminous data, big data technology can be divided into four prominent fields (*Kitchin, 2014*) .

- Data Storage

This component of analytical big data offers a variety of ways through which tremendous data generated from various sources in e-learning can be accumulated.

Hadoop: Big data obtained from heterogeneous sources can be gathered in Hadoop framework. This framework is developed to amass and manage data in a distributed data processing environment with commodity hardware. It is based on map reduce paradigm. Haddop framework gives us away to pile up enormous data and ways to examine the data pattern and associations existing in different machines with superior rapidity and low price for making good decisions.

MongoDB: It is a NoSQL Document Databases that gives a substitute to relational schema. That is prominently used in relational databases. MongoDB imparts flexibility to tackle a large variety of datatypes and hefty amount of data across distributed architectures.

RainStor: It is also a database management system developed by software company named as "Rainstor" . It has capability to maintain and analyze large volume of data for large organizations. It employs deduplication methods to systematize the process of keeping hefty quantity data for reference.

Hunk: It allows to retrieve data using virtual indexes of remote Hadoop clusters and allows to utilize dSplunk Search Processing Language for analysis. It is used for reporting and visualizing large amounts of data from Hadoop and NoSQL data sources.

- Data Mining

It is an essential field which is used to extract the vital information from the stored data. Broadly, data mining provides three different technique namely supervised learning, unsupervised learning and association mining. Various tools are used to apply data mining techniques. Some of them are described below.

Presto is an open source distributed query engine which is able to run user friendly analytic queries against various data sources varying in size from gigabytes to petabytes. It offers retrieving data from various databases such as relational databases, Cassandra, and various other data stores as Hive.

RapidMiner is a centralized key that is a robust and good graphical user interface (GUI). This GUI facilitates to design advanced workflows. This tool is able to deliver, and maintain predictive analytics. Also, it has support of scripting in many languages for developers..

Elastic search is a powerful search engine using the Lucene library. It gives a full-text, multitenant-capable and distributed search engine having an hyper text transfer protocol web interface and schema-free JSON documents.

- Data Analytics

Various kind of analysis using soft computing as well as other intelligent techniques in various applications can be provided by employing the different tools. For example, Apache Kafka, a distributed streaming platform provides three main functionalities namely publisher, subscriber and consumer. Splunk is another one that helps to catch, index, and correlate real-time data in a searchable repository. Through that it is used to create reports, alerts, dashboards, graphs another data representation. Splunk can be used to manage different applications. It also can be employed for business and web analytics as well as security and compliance. KNIME is also a tool which is used to selectively execute few or every analysis step, create data flows, and investigate output, models, and interactive views. This tool is based on Eclipse is developed in Java and employs its extension mechanism to add plug-ins providing other functionality. Apache Spark is also open source framework that gives in-memory computing functionality to provide speed, a generalized execution model to assist various applications. It supports API in different languages like Java, Scala, and Python for ease of development. Apache Flink is competitor of Spark which provides the functionalities similar to Spark but uses mini-batch streaming processing rather than pure streaming processing Moreover, R is a tool for analytics, free software environment for statistical/mining techniques and graphics. It provides R language for writing the code for data science analyst, forensics analyst, statisticians and researchers to develop methods for getting solutions . It also provides the support for Hadoop and Hive.

- Data Visualization

To visualize the data from broad perspective of business, Tableau is a very efficient and powerful tool. It is a fastest growing visualization tool which is frequently applied in the business intelligence and online shopping, bio-chemical industries and academia for research purpose. Tableau is very speedy while analyzing the data. It provides different ways like dashboards, worksheets and others to visualize. Plotly is another library that is mainly used to make creating graphs faster and more efficient. It can also be used to style interactive graphs with Jupyter notebook.

3. SOFT COMPUTING APPROACHES

SC approaches can be studied in three major components:

3.1 Fuzzy Logic

Fuzzy logic (FL) algorithm helps to handle complex problems having uncertainty. Uncertainty can be visualized in various forms as not clear, unknown, random, not sharp, imprecise, approximate, vague, ambiguous and other forms (Ross, 2005). To understand the fuzzy concept, Zadeh (Ross et al., 2002) classified three statements into three different concepts as Vague, Fuzzy and Probability E.g;

Statement 1: He will do this work soon. => **Vague** statement (does not give any information about how much time)
Statement 2: He will do this work in few days. => **Fuzzy** statement (it has uncertainty but gives some notion of time in which he can finish the work)
Statement 3: I will do this work soon within 2 days from 15/06/2020. => **Probability** statement as it has uncertainty with quantifiable imprecision

Hence, fuzzy logic theory is able to give approximate, fast but not exact solutions to those problems where analytical solution or numerical relations is lacking. To handle this uncertainty, fuzzy logic considers multi-valued logic i.e. any value between 0 and 1[0 and 1 both are inclusive]. Typically, a fuzzy system considers three major steps as fuzzification, fuzzy rule base and fuzzy inference mechanism for finding solution for the problem using fuzzy logic.

3.1.1 Fuzzification

Fuzzification is the means of converting crisp input (variables) to fuzzy input variable. It involves defining input variable/variables with its membership value. These variables are known as linguistic variables (Zadeh, 1975). The values in these variables are words or sentences in natural language. E.g. Temperature is **linguistic variable** (Zadeh, 1975; Meier et al. 2008) if it consists of values as hot, cool, warm, comfortable in natural language.

A linguistic variable is defined by a quintuple (V, T, U, R, S) where V is the name of the linguistic variable, T is the set of terms of V (each term of V is a fuzzy variable), U is the universe of discourse, R is a syntactic rule for producing the name of the terms, and S is a semantic rule for relating each term with its meaning, that is, a fuzzy set defined on U. E.g.

V can be considered as a linguistic variable having the name (label) "Temperature " with U= [-60,60]. Then terms of this variable, T (Temperature) can be taken as PostiveHigh, PositiveLow, NegativeLow, NegativeHigh, and Zero. Every term in the set T is a fuzzy set. R is a syntactic rule which spawns terms of V and S is the rule that can be defined (using the concept of fuzzy set) using (1).

$$S (PositiveLow) = \{(u, \mu_{PositiveLow} (u)) \text{ where u belong to the set U}\} \tag{1}$$

where, PositiveLow is a **fuzzy set**/fuzzy variable which can be defined mathematically by assigning to each possible individual (u) in the universe of discourse (U) a value representing its degree (grade) of membership (μ) in the fuzzy set. This degree of membership lies between 0 and 1 means and can be calculated from using one of the membership functions. These functions include a vast variety of functions namely triangular, trapezoidal, gaussian, generalized bell, sigmoidal and others [8].

Figure 1 shows different membership functions as triangular/ trapezoidal function to assign membership value (μ) to different fuzzy sets for "Temperature" variable. x-axis in Figure 1 is providing temperature from the universe(U). Membership function corresponding to different terms of "Temperature" variable (V) namely PostiveHigh, PositiveLow, NegativeLow, NegativeHigh, and Zero are represented on y-axis as shown in Figure 1.

Figure 1. Membership functions for "Temperature" (linguistic variable)

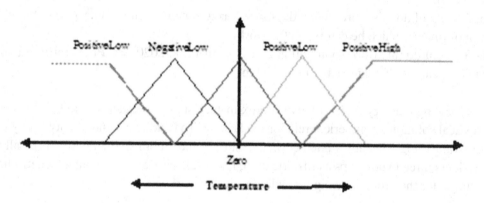

Various set operations like crisp set can also be made on fuzzy set. Let universe of discourse(U) be set of temperatures as {10,20,30}, fuzzy set Hot Weather (H)= {(10,0.2), (20,0.4),(30,0.7) },and Cold Weather (C) = {(10,0.8), (20,0.6),(30,0.1) } then,

Union: $H \lor C = \{u, \max (\mu_H (u), \mu_C (u))\} = \{(10, 0.8), (20, 0.6), (30, 0.7)\}$
Intersection: $H \land C = \{u, \min (\mu_H (u), \mu_C (u))\} = \{(10, 0.2), (20, 0.4), (30, 0.1)\}$
Complement: $H' = \{u, 1- (\mu_H (u)\} = \{(10, 0.8), (20, 0.6), (30, 0.3)\}$
$C' = \{u, 1- (\mu_C (u)\} = \{(10, 0.2), (20, 0.4), (30, 0.9)\}$
Difference: $H/C = H \land C'$ and $C/H = C \land H'$

Additionally, fuzzy relations can be defined on fuzzy sets. If C and D are fuzzy sets on the universe of discourse X and Y respectively, relation R= C x D which is subset of X x Y, whose membership function is computed by using (2).

$$\mu_R (x,y) = \mu_{C \times D} (x,y)) = \{min((\mu_C (x), \mu_D (y))\} \tag{2}$$

Basic operations discussed for fuzzy sets can also be applied on fuzzy relations. Moreover, another popular operator is fuzzy composition. A fuzzy composition(C) can be defined using two common forms namely max-min and max-product shown by (3) and (4) if P and Q be two relations mapping from universe R to universe S and from universe S to universe T respectively.

$$C = P \circ Q = max \ s \ \epsilon \ S \ \{min \ ((\mu_P (r, s), \mu_Q (s, t))\} \tag{3}$$

$$C = P \circ Q = max \ s \ \epsilon \ S \ \{\mu_P (r,s) * \mu_Q (s, t))\} \tag{4}$$

Example: Fuzzy composition operation can be used to find the association of animals with the different symptoms of diseases. Let A = {A1, A2, A3} and D = {D1, D2} represent a set of 3 different animals and a set of 2 animal diseases respectively. In addition to this, there is another set S = {S1, S2} which shows the symptoms of diseases. Let P and Q be two fuzzy relations defined as below

$$\text{Fuzzy Relation P} = A \times D = \begin{matrix} 0.1 & 0.2 \\ 0.3 & 0.6 \\ 0.0 & 0.1 \end{matrix} .$$

$$\text{Fuzzy Relation Q} = D \times S = \begin{matrix} 0.9 & 0.8 \\ 0.7 & 0.5 \end{matrix} .$$

$$\text{Fuzzy composition using max-min using (3)} = P \circ Q = \begin{matrix} 0.2 & 0.2 \\ 0.6 & 0.5 \\ 0.1 & 0.1 \end{matrix} .$$

Fuzzy composition using max-product using (4) = P ∘ Q = $\begin{matrix} 0.14 & 0.10 \\ 0.42 & 0.30 \\ 0.07 & 0.05 \end{matrix}$ .In fuzzification process, grade of membership can also be computed using method of intuition, inference methods, neural network, genetic algorithm, rank ordering and others.

3.1.2 Fuzzy Rule Base

Fuzzy Rule base is a database of if-then rules known as fuzzy rules. These rules can be represented as fuzzy relation (R) using (5) which is equivalent to fuzzy implication shown by (6).

$$\text{R: \textbf{If service is GOOD} then } \textit{tip is HIGH} \tag{5}$$

$$R: S_{GOOD} \rightarrow T_{HIGH} \tag{6}$$

Where GOOD and HIGH are the fuzzy sets over the universe of discourses S and T respectively. Bold part and italic part in (5) is known as antecedent (premise) and consequence (conclusion) respectively. Antecedent part in a fuzzy rule can have more than one antecedent part connected by and ($\wedge$)/or ($\vee$) operator. A fuzzy relation R is equal to (GOOD x HIGH) $^{\vee}$ (GOOD' x T) and membership function is computed by (7).

$$\mu_R \text{ (service, tip)} = \max \{(\mu_{GOOD} \text{ (service)} ^{\wedge} \mu_{HIGH} \text{ (tip)}), (1 - \mu_{GOOD} \text{ (service)})\} \tag{7}$$

This fuzzy relation can be used to find the consequent part if a new antecedent part (if service is **POOR**) is given using composition operator between fuzzy set **POOR** and relation matrix R obtained from (7) discussed in above section. There exists if-then-else form of fuzzy rules as well (Ross, 2005).

Number of feasible fuzzy rules in database is dependent on number of linguistic variables (input) and number of terms (linguistic states) present in each fuzzy set and then can be denoted by employing a fuzzy rule base matrix. For example, if there are two linguistic variables, **service** which takes three values as GOOD (G), BAD (B), and SATISFACTORY(S) and **food quality** which takes three values EXCELLENT (E), FAIR(F), UNSATISFACTORY (U) then total count of possible fuzzy rules (using "AND" in antecedents) in fuzzy rule base will be 3*3=9.

3.1.3 Fuzzy Inference Mechanisms

Once set of fuzzy rules is designed, it can be used to infer consequent part by employing fuzzy inference mechanisms if a new antecedent (input) is presented in fuzzy system. There are two most popular approaches namely Mamdani and Sugeno(Ross, 2005). The first approach i.e. Mamdani approach is suitable when consequent part of fuzzy rules is a fuzzy set. It employs max-min/ max-product method to infer the information from each rule corresponding to given inputs. Consequently, corresponding output fuzzy function from each fired inference rule is obtained. The output fuzzy functions from every fired rules corresponding to inputs are found. As the output received is a fuzzy, hence one of the defuzzification methods such as maxima methods, centroid methods and weighted average method (Ross, 2005) is used to compute the crisp input. Second one, Sugeno is used when consequent part of rules can be expressed as a polynomial function of input variables. As this function is a crisp function, the output obtained after fired rules need not be defuzzified. Hence, result in Sugeno model can simply be calculated by a weighted average method (Ross, 2005). Weight against each fired rule can be computed by antecedent part.

3.2 Artificial Neural Networks

Artificial neural network (ANN) aims to mimic the human's biological neural network which consists of cell body connected with axon and dendrites having synaptic inputs with different strength.

Figure 2 shows that how ANN can be modeled by considering the features/ variables v_1, v_2 and v_3 as neurons (synaptic inputs) having the weights/strengths s_1, s_2, and s_3 respectively(synaptic weights). It also has bias weight (b) as an input. "$\sum$" (Sum) computes sum of weighted input from all input neurons along with the bias using (8) and apply activation function (AF) over it to make a decision (output).

Figure 2. A basic ANN model

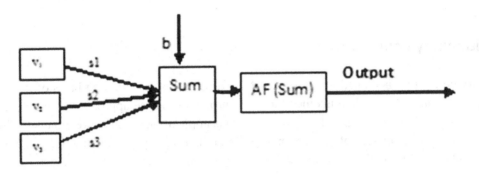

There are a various activation functions(AF) such as threshold, soft margin, sigmoid, hyperbolic tangent function, rectified linear unit, leaky linear unit and others to find the final output.

$$\text{Sum} = \sum(v_i . s_i) + b = (v_1 . s_1) + (v_2 . s_2) + (v_3 . s_3) + b \qquad (8)$$

ANNs have ability to learn from examples (data) and gives the approximate solutions. These networks can work as both supervised as well as unsupervised learners in various applications such as topic modeling, MRI Image classification for different diseases etc. These networks may be either single/multiple feed forward networks or single/multiple recurrent network.

A fundamental feed forward neural network such as Perceptron (Sivanandam & Deepa, 2007) has only two layers. One is input layer having number of neurons depending on the input variable/features in the problem and second one is output layer which gives us the output(also has neurons). Single layered network are not apt to solve XOR type of problems which are non-linear in nature. While, a network with hidden layers having hidden neurons in between input layer and output layers is known as multilayer neural network and has the ability to solve non-linear problem like XOR. A popular network of this kind of network is Multi-layer Perceptron. Although, many hidden layers may be used to get the solution, it is proved by the researchers that only single/one hidden layer is able to solve non-linear problems (Haykin, 2010). A feed forward network with at least one feedback loop (output is fed back to each input neuron of ANN is known as recurrent neural network. A popular example of such kind of network is long term short term memory (LSTM) that is being used heavily for times series data such as chat bots, question answering systems, voice recognition etc.

The neural networks use a variety of learning rule such as hebbian, competitive, boltzmann, backpropgation and other for training/ learning the networks. These are susceptible to various parameters such as learning rate, momentum factor and others. Convergence of a neural network depends on learning rate as well as momentum factor. Learning rate lies in between 0 and 1 and should be chosen carefully / empirically which is used in weight updation process. Momentum factor is used in backpropgation learning for faster convergence.

Recently, deep learning neural networks (Aggarwal, 2018) have emerged which has several hidden layers between input and output layers. It is also being used in various applications such as image classification, machine translation, IoT forensics and others. Convolution neural network, Alexnet, VGG 16, Resnet and others are widespread deep neural networks for the problems where a large amount of data with numerous features is present. In practice, deep learning network are equipped with inherent feature engineering.

3.3 Evolutionary computing

Evolutionary computing is coined for those set of approaches that have strong basis of natural evolution of a population and provide outcomes for given problems. These approaches are nature-inspired approaches toward optimization problems. It has various applications such as weapon detection, drug-target prediction, and discovery of interaction disease prediction, topic modeling and many others. In general, evolutionary computing algorithms typically work in following steps:

Step1: Initialize the population.
Step 2: Evaluate the individuals using fitness function.
Step 3: Terminate if convergence criteria is met else go to Step 4.
Step 4: Apply selection
Step 4: Do variation and goto Step 2.

Evolutionary computing techniques take account of Genetic Algorithms (GA), Genetic Programming (GP), Grammatical Evolution (GE), and Evolutionary Algorithms (EAs) (Volta et al., 2000; Sen, 2015; Sloss & Gustafson, 2020). Genetic algorithms is the most popular approach, based on idea of natural selection gives possible solution of a genetically formulated problem presented in the form of chromosomes. GA uses key operators as reproduction, crossover, selection, and mutation. GA procedure needs some key parameters for its implementation as population size, number of generations, crossover probability as well as mutation rates. The study done by (Hermawanto, 2013) shows a working example of genetic algorithm for small mathematical function having four variables. Similar to GA, Memetic Algorithm (Bagavathi & Saraniya, 2019) is developed that is motivated from Dawkins' notion of a meme and includes non obligatory local search process. This approach selects a cluster of memes as an initial population and progress towards optimal solution by applying crossover and mutation operator by employing personal experience of the memes. Memetic algorithms converge faster as compared to GA because of its local search process. GP aims to find out the optimal executable program to meet its objective function. Similar to GP, GE approaches are a special type of GA uses genetic operators to an integer string, subsequently mapped to a program (or similar) through the use of a grammar. Further, evolutionary al algorithms use the problem dependent structures and extra natural for the task as compared to GA. In EA, the genetic operators take original structure and solve the problem. EA methods include swarm intelligence algorithms, evaluation strategies, evolution programming and others (Volta et al., 2000; Bagavathi & Saraniya, 2019). These approaches differ from each other the way it represent the individuals in the populations. E.g. GA presents individuals in the form of chromosome, GP and GE employ tree and Backus-Naur Form grammar (Sen, 2015), and particle swam intelligence (one of swarm intelligence algorithm) uses particles (Bagavathi & Saraniya, 2019).

Typically, EA algorithms aim to optimize i.e. minimize/maximize the objective function. There may be single or multiple objective functions depending on the problem to be modeled. The class of approaches that tackle multi-objective problems called as multi-objective evolutionary algorithms (Deb, 2001).

4. HYBRID SOFT COMPUTING

We discussed a set of problem-solving techniques under the umbrella of soft computing such as Neural network, genetic algorithm, and Fuzzy logic. Each of these techniques has been applied in various application domains to solve real world complex problems. These techniques have different reasoning and searching method. So, it is difficult to determine the appropriate model for a given application. There are some techniques which uses a combination of techniques to improve upon the limitation of each of this approach. Researchers have analyzed combinations of soft computing technologies for further improvement like use of Fuzzy logic to decide neural network as well as genetic algorithm parameters.

A hybrid soft computing technique which combines two soft computing approaches has been applied (Tahmasebi & Hezarkhani, 2012). A combination of Artificial neural network and Fuzzy logic is applied. Genetic algorithm is also applied for optimization of network parameters. Shigeyasu Kawaji also applied hybrid soft computing approach for identification of systems (Kawaji, 2002).

5. APPLICATION OF SOFT COMPUTING IN BIG DATA

Big data is generated from various sources. This vast amount of data does not only symbolize about the size of data but also the intelligence and values it contains in it. The business organizations get value from it in terms of decision support systems, develop innovative products and analyze and predict customer needs and behavior and competencies related to growth of business. Government organization also use the power of big data to improve national security and overcome national challenges like terrorism, natural disasters, providing health care facilities etc. It will help them to better serve their citizens by preventing fraud and crime and increase citizen engagement in public affairs. There are many goals which we can achieve with the help of vast amount of data available to us but it also brings new challenges like security, privacy, need for new technology as well as human skills. There is strong need for efficient methods to perform accurate and timely analysis of the data set available in various fields (Kim et al., 2014).

The government has availability of huge data about the citizens from different sources like healthcare, financial planning, buying behavior makes it easy for them to plan and manage resources accordingly. Each country wants to make future plan based on the problems they are facing. Japan has used large data available from tsunami, earthquake and nuclear power plant disaster for reconstruction of affected areas. The availability of big data helps countries to establish administrative analytics, design required infrastructure and plan for welfare benefits. Different departments or ministries like Forestry, food and agriculture utilize the huge data available to them for betterment of services (Kim et al., 2014).

The field of artificial intelligence portrays technologies which try to mimic the natural intelligence behavior of humans and animals. Complex and vague problems are solved by artificial intelligence. Soft computing and the computational intelligence are popular in Artificial intelligence. It is applied in various domains like healthcare, finance, agriculture, military applications, video games and many more. Soft computing includes several techniques like fuzzy logic approach, artificial neural networks, evolutionary computation and probabilistic reasoning (Omolaye et al., 2017).

In this section, we will discuss about the applications of soft computing techniques in the field of agriculture for plant disease detection.

Soft Computing in Agriculture

Food is essential for human body which comes from agriculture. However, agriculture is an important source of economy for a country. There are many issues in the field of agriculture like plant diseases. Plant diseases impact the quantity as well as the quality of plant produce. If the advancement of technology can give an early insight about these, then it will be very beneficial for us. Artificial neural networks (ANN), genetic programming and fuzzy logic are the Soft computing methods which can be used as an alternative method for plant disease identification (Singh & Misra, 2017), (Ghaiwat &Arora, 2014) (Pujari etal., 2015),(Huang et al., 2018),(Gautam et al., 2020).

Plant Disease Detection

Plant diseases occur due to fungi, virus and bacteria etc. It is a common practice to call the experts for detection of diseases in plant. A team of agricultural experts visit the agricultural land and do the manual observation regularly for a period of time. So, this is very time consuming and costly process. Most of the time, farmers are not able to bear the expenditure on this early and timely disease detection process. The advancement of technology can serve as a tool which can automatically identify the disease by observing the images of the infected plants. This process is easier, cheaper as well as accurate. Now days, robots are also available which guide the whole plant disease identification process and takes care about it.

In general, when plant is infected, it develops some spots on the leaves or the color of affected area changes. The images of plants can be compared to find out the disease. Image processing is used to figure out the disease affected areas of leaves. The process of assignment of a label to each pixel is known as image segmentation. The output of image segmentation is set of segments that cover the whole image.

In the first step, the leaf images are captured through digital camera. The in the next step, these captured images are preprocessed to remove any distortion and enhance the image quality. During preprocessing, image clipping is performed which separates the image from its background. Image enhancement is performed with image smoothing. Image smoothing improve the visual quality of images while the contrast is enhanced through image enhancement. (Singh & Misra, 2017)

Authors describe about different classification algorithms for plant leaf disease identification through image processing techniques. The classification techniques like k-Nearest Neighbor Classifier, Support Vector Machine, Artificial neural network, Self-organizing maps, probabilistic neural network and Fuzzy logic have been discussed along with the issues associated with each algorithm. The other soft computing methods can also be used as an alternative method for plant disease identification (Ghaiwat &Arora, 2014).

Fungi takes its food from the plant on which it lives. It damages the plant by creating rusts, scabs and blotches. Authors have conducted early detection of fungal diseases on various crops using image analysis. They have applied algorithms on four types of crops viz. Fruit crop, vegetable crop, commercial crop and cereal crop. Neural network, SVM and other algorithms have been applied for classification purpose (Pujari etal., 2015).

Precision agriculture is farming concept based on establishing a decision support system for better crop management. It is also known as satellite farming. The data obtained from more than thousand active satellite orbiting earth provide data about earth surface. This data is captured every second and gets stored. This large-scale data generated from these sources is used for agricultural remote sensing which considers inter and intra field variability. Author describes the process of big data obtained from remote sensing of agricultural data),(Huang et al., 2018).

The temperature is an influential factor in irrigation and agriculture. Various activities related to agriculture needs to be planned according to temperature. Soft computing models have been used by various researchers to predict the air temperature. The study applies Adaptive neuro-fuzzy inference system for prediction of air temperature. Two optimization algorithms Genetic algorithm and ant colony optimization algorithm have been used along with Adaptive neuro-fuzzy inference system as they have better performance and reasonable convergence speed in the optimization of complicated phenomena or large computational tasks (Gautam et al., 2020).

Soft Computing for Smart Cities

With the technological advancement in the field of information and communication technology and a need for sustainable development of cities, the concept of smart cities is emerging. Internet of Things (IoT) has become an integral part of smart cities. IoT is all about network of smart connected devices which facilitates in smart and intelligent devices and services. IoT also helps in collection of large-scale data from different locations. IoT is used in smart homes to control home appliances, maintain temperature and improve security for the smart community. IoT is commonly used for smart transport in vehicle tracking, smart parking and in providing security solutions (Omar et al.,2020).

The field is gaining popularity and there is need to analyze the huge amount of data available. Researchers have applied soft computing techniques like ANN, deep neural network, fuzzy logic which reduce the complexity of large-scale data and are helpful in extracting information from this big data obtained from the resources.

Traffic Congestion Monitoring and Control System in Smart Cities

With the growth in population, the number of vehicles on the roads are also increasing day by day all. This problem is being faced by almost every country of the world. In case of narrow roads, this problem increases many folds if the traffic is not controlled. With the advent of smart cities, the traffic management problem needs to be addressed very carefully. The traffic congestion also results in increase of air pollution and loss of valuable time and money. Therefore, a smart system is required which can figure out traffic congestion on the road and assist the users. It is the need of the hour to work upon Intelligent transportation system which can monitor and manage the traffic congestion so that the travel time and air pollution can be reduced and there should be smooth mobility of vehicles (Omar et al.,2020), (Elleuch et al.,2016).

Intelligent traffic monitoring and control system is generally managed by the government. This serves as a monitoring system, which monitors if the people operating vehicle are following traffic rules or not. Simultaneously, it monitors the traffic congestion state on roads in real time and the management of traffic is done through its decision support system. By determining the congestion status on different roads, it will help in guiding alternate routes to reach to destination. It will also help the government to better traffic management by making future plans like construction of fly overs etc. (Ashifuddin & Rehena.,2019).

To better manage traffic, instead of conventional fixed time traffic lights, the fuzzy logic-controlled traffic lights have been suggested. A simulation study has been conducted to illustrate intelligent fuzzy based system for traffic signal control (Abiyev et al., 2017). Another study also emphasis on using intelligent signal control where a combination of different signal control strategies are combined using fuzzy concept in hardware device. The simulation results depict a comparison of various control strategies in comparison with Fuzzy based traffic light control strategy (Jin et al., 2016).

ANN in Traffic Management

Researchers have proposed an efficient traffic management system which classifies categorizes the on-road traffic into three categories depending upon the congestion on the road. The three categories of congestion is High, medium and free flow. To estimate congestion level, certain information is required like number of vehicles present on road at a particular time along with the speed of vehicles. This information is captured with the help of sensors fitted on the road. Artificial neural network is used to assess the level of congestion on the road segments (Fadlullah et al.,2017).

The traffic monitoring and controlling system has three major components. The first part is related to collection of traffic data. The traffic data is collected with the help of sensors installed on the road. The sensors capture the number of vehicles and speed of each vehicle. The captured data is sent and stored in remote data analysis unit preferably to an online cloud service. This data is used to calculate the average speed of the vehicles and traffic density of the road for better planning and management.

Authors have proposed a traffic monitoring and controlling system using artificial neural network. It provides the congestion status of various road segments. Artificial neural network is applied in that the input layer accepts two traffic parameters viz. speed of vehicle and traffic density. The ANN model determines the congestion status of different roads. (Fadlullah et al.,2017).

Studies have been conducted to control network traffic as well. The routing protocols guide the network traffic movement. However, that cannot utilize the previous experience data to avoid same problems to occur in future. Therefore, there is an essential requirement for network traffic control to avoid congestion. The deep learning, a machine learning technique, has been proved fruitful in many disciplines. Convolutional neural network has been applied in network traffic control such as suggesting routing methodology in the wireless networks. Authors have applied deep convolutional neural network for introducing intelligence in network traffic control and management.

They obtained better performance in terms of average delay and packet loss rate in comparison to existing routing methods (Tang et al., 2017).

Soft Computing in Software Domain

Generally, we develop code to automate various applications. Developers contribute towards the filed in this way. In any organization or in an opensource development environment, we have huge amount of data generated in the process of development. This data can be the list of bugs reported over a period of time or the different versions of software developed, from the communication among the developers. This huge amount of data can serve in various analysis and outcomes which can facilitate the development process in identifying the error prone modules present in the source code or identifying appropriate developer who can fix the bug in less time or predicting the future bugs. The analysis of software bug reports has been conducted by various researchers in correctly labelling the issue reports and software fault prediction. Soft computing techniques have played a big role in solving these issues and provide a solution.

Software Fault Prediction

A reliable software is one which has as few bugs present in it so that there is less number of failures. Timely identification of the bugs present in the source code is important so that those errors can be fixed. It has been observed that some software modules are more prone to failures as compared to others. So, timely identification of these modules will give time to further test the software. Author has applied different soft computing methods such as artificial neural network, Support Vector machine to predict the fault prone modules. They have also applied hybrid soft computing method called ANFIS- Adaptive neuro Fuzzy Inference system (Tang et al., 2017).

Similarly, the concern of mislabeling of issue report leads to justification of accuracy of various studies which considers the mislabeled dataset for their studies. The identification and assignment of labels to software issue reports is also performed by researchers. Fuzzy approach from the soft computing domain is applied for the assessment of label information. A comparison among the performance achieved with machine learning algorithms and fuzzy approach is performed which shows that fuzzy approach performs better as compared to machine learning algorithms (Chawla & Singh, 2017).

Soft Computing in Stock Market Domain

Stock market is one of the most attractive and profitable investment arenas. The prediction of stock prices and movement can open enormous opportunities for investors and also helps the organizations in determining various decisions related to the areas of possessions, acquisition, advertising, planning as only using historical data about the stock does not accurately predict the future prices. It is also said that the stock prices are unpredictable. The stock data are most challenging as because of its dynamic nature. The companies are linked with each other via various relationships. So, the change of stock prices of a particular organization would also be affected by organizations that are linked (Rajab & Sharma, 2019).

Stock Value Prediction

The stock value prediction is an interesting and required field. The main intention of stock value prediction is to facilitate the organization for various planning and reduce the risk in decision making. Many researchers have worked on stock value prediction. Different models have been selected for the purpose. Different soft computing models have been applied.

Mohammed Siddique et al applied Artificial neural network model optimized by particle Swarm optimization for predicting next day high price. They have experimented on yahoo stock value and Microsoft stock value (Siddique et al., 2017). Chao Shi et al applied support vector machine (SVM), and artificial neural network (ANN) and hidden Markov model (HMM) (Shi & Zhuang, 2019). Yingmei Chen et al applied graph Convolutional Neural Networks for Stock Price Prediction (Chen et al., 2018).

6. EXPERIMENTATION AND RESULTS

Experiments have been carried out to illustrate the use of one of soft computing techniques. Multilayer Perceptron (MLP) which is one of the neural network models is applied on Bank Marketing data set. This data set was taken from UCI repository [Moro et al., 2014]. MLP is applied as classification technique using Weka tool. Classification accuracy achieved by MLP was 88.18% and 86.88% by Naïve-Bayes classifier. Experiments carried out by ten-fold cross validation depict that the use of MLP as a neural network technique over Naïve-Bayes classifier has produced better results.

7. RESEARCH CHALLENGES

Artificial neural network and Fuzzy logic has been successfully applied for solving various problems in different domains. However, both the methods do not always produce the best results. This is due to the reason that the performance of these algorithms depends on several factors. While using artificial neural network, the performance of the algorithms depends upon various factors such as number of hidden layers, learning rates, assignment of weights. Presence of many layers and nodes in hidden layers causes the network to be more complex. The performance of ANN is impacted by the weights assigned in it. The weights are also controlled by network architecture. So, deciding the architecture is also an issue while designing artificial neural network.

Fuzzy logic works with the help of membership function. There are various membership functions available. One of the issues with using fuzzy technique is choosing the most appropriate membership function.

8. CONCLUSION

Soft computing has gained much familiarity and importance. With the notable advancement in technology, new avenues have been crated. As a result, abundance data sources and the data availability have also opened a new challenging environment to extract useful information from them. Soft computing techniques such as fuzzy logic, neural network and evolutionary algorithms have been applied to help solve the issues related to different domains. The work proposed by researchers also suggests that the future work is going to belong to soft computing category.

There are many applications where soft computing is successfully applied to solve the problem accurately. Soft computing has been applied in various domains. This paper focuses on different soft computing techniques applied in the domain of Agriculture, smart cities, software and stock market. In particular, it discusses the plant disease identification in the field of agriculture and from the smart cities; it talks about traffic congestion management and control. The work gives an insight into various soft computing techniques, methodologies and how these computing techniques are applied to solve issues related to different application areas.

This chapter also discusses hybrid methods like genetic-fuzzy and neuro fuzzy. Hybrid methods overcome the limitations of the single method. By using fuzzy approach along with neural network, genetic algorithm and support vector machine, the performance improves.

REFERENCES

Abiyev, R. H., Ma'aitah, M., & Sonyel, B. (2017, December). Fuzzy Logic Traffic Lights Control (FLTLC). In *Proceedings of the 2017 9th International Conference on Education Technology and Computers* (pp. 233-238). Academic Press.

Aggarwal, C. C. (2018). Neural networks and deep learning. Springer.

Ashifuddin Mondal, M., & Rehena, Z. (2019, May). Intelligent Traffic Congestion Classification System using Artificial Neural Network. In *Companion Proceedings of the 2019 World Wide Web Conference* (pp. 110-116). Academic Press.

Bagavathi, C., & Saraniya, O. (2019). Evolutionary Mapping Techniques for Systolic Computing System. In Deep Learning and Parallel Computing Environment for Bioengineering Systems (pp. 207-223). Academic Press.

Bonissone, P. P., Chen, Y. T., Goebel, K., & Khedkar, P. S. (1999). Hybrid soft computing systems: Industrial and commercial applications. *Proceedings of the IEEE, 87*(9), 1641–1667. doi:10.1109/5.784245

Chawla, I., & Singh, S. K. (2017). A fuzzy-based approach for bug report categorisation. *International Journal of Intelligent Systems Technologies and Applications, 16*(4), 319–341.

Chen, Y., Wei, Z., & Huang, X. (2018, October). Incorporating corporation relationship via graph convolutional neural networks for stock price prediction. *Proceedings of the 27th ACM International Conference on Information and Knowledge Management*, 1655-1658.

Cianchetti, M., Laschi, C., Menciassi, A., & Dario, P. (2018). Biomedical applications of soft robotics. *Nature Reviews. Materials, 3*(6), 143–153. doi:10.103841578-018-0022-y

Das, H., Naik, B., & Behera, H. S. (2020). A Hybrid Neuro-Fuzzy and Feature Reduction Model for Classification. *Advances in Fuzzy Systems, 2020*, 2020. doi:10.1155/2020/4152049

Deb, K. (2001). *Multi-objective optimization using evolutionary algorithms* (Vol. 16). John Wiley & Sons.

Elleuch, W., Wali, A., & Alimi, A. M. (2016, December). Intelligent Traffic Congestion Prediction System Based on ANN and Decision Tree Using Big GPS Traces. In *International Conference on Intelligent Systems Design and Applications* (pp. 478-487). Springer.

Erturk, E., & Sezer, E. A. (2015). A comparison of some soft computing methods for software fault prediction. *Expert Systems with Applications, 42*(4), 1872–1879.

Fadlullah, Z. M., Tang, F., Mao, B., Kato, N., Akashi, O., Inoue, T., & Mizutani, K. (2017). State-of-the-art deep learning: Evolving machine intelligence toward tomorrow's intelligent network traffic control systems. *IEEE Communications Surveys and Tutorials, 19*(4), 2432–2455.

Gautam, K., Puri, V., Tromp, J. G., Nguyen, N. G., & Van Le, C. (2020). Internet of Things (IoT) and Deep Neural Network-Based Intelligent and Conceptual Model for Smart City. In *Frontiers in Intelligent Computing: Theory and Applications* (pp. 287–300). Springer.

Ghaiwat, S. N., & Arora, P. (2014). Detection and classification of plant leaf diseases using image processing techniques: A review. *International Journal of Recent Advances in Engineering & Technology, 2*(3), 1–7.

Gupta, B. B., Agrawal, D. P., Yamaguchi, S., & Sheng, M. (2020). *Soft computing techniques for big data and cloud computing.* Academic Press.

Haykin, S. (2010). *Neural Networks and Learning Machines, 3/E.* Pearson Education India.

Hermawanto, D. (2013). *Genetic algorithm for solving simple mathematical equality problem.* arXiv preprint arXiv:1308.4675.

Huang, Y., Chen, Z. X., Tao, Y. U., Huang, X. Z., & Gu, X. F. (2018). Agricultural remote sensing big data: Management and applications. *Journal of Integrative Agriculture, 17*(9), 1915–1931.

Jin, J., Ma, X., Koskinen, K., Rychlik, M., & Kosonen, I. (2016). Evaluation of fuzzy intelligent traffic signal control (FITS) system using traffic simulation. In *Transportation Research Board 95th Annual Meeting, Finland* (p. 11). Academic Press.

Kawaji, S. (2002). Hybrid soft computing approaches to identification of nonlinear systems. *IFAC Proceedings Volumes, 35*(1), 187-192.

Kim, G. H., Trimi, S., & Chung, J. H. (2014). Big-data applications in the government sector. *Communications of the ACM, 57*(3), 78–85.

Kitchin, R. (2014). The data revolution: Big data, open data, data infrastructures and their consequences. *Sage (Atlanta, Ga.).* Advance online publication. doi:10.4135/9781473909472

Meier, A., Schindler, G., & Werro, N. (2008). Fuzzy classification on relational databases. In *Handbook of research on fuzzy information processing in databases* (pp. 586–614). IGI Global.

Moro, S., Cortez, P., & Rita, P. (2014). A data-driven approach to predict the success of bank telemarketing. *Decision Support Systems, 62*, 22–31.

Omar, T., Bovard, D., & Tran, H. (2020, April). Smart Cities Traffic Congestion Monitoring and Control System. In *Proceedings of the 2020 ACM Southeast Conference* (pp. 115-121). Academic Press.

Omolaye, P. O., Mom, J. M., & Igwue, G. A. (2017). A Holistic Review of Soft Computing Techniques. *Applied and Computational Mathematics, 6*(2), 93.

Pujari, J. D., Yakkundimath, R., & Byadgi, A. S. (2015). Image processing based detection of fungal diseases in plants. *Procedia Computer Science, 46*, 1802–1808.

Rajab, S., & Sharma, V. (2019). An interpretable neuro-fuzzy approach to stock price forecasting. *Soft Computing, 23*(3), 921–936.

Ross, T. J. (2005). *Fuzzy logic with engineering applications.* John Wiley & Sons.

Ross, T. J., Booker, J. M., & Parkinson, W. J. (Eds.). (2002). *Fuzzy logic and probability applications: bridging the gap.* Society for Industrial and Applied Mathematics. doi:10.1137/1.9780898718447

Sanchez, E., Shibata, T., & Zadeh, L. A. (1997). *Genetic algorithms and fuzzy logic systems: Soft computing perspectives* (Vol. 7). World Scientific. doi:10.1142/2896

Santana, E. F. Z., Chaves, A. P., Gerosa, M. A., Kon, F., & Milojicic, D. S. (2017). Software platforms for smart cities: Concepts, requirements, challenges, and a unified reference architecture. *ACM Computing Surveys (Csur)*, *50*(6), 1–37.

Sen, S. (2015). A survey of intrusion detection systems using evolutionary computation. In *Bio-inspired computation in telecommunications* (pp. 73–94). Morgan Kaufmann.

Shi, C., & Zhuang, X. (2019). A Study Concerning Soft Computing Approaches for Stock Price Forecasting. *Axioms*, *8*(4), 116.

Siddique, M., DebdulalPanda, S. D., & Mohapatra, S. K. (2017). A Hybrid Forecasting Model For Stock Value Prediction Using Soft Computing. *International Journal of Pure and Applied Mathematics*, *117*(19), 357–363.

Singh, V., & Misra, A. K. (2017). Detection of plant leaf diseases using image segmentation and soft computing techniques. *Information Processing in Agriculture*, *4*(1), 41–49.

Sivanandam, S. N., & Deepa, S. N. (2007). *Principles of soft computing (with CD)*. John Wiley & Sons.

Sloss, A. N., & Gustafson, S. (2020). 2019 Evolutionary algorithms review. *Genetic Programming Theory into Practice*, *17*, 307–344.

Tahmasebi, P., & Hezarkhani, A. (2012). A hybrid neural networks-fuzzy logic-genetic algorithm for grade estimation. *Computers & Geosciences*, *42*, 18–27.

Tang, F., Mao, B., Fadlullah, Z. M., Kato, N., Akashi, O., Inoue, T., & Mizutani, K. (2017). On removing routing protocol from future wireless networks: A real-time deep learning approach for intelligent traffic control. *IEEE Wireless Communications*, *25*(1), 154–160.

Volta, G., Jaeger, E. P., Vazquezmontiel, S., & Hibbs, R. (2000). Introduction to evolutionary computing techniques. In *Proceedings of the electronic Technology Directions to the* (pp. 122-127). Academic Press.

Zadeh, L. A. (1975). The concept of a linguistic variable and its application to approximate reasoning-III. *Information Sciences*, *9*(1), 43–80. doi:10.1016/0020-0255(75)90017-1

Zhou, Z. H., Chawla, N. V., Jin, Y., & Williams, G. J. (2014). Big data opportunities and challenges: Discussions from data analytics perspectives [discussion forum]. *IEEE Computational Intelligence Magazine*, *9*(4), 62–74. doi:10.1109/MCI.2014.2350953

Chapter 3
Emerging Trends of Big Data in Cloud Computing

Poonam Nandal
https://orcid.org/0000-0002-2684-4354
Manav Rachna International Institute of Research and Studies, India

Deepa Bura
Manav Rachna International Institute of Research and Studies, India

Meeta Singh
https://orcid.org/0000-0003-4175-467X
Manav Rachna International Institute of Research and Studies, India

ABSTRACT

In today's world where data is accumulating at an ever-increasing rate, processing of this big data was a necessity rather than a need. This required some tools for processing as well as analysis of the data that could be achieved to obtain some meaningful result or outcome out of it. There are many tools available in market which could be used for processing of big data. But the main focus on this chapter is on Apache Hadoop which could be regarded as an open source software based framework which could be efficiently deployed for processing, storing, analyzing, and to produce meaningful insights from large sets of data. It is always said that if exponential increase of data is processing challenge then Hadoop could be considered as one of the effective solution for processing, managing, analyzing, and storing this big data. Hadoop versions and components are also illustrated in the later section of the paper. This chapter majorly focuses on the technique, methodology, components, and methodologies adopted by Apache Hadoop software framework for big data processing.

DOI: 10.4018/978-1-7998-6673-2.ch003

INTRODUCTION

The ceaseless increment in the volume and detail of information caught by associations, for example multimedia, Internet of Things (IoT) and the ascent of web-based social networking which has delivered an overpowering stream of information in either organized or unstructured arrangement. Information creation is happening at are line rate, alluded to here in as large data, and has developed as a broadly perceived pattern. Enormous information is evoking consideration from the Academics, governmental organizations, and industries. Enormous information is portrayed by three aspects: (a) data which is used is huge, (b)data which is in use could not be handled with the existing traditional databases, and (c) frequency of data generation, storage, organization and management. However, this enormous information which is generated by big data is changing the way one use to handle business, science, finance, engineering, healthcare, and in the end, the general public. The main focus of Big Data concepts deals with the information of stockpiling the data and using various data mining innovations which have changed the way of information was held by various organizations Olofson and Eastwood (2011). The frequency at which Big Data is increasing is immense. A noteworthy test for data scientists and enthusiasts is that the frequency of data generation is surpassing the capacity to configure as well as implement Big Data in Cloud Computing platform. Its role is no more restricted for managing workloads only, but also for the analyzing the data stored in it.

Cloud computing is a standout amongst one of the most efficient technologies which are used for administration for big business applications and with time has turned itself into a capable design to perform extensive as well as massive scale complex computation. The benefits of Cloud computing incorporate virtualized resources, security, parallel processing capabilities and data administration and its combination with the Data storage. The benefits of Cloud computing platform also comprise cost reduction as the hardware resources are being virtualized and managed effectively, also this helps in providing provisioning, automated task functioning and various other benefits which imparts to efficient administration and better client access Lu and Yang (2013).

With the increase in computational resources to handle and process big data, the data is not only becoming critical for making business decisions but also more valuable in terms of being more comprehendible to the computer. TeraBytes of data is being generated by social networking sites daily. With the increase in shift from traditionally storing data to using cloud platform and paying as per use. The application we use today makes use of various tools which enhances its capacity to store, apprehend, manage and process data that is generated by each one of us, be it of any form that is structured, unstructured or semi structured. There have been remarkable efforts by researchers, data scientists and enthusiasts in the field of big data managing which has resulted in where we are standing today in terms of processing data. Researches in data handling technologies, data mining platforms, file processing system, artificial intelligence, machine learning all are enhancing the way we treat and manage the data we generate daily.

A portion of the main adopters of big data in cloud computing are clients, who used Hadoop technology for processing and storing large data sets which is exceptionally adaptable and versatile platform provided by the cloud vendors like Amazon AWS, IBM and Microsoft Azure, Liu and Chen (2013). Virtualization is one of the base advances material which is extensively used in cloud. It is known as basically creating a logical layer of abstraction which could be hardware related, computer networks or storing data, which helps in enhancing the efficiency of cloud. Singh et al. (2017) compared various load balancing techniques and gave the advantages and disadvantages of each technique.

The objective of this paper is to analyze and have complete knowledge of the status of big data in cloud computing, conditions influencing decision making and the definitions, qualities and grouping all the information regarding the latest researches and work done by the enthusiasts in this platform. This research paper also discusses the basic concepts governing big data, cloud platform, Hadoop technology and various innovations and researches done by the scientists. Even though investigating the difficulties and challenges which are yet to be resolved in this field, this paper also talks about concentrating on the versatility, availability, information uprightness, data transformation, data integration, heterogeneity of data, data integrity and privacy, legal and administrative issues, and also, administration. In this paper we adhere to state various researches conducted by various researchers, characteristics, history, real time application as well as challenges which are still there to be upgraded so as to make the platform even more efficient for a better world. Various technologies, terminologies, emergence and challenges of big data and cloud processing with its various tools and functionalities are explained in later section of this paper.

RELATED WORK

Big data and cloud computing are interrelated to each other, so much work has been done in both these fields to bring out the best in both areas.

Since the concept of big data is mainly related to the idea of storing vast amount of data and cloud computing is often seen as a means of storing this large amount of data and accessing them easily, so many solutions were thus proposed to solve this problem of handling enormous data. Ghemawat et al. (2003) made an attempt to give solutions in order to provide scalability and robustness required by some cloud services in the form of Google File System. The concept of big data analytics uses Map reduce programming model to generate and process big data. An open implementation of this model is Hadoop which uses the Hadoop Distributed File System (HDFS), which is used to replicate datasets. Thusoo et al. (2010) made use of this Hadoop technology in order to process Facebook's large data sets, for which an analytics platform was built. Cloud technologies also had some drawbacks, and keeping this in mind Ananthanarayan and Menache (2009) took up POSIX- based file systems to use as data storage for cloud applications. Zhang et al. (2010) used Hadoop cloud computing techniques in order to process many sequences of images of living cells by using the concept of MATLAB.

Sometimes it is required to integrate numerous data sources, so Cohen et al. (2009) provided a parallel database model for analyzing and integrating the several data sources and this database design supports SQL and MapReduce for combining data sources. Birst provided SaaS as a solution which offered analytics functionalities and business analytics infrastructure which gave customers a model to move gradually from on premise analytics to cloud analytics infrastructure. Lee et al. (2011) had also presented a survey describing features, benefits and some limitations of MapReduce in parallel data analytics.

Cloud is seen as a platform to remotely store the data and access that data with on demand advanced applications offered by cloud servers. Generally, data is outsourced on cloud which usually reduces the burden of maintaining the data and the user is relieved, but what about the integrity of data. The question arises is the integrity of data maintained? In some cases, yes while in others it is a big no, hence to preserve the integrity of data a new scheme was enabled which allowed users to verify whether their data was maintained with correctness or not. The user's auditability for the data stored in cloud was very important in order to ensure the user's that their data was preserved in the cloud by the cloud servers. Ateniese et al (2007) took up this scheme of public auditability in their "provable data possession" model to ensure the possession of data on storages which were untrusted. But when their technique was used directly, the protocol proved to be inefficient as data may lead to the auditor. Juels et al. (2007) defined a "proof of retrievability" model in which possession and retrievability of data where ensured by spot checking and some error correcting codes. But this scheme also didn't work well because the numbers of audits were limited. While many schemes provided methods for correct and efficient auditing of data stored remotely on cloud, but neither of the schemes helped in maintaining privacy preserving public auditing in cloud. Wang et al. (2009) introduced four algorithms to certify the veracity of data in cloud environment. They considered batch auditing method which if adopted and implemented properly can reduce the cost of computations whenever a Third-Party Auditor (TPA) is dealing with enormous number of audit delegations. Godara et. al. (2018), Godara and Singh (2017), Godara and Singh (2014), Bura and Choudhary (2020), Godara and Singh (2015) Bura and Chaudhary(2020) defined a technique wherein how various changes can be identified, this could help in implementing and proposing various techniques in Big Data.

Scalability is often seen a challenge in the field of big data and cloud computing and many researchers worked to solve this problem of handling the ever-increasing amounts of data by the storage systems in a proper manner. Wang et al. (2009) had projected a new scalable data cube analysis technique named HaCube in order to overcome the challenges of vast amount of data. HaCube is basically an extension of MapReduce and it uses some features of MapReduce. The biggest advantage of HaCube is that it is much faster than Hadoop in view maintenance. Bura et al. (2018) discussed how load can be balance in cloud by comparing different types of techniques. These techniques can be helpful in managing data in cloud. Mehra et al. (2018) analyzed the aspects of security in cloud which is also one of the essential aspects of big data in cloud.

BIG DATA

"Big Data" the term itself includes so many concepts, algorithms that are not only vast in explanation but would require much time to understand. Stergiou et. al.(2020) demonstrated that Big Data refers to so many things like Exabyte's of size, large sets, storage, analytics, technology, implementations, management, visualizations, approaches, challenges, processes, critiques, paradigms, trends, market use, past relation, researches, software's, cost, initiatives, insights, complexities and at the end USER that is we . we in this world are making efforts to make our work as easy as possible. We all love a life where complex things like 15 digits calculations occur instantly (calculator), where things like complex multiplication could be converted to simple additions and subtractions(log tables) for an instance. Constantly we the "HUMAN" are trying hard to create a world which will manage everything with ease. With the evolution of human themselves, we tried to build home for shelter, we tried to build a workplace which suits our environment from very basic that is from electric sharpener to the real-time robots, from electric cars to automated homes, from automated medical diagnosis to online shopping etc. Our lives are changing day by day and every day we are trying to make our lives bit easier than yesterday.

The term big data came into picture to deal with complexities of ever-increasing data. Figure 1 below explains about various characteristics of Big Data. Different people define big data in their own terms. Some define big data as enormous and ever-increasing data, and some defined it in terms of managing vast amounts of data with efficiency and flexibility. Big Data refers to firm's ability to store, process and access all the information which is important for an enterprise to operate effectively, make decisions,

Figure 1. Characteristics of Data

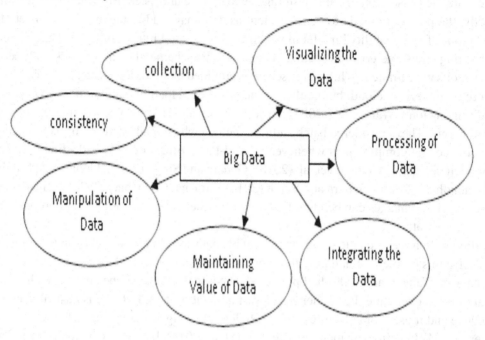

reduce risks and serve the customers. The term big data was very first used in 1990's which not only signifies rapidly expanding data volumes but also the ability to effectively manage data that has ever existed, Lam (2010). Big data has been very eminent in influencing better decision-making capability for companies, government, nonprofit organizations etc. Not only volume but the velocity with which the data is increasing rapidly in this era is also a big challenge. International Data Corporation (IDC) in 2012 estimated that 2.8 zettabytes of personal data is generated and will double its volume by 2015.

History of Big Data

The past of Big Data as a term is brief, yet a considerable lot of the developments it is based on were laid long prior. Well before PCs were ordinary and not like how they look now, the likelihood that we were making a regularly growing assemblage of learning ready for investigation was prominent in the scholarly world. It is difficult to overlook, our increasing size to stock and breakdown data has been a progressive advancement, in spite of the fact that things unquestionably accelerated toward the finish of the most recent century, with the innovation of computerized stockpiling and the web. History of Big Data started with the evolution of internet or World Wide Web (in 1991) which became a medium for sharing information. In 1995 with emergence of Java i.e. a robust and one of the popular languages of all time was used in making applications which were a source of generating, recording and storing web traffic Bura et al.(2017). With the launch of Wikipedia which is a crowd sourced encyclopedia which approximately had 1 million articles by end of 2004. Social networking sites like LinkedIn and Facebook had 260 million users and 1.15 billion users respectively in year 2013. Soon the devices connected via internet exceeded world's population. With the introduction of open source software i.e. Apache Hadoop project which was based on MapReduce paradigm for processing large sets of data, laid the foundational part for almost every Big Data strategy and is functional till date.

Laney (2012) gave the concept of 3 V's in his research publication which is illustrated below:

1. Volume: the first V of Big Data deals with the volume of data being generated from different sources in structured or unstructured form.
2. Velocity: The second V of Big Data deals with speed at which data is being generated and the speed with which it is moving from one platform to another.
3. Variety: The third V deals with different forms of data being created everyday. Big Data is mainly categorized in:

Structured Data: Structured data refers to the data that is stored in most organized format such as in relational database management systems. This kind of data is mostly beneficial for companies because working on such kind of data consumes less energy and time. Example of this kind of data is numbers, strings, dates and spread sheets.

Unstructured Data: Unstructured data refers to the data that is generated from different multimedia. Managing of this kind of data becomes difficult for the companies because there is no structured organization of data and it consumes lot of time. Examples of unstructured type of data includes word documents, e-mail messages, pictures, audio and video files, power point presentations, web pages etc.

Semi Structured Data: Semi structured data refers to the data that lies between structured and unstructured data. It may include data from NoSQL databases and various XML documents. Further as the concept of big data evolved 6 more V's were included which are illustrated below, Khan et al. (2014). Also, Figure 2 illustrates about the various nine V's of Big Data. These are:

1. Value: Anything that exists without proper usage and worth is completely useless. If not implemented properly then is of no use.
2. Veracity: With ever increasing generation of data there is a need to maintain the data with full control, accuracy and trustworthiness. Due to different forms of data being created quality and reliability of data must be ensured. Big Data analytics allow the users to work with different kind of data and also assures correctness of data.
3. Volatility: When we discuss unpredictability of Big Data, we can without much of a stretch review the maintenance approach of organized information that we actualize each day in our organizations. When maintenance period terminates, we can without much of a stretch wreck it. For instance: an online internet business organization might not have any desire to keep a one-year client buy history. Since following one year and default guarantee on their item terminates so there is no probability of these information reestablish ever .
4. Visualization: visualization deals with exploring as well as understanding the data in a similar way as the brain of a human process it. This usually refers to analyzing the data in graphical form so that it is easy to read, interpret and is easy to comprehend. The understanding of big data could be better explained to people in forms of graphs, and pie charts instead of reports and theoretical papers.
5. Validity: It deals with maintaining the integrity of big data. It usually requires accurateness and completeness of the data stored in it. The right decisions could be well influenced by the validity of the data.

6. Variability: it is always said that data flow can at times be very inconsistent along with maintaining its value. It could be very challenging to maintain rather manage the data(especially unstructured form).

Figure 2. Characteristics of Data

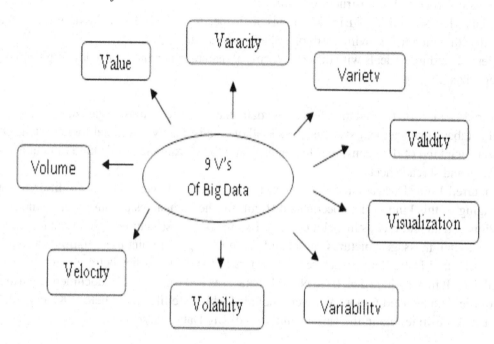

As the data was increasing at exponential rate so managing, storing and processing of Big Data possessed a big challenge. There was an alarming need for new technology which could revolutionize the way we process data. After so many researches data scientists were trying their best to evolve a technology which was not only faster in processing but also is reliable in use. One of those inventions was Apache Hadoop project which is till date eminent in handling and processing Big Data. It's working and functionalities are explained in detail in the paper below.

HADOOP

Hadoop is a framework written in Java and is an open source project of Apache. It was developed by Doug Cutting and Mike Cafarella in the year 2005. It is used for processing large datasets in the form of distributed computing.

Hadoop came a long way in its usage, accepted and implemented by many big organizations. With its capability of managing data extensively and providing scalability to its users and developers, hadoop became popular among developers, users and organizations thus paving way for its versions. Hadoop version 1.0 contains Hadoop Distributed File System (HDFS) followed by MapReduce cluster management for big data processing, pig for managing data flow and hives for summarizing data, analyzing it and performing SQL querying. Whereas in Hadoop 2.0 components comprises of Hadoop Distributed File System 2 (HDFS2), YARN (Yet Another Resource Negotiator) which is used for managing clusters in Hadoop, Tez which basically provides an extendible framework for high performance and iterative batch as well as data processing or could be considered as an execution engine in hadoop, MapReduce, Hives, Pig and also includes services like HBase (Hadoop Base). Hadoop has two versions exclusively named as Hadoop Version 1.0 and Hadoop Version 2.0 which are explained below:

Hadoop Version 1.0

Hadoop Version 1.0 comprised of two parts:

1. Data Processing Framework: This framework makes uses of two components called mapper and reducer. The main task of mapper is generation of data and on the other hand reducer performs the task of generating output from input data. Both the components are fault tolerant and perform their tasks independent of each other.
2. Data Storage Framework: This is known as HDFS and is used to store and process data.

Hadoop Version 2.0

Later on Hadoop Version 2.0 was introduced which was implemented on another framework entirely different from Hadoop Version 1.0. Hadoop Version 2.0 used a new technology called YARN an acronym for Yet Another Resource Navigator. YARN provided many advantages over Hadoop Version 1.0 like flexibility, efficiency and scalability for applications.

It is able to run any application with the help of Application Manager and is not only concentrated to MapReduce only. Also, the mandatory requirement for programming expertise is also not here that is the Map Reducing for data processing was no longer the only option. It also not only supported batch processing but real time processing.

There were many differences between the versions of Hadoop which are enlisted with the help of a Table 1 which is explained below:

Table 1. Difference of Hadoop 1.0 and Hadoop 2.0

S.No	Hadoop 1.0	Hadoop 2.0
1	This version supported only MapReduce Framework to run and process data which was stored in HDFS systems. Thus, disallowing any other application to process HDFS cluster	This version came up with YARN which allowed both MapReduce and other applications like Spark to access the HDFS cluster
2	Only a single name node was present in order to track the data storage in a cluster. Thus, in case if this Name Nodes crashes then whole cluster of Hadoop will also go down.	Multiple name nodes to manage the data. Thus, in case failure of one name node occurs, it doesn't affect the whole cluster.
3	Was built exclusively for UNIX systems, so didn't support the Windows platform.	Native support for Windows was added.
4	Less scalable as it was limited to only 4000 nodes per cluster	More scalable. Could support 10000 nodes per cluster.
5	Supports the concept of slots. These slots could run only a Map or Reduce task only.	Supports the concept of containers. Could run generic tasks.

Components of Hadoop

Hadoop is formed by various components which have their own roles to play when it comes to functioning of Hadoop. It has various components for data processing, managing, manipulating and storing. Different components of Hadoop are given in Figure 3.

Figure 3. Components of Hadoop

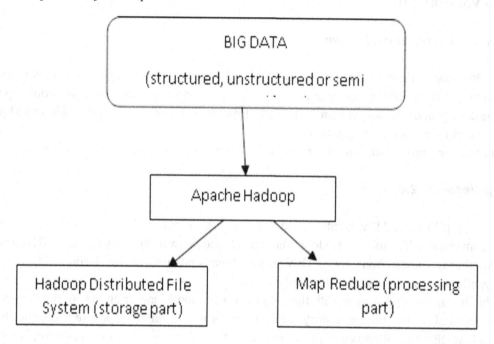

MapReduce Framework

In past times Google had implemented many computation techniques to process vast amounts of raw data, derived data, request logs, structured data, unstructured data, semi structured data etc. These computations were simple in implementation but as input datasets were large and the data had to be processed across thousands of machines, it became difficult to distribute data, parallelize data, failures couldn't be managed easily. In order to solve all these major complexities a new abstraction was designed by Google in its research paper. This abstraction allowed computations to be carried out easily, but it provided an added advantage of hiding the details of distribution of data, parallelization of data and fault tolerance. The new designed abstractions were inspired by two primitives from Lisp language. These were map and reduce primitives. In each of the computations a "map" operation is applied to a logical "record" in the input dataset which generated intermediate key/value pair. In order to derive an output, a reduce operation is applied to all those input values which have the same key. The uses of these maps and reduce functions allowed to parallelize vast computations efficiently and easily. The biggest advantage of map reduce framework is that it is beneficial for all the programmers who have no experience in dealing with parallel and distributed systems by letting them utilize the resources of large distributed systems. Figure 4 illustrates framework of MapReduce.

1. The very first step is to divide the large dataset into multiple chunks that is sent as an input to framework.
2. After the division of dataset, framework creates master and various workers processes. These workers processes are then executed remotely.
3. Map worker makes use of map function in order to extract the data which is present on server and generates a key pair for the extracted data.
4. The data is divided in various regions by map worker which makes use of partitioner function to do this task.
5. After the completion of work by map workers an instruction is sent to reduce workers so that they can start their work. The reduce workers generate a request in order to get the key pair from map workers.
6. A reduced function is called for each unique key. The reduced function helps in generating output to file.
7. At the end when all the work is done both by mapper and reducer the control is then transferred to user by master.

Figure 4. Framework of MapReduce

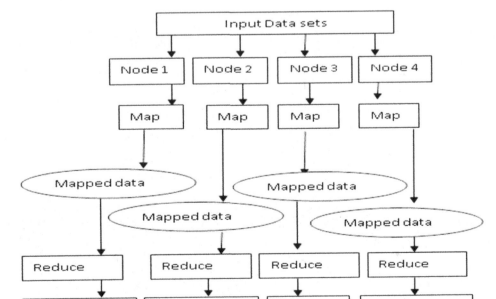

Hadoop Distributed File System (HDFS)

It is a part of the Apache project which marks its origin as an infrastructure to the web crawler which was an open source Apache Nutch. It is a distributed type of file system which has high fault tolerance and could be run on commodity hardware resulting in low cost for the hardware. The main goal of HDFS is to detect faults and then recover from these faults automatically and quickly. This file system consists of many servers' machines where pieces of data are stored. There is always a possibility that some or the other component won't be functional due to hardware failure. This type of file system is could be used more for batch processing while not for use by user interaction. Applications which can run on file system require streaming access for the data sets. A typical size for the HDFS file ranges from Gigabytes to Terabytes and is tuned well to work with large files. It supports millions of files as a single structure. HDFS model of files is based on the concept of read many and write once approach. Here if a file is created, written and is then closed, hence the file need not change. This helps in maintaining data coherence and also helps in enabling high data access throughput. Moving data is comparatively expensive than moving computation. Hence HDFS follows this technique. It is always suggested that the application requesting computation on some data is efficient when the data is near the computational resource and especially when the size of the file or data being operated on is huge. Hadoop Distributed File System works by providing an interface for applications to migrate and perform computation where the data is actually present or stored. HDFS file systems has been designed such that it could be easily be ported from one platform to other which helps in adoption of HDFS for processing and implementing large data sets of applications by users irrespective of the platform applications are developed in. This type of file system uses master slave architecture where a single cluster of an HDFS consists of Name Node and number of Data nodes. Here Name node serves as a master node which manages namespace in the

Figure 5. Hadoop Distributed File System

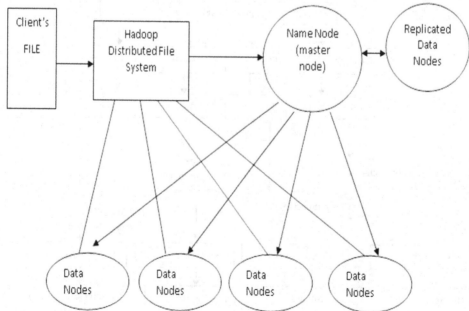

file system, while Data nodes are present usually in a way so that, there is one Data node per Name node in the cluster. This helps in storage management in the file system. Large clusters are used by Hadoop Distributed File System to store a large number of files reliably. Figure 5 demonstrates Hadoop Distributed File System and some of the advantages of MapReduce Framework is given in Table 2.

Table 2. Advantages of MapReduce Framework

Features	Advantages
Increased Speed	Due to the introduction of MapReduce Framework, the speed of processing became very fast. MapReduce introduces parallel processing which implies that complex problems which used to take lot of days to process can now be processed in few hours or minutes.
Efficiently Scalable	Hadoop make use of Mapreduce to process huge amount of data ranging from terabytes to petabytes using Hadoop Distributed File System.
Fault Tolerance	Failures are unavoidable in a system .Mapreduce helps in recovery of the data when one machine with data is not available, it will simply make use of another machine which has a copy of same value or key pair which is used to solve the same sub task. Also, the job tracker is used for maintaining and keeping job record.
Reduced data circulation	One of the major things that governs the faster efficiency and computational speed of Hadoop is that it moves computation to data and not the data to computation. In Hadoop processing occurs on the nodes where data is residing.
Reduced complexity	Mapreduce framework and HDFS file system are platform independent that is a programmer or a developer could make of any programming language for developing applications and process them using hadoop technology.

Hadoop Common

Hadoop common is also known as Hadoop core which is basically a collection of common libraries as well as utilities that are required for supporting other Hadoop components or modules for proper functioning of the software technology. Here Hadoop modules include Hadoop Distributed File System (HDFS), MapReduce Framework and Hadoop YARN. This package helps in providing basic services and essential processes. Hadoop common also is provided with proper documentation and source code.

Apache HBase:

Apache HBase stands for Hadoop Database which applies scalable and distributed storage of big data. HBase was modeled on BigTable Google's Database. It could be considered as non relational, scalable and fault tolerant data base. It is eminent in providing real time write or read access to the data. HBase make use of the zookeeper which could be used for providing configuration information in a centralized manner for managing any sort of partial. It is also used for storing multidimensional maps in terms of tables where each column and row is identified uniquely by its value. Here each table is composed of a region and consists of pair of start and end keys.

Apache Hives

Apache hive is a software project which is a data warehouse and is build on the top of Hadoop which provides analytics on huge data sets, the summarization of data as well as querying processes. Hadoop stores data in various file systems and Databases which could be queried by a SQL like interface provided by Hives. Mostly all the data warehouse applications works on SQL based languages used for querying of data. Thereby, Hives facilitates the portability of the applications which are SQL based to Hadoop. Hives eases aggregation of data visualizing tool and different business approaches with the hadoop software. The tools available by hives allow the user to structure, analyze or explore the data so as to get meaningful business insights. Today hives are used and is developed by many companies like Facebook, Financial Industry Regulatory Authority(FINRA) and Netflix.

HISTORY OF HADOOP

Hadoop was developed by Doug Cutting and Mike Cafarella. The birth of Hadoop was not so simple and straight. Right before hadoop was born Doug had 2 projects in hand which actually marked the birth of Hadoop. Doug first project Lucene was named after his wife which was a apache project. Lucene was an open source library which supports applications that require full featured text indexing. Nutch was also proposed by Doug as an extension of Lucene. The Nutch helps the developers in building web search engines by having Lucene as its main component. Nutch has many other components like Web crawler, parsers that are usually required for building a web search engine. Nutch's basic challenge was scalability. In 2004, Google in its paper described the concept of MapReduce and Google file system . Doug after studying about these two technologies decided that these two technologies could help in solving problem of scalability. Doug and his team then started a new framework and this was ported to Nutch. This implementation helped in increasing the scalability of Nutch. This new implementation and extension of Nutch was termed as Hadoop.

   Some features of hadoop are explained. It can handle large sets of unstructured, semi structured and structured form of data. Hadoop has low latency and high throughput with non- immediate response time as it operates on massive data which follow Batch Operations. It cannot be compared with that of Relational Database Management Systems as it complements various processing techniques like Online Transaction Processing (OLTP) and Online Analytical Processing (OLAP). It also follows a simple architecture. Hadoop works best with large datasets and large files, however it is not good for processing and handling of small files. It treats and manipulates data independently and cannot work well when data is dependent.

Advantages of Hadoop

There were many disadvantages or limitations of traditional file processing system. As data was increasing at a buzzing rate there was not only urge but need of new technology which could solve the problem of handling ever increasing data. Hadoop was one of those technologies that revolutionized the way to handle big data. The main advantages of Hadoop are described below:-

Simplicity:-The hadoop platform has a simple architecture which in turn helps it's users to write and perform their codes efficiently, quickly and with utmost level of ease.
Scalability:-Refers to the ability of a computer system, process or a network to handle increasing amount of data with efficiency. Hadoop works in a clustered environment and by adding more nodes to the cluster, it helps to handle enormous amount of data in a scalable manner.
Fast Accessibility: - The speed of processing in environment of hadoop is quite fast when compared to conventional systems.

Flexibility: - The hadoop platform is flexible because it allows the user to work with all difficult forms of data. It also helps in deriving meaningful business insights from social media, emails etc.

Fault Tolerance: - The greatest advantage of hadoop platform is that it is highly fault tolerant. Replication of data is performed in hadoop environment, as in whenever any data is submitted to a node, and then the same data is replicated to other different nodes in the cluster. This ensures that if any node is failed the data is not lost.

RELATIONSHIP BETWEEN BIG DATA AND CLOUD COMPUTING

Cloud and Big data work together to achieve the feasibility in order to access the data in an effective manner. Big Data was mainly incorporated to solve the issues that business organizations were facing . In fact, Big Data aims to achieve business value by deploying the current application analytics. Cloud Services and big data usually work hand in hand as both aims to achieve feasibility of accessing the data, management of data in appropriate manner and availability of data as and when required by the end user. Every technology requires a architecture to be built before it comes into implementation. The main force behind adopting the technology of big data in business is benefits that company will get, such as better productivity and outcome, security and allowing the data to be processed in parallel manner also Cloud acts as an effective platform to analyze the data for manipulation. Further this paper progresses with the detailed explanation of cloud.

Big Data and Cloud Computing are two different technologies that are providing various benefits to the IT industries in their own terms. Both of them are valuable to the companies if implemented properly. Today most of the industries want both of these technologies to work together so as to have a beneficial output. The major application of big data is in Big Data Analytics. Industries are able to analyze and derive better results when they utilize cloud for dealing with vast variety of unstructured and structured data. The biggest advantage of cloud computing is that it helps in reducing the cost of resources involved in dealing with big data analytics which in turn helps small and medium sized enterprises. One of the major problem associated with big data is integration of data from various sources, but by incorporating cloud into usage this problem can be easily solved. Moreover the infrastructure provided in cloud environment is quite flexible and scalable that helps in managing and analyzing the different large sets of data. A major implementation of processing of big data in cloud is MapReduce Framework. Both cloud and big data work hand in hand to provide VALUE to the enterprise by bringing the overall cost down to some extent. According to a survey in 2014, it was predicted that combining of big data and cloud transformed the entire working of organizations. Also cloud mainly public cloud provides an easy access to large datasets across the world. Cloud platform posses the feature of elasticity due to which storage needs can be dynamically expanded and shrinked according to the requirement. Also due to the easy availability of storage in cloud and infrastructure it has become easier for business to gather information from dozens of resources and provide a more clear picture about the information being processed.

CLOUD COMPUTING

Whenever a new product or technology is launched in market, then the industry or people accept the product only when it provides the best features and benefits. One such technology which emerged as a boom in the IT industry was cloud computing technology. The concept of cloud computing was brought into the industry was Joseph Carl Robnett Lickliden in 1960's, with the sole aim of connecting people and their data at anytime and from anywhere. This technology of cloud assures a reliable hardware, software and services over the Internet. The basic principle behind the cloud computing technology is to offer storage and computing software as a service. Cloud cannot be confined in one definition. Many researchers's expressed their views and explained the concept of cloud in their own terms. Cloud computing may be regarded as consolidation of well-defined admix which could be accessed anywhere on-demand and charged as per usage. The word "cloud "here implies that the data is accessible to the user everywhere and anywhere while computing refers to the consistent development of software's and application programs. It can also be regarded as a evolving paradigm or a model which facilitate us with pervasive, user-friendly, on-demand accessing network and pool of computing resources like storage, applications, servers, services and network . Cloud computing integrate virtualization, big data, internet services and condemned application deployment. The main goal of cloud computing is to provide ease of access of various services that could be used on demand and as per usage. Major companies like Microsoft, Citrix, Google, Amazon, IBM, Rackspace, Joyent, VMware etc. are facilitating users with cloud services. Cloud technology basically allows IT organizations to concentrate on their mainframe business without taking any tension about the availability of resources and infrastructure.

MIGRATION TO CLOUD

21'st century is termed as the age of information. Systems designed traditionally were used to create, manage and store data. In earlier times, IT industries relied on physical infrastructure for storage of their data. But with the evolution of enormous data, the industries started facing many problems. Some of the shortcomings of physical infrastructure were:-

1. **Sizing of physical infrastructure:** Everyday with the advancement in technology, new requirements have to be setup which requires the resize of already setup physical infrastructure. If in case the requirement goes down, then the extra infrastructure remains unutilized which results in inherent loss.
2. **Security:** There was no efficient management of data center's due to which security of data was at risk.
3. **Managing the Assets**: Due to the risk in enormous data it became almost impossible to manage and track all physical server assets. This increase in data led to increase in number of servers. Moreover, the different infrastructure and heterogeneity between these infrastructures didn't allow it to run any common applications that could keep track of these assets.

These shortcomings resulted in the need of virtualizing the existing infrastructure . Moreover, the emergence of cloud computing technologies was marked with evolution of mainframe computers in 1950s where multiuser concept was used for accessing central computer. Since the cost of maintenance is high for mainframe computers that is why using and installing it for every employee of a company was not at all viable as memory and resource demand for each employee varies.

ADVANTAGES AND DISADVANTAGES OF BIG DATA AND CLOUD COMPUTING

Cloud Computing and Big Data are the buzz words of the computer science field. The techniques available in both the area have been widely used by the researchers, academicians, industrialist etc. In industry also there are many tasks which use the techniques of cloud computing and big data like mining, prediction, data analysis, storage, etc. Although the use of techniques from both the fields have been increasing exponentially as they have advantages but along with the advantages, the disadvantages also occurs.

In cloud computing, users get the felexibilty for growth, efficient recovery, accessibility with easy implementation. But, there are issues of bandwidth, redundant data also.

CONCLUSION

As the size of data is expanding, different kinds and different volumes of data is being generated. To manage vast amount of data and in order to bring maximum profits from their business cloud services were seen as the best solution for these enormously large bundle of datasets. Various Cloud services helped in storing, analyzing and managing the big data. In this paper we discussed the term big data in broad terms and how cloud helps in effectively handling this large amount of data. The different techniques that were proposed in order to help solve the bundle of data sets with least complexity were also discussed and these included MapReduce Framework, Hadoop. Moreover how these two terms are related to each other is also discussed in this study. Some of the challenges being faced like scalability, privacy, quality of data, were also highlighted. Much work is being done in this field so as to bring out the best in both and to have optimum solutions for handling the data. There is a need for researchers, scholars and practitioners to work in this field in order to collaborate big data and cloud in better way so that the problems still that are being faced by end user gets solved.

REFERENCES

Ananthanarayanan, G., & Menache, I. (2016). Big data analytics systems. In S. Cui, A. Hero III, Z. Luo, & J. Moura (Eds.), *Big Data over Networks* (pp. 137–160). Cambridge University Press. doi:10.1017/CBO9781316162750.006

Ateniese, G., Burns, R., Curtmola, R., Herring, J., Kissner, L., Peterson, Z., & Song, D. (2007). *Provable data possession at untrusted stores*. Cryptology ePrint Archive, Report 2007/202. https://eprint.iacr.org/

Birst Inc. (n.d.). http://www.birst.com

Bura, D., & Choudhary, A. (2020). Enhancing Information Retrieval System Using Change-Prone Classes. In *Critical Approaches to Information Retrieval Research* (pp. 40–68). IGI Global.

Bura, D., & Choudhary, A. (2020). A novel change impact model for enhancing project management. *International Journal of Project Organisation and Management*, *12*(2), 119–132.

Bura, D., Choudhary, A., & Singh, R. K. (2017). A Novel UML Based Approach for Early Detection of Change Prone Classes. *International Journal of Open Source Software and Processes*, *8*(3), 1–23.

Bura, D., Singh, M., & Nandal, P. (2018). Analysis and Development of Load Balancing Algorithms in Cloud Computing. *International Journal of Information Technology and Web Engineering, 13*(3), 35–53.

Cohen, J., Dolan, B., Dunlap, M., Hellerstein, J. M., & Welton, C. (2009). MAD skills: New analysis practices for big data. *Proceedings of the VLDB Endowment International Conference on Very Large Data Bases, 2*(2), 1481–1492.

Ghemawat, S., Gobioff, H., & Leung, S.-T. (2003). The Google File System. In *Proceedings of the 9th ACM Symposium on Operating Systems Principles (SOSP 2003)*. ACM.

Godara, D., Choudhary, A., & Singh, R. K. (2018). Predicting Change Prone Classes in Open Source Software. *International Journal of Information Retrieval Research, 8*(4), 1–23.

Godara, D., & Singh, R. (2014). A new hybrid model for predicting change prone class in object oriented software. *International Journal of Computer Science and Telecommunications, 5*(7), 1–6.

Godara, D., & Singh, R. K. (2014). A review of studies on change proneness prediction in object oriented software. *International Journal of Computers and Applications, 105*(3).

Godara, D., & Singh, R. K. (2015). Enhancing Frequency Based Change Proneness Prediction Method Using Artificial Bee Colony Algorithm. In *Advances in Intelligent Informatics* (pp. 535–543). Springer.

Godara, D., & Singh, R. K. (2017). Exploring the relationships between design measures and change proneness in object-oriented systems. International Journal of Software Engineering. *Technology and Applications, 2*(1), 64–80.

Juels, A., Burton, J., & Kaliski, S. (2007). Pors: Proofs of retrievability for large files. *Proc. of CCS'07,* 584–597.

Khan, M. A., Fahim Uddin, M., & Gupta, N. (2014). Seven V's of Big Data. *Proceedings of 2014 Zone 1 Conference of the American Society for Engineering Education (ASEE Zone 1),* 3-5.

Lam, C. (2010). *Hadoop in action.* Manning Publications Co.

Laney, D. (2012). *The importance of 'Big Data': A Definition.* Gartner.

Lee, G., Chun, B.-G., & Katz, R. H. (2011). Heterogeneity-Aware Resource Allocation and Scheduling in the Cloud. In *Proceedings of the 3rd USENIX conference on Hot topics in Cloud computing (HotCloud 2011).* USENIX Association.

Liu, C., Ranjan, R., Zhang, X., Yang, C., Georgakopoulos, D., & Chen, J. (2013, December). Public auditing for big data storage in cloud computing--a survey. In *2013 IEEE 16th International Conference on Computational Science and Engineering* (pp. 1128-1135). IEEE.

Lu, C. W., Hsieh, C. M., Chang, C. H., & Yang, C. T. (2013, July). An improvement to data service in cloud computing with content sensitive transaction analysis and adaptation. In *2013 IEEE 37th Annual Computer Software and Applications Conference Workshops* (pp. 463-468). IEEE.

Mehra, N., Aggarwal, S., Shokeen, A., & Bura, D. (2018). Analyzing Cloud Computing Security Issues and Challenges. In *Progress in Computing, Analytics and Networking* (pp. 193–202). Springer.

Owais, S. S., & Hussein, N. S. (2016). Extract Five Categories CPIVW from the 9V's Characteristics of the Big Data. *International Journal of Advanced Computer Science & Applications, 1*(7), 254–258.

Singh, M., Nandal, P., & Bura, D. (2017, October). Comparative Analysis of Different Load Balancing Algorithm Using Cloud Analyst. In *International Conference on Recent Developments in Science, Engineering and Technology* (pp. 321-329). Springer.

Stergiou, C. L., Plageras, A. P., Psannis, K. E., & Gupta, B. B. (2020). Secure machine learning scenario from big data in cloud computing via internet of things network. In *Handbook of Computer Networks and Cyber Security* (pp. 525–554). Springer.

Thusoo, A., Shao, Z., Anthony, S., Borthakur, D., Jain, N., Sarma, J. S., Murthy, R., & Liu, H. (2010). Data warehousing and analytics infrastructure at Facebook. In *Proceedings of the 2010 international conference on Management of data*. ACM.

Villars, R. L., Olofson, C. W., & Eastwood, M. (2011). Big data: What it is and why you should care. *White Paper, IDC, 14*, 1-14.

Wang, C., Wang, Q., Ren, K., & Lou, W. (2009). Ensuring Data Storage Security in Cloud Computing. *Proc. of IWQoS'09.*

Zhang, X., Zhang, E., Song, B., & Wei, F. (2010). Towards Building an Integrated Information Platform for Eco-city. *Proceedings of the 7th International Conference on e-Business Engineering (ICEBE 2010)*, 393–398.

Chapter 4
Machine Learning for Big Data

Supriya M. S.

https://orcid.org/0000-0003-3465-6879
Ramaiah University of Applied Sciences, India

Keerthana Sasidaran
Ramaiah University of Applied Sciences, India

ABSTRACT

Big data and machine learning currently play an important role in various applications and in research. These approaches are explored in depth in this chapter. The chapter starts with a summary of big data and its implementation in a number of fields, and then deals with the problems that big data presents and the need for other technology to resolve these issues/challenges. Big data can best be used with the aid of the machine learning model, even though they are not directly related. Thus, the paradigms of machine learning that support big data can be combined with big data technology, thus providing insight into a range of big data machine learning approaches and techniques. Although big data cannot rely solely on the few paradigms of machine learning, the underlying problems are addressed. New machine learning algorithms are needed that can explore the full scale of the big data process and enable software engineering firms to come up with better solutions.

INTRODUCTION AND BACKGROUND

The proper investigative frameworks can tackle complex issues, settle on discerning choices, improve application interface and furthermore produce financially savvy execution. Enormous information is a terminology used for big data indexes having increasingly differed and compound structure through the challenges of setting away, dissecting and foreseeing for additional processes. The process of analysis into huge methods of data to reveal hidden examples and mysterious associations named as big data analytics. These valued data for organizations with the assistance of cumulative extravagant and additional thoughtful little of knowledge and in receipt of a favourable position over the opposition. Thus, usage of big data has to break down and implemented as exactly as might be anticipated underneath the environments. Calculation and stowage, robotics and sensor technology are therefore hefty. It is therefore

DOI: 10.4018/978-1-7998-6673-2.ch004

important to develop intelligence systems that deals with real-time and past data in order to maintain the performance of these technologies. Thus, big data analytics research play a vital role in data mining and data processing (Bendre & Thool, 2016).

The Internet of Things (IoT), maintains gathered data over the internet after various devices along with sensor network is on the growth. RFID tags captures transaction data that perform on products such as goods conveyed via supply chain. Big data also applies in dynamic and bursting knowledge on social media platforms. According to the International Data Corporation (IDC) report, the innovation in big data and administration industry is quickly rising field wherein billions of dollars will be put resources into the not so distant future on the general business. According to IDC director's view, the growth through IT (Information Technology) companies will increase rapidly in means of clients and their offer market. It predicts that the technology like big data and its service industry will rise at a combined annual growth rate of 26.24 per cent, to hit $23.8 billion by 2016, in 2018 it may reach $41.52 billion and up to $48.6 billion in 2019 (Bendre & Thool, 2016).

Big data should be capable of providing certain resources, methods and processes for loading, extracting and improving handling using equal computing capacity for widespread compound operations and surveillance. Designing a big data framework for examining, handling and keeping missing information will bring about a development of particular problems since multifaceted nature of huge data. Mainly, gathering and integrating data with dispersed locations is a difficult task because of the several independent data sources and a vast ability. Hence, there is a need for system that can possibly deal with handling and big data processing and similarly trail the reassurance of the performance properties in terms of accessing speed, scalability, recovery, and privacy. The big data must effectively extract information from a large data-sets at various levels, so that features can be exposed in order to improve decisions taken and obtain more benefits in realistic and non-realistic environments.

The revolutionary steps of big data is characterised into three components (Sagiroglu & Sinanc, 2013):

Variety: The classification of big data is categorised into structured, semi-structured and unstructured. The type of inserting the data into a tagged warehouse can be called as structured data that can be easily sorted whereas, the process is random and difficult to analyse in unstructured data. On the other hand, semi-structured has tags that can separate data element though has no fixed fields

Volume: At present, the size of the data is usually in terabytes and petabytes. The fabulous scale and ascent of information surpasses customary store and examination methods

Velocity: Not only big data uses this component but also other processes. For time fewer processes, as big data enhances that organizational value by streaming

Machine Learning is the investigation of computational strategies for execution upgrade through motorizing data obtaining for a fact. Expert output requires comprehensive domain-specific expertise, and hundreds of machine learning expert systems have been developed by software engineering have been widely used in industries. On the other side, big data is rapidly making its progress in various domains, its significance is in using the novel ideas to present solutions to the challenges stands epic. Present world lives with enormous data. In previous days, machine learning systems have been broadly embraced in various monstrous and complex information escalated fields, for example, medication, stargazing, science, for these methods give potential answers for mine the data covered up in the information. As the ideal opportunity for big data is coming, the assortment of informational indexes is so huge and complex that it is hard to manage utilizing customary learning techniques since the built up procedure of gaining from ordinary informational collections was not intended to and won't function admirably with huge data.

MACHINE LEANING AND BIG DATA: REAL-TIME APPLICATIONS

Utmost instances of extensive usage of data are initiated in the following applications after penetrating for thousands of electronic records that are obtainable on various sites of big data.

Healthcare

The data gathered here in this healthcare are naturally mind boggling and usually requires a more space in PC memory. The big data can be a prerequisite in healthcare systems in order to analyse the data produced, that may require a testing ahead of considering it practically. The benefit of applying data mining of health information technology to big data is the technical resources are available to address big data difficulties such as high dimensionality and class inequality. The big data and e-Health Service (BDeHS) method is to carry services in health care and data management information into the environments for improved torrent preparing, authoritative administration, and administrative consistence.

The world's largest healthcare partnership is in the US, with over 2700 integrated healthcare and hospitals systems, per 400,000 doctors and 90,000 non-acute maintenance services. The health of patient analytics will be tracked by further 330 hospitals, and performance enhancement is tracked by exchanging data between hospitals. Using equipment for IoT, and analysis allows for simple examination of which patients need urgent care. IBM has taken an initiative through is platform to help healthcare entities improve their healthcare, over 3000 cases were successfully completed (Bendre & Thool, 2016).

Predictive research helps doctors and clinicians to concentrate on optimal quality and patient treatment, providing a constructive system to tackle patient concerns before they are sick. Wearable devices and monitors utilize data to monitor patient safety in real time, identifying patterns or warning flags that might possibly predict a hazardous health condition like cardiac arrest. Advances in cognitive technology can aid a diagnosis by processing increasingly vast amounts of medical and health care data, finding trends and joining the dots to improve treatment and care (Software, 2020).

Government

Perhaps, the greatest datum sources is the assortment of projects, offices, and administrations that an administration gives to its residents. Such information originate from various government divisions like police offices, transport offices, military associations, national security organizations, rural offices, income offices, ecological and social government assistance offices, insight offices, and other government offices. Big data examination instruments can rapidly and dependably get data from these accessible information and propose a substantially more productive method for upholding the arrangements. Semi-organized and unstructured e-administration information are still in simple structure and subsequently should be converted into advanced arrangement with the goal that dynamic can be effectively put away, prepared and traded in the open intrigue. Resistance, security and police organizations screen the ever-expanding dangers of fear based oppressor assaults and ever-expanding outlines of wrongdoing (Bendre & Thool, 2016).

Transportation

The transportation and automobile activities such as routes, traffic data, positions, GPS, thus requiring a large data system. The system that are GPS-based can assist in controlling traffic and evade road mishaps. With creative transport solutions, the big data analytics program will route and enhance transportation services. New architecture for data transportation can be designed to capture, manage by storing data flow over a period of time to find the link sections necessary for transport schedules.

On behalf of instance, inward feeds obtained from 560 cameras across the city with 360 remote services are combined into a server to display on a tiled screen wall of 80 square metres. The map is contrasted with real-time information that has 120 layers, such as GPS monitoring of the buses, local and official city traffic. The seven-day study, over 400 workers operating in shifts 24 hours a day, increases productivity and safety quality in the city for even day-to-day transport service (Bendre & Thool, 2016).

Marketing

Several shopping stations and ads on social media inspire consumers to shop online, these online stores and administrations give consumers with guidance to choose the product of their prime and can support in comparing goods and prices. A huge amount of data is produced in the trade and consumer product atmosphere while consumes are engaged online, social media, and broadcast advertising, also an on-line customer data. Additionally, some purchased product details, online shopping, bills, pricing, sales quotes, and consumer goods. To improve the business, sellers need a colossal volume and assortment of information to gather, store, oversee and investigate for consumer loyalty. Merchants can address large information challenges by creating significant bits of knowledge to improve marketing campaign efficiency, optimize assortment and decision making, and avoid distributing and operating difficulties. New technologies are intended to yield advantage of big data and permit industries to get benefit from trade and sales change, counting providing a better shopping understanding, creating better retail and networking. Thus, by analysing these data, the industries easily find customer requirements (Bendre & Thool, 2016).

Banking

The needs for changing financial administrations and security in banking is provided by the big data analytics. The key destinations in this part are to fabricate a client centric organization, advance business hazard the executives, enhance business security the board, improve productivity and smooth out tasks, streamline offers and strategically pitch. Enormous information examination will give improved item and administration the executive's approaches for perceiving banks' requirements for clients and workers. In this field, the utilization of measurable techniques and employment booking utilizing conveyed and equal preparing to deal with and process exchanges forestalls exchange stalemate and disappointment. By utilizing content and portable examination, banks can give advance, reserve funds, premium and record arrangements related arrangements for buyer profitability, maintenance, and fulfilment as indicated by the accessible information. Large information engineering is fit for incorporating, approving, improving and breaking down the information got from the distinctive source frameworks as experienced in the financial practice through different Big Data Analytics procedures. Simultaneously, it meets the various measures for information mix, transmission and handling coordination generally experienced inside a worldwide money related establishment (Bendre & Thool, 2016).

Global Diversification of Machine Learning

The price of artificial intelligence machines would decrease with developments in new technology and an increase in the production rate, thus being embrace globally. Due to big difference in culture, ethnicity, language, and political affiliations, it is important to train artificial intelligence machines differently. Thus, we will enter the global market through machine learning and big data without harming people's feelings (Software, 2020).

Automotive

The automotive industry is taking actions to distinguish itself in the face of strong competition by using big data analytics and machine learning technologies to boost production, marketing and consumer experience before, during, and after purchase.

Using statistical models to historical data aids automakers determine the effect of previous marketing activities in identifying potential plans for increasing investment returns. Predictive analytics helps suppliers to track and exchange critical information with dealerships about possible vehicle or component failures, thereby reducing the cost of consumer maintenance (Software, 2020).

Predict Future Developments

Machine learning in big data helps to link computers with huge data sets, allowing them learn new things by themselves. Using machine learning algorithms to evaluate big data helps companies predict future business patterns (Software, 2020).

ENCOUNTERS IN BIG DATA

The size, velocity, and variety of information delivered after the varied sensors and sources hint to diverse huge information and stage difficulties. The Transaction Processing Performance Council (TPPC) sets gauges for advancing quick, secure, and dependable information base preparing and online business exchange over the system. The multifaceted nature of enormous information frameworks faces the accompanying issues (Bendre & Thool, 2016).

System Complexity: Big data infrastructure consists several set of distributed device networks. Therefore, system and device organisation is a challenging job. There's no clear single structure for modelling this whole network.

Variety of Applications: The architecture represents program factors like managing big data, different data, and modules of applications. Since, extracting the information from vast quantities of data is difficult job.

Scale of Data: Data gathered from different sources are tough to classify, as the data structure is dissimilar and entire data are interrelated.

System Evolution: As the data proportions grows every passing day, a novel technical assessment is necessary, beside with new data sources. Designing a novel interface for the individual applications is a daunting job.

MACHINE LEARNING INCORPORATION WITH BIG DATA USING SIGNAL PROCESSING TECHNIQUES

It is only that signal processing is of most elevated significance to opportune large information applications like ongoing clinical imaging, slant investigation from online internet based life, savvy urban communities and may others. Underneath, Artificial Intelligence (AI) with Signal Processing (SP) strategies for handling of big data are used. An overview of the representative work is as follows (Qiu et al., 2016).

Statistical Learning for Big Data Analysis: It is without question this is a period of information storm wherever gaining from these a lot of data via focal processors and capacity units appears to be infeasible. Henceforth, the signal processing and factual learning devices must be rethought. It is smarter to perform learning progressively for the approach of spilling information sources, regularly devoid of opportunity to return to previous sections. Big data errands applicable to SP primarily involve huge scope, anomalies and missing qualities, continuous requirements, and distributed storage. We need to confront incredible big data challenges like expectation and determining, purging and ascription, dimensionality decrease, relapse, arrangement, and bunching. As far as these undertakings and difficulties, excellent prototypes and enhancement with the signal processing and learning methodology for to incorporate big data equally and decentralized, information versatile, strong, brief, and scanty innovations (Qiu et al., 2016).

Convex optimization for big data analytics: Although the significance of convex formulations and optimization has improved intensely in the over a years and employing these formulations in an extensive several applications of signal processing, In context of big data, it is quite difficult to deal with the optimization problems due to hug data size, consequently reinvention of convex optimization is in need. (Qiu et al., 2016) Studied new developments in convex optimization algorithms personalized for big data, taking as decisive aim to evidently decrease the computational, storage, and communication blockages. As an instance, advancement issue with big data detailed as

$$F^* = \min_x \{F(x) = f(x) + g(x); x \in R^p \tag{1}$$

Where f and g are represent convex functions. To acquire an optimal solution x * of (1) and the necessary suppositions on f and g, the creators introduced three effective enormous information estimate strategies, including first-request techniques, randomization and parallel and distributed computation. They alluded basically to the versatile, randomized, and equal calculations for analytics in big data. Moreover, used for the advancement issue, ADMM can give a straightforward appropriated calculation to comprehend its composite structure, by utilizing incredible enlarged Lagrangian and double deterioration strategies. Despite the fact that there are two provisos for ADMM, i.e., one is that shut structure answers don't generally exist and the other is that no intermingling ensures for in excess of two advancement target terms, there are a few new answers for address the two burdens, for example, proximal angle strategies and equal processing .Precisely, from machine learning viewpoint, those distributed mechanisms like versatile, equal, and circulated systems are additionally required, and a few utilizations of utilizing the ongoing curved improvement calculations in learning techniques, for example, bolster vector machines and chart learning have been showed up lately (Qiu et al., 2016).

Stochastic Approximation for Big Data Analytics: Apart from the fact that huge numbers of internet learning strategies were created inside the AI discipline, they had solid associations with workhorse SP procedures. Ongoing advancements in internet learning for big data investigation were introduced, where it underlined the associations and contrasts amid web based learning techniques and about conspicuous measurable SP devices, for example, stochastic guess (SA) and stochastic slope (SG) calculations. From one perspective, the fundamental takes a shot at SA, for example, by Robbins–Monro and Widrow calculations, and the workhorse behind a few traditional Signal processing devices, for example, LMS and RLS calculations, conveyed rich potential in present day learning assignments for enormous data analytics. Then again, it was likewise exhibited that internet learning plans together with irregular testing strategies were required to assume dynamic jobs in illuminating enormous scope streamlining assignments. In plot, the ongoing advances in web based learning strategies and a few SP procedures referenced have the one of a kind and integral qualities with one another (Qiu et al., 2016).

MACHINE LEARNING PATTERNS FOR BIG DATA

Deep Learning

It is a framework from the family of machine leaning that constitutes representation. The example research is generally called feature learning (L'heureux et al., 2017). This algorithm has a specified way to use data representations to perform tasks instead of external data features. It alters data into abstract illustrations which allow learning of the features. Those representations are then used in a deep learning system to accomplish the tasks of machine learning. The scope for feature engineering is limited as the features are learned directly from the results. In the sense of Big Data, due to the difficulties associated with this process (L'heureux et al., 2017), the opportunity to circumvent feature development is seen as an incredible advantage.

Deep learning utilizes a various levelled learning method indistinguishable from that of neural systems to remove information portrayals from information. It uses a few concealed layers, with the information go through each layer, non-straight changes are utilized. These portrayals involve elevated near complex deliberations of the information (L'heureux et al., 2017) . Every layer endeavours to isolate the variables of variety inside the information. As the yield of the last layer is just a change of the first information, it tends to be used as a contribution to other AI calculations also. This type of learning calculations can catch different phases of reflections, along these lines this kind of learning is a perfect response to the issue of picture grouping and acknowledgment (L'heureux et al., 2017).

Deep learning engineering is flexible and able to assemble utilizing a huge number of parts: Self-encoders and constrained Boltzmann machines are regular structure squares (L'heureux et al., 2017). Auto-encoders are solo calculations that can be utilized for some, reasons, similar to inconsistency location, yet they clearly fill in as an antecedent stage for neural systems in the feeling of big data (L'heureux et al., 2017). They work over backpropagation, trying to set their target yields as their information, so it's possible to self-encode by themselves. These devices are inseparable by the use of stochastic instead of deterministic methods. Profound conviction systems are another case of deep learning calculations are (L'heureux et al., 2017).

However, fewer representations allows these kind of algorithms to be flexible enough to adapt the changing data. Due to abstracted data, the various data structures and bases have no immediate effect on the performance of the algorithm, making deep learning an ideal possibility to counter data heterogeneity (L'heureux et al., 2017).

Remarkably, both supervised and unsupervised learning can be used for deep learning (L'heureux et al., 2017). This is likely because of the very idea of the technique; Extract global connections and patterns from data due to their reliance on high level abstractions. It is an extraordinary bit of leeway in the feeling of big data, as it makes the algorithms less inclined to the topic of veracity difficulties (L'heureux et al., 2017). Also, its different layers of non-direct changes address the test of non-linearity in the information. Deep compression was suggested to speed up planning without loss of accuracy (L'heureux et al., 2017).

Deep learning is sufficient in all accounts to solve some of the difficulties already described, such as feature engineering, non-linearity, noisy and dirty data, data heterogeneity and data vulnerability, according to the characteristics listed above. However, these algorithms are not fundamentally designed for incremental learning (L'heureux et al., 2017) and are vulnerable to the problem of data velocity. In spite of the fact that they are particularly well suited for managing more datasets with troublesome issues, they don't do as such in a computationally productive way. These algorithms can also become infallible for data that has high-dimensionality (L'heureux et al., 2017).

Online Learning

The response to the large-scale processing by online learning is an example of machine learning to address the gaps in efficacy produced in the use of big data. It can be used as a replacement for batch learning, the model that traditional machine learning usually uses. Data is processes in batches in case of batch learning, and needs the full dataset to be eligible for sample model Also, the model can no longer be altered once it has been produced. This makes it impossible for the following definitions to tackle the dimensions of big data (L'heureux et al., 2017):

Volume: Sometimes, computationally efficient to process at once a very broad data volume
Variety: An obligation to make sure that the full data is accessible at the commencement of the process cycle, restricts the use of data from multiple sources
Velocity: At the time of analysis, the necessity to access the entire dataset neither allow real-time analyses nor the data from multiple sources
Veracity: Impediments to results caused by bad data veracity are extremely important as the modification of data is not possible

Alternatively, online learning uses planning data sources and models will train on a single event (L'heureux et al., 2017). This "Learn-as-you-go" approach increases time taken to load and process, since the data do not need to be in memory completely. Thus, huge amount of data can be processed, removes the modularity curses, and enables real-time processing (L'heureux et al., 2017).

Moreover, the "web" descriptor also imitates the idea that this concept supports its application unceasingly; this can be altered as the algorithm sees right. Its flexibility considers several count of dirty and noisy data, imbalances in the classes and floating ideas. (L'heureux et al., 2017) Proposed, of course, a series of online subsets of powerful sequential learning machines.

This style of learning can solve big data speed problems well its step-by-step learning design facilitates data usability, real-time processing, and concept participation difficulties. As an example, this model is used to deal with inventory data forecasts as the stock market constantly develops and grows quickly. The scale, layout and variety issues are still unresolved. However, the online learning process does not easily fit all machine learning algorithms (L'heureux et al., 2017).

Local Learning

Local learning was initially suggested in 1992 by Bottou and Vapnik (L'heureux et al., 2017), and is a technique that gives a replacement for traditional global learning. Global learning is used by machine learning algorithms, conservatively, by techniques such as generative learning (L'heureux et al., 2017). This method includes using a model to re-generate the input data, based on the underlying data distribution. It essentially tries to study the full dataset, while local learning is just anxious with interesting subsets. It can therefore be called a semi-parametric approximation of a global model. This hybrid, parametric model's stronger but less restrictive assumptions on small variation and distortion (L'heureux et al., 2017). As an example, the prediction about the energy consumed by the customers is a characteristic example of where local learning can be useful. Creating a model for customers alike may be useful for building one model for each customer or same model for all the customers (L'heureux et al., 2017). As per (L'heureux et al., 2017) newly developed a random local vector supporting machine parallel learning algorithm that was a lot better than the one standard SVM algorithm to address the issues related to volume, thus indicating to ease some big-data problems with the help of local learning. Local learning in various statistical studies actually outdid global precision and quantitative preparation.

Distributing the problem in controllable data sections decreases the data size be processed and loaded possibly at once into the memory; thus the model decreases the modularity curse. Models are not even influenced by the problems related to class imbalances and location of data as regards the location of each cluster. Recent research has shown that, when dealing with imbalanced datasets, the effect of local learning is always better than global learning (L'heureux et al., 2017).

As a consequence, a local technique will ease the burden of the modularity curse, class inequality, variation and bias, and data locality. Nevertheless, matters of dimensionality and velocity have yet to be addressed, such as concept drift among others. Overall, the local strategies remain largely unexplored in the big data context; it's possible to encounter the challenges by learning the model's effect on speed and accuracy (L'heureux et al., 2017).

BIG DATA TOOLS AND TECHNOLOGIES

Hadoop 3.0, Hadoop Ecosystem (HE), Spark 2.3 are the widely used big data technologies illustrate this section. You may categorise the prevalent big data tools as Stream processing tools, Interactive query processing tools. Another subcategories of tools, the large data infrastructure such as the tools for data ingestion, container orchestration and messaging systems is nevertheless applicable (Rao et al., 2019).

Hadoop Integrated Environment

Hadoop is a Distributed File System (HDFS) used with a MapReduce programming model to analyse massive data sets. MapReduce is a programming language that is utilised to cost-effectively process and analyse the big data. Hadoop offers expandability, computational power, and storage. HDFS is Hadoop's file system component that keeps the blocks identified as file system metadata. HDFS comprises the node of name and the node of info. HDFS functions as a system of master-slaves. An HDFS cluster has a solitary node, a master server that completes the nomenclature and directories of the file system in the method of a hierarchy. Two files are used as data node (Hussain, Sanga, & Mongia, 2019). Yarn offers a dissimilar processing system, e.g. interactive processing, graph processing, stream processing, and batch processing. MapReduce is a Hadoop framework wherein two components are mapping task first and reduces task. Formerly one divides a set of data and transforms it to one more set of data and afterwards one takes the result from the map and joins that data into a main pair into a reduced set of tuples. The popular hadoop includes libraries and directories (Hussain, Sanga, & Mongia, 2019).

Hadoop 3.0 Ecosystem (HE 3.0)

HE is an interconnected framework through many necessary tools of data processing that offer storage, access mechanism, and data managing services based on vendor necessities. It permits for synchronisation between customers, aggregators, integrators and providers of data (Rao et al., 2019).

HE 3.0 Features

Erasure Coding (EC)

Instead of exploiting duplication, HDFS supports Erasure Coding (EC) in HE 3.0 to substantially reduce storage space (Rao et al., 2019). In HDFS, the replication factor is three, which is costlier. The 3x HDFS method of replication causes overhead in storage space and network capital to 200% (Rao et al., 2019). Therefore, rather than utilizing replication, use EC method is a safer solution, which ensures fair tolerance of fault with limited storage space (Rao et al., 2019) .

Multiple NameNodes

One more enhanced characteristic in Hadoop 3.0 is that numerous NameNodes are supported. Hadoop 2.0 has a single ANN, the tolerance for the fault is a single SNN and a quorum version of three JNS is obtained by replication. Hadoop 2.0 is able to manage any device node drop. Though, Hadoop 3.0 upholds several standby NameNodes to attain a greater level of fault-tolerance for certain peculiar deployments (Rao et al., 2019).

Data Lake and Aliyun

HE 3.0 backs Hadoop's alternate well-matched file systems: Azure Data Lake13 and Aliyun Object Storage System (Aliyun OSS), 14 an Alibaba Cloud file system (Rao et al., 2019).

Intra-DataNode Balancer

HE 3.0 is one more essential function identified as Intra-DataNode Balancer that manages the skewedness when incrementing or deleting the DataNode discs (Rao et al., 2019).

Apache Spark 2.3

Platforms centred on MapReduce remain ideal for running commodity with applications for large-scale clusters. MapReduce-based systems adopt the acyclic data flow principle and thus ineffective to manage iterative duties in parallel operations. Apache Spark is a Scala-written swift cluster computing system in memory that handles both iterative and interactive jobs by attaining extraordinary expandability and acceptance to fault (Rao et al., 2019). Spark is well-matched with Apache Hadoop in functions and storage. Spark is in memory which additional gain that a fine data storage cap is reached with I/O modification (Rao et al., 2019).

Stream Processing Systems

These systems portray a vital character in offering valued customer data and authorising productions to make suitable and swift results. Stream programming tools process live sources of data and yield outcomes that are low in latency. Applications needed for stream processing are usually represented as acyclic guided chart with vertices that indicate data flow channel among operator means operators and edges (Rao et al., 2019).

Distributed Stream Processing Systems

Apache Storm

Apache Storm (Rao et al., 2019) is a distributed, tolerant fault computer device, designed to stream huge volumes of data. A stream is the essential characteristic at Storm. It can be an incessant sequenced tuple list that gets measured in a distributed method (Rao et al., 2019). A stream as a pattern consisting of info in tuples on different arenas. Apache Storm consists basically of three abstractions. They are topologies, bolts and spouts. A spout in a computational method is the origin of streams. A spout produces its own streams, reads messaging data, or produces streams from external streaming APIs, reading the data. A bolt measures many input streams and generates many output streams. The information is sent to one or more bolts through a spout. A bolt produces data that is from the spout and processes number of data sources chosen to deliver the current data flows (Rao et al., 2019 . The topology is a network of spouts and bolts, with either a sputum or a bolt at each node. A topological edge means a bolt subscribing to another source of information from sputum or bolt production. (Rao et al., 2019).

Simple Scalable Streaming System (S4)

S4 is an all-purpose, dispersed, MapReduce driven stream processing engine built at Yahoo (Rao et al., 2019). It is an expandable, partly defect-tolerant, pluggable architecture which is utilised to manage limitless and unlimited data streams. In S4, the rudimentary computational units are cluster-distributed computing components (PEs). The transmission of message amongst the PEs takes place in the method of data events. The design, sorting, key and key values of the components recognise an instance of PE. Every PE absorbs events which match the value of the key. Processing Nodes (PNs) are logical hosts for PEs that are responsible to receive, encode, transmit and generating output events. S4 attains part fault-tolerance, if there is no user-mentioned state fall-back feature in PEs, then during the handoff the states connected to unsuccessful PEs and info disappeared (Rao et al., 2019).

Interactive Analytical Processing Tools

This includes Big Data tools, which are interactive computational analysis tools that resolve the need to communicate with various instruments to control large datasets of diverse applications. Users can access and perform data analysis in an interactive environment using interactive tools (Rao et al., 2019).

Apache Tez offers a combined framework for creating expandable, effective data-flow-centric engines. Apache Tez is valuable for creating engines that are purpose-built that processes data with specific needs. These APIs have the task of regulating frameworks in order to model the physical and logical semics with less code for data flow graphs. Tez isn't an engine, instead a component library that is utilised to create data flow-based engines.

Hive was first established by Facebook and take on by a variety of other companies such as Amazon, Hortonworks (Rao et al., 2019). It is a data warehouse key that denotes enquiries with alike qualities of SQL in a declarative language named as HiveQL. Hive's key tasks are to transform HiveQL into MapReduce jobs and to execute those jobs utilising Hadoop (Rao et al., 2019). Hive aims to perform ad hoc searches, collect data and evaluate big data.

Impala is an ad hoc open-source querying technique, which in HE uses SQL (Rao et al., 2019). Impala has its own architecture and runs daemons, as opposed to Hive, on any cluster node. Impala uses an alternative to MapReduce MPP generator. (Rao et al., 2019) Impala allows you to easily query the data from HDFS or HBase tables, which increase the ability of Hadoop to combine different data types with the scheme during operation. It includes input data which includes types of data, partition names that use the metastore Hive. Impala is high in its I / O subsystem calculating capabilities (Rao et al., 2019).

Data Ingestion Tools

The mechanism by which data is collected and processed into a data storage is termed as a data ingestion. A successful process of ingestion of data begins by harmonising data sources, approving all documents and directing info to the precise destination (Rao et al., 2019). Data ingestion tools like Flume, Sqoop, and Chukwa performs a critical part in transporting data to Hadoop from database.

Sqoop transports enormous amounts of structured data among Hadoop databases (Rao et al., 2019). Sqoop allows the ingress and distribute of data to HDFS from outside sources. It also coordinates with Oozie to plan and mechanize transactions for ingress and distribute. The method of importing into Sqoop takes place in two phases (Rao et al., 2019).

Apache Flume is a secure, distributed and accessible data ingestion framework for storing, merging and uploading huge quantities of data streams like events, log data and others to a centralised data store from several different data sources. It has an easy, modular architecture which gives online analysis of data streams (Gürcan & Berigel, 2018).

DISTRIBUTED MACHINE LEARNING TOOLS

Mahout

Apache Mahout (Rao et al., 2019) aims to construct and improve machine learning algorithms that can be extended. The Mahout 0, 13.0 environment includes Mahout-Samsara environment, Scala variation for Spark algorithms 6 and Samsara Apache environment 7 and H2O.8, and the sparse matrix, vector computing compatible with MLlib Spark environment. The Framework of Samsara includes Stochastic Singular Value Decomposition (SSVD), Stochastic Main Component Analysis (SPCA), distributed Cholesky QR, DALS, and Collaborative Similarity Filtering among items and rows and Naive Bayes algorithms for classification of objects. Nevertheless, the preceding form of Mahout contains a range of conventional grouping, clustering, themed models, collaborative philtres, dimension reduction, and mining of association rules (Rao et al., 2019).

Spark MLlib

Apache Spark comprises of an ML algorithm library, identified as MLlib. The DataFrame API enables rich functional integration amongst spark applications by executing different relational operations on RDDs (Rao et al., 2019). Spark.ml consists of the API pipelines to build, monitor and manage pipelines, while spark.mllib consists of many ML algorithms and utilities. Ensuing are the presently obtainable algorithms in Apache Spark (Rao et al., 2019).

The developments in Apache Spark 2.2 are ALS algorithms for top-k references for every users, LinearSVC for data organization utilising vector support machines, and presently logistic regression supports coefficiency constraints during data training (Rao et al., 2019). ALS algorithm's aim is to approximate the rating matrix into two lower-rank matrices product. But in version 2.2 of Spark, to fit the default ALS API setting the method DeveloperApi ALS.train()sets the default value of regParam as 0.1 instead of 1.0 (Rao et al., 2019) . The ALS method would also not impact users, because it is labelled with DeveloperApi. The MLlib has the ensuing fresh qualities and advances to present algorithms in the latest version Spark 2.3 (Rao et al., 2019).

In Spark 2.3, all existing equipped models and pipelines now operate with organized streaming jobs to produce output results while running MLlib models and pipelines.

Break API Changes The class and logistic regression models' hierarchy has been updated to be more sleek and remarkable in order to provide multi-tier overview support. This property is a user code breaking shift that flings the Logistic Regression Training Summary (LRTS) into a Binary Logistic Regression Training Summary (BLRTS) (Rao et al., 2019). Logistic Regression is a well-acknowledged and specific instance of generalised linear models which guesses the likelihood of a result. Logistic regression can be employed in spark.ml to forecast a binary out-turn using binomial logistical regression, or it can be employed to forecast a multi-class out-turn using multinomial regression. The LRTS presents a Logistic Regression Model description. A further measure such as ROC curve is possible in the case of binary classification. Utilising binary Summary method in spark ML classification (Rao et al., 2019) to trigger the binary summary. The option between LRTS and BLRTS may be defined by a family parameter. Spark can make sure of the correct alternative between LRTS and BLRTS though by keeping the parameter unset (Rao et al., 2019).

MACHINE LEARNING TOOLS BASED ON CLOUD

Microsoft Azure ML

Azure ML Studio is a cloud-based, collaborative, drag-and - drop, fully controlled application and visual workspace platform for designing, testing and deploying user data predictive analytics tasks in the Microsoft Azure cloud.9 Azure ML Studio consists of a graphical framework to handle ML tasks, a series of pre-processing modules, a group of ML algorithms and an API interface to reveal an interface to a model. This studio contains of a great number of ML algorithms that facilitate input data, performance, preparation and visualisation with modules that help. Applying these functions, after some iterations, a user can create a predictive analytics assessment and apply it to prepare the user model (Rao et al., 2019). This technique has a wide variety of algorithms that can be grouped into families-regression, classification, clusters and the detection of anomalies. Azure ML involves Azure ML API service that offers a web service hosting environment for Azure ML to function in the execution of ML experiment evaluations and development. Azure ML is made up of two kinds of Web services. These are Batch Execution Service (BES) and Request-Response Service (RRS). RRS is an extendable, down-time service that offers an interface to ML Studio's stateless models. BES is an asynchronous service which collects a lot of data. The measurement purpose is to deliver the output of a prophetic web service. However, Azure ML has some inconveniences. Azure ML doesn't support python and R, which is a shortage of enacting APIs. The range and storage limitations of data sets are further shortcomings. During function normalisation, data types can be generalised to higher datasets, restricted to 10GB maximum (Rao et al., 2019).

IBM Watson ML

This offers a cloud service that connects a local user environment to an IBM server with a fusion approach. Watson ML is an ML API for user templates that are used for printing, designing and labelling. Users must conduct two main ML activities, training and scoring. Training data is utilised for the creation of an ML model. The analysis of an algorithm by learning data is called a training course. The operation's performance is recognized as a model that contains the coefficients learned from mathematical expressions. The procedure which is applied by a trained model to forecast a consequence is known as scoring. The Watson ML's core focus is the implementation of a standard. But Watson ML is combined with IBM SPSS Modeler, Data Science Expertise to work with ML models and pipelines using ML API (Rao et al., 2019). Most of the models to study from ML, data mining, and computational algorithms in different models. IBM Watson Studio is employed to increase output by creating a distinctive environment in which a set of people can collaborate to develop and deploy AI with the best open source and IBM applications. It also provides developers, data scientists, science experts a range of tools to team up and operate design data, create and organize the data obtained from models (Rao et al., 2019).

CURRENT ISSUES WITH MACHINE LEARNING FOR BIG DATA

Amid ML's current challenges on big data, advancing the effectiveness for iterations is a major issue. At present there are no specific machine learning algorithms proposed. The tools of big data usually do batch-mode computation and cannot handle tasks that involves the process to carry iteratively and the operations which deals with huge data dependency. Iterative subtasks supervise both algorithm groups. Improving the distribution of cluster resources among several working loads of iterative algorithms must be dynamic, which sequentially includes: (a) forecasting the iterations count and (b) forecasting the time taken for each repetition (Zhou et al., 2017). The Hadoop architecture can evade, and handle, very sluggish or straggler errands at runtime. With MapReduce and fault tolerance spark (Zhou et al., 2017) supports cache data between iterations in memory similarly, on the another note, approaches have already been progressed to progress big data proficiency in computation without overlooking machine learning execution, that has just little bits of data instead of all information in quick memory and predictor is formed on each tiny piece, which joins all predictors together (Zhou et al., 2017). Graph-based architectures and big data in-memory tools were also created to decrease cost of I / O and to enhance iterative processing (Zhou et al., 2017).

The challenge is to limit the response with classificatory. The ideal classification chain learning at runtime has shown to be a multi-player bandit problem with negligible reactions (Zhou et al., 2017). To permit the ideal classifier chain learning (Zhou et al., 2017), it doesn't require local classifiers that are distributed to exchange any information with the exception of confined reaction to mining results (Zhou et al., 2017).

To tackle the speed characteristic of big data in machine learning. Current responses are unintended to address changeable streams for the study of big data (Zhou et al., 2017). A machine learning system essentially be in a position to handle incessantly through the arrival of altering data. Lifelong learning of computers is in deviation from conventional one-shot learning (Zhou et al., 2017). Thus, web based learning has been misused to render piece techniques efficacious and versatile for huge scope learning applications. For instance, to deal with three web based learning undertakings, two diverse online part ML calculations – Fourier Online Gradient Descent and Nystrom Online Gradient Descent calculations were found: regression binary classification and multi-class classification. An applications in real-time needs the work to be completed in a stipulated amount of time frame otherwise the outcome of those processes would be insignificant like earthquake forecast, stock market forecast and autonomous exchange systems that are based on agents, and many others. In such time-sensitive conditions, the true data value rest on on the freshness of information that should be handled in real time (Qiu et al., 2016).

High speed data can be learnt by a capable key approach like online learning. It's a is a deep-rooted learning model whose plan is to study one occurrence at a moment, rather than learning that's based on offline, the whole information needed to train the data should be gathered. This successive learning system works with big data to ensure that the present machines are incapable to store the entire data in the memory. A new learning algorithm has newly been named an extreme instructor (ELM) for hidden layer feeding neural networking networks (SLFNs) has been suggested to speed up learning (Qiu et al., 2016 . ELM delivers very fast learning speed, improved generalization performance and with the least amount of humans in comparison to some other traditional learning algorithms. ELM thus has significant advantages in the process of high data speed (Qiu et al., 2016).

One more challenge is to attend to the diversity feature of big data in ML. The majority previously developed machine algorithms can only receive a particular kind of input, like numerical, text or images. Data that may be utilized for a solitary ML objective in a few circumstances could come in various sorts and formats. That will possibly lead to outbreak of learning characteristics, and is many a times stated as a challenge of "Big Dimensionality"(Zhou et al., 2017. Consider an example, single ML algorithm may want to learn from a mix of huge data capacity and data stream with high-speed or huge data capacity with image, text, acoustics, and movement qualities (Zhou et al., 2017).

The huge diversity of data creates interests and challenges in big data. This is caused from the occurrence that data usually comes from numerous bases and are of diverse types. The development of heterogeneous, high-dimensional and nonlinear data using diverse representative procedures is facilitated by structured, semi-structured and even fully unstructured databases. Studying with these kind of datasets, the remarkable difficulty is achievable and even before we hit them fully, the indicator of difficulty cannot be conceived (Qiu et al., 2016).

The data integration is method used in heterogeneous data that helps to blend the data that resides in various bases and give the user a united sight of these data. The data integration problem can be well addressed by studying data representations obtained from an individual data sources (Qiu et al., 2016). Therefore, representation learning is favourable. (Qiu et al., 2016) Suggests a theory of data fusion established on statistical learning for the heterogeneous data that fall under a spectrum of two-dimension. Furthermore, deep learning approaches are exposed to be extremely efficient in combining various sources data. For instance, deep learning algorithms proposed by (Qiu et al., 2016) is to study a united portrayal that adds compressed image and text data that are real-valued (Qiu et al., 2016) .

One more problem related with high diversity data are they are high dimensional and nonlinear, like global stellar, spectra climate patterns and human gene distributions. In order to handle data with high dimension, the decline in dimension is an efficient solution through the discovery of important low-dimensional structures hidden in their commentary. Usual methods use feature extraction to decrease the dimensions of data. As an example, (Qiu et al., 2016) offered a local-learning selection algorithm for the function to analyse the data that are high in dimension. To reduce the dimensionality of data, Principal component analysis (PCA), locally linear embedding (LLE), linear discriminant analysis (LDA) and Laplacian Eigen maps machine learning algorithms can be used (Qiu et al., 2016) . Lately, matrix with low-rank portrays more vital part in analysis of large-scale data and in reduction of dimensionality (Qiu et al., 2016). The issue of recovering a low-rank matrix is an important obstacle with machine learning applications (Qiu et al., 2016). Consider a simple instance of with high-dimensional data processing low-ranking matrix recovery algorithms. Let's presume that a large data matrix N is provided, and let's know that it can be decomposed as N = M + Λ total of a single, where M is in a low-level ranking. Because the low-dimensional column or row space of M is not unknown, the matrix M of the data matrix N needs to be strengthened and the problem can be framed as a regular PCA (Qiu et al., 2016):

$$\min \left\| M \right\|_* . \tag{2}$$

$$\{M\} \tag{3}$$

$$s.t. \left\| N - M \right\|_F \leq \varepsilon \tag{4}$$

The above issue demonstrates the key task of the matrix recovery analysis of processing the data that are highly dimensional that can be proficiently resolved by several current algorithms counting Augmented Lagrange multipliers (ALM) algorithm and Accelerated Proximal Gradient (APG) algorithm (Qiu et al., 2016) . Concerning data that accepts non-linear characteristics connected to various kernel-based learning means possibly give creditable answers (Qiu et al., 2016).

Low value density and diversity are another problem. Actually, by abusing an array of learning approaches to examine large datasets, the last objective is to obtain useful info from huge quantities of data in categories that are advantageous commercially. Thus, value is likewise measured as a striking qualities of big data (Qiu et al., 2016). Nevertheless, it is not clear whether it is possible to obtain large quantities of low dense data. For instance, cops can manage criminal cases by frequent access to several surveillance videos. Regrettably, a limited usage data frames are often concealed in a big quantity of video sources (Qiu et al., 2016).

In order to carry out certain tasks, Knowledge Discovery in Databases (KDDs) and data mining technologies will come into effect, because these technologies offer conceivable answers in order to obtain the necessary information hidden in the vast data (Qiu et al., 2016) . These technologies can also be incorporated in IoT. In particular, it was discussed in detail in terms of classification, clustering and frequent pattern technologies to gain importance from enormous IoT data, infrastructures and services (Qiu et al., 2016).

The variation in data significance, that is, the commercial value of various data varies meaningfully and even the similar data have different importance when judging from various perceptions or situations, is an additional difficulty related to the value of big data. Any new cognitive technology should therefore be built to improve the adaptability and intellectuality of present learning systems. The most striking case of these tools is "Watson"(L'heureux et al., 2017) from IBM, which is made of various subsystems that use various machine learning techniques with a strong cognitive capacity to investigate the question and achieve the very likely response. Some features such as learning, change, interaction and awareness make Watson's ability to be intelligent and more capable of computerized data management. The age of cognitive computing is anticipated to arrive (Qiu et al., 2016).

APPLICATIONS AND FUTURE DIRECTIONS

Much current research on ML for big data concentrated with features of volume, velocity and variety, while not much work has been done to tackle the left over two features of big data: veracity and value. To manage data veracity, one assuring way is to build algorithms that are able of evaluating data or data sources' trustworthiness or integrity so as to sort unreliable data in the course of pre-processing; and one more way is to construct latest ML paradigms that can infer with inaccurate and contradictory data. To appreciate the importance of big data in decision support, the users should be assisted to comprehend the ML outcomes and the reasoning behind the individual system's decision. Understandable ML would therefore be a major field of potential study. In this connection, we also have to address fundamental work in helping people in the loop to obtain large quantities of interpreted data efficiently, for example, through crowd-tracking. We need to evaluate an algorithm based not just on its predictive accuracy and extensibility, but also on its total capacity to help end users carry out their tasks. In addition, more open research questions comprise: (1) The way to defend data privacy when executing ML; (2) The way to make ML more asserting in order to make it simpler for non-experts to identify and communicate with; (3) how to include typical domain information in ML; and (4) The way to develop modern big data ML architecture that offers seamless decision support based on actual scrutiny of huge quantities of varied data that might not be accurate (Zhou et al., 2017) .

In synopsis, ML is indispensable to address the issues raised by big data and to discover secret patterns, information, and visions from big data to turn the promise of the latter into real value for business decision-making and scientific research. The ML and Big data marriage leads to a stable future inside a modern boundary (Zhou et al., 2017).

Environment and Water Management

Big data will change methodological studies by EWM researchers deeply. The benefit of big data can only be maximised when there is a relatively low price of enough automated data wrangling and cleaning.

The next big data Wave answers should be developed and created by people who comprehend the issues and meaning, and not only by those who comprehend the algorithms. A way to do this is by promoting cooperation between data scientists, domain experts, governments, the public, and the private sectors. It is as well vitally significant to coach the following generation of EWM researchers from the beginning to become more competent and semantically lush in data science, duplicable data items. Scientific evidence, as recommended by (Sun & Scanlon, 2019) must be linked to provenance to assist in analysis and confidence, and definition of approaches to back duplicability.

The journey toward smart data would involve a various operating measures from the existing one, AI and automated execution and one predicated. The possible prize related with including EWM also has huge data and DL, considering the growing humanitarian effort in disaster relief, thanks to an enhanced and faster information source. This means that EWM needs to improve situational awareness skills substantially, contributing not just to a greater ability to anticipate short-term changes but likewise an improved comprehending of the incremental changes faced by the Earth system with regard to environmental factors and human pressure (Sun & Scanlon, 2019).

Health and Safety Inspection

Big data and machine learning is used choosing artefacts of inspection Supervised and unsupervised learning algorithms need a large amount of data, both with regards to the number of observations and the number of variables, typically denoted to as 'features.' Some labour inspectors gather and store enormous quantities of data relevant to their objects of investigation and investigation. The available data typically includes company specific characteristics such as number of staff, age of company, industrial classification, number of previous inspections, consequences of previous inspections, accident reports. In addition, the volume of data rises day by day as new inspection reports are published. In theory then, the problem of targeting high-risk businesses by using big data should be well suited for machine learning algorithms nevertheless at initial look. However there are a few influential exclusions, which all show that big data and machine learning are of great importance to the labour inspectors to deal with the issue of high-risk goods.

For example, a research study explores the aptitude or more specifically, the aptitude of machine learning activities to predict workplace mishaps; falls at ground level. The downside to this study is that the qualities used in algorithms are generally not the type of data labour inspectors have, given their fairly accurate predictions (Dahl & Starren, 2019).

Smart Buildings

A world of appliances that meet your requirements and do exactly what you want them to do by pushing a button is the Smart Buildings pledge. As SBs and their inhabitants make a massive amount of streaming data, researchers look to ML and big data Analytics methods to manage, process, and gain insights from this big data. Though new technological improvements which make the idea of SBs possible, there are nonetheless a variability of tasks in the field of SBs which restrain large-scale real-world systems. The tasks will soon become an important driving force for development in industrial and academic SB research (Qolomany et al., 2019).

Future Computing

Computational Optimization

(Jeong, Hassan, & Sangaiah, 2019) created a parallel algorithm for the graphics processing unit (GPU), precisely to accelerate the procedure of weighting data gravity classification characteristics. Snag confronted by reducing classification model's computational complexity Centered on gravitational data using GPU.

Privacy and Security

(Jeong, Hassan, & Sangaiah, 2019)Put forward fingerprinting technique that uses radio frequency to recognize genuine devices to resolve security problems linked to wireless devices that includes grouping of the dimension reduction process and the classifier to fulfil the application requirements.

Optimized Data Processing and Sharing

The answer to the recursive fuzzy linear regression model with transfer tolerances was developed to assess the functional relationship between passengers (Qolomany et al., 2019). Experimental findings indicate that the cost of locating the actual bike and delaying traffic lights are more difficult to distance, whereas typical cyclists are afraid of the time cost for locating the actual bike (Qolomany et al., 2019).

CONCLUSION

Machine Learning is the investigation of computational strategies for execution upgrade through motorizing data obtaining for a fact. Expert output requires comprehensive domain specific expertise, and hundreds of machine learning expert systems have been developed by software engineering have been widely used in industries. Machine learning enhances the usage of automation in the process of software engineering, in turn reduces the time consumption with automated techniques to improvise precision or efficiency through the discovery and exploitation of regularities in training data. On the other side, big data is rapidly making its progress in various domains, its significance is in using the novel ideas to present solutions to the challenges stands epic. At present, we are living in a world where enormous amount of data is generated with ever increasing scales. In previous days, machine learning systems have been broadly embraced in various monstrous and complex information escalated fields, for example, medication, stargazing, science, for these methods give potential answers for mine the data covered up in the information (Qiu et al., 2016). The need at present is to construct efficient intelligent models that will help with future demands, in line with the development of energy-efficient data models essential for various data-intensive areas incorporated by most industries, as they affect several related industries. Software engineering companies can deliver better solutions in a fixed timeframe using big data and emerging machine-learning technologies. The need for machine learning that contributes to market adoption will be increased further.

REFERENCES

Bendre, M. R., & Thool, V. R. (2016). Analytics, challenges and applications in big data environment: A survey. *Journal of Management Analytics*, *3*(3), 206–239. doi:10.1080/23270012.2016.1186578

Bhatnagar, R. (2018, February). Machine Learning and Big Data processing: a technological perspective and review. In *International Conference on Advanced Machine Learning Technologies and Applications* (pp. 468-478). Springer. 10.1007/978-3-319-74690-6_46

Dahl, Ø., & Starren, A. (2019). *The future role of big data and machine learning for health and safety inspection efficiency*. EU-OSHA.

Gürcan, F., & Berigel, M. (2018, October). Real-Time Processing of Big Data Streams: Lifecycle, Tools, Tasks, and Challenges. In *2018 2nd International Symposium on Multidisciplinary Studies and Innovative Technologies (ISMSIT)* (pp. 1-6). IEEE.

HussainT.SangaA.MongiaS. (2019). Big Data Hadoop Tools and Technologies: A Review. Available at SSRN 3462554. doi:10.2139srn.3462554

Jeong, Y. S., Hassan, H., & Sangaiah, A. K. (2019). Machine learning on big data for future computing. *The Journal of Supercomputing*, *75*(6), 2925–2929. doi:10.100711227-019-02872-z

L'heureux, A., Grolinger, K., Elyamany, H. F., & Capretz, M. A. (2017). Machine learning with big data: Challenges and approaches. *IEEE Access: Practical Innovations, Open Solutions*, *5*, 7776–7797. doi:10.1109/ACCESS.2017.2696365

Qiu, J., Wu, Q., Ding, G., Xu, Y., & Feng, S. (2016). A survey of machine learning for big data processing. *EURASIP Journal on Advances in Signal Processing*, *2016*(1), 67. doi:10.118613634-016-0355-x

Qolomany, B., Al-Fuqaha, A., Gupta, A., Benhaddou, D., Alwajidi, S., Qadir, J., & Fong, A. C. (2019). Leveraging machine learning and big data for smart buildings: A comprehensive survey. *IEEE Access: Practical Innovations, Open Solutions*, *7*, 90316–90356. doi:10.1109/ACCESS.2019.2926642

Rao, T. R., Mitra, P., Bhatt, R., & Goswami, A. (2019). The big data system, components, tools, and technologies: A survey. *Knowledge and Information Systems*, *60*(3), 1–81. doi:10.100710115-018-1248-0

Sagiroglu, S., & Sinanc, D. (2013, May). Big data: A review. In *2013 international conference on collaboration technologies and systems (CTS)* (pp. 42-47). IEEE.

Software, D. (2020). Available: https://medium.com/app-affairs/9-applications-of-machine-learning-from-day-to-day-life-112a47a429d0.

Sun, A. Y., & Scanlon, B. R. (2019). How can Big Data and machine learning benefit environment and water management: A survey of methods, applications, and future directions. *Environmental Research Letters, 14*(7), 073001. doi:10.1088/1748-9326/ab1b7d

Zhou, L., Pan, S., Wang, J., & Vasilakos, A. V. (2017). Machine learning on big data: Opportunities and challenges. *Neurocomputing, 237*, 350–361. doi:10.1016/j.neucom.2017.01.026

Chapter 5
Big Data in Cloud Computing

Jayashree K.
Rajalakshmi Engineering College, India

Swaminathan B.
iD https://orcid.org/0000-0002-0822-3087
Rajalakshmi Engineering College, India

ABSTRACT

The huge size of data that has been produced by applications that spans from social network to scientific computing is termed big data. Cloud computing as a delivery model for IT services enhances business productivity by reducing cost. It has the intention of achieving solution for managing big data such as high dimensional data sets. Thus, this chapter discusses the background of big data and cloud computing. It also discusses the various application of big data in detail. The various related work, research challenges of big data in cloud computing, and the future direction are addressed in this chapter.

1. INTRODUCTION

In the past few years cloud computing has been developing rapidly and it is a novel computing archetype that has the ability to provide various services on request (Alfazi et al, 2017). It supports self-service through no or slight retailer facilitation and it offers an efficacy archetypal of resources where companies merely pay for their utilization. Sharing of resources leads to cost of computing much lower (Gupta et al, 2012). The elasticity, low upfront investment, pay per use are few of the foremost facilitating features that makes the cloud computing the universal platform for installing parsimoniously reasonable enterprise organization settings (Venkatesh et al, 2015).

Big data is a data exploration approach supported by inventive tools which provision high-velocity data seizure, storage, and exploration. Data production rate has been growing rapidly during the recent years. Certain corporate examples of big data are social network content, cell phone particulars, transactional information, fitness archives, commercial official papers, and weather data. (Balachandran & Prasad, 2017). It can be useful in smart cities to mine and analyse the data from an enormous size of data (Jayashree et al, 2019). Data are produced from many origins such as medical devices, sensors or

DOI: 10.4018/978-1-7998-6673-2.ch005

associated instruments. To store and analyze the data that has been generated big data technologies can utilize cloud computing (Gholami & Laure, 2016).

Cloud computing has several inherent capabilities such as quantifiability, flexibility, metered pay-per-use capability, sharing, data dependability, easier preservation that offer real opportunities for big data (Hanan Elazhary 2014).

The rest of this chapter is structured as: Section 2 delivers a broad-spectrum summary of big data and its applications and cloud computing, related works are discussed in Section 3. The challenges of big data in cloud computing is deliberated in Section 4. Future research directions are described in Section 5 and the conclusion of the chapter is briefed in Section 6.

2. BACKGROUND

2.1 Bigdata

Neves describes the five aspects such as Volume, Variety, Velocity, Value and Veracity. Volume defines the dimensions of datasets that a big data method convention with. Variety deals with that data arises in all kinds of presentations such as from organized, numeric data in customary databases to unstructured text documents, electronic mail, video, audio, and business contacts (Wadhwani K & Wang, 2017). Velocity denotes to the period in which big data can be processed (Hadi et al, 2016). Value deals with the accurate value of information. Veracity denotes to the reliability of the data, addressing data privacy, consistency, and accessibility.

2.2 Big Data and its Applications (kiran et al 2015)

Big data are classified such as structured and unstructured.

1.   Structured Data

Words and numbers that can be certainly categorized and examined belongs to structured data. Structured data are produced by things like network sensors, smart phones, trades data, and global positioning system devices.

2.   Unstructured Data

Unstructured data comprise further multifarious data, such as consumer analyses from merchandisable websites, photos and other multimedia, and remarks on social networking sites. Separation of these data and grouping are not easy and numerical analysis are also difficult.

Some areas of big data computing are portrayed in the subsequent texts (Kune et al, 2016).

Scientific surveys: Data obtained from different sensors are studied to extract the suitable information for communal profits.

Health care: Medical care groups might figure the localities from where the infections are spreading in order to avoid more spreads (Mayer & Cukier 2013). Clinical decision support methods, specific analytics applied for patient summary, custom-made medicine, examine disease patterns, improve public health.

Governance: In transport sectors by means of real-time transportation data to calculate traffic patterns, and modernize communal transport schedules.

Stock: A private stock trade in Asia utilizes indatabase analytics to build up an exhaustive framework to detect abusive trading patterns to detect fraud in private stock trade.

Web analytics: Several websites are experiencing millions of unique visitors per day, thus creating a large range of content. Increasingly, companies want to be able to mine this data to understand limitations of their sites, improve response time, offer more targeted ads, and so on. This requires tools to perform complicated analytics on data that far exceed the memory of a single machine or even in cluster of machines.

2.3. Cloud Computing

Cloud paradigms include various services such as Software as a Service (SaaS), Platform as a Service (PaaS), and Infrastructure as a Service (IaaS) (Agrawal et al, 2011).

There is extensive amount of replacements for commerce by means of the cloud for PaaS (Purcell et al, 2013). PaaS is used to deliver platforms for the improvement and custom of concord applications. PaaS solutions contain application project and enhancement tools, versioning, incorporation, deployment and hosting, state running, and other associated enhancement tools (Geczy et al, 2012). Trades achieve price redeeming by means of PaaS from end to end regularization and great consumption of the cloud-based phase through an amount of applications. Further benefits of utilizing PaaS are endorsing shared services, refining software security, and bringing down ability prerequisites required for new frameworks improvement.

SaaS offers companies by means of applications that are kept and run on simulated servers within the cloud. Advantages of utilizing SaaS are simpler programming, programmed updates and fix organization, programming similarity through the trade, simpler cooperation, and worldwide openness. SaaS offers companies examining big data demonstrated software elucidations meant for statistics analysis.

Services offered to enterprises over the IaaS prototypical incorporate disaster rescue, data center and storing as a provision, virtual desktop organization, and cloud bursting. Virtualization is generally utilized in IaaS cloud in order to blend/break down actual resources in an ad-hoc mode to encounter evolving or diminishing resource request from cloud clients (Santosh Kumar and Goudar, 2012). Advantages of IaaS comprises expanded monetary adaptability, selection of services, business liveliness, practical versatility, and expanded security.

2.4 Big Data in Cloud

Big data in clouds is an innovative data-intensive platform for rapidly creating the analytics and installing in excess of an elastically accessible organization. They are generally categorized as:

Public big data clouds: Wide-ranging data association and handling over the flexibly accessible clouds substructure. The resources are functioned over Internet as pay-as-go computing prototypes. The examples are Amazon big data computing in clouds, Windows Azure HDInsight, RackSpace Cloudera Hadoop, and Google cloud platform of big data computing.

Private big data clouds: Arrangement of big data policy within the venture above a virtualized framework, with a more prominent mechanism and security to the particular organizations.

Hybrid big data clouds: Incorporation of public and private big data clouds for versatility, catastrophe rescue, and abundant accessibility. In this arrangement, the private chores can be transferred to the communal arrangement through uttermost loads.

2.5 ADVANTAGES OF BIG DATA AND CLOUD COMPUTING (ISLAM & REZA 2019)

Agility

It is likely to offer several arrangements with all the essential resources rapidly.

Elasticity

A cloud platform can dynamically increase to deliver storage for continually growing data.

Reducing Expense with Big Data in the Cloud

With the cloud computing, the accountability moves to the cloud suppliers and the enterprise merely devise to emolument for the storing space and power consumption.

Compact Intricacy

Several process of big data solution comprises many constituents and incorporations. Cloud computing delivers the likelihood to establish these constituents, therefore decreasing intricacy and expanding the profitability of the big data investigation group.

3. RELATED WORK

The combination of big data and cloud computing has long term profits of together acuities and performance (Chandrashekar et al, 2015). Cloud services can deal wide extents of data through fast latency and real time handling of the data that has been collected. There are presently a small number of incorporated cloud environments for big data investigation.

In digital domain, data are produced from several bases and the quick change as of digital innovations devises to the evolution of big data (Acharjya & Ahmed, 2016). It delivers progressive innovations in various arenas through assortment of huge datasets. Talia, 2013 indicated that finding appropriate data as of from huge amounts of data involves adaptable analysis procedures to produce suitable outcomes. Effective data investigation tools in addition to skills are necessary to deal with specific data. Every procedure enactment stops to rise directly through collective computational means. Several challenges of big data comprise Heterogeneity, Incompleteness, versatility, Timeliness, Privacy and Security have been addressed in this chapter (Jayashree & Abirami, 2018).

As researchers keep on examining the concerns of big data in cloud computing, different issues in big data handling emerge through the interim data study methods. The speediness of torrent data received as of dissimilar data sources need be managed and associated through historic information within a specific timeframe. Specific data bases might comprise dissimilar strategies that creates the coordination of numerous bases meant for examination a multifarious stint.

Research exertions formulated toward making a big data management framework for the cloud. Khan et al, 2015 have suggested a data exemplary as well as offers a schema for big data in the cloud and endeavors for the facilitation toward requesting data on behalf of the consumer. Ortiz et al, 2015 reconnoitered the utilization of a suggested combined Hadoop and MPI/OpenMP system and in what way the accompanying can expand speed and performance.

Cohen et al, 2009 provided a parallel database design aimed at analytics that provisions SQL and MapReduce scripting arranged in the top of a DBMS towards incorporating numerous data bases. Data handling as well as analytics abilities stay stirring in the direction of Enterprise Data Haylofts, otherwise organized in data centers to ease reprocess through several data collections (Jensen et al, 2012).

4. CHALLANGES OF BIG DATA IN CLOUD COMPUTING

Hashem et al, 2015 have depicted several significant research challenges, contains versatility, accessibility, convenience, data reliability, data conversion, data value, data diversity, secrecy and authorized concerns, and regulatory governance.

4.1 Data Staging

Utmost significant exposed research concern about data staging stays associated towards the assorted nature of data. Statistics collected as of diverse bases will not have an organized arrangement. Changing and cleaning aforesaid indistinct data beforehand stocking them into the warehouse for analysis are motivating tasks.

4.2 Distributed Storage Methods

A number of elucidations was suggested towards storing and recovering huge volumes of data. Specific elucidations were pragmatic in a cloud computing environs. Though, some concerns obstruct the efficacious execution of specific elucidations, containing the ability of recent cloud technologies offering needed size and great enactment to treatise enormous aggregates of data, development of current file structures in place of the capacities required through data mining solicitations, in addition to, by what means data can remain kept in such a way that they be able to be simply recovered and migrated amongst servers.

4.3 Data Analysis

The determination of a suitable exemplary used in place of extensive data exploration remains critical.

Data Security

The safety coercions are expanded through the volume, velocity, and variety of big data. Additionally, some coercions and concerns, such as secrecy, concealment, reliability, and accessibility of data, occur in big data by means of cloud computing platforms. Hence, data safety need remain stately after data are subcontracted towards the cloud provision suppliers. The cloud need furthermore evaluation by fixed interims to secure the aforementioned beside coercions.

Manogaran et al 2016 have portrayed the safety tasks related by means of big data in cloud computing. Big data safety in the cloud computing is vital owing towards the accompanying concerns as:

1. To safeguard and avert vast mass about trusted commerce, government, or controlling data from malevolent invaders and progressive coercions
2. Absence of responsiveness and standards almost in what way cloud provision suppliers firmly preserving the massive disk space plus removal of remaining big data,
3. Absence of guidelines approximately examining and recording of enormous data in public cloud
4. Consumers who does not even graft for the association, yet can take complete control in addition to perceptibility into past of business data.

5. FUTURE RESEARCH DIRECTIONS

Skourletopoulos et al 2017, have deliberated several open research concerns comprising seizure, storing, handling, cleaning, investigation, gathering information, examine, distribution, conception, demanding and secrecy of the precise huge capacities of data. The research future direction could be

*   Data storage and management
*   Data broadcast and curation
*   Data handling and exploration
*   Data secrecy and security

6. CONCLUSION

Cloud computing environments remain made for wide-ranging perseverance workloads plus resource sharing that remains used towards deliver elasticity on request. Thus, the cloud computing environment appears to stay well appropriate for big data. Data storage with cloud computing stays a reasonable choice for trivial to moderate sized industries in view of the usage of Big Data analytic techniques (Zanoon et al, 2016). Therefore, this chapter deliberates the background of big data and cloud computing. It likewise addresses the challenges associated to big data in cloud computing.

REFERENCES

Acharjya, D.P., & Ahmed, K.P. (2016). A Survey on Big Data Analytics: Challenges, Open Research Issues and Tools. *International Journal of Advanced Computer Science and Applications, 7*(2).

Agrawal, D., Das, S., & Abbadi, A.E. (2011). *Big Data and Cloud Computing: Current State and Future Opportunities*. EDBT.

Alfazi, Abdullah, Sheng, Quan, Babar, Ali, Ruan, Wenjie, & Qin. (2017). Toward Unified Cloud Service Discovery for Enhanced Service Identification. *The 6th Australasian Symposium on Service Research and Innovation (ASSRI'17).*

Balachandran, B., & Prasad, S. (2017). Challenges and Benefits of Deploying Big Data Analytics in the Cloud for Business Intelligence International Conference on Knowledge Based and Intelligent Information and Engineering Systems. *Procedia Computer Science, 112,* 1112–1122. doi:10.1016/j.procs.2017.08.138

Chandrashekar, R., Kala, M., & Mane, D. (2015). *Integration of Big Data in Cloud computing environments for enhanced data processing capabilities. International Journal of Engineering Research and General Science.*

Cohen, J., Dolan, B., Dunlap, M., Hellerstein, J. M., & Welton, C. (2009). MAD skills: New analysis practices for big data. *Proceedings of the VLDB Endowment International Conference on Very Large Data Bases, 2*(2), 1481–1492. doi:10.14778/1687553.1687576

Elazhary. (2014). Cloud Computing for Big Data MAGNT Research Report. Academic Press.

Geczy, P., Izumi, N., & Hasida, K. (2012). Cloudsourcing: Managing cloud adoption. *Global Journal of Business Research, 6*(2), 57–70.

Gholami, A., & Laure, E. (2016). Big data security and privacy issues in the cloud. *International Journal of Network Security & Its Applications, 8*(1).

Gupta, R., Gupta, H., & Mohania, M. (2012). Cloud Computing and Big Data Analytics: What Is New from Databases Perspective? *LNCS, 7678,* 42–61.

Hadi, H.J., Shnain, A.H., Hadishaheed, S., & Ahmad, A.H. (2015). Big Data and Five V'S Characteristics. *International Journal of Advances in Electronics and Computer Science, 2*(1).

Hashem, I. A. T., Yaqoob, I., Anuar, N. B., Mokhtar, S., Gani, A., & Ullah Khan, S. (2015). The rise of "big data" on cloud computing: Review and open research issues. *Information Systems, 47,* 98–115. doi:10.1016/j.is.2014.07.006

Islam, M., & Reza, M. (2019). The Rise of Big Data and Cloud Computing. *Internet of Things and Cloud Computing., 7*(2), 45–53. doi:10.11648/j.iotcc.20190702.12

Jayashree, K., & Abirami, R. (2018). Big Data Technologies and Management Innovative in Applications of Knowledge Discovery and Information Resources Management. IGI Global Publisher.

Jayashree, K., Abirami, R., & Babu, R. (2018). A Collaborative Approach of IoT, Big Data, and Smart City in Big Data analytics for Smart and Connected Cities. IGI Global Publisher.

Jensen, D., Konkel, K., Mohindra, A., Naccarati, F., & Sam, E. (2012). *Business Analytics in the Cloud.* White paper IBW03004-USEN-00, IBM.

Khan, I., Naqvi, S. K., Alam, M., & Rizvi, S. N. A. (2015). Data model for Big Data in cloud environment. *Computing for Sustainable Global Development (INDIACom), 2nd International Conference,* 582–585.

Kiran, J. S., Sravanthi, M., Preethi, K., & Anusha, M. (2015). Recent Issues and Challenges on Big Data in Cloud Computing. IJCST, 6(2).

Kumar & Goudar. (2012). Cloud Computing – Research Issues, Challenges, Architecture. *Platforms and Applications: A Survey International Journal of Future Computer and Communication, 1*(4), 356-360.

Kune, R., Konugurthi, P. K., Agarwal, A., Chillarige, R. R., & Buyya, R. (2016). The anatomy of big data computing Journal of Software. *Practice and Experience, 46*(1), 79–105. doi:10.1002pe.2374

Manogaran, G., Thota, C., & Kumar, M. V. (2016). MetaCloudDataStorage Architecture for Big Data Security in Cloud Computing. *Procedia Computer Science, 87*, 128–133. doi:10.1016/j.procs.2016.05.138

Mayer, V. V., & Cukier, K. (2013). *Big Data: A Revolution That Will Transform How We Live, Work and Think.* John Murray Press.

Neves, Schmerl, Camara, & Bernardino. (2016). Big Data in Cloud Computing: Features and Issues. *Proceedings of the International Conference on Internet of Things and Big Data, 1*, 307-314. 10.5220/0005846303070314

Purcell, M.B. (2013). Big data using cloud computing. *Journal of Technology Research,* 1-7.

Reyes-Ortiz, J., Oneto, L., & Anguita, D. (2015). Big Data Analytics in the Cloud: Spark on Hadoop vs MPI/OpenMP on Beowulf. *Procedia Computer Science, 53*(1), 121–130. doi:10.1016/j.procs.2015.07.286

Skourletopoulos, G., Mavromoustakis, C.X., Mastorakis, G., Batalla, J.M., Dobre, C., Panagiotakis, S., & Pallis, E. (2016). Big Data and Cloud Computing: A Survey of the State-of-the-Art and Research Challenges. In Advances in Mobile Cloud Computing and Big Data in the 5G Era. Studies in Big Data (Vol. 22). Springer.

Talia, D. (2013). Clouds for scalable big data analytics. *Computer, 46*(5), 98–101. doi:10.1109/MC.2013.162

Venkatesh, H., Perur, D.S., & Jalihal, N. (2015). A Study on Use of Big Data in Cloud Computing Environment. *International Journal of Computer Science and Information Technologies, 6*(3), 2076-2078.

Wadhwani, K., & Wang, Y. (2017). *Big Data Challenges and solutions.* Technical Report.

Zanoon, N., Al-Haj, N., & Khwaldeh, S. (2017). M Cloud Computing and Big Data is there a Relation between the Two: A Study. *International Journal of Applied Engineering Research, 12*(17), 6970–6982.

Chapter 6
Big Data Analytics in Healthcare:
A Developing Country Survey

Sam Goundar
https://orcid.org/0000-0001-6465-1097
The University of the South Pacific, Fiji

Karpagam Masilamani
The University of the South Pacific, Fiji

Akashdeep Bhardwaj
https://orcid.org/0000-0001-7361-0465
University of Petroleum and Energy Studies, India

Chandramohan Dhasarathan
https://orcid.org/0000-0002-5279-950X
Madanapalle Institute of Technology and Science, India

ABSTRACT

This chapter provides better understanding and use-cases of big data in healthcare. The healthcare industry generates lot of data every day, and without proper analytical tools, it is quite difficult to extract meaningful data. It is essential to understand big data tools since the traditional devices don't maintain this vast data, and big data solves the major issue in handling massive healthcare data. Health data from numerous health records are collected from various sources, and this massive data is put together to form the big data. Conventional database cannot be used in this purpose due to the diversity in data formats, so it is difficult to merge, and so it is quite impossible to process. With the use of big data this problem is solved, and it can process highly variable data from different sources.

DOI: 10.4018/978-1-7998-6673-2.ch006

INTRODUCTION

Information Technology plays a vital role in today's industries by acting as a business enabler. The amounts of data currently generated by the businesses are massive and increasing exponentially. Especially the data produced in the healthcare industry is quite huge due to various forms of data such as audio and video files, images and other types of data, which are very crucial and valuable. Because of the ongoing substantial increase in the data, the traditional storage devices slowly become obsolete due to their limitations in computing. Thus, the concept of Big Data has evolved to overcome the boundaries of the legacy storage system. Big Data is just raw data collected from different sources, which will not be able to perform any analytics or decision making for the businesses.

Healthcare industry needs to collect and analyse a vast amount of data for enhancing the efficiency and effectiveness of medical treatment and share new treatment methods within the medical fraternity promptly. Hence, the data has to be analysed efficiently within minimum time. To compute and validate the vast amount of data, Big Data Analytics is needed. Moreover, Big Data Analytics will be very useful in the healthcare industry for developing countries to increase the quality of treatment by curing the diseases quickly and prevent the recurrence of the diseases. Big Data Analytics can discover the disease pattern and disease outbreaks. Some of the Big Data analytical tools in the healthcare industry can reduce the cost, prevent the disease and get the potential benefits. The combination of Big Data and Analytics in healthcare can prevent risk portfolios faster and detect fraud.

According to Technopedia Target (2019), Big Data is defined as large volume of data, which are in the formats of structured, unstructured and semi-structured, which is complex for existing machine and software technologies to analyse. The cost effective, enhanced insights and decision making is the main target for the Big Data. As per Health IT Analytics (2020), Big Data in healthcare refers to electronic health data sets that are so large, complex, and difficult to manage with traditional software and/or hardware; nor can this be managed with traditional or common data management tools and methods.

Characteristic of Big Data

Big Data has specific characteristics illustrated by 'Five Vs' (Vartika et al., 2020). They are Volume, Velocity, Variety, Value, and Veracity, which is symbolically known as five V's.

- **Volume**: The amount of data in healthcare, which are in the forms of reports, scan images and X- rays.
- **Velocity**: Velocity is the speed at which data is collected from healthcare. This also includes comments via Social media as user views, posts in case of epidemic natural disaster, RFID tags, sensors, smart metering.
- **Variety**: The data, which is collected from the analysis of patients for effective treatments. The formats in which the data are produced are variety. The three formats of Big Data are structured, unstructured and semi-structured. Structured data is in common spreadsheet format which is easy for computing whereas Unstructured data are such as Electronic Medical Report, CDSS, Physician prescription, image, texts, audio and videos and are complicated for processing (Revanth Sonnati, 2017).
- **Value**: The data, which are produced in healthcare from social media sometimes, can be of fake news. The patients should always provide genuine data, which is very important for analysis. The

patients' data collected are still of high value, and it should be of quality for the medical industry. Electronic Medical Report and Electronic Health Record are valuable for better analysis.

- **Veracity**: Health is the main factor for everybody in this world. In healthcare, all the data generated are precious and vital because it has the patients' report history. In case the data loss happens, the patient's life may become miserable. It should be kept very careful to get better results. The medical reports have some specific information, which should be of trustworthiness.

Benefits of Big Data Analytics

Big Data Analytics in Healthcare industry (Big Data, 2020) helps the doctors, patients, insurance providers, machines, financial department, and researchers and so on. The advanced techniques can help to enhance the decision-making capacity of the top management in health care through the following ways. Electronic Medical Record the main benefits of Big Data where all the formats are evaluated for adequate care. Patient Profile Analytics consider the individual patient's activity with the proactive approach. The data analytics approach efficiently included in Genomics Analytics as a part of regular medical decision process. Fraud Analysis is an effective analysis can help reduce Fraud, Waste, and Abuse (Berke, 2020). Safety monitoring does real-time analysing of patients in the hospital supports the safety monitoring and negative event prediction.

Opportunities to Cost Reduce

When the patient is having some problem, the doctor will find the solution by viewing his medical reports. When the patient is not cured or not satisfied with that diagnosis, he might go to the second opinion, as presented by Patel et al. (2016). In that situation, the doctor should not recommend the patients to do all the tests again from the beginning. If they avoid this condition, they can reduce the cost in the healthcare industry. The population of a country can be helpful to reduce the cost of medical treatment. BDA can prevent the disease outbreak in advance. To develop the coordination of care, there should be an increase in generating the products but a decrease in the overlapping of data. Predicting the behavior of the individual patient and giving the appropriate medicine can reduce the cost. Considering the patient's symptoms in advance can prevent the disease much more comfortable than they become worse. Wang. et al. (2018) minimized the cost of healthcare. The comparison of randomized controlled trial with Electronic Medical Record has found a solution for identifying and tracking the patient's patterns in type 2 diabetes.

Challenges of Big Data Analytics

There are several challenges in Big Data Analytics in Healthcare. Data management is the target goal for Big Data analytics. Without the proper maintenance of data management in Big Data, the Big Data analytics cannot be achieved. Therefore, data provided by the health care such as the patient's history, reports, Electronic Health record should have complete data without any missing information, unreliable, inaccessible or incomplete data as presented by Jasleen Kaur Bains (2016). The right data management can have good results for decision making for the patients.

Nivdita Das (2018) researched on patients' personal information being saved and any mislead of data can affect the patient's life. Some healthcare providers, physician, Hospitals are restricted to share the patient's data. It is confidential between the patients and management. Therefore, it is difficult for Big Data Analytics to perform their job. Significant investments are needed to develop the Big Data Architecture. Creating the BDA Architecture is costly. As it required high-qualified data scientists to support the design, implementation, which is the biggest, challenges of Big Data Analytics. Security is the first concern in many industries including healthcare. In healthcare, it is essential to consider the security of the patients' records. To get the best clinical decision result, BDA has to analyse the large volume of data; then it can prevent the desired effect and can suggest the alternative treatment.

Literature Review

According to Ristevski et al. (2018), using the tools and techniques in healthcare like Hadoop will allow users to analyse the patient's information, measure the risk and predict the outcomes of patients. MapReduce platforms with Hadoop will overcome the problem of the utilization of drugs, fraud detection, and assist diagnosis even in real time.

According to Vishnu Basuthkar (2016), Big Data analytics has many tools to support each other in processing and execution. The execution of big tools is a big challenge. The author concluded that using various tools in Healthcare, Big Data would solve the problem and improve the individual patient diagnosis.

Suzie et al. (2014) researched on the concurrence of big data analytics in healthcare listed many challenges like lack of appropriate IT infrastructure, lack of knowledge in big data domain, financial costs, a security issue, missing information, irregular history record. The solution is to implement the data governance, employing the skilled person, information sharing to be done by data encryption and make use of cloud computing.

According to Praveena et al. (2018), Big Data was founded in 1990, but recently over the last five years, it has been widely used by many organizations for their business profits. Big data architectural frameworks are used to overcome the comparative review analysis and various characteristic of big data tools. Numerical, analytical tool R is used for the comparative analysis.

According to the authors Sachin et al. (2019), finding the exact tools and algorithms is a challenging task. To improve the healthcare delivery quality of the medicine and cost reduction analytical tools like data mining and artificial intelligence have been used. This paper reviewed various tools like Apache Hadoop, MapReduce, HDFS, Hive, and Pig and so on. The algorithms like classification, CNN, Neural network and Apriori to help the diagnosis and predict the medical decision making better. As a result, they found classification algorithm C5.0 is faster in speed, memory, performance and calculating the accuracy is high for dental implant therapy. Implementing cloud computing in healthcare will be much more comfortable, its scalability and it is also highly secured, pay as you go, which will reduce the cost. It will be future research in healthcare.

Sarwar et al. (2017) revealed a hybrid approach is better than using the existing modify approach. The hybrid approach can store data and process large data in a distributed environment. The challenging task is collecting data from different sources, which are in different formats like structured, unstructured and semi-structured. Hadoop plays a vital role, as the tools are open source thus diagnosis will be more straightforward.

According to Palanisamy et al. (2017), computational intelligence is used to improve the recommendation in healthcare such as prognosis screening, diagnosis, image processing, signal processing, and genomics. Hadoop framework was developed to process large scale and real-time, but it was a failure for intensive care units. The clinical setting cost and time to the delivery recommendation in genomics are critical problems. In signal processing, the alerts system failed due to lack of information of the patient, accurate historical record. The involvement of new data is the challenge. Schizophrenia patients and single nucleotide polymorphism data have adopted the hybrid machine-learning algorithm.

According to Adjei et al. (2018) Ghana, which is the developing countries in West Africa. The number of hospitals in Ghana produces a large amount of data, but there is proper tools or data warehouse to store that data for medical analysis. They did the comparison with five developed countries, who have adopted the big data ecosystem for their benefits, and they proposed the big data architectural framework, So Government assumes that implementing big data in Ghana will support the patients and healthcare industry effectively.

According to Archenaa et al. (2018), the volume of data produced cannot be stored in hard copy or traditional database management system. The Deployment of Big data in healthcare will lead to reducing cost in clinical decision support, disease surveillance, and population health management. By 2020, the data produced alone by US healthcare will be expected between Zettabyte and yottabytes.

Bhattacharjee *et al.* (2019) Smart Internet of Things (IoT) applications require real-time and robust predictive analytics, which are based on Machine Learning (ML) models. Building ML models from Big Data is not only time-consuming, but developers often lack the needed expertise for feature engineering, parameter tuning, and model selection. The proliferation of ML libraries and frameworks, data ingestion tools, stream and batch processing engines, visualization techniques, and the range of available hardware platforms further exacerbates the system design, rapid development, and deployment problems. Finally, resource constraints of IoT require that the execution of the analytics engine be distributed across the cloud-edge spectrum. To overcome these daunting challenges, we present Stratum, which is an event-driven Big Data-as-a-Service offering for IoT analytics lifecycle management. Stratum provides users with an intuitive, declarative mechanism based on the principles of model-driven engineering to specify the application and infrastructure requirements. It automates the deployment via generative programming principles. This paper highlights the problems that Stratum resolves, demonstrating its capabilities using real-world case studies.

Jesi et al. (2019) designed and implemented Lepida ScpA Big Data infrastructure. Our goal is to provide the Regional PA with proper tools to address future challenges such as planning the allocation of resources and creating new business models involving public and private organizations. The authors first designed of the infrastructure started from a specific scenario and addresses a particular aspect: ingesting the Regional public WiFi data traffic and gathering interesting analytics. The authors also describe the challenges faced and the choices made during the process and the results achieved.

Smart city is a developed urban city that includes intelligent systems to improve the quality of citizens' life by providing the smart services the smart services that are equipped and focused including mobility, transport, technologies energies, buildings and governance. These services are enhancing the smartness of living at the same time we also need a smart service that handle the emergency smartly and in the area of smart emergency services are neither witnessed nor addressed in the smart city scenario. The road accidents are inevitable in the smart city though and it is contemplated to be one of the emergency services that need to be given more important to save the life and require quick smart services. Al-Salami et al. (2019) addressed the important of emergency services particularly at the time of road accident in the smart environment. This smart emergency services works in perceptive actions of IoT sensors and call for actions that required saving the life of injured and provide intelligent emergency supports to bring back the smart city usage for others rapidly. The system experiments and provide prototype of smart emergency services using IoT sensors, Arduino with Raspberry Pi setup, CoolTerm. The data that are observed during the experiments are analysed using Apache Zeppelin Bigdata analytical tools. The conclusive result of analytical data to be transmitted wirelessly to enable the required smart emergency services ranging from hospitals ambulances, fire, traffic, cleaning services to services that are bring the smart city back to function normally. The project also emphasizes that the IoT and Big Data bonds closely woven prospects of smart emergency systems.

Data are generated and stored in databases at a very high speed and hence it need to be handled and analysed properly. Nowadays industries are extensively using Hadoop and Spark to analyse the datasets. Both the frameworks are used for increasing processing speeds in computing huge complex datasets. Many researchers are comparing both of them. Now, the big questions arising are, Is Spark a substitute for Hadoop. Is Hadoop going to be replaced by spark in mere future? Spark is "built on top of" Hadoop and it extends the model to deploy more types of computations, which incorporates Stream Processing and Interactive Queries. No doubt, Spark's execution speed is much faster than Hadoop, but talking in terms of fault tolerance, Hadoop is slightly more fault tolerant than spark. In this article comparison of various Bigdata analytics tools are done and Hadoop and Spark are discussed in detail. This article further gives an overview of Bigdata, spark and Hadoop issues. In this survey paper, Jaiswal et al. (2020) discussed and resolved the issues and approaches of spark and Hadoop.

Need to Use Big Data Analytics in Healthcare

Big Data is just a raw data from the healthcare with that data we cannot get any meaningful insight and decision-making it is considered useless data. Big data analytics analyse the history of a patient's data. Big Data analytics has the potential to make raw data into useful data for better decision making, helps to reduce costs, improve the patient's treatments, use analytics tools to predict the disease before its effect the patients, reduce the re-admission costs, improve the quality of healthcare as presented by Priyanka et al. (2014). Medical data is needed to find the disease in advances, and it can control drug usage at the required level and not get any complication because of consuming the overdoses of drugs. The patients on the particular disease cannot be predicted but the common disease outbreaks disease can be predicted by analysing the search engines. The doctors cannot be up to date in the healthcare industry as every day the new disease is found by some of the medical scientists. Using big data analytics, it will easier to analyse the symptoms or any outbreaks of disease in the specific place.

The hospitals need to be supervised by the professionals for their cleanliness and public patients' safety. As especially the government hospitals or health centres, which provide the fewer costs of treatments, should be taken care of by the government professionals. Immediate action can be given to the hospitals, which are not in proper conditions. The doctors can give the absolute solution to the new patients from their past patient's experiences and if the symptoms are same as well. For the more significant improvement in medication given to the particular patients should be examined through their analysis of drug doses. Even in a government military hospital, big data analytics is used to find traumatic brain disease, and other Military hospitals are using data analytics to suggest treatment with their historical data. To improve the clinical and quality standard, CMS uses the data analytics.

Minimize Costs by Utilizing Big Data Tools in Healthcare

Hospitals want to reduce the number of ER visits or Emergency visits of patients. They believe that it increases health care costs and sometimes does not lead to better outcomes for patients. For example, a man suffering from acute abdominal pain comes to an emergency room. The doctor will try to figure out the cause of the problem such as kidney stone or appendicitis or something else. Now if he has a way of knowing the patient's past medical results, he could begin the treatment as soon as possible. The examination would take less time and would cost less money.

Some Real Life Examples

When the patient is having some problem, the doctor will find the solution by viewing his medical reports. When the patient is not cured or not satisfied with that diagnosis, they might go to the second opinion. In that situation, the doctor should not again recommend the patients to do all the tests repeatedly from the beginning. By avoiding this condition, they can reduce the emerging visits cost in the healthcare industry. Wearable sensors can be used in real time for monitoring the patient from home. Many tools in healthcare can minimize the patients' regular check-up physical visit to the hospitals, as mentioned by 18 Examples of Big Data in Healthcare that can save people (2020).

Predictive analytics can reduce half of the cost for patients, payers, providers, health insurance in healthcare. Predictive analyse is the most critical methods to implement in healthcare. Prediction is more potent than being affected. The researchers need the patients' data for powerful predictive analysis as per Akshita Kapoor (2018). The patient's record is stored in the paper documents, which is complicated to do the analysis. If there is no proper maintenance and update made to the patient data, it wastes time and cost of the management team.

Now the adoption of big data in health care uses the electronic health record, the data are stored securely, and the doctors, management, etc make modification faster. The advanced analytics can be used to cure cancer. By collecting the data from different healthcare institution for analysing helps healthcare industry so using Hadoop with master and slave nodes it can be possible in storing in Hadoop Distributed file system.

Traditional Analytical Tools and Big Data Analytical Tools

The traditional analytical tools are becoming user-friendly and transparent. The user interfaces of traditional tools are different, but algorithms and approaches are considered the same. During real-time streaming waveforms, the standard database like relational database management system or ORDMS are hard to process and cannot manage the large-scale data. Traditional data warehouses have played a vital role in a decision support system. The big issues in traditional analytical tools are stored as mentioned by Why Traditional Marketing Analytics Tools Fail and What to do about it (2019).

The conventional tools are not flexible, not reliable, and not scalable and not distributed which cannot store the data for more than three days. The most significant advantages of big data analytical tools are stored. It can save a large volume of data more than Terabytes or Exabyte. The Big Data Tools are immensely harder, programming intensive and require the application of a variety of skills; the proprietary vendor has become less support because of the use of open source software tools.

Uses of Open-Source Tools in Healthcare

Apache Hadoop is an open-source tool used widely in healthcare. It is a software library and applied for a distributed process for parallelism. In healthcare usage of open source, devices can be faster than the traditional approaches, and open-source tools are less expensive for management as well as for the public sector. The full complete views for gathering the data from different resources in different formats are integrated. The open-source tools will act to real-time or near real-time data such as data from wearable heart or glucose monitors. The data warehouses do not have the quality to separate the data, which leads to increase the work of the traditional machine and need large storage access.

Storage costs are reduced by automatically deciding whether to store or discard incoming data as it arrives in Big Data Analytics. The open sources tools help to find and respond to critical events by sending the information related to the patient's condition message to a clinician. If the patient does not fill the complete information of his history and prescription, it would be detected. The regulations and policies are changeable in healthcare insurance [38]. Therefore, these tools can manage the changes made in healthcare, and they can adopt the procedures according to them in any situation. The data in healthcare such as protecting the individual health information and identifiable information are highly important for their security and privacy requirements.

Methodology

This project is based on a qualitative research approach. Information is gathered from Online Research, and online research is conducted for the literature review. The main search engine was Google. Significant resources are extracted from sites like "Google Scholar," "IEEE," "Scientific Journals." Many other places are also used for the research. The resource will include Journals, Publications, Case Studies, and Books. Media – News websites and broadcasting sites are visited to gather news on the inclusion of big data in healthcare and its outcomes.

Some Big Data Tools

Big data has different platforms and tools to process their work. One of the formats in healthcare is structured data where all the data are stored in a proper spreadsheet. In big data, "big table" is used to store all the structured data, which was developed by the Google file system. Google distributed file system and MapReduce plays a vital role. In healthcare saving, a large amount of information is the biggest problem. Involving cloud computing into big data has significant benefits because of its distributed storage capacity.

Using cloud computing to healthcare will solve the problem of storage techniques for large-scale processing. Cloud computing has a large data center where storage and handling will be much more comfortable compared to the other traditional data warehouse. Infrastructure management is not required for any organization as it is located in remote places. The big data combining with the cloud has some providers who are Google cloud services, Amazon S3, Microsoft Azure. Two primary tools widely used are Apache Hadoop and MapReduce.

Apache Hadoop is an open source software framework, and it is the biggest platform for massive data sets for storing on computer clusters built from commodity hardware. The other tools of Apache will also support the healthcare industry. Map Reduce is a programming model for distributed processing of large data sets. Apache Hadoop and Map Reduce are efficient in a fault tolerant and data processing. It is the most commonly used software framework. Hadoop divides the job to the Map Reduce. The first task was given to Hadoop; it has the master nodes and slave nodes. The master node of Hadoop breaks the job into smaller sub-nodes then it processes to Map Reduce.

MapReduce is a software framework for distributed processing of the vast amount of structured and unstructured data sets. Two tasks in MapReduce are Map task and reduce task. Each task has the input and output value. The Map tasks take a set of data as an input and convert into a structured set as an output. The output of the Map task is taken as input of Reduce task. Two task was performed in the map task and reduce task. It is highly scalable, faster and simpler. HDFS is a Hadoop Distributed File System and is an open-source framework building on the top of the Hadoop and its support on cloud processing.

Apache Mahout is a project to produce free implementations on distributed and scalable machine learning. Machine learning algorithm and data mining are the main purposes of Apache Mahout. It provides many algorithms like clustering, collaborative filtering, classification, frequent pattern mining and so on. This algorithm will discover the meaningful pattern for large datasets. All data are stored in HDFS.

Apache Pig, handle all kinds of data and bulk amount of data stored in the Hadoop distributed file system are used for analysing and querying. It is because of its high-level language. It is same as SQL but uses its Language, which is PigLatin. It does the modification, filtering and changes into a standard format. Features of Pig is automatic execution, creates own function and optimization opportunities.

Apache Hive is a Data warehouse infrastructure built on top of Hadoop for providing data summarization. It has a specific language, which is known as HiveQueryLanguage. The primary purpose of Hive is to query and analyse a large volume of datasets stored in Hadoop. The Hadoop will execute the translated SQL queries from Hive to MapReduce.

Apache HBase is developed to store the structured formats like excel with lots of rows and columns. It is a distributed database and manages the Hadoop cluster. When there is a call from a customer, it does the reading, writing, updating and deleting in Hadoop cluster. It works with NoSQL database built on top of Hadoop.

Apache Cassandra is an open source distributed database management system. Apache Cassandra is a database, which has high functional availability, scalability, and multiple datacentres are replicated in case of failure. It is fault tolerance, low latency and the favourite in large productions of providers and it is professionally supported.

Apache Spark is the cluster-computing framework. Spark is very useful for both real-time processing, batch processing, and advanced analytics. Spark is million times faster than any other tools in Hadoop platform. Some of the organizations were adopting the Spark for their data execution. Compare to MapReduce; Spark proves very fast, scalable and elastic to data scientists and data analysts.

Big Data Tools Used in Healthcare

Hadoop plays a vital role in healthcare. In Atlanta, the children's healthcare has used Hadoop ecosystem components such as Flume, Sqoop, spark, Impala to analyse the patient's behavior signs. The patients from the ICU units had sensor-based beds to monitor their blood pressure, heartbeat and respiratory rate, so it makes the doctor and nurse to aware the patient's condition when there is a dangerous condition [8]. Data mining and medical informatics are used to reduce the cost, improve healthcare and decision-making. Big data in clinical genomics analysis can detect HIV patients.

Apache Mahout is used in predicting the risk of readmission of congestive heart failure. Personalized treatment care is given to the individual. [18] Using Apache mahout framework, the Hadoop file system has the collected data from different sources, which is pre-processed. The pre-processed data is passed to Mahout as an input data using a random algorithm. Hadoop is used to treat cancer. Cancer is hard to be cured because each patient has a different pattern and different types of gene. If we find the drug to cure cancer, it will support only a few patients whereas for others it will not be effective.

Hadoop will collect the data and analysis the cancer types present in each patient and it can be a solution to cure cancer practically. Hadoop using MapReduce can achieve the parallelization and allocation the job to the Map and Reduce. The development of personalized medicine for a cancer patient is the main project for the UK. To minimize the amount of money in health, to manage the people at risk and to give the best clinical support and to find the best solution for medical practitioners and clinicians, the Clever land clinic has adopted the analytical tools Hadoop and data mining technology. To provide a better solution for the healthcare insurance in handling the particular information about patients for their analyse they have to come through an extensive process of time. Using Apache Pig, Hive and MapReduce large volume of data can be generated quickly and quickly for better and faster results. Healthcare insurance has competitors among other to earn profits.

Business Intelligence analyzes history and gives the best effect to improve the insurance companies. Sepsis is the disease that affects the people in the US. The Dignity Health is the most popular healthcare in the US, which produces more than terabytes of data from more than 30 hospitals. The community found that compare to breast cancer, AIDS and propagate cancer the people die more from Sepsis disease. Lack of analytical tool is a significant issue. Because the amount of data generated is not processed in, a meaningful way and no predictive treatments have accepted. Therefore, the Dignity healthcare has adopted the Hadoop technology to solve the problem of Sepsis. Now the patients have a predictive method for curing [eight].

Architectural Framework

This architectural framework in Figure 1 depicts the conceptual architecture of Big Data Analytics.

Business intelligence tools are used for traditional analytics. The algorithms and models are the same for traditional and Big Data analytics. In traditional analytics, batch processing is very flexible. However, execution in Big Data analytical tools is different from traditional analytical instruments. They do

Figure 1. Applied Conceptual Architecture of Big Data Analytics

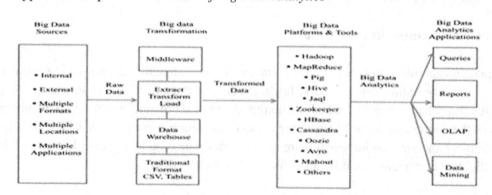

parallelized processing and split the job to other analytical tools. Some of the devices in Big Data has provided the benefits for the healthcare industry to get better decision making. Big Data ecosystem such as Apache Hadoop is the most commonly used tools, which are provided by the Google File system.

Most the big organization has adopted the Big Data tools for their business growth. There are four layers in healthcare: Data source layer, transformation layer, Big data platform layer, Analytical layer and where all the data are gathered from input and output data from an electronic health record, clinical records, scanning records, etc. from a different format, sources, locations, healthcare institutions. All these raw data are required to be transformed and pre-processed for the meaningful data.

The solution to store these data can be data warehouses or web service joining the service architecture. The sources for data sources layer can be from social media like twitters, Facebook, machine to machine like sensors, vital patient signs. Normally the ingestion process is some level of analysis, sorting, and labelling takes place. ETL stand for extract, transform and load and this term conventionally refers to legacy data and warehousing processes. In Big data platform layer the big data tools used for storing, filtering, modifying and updating for real time and batch process. The analysis layer is very complex to perform.

It needs the knowledge of the big data tools. The data scientists are highly qualified professional know about the benefits of big data tools. In analysis layer, the analysis engine works with algorithms, methods, tools for storing and execution. The queries, data mining, online analytical process and reports are the results from raw to valuable data. Few of the same concepts apply to data entering the big data system. It is believed that the implementation of big data analytics by healthcare organizations might lead to a saving of over 25% in annual costs in the coming years. Better diagnosis and disease predictions by big data analytics can enable cost reduction by decreasing the hospital readmission rate.

FUTURE RESEARCH AND RECOMMENDATIONS

Big Data Analytics has played an essential role in healthcare using their tools in real time. More effort is needed to implement big data analytics in healthcare, as it is the most critical feature of a healthy life. The new techniques and technologies are increased in healthcare for the patients, doctors, pharmacies, etc. There is no real time application in healthcare in developing countries. The remote computing should be taken into the critical factor for developing healthcare in developing countries.

The data-mining algorithm can be used to analyse the history and extract the meaningful information. The big data analytical tools can make a big difference in Developing countries. The Big Data and Analytical tools have given a better business solution. It motivated the people as well as the healthcare industry. Most of the above research was done in developed countries.

In Developing countries, big data tools can prevent the Diabetes Mellitus. It can have the chance to reduce the number of people being affected by this disease. In this whole world, developing countries has ranked number one in Diabetes. There are three types of Diabetes. The type1 is the starting stage of diabetes mellitus, which can be cured by insulin. The type2 is an elaborate stage in which the patient cannot be cured by taking insulin and type3 is gestational diabetes, which is mostly affected by the pregnant women. In Developing countries, one and a half year baby has type1 diabetes, and a twelve-year-old boy got type2 diabetes. Most of the women are affected by diabetes than men.

CONCLUSION

In a country like Developing countries where the health care system is highly decentralized, Big Data analytics will play a significant role in collecting data from various healthcare service providers, correlating and analysing the same to determine the gravity of various illnesses and implement prompt and useful corrective and preventive measures. This research found that data stored in a traditional database does not give the actual benefits for a large amount of data. Implementing Big data and its tools in healthcare have produced the significant advantages and reduced the cost. Thus, we conclude that the use of big data will help Developing countries in providing them better treatments by the use of this technology.

REFERENCES

Adjei, E., Otoo D., Gyamfi, K. (2018). Towards a Big Data Architectural Framework for Healthcare in Ghana. *Communications on Applied Electronics (CAE), 7*(12).

Al-Salmi, J., & Al-Foori, A., YasirAl-Jahwari, A., Hajamohideen, F. (2019). Smart emergency — A contextual framework for cognitive understanding of IoT devices using big data analytics. *2nd Smart Cities Symposium (SCS 2019)*, 1-4. 10.1049/cp.2019.0233

Archenaa, J., & Mary Anita, E. (2018). A Survey of Big Data Analytics in Healthcare and Government. *Procedia Computer Science, (50)*, 408–413.

Bains, J. K. (2016). Big Data Analytics in Healthcare- Its Benefits, Phases and Challenges. *International Journal of Advanced Research in Computer Science and Software Engineering, 6*(4), 430–435.

Basuthkar, V. (2016). A Survey of Cost-Effective Big Data in Healthcare Applications. *International Journal of Computers and Applications.*

Berke, L. (n.d.). *Lindsey Berke*. Retrieved December 11, 2020, from https://www.dimins.com/blog/2020/03/02/big-data-healthcare

Bhattacharjee, A., Barve, Y., Khare, S., Bao, S., Kang, Z., Gokhale, A., & Damiano, T. (2019). STRATUM: A BigData-as-a-Service for Lifecycle Management of IoT Analytics Applications. *IEEE International Conference on Big Data (Big Data)*, 1607-1612. 10.1109/BigData47090.2019.9006518

Bigdata. (2020, June 26). *Which Are The Real Benefits of Big Data?* Retrieved August 11, 2020, from https://bigdataanalyticsnews.com/real-benefits-of-big-data/

Das. (2018). Big Data Analytics for Medical Applications. *International Journal of Modern Education and Computer Science.*

Examples of Big Data In Healthcare That Can Save People. (2020, October 21). Retrieved November 6, 2020, from https://www.datapine.com/blog/big-data-examples-in-healthcare

Jaiswal, A., Dwivedi, V., & Yadav, O. (2020). Big Data and its Analyzing Tools: A Perspective. *6th International Conference on Advanced Computing and Communication Systems (ICACCS)*, 560-565, 10.1109/ICACCS48705.2020.9074222

Jesi, G., Gori, E., Micocci, S., & Mazzini, G. (2019). Building Lepida ScpA BigData Infrastructure. *Big Data, Knowledge and Control Systems Engineering (BdKCSE)*, 1-9, . doi:10.1109/BdKCSE48644.2019.9010604

Kapoor, A. (2018, June 9). *Real world applications of big data in healthcare*. Retrieved June 22, 2020, from https://medium.com/the-research-nest/real-world-applications-of-big-data-in-healthcare-5c84696fd3d4

Kent, J. (2020, September 14). *How Big Data Analytics Models can impact Healthcare Decision-Making*. Retrieved September 20, 2020, from https://healthitanalytics.com/news/how-big-data-analytics-models-can-impact-healthcare-decision-making

Mehta, N., & Panditb, A. (2018). Concurrence of big data analytics and healthcare: A systematic review. *International Journal of Medical Informatics*.

Palanisamy, V., & Thirunavukarasu, R. (2017). *Implications of big data analytics in developing healthcare frameworks – A review*. School of Information Technology and Engineering.

Patel, S., Patel, A. (2016). A Big Data Revolution in Healthcare sector: Opportunities, Challenges & Technological Advancements. *International Journal of Information Sciences and Techniques, 6*(1).

Praveena, M., & Kameswara, R. (2018). Survey on Big data analytics in Healthcare Domain. *IACSIT International Journal of Engineering and Technology*.

Priyanka, K., & Kulennavar, N. (2014). A Survey on Big Data Analytics in Health Care. *International Journal of Computer Science and Information Technologies, 5*(4), 5865–5868.

Ristevski, B., & Chen, M. (2018). Big Data Analytics in Medicine and Healthcare. *Journal of Integrative Bioinformatics, 15*(3). Advance online publication. doi:10.1515/jib-2017-0030 PMID:29746254

Sachin, K., Gunasekaran, A., Goswami, M., & Manda, J. (2019). A systematic perspective on the applications of big data analytics in healthcare management. *International Journal of Healthcare Management, 12*(3).

Sarwar, M., Hanif, K., Talib, R., Mobeen, A., & Aslam, M. (2017). A Survey of Big Data Analytics in Healthcare. *International Journal of Advanced Computer Science and Applications*.

Sonnati, R. (2017, March 3). Improving Healthcare Using Big Data Analytics. *International Journal of Scientific & Technology Research, 6*(3).

Suzzie, A., & Apenteng, A. (2014). Big Data: A Tool for Development in Developing Nations. *International Journal of Scientific and Research Publications, 4*(5).

V. (2019, January 10). *5 V's of Big Data*. Retrieved June 5, 2020, from https://www.geeksforgeeks.org/5-vs-of-big-data

Wang, Y., Lee, K., & Terry, A. (2018). Big Data Analytics: Understanding its capabilities and potential benefits for healthcare organizations. *Technological Forecasting and Social Change, 126*, 3–13. doi:10.1016/j.techfore.2015.12.019

What is Big Data? - Definition from Techopedia. (n.d.). Retrieved December 11, 2020, from https://www.techopedia.com/definition/27745/big-data

Why Traditional Marketing Analytics Tools Fail and What to do about it. (2020, November 2). Retrieved July 24, 2020, from https://www.pointillist.com/blog/why-traditional-marketing-analytics-tools-fail

Chapter 7
Big Data With IoT for Smart Farming

Supriya M. S.

ⓘ https://orcid.org/0000-0003-3465-6879

Ramaiah University of Applied Sciences, India

Meenaxy Roy

Ramaiah University of Applied Sciences, India

ABSTRACT

Smart farming may also be called digital farming. The world is changing and digitizing at a quick rate. So all the work from agriculture to the stock market will become more productive and faster. Speed and efficiency play a key role in coping with the rapid pace of life and growing population. Smart agriculture has removed many of the problems faced by farmers during the conventional farming process. Several technologies are useful in this field, which make them work comfortably. Productivity in all areas of this sector can be increased with the aid of new technologies such as IoT and big data. Data can be accessed and analyzed from any part of the world with the help of IoT devices. The chapter offers insight into technology, such as big data and IoT, its applications in smart farming, as well as future innovations and opportunities.

INTRODUCTION AND BACKGROUND

Day by day due to massive population growth, the need to feed the population is increasing. Agriculture supports in country's growth. Hence, farming is play very crucial part to maintain the balance in the country's economy (Altieri & Koohafkan, 2008). Thus the expanding population can be fed with farming that includes information and communication technologies into machinery, equipment and sensors that are used in agriculture manufacturing system. Technological development like the usage of electronic devices and data transmission system has created essential changes in the agriculture process (Pivoto et al., 2018).

DOI: 10.4018/978-1-7998-6673-2.ch007

The researchers have drawn attention to demographic patterns including ageing populations and continuing movement of people from rural to urban areas. In addition to the trends, there are few more factors which compelled the researchers to come up with the advanced technologies is the unpredictable climate change (Pivoto et al., 2018). The climate changes are so drastically unpredictable which in return cause the crop destruction and huge loss to the farmers and economy. Agriculture is undergoing through many technological changes with the policy makers around the world (Pivoto et al., 2018). The technologies like artificial intelligence, robotics, Internet of Things (IoT) and many more can be incorporated in agriculture. To deal with the climatic change, in 1999, member of Radio Frequency Identification Development (RFID) community introduced IoT concept (Shete & Agrawal, 2016). The mobile phone usage and other technologies have made the concept of IoT more relevant. With the help of internet cities and administrative authority will be able to get the information not only from city environments but also from remote areas. There are many hardware platforms to support the interfacing of huge variety of sensors like humidity sensors, temperature and pressure sensors and light intensity sensors which can collect the required information and data, these sensors play a vital role in the agriculture field too. These data can be uploaded to the server so that the authorize people can access it (Shete & Agrawal, 2016). This helps to know about the environment, which in return helps the farmers to grow crops accordingly. This also helps the authorize people in making quality decision.

Smart farming is also about bringing change in other industries like the dairy farm. The researchers are also concerned about the dairy products. The innovation forces which drive smart dairy farming currently fall into three key categories. The robotic milking, automated feeding and the quality of the product. The quality of the product is the crucial point which needs lot of attention. Robotic milking is not a new concept, it has been used since the 1990s. This concept has reduced the labour cost and made it much more efficient, both money and time can be saved. The actual creativity is the intelligence behind it, the automation has reduced the labour cost and the primary motivation behind various industries is the intelligence software, and the large scale farming industries are no different. It is also very difficult to find labours as you need to wake up early and work late. It is also not the most ambient environment as it doesn't smell nice like the other air conditioned room (Grogan, 2012). All the industries are changing to cope up with the increasing world population as well as with the global market. Robotic milking has almost completed second decades in dairy farming. The technology behind this is based on the development of sensors and robotic grabber engineering (Grogan, 2012). The software that interfaces into it is the real next technology in dairy farming. This is mainly into the herd management that firstly collects the information and the data. It then analyses the farmers' data generating the different profiles that are returned to automatic milking. The cows are also sent to feeding and cleaning that are often wireless (Grogan, 2012).

Therefore, not only the agriculture field but also dairy farming is taking steps towards the smart farming. Smart farming will help us to lead life in more efficient and comfortable way. Increasing farm productivity is important as it also increases the farm profitability. It is no secret that with the increasing population we need to fuel up the growth of food production to meet the demand. To increase the food production it is important that to understand the weather and climatic condition. There is a need to understand various soil, fertilisation and irrigation condition. Throughput can be improved by knowing the type of crop will grow under the best suitable condition which is soil, fertilisation and irrigation condition. Crop recommendation will need data collected from the field based on the environmental condition. The same data-driven method can be used to understand the climatic condition, resource concern like water, labour and energy shortages. As per United Nation's Food and Agriculture Organisation, the production in food have to increase by 60 per cent to cope up with the expanding population which is supposed to be 9 billion by 2050 (Grogan, 2012).

Through day, both agriculture and farming are confronted by a variety of challenges. Smart farming uses Information and Communications Technology (ICT) and IoT to make the traditional farming more efficient. Overall, the efficiency and productivity of the crops can be improved in an agricultural domain with the help of emerging electronic devices (Barreto & Amaral, 2018). Thus it's possible to feed a larger population with the technology like smart farming.

CHALLENGES IN SMART FARMING

Smart farming can also refer to as digital agriculture. The world is changing at a high pace, making everything digital. So that all the works from agriculture to the stock market become more efficient and fast. To cope up with the high pace of life and the growing population, speed and efficiency play a vital role. Smart farming has eliminated many problems which farmers were facing during the traditional way of farming. With the help of smart farming farmers are able to do those things which they have always wished for. Farmers are able to know the climatic conditions for the upcoming years beforehand. They are also able to know about the weather which helped them tremendously. This is not all about it, farmers can get to understand their soil condition which helped them to plant crops and deal with plantation more effectively. Smart farming is the reality that each farmer has ever dreamt of. But there is always bane and boon to every aspect of things. The challenges are the legal and regulatory framework which goes around the data collection and sharing the information about the agricultural data (Wiseman et al., 2019). Farmers are embracing the robotic technologies and digitalization which have transformed the way they used to farm. Some of the farmers have still mixed feelings to indulge in smart farming. The challenges these farmers are facing is moral and ethical. The questions arises that how much other influencers will have access over the information and data, price, measure and support that will indeed decide if it can happen in future or not. The progression of modernisation is inevitable in agriculture but the concern is that how much it is secure. These technologies can be very useful until the information and data are not misused (Wiseman et al., 2019).

The farmer's needs are neglected during the hyperbolic discussion of the intelligent agriculture and digital technologies. Farmer's concern should be taken at first before anything else. First, the review of the issues posed by omnipresent data collection, sharing and usage of agricultural data should be handled carefully. There is no particular law or framework which ensures the security of this data. There should be some proper law and regulations over the access, data ownership and use of the data, can be done up to certain limit. This law will ensure the safety and security of the farmers.

While there are presently no lawful or administrative structures that are focused on farming information explicitly, the existing more extensive lawful and administrative structures around information assortment both advise and are educated by worries over information proprietorship, access and use (Wiseman et al., 2019). So whether or not, the farmers are willing to give up their information and data became the main concern. As over the time, all have seen that the leaks of information is happening a lot, most of the farmers' information also shared with third parties for money. The misuse of the data and information is increasing. These misuses of information have made trust issue between the people. An absence of trust in the way information is overseen has become some portion of an ordinary discussion among people and a wide scope of businesses.

One more challenge is that if the farmers are not well trained then due to lack of knowledge, nurturing and maintenance of the plant becomes very difficult. Thus, the technology incorporated in smart farming should ease these difficulties.

Agricultural profitability can be improved by increasing agricultural productivity and to meet fast growing food needs driven by rapid global population growth. The recognition and prediction of crop production under a variety of environmental conditions can help to improve farm productivity. Crop recommendations presently depend on accumulated field data studies capturing crop production under a different environmental conditions. But the collection of crop performance data is now slow, as studies on crop are often carried out in remote and distributed areas, typically collected physically. Moreover, the quality of the crop performance data collected physically is very less as the previous conditions are not considered, but is crucial to filter out the information collected that leads to unnecessary conclusions. Thus there is a need of IoT technologies that are wireless sensor networks, network-connected weather stations, cameras, and smart phones to collect crop performance and environmental data. The data composed over these IoT devices were then used to analyse and remove the unwanted data, also to give personalised recommendations for growing crops in any specific farm (Wolfert et al., 2017).

As there were some demerits in smart farming, the farmers were sceptical to opt this opportunity. But the traditional farming can't feed the fast growing population. IoT makes it more secure and efficient. Few advantages of using IoT is listed as below: (Patil et al., 2012)

- Increased efficiency in selection of inputs such as soil, fertilizer, pesticides and many more
- Reduction in production cost
- Cost-Effectiveness
- Food safety
- Environment Protection
- Sustainability

INCORPORATING BIG DATA AND IOT FOR SMART FARMING

The emerging IoT technology can solve most of the issues in smart farming. The IoT is the most efficient way to resolve these problems. IoT have evolved from many different building blocks like sensors, software networks and other electronic devices (Tzounis et al., 2017). The population is increasing at an exponential rate, so does the need for food. The growing food demand not only for quantity, but also for quality, this has raised the demand of the strengthening and industrialisation in agriculture sector. The IoT is the family of promising technologies which can handle these issues in an efficient way. In 1999, British visionary Kevin Ashton coined the terminology "Internet of Things". As the phrase reveals, IoT model will provide a technological universe, which eases the most of the tasks with the help of sensors. Regular instruments and equipment enhanced by the capabilities of processing power and system management will have the option to assume a job, also as single units or as a dispersed working together multitude of heterogeneous gadgets (Tzounis et al., 2017).

Security is one of the concern that hesitate farmers to indulge in smart farming. An advantages of Information and Communication Technologies (ICT) with IoT have increased the precision in smart farming. Utilizing drones, robots, smart data, smart security devices for seed traits and to treat soil conditions, and other novel frameworks propose uncommon comforts and enhancements to deal with the quality factor in agricultural farming. In spite of having so many advantages, it comes with a inherit risk of cyber leaking of data and information. Still most of the companies and food departments are not investing much to the cyber security. Nonetheless the likelihood of cyber agro terrorism have started to concern the sector. A cyber-attack can cause wreckage of food and agriculture Company. Intelligent farming depends on Cyber Physical System (CPS)-based intelligent networks. The CPS can do operations such as monitor, coordinate and integrate by computer and communication system, interaction with the outside world is done with the help of network agents, which consists of sensors, actuators, communication devices and control processing units.

In order to help the remote irrigation system, (Zamora et al., 2019) proposed an approach called cyberisation of Solar Photovoltaic Water Systems (SPVWS). The platform proposed here assists in communication between the green house and cloud that corresponds to operational and supervisory level. With the help of this architecture, the farmers can observe and succeed the activities of SPVWS.

For instance, sensors can collect information on the soil, moisture, fertilisation and the weather and transmit it to the wireless network in real time. These all helps in providing information about the weather condition, soil quality, livestock, logistic and many others. (Jayaraman et al., 2016) Proposed an IoT based platform that can collect data associated with environment, fertilization and irrigation. It can process it and remove unwanted data such that productive crop recommendations can be done to that specific farm. It eases the integration of various IoT devices with the help of this platform. (Ahmed, De, & Hussain, 2018) Proposed a cross-layer-based channel access and routing solution to minimize operation of sensing and actuation so as to reduce the latency in the network.

The Agricultural Electronic foundation (AEF) is an international union which works on research, design and manufacturing of machines and systems required for agriculture. It is deeply involved in accurate agricultural technologies that is validated by ISOBUS whose ongoing declaration advance towards a time critical systems administration dependent on the Ethernet and broad reach physical layer, will empower fast interchanges in machines used for agriculture, support procedures on the homestead and empowering disseminated control frameworks, and in this way an IoT worldview.

To recognize and evaluate the contact criteria and agricultural areas requirements, the environmental structure needs to be discussed properly. Most of the countries have large fields which need extensive cultivation of maize, rice, soy beans and sugarcane (Bacco et al., 2018). For this huge machines are needed which require direct connection with the real time communication so that it can be used very efficiently. Real time communication should work parallel so that we can get the data from the farm and update it even there is a constraints on time limit. Unmanned ground vehicles Unmanned Ground Vehicles (UGV) support farmers to reduce the manual effort. In UGVs, tractors can automatically plant seeds more accurately. Then harvesters guided by GPS reap the seeds with high precision (Bacco et al., 2018).

Remote sensing techniques are using UAV in constant progress and the use of tiny MEMS sensors. The use of powerful processors, small GPS modules and range of digital radios tries to make drone more efficient by making them compact, cost effective and easy to operate. Within a short period of time UAVs have become an important tool in many application fields. Drone is more convenient because unlike the terrestrial vehicle, drone updates prescription map in real-time. So the main purpose of UAVs and UGVs is the communication. In fact these techniques are used to collect multispectral images (Bacco et al., 2018). These operation are crucial as it helped in evolution of variable rate in treatments. It's one of the important features is precision in farming (Bacco et al., 2018).

Computer vision is experiencing revolution in today's world. The increasing use of UAVs and UGVs has led the path for the development in deep learning architectures and specifically in Convolutional

Neural Networks (CNNs). Increasing use of UAVs and UGVs and decreasing cost of the same have drawn attention in application for monitoring crop state. Machine vision system can work in or outside the visible spectral bands. These machines are associated with IoT devices. Machine vision frameworks can be supplemented with the utilization of CNNs, Where UAV-procured paddy field imagery at low altitudes is used to plan CNNs and determine the paddy field yield. The classification of grass and measurement of weed infestation can be done by deep learning technology (Bacco et al., 2018).

This technology enables smart farm to collect information and data to work upon it. This increase the operational performance by analysing the collected data and taking actions upon those analysed data which will increase the productivity or streamline operations.

Usage of these technologies also reveals and improves the likelihood of misuse of data which will affect the estimated result with the actual result. It can also be the reason of security breach. In order to have better work efficiency in smart farming, IOT can play a vital role. This help people to get the required information about the weather to the soil. Given a huge variety of niche equipment, it is not a shock anymore that IOT in agriculture have provided varied and also lot of benefits which are generated to a specific requirement. This requires highly precise equipment in order to get information and data (Barreto & Amaral, 2018).

In the cyber physical management process smart farming focuses on the application of information and communication technology. The researchers have drawn attention to demographic patterns including ageing populations and continuing movement of people from rural to urban areas. This growth will be made possible by new technologies like the internet of things and cloud computing and bring robotics, artificial intelligence into the picture enabled (Kamilaris, Kartakoullis, & Prenafeta-Boldú, 2017). IoT collects large amount of data that are supposed to be examined and use to make decisions. With huge size data and information can be collected and analysed meticulously. As the smart machines are used in the farming, with these there will be also some growth in terms of quantity and scope. These will make more smart farming as data driven and data enabled (Kamilaris, Kartakoullis, & Prenafeta-Boldú, 2017).

Clod computing is emerging in IT world in which the computation is dynamically scalable and often virtual resources are provided as a service over the internet (Patil et al., 2012). There is affinity towards cloud computing because of the some advantages it has (Hori, Kawashima, & Yamazaki, 2010):

- Reduction in initial investment
- Limitless resource allocation
- Maintenance and up gradation is perform at the back-end
- It provides easy and quick development which also includes cooperation with the other cloud platforms
- Increased opportunities for global service development

Machines are armed with all kinds of sensors which can measure the data in the environment in order to know the behaviour of the machine. This can differ from comparatively simple feedback mechanisms to deep learning algorithms, for example from thermostatic regulating temperature to implementing the right crop protection strategy. This is used by consolidating with other, external sources of big data such as weather or market data with other farms. It is difficult to give definition for big data, however generally it can be define in term for data sets that are very large and complex. Hence the traditional processing application is inadequate. A set of techniques and technology are required by big data to reveal the insights of datasets which are diverse, complex and massive with the integration of the new forms (Wolfert et al., 2017).

The Data FAIRport initiative highlights more operational dimension of Big Data. The Fairport provides the FAIR principle that the data should be findable, accessible, interoperable and reusable. This also suggests the significance of metadata that means "data about the data". This includes time, location and standard used. Both the big data and IoT are emerging concepts, so it is expected that the application and implication for this research and development is not widely spread (Wolfert et al., 2017).

Further, context can be characterized as the data collected by IoT devices is utilized to describe the entities of substances (for example regardless of whether an individual, spot or object) and It is considered applicable to the real-time contact between a client and an application, including the client and the application itself (Ge, Bangui, & Buhnova, 2018). Since this context is important to the place, time, personnel status and environmental settings. For this IoT becomes a primary source of contextual data with huge amount of volume, variety and velocity. This can bring many challenges to the IoT. With the help of big data we can resolve these issues. Big data have brought some substantial transformation to its high influence and application in various sectors.

The convergence of big data and IoT created huge opportunities to build services for complex systems such as smart cities. Many big data technologies have emerged to help process large amounts of data. However, the IoT have created significant vast changes at the process of collecting different and huge amount data. Big data, on the other hand, created visible improvements and introduced new opportunities to build new IoT technologies for the industries and academia.

IoT domains have been centre of attention for many researchers, it helped enormously in agricultural field. With the benefits of IoT technologies people have increased the quality of the product and fulfilled the satisfaction of the end-users. As an instance, IoT have helped lot an important role to play in order to protect the crops from rodents or insects. In order to handle all these activities efficiently and to find optimum environmental conditions, cloud systems are useful in storing and analysing confidential information, which in return can increase efficiency and save resources (Ge, Bangui, & Buhnova, 2018).

IOT AND BIG DATA TECHNOLOGIES WITH ARCHITECTURE

There are lot of technologies that are involved in IoT agriculture solutions. This makes it is hard to have an explicit discussion. So here are some examples of core technologies:

Cloud and Edge Computing

Cooperation of IoT and cloud computing have unavoidable access to the shared resources in agriculture. To get information upon a request over the network and this can be executed b cloud computation which plays a crucial role in agriculture (Sundmaeker et al., 2016). There are some protocols like IPv6 and 6LoWPAN. These are the last layer of generalisation that permits the advancement of numerous applications. The communication protocol deployed in this layer can monitor various parameters of agriculture which incorporates irrigation monitoring, weather information, soil moisture textures. Application Layer – More energy limitations and rigorous computation makes to come up with some substitutes of lightweight protocols on application layers are CoAP, MQTT, AMQP and HTTP. CoAP protocol runs on UDP, and operates on architecture of appeal and reply and HTTP is very well-known global design.

IOT Agriculture and Network Platform

The IOT agriculture refers to both the cloud model and the big data analytics model-

Big data Analytics model- This helps to get the meaningful and required information is obtained from the huge amount of data. This meaningful information can be extracted from different forms of data. The disease management of crop and crop growth model are formed from the data. This study assists farmers in providing decision support services. Productivity of crop and optimization of crop expenses can be increased. The network platform includes 6 components (Farooq et al., 2019)

- Farmer experience
- Big Data Analysis
- Sensing and Monitoring
- Storage Services
- Communication Protocol
- Physical Implementation

IOT Agricultural Network Architecture

This network is the primary component of IoT in the agricultural sector. It proposes a blueprint for the design of physical part as well as its working standards and procedures. Most of IOT's framework has 4 architectural layers (Farooq et al., 2019)

- Network Layer – It is an imperative innovation for accuracy farming. This layer is also responsible for the transmission of information to the application layer. The two versions are IPv4 and IPv6. IPv4 appeared because of expanding the huge number of addressable gadgets. On the other hand, development of IPv6 was normal which progressively build up on all systems networking gadgets.
- Application Layer- Energy restrictions and tough calculation required through the IoT devices there are numerous trivial protocols on application layer such as CoAP, MQTT, AMQP, and HTTP (Farooq et al., 2019)
- Physical and Mac Layer – Final layer of agricultural network architecture used to get various parameters actuated and sensed (Farooq et al., 2019)
- Transport Layer/host layer- In this layer the information is sent to IOT devices directly. The main purpose of this layer is to collect and encapsulate the information and data obtained through the sensor layer (Farooq et al., 2019)

APPLICATIONS OF IOT AND BIG DATA IN SMART FARMING

The following are the farming applications which assists in improving and building up the agricultural practices.

Precision Farming - This assists the farmers to automate the system which can help to save lot of time. It helps to improve and optimise the productivity of the agriculture in all potential ways to amplify the output so as to create smart cropping system. To enhance the crop productivity a relation between the Information was given on the agricultural environment and crop statistical analysis, which helped collect crop data. Different sensors have been deployed to get information about soil fertility, weather condition, and moisture level.

- Monitor Climate Conditions – It is very crucial to monitor the conditions of climate in agriculture. Climate is one of the most crucial factors for agriculture. It provides a tremendous help to the farmers to have knowledge about the future climate condition, so that they can planned accordingly which plant to grow. The weather parameters being tracked include humidity, temperature, and direction of the wind, air pressure and much more.
- These parameters are sent to cloud servers for the analysis, because of the analysis new information and data are emerge which help to increase the productivity of the agriculture. Weather stations are the most common agricultural equipment used to observe distinctive atmosphere conditions. US Food and Agriculture Organization (FAO) has been characterized a climate related methodology called Climate Smart Agriculture (CSA) which encourages the users to change agricultural systems by spotting environmental circumstances (Farooq et al., 2019)
- Soil Patterns – It is one among important practises for analysis over the period of time in agriculture as well as industries. In soil observing there are numerous ecological problems that influences production of crop. If these kinds of problems can be studied precisely, understanding of farming patterns and process will be lot easier. In monitoring soil patterns includes soil fertility, soil humidity, moisture, temperature and many more (Farooq et al., 2019)
- Pest and crop disease monitoring – One of the main causes of revenue and production loss is due to crop failure. The use of IOT have helped farmers to collect information about the crop disease in early stage. Predicting about the crop disease at beginning stage helps the farmers to collect revenue and spare the crop from pest outbreaks. IOT based monitoring system were developed. These systems can detect different diseases in different crops such as rice, wheat etc. Another IOT based monitoring system does the detection of wild animals to protect the crops from them. Attacks by wild animals are also the reason for land contradiction. So, these IOT based system helps a lot to overcome these problems. The parameters which is observed includes temperature, humidity, and wind pressure (Farooq et al., 2019)

Livestock Monitoring - Ideal condition or climate conditions which ingest huge amount of environmental conditions leaves negative effect on the efficiency of creatures which is a significant issue for some researchers. On the other hand, demand of high-quality dairy product, it becomes high time for the livestock management. IOT helps to increase the quality as well as quantity of the livestock. This helps those farmers as they undergo huge amount of loss every year. In any case, IOT based livestock management solutions assists farmers to improve the cultivating standards, domesticated animals' conditions and dairy items (Javaid et al., 2018).

Existing Agriculture Techniques

Existing techniques are not able to fulfil the need for this generation as there are some lagging in the processor speed, data storage space, availability, reliability, scalability and many more. In reality, even assets that are used in PC-based farming systems are not used productively. In order to address the issue of current agricultural systems, a cloud-based autonomous information system needs to be built that transmits agriculture as a service (Gill, Chana, & Buyya, 2017). This is a cloud based autonomic agriculture service which is called Aaas. This can manage various data based on agriculture on different types of domains. QoS boundaries (budget and processing time) must be distinguished prior to the allotment of assets. AaaS is the key component that guarantees that the asset director can serve enormous measure of solicitations without disregarding SLA terms and powerfully deals with the assets dependent on QoS necessities recognized by QoS manager (Gill, Chana, & Buyya, 2017). AaaS services has been partitioned into three kinds: SaaS (Software as a Service), PaaS (Platform as a Service) and IaaS (Infrastructure as a Service). In SaaS, with the help of UI the user can associate with the system. The application Aaas includes two subsystems are-

- User
- Cloud

User Subsystem - This subsystem gives a UI, where diverse sort of user interface with AaaS to give and get valuable data about farming dependent on various spaces. Nine type of information of various domain is included- crop, weather, soil, pest, fertilizer, productivity, irrigation, cattle, and equipment and three categories based on user:

- Agriculture expert
- Agriculture officers
- Farmers

The agriculture expert shares proficient information by noting rancher inquiries and updates the AaaS information base dependent on the most recent exploration done in the field of farming regarding their space. Agriculture officials are the administration authorities that give the most recent data on novel policies of agriculture, plans, and legislature rules. Rancher is a substantial AaaS material that can make the most of it by asking questions and having automatic responses after review (Gill, Chana, & Buyya, 2017).

Cloud Subsystem – It contains the stage where agriculture service is facilitated on a cloud. Insights regarding users and agriculture data are put away in a repository of cloud in various classes for various fields with ID number. The data is checked, analysed, and handled consistently through AaaS (Gill, Chana, & Buyya, 2017).

CHALLENGES OF IOT AND BIG DATA FOR SMART FARMING

The Internet is continually growing and changing. IoT embeds some Internet-connected knowledge which help to have better communication, exchange of information and increase decision making capacity. IoT can change future of smart farming. It can bring enormous differences eases peoples' life and contented. But IoT have some drawbacks.

- The development of broad monopolies from a socio-political perspective agri-food and farmers' reliance on larger businesses becomes possible big data concerted in the hands of large agribusinesses restrict the technology capacity, lone improvement of capacities and business benefits a limited enterprises (Zhang et al., 2014)

- Concern about who owns the data and who poses concerns about privacy can monetize it. Farmers are worried that knowledge on cultivation, seed companies or rival farms may be misused (Zhang et al., 2014)
- Big data processing and analysis have posed concerns health, precision and access
- Unbalanced technology and lack of skilled analyst in developing countries to handle the technologies (Zhang et al., 2014)
- Information on the ground truth is required products and services assessment in different physical and conditions or conditions of weather but developers have limited access to this (Zhang et al., 2014)
- To Name and Manage Identity- IoT connects billion of objects to offer information and also give innovative services. For giving information or services according to the request send by the user, it needs to have unique identity and naming management (Khan et al., 2012).
- Interoperability and Standardization – Various manufacturers make their own devices and then provide their own services. But sometimes these services are not accessible for other. So standardization is significant in offering interoperability to the objects and sensor devices (Khan et al., 2012).
- Safety and Security of Devices – IoT comprises of enormous number of insights object all over the world. It is also necessary to prevent this information and data from the intruder's access. It can cause a huge catastrophe, if all the information gets leak to the world (Khan et al., 2012).
- Information privacy- The IoT practises various technologies to identify an object. It is important to make sure that no unauthorised people can access those information (Khan et al., 2012). Confidentiality and Encryption of Data-The sensor systems do independent measurement and sensing. Then, pass data through the transmission network to the information processing unit. It becomes very compulsory to have proper encryption mechanism so that it can provide the confidentiality. Thus it can guard the data from the externals (Khan et al., 2012).
- Spectrum – To transmit data, specific spectrum is required to transfer data. This will enable billions of sensors to communicate with each other.
- Network security – Large number of data are sent over the wireless network. These data should be safe and secured so that no external interference should be there (Khan et al., 2012).
- Business Issues (Zhang et al., 2014):
  - Cost: The setup and running cost of IoT devices
  - Business models: IoT devices accumulates the data and farmers supports revenue generation models
  - Lack of adequate knowledge: The farmers situated in rural areas will lack knowledge about use of IoT in agriculture
- Technical issues (Zhang et al., 2014):
  - Interference: Massive IoT devices can cause interference in particular with IoT devices which use the unlimited spectrum, such as ZigBee, Wi-Fi, Sigfox and LoRa, for agricultural purposes and for another purposes. This could result in data loss and decrease the IoT ecosystem reliability.
  - Security and privacy: The lack of adequate protection will result in loss of data, Privacy Bridge and raw information on on-the-ground constraints and other rational properties which can affect the competitive benefits of owners of reserved property.

- Reliability: An IoT devices should be able to operate in harsh environment that challenges reliability.
- Scalability: Intelligent IoT management system has to be created as large number of IoT devices has to be managed by existing gateways and protocols
- Localization: For the implementation of IoT devices there are many aspects to consider. These considerations include the ability to support the IoT system and play features that can be wherever and be associated to or without configuration or other devices like gateways, with no or limited configuration.
- Resource optimization: Due to various farmer sizes and the type of sensors necessary to track agricultural variables for specific crops and animals, this is especially challenging.
- Choice of technology: IoT technology is the best option this is a major challenge because a great deal is needed for investment new technology rollout, as most of them are still under pilot test.
- Sector issues (Zhang et al., 2014):
  - Regulatory Challenges: Each countries will have unique regulations, therefore, the legal frameworks and regulations has to be properly maintained between the farmers and the companies as it may pose a serious problem
  - Interoperability challenges: Lot of IoT devices will be connected with each other and thus, interoperability poses a concern as it needs to be managed well.

FUTURE TRENDS AND OPPORTUNITIES

The need for high data rates, low latency and spectrum performance are vital considerations in IOT with the fifth generation of networks (5G). There is also need of coexistence of different networks. To incorporate all of the mentioned requirements, there is a need of Artificial Intelligence (AI). AI is very useful as it helps to understand the pattern and extract data. By understanding the pattern, it can make logical decisions and can prescribe action to end devices.

- Energy Efficiency – to make greener perspective of 5G network, there is two aspects-
- In loaded case there should be energy- efficient data transmission.
- Consumption of low energy by idle scenarios like sleep ratio and sleep duration.

Intelligence is not necessarily needed for technologies but it can bring revolution in daily life. With the help of intelligence everything becomes easy to work. Interference begins with the autonomous existence of technology which will ensure the Qos for the society as well as business thus having a direct impact on human beings. The big data which is produced from the IoT will work intelligently with help of 5G network based IOT devices (Javaid et al., 2018). To make the system self-configured, self- adaptive, self-organised, and the devices should be connected to the intelligence to make conclusions in an organised way. The data are actually unstructured and can be submitted to the cloud in order to minimise latency and computational complexity. But if in any case legacy system has already connected intelligence, it can analyse on the basis of the pattern and give decision based on that, which will make it structured and reduce the duplications to limit computational complexities (Javaid et al., 2018). The following areas can be identified under this section (Elijah et al., 2018).

Technological

- Deployment of LPWA Technologies: This technology offers a long-range and low-power application thus enabling large-scale applications pilot test in the field of agriculture
- Universal Platform: This makes it possible to change a device to accommodate, Manage and control of different applications of crops and animals for sale to local shops and goods. It is free of geographical and technological gaps and regional limitations and can be used for many IoT enablers in forestry.
- Security: More research is need to make IoT devices work with new security algorithms like signcryption and many more.
- Spectral and Energy Efficiency: New innovations are being developed as more LPWA complaint solutions are being introduced can support higher results, high path loss, long distance coverage connection budget and extended battery life are needed
- Quality of Service: Desire to make sure an appliance that will be able to use IoT to send vital data any communication technology remains an available research area. The use of NB-IoT technology assures connectivity related with LoRa, strong QoS. There must be more jobs in the provision of QoS-assuring mechanism the various network layers of IoT
- Artificial Intelligence and DA: Further analysis is planned to model crop growth using artificial intelligence and management of diseases based on farm and climate data. For example, machine learning is used for disease recognition from smart-phone photos. Large quantities of data can be processed by DA that is faster than the IoT time are anticipated to be produced.
- Privacy-Preservation: Endwise privacy protection techniques that permits data to be collected while retaining individual privacy were proposed to resolve the IoT data infringement issues
- Data Compression: It needs a lot of attention as there are involvement of transmission of images and video.
- Real Time Monitoring: Since the field needs to deploy several sensors to monitor in real-time, a modest network governance protocol should be developed to facilitate less crowded messaging between objects and servers. Present protocols are particularly designed for network devices and can cause high network overhead and data traffic as well as improve IoT devices' power requirements.

Application Level

At present, IoT devices, software systems and networking technologies which offers cost-effective IoT deployments are being developed and investigated. Much of the experimental work includes prototyping and small-scale experimentation. In order to assess the usability of IoT technologies in agriculture, large scale pilots are required (Wiseman et al., 2019). In the future, the whole supply chain and agri-food projects are to involve more large-scale pilots, not just in developed countries, but also in developing countries.

Business and Marketing

- Cost Reduction: Optimized energy use the costs for IoT solutions are expected to be reduced, physical size reduction and huge performance. Future work will lead to cheaper construction sensors, hybrid study of various implementation scenarios, use of licensed and unlicensed combined to reduce the installation and communication technologies costs of service.

- Policies and Regulations: Attention is needed for the implementation of IoT policies and standardization in agriculture. Government level engagement or Department of Agriculture should be guaranteed when occupied on IoT policies and rules in agriculture that might vary from across regions.

CONCLUSION

It is known that agriculture plays a crucial role in every society. With the increasing population, the need to feed people also increases. It is possible to achieve these goals, it is important to use a right technology for more benefits. IoT can bring innovation of smart farming, increase in production of crops can be achieved. With the help of IoT, people can get information about the weather, soil, fertiliser and many others. This will hugely improve the quality and quantity in the production of crops. The unpredictable nature of climate has immense impact on crops. It can destroy the crops in a moment. But with the involvement of IoT technologies people can solve those issues at some extent. However, IoT when incorporated with big data can bring much more enhancements in this field. The huge amount of data collected by IoT devices can be managed with the help of big data technology. Therefore, IoT in smart farming with the help of big data can resolve many issues and have created enormous opportunities to develop in the field of smart farming. There are also some future opportunities in the field of smart farming with the help of IOT. Bringing 5G networks and intelligence will bring gigantic changes in the agriculture. It can be used to abolish the hunger of the poor people across the world.

REFERENCES

Ahmed, N., De, D., & Hussain, I. (2018). Internet of Things (IoT) for smart precision agriculture and farming in rural areas. *IEEE Internet of Things Journal, 5*(6), 4890–4899. doi:10.1109/JIOT.2018.2879579

Altieri, M. A., & Koohafkan, P. (2008). Enduring farms: climate change, smallholders and traditional farming communities (Vol. 6). Penang: Third World Network (TWN).

Bacco, M., Berton, A., Ferro, E., Gennaro, C., Gotta, A., Matteoli, S., & Zanella, A. (2018, May). Smart farming: Opportunities, challenges and technology enablers. In *2018 IoT Vertical and Topical Summit on Agriculture-Tuscany (IOT Tuscany)* (pp. 1-6). IEEE.

Barreto, L., & Amaral, A. (2018, September). Smart farming: Cyber security challenges. In *2018 International Conference on Intelligent Systems (IS)* (pp. 870-876). IEEE. 10.1109/IS.2018.8710531

Elijah, O., Rahman, T. A., Orikumhi, I., Leow, C. Y., & Hindia, M. N. (2018). An overview of Internet of Things (IoT) and data analytics in agriculture: Benefits and challenges. *IEEE Internet of Things Journal, 5*(5), 3758–3773. doi:10.1109/JIOT.2018.2844296

Farooq, M. S., Riaz, S., Abid, A., Abid, K., & Naeem, M. A. (2019). A Survey on the Role of IoT in Agriculture for the Implementation of Smart Farming. *IEEE Access: Practical Innovations, Open Solutions, 7*, 156237–156271. doi:10.1109/ACCESS.2019.2949703

Ge, M., Bangui, H., & Buhnova, B. (2018). Big data for internet of things: A survey. *Future Generation Computer Systems*, *87*, 601–614. doi:10.1016/j.future.2018.04.053

Gill, S. S., Chana, I., & Buyya, R. (2017). IoT based agriculture as a cloud and big data service: The beginning of digital India. *Journal of Organizational and End User Computing*, *29*(4), 1–23. doi:10.4018/JOEUC.2017100101

Grogan, A. (2012). Smart farming. *Engineering & Technology*, *7*(6), 38–40. doi:10.1049/et.2012.0601

Hori, M., Kawashima, E., & Yamazaki, T. (2010). Application of cloud computing to agriculture and prospects in other fields. *Fujitsu Scientific and Technical Journal*, *46*(4), 446–454.

Javaid, N., Sher, A., Nasir, H., & Guizani, N. (2018). Intelligence in IoT-based 5G networks: Opportunities and challenges. *IEEE Communications Magazine*, *56*(10), 94–100. doi:10.1109/MCOM.2018.1800036

Jayaraman, P. P., Yavari, A., Georgakopoulos, D., Morshed, A., & Zaslavsky, A. (2016). Internet of things platform for smart farming: Experiences and lessons learnt. *Sensors (Basel)*, *16*(11), 1884. doi:10.339016111884 PMID:27834862

Kamilaris, A., Kartakoullis, A., & Prenafeta-Boldú, F. X. (2017). A review on the practice of big data analysis in agriculture. *Computers and Electronics in Agriculture*, *143*, 23–37. doi:10.1016/j.compag.2017.09.037

Khan, R., Khan, S. U., Zaheer, R., & Khan, S. (2012, December). Future internet: the internet of things architecture, possible applications and key challenges. In *2012 10th international conference on frontiers of information technology* (pp. 257-260). IEEE. 10.1109/FIT.2012.53

Patil, V. C., Al-Gaadi, K. A., Biradar, D. P., & Rangaswamy, M. (2012). Internet of things (Iot) and cloud computing for agriculture: An overview. Proceedings of agro-informatics and precision agriculture (AIPA 2012), 292-296.

Pivoto, D., Waquil, P. D., Talamini, E., Finocchio, C. P. S., Dalla Corte, V. F., & de Vargas Mores, G. (2018). Scientific development of smart farming technologies and their application in Brazil. *Information Processing in Agriculture*, *5*(1), 21–32. doi:10.1016/j.inpa.2017.12.002

Shete, R., & Agrawal, S. (2016, April). IoT based urban climate monitoring using Raspberry Pi. In *2016 International Conference on Communication and Signal Processing (ICCSP)* (pp. 2008-2012). IEEE. 10.1109/ICCSP.2016.7754526

Sundmaeker, H., Verdouw, C. N., Wolfert, J., & Freire, L. P. (2016). Internet of food and farm 2020. In *Digitising the Industry* (Vol. 49, pp. 129–150). River Publishers.

Tzounis, A., Katsoulas, N., Bartzanas, T., & Kittas, C. (2017). Internet of Things in agriculture, recent advances and future challenges. *Biosystems Engineering*, *164*, 31–48. doi:10.1016/j.biosystemseng.2017.09.007

Wiseman, L., Sanderson, J., Zhang, A., & Jakku, E. (2019). Farmers and their data: An examination of farmers' reluctance to share their data through the lens of the laws impacting smart farming. *NJAS Wageningen Journal of Life Sciences*, *90*, 100301. doi:10.1016/j.njas.2019.04.007

Wolfert, S., Ge, L., Verdouw, C., & Bogaardt, M. J. (2017). Big data in smart farming–a review. *Agricultural Systems*, *153*, 69–80. doi:10.1016/j.agsy.2017.01.023

Zamora-Izquierdo, M. A., Santa, J., Martínez, J. A., Martínez, V., & Skarmeta, A. F. (2019). Smart farming IoT platform based on edge and cloud computing. *Biosystems Engineering*, *177*, 4–17. doi:10.1016/j.biosystemseng.2018.10.014

Zhang, Z. K., Cho, M. C. Y., Wang, C. W., Hsu, C. W., Chen, C. K., & Shieh, S. (2014, November). IoT security: ongoing challenges and research opportunities. In *2014 IEEE 7th international conference on service-oriented computing and applications* (pp. 230-234). IEEE. 10.1109/SOCA.2014.58

Chapter 8
Data Analytics and Its Applications in Brief

Nilesh Kumar Sahu
https://orcid.org/0000-0003-1675-7270
Birla Institute of Technology, India

Manorama Patnaik
https://orcid.org/0000-0003-4035-2468
Birla Institute of Technology, India

Itu Snigdh
Birla Institute of Technology, India

ABSTRACT

With an ever-increasing amount of data created, it has become a major challenge for infrastructures and frameworks to process a lot of information inside stipulated time and resources. So as to effectively extract from this information, organizations are required to discover new devices and strategies in particular for large information preparation. Therefore, data analytics has become a key factor for organizations to uncover hidden data and accomplish the upper hand in the market. As of now, tremendous distributions of larger data and information processing make it hard for experts and specialists to discover points they are keen on and track forward-thinking. This chapter puts forth an outline of data analytics, extension, and discoveries just as opportunities emancipated by analysis of data. The chapter also deals with various applications of data analytics which include applying an algorithmic or mechanical procedure to infer bits of knowledge, for instance, going through a few informational collections to search for significant connections between one another.

DOI: 10.4018/978-1-7998-6673-2.ch008

INTRODUCTION

Data Analytics is the branch of Machine Learning which deals with exploring the raw data in order to extract some conclusive conclusions. It involves studying the past and historical data to research future trends, to analyse the effects of decision taken by the organisation or events, or to evaluate performance of the given scenarios(Bertsimas et.al., 2014; Chong et.al., 2015). Today Data analytics are used by everyone especially Researchers, Institutions, Industries and even by small entrepreneurs to make better decisions. It totally depends upon the conclusion or say inference drawn from the data.

Data Analytics (DA) is the way towards looking at informational indexes so as to make inferences about the data they contain, progressively with the guide of particular frameworks and programming (Iqbal et.al., 2020). Data Analytics advancements and procedures are generally utilized in business enterprises to empower associations to settle on progressively educated business choices and by researchers and analysts to check or invalidate logical models, speculations and theories (LaValle et.al., 2011). Some examples include Analysis about customer buying habits, Bank customer satisfaction and similar survey-based analysis.

Data

Data is defined as Raw facts and figures collected for reference and analysis. Generally, data is divided into two types, Structured data and Unstructured data as shown in Figure 1.

Figure 1. Types of Data

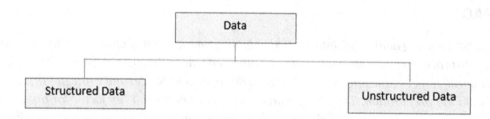

Structured data are those data which are highly organised and are easily searchable and traceable. These data contain only one data type like Text data, Numerical data, and the likes (Hu et.al., 2014). Examples included in this category are Bank credits and deposits data.

Unstructured data are those data which are not properly organised and are not easily searchable. These types of data consist of mixed type data i.e. Data consisting of numbers, text, video, images, for example, Bank customer satisfaction, comments on varied posts on the internet.

Primary data is the data collected by researchers or organisations for a specific task and Secondary data refers to data collected by someone else for some other task (Mohammadi et. al., 2018), (Khan et. al., 2015).While Secondary Data collected by a Scholar for his project work is an example of primary data, the same data if is being used by some other Organisations or Industries becomes Secondary Data. Thus, on the basis of sources of data, data are divided into classes as outlined in Figure 2.

Figure 2. Types of Data on basis of its sources

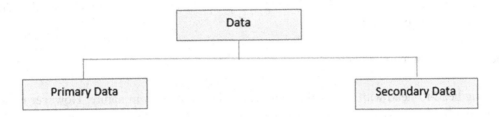

Analytics

Analytics is defined as the process of conducting logical analysis of data (Ohlhorst et.al., 2012) from a large set of business data using mathematics and statistics. Data analytics procedures can uncover patterns and measurements that would somehow be lost in the mass of data. This data would then be in shape of being utilized to streamline procedures for building the general productivity of a business or framework.

How can Data Help Anyone?

Past and historical data help us to derive insight which will help researchers, industries, or organisations to take better decisions in the following ways:

1. Help us to identify new growth opportunities
2. Drive innovation and innovative ideas
3. Operate businesses and organisations more efficiently.
4. Identify new risks and their mitigation.

Data analytics is an expansive term that includes numerous assorted kinds of analytical information. Any kind of data can be exposed to information investigation strategies to get the knowledge that can be utilized to improve things (Tsai et.al., 2015). For instance, manufacturing or production organizations regularly record the runtime, personal time, and work line for different machines. This data is afterwards broken down as information so as to readily schedule remaining tasks at hand for the machines' maximal performance nearing the top limit.

Data analytics can do substantially more than call attention in gaming organizations as they use analytical information to set prize calendars for players that keep most of the players dynamic in the game. Content organizations utilize a large number of similar information examination to keep you clicking, viewing, or re-arranging substance to get another view or another snap (Qin et.al., 2014).

DATA ANALYTICS IMPACTING BUSINESS TODAY

(Russom et.al., 2011), (L'heureux et.al., 2017)

1. It helps business to launch new products and services.

Today business uses past historical data to analyse the buying habits of the customers and using those analysis it also helps the business to launch new products and services which would be liked by the customers (Russom et.al., 2011).

2.   It helps in creating new markets.

Competing head-to-head with an existing market can be a cutthroat in nature. However rather than directly shifting from the existing market to a new market can be a risky bet since it requires both tremendous amounts of capital and the time to build. So, studying the past data will help the organisation to take decisions carefully. For example, for analytical questions like how many years it took for the market to move from landline phone to mobile phone and then smartphones, needs to be considered for identifying market trends towards adaptation to newer technology.

3.   Disrupting existing market.

It is same as creating a new market. Here too, past historical data are used to launch new products which disrupts the current market. For example, before Digital Camera, reel camera was famous, and Kodak was leading the Camera market then but as soon as the digital camera was launched the existing reel markets were disrupted.

4.   Driving increased efficiency.

Today each and every organisation wants to lead the market in their respective field and for that they have to increase their efficiency which can only done through logical analysis done on their past sales and production.

Data Analytics as an Aid in Decision Making

Combining both past historical data and insight can help in making new decisions. Previously organisations as well as independent researchers' decisions towards their respective growth were totally based on their insights. whether to go forth with a decision or against. However, at times these insights needed a background for success and to make the decision in favour, today it has become necessary to combine both the analysis of historical data and insight for making new decision. This would not only reduce the burden on one's insight and belief for judgement, rather provide a support with analytical data in case something was to go wrong (Ferraris et.al., 2019).

Process Involved in Data Analysis

Before a conclusion can be inferred from the analysis of data available, there are a number of varied processes involved. The analysis of Data (Watson et.al., 2014) from the raw data can be illustrated as follows:

Determining the Data Requirement

In this step we mainly focus on the problem statement which needs to be solved, and on the basis of the particular problem we try to determine the relevance of the data. We need to identify which data would be critical in order to find the solution to the given problem. Some problem statements require huge amount of historical data for instance, data pertaining to last 10 to 20 years, while some problem statements require a small amount of data like considering data of the past 2 years.

Collecting the Data

After determining the data required for solving the problem, the next step is to collect those data which would help in doing analysis. These data can be either collected from data repositories, wherever, depending upon the problems. Sometimes data are gathered through surveys in which customers or the service user give their valuable opinions which are then collated as the 'data'. There are other instances where the run-time operational data from organisations are collected for analysis purpose.

Organising Data

In this step, Data are organised and restructured depending upon the requirement of data for the given problem. The data therefore needs to be sorted, filtered and organised as each and every data collected would not be relevant enough to be used.

Cleaning Data

In this step, Data are cleaned by removing the unwanted and noisy data which are of no use and are not going to take part in decision making.

Analysis Data

This is the last and most important step in which Statistics and different mathematic tools are used to derive some useful conclusion which would solve the problem.

The Four Aspects of the Data Analytics and Framework

According to PWC (the global Data Analytic company) there are four aspects of the data and analytics framework (Kaisler et.al., 2013)

Discovery – 'Observation to Information'

Here, first of all problems are defined, Data are collected and explored and analysis are done on collected data.

Insight – 'Information to Insights'

In this step new techniques are applied on both existing data and new data to generate insights. The most important thing in this step is collecting insight as much possible.

Decisions/Actions

The insights gathered in the previous step are used here to make decisions and obtain recommended actions and execute the plan.

Outcomes

In this step, the desired outcome is reviewed for the long-term decisions and their impacts on the organisation.

Types of Data Analytics

The five types of data analytics as shown in Figure 3 illustrate the basic operations performed and tools used on data(Tsai et.al., 2015);

Figure 3. Types of Data Analytics

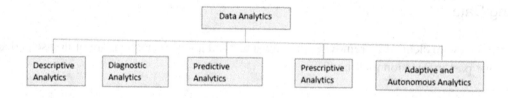

Descriptive Analytics – 'What Happened'

Summarising the existing data using the existing Intelligence tools to better understand what has happened.

Diagnostic Analytics – 'Why did it Happen'

In diagnostic analytics, we focus on past or historical performance to determine what has happened and why did it happen.

Predictive Analytics – 'What Could Happen'

As the name suggests, it's totally focused on future prediction, i.e. predicting the possible outcome using the statistical tools and Machine Learning.

Prescriptive Analytic– 'What Should be Done'

Prescriptive analytic is a part of predictive analytics which emphasizes on the recommended actions which should be taken for better analysis and result.

Adaptive and Autonomous – 'How to Adapt to Changes'

The future of analytics is going to be Adaptive and Autonomous i.e. the model is going to learn from past data and day to day updated data for better analysis. As inferred by the name 'Autonomous', data analysis should not involve any human interference. Autonomous analytics is the application of ML to enhance human judgements. For example, let us consider a scenario where a weak student was very much worried for the upcoming exam which was due just 10 days, so he went to his teacher for his help. The teacher suggested the student to collect old notes and last ten to fifteen-year's question papers. Now, using the data of last few years question paper the student would get an idea regarding the relevance and importance of the chapters as to which would be carrying more marks and which to be focused more. This method is called Descriptive Analytics. The next time the student would be able to estimate the probability of questions to be asked using AI and Machine Learning techniques. As the student is able to successfully predict the questions on the basis of their patterns, this is called predictive analytics. Further after getting and estimating the probability, the student gets an insight on which chapter should be focused more and more time to be spent, which is called prescriptive analytics.

Now, from the next time AI and Machine Learning will be used to predict the questions for the next upcoming examination and this is called Adaptive and Autonomous Analytics.

Where Data and Analytics is Used

The Organisation, Institutions, Educational Institute, business, Industries and other sectors, where discovering new patterns and gaining new insights helps them to grow and outstand them from others(Vera-Baquero et.al., 2013).

Data and Analytics in Different Sectors

Health Industry

Data Analytics helps in predicting epidemics and its overall impact. It also helps in preventing disease and spreading of viral disease with better analysis and details. Today Data analytics is helping in optimizing the treatment selection for treating many diseases (Roski et.al., 2014), and is also helping in Lifestyle improvement of people with a better customer service. Today many researchers are working in developing and employing better Artificial Intelligence tools using Machine Learning, Data Analytics to provide better prediction of disease at an early stage.

Online Shopping

Data analytics helps the ecommerce sites to attract, recommend and trace out their potential buyers by know their buying habits. Tis also helps them to lure such customers with better offers. Old historical data are taken here for consideration which helps the industry to know their customers very well and recommending the right products and offers which will unknowingly compel them to buy those products.

Educational Institutes

Education plays a vital role in a country's overall growth. Nowadays the Education sector has become more challenging due to rapid growth and evolution in the modes of teaching. At present Colleges and University want to select only excellent students for the courses provided and Data Analytics plays a vital role in deciding this. Data Analytics also helps in analysing student's progress and finding out the student's finest and weakest part (Parwez et.al., 2017).

Hiring Agencies:

In the present day, many organisations depend upon data analytics for hiring good candidates for their organisation. After having the screening tests, organisations resort to analytics for discovering the strongest and weakest of the candidates. According to those analysis, they hire candidates for different departments as every department do not require similar candidature qualities.

Key Factors Increasing the Relevance of Data and Analytics (Bakshi et.al., 2012)

1. Enormous amount of data being generated in day-to-day life recur to technology advancement.
2. Data plays an important part making decisions and implementing them.
3. Dramatic reduction in the cost of infrastructure and tools used for analysis.

Big Data

Collection of large and complex data which are difficult to process using the basic Database Management tools or traditional data processing tools. It is combination of structured, semi structured and unstructured data either collected from primary source or secondary source which is mined for gathering information which is used for developing models and doing analysis.

4 V'S OF BIG DATA ARE (SPANGENBERG ET.AL., 2015)

Volume

Size/ amount of generated dataset. Today Organisations collect data from different sources which includes business transaction, IoT devices, Social media and many more. Some examples are Transactional Databases, Unstructured data from social media, Sensors and Machine to Machine data.

Velocity

Velocity means the speed at which data are generated. With enormous growth in the field of Internet of Things, today lots and lots of data are being generated by sensors, smart meters and RFID tags each and every seconds.

Variety

As huge amounts of data are being generated, data comes in different formats. Data like structured data, numeric data, unstructured, text, emails, audio, videos etc.

Veracity

Veracity refers to the quality of data, because data are being generated from different sources and it is very difficult to clean and transform them. Data consists of biasness, noise and abnormalities which is to be handled carefully.

Data Visualization Tools Needed for Data Analytics

Different tools are needed for different analytics.
Descriptive and Diagnostic Analytic tools:

- SQL
- Tableau
- QlikView
- Hadoop/Spark
- Microsoft Access
- SAS, Python, R and various statistical package within them.

Predictive and Prescriptive analytics tools:

- SAS, R, Python
- Vensim, Any logic
- Gurobi, River Logic
- Scikit-learn, TensorFlow, Theano
- Machine Learning, Deep Learning
- NLTK

CONCLUSION

Data analytics applications include something other than breaking down information. Especially on cutting edge investigation ventures, a significant part of the necessary work happens forthright, in gathering, coordinating and getting ready information and afterward creating, testing and re-examining expository models to guarantee that they produce precise outcomes. Notwithstanding information researchers and other information experts, investigation groups frequently incorporate information builds, whose activity is to help prepare informational indexes for examination.

Data Analytics advancements and procedures are generally utilized in business enterprises to empower associations to settle on progressively educated business choices and by researchers and analysts to check or invalidate logical models, speculations, and theories (LaValle et.al., 2011). Some examples include Analysis about customer buying habits, Bank customer satisfaction and similar survey-based analysis.

REFERENCES

Bakshi, K. (2012, March). *Considerations for big data: Architecture and approach. In 2012 IEEE aerospace conference.* IEEE.

Bertsimas, D., & Kallus, N. (2014). *From predictive to prescriptive analytics.* arXiv preprint arXiv:1402.5481.

Chong, D., & Shi, H. (2015). Big data analytics: A literature review. *Journal of Management Analytics*, 2(3), 175–201. doi:10.1080/23270012.2015.1082449

Das, T. K., & Kumar, P. M. (2013). Big data analytics: A framework for unstructured data analysis. *International Journal of Engineering Science and Technology*, 5(1), 153.

Ferraris, A., Mazzoleni, A., Devalle, A., & Couturier, J. (2019). Big data analytics capabilities and knowledge management: Impact on firm performance. *Management Decision*, 57(8), 1923–1936. doi:10.1108/MD-07-2018-0825

Hu, H., Wen, Y., Chua, T. S., & Li, X. (2014). Toward scalable systems for big data analytics: A technology tutorial. *IEEE Access: Practical Innovations, Open Solutions*, 2, 652–687. doi:10.1109/ACCESS.2014.2332453

Iqbal, R., Doctor, F., More, B., Mahmud, S., & Yousuf, U. (2020). Big Data analytics and Computational Intelligence for Cyber–Physical Systems: Recent trends and state of the art applications. *Future Generation Computer Systems*, 105, 766–778. doi:10.1016/j.future.2017.10.021

Kaisler, S., Armour, F., Espinosa, J. A., & Money, W. (2013, January). Big data: Issues and challenges moving forward. In *2013 46th Hawaii International Conference on System Sciences* (pp. 995-1004). IEEE.

Khan, Z., Anjum, A., Soomro, K., & Tahir, M. A. (2015). Towards cloud based big data analytics for smart future cities. *Journal of Cloud Computing*, 4(1), 1–11.

L'heureux, A., Grolinger, K., Elyamany, H. F., & Capretz, M. A. (2017). Machine learning with big data: Challenges and approaches. *IEEE Access: Practical Innovations, Open Solutions*, 5, 7776–7797. doi:10.1109/ACCESS.2017.2696365

LaValle, S., Lesser, E., Shockley, R., Hopkins, M. S., & Kruschwitz, N. (2011). Big data, analytics and the path from insights to value. *MIT Sloan Management Review*, 52(2), 21–32.

McAfee, A., Brynjolfsson, E., Davenport, T. H., Patil, D. J., & Barton, D. (2012). Big data: The management revolution. *Harvard Business Review*, *90*(10), 60–68. PMID:23074865

Mohammadi, M., Al-Fuqaha, A., Sorour, S., & Guizani, M. (2018). Deep learning for IoT big data and streaming analytics: A survey. *IEEE Communications Surveys and Tutorials*, *20*(4), 2923–2960. doi:10.1109/COMST.2018.2844341

Ohlhorst, F. J. (2012). *Big data analytics: turning big data into big money* (Vol. 65). John Wiley & Sons. doi:10.1002/9781119205005

Parwez, M. S., Rawat, D. B., & Garuba, M. (2017). Big data analytics for user-activity analysis and user-anomaly detection in mobile wireless network. *IEEE Transactions on Industrial Informatics*, *13*(4), 2058–2065. doi:10.1109/TII.2017.2650206

Qin, S. J. (2014). *Process data analytics in the era of big data*. Academic Press.

Roski, J., Bo-Linn, G. W., & Andrews, T. A. (2014). Creating value in health care through big data: Opportunities and policy implications. *Health Affairs*, *33*(7), 1115–1122. doi:10.1377/hlthaff.2014.0147 PMID:25006136

Russom, P. (2011). Big data analytics. *TDWI Best Practices Report, 19*(4), 1-34.

Spangenberg, N., Roth, M., & Franczyk, B. (2015, June). Evaluating new approaches of big data analytics frameworks. In *International Conference on Business Information Systems* (pp. 28-37). Springer. 10.1007/978-3-319-19027-3_3

Tsai, C. W., Lai, C. F., Chao, H. C., & Vasilakos, A. V. (2015). Big data analytics: A survey. *Journal of Big Data*, *2*(1), 1–32. doi:10.118640537-015-0030-3 PMID:26191487

Vera-Baquero, A., Colomo-Palacios, R., & Molloy, O. (2013). Business process analytics using a big data approach. *IT Professional*, *15*(6), 29–35. doi:10.1109/MITP.2013.60

Watson, H. J. (2014). Tutorial: Big data analytics: Concepts, technologies, and applications. *Communications of the Association for Information Systems*, *34*(1), 65. doi:10.17705/1CAIS.03465

Chapter 9
Data Visualisation in Business

Remya Lathabhavan

https://orcid.org/0000-0002-4666-4748
VIT University, India

K. M. S. V. D. Akshar
VIT University, India

ABSTRACT

The main objective of data visualization is to communicate information clearly and effectively through graphical means. It doesn't mean that data visualization needs to look boring to be functional or extremely sophisticated to look beautiful. To convey ideas effectively, both aesthetic form and functionality need to go hand in hand, providing insights into a rather sparse and complex data set by communicating its key-aspects in a more intuitive way. This chapter analyses the following aspects of data visualisation. First, it describes data visualisation. Second, it describes the importance of data visualisation in business. Third, it describes different types of data visualisation methods used in business and familiarises some tools available for data visualisation. Last, it describes the recent developments in data visualisation and its future research directions.

INTRODUCTION

Data visualization describes the attempt to assist individuals or organisations recognise and analyse the importance of data by allocating it in a visual context. Data visualisation is the communication of information using graphical representation (Knaflic, 2015). Thus, it is a process of changing information into a visual form and help the user to discover, recognise and examine the data and helps to take decision based on that (Murray, 2017).Since pictorial representation is easy to learn, represent and understand, they played a key role in communication and information sharing much before the formulation of written languages (Chen et al., 2008). The other methods for data interpretation such as information graphics, information visualization, scientific visualization, exploratory data analysis and statistical graphics etc. show close similarity with data visualisation.

DOI: 10.4018/978-1-7998-6673-2.ch009

In the contemporary world, data visualisation represents as the present-day alternative of visual communication. It consists of the generation and study of the visual representation of data. In visual representation context, it will be easier to understand and interpret it for business compared to going thorough tons of data every day. The issues arise on text-based data, such as non-detection of patterns, trends and correlations in some cases, can be resolved and analyse easily with data visualization tools(Ward et al., 2017). These functionalities make data visualisation as a favourite area among both academicians and practitioners. Most importantly, data visualisation is a combination of visualisations of Science and information(Post et al.,2002).Data visualisation in business is still exploring new avenues as it eases the business decision making and make it more perfect(Zheng, 2017). This paper mainly gives an overview of the importance, the types and tools of the data visualisation.

IMPORTANCE OF DATA VISUALISATION IN BUSINESS

There are huge importance and benefits for data visualisation. That includes quicker action, identifying patterns, better analysis, finding connection and emerging trends (Kirk, 2016).

Quick action The human brain has the capacity to recognise and analyse visual information much faster than text-based data and this will lead to quicker action. It also helps managers and higher authorities alert promptly of new data changes and take appropriate decision accordingly.

Identifying patterns A visual representation of data recognise quickly correlations and find link between the different functionalities and performance.Visualised data helps out to find out market trends very easily and thus help for boosting profitability and competitive advantage. Understanding and analysing these patterns allows the analysts and decision makers to give attention on key areas which demands focus in data, hence help them to recognise the importance of that selected areas to run business successfully.

Better analysis Data visualisation leads to key dialogue on the business including the pace of improvement, expansion, and direction of business. Efficient data visualisation should be informative, efficient, appealing, interactive and predictive (Kirk, 2016). It also helps to analyse reports regarding different functions of management such as marketing, finance etc. Considering the analysis, the decision makers can check the functions that need a focus to enhance profit, and thus making the business efficient .

Finding connections and errors By arranging data visuals in a purposeful way, it helps the users to understand the relations in a single view. Spotting out errors in data is much easier in data visualisation. Such prompt actions of data visualisation to spotting erroneous data helps user to remove that particular data from analysis and to avoid wrong actions on predictions.

Emerging trends Data visualization helps to understand and analyse the new changes and trends in business to produce quality goods and services . This also helps to identify the issues before it arise. Being highly efficient among the current techniques, it helps to increase the effectiveness and efficient nature of the business.

DATA VISUALISATION METHODS IN BUSINESS

Data visualisation methods can be broadly classified into- data visualisation methods for two dimensional area, multidimensional, hierarchical data visualisation, network data models and temporal visualization. Figure 1 depicts the types of data visualisation methods.

Figure 1. Data visualisation methods

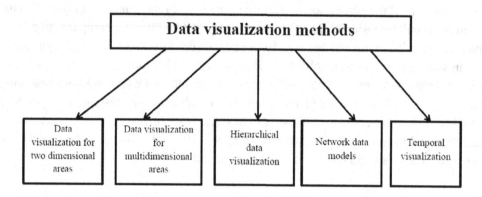

Data Visualisation for two Dimensional Areas

Two dimensional area visual forms are geospatial in nature . They represent particular place or location in the world. This include **area or distance cartogram, choropleth** and **dot distribution map**.

Area or distance cartograms are the impressions of some parts of maps, representing some additional parameters of importance for that business or entity. These parameters may include frequency of business ventures, demography, planation details, population size, travel times and any other variables.

Cartograms combine mathematical and regional information in thematic maps, in which regions are scaled in proportion to some statistic such as sales, production etc (Nusrat & Kobourov, 2016). Thus it help to gain insights into particular business activities in a specific area.

Choropleth is a map colored in combination of different colors depending on the level of the considered variable, such as profit level per organization, sales level per district and biggest inventory stocks per country etc. Choropleths are very useful in representing the changes of the represented measurement, across a particular geographic area.

Dot distribution map is the data visualization method which pass on information using the dots to highlight the degree of existence of the variable under consideration within the area(Berg et al., 2004). Figure 2 depicts the area cartogram, choropleth and dot distribution map

Multidimensional Data Visualization

Multidimensional data visualization consists of pie chart, histogram, scatter plot etc. The pie chart is among the most widely methods for representing data. It divides into different sectors representing numerical values. These values are calculated proportional to each sector and represent using corresponding angle and arc length in each sector. Hence the users can identify very easily data given. The histogram is a set of rectangles which visualize the time periods and the parameter values, normally represent as width and height respectively. These width and height help vividly to understand the parameter adjustments. Its also a commonly used method and easily understandable by the users.

The scatter plot is the form of data visualization which represent parameter values using two sets of unconnected dots (Shao et al., 2016). Uses of scatter plots are to observe and show relationships between

Figure 2. Area or distance cartogram, choropleth and dot distribution map

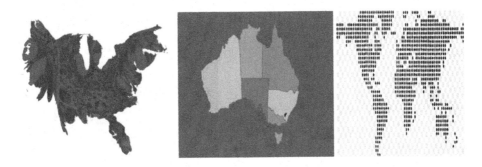

two numeric variables. It also shows patterns when the data are taken as a whole. Figure 3 represents pie chart, histogram and scatter plot.

Figure 3. Pie chart, histogram and scatter plot

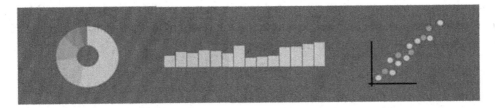

Hierarchical Data Visualization

Hierarchical data visualization is important in cases where the comparison of one set of data values with another one or more data value sets are done. This includes dendrogram, sunburst chart and tree diagram.

A dendrogram represents clustering of different data sets in hierarchical form and assist to understand the relationship at a glance (Phipps, 1971). It tries out the best way to allocate objects to clusters. A sunburst chart, also called as a ring chart, is a partition chart with radial orientation that supports visualizing large or small hierarchies without requiring scrolling or other interaction (Smith et al., 2014). In simple terms, it is a pie chart with concentric circles which represents the hierarchy of data values. The tree diagram represents the tree-like relations within the data structure, either in the upside down or from the left to the right patterns, extending an easier interpretation (Binder et al., 2015). Figure 4 depicts dendrogram, sunburst chart and tree diagram.

Network Data Visualization Techniques

Network data visualization techniques describe the pattern of how various data sets compare and relate to each other. It consists of alluvial diagram, node link diagram and matrix diagram. An alluvial diagram is like a flow diagram which describes changes in the data over a period or under certain situations. It

Figure 4. Dendrogram, sunburst chart and tree diagram

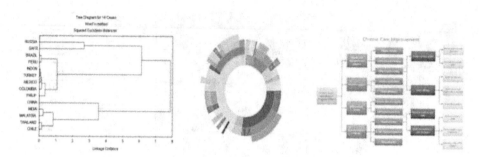

enables users for an easy and quick understanding of data pattern and analyze the relationships between the between the different data variables (Yeung, 2018).

A node-link diagram is a circular image with dots and lines. The dots act the data nodes and lines represents the links between the nodes (Keller et al., 2006).This helps understand and analyze the relations between the data and recognize how results are based on respective data. A matrix diagram or chart is used when there are numerous data connected to one another with any relationship (Miner, 2002). Hence, in its representation, the data set positions and the relations will be visible. Figure 5 represents alluvial diagram, node link diagram and matrix diagram

Figure 5. Alluvial diagram, node link diagram and matrix diagram

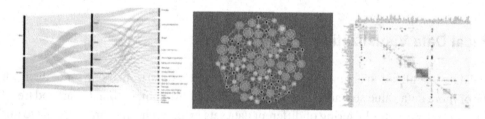

Temporal Visualizations

Temporal visualizations has a visual similarity with simple linear graphs. It consists of a start and finish time. It projects as a descriptive image showing the variable adjustment over time because some of the data measured might overlap over time.It includes connected scatter plot, polar area diagram and time series. Connected scatter plot is the pictorial representation of values for two variables taken from a data set. As the name indicate, in the connected scatter plot, there is a line which connects the scattered values throughout the plot. (Haroz et al., 2016). Polar area diagram is visually similar to a standard pie chart, but differs on the evaluation on the size of the sector by considering the distance from the center, instead of the arc length and angle in pie chart(Sadeghi Bigham et al., 2008). Hence, a sector extended far away from the center might be more important than sector which has less distance. A very good example for continuous data estimation and prediction over a stretched period is time series (Eichler,

2007). The computer memory usage graph, the number of webpages visited in a week and abundance of other past data are best visualized using these techniques. Figure 6 depicts the connected scatter plot, polar area diagram and time series

Figure 6. Connected scatter plot, polar area diagram and time series

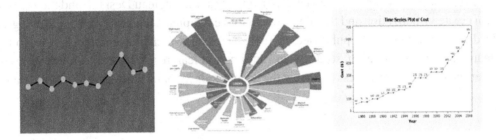

TOOLS FOR DATA VISUALISATION

Tableau

Tableau is a very powerful and popular tool used for Data visualization in the companies for business intelligence. It aids in converting massive and complicated data into meaningful insights. The data analysis process is very fast with Tableau and the visualizations are represented in the form of dashboards or worksheets. The illustrations in Tableau are such that anyone in the managerial chain can interpret the meaning, also even non-technical people can easily learn and create dashboards themselves. Some great features of Tableau are "Data Collaboration", "Real-time analysis", "Data mixing". Tableau doesn't require little technical knowledge which led to its wide popularity among managers, researchers, and companies.

There are different products under Tableau: Tableau Desktop, Tableau server, Tableau online and Tableau public.

Tableau Desktop It has many features like coding, live data analysis, customization of dashboards. It has everything to create an end-to-end data analysis report

Tableau server This tool is designed to help share the reports, dashboards created in Tableau desktop to other tableau users. The dashboard should be first published in Tableau Desktop and then is accessible to intended users via Tableau server

Tableau online It is like Tableau server, but the data is hosted on the cloud maintained by Tableau. This tool has a large set of APIs and 3rd party integration support like google analytics, salesforce API, amazon aurora etc.

Tableau public It is the cost-free version of Tableau. The workbooks or dashboards created cannot be locally stored, it can be stored online which is publicly available for anyone to use. So for people who want to learn, this is the ideal tool

Tableau Reader This is used just for viewing the dashboards created using Tableau Desktop or Public version. Filtering is allowed but modifying isn't. it is basically like read/view mode.

Only Tableau Desktop and Tableau Public are for data analysis and dashboard creations, the rest are for sharing the visualizations and dashboards.

How does Tableau Actually Work?

Tableau can extract data from any platform such as from as simple as Excel to Google and Amazon cloud. It can also extract data from complex databases such as Oracle. When we open Tableau software, there are many data connectors that allow us to extract the data from different sources, the number of data connectors and variety of them will be dependent on the license version of the software.

The extracted data can now be analyzed and played within the Tableau Desktop and the Data analyst/engineer can create visualization and the files are sent to the recipients who can view them using Tableau reader. The dashboards can also be published on Tableau Server, which is an enterprise-level tool, which provides features like collaboration, security, and automation features. With Tableau Server, users have a better experience as they can access and view the dashboards in many platforms like mobile and email

QlikView

QlikView is a business intelligence tool which allows users to build analytics apps with the help of inferences and data. It makes easy for companies to adapt changes in requirements. QlikView's "Associative Data Indexing Engine" can be used to identify hidden patterns in the data to make data backed decisions. This software can be used with multiple data sources at the same time to develop complex visualizations. QlikView has custom data connectors and open API's to make it easy for users to transfer data from multiple systems. The open API of this software can connect to almost any other software for analysis purposes. Users can choose to deploy the models in the cloud or on their own server, this feature is most useful for companies with low hardware capacity. It also has excellent features for collaboration making it an effective tool to work on data as a team.

Some of the popular features of QlikView are: (Some of them are patented)

Colors for visual relationship Usually the relationship between data is portrayed using lines/shapes/arrows, but in this tool colors are used. Related data is shown in some specific colors different to unrelated data.

Data is stored in RAM The analysis, data and computations are all placed in the RAM (Random access memory) of the server to make it quick for users to generate or view reports. This enhances the user experience as well as load time.

Compression of Data We almost always don't need all the available data for analysis purposes, and as QlikView is heavily dependent on data, the data is compressed into a small size going up to 10% of its actual size.

Computations are done on the fly As RAM is used, the values can be instantly used without the need to store them internally and retrieving it, this enables faster computation.

Data Association is automated This tool tries to figure out the relationship amongst the data automatically without having the user manually relate everything. This applies to the whole dataset, however a review of the relations formed by the tool is highly advised.

Some benefits unique to QlikView are:

Integration and Flexibility QlikView gives users almost all the tools or functionalities required to set up the workspace and also process the data as required. There are custom scripts to develop apps or use the "workbench" for extensive development.

Security Generally sensitive and confidential corporate data is used for analysis purposes, so security is very much needed. QlikView takes total charge of permissions, access, and management of data. It provides in depth control of the layouts and dashboards by assigning roles to users and scope of the roles.

Collaboration Reports/layouts/dashboards which are created in QlikView are all shareable. They can be shared using the cloud or via the company server or give rights to those users in the software to view the visual.

Data Discovery It has custom connectors which can be installed when required to retrieve data from other widely used systems such as Teradata, Salesforce, Hive etc. This makes QlikView suitable from small data processing to enterprise level data analysis.

Although the initial investment is high, they have released a similar software named Qliksense with Saas model to eliminate the initial investment problem.

Power BI

It is used to gather inferences and generate reports using a company's data. It can incorporate a lot of data sources at the same time and cleans the data so that it is visually appealing/easier to understand. This tool is not only useful to find the past inferences from the data, but also predict the future. It has a lot of Machine learning features embedded, which can be used to find patterns in data which can then be used to simulate "what if" situations. These features all combined allow users to create forecasts and prepare contingency plans.

The main components of Power BI are:

Power Q&A It has the capability to comprehend queries using natural language and answer using data. Queries regarding the data can be asked just the way we interact with Alexa or any other voice assistant.

Power Pivot This is meant for modelling the data. Here there are multiple ways to model our data specific to our application.

Power Map This is used to create awesome 3D visualizations of data; these are used when we have complex datasets and many parameters to handle.

Power View This functionality can be used to create charts, maps, and graphs using the data, each visual can be deeply customized and changed to suit our requirements.

Power Query It is used to merge, transform, and improve the data from multiple and different sources.

Popular benefits of using Power BI are includes usuage and processing of massive amounts of data, inbuilt ML models help in analyzing the data as well as make probabilistic predictions. As this tool is cloud based, there are frequent updates and features which make the tool more powerful as well help in getting more insights. Also, outstanding personalization capabilities allow users to design dashboards as they wish and also present them appropriately to different groups of audience. Power BI integrates with all other related Microsoft products as well as with other software such as Google analytics, SAP, Hadoop, Salesforce etc. Finally, high level of security is achieved using micro controlling features on accessibility.

There are several versions/variants of Power BI out there designed for specific user groups such as Power BI Desktop (for medium to small businesses), Power BI Service, Power BI Premium(for large enterprises), Power BI Report Server (for organizations which deal with highly sensitive data and do not prefer to store on the cloud), Power BI Embedded, Power BI Mobile (for managers who need to check on the data frequently on the fly).

RECENT DEVELOPMENTS IN DATA VISUALISATION IN BUSINESS

Business data visualization reflects its superiority and uniqueness with some of its notable features while compare to some related fields such as information visualization, illustration, scientific visualization (discussed together with computer graphics and VR), and simulation. Here we mention the comparison these fields taking three parameters- content, visual forms/tools and purpose.

Content – Business data visualisation includes data which are measurable and metrics.Key performance indicators (KPIs) are also an important feature of this. While information visualisation includes all types of information, measurable and qualitative, illustration includes processes, structures concepts, ideas. Contents in scientific visualisation are mostly real time cases, formulas and statistical functions. Simulation includes calculated data based on formulas or rules (Zheng, 2017).

Visual forms/tools - Charts, diagrams, dashboards are the tools used in business data visualisation. Information visualisation represents data through infographics and illustrational diagrams. Scientific visualisation tools are computer generated graphics and 3D virtual reality. Simulation uses animated diagram or virtual reality (Zheng, 2017).

Purpose- Business data visualisation purposes are data exploration, analysis and decision making. While information visualization sticks on information search, artistic displays, usual communication and storytelling, illustration purposes are making the content more indulging and easier to understand the complexity. The purpose of scientific visualisation caters recreate or simulates the real world entity or process, or visualize an algorithm effect. Simulation demonstrates the effect of situations under certain rules (Zheng, 2017).

Thus data visualization has been one of the growing forces driving the Business Intelligence (BI) industry. As an important part of modern business intelligence systems and platforms, business data visualization closely impacts the normal BI and analytics trends. Some of the notable recent trends in BI where data visualisation plays unprecedented impact are Self-service BI, embedded BI and mobile BI.

Self-service BI: This is also known as Personal BI which features control in the hands of users, especially power users. This highly skilled users in using technology applications in business tasks, and they often need instant results. For this, some of the tools like Tableau and Power BI have quickly risen to satisfy this need using a visualization-driven approach and gained wide recognition(Abelló et al., 2013).

Embedded BI: Embedded BI emphasizes the analytics and data presentation as an integral part of an application. It delivers standard reports and dashboards in a more efficient way to satisfy the most common needs. The analytics component has become a competitive component of many business systems(Grublješič & Jaklič, 2015).

Mobile BI: Mobile computing drives the evolvement of BI and data visualization to be more accessible on multiple devices. Access to information though portable devices such as tablets is increasing in many industrial environments where individuals involved in regular activities related to health care, sales and sports. The major influence from mobile computing is the interaction method of touch-oriented interfaces(Verkoou & Spruit, 2013).

The job market of data visualisation seems to be in booming stage now. Also career development in the fields related to data analysis and visualization have seen an impressive trend. Hence, the demand for multi-skill capacity and and integrative experience will increase over time.

FUTURE RESEARCH DIRECTIONS

This chapter would also provide some future research directions in this area. First, future studies can focus on empirical perspective on connecting data visualisation with different business aspects. This can provide better realistic view on the applied business approach. Second, future studies can consider the perception of users, employees, analysts, researchers and practitioners for exploration different views on this area. Third, comparative studies among different industrial application using data visualisation can also widen up the area of research. Last, more factors on technical and usability aspects can be considered for future studies for extracting the unexplored areas of data visualisation.

CONCLUSION

Data visualisation becomes as inevitable method in global business. It provides an easy understanding for huge volume of data. The chapter described importance of data visualisation, its types, some tools, recent developments and future research directions. As global business moves towards more technological realm and geographical distances are shrinking due to technology, data visualisation has more acceptance and popularity.

REFERENCES

Abelló, A., Darmont, J., Etcheverry, L., Golfarelli, M., Mazón, J. N., Naumann, F., Pedersen, T. B., Rizzi, S., Trujillo, J., Vassiliadis, P., & Vossen, G. (2013). Fusion cubes: Towards self-service business intelligence. *International Journal of Data Warehousing and Mining*, *9*(2), 66–88. doi:10.4018/jdwm.2013040104

Binder, K., Krauss, S., & Bruckmaier, G. (2015). Effects of visualizing statistical information – an empirical study on tree diagrams and 2 × 2 tables. *Frontiers in Psychology*, *6*(August), 1–9. doi:10.3389/fpsyg.2015.01186 PMID:26379569

Chen, C., Härdle, W., Unwin, A., & Friendly, M. (2008). *A Brief History of Data Visualization*. doi:10.1007/978-3-540-33037-0_2

De Berg, M., Bose, P., Cheong, O., & Morin, P. (2004). On simplifying dot maps. *Computational Geometry*, *27*(1), 43–62. doi:10.1016/j.comgeo.2003.07.005

Eichler, M. (2007). Granger causality and path diagrams for multivariate time series. *Journal of Econometrics*, *137*(2), 334–353. doi:10.1016/j.jeconom.2005.06.032

Grublješič, T., & Jaklič, J. (2015). Conceptualization of the business intelligence extended use model. *Journal of Computer Information Systems*, *55*(3), 72–82. doi:10.1080/08874417.2015.11645774

Haroz, S., Kosara, R., & Franconeri, S. L. (2016). The Connected Scatterplot for Presenting Paired Time Series. *IEEE Transactions on Visualization and Computer Graphics*, *22*(9), 2174–2186. doi:10.1109/TVCG.2015.2502587 PMID:26600062

Keller, R., Eckert, C. M., & Clarkson, P. J. (2006). Matrices or node-link diagrams: Which visual representation is better for visualising connectivity models? *Information Visualization, 5*(1), 62–76. doi:10.1057/palgrave.ivs.9500116

Kirk, A. (2016). *Data visualisation: a handbook for data driven design.* Academic Press.

Knaflic, C. N. (2015). *Storytelling with data: A data visualization guide for business professionals.* Academic Press.

Miner, A. S. (2002). Efficient solution of GSPNs using canonical matrix diagrams. *Proceedings 9th International Workshop on Petri Nets and Performance Models*, 101–110. 10.1109/PNPM.2001.953360

Murray, S. (2017). Interactive Data Visualization for the Web. O'Reilly, Canada. doi:10.1017/CBO9781107415324.004

Nusrat, S., & Kobourov, S. (2016). The State of the Art in Cartograms The State of the Art in Cartograms. *Computer Graphics Forum, 35*(3), 1–24. doi:10.1111/cgf.12932

Phipps, J. B. (1971). Dendrogram Topology. *Systematic Biology, 20*(3), 306–308.

Sadeghi Bigham, B., Mohades, A., & Ortega, L. (2008). Dynamic polar diagram. *Information Processing Letters, 109*(2), 142–146. doi:10.1016/j.ipl.2008.09.018

Shao, L., Schleicher, T., Behrisch, M., Schreck, T., Sipiran, I., & Keim, D. A. (2016). Guiding the exploration of scatter plot data using motif-based interest measures. *Journal of Visual Languages and Computing, 36*, 1–12. doi:10.1016/j.jvlc.2016.07.003

Smith, A., Hawes, T., & Myers, M. (2014). Interactive Visualization for Hierarchical Topic Models. *Proceedings of the Workshop on Interactive Language Learning, Visualization, and Interfaces*, 71–78. 10.3115/v1/W14-3111

Verkoou, K., & Spruit, M. (2013). Mobile business intelligence: Key considerations for implementations projects. *Journal of Computer Information Systems, 54*(1), 23–33. doi:10.1080/08874417.2013.11645668

Ward, M., Grinstein, G., & Keim, D. (2017). Interactive Data Visualization. CRC Press. doi:10.1016/B978-0-12-809715-1.00007-9

Yeung, A. W. K. (2018). Data visualization by alluvial diagrams for bibliometric reports, systematic reviews and meta-analyses. *Current Science, 115*(10), 1942–1947. doi:10.18520/cs/v115/i10/1942-1947

Zheng, J. G. (2017). Data visualization in business intelligence. In Global Business Intelligence (pp. 67–82). doi:10.4324/9781315471136-6

Chapter 10
Application of Econometrics in Business Research:
An Analysis Using Business Data

Jhumur Sengupta

Dinabandhu Andrews College, Calcutta University, India

ABSTRACT

The last few years have seen great developments in econometrics for a better understanding of economic phenomena. The range of areas in which econometric models are successfully applied has steadily widened including finance and business management. Econometric analysis is concerned with the quantitative relationships between economic variables and it can provide an important input into the decision-making process. The range of areas in which econometric models are successfully applied has steadily widened including finance and business management. Econometrics has enhanced our understanding of the way the managerial decision works. Econometrics is used in doing quantitative analysis of actual economic phenomena based on theory and observations. An economic model is based on a set of assumptions to simplify the complex economic phenomena. This chapter is an attempt to review the application of econometrics using business data. The main objective of this chapter is to chart the application of this science in various fields of business management.

INTRODUCTION

Econometric analysis is concerned with the empirical relationship between economic variables. It applies techniques for analyzing various economic theories. Although econometrics has been evolved from Economics discipline, it has application in various fields of management. Econometrics as a tool has enhanced the ability of managerial decision making process.

Econometrics has its applications in various fields of management. Econometrics as a tool for data analysis was recognized way back in 1969 when two Econometricians R. A Frisch and J Tinbergen got Nobel prize for their works related to multicollinearity and for generating an econometric model. Later in 2003, Robert F Engle and Clive J Granger received Nobel prize for their contributions on seasonal

DOI: 10.4018/978-1-7998-6673-2.ch010

volatility and non-stationarity in financial time series data. Engle focused his work on ARCH (Auto Regressive Conditional Heteroscedasticity) which is useful in the study of volatility of asset prices in financial markets. Granger made special contribution in developing the methods of cointegration which is useful in analyzing financial data.

In recent times, global recessions, increasing cost of production, declining profit margins and volatile business environment are the challenges faced by companies in today's competitive world. In these circumstances, the research and innovations are used as tools for coping up with the uncertain business environment. With the help of real data, firm managers try to find out solutions for increasing efficiencies and reducing costs. Therefore, econometric analysis has become the most useful technique for analyzing business data in order to forecast and about future.

The chapter provides an idea on the application of econometrics in different areas of management. The present Section 1 of this chapter explains the concepts used in econometric analysis. In section 2, the theoretical framework is discussed. In section 3 methodologies used in the chapter have been explained. Section 4 discusses the background literature. Section 5 illustrates the econometric results using data and section 6 concludes.

In the first issue of Econometrica Fisher (1933), explained that the objective of econometric analysis is to make unification between theory and empirics.

Econometric analysis may be done in two ways -Classical Econometrics and Bayesian Econometrics. In classical type, the focus is on estimator. In Bayesian analysis, a posterior density function is obtained.

THEORETICAL FRAMEWORK

Econometric analysis is used by companies for planning and model building. The steps involved in doing Econometric analysis include-

Statement of theory and hypothesis - The starting point is to make statement of theory. For example, in economics, output of a firm is a function of labour.

Collection of data - For empirical analysis data is collected from various sources.

Specification of Model - In econometrics various types of linear and non linear models are used. For example, the relationship between output and labour can be expressed in terms of a linear relationship: $OUTPUT = b_1 + b_2 LABOUR$ where b_1 and b_2 are the parameters of the linear function. The slope b_2 measures the change in OUTPUT for one unit change in LABOUR. In addition to labour there may be other factors affecting output decisions. By capturing the influences of all other variables affecting OUTPUT by U, the above equation is modified as $OUTPUT = b_1 + b_2 LABOUR + U$ where U represents the random error term. This equation represents an econometric model. More precisely, it is an example of what is known as a linear regression model. In the above model, the left-hand side variable is called the dependent variable and the right-hand side is called the independent variable.

Estimation of parameters – Based on the sample data on OUTPUT and LABOUR, one can estimate the parameters of the model namely, b_1 and b_2. The above linear regression model can be estimated by various techniques, such as, ordinary least square, generalized least square, general method of moments, simultaneous equation model.

Hypothesis Testing- After estimating the parameters, hypothesis testing is performed. That is, one may want to find out whether the estimated model makes economic sense and whether the results obtained conform to the underlying theory. In this case, the theory postulates a positive relationship between output and labour. If estimation result shows a positive relationship, then one can say that the statistical results are in conformity with the hypothesis.

Forecasting- The estimated model can be used in predictions about the future. Various forecasting techniques such as qualitative, time series projections are used for making predictions on future trends of events such as inflation, interest rates, employment levels as all these factors are important for making business decisions.

In the present paper the different econometric models used in various fields of management have been explained and then a review of relevant research papers is made.

Figure 1.

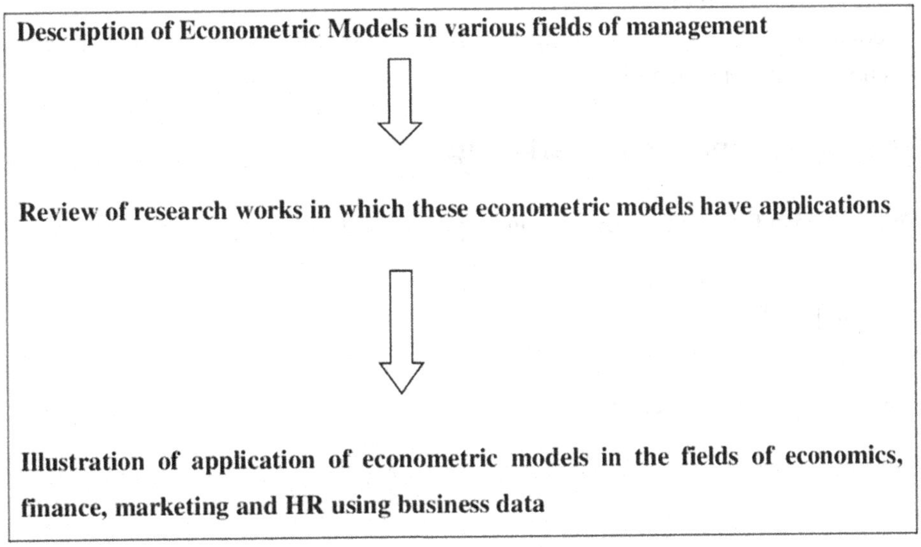

Description of Econometric Models in various fields of management

Review of research works in which these econometric models have applications

Illustration of application of econometric models in the fields of economics, finance, marketing and HR using business data

METHODOLOGY

The approach used in the present chapter is mainly descriptive and exploratory in nature. The various econometric models used in different fields of study are also specified in the present chapter.

USE OF ECONOMETRIC MODELS IN MARKETING

VAR Model Used in Marketing

A VAR model describes the evolution of a set of k variables (called endogenous variables) over the same sample period (t = 1, ..., T) as a linear function of past evolution.

VARX model is a modified version of VAR in which we consider a VAR model along with exogenous variables. A VARX model is represented by

$$Y_t = a_0 + a_1 Y_{t-1} + \ldots + a_p Y_{t-p} + b_1 X_{t-1} + \ldots + b_q X_{t-q} + U_t \tag{1}$$

where $\{X_t\}$ is a vector of exogenous variables, a_0 is a vector of intercepts, the a_j's are coefficient matrices, the b_i's are coefficient matrices, and U_t is the vector of errors.

The ARMA Model in Univariate Time Series Analysis

$$Y_t = a_0 + a_1 Y_{t-1} + a_2 Y_{t-2} + \ldots\ldots + a_p Y_{t-p} + b_1 U_{t-1} + b_2 U_{t-2} + \ldots\ldots + b_q U_{t-q} \ldots\ldots \tag{2}$$

Where Y_{t-p} : Y in period t-p

$\quad U_{t-q}$: Error term of (t-q) th period

The above equation represents Auto Regressive Moving Average process with order p and q.

Y_t may be sales or advertisement data.

Impulse Response Function in Marketing

Vidale and Wolfe (1957) formulated advertising response models.

$$\dot{S} = \rho X [1 - (s/m)] - \lambda S \ldots\ldots \tag{3}$$

Where S: sales rate (sales per period)

$$\dot{S} = \frac{dS}{dt}$$

X: advertising rate
ρ: response constant
λ: decay constant
m: saturation sales rate

The impulse response of sales (S) to an amount spent on advertisement expressed by

$$\Delta S(t) = S(t) - S(0)e^{-\lambda t}$$
$$= [m - S(0)][1 - e^{-\rho X/m}]e^{-\lambda t} \tag{4}$$

Here impulse response function is an exponential function with a decay constant λ

State Space Model in Marketing

State space model is formulated by using Bayesian framework.

αt State vector which is unobserved.

W_t: The explanatory variables which explain the probability that customer switches from one state to another state

V_t: The output variables which characterize customer behavior.

The output variables V_u^t may be various behaviors of customer such as number of products browsed, number of purchases made online and offline.

Gaussian State Space model in linear form can be expressed by two equations, namely, state equation and observation equation.

State Equation:

$$\alpha_{t+1} = T_t\alpha_t + R_t\xi_{t,} \quad \xi_t \sim NID(0,Q_t) \tag{5}$$

Observation Equation:

$$V_t = W_t\alpha_t + \varepsilon_t \quad \varepsilon_t \sim NID(0,H_t) \tag{6}$$

The unobserved state αt can be estimated with Kalman filter.

Logistic Regression in Marketing

In logistic regression the dependent variable is categorical in nature.

$$P_i = E(Y=1/X_i) = \frac{1}{1+e^{-(\beta_0+\beta_1X_1+\beta_2X_2+\ldots+\beta_nX_n)}} \ldots\ldots \tag{7}$$

The above equation represents logistic distribution function. From the logistic distribution function

we can estimate odds ratio, $\dfrac{P_i}{1-P_i}$

For estimating logit model we consider

$$L_i = \ln(\frac{P_i}{1-P_i}) = \beta_0 + \beta_1X_1 + \beta_2X_2 + \ldots\ldots\ldots + \beta_nX_n + U_i \ldots\ldots\ldots \tag{8}$$

Using the estimated P_t we can obtain

$$\hat{L}_i = \ln(\frac{\hat{P}_i}{1-\hat{P}_i}) = \hat{\beta}_0 + \hat{\beta}_1X_1 + \hat{\beta}_2X_2 + \ldots\ldots\ldots + \hat{\beta}_nX_n \ldots\ldots\ldots \tag{9}$$

USE OF ECONOMETRIC MODEL IN FINANCE

The Capital Asset Pricing Model (CAPM) in Finance

$$ER_i = R_f + \beta_i(ER_m - R_f) \dots\dots\dots\dots \tag{10}$$

ER_i: Expected return from stock i
R_f: Risk free rate

$(ER_m - R_f)$: Market risk premium. It is the expected return which is expected from the market above R_f. In this model, βi measures the effect of market risk premium on expected return.

If a stock is riskier, then βi$_>$1, otherwise, βi$<_1$

Multifactor Model in Finance

$$R_i = a_i + \beta_m R_m + \beta_1 F_1 + \beta_2 F_2 + \beta_3 F_3 + \varepsilon_i \dots\dots\dots\dots \tag{11}$$

where R_i: Return of security i

R_m: Market return
βi It is the β with respect to each factor including the market
εi: Error term in multifactor model

Arbitrage Pricing Theory (APT) in Finance

For a well diversified portfolio,

$$E(R_p) = R_f + \beta_1 F_1 + \beta_2 F_2 + \beta_3 F_3 + \dots\dots + \beta_n F_n \dots\dots \tag{12}$$

$E(R_p)$: Expected return
R_f: risk free rate of return
βn Coeffficient of asset's return to the particular factor
F_n: nth factor

Ross & Roll specify certain factors in APT. These are change in inflation, change in level of level of industrial production, change in interest rates.

GARCH(p,q) Model for Measuring Volatility in Finance

$$\sigma_i^2 = \alpha_0 + \alpha_1 U_{t-1}^2 + \dots\dots\dots + \alpha_p U_{t-p}^2 + \beta_1 \sigma_{t-1}^2 + \dots\dots\dots + \beta_p \sigma_{t-p}^2 \dots\dots\dots \tag{13}$$

$\alpha 0$ coefficient of the intercept

αi coefficient of ARCH component

βi coefficients of GARCH component

The GARCH (1,1) model can be written as

$$\sigma_i^2 = \alpha_0 + \alpha_1 U_{t-1}^2 + \beta_1 \sigma_{t-1}^2 \ldots \ldots \tag{14}$$

USE OF ECONOMETRIC MODELS IN HUMAN RESOURCE MANAGEMENT

Panel Data Regression

For measuring the impact of HRM practices on productivity, panel data regression may be applied.

$$Y_{it} = \beta_0 + \beta_1 X_{1it} + \beta_2 X_{2it} + \beta_3 X_{3it} + U_{it} \ldots \ldots \ldots \tag{15}$$

Y_{it}: productivity of ith firm for period t

X_{1it}: incentive pay applied in firm i in period t

X_{2it}: A measure of team work in ith firm at period t

X_{3it}: A measure of careful hiring strategy of ith firm at period t

Productivity Measurement & Use of Dummy Variable Regression

$$Y_{it} = \beta_0 + \beta_1 X_{it} + \varepsilon_{it} \ldots \ldots \tag{16}$$

Y_{it}: Monthly measure of average daily output for workers in a company

X_{it}: A change from hourly pay to piece rate pay from hourly pay. X_{it} is a dummy variable (0 or 1).

USE OF ECONOMETRIC MODELS IN OPERATIONS MANAGEMENT

The operational efficiency of a firm is defined by its supply chain management. Supply chain management mechanism is commonly measured by inventory turnover (IT). In order to determine supply chain management, a panel data analysis can be conducted in which IT acts as dependent variable. The determinants of IT are ratio between gross margin/mark up, capital intensity (CI) and sales surprise (SS). The regression model is represented by

$$\log IT_{it} = F_i + C_t + b_2 \log\left(\frac{GM}{MU}\right)_{it} + b_3 \log CI_{it} + b_4 \log SS_{it} + \mu_{it} \ldots \ldots \ldots \tag{17}$$

Where, F_i and C_i are firm and year specific effect

$$IT_{it} = \frac{CGS_{it}}{\frac{1}{n}\sum Inv_{it}}$$

where CGS_{it} represents costs of goods sold by firm i in period t and Inv_{it} represents the inventory valued at cost of the frim

$$GM_{it} = \frac{S_{it} - CGS_{it}}{S_{it}}$$

where S_{it} measures the sales

$$CI_{it} = \frac{\sum GFA_{it}}{\frac{1}{4}\sum Inv_{it}}$$

where GFA_{it} represents gross fixed assets (land, property, equipment)

SS_{it} represents sales surprise by firm i in period t measured by Holt's Linear smoothing method

The above panel data regression model can be run by fixed effect method.

APPLICATION OF ECONOMETRICS IN BUSINESS RESEARCH

Macro Economics

Econometrics is widely used in the study of business cycle. Using time series data, Clement Juglar (1819-1905) made a study on business cycle. He discovered an investment cycle of about 7-11 years duration. The investment cycle is called the Juglar cycle. Kitchin, Kuznets and Kondratieff invented the inventory cycle of 3-5 years duration, the building cycle of 15-25 years duration and the long wave of 45-60 years duration, respectively. Long and Plosser (1983), Kydland and Prescott (1982), and Hansen (1985) investigated business cycle using general equilibrium models. In recent years, Dynamic Stochastic General Equilibrium (DSGE)[1] models are widely used in the recent Real Business Cycle (RBC) analysis. Applications of econometrics using time series analysis and forecasting technique are found in the study done by Faust and Wright (2013).

Marketing

Time series models are widely used in market research.

Forecasting in Marketing Using Time Series Models

Forecasting is an important technique in market research. In order to measure the dynamic effects of advertising, the *p*-percent duration interval model is used. Tellis *et al.* (2000) and Chandy *et al.* (2001) use the *p*-percent duration interval model in finding the impact of advertisement on sales.

In market research, Bass model (1969) is used for studying adoption. Boswijk and Franses (2005) modified the Bass regression model by incorporating heteroskedastic errors and by considering short-run deviations from the S-shaped path of the diffusion pattern of adoption. Xie et al. (1997) and Naik et al. (1998) made the Kalman filter estimation of dynamic models.

Multivariate Time Series in Market Research

Multivariate time series models are considered in market research in which one variable is explained by more than one variable. Models which involve endogenous variables are also considered in multivariate analysis. Vector Auto Regressive Models with exogenous variable (VARX), Structural VAR models (SVAR) are used in market research.

Univariate Time Series Analysis in Market Research

In Univariate time series process Auto Regressive process (AR) is used. [for example, sales are affected by the sales in the previous period]. Univariate analysis also considers Moving Average process (MA) which assumes that a random shock at (t-1) affects sales levels at time t. Auto Regressive Moving Average (ARMA) combines AR and MA in which past sales and past random shocks affect sales in the present period.

Using time series data, Lal and Padmanbhan (1995) examine the relationship between market share and promotional expenditure. As per their findings market shares for most of the products are stationary, that is, mean, variance, covariance of market share series is independent of time. In market research, persistence modeling and state space models are the two widely used time series techniques.

Persistent Modeling

persistent modeling is used for measuring long term response of a marketing strategy like an unexpected increase in advertising support or a price promotion. Persistence modeling involves a multi step process. In the first step, unit root test is conducted for checking stationarity. In this type of modeling impulse response functions (IRFs) are used for measuring the incremental effect of a one unit shock in one variable on the future values of the endogenous variables.

Using persistence modeling technique, Chowdhury (1994) finds no long run relationship between UK aggregate advertising spending and a series of macro-economic variables. Dekimpe and Hanssens (1995) show that market-share series is mostly stationary. Dekimpe et. al. (1999) prove that introduction of new product causes change in loyalty patterns of customers.

State Space Models for Estimation of Dynamic Models

Linear state space models are expressed by two sets of equations. State-space models assumes two equations-state equation and observation equation. State equation considers a vector which is unobserved. Models of purchase timing and quantity that are affected by unobserved household inventories are examples of state space models. Xie et al. (1997) and Putsis (1998) use state-space models which used Kalman filter[2] (Hamilton 1994, Harvey 1990) to estimate time-varying parameters in the context of new product sales.

logistic Regression

Application of logistic regression in market research is divided into two categories- customer based studies and firm based studies.

Customer Based Studies

Berkowitz et al. (1997) describe the five stages through which consumers pass through in making choices. The stages as mentioned in their papers are- problem recognition, information search, evaluation of alternatives, purchase decision and post-purchase behavior. Using logistic regression, Hoque and Lohse (1999) analyze the information search cost for designing interfaces for electronic commerce. Using logistic regression, Lee (2002) examines the effect of advertisement on brand choice.

Firm Based Studies

Firm based studies take into consideration environmental, organizational, interpersonal and individual factors that firms consider in making business decisions. Ekeledo and Sivakumar (2004) study the impact of knowledge, business experience, specialized asset and firm size on business decision. In their study they use logistic regression. Farley et. al. (2004) considers organizational influences and examines the impact of marketing mix variables on choosing business to business financial services. Using logistic regression. Heide (2003) tries to find out whether a firm relied on a single supplier or multiple suppliers.

Pauwels et al. (2004) identified a number of challenges that needs to be addressed through econometric modelling. The areas in market research which are still under researched are- asymmetries in market response, temporal aggregation between the different variables and incorporation of Bayesian inference procedures in time series.

Finance

With the rise in uncertainty in global market, financial econometrics has gained importance for better risk management and for understanding financial volatilities in a better manner. Multivariate modeling is used in financial econometrics for asset pricing, portfolio selection, option pricing, hedging, and risk management. A large strand of the literature deals with asset pricing and optimal trading of large portfolios.

Capital Asset Pricing Model

The capital asset pricing model (CAPM) predicts the relationship between risk and expected return on an asset. CAPM states that expected return of an asset over a risk free bond is a multiple of the excessive return of the market portfolio.

Markowitz shows that investor's portfolio selection depends on expected return and variance of return. Sharpe and Linter show that the expected return on an asset is the sum of return on risk free asset and *beta* times expected return on market portfolio over risk free asset. CAPM is used for measuring cost of capital and event study.

According to Fama and French (2004), CAPM is used for assessing the performance of managed portfolios like mutual funds. CAPM was tested empirically by Black, Jensen, Scholes (1972) and Fama, Macbeth (1973) for the 1926-1968 period. More recent studies by Reinganum (1981) and Lakonishok and Shapiro (1986) for the period 1960 and 2000 do not find relation between asset's risk and the average return.

Multifactor Model

Fama and French (1993) formulate this model. The model considers additional factors like firm's size and firm's book value. The additional factors in multifactor model improve the explanatory power of CAPM. In this model, the stocks are grouped into portfolios on the basis of the firm size and firm's book-to-market value. Some macroeconomic variables are also used to explain variation in stock returns. Chen, Roll and Ross (1986) examine multifactor model.

Arbitrage Pricing Theory

Arbitrage Pricing Theory (APT) was formulated by Ross (1976). It explains the relationship between return and risk. The arbitrage pricing theory assumes that a security return is a linear function of a set of factors.

According to APT, the risk premium for an asset is related to the risk premium for each factor. Using daily data for the period 1962 -72, Roll and Ross (1980) test APT for equities listed on the New York Stock Exchange. Chen (1983) also tests APT on stocks listed on New York Stock Exchange. He uses daily return on stocks for the period 1963 to 1978. By making a comparison between CAPM and APT, he concludes that APT outperformed CAPM. Ostermark (1989) finds that APT is better than CAPM in explaining stock returns. He uses Finnish and Swedish data for making comparison. Yli-Olli *et al.* (1990) identify three stable factors common for Finland and Sweden. They use monthly data for the period 1977 to 1986. Martikainen *et al.* (1991) find out the factors that affect Finish Stock returns in two time periods 1977-81 and 1982-86. They first use principal components analysis and varimax rotation to get the factor loadings. Then they apply OLS regressions considering factor loadings as independent variables and the average stock as dependent variable.

Pricing of Financial Derivatives

Financial derivatives are of different types- options on stocks, stock indices, bonds, bonds indices, futures on commodities and currencies. In doing option pricing, the well known Black Scholes formula is used.

According to Black Scholes formula, the price of option depends on stock price, risk free rate of interest, the time to maturity, volatility. In this model, volatility and risk-free interest rate are considered as constant. Literature on determination of option pricing empirically is found in papers by Engle (1982), Bakshi et al. (1997), Bates (2000), Chernov and Ghysels (2000), Chernov et al. (2003) and Eraker et al. (2003) which contribute to the estimation of option pricing.

Volatility Forecasting

Volatility is one of the most important variables in the pricing of financial derivatives. Using data on daily returns for 2004 to 2009 and applying the method EGARCH, Olowe (2009) find persistent volatility in Nigerian stock market return. Peng et. al (2017) find that past returns of NEKKEI influences current period returns. They analyze data for the period January 2000 to March 2016 using EGARCH model.

Taylor (1987) analyzes high, low, and closing prices to forecast the volatility of one to twenty days DM/$ futures and it is found that a weighted average which is a composite forecast is the best outcome. Alford and Boatman (1995) find that use of historical volatility as volatility estimates of firms of same size in the same industry gives a good volatility forecast. According to Alford and Boatman (1995), Figlewski (1997), and Figlewski and Green (1999), a long enough estimation period is required for making a good volatility forecast. Akigray (1989) uses GARCH model for volatility forecasting. Bali (2000) shows that non linear GARCH model is good enough for forecasting one-week ahead volatility of U.S. T-Bill yields. Using EGARCH model, Charles Cao and Ruey Tsay (1992), Ronald Heynen and Harry Kat (1994), Lee (1991), and Adrian Pagan and G. William Schwert (1990) measure the volatility of stock indices and exchange rates.

Non Parametric Techniques

Non parametric technique is used to estimate stock return, volatility and state price densities of stock prices and bond yields. It is used for valuation of bond price and stock options.

Arrow and Debreu used time state preference model which is a non parametric technique to study investment under uncertainty. Ait-Sahalia and Lo (1998) apply multivariate Kernel regression technique to develop state price density (SPD). SDP provides information on preferences and asset price dynamics.

Econometrics in Human Resource Management

Jac Fitz-enz (1984) makes the first national study on HR matrices. Fitz-enz measures the efficiency and effectiveness of HR functions. The study identifies the basic formulas for identifying costs and benefits from employee turnover, methods of recruitment and training learning curves.

Ichniowski and Shaw (2003) use insider econometrics which requires field study and application of econometrics to measure the effect of HR practices on firm performance. Insider econometrics is to understand differences in firms' decisions and to examine the impact of different decisions of firms on economic performance. Insider Econometrics research is undertaken either as single firm studies or as multi-establishment studies.

HR Practices and Single Firm Performance

Recent applications of econometrics in business research includes the work done by Frank and Obloj (2014) which examines the impact of human capital on retail banking performance. Cabral and Lazzarini (2015) study the efficiency of mechanisms undertaken by the department of police. A number of recent studies deals with the effect of HR practices on a single firm's productivity. Roberts (2013) examines the impact of new HR practices on productivity. Hoffman and Burks (2017) examine the effect of employees training on their productivities.

Wright et. al. (2005) examine the effect of HR practices on organizational performance. The study finds that the impact of HR practices on organizational performance disappears if the past performance is considered.

Huselid et. al. (1996) undertake a field study on senior HR executives and measure the capabilities of HR staffs. They find that the correlation between HR capabilities and future performance is significantly high.

David Guest et. al. (2003) find a strong positive relation between HR management index and firm performance but this relationship disappears when past performance of the firm is taken into consideration. Benjamin Schneider et. al. (2003) study the impact of employee attitude on firm performance. They find that the impact is positive but it becomes opposite when they consider past firm performance as additional explanatory variable.

Ichniowski Shaw and Prennushi (1997) collect US data on 36 manufacturing units and examine the effect of HR management on productivity. They find that sophisticated HR system has a favorable effect on productivity. They find that more sophisticated HR practices lead to higher prime yield rate.

Based on National Employer Survey data and the Census Bureau's Research data Cappelli and Neumark (2001) show that high performance work practices increase sales per worker and labor costs.

Study on the Effect of Incentive Pay on Productivity

Lazear (2000) examines the effect of monetary incentives on employee performance. The study finds that worker productivity is 44% higher when the firm implements piece rate pay. Bandiera, Barankay, and Rasul (2005) examines the impact of change in piece rate pay on firm performance. Using panel data on 142 workers for 108 days, the paper finds that the average productivity of workers rises by 58% when firm switches to a new piece rate pay.

Hamilton, Nickerson and Owan (2003) study the impact of team work on productivity in apparel industry. The result of the study shows that productivity increases when workers shift to team work.

Within Industry Studies

A study by Ichniowski, Shaw, and Prennushi (1997) and another study by Gant, Ichniowski, and Shaw (2002) examine productivity of finishing lines within integrated steel mills. They identify that innovation policy is the most effective in recruitment and selection policies, compensation, teamwork, communication and employee training policies. With panel data of 36 steel mills over years for each finishing line, they find that highly innovative HR practices achieve the highest productivity levels.

Henderson and Cockburn (1996) study productivity of research activities undertaken by pharmaceutical industry using 5,000 annual observations on research projects. Productivity of research activity is measured by patents and the management treatments (which have impact on productivity) are measured by firm's expenditures per project and scope of research. The authors find a positive effect of research expenditures on the given project on research productivity. The scope of the firm measured by the number of large research projects also improves the productivity.

Effects of Treatments in Different Organizations

Hamilton et al. (2003) study the effect of team management on productivity as a whole. Using panel data on 34 steel mills for 5 years, Boning, Ichniowski, Shaw (2007) study productivity in mini mill sector. The study shows that by adopting problem solving skills, the quality of bars produced improved.

Inventory Modeling

Inventory modeling is used for empirical study in operations management. Gaur et al. (2005) find that inventory turnover for retailing firms is positively related to capital intensity and sales surprise and inversely related to gross margins.

Another study by Gaur et al. (1999) explain that improvement in financial performance of retailing companies comes from operational strategies that may involve low or high product margins and low or high inventory returns in different segments. Gaur and Kesavan (2006) examine the effects of firm size and sales growth on inventories.

Rajagopalan and Malhotra (2001) examine the impact of introduction of just-in-time (JIT) practices and information technology (IT) system implementations on inventory management. They find that material and work in process inventories decreased in most of the two-digit Standard Industrial Classification (SIC) industries between 1961 and 1994.

Chen et al. (2005, 2007) find out decline in trends for relative inventories in manufacturing and wholesale sectors between the period 1981 and 2003. They find a mixed evidence in the retailing sector. Lai (2005) find that inventory levels do not have any impact on firm value.

Roumiantsev and Netessine (2005) examine the impact of mean sales, sales uncertainty and product margins on inventories of firms. Singhal (2005) finds that the negative effect of excess inventory on stock market is significant. Roumiantsev and Netessine (2005) do not find any effect of return on assets on inventory levels but find that the speed of change in inventory management has impact on earnings of firms.

Using survey and secondary plant-level data, Lieberman et al. (1999) find that both technological and managerial factors have favorable effects on inventory levels.

By using a combination of three databases – Edgar, COMPUSTAT and Bureau van Dijk Lai(2006) finds that public infrastructure has positive effect on inventory management.

Inventory is also studied in the field of macroeconomics. Ramey and West (1999) suggest that models of stock-adjustment and production-smoothing relate inventory with production, sales and GDP.

A research paper by Thomas and Zhang (2002) analyzes the impact of changes in balance sheet items on stock returns. They find a negative relationship between accruals and future abnormal return due to inventory changes.

The main limitation of inventory management study is that most of the empirical studies on inventories have been largely limited to the US economy and these studies do not analyze the different types of inventories.

ILLUSTRATION OF APPLICATION OF ECONOMETRICS USING BUSINESS DATA

In order to analyze data using different econometric techniques, software packages like STATA, R, SPSS, Eviews are used by business data analysts. In this chapter, I have shown econometric outcomes in different fields of management using STATA.

Application in Marketing - Vector Auto Regression Model on Time Series data on Sales and Advertisement Expenditure

The above result shows the effect on past sales and advertisement expenditure on current period sales. The analysis is based on annual data from 1980 to 2017. Here past sales data for a period of 5 years and current year's advertisement expenditure data have been considered as explanatory variables. The result shows that the sales data with a lag of one year and two years have positive and significant impact on sales of current period. But sales data with a lag of 3, 4 and 5 are insignificant on current year's sales. The impact of current year's advertisement expenditure on current year's sales is positive but it is not statistically significant.

Table 1. Effect of Advertisement on Sales[3]

```
Sample: 1980 - 2017
      sales I coefficient. S.E z P>Izl [95% Confidence Interval]
      --------------+----------------------------------------------------------------
      Sales(t-1) I 1.282929 .1568499 8.18 0.000 .9755089 1.590349
      Sales(t-2) I -.4933554 .2473497 -1.99 0.046 -.9781519 -.0085589
      Sales(t-3) I .099828 .2532752 0.39 0.693 -.3965823 .5962383
      Sales(t-4) I .3912463 .2420792 1.62 0.106 -.0832202 .8657127
      Sales(t-5) -.283835 .1627752 -1.74 0.081 -.6028685 .0351984
      advt I .0006622 .0352316 0.02 0.985 .0683905 .0697149
      _cons I 146.1706 512.8316 0.29 0.776 -858.9609 1151.302
```

Application in Human Resource Management - Dummy Variable Regression on Panel Data on Average Daily Output by per Worker

In the above results, the impact of a switch of pay structure to piece rate pay from hourly pay on average daily output per worker have been reported. It is evident from the above results that a change to piece rate pay from hourly pay has favorable impact and it is significant in fixed effect as well as in random effect model. Panel data on 55 firms in handicrafts industry for a period of 5 years (2005-2010) have been considered for the analysis.

Application in Finance – CAPM

It is observed from the above result that coefficient of market risk premium is positive and it is less than 1 (0.031454). Therefore, it can be inferred that SBI stock is less risky than the market.

Table 2. Effect on Daily Output Per Worker(Fixed Effect Result)[4]

```
Number of firms = 55
Number of years = 5
---------------------------------------------------------------------
dailyoutputperworker Coefficient. S.E t P>ltl [95% Confidence Interval]
-------------+-------------------------------------------------------
switchfrompay | .0166562 .0068923 2.42 0.019 .0028057 .0305068
_cons | 9.625818 .0055479 1735.04 0.000 9.614669 9.636967
------------ --+-------------------------------------------------------
Random Effect Result
Number of firms = 55
Number of years = 5
---------------------------------------------------------------------
dailyoutputperworker | Coefficient. Std. Err. z P>lzl [95% Confidence Interval]
-------------+-------------------------------------------------------
switchfrompay | .0205659 .0069543 2.96 0.003 .0069358 .034196
_cons | 9.622975 .0094764 1015.47 0.000 9.604401 9.641548
```

Table 3. Calculation of Coefficient of risk premium for State Bank of India

```
R² = 0.0004
Adj R² = -0.0602
---------------------------------------------------------------------
ri | Coefficient. S.E t P>ltl [95% Confidence Interval]
-------------+-------------------------------------------------------
rf | .2979653 4.744059 0.06 0.950 -9.353895 9.949825
riskprem | .031454 .299989 0.10 0.917 -.5788782 .6417861
_cons | -1.268879 23.5676 -0.05 0.957 -49.21751 46.67976
```

Application in Economics- Data on Income and Education (Measured by Years of Education) of Households

The above result shows the impact of education on income which is measured by the years of education on income per capita of households. It is observed from the result that the impact of education on income is 1.40 at 1% level of significance. The model explains 63% of variation.

Table 4. Effect of Education on Income

```
Number of Households = 30
R² = 0.6300
Adj R² = 0.6168
---------------------------------------------------------------------
inc | Coefficient S.E t P>ltl [95% Confidence Interval]
-------------+-------------------------------------------------------
edu | 1.396394 .2022426 6.90 0.000 .9821189 1.810669
_cons | 6.123529 .4784823 12.80 0.000 5.143402 7.103655
---------------------------------------------------------------------
```

CONCLUSION

The fast-changing global economic environment makes it difficult for out-of-sample forecasts and for other econometric analysis. An econometric model which performed well in the past does not necessarily forecast well in the future if there is a structural break. The volatility model proposed by Engle (1982) is generally used to forecast volatility over time using historical asset returns. But dynamic economic system imposes a challenge for forecasts.

Second limitation in econometric analysis is the availability of reliable data. The success of empirical study depends on the quality of data. The data may be wrongly measured or may correspond to variables improperly. Further, selection of sample may be biased.

Thirdly, econometric model can only capture the most important factors in a business, but the observed data is the outcome of many unaccountable factors.

Fourthly, application of time series analysis in various fields is not free from Lucas Critique. Lucas critique states that policy changes from time to time alter the parameters. It makes the parameter estimates less reliable.

Another limitation is that econometric analysis is based on prior assumptions and hypotheses. The assumptions help to reduce complex social phenomena and it makes data analysis easier. But this simplification involves abstraction which may be far from reality. By taking these limitations into consideration, econometrics is used as a tool for doing business research.

REFERENCES

Akigray, V. (1989). Conditional Heteroscedasity in Time tock of Stock Returns: Evidence and Forecasting. *The Journal of Business*, *62*(1), 55–80. doi:10.1086/296451

Alford, A. W., & Boatsman, J. R. (1995). Predicting Long-Term Stock Return Volatility: Implications for Accounting and Valuation of Equity Derivatives. *Acc. Rev.*, *70*(4), 599–618.

Bakshi, G., Cao, C., & Chen, Z. (1997). Empirical performance of alternative option pricing models. *The Journal of Finance*, *52*(5), 2003–2204. doi:10.1111/j.1540-6261.1997.tb02749.x

Banker, R. D., & Khosla, I. S. (1995). Economics of operations management: A research perspective. *Journal of Operations Management*, *12*(3-4), 423–435. doi:10.1016/0272-6963(95)00022-K

Bartel, A. P. (2004). Human Resource Management and Organizational Performance: Evidence from Retail Banking. *Industrial & Labor Relations Review*, *57*(2), 181–203. doi:10.1177/001979390405700202

Bass, F. M. (1969). A new product growth model for consumer durables. *Management Science*, *15*(5), 215–227. doi:10.1287/mnsc.15.5.215

Bass, F. M. (1969). A New Product Growth for Model Consumer Durables. *Management Science*, *15*(5), 215–227. doi:10.1287/mnsc.15.5.215

Bates, D. (2000). Post-87 crash fears in S&P 500 futures options. *Journal of Econometrics*, *94*(1-2), 181–238. doi:10.1016/S0304-4076(99)00021-4

Berkowitz, E. N., Kerin, R. A., Hartley, S. W., & Rudelius, W. (1997). *Marketing* (5th ed.). McGraw-Hill/Irwin.

Black, F., Jensen, M., & Scholes, M. (1972). The Capital-Asset Pricing Model: Some empirical tests. In Studies in the Theory of Capital Markets. Praeger Publishers Inc.

Black, F., Jensen, M., & Scholes, M. S. (1972). The Capital Asset Pricing Model: Some Empirical Findings. In M. Jensen (Ed.), *Studies in the Theory of Capital Markets* (pp. 79–124). Praeger Publishers.

Bloom, N., Eifert, B., Mahajan, A., McKenzie, D., & Roberts, J. (2013). Does management matter? Evidence from India. *The Quarterly Journal of Economics, 128*(1), 1–51. doi:10.1093/qje/qjs044

Boswijk, H., & Franses, P. (2005). On the econometrics of the bass diffusion model. *Journal of Business & Economic Statistics, 23*(3), 255–268. doi:10.1198/073500104000000604

Cabral, S., & Lazzarini, S. G. (2015). The "guarding the guardians" problem: An analysis of the organizational performance of an internal affairs division. *Journal of Public Administration: Research and Theory, 25*(3), 797–829. doi:10.1093/jopart/muu001

Cao, C. Q., & Tsay, R. S. (1992). Nonlinear time-series analysis of stock volatilities. *Journal of Applied Econometrics, 7*(S1), S165–S185. doi:10.1002/jae.3950070512

Cappelli, P., & Neumark, D. (2001). Do "High-Performance" Work Practices Improve Establishment-Level Outcomes? *Industrial & Labor Relations Review, 54*(4), 737–775.

Chandy, R. K., Tellis, G. J., MacInnis, D. J., & Thaivanich, P. (2001). What to say when: Advertising appeals in evolving markets. *JMR, Journal of Marketing Research, 38*(4), 399–414. doi:10.1509/jmkr.38.4.399.18908

Chandy, R. K., Tellis, G. J., MacInnis, D. J., & Thaivanich, P. (2001). What to say when: Advertising appeals in evolving markets. *JMR, Journal of Marketing Research, 38*(4), 399–414. doi:10.1509/jmkr.38.4.399.18908

Chen, H., Frank, M., & Wu, O. (2005). What Actually Happened to the Inventories of American Companies between 1981 and 2000? *Management Science, 51*(7), 1015–1031. doi:10.1287/mnsc.1050.0368

Chen, H., Frank, M., & Wu, O. (2007). US Retail and Wholesale Inventory Performance from 1981 to 2004. *Manufacturing & Service Operations Management, 9*(4), 430–456. doi:10.1287/msom.1060.0129

Chen, N., Roll, R., & Ross, S. A. (1986). Economic Forces and the Stock Market. *The Journal of Business, 59*(3), 383–403. doi:10.1086/296344

Chen, N.-F. (1983). Some Empirical Tests of the Theory of Arbitrage Pricing. *The Journal of Finance, 38*(5), 1393–1414. doi:10.1111/j.1540-6261.1983.tb03831.x

Chernov, M., Gallant, A. R., Ghysels, E., & Tauchen, G. (2003). Alternative models for stock price dynamics. *Journal of Econometrics, 116*(1-2), 225–257. doi:10.1016/S0304-4076(03)00108-8

Chernov, M., & Ghysels, E. (2000). A study towards a unified approach to the joint estimation of objective and risk neutral measures for the purpose of option valuation. *Journal of Financial Economics, 56*(3), 407–458. doi:10.1016/S0304-405X(00)00046-5

Chow, G. C. (1960). Tests of Equality between Sets of Coe¢ cients in Two Linear Regressions. *Econometrica, 28*(3), 591–605. doi:10.2307/1910133

Chowdhury, A. R. (1994). Advertising Expenditures and the Macro-Economy: Some New Evidence. *International Journal of Advertising, 13*(1), 1–14. doi:10.1080/02650487.1994.11104557

Dekimpe & Hanssens. (1995b). Empirical Generalizations about Market Evolution and Stationarity. *Marketing Science, 14*(3,2), G109-G121.

Dekimpe, M. G., & Hanssens, D. M. (1995a). The Persistence of Marketing Effects on Sales. *Marketing Science, 14*(1), 1–21. doi:10.1287/mksc.14.1.1

Dekimpe, M. G., & Hanssens, D. M. (1999). Sustained Spending and Persistent Response: A New Look at Long-Term Marketing Profitability. *JMR, Journal of Marketing Research, 36*(4), 397–412. doi:10.1177/002224379903600401

Dekimpe, M. G., & Hanssens, D. M. (2000). Time-series Models in Marketing: Past, Present and Future. *International Journal of Research in Marketing, 17*(2-3), 183–193. doi:10.1016/S0167-8116(00)00014-8

Ekeledo, I., & Sivakumar, K. (2004). International market entry mode strategies of manufacturing firms and service firms: A resource-based perspective. *International Marketing Review, 21*(1), 68–101. doi:10.1108/02651330410522943

Engle, R. (1982). Autoregressive Conditional Hetersokedasticity with Estimates of the Vari-ance of United Kingdom In.ation. *Econometrica, 50*(4), 987–2008. doi:10.2307/1912773

Eraker, B., Johannes, M. S., & Polson, N. G. (2003). The impact of jumps in returns and volatility. *The Journal of Finance, 53*(3), 1269–1300. doi:10.1111/1540-6261.00566

Fama, E. F., & French, K. R. (1993). Common Risk Factors in the Returns on Stocks and Bonds. *Journal of Financial Economics, 33*(1), 3–56. doi:10.1016/0304-405X(93)90023-5

Fama, E. F., & French, K. R. (2004). The CAPM: Theory and Evidence. *The Journal of Economic Perspectives, 18*, 25–46. doi:10.1257/0895330042162430

Fama, E. F., & MacBeth, J. D. (1973). Risk, Return, and Equilibrium: Empirical Tests. *Journal of Political Economy, 81*(3), 607–636. doi:10.1086/260061

Farley, J. U., Hayes, A. F., & Kopalle, P. (2004). Choosing and upgrading financial services dealers in the US and UK. *International Journal of Research in Marketing, 21*(4), 359–375. doi:10.1016/j.ijresmar.2004.08.001

Faust & Jonathan. (2013), Forecasting Inflation. In *Handbook of Economic Forecasting*. New York: Elsevier.

Fisher, I. (1933). Report of the Meeting. *Econometrica, 1*, 92–93.

Gaur, V., Fisher, M., & Raman, A. (1999). *What Explains Superior Retail Performance?* NYU Working Paper No. OM-2005-03.

Gaur, V., Fisher, M., & Raman, A. (2005). An Econometric Analysis of Inventory Turnover Performance in Retail Services. *Management Science*, *51*(2), 181–194. doi:10.1287/mnsc.1040.0298

Gaur, V., & Kesavan, S. (2006). The Effects of Firm Size and Sales Growth Rate on Inventory Turnover Performance in the U.S. Retail Sector. In N. Agrawal & S. Smith (Eds.), *Retail Supply Chain Management*. Kluwer Publishers.

Green, T. C., & Figlewski, S. (1999). Market risk and model risk for a financial institution writing options. *The Journal of Finance*, *54*(4), 1465–1499. doi:10.1111/0022-1082.00152

Guest, D., Michie, J., Conway, N., & Sheehan, M. (2003). Human Resource Management and Corporate Performance in UK. *British Journal of Industrial Relations*, *41*(2), 291–314. doi:10.1111/1467-8543.00273

Hamilton, B., Nickerson, J., & Owan, H. (2003). Team Incentives and Worker Heterogeneity: An Empirical Analysis of the Impact of Teams on Productivity and Participation. *Journal of Political Economy*, *111*(3), 465–497. doi:10.1086/374182

Hamilton, J. D. (1994). *Time Series Analysis*. Princeton University Press. doi:10.1515/9780691218632

Hansen, B. E. (2001). The New Econometrics of Structural Change: Dating Breaks in U.S. Labor Productivity. *The Journal of Economic Perspectives*, *15*(4), 117–128. doi:10.1257/jep.15.4.117

Hansen, G. D. (1985). Indivisible Labor and The Business Cycle. *Journal of Monetary Economics*, *16*(3), 309–327. doi:10.1016/0304-3932(85)90039-X

Heide, J. B. (2003). Plural governance in industrial purchasing. *Journal of Marketing*, *67*(4), 18–29. doi:10.1509/jmkg.67.4.18.18689

Hendricks, K., & Singhal, V. (2005). Association Between Supply Chain Glitches and Operating Performance. *Management Science*, *51*(5), 695–711. doi:10.1287/mnsc.1040.0353

Hoffman, M., & Burks, S. V. (2017). *Training contracts, employee turnover, and the returns from firm-sponsored general training* (NBER Working Paper series No. 23247).

Hoque, A., & Lohse, G. L. (1999). An information search cost perspective for designing interfaces for electronic commerce. *JMR, Journal of Marketing Research*, *36*(3), 387–395. doi:10.1177/002224379903600307

Huselid, M., & Becker, B. (1996). High Performance Work Systems and Firm Performance: Cross-Sectional Versus Panel Estimates. *Industrial Relations*, 635–672.

Huselid, M. A., & Becker, B. E. (1997). *The impact of high performance work systems, implementation effectiveness, and alignment with strategy on shareholder wealth. Academy of Management Best Papers Proceedings*. doi:10.5465/ambpp.1997.4981101

Ichniowski, C., Levine, D. I., Olson, C., & Strauss, G. (1996). What Works at Work: Overview and Assessment. *Industrial & Labor Relations Review*, *35*, 299–334.

Ichniowski, C., & Shaw, K. (forthcoming). Insider Econometrics: A Roadmap to Estimating Empirical Models of Organizational Performance. In R. Gibbons & J. Roberts (Eds.), *The Handbook of Organizational Economics*. Princeton University Press.

Ichniowski, C., Shaw, K., & Prennushi, G. (1997). The Effects of Human Resource Management Practices on Productivity: A Study of Steel Finishing Lines. *The American Economic Review, 87*, 291–313.

John, B. (1990). Benefit segmentation for fund raisers. *Journal of the Academy of Marketing Science, 18*(1), 77–86. doi:10.1007/BF02729764

Kothari, S. P. (2001). Capital Markets Research in Accounting. *Journal of Accounting and Economics, 31*(1-3), 105–231. doi:10.1016/S0165-4101(01)00030-1

Kotler, P. (2000). *Marketing Management*. Prentice-Hall.

Kydland, F., & Prescott, E. (1982). Time to build and aggregate Fluctuations. *Econometrica, 50*(6), 173–208. doi:10.2307/1913386

Lai, R. (2005). *Inventory and the Stock Market*. Working paper, Harvard University.

Lai, R. (2006a). *The Geography of Retail Inventory*. Working paper, Harvard University.

Lai, R. (2006b). *Does public infrastructure reduce private inventory?* Working paper, Harvard University.

Lakonishok, J., & Shapiro, A. C. (1986). Systematic risk, total risk and size as determinants of stock market returns. *Journal of Banking & Finance, 10*(1), 115–132. doi:10.1016/0378-4266(86)90023-3

Lal, R., & Padmanabhan, V. (1995). Competitive Response and Equilibria. *Marketing Science, 14*(3), G101–G108. doi:10.1287/mksc.14.3.G101

Lazear, E. P. (2000). Performance Pay and Productivity. *The American Economic Review, 5*(5), 1346–1361. doi:10.1257/aer.90.5.1346

Lee, A. Y. (2002). Effects of implicit memory on memory-based versus stimulus-based brand choice. *JMR, Journal of Marketing Research, 39*(4), 440–455. doi:10.1509/jmkr.39.4.440.19119

Lieberman, M. B., & Demeester, L. (1999). Inventory Reduction and Productivity Growth: Linkages in the Japanese Automotive Industry. *Management Science, 45*(4), 466–476. doi:10.1287/mnsc.45.4.466

Lieberman, M. B., Helper, S., & Demeester, L. (1999). The Empirical Determinants of Inventory Levels in High-Volume Manufacturing. *Production and Operations Management, 8*(1), 44–55. doi:10.1111/j.1937-5956.1999.tb00060.x

Lintner, J. (1965). The Valuation of Risky Assets and the Selection of Risky Investments in Stock Portfolios and Capital Budgets. *The Review of Economics and Statistics, 47*(1), 13–37. doi:10.2307/1924119

Louis, E. (1995). *Contemporary Marketing*. Dryden Press.

Martikainen, T., & Ankelo, T. (1991). On the instability of financial patterns of failed firms and the predictability of corporate failure. *Economics Letters, 35*(2), 209–214. doi:10.1016/0165-1765(91)90171-G

Naik, P. A., Mantrala, M. K., & Sawyer, A. (1998). Planning Pulsing Media Schedules in the Presence of Dynamic Advertising Quality. *Marketing Science, 17*(3), 214–235. doi:10.1287/mksc.17.3.214

Obloj, T., & Frank, D. H. (2014). Firm-specific human capital, organizational incentives, and agency costs: Evidence from retail banking. *Strategic Management Journal, 35*(9), 1279–1301. doi:10.1002mj.2148

Östermark, R. (1989). Predictability of Finnish and Swedish stock returns. *Omega, 17*(3), 223–236. doi:10.1016/0305-0483(89)90028-5

Pauwels, K. (2004). How Dynamic Consumer Response, Dynamic Competitor Response and Expanded Company Action Shape Long-Term Marketing Effectiveness. *Marketing Science, 23*(4), 596–610. doi:10.1287/mksc.1040.0075

Pechmann, C. (1996). Do consumers overgeneralize one-sided comparative price claims, and are more stringent regulations needed? *JMR, Journal of Marketing Research, 33*(2), 150–163. doi:10.1177/002224379603300203

Punj, G., & Brookes, R. (2002). The influence of pre-decisional constraints on information search and consideration set formation in new automotive purchases. *International Journal of Research in Marketing, 19*(4), 383–400. doi:10.1016/S0167-8116(02)00100-3

Putsis, W. P. Jr. (1998). Parameter variation and new product diffusion. *Journal of Forecasting, 17*(3-4), 231–257. doi:10.1002/(SICI)1099-131X(199806/07)17:3/4<231::AID-FOR695>3.0.CO;2-L

Rajagopalan, S., & Malhotra, A. (2001). Have US Manufacturing Inventories Really Decreased? An Empirical Study. *Manufacturing & Service Operations Management, 3*(1), 14–24. doi:10.1287/msom.3.1.14.9995

Ramey, V., & West, K. (1999). Inventories. In Handbook of Macroeconomics (Vol. 1). Elsevier Science.

Reinganum, M. R. (1981). Misspecification of capital asset pricing: Empirical anomalies based on earnings' yields and market values. *Journal of Financial Economics, 9*(1), 19–46. doi:10.1016/0304-405X(81)90019-2

Roll, R., & Ross, S. (1980). An Empirical Investigation of the Arbitrage Pricing Theory. *The Journal of Finance, 35*(5), 1073–1103. doi:10.1111/j.1540-6261.1980.tb02197.x

Ross, S. (1976). The Arbitrage Theory of Capital Asset Pricing. *Journal of Economic Theory, 13*(3), 341–360. doi:10.1016/0022-0531(76)90046-6

Roumiantsev, S., & Netessine, S. (2005a). *What Can Be Learned from Classical Inventory Models: a Cross-Industry Empirical Investigation.* Working paper, University of Pennsylvania.

Roumiantsev, S., & Netessine, S. (2005b). *Should Inventory Policy Be Lean or Responsive? Evidence for US Public Companies.* Working paper, University of Pennsylvania.

Sahalia, Y. A., & Lo, A. W. (1998). Non parametric estimation of state price Densities implicit in Financial asset Prices. *The Journal of Finance, 53*(2), 499–547. doi:10.1111/0022-1082.215228

Schneider, B., Hanges, P. J., Smith, D. B., & Salvaggio, A. N. (2003). Which Comes First: Employee Attitudes or Organizational Financial and Market Performance? *The Journal of Applied Psychology, 88*(5), 836–851. doi:10.1037/0021-9010.88.5.836 PMID:14516248

Sharpe, W. (1964). Capital Asset Prices: A Theory of Market Equilibrium under Conditions of Risk. *The Journal of Finance, 19*, 425–442.

Singhal, V. (2005). *Excess Inventory and Long-Term Stock Performance.* Working paper, Georgia Institute of Technology.

Taylor, S. J. (1987). Forecasting the volatility of currency exchange rates. *International Journal of Forecasting, 3*(1), 159–170. doi:10.1016/0169-2070(87)90085-9

Tellis, G. J., Chandy, R., & Thaivanich, P. (2000). Which ad works, when, where,and how often? Modeling the effects of direct television advertising. *JMR, Journal of Marketing Research, 37*(1), 32–46. doi:10.1509/jmkr.37.1.32.18716

Thomas, J., & Zhang, H. (2002). Inventory Changes and Future Returns. *Review of Accounting Studies, 7*(2/3), 162–187. doi:10.1023/A:1020221918065

Unnava, H. R., & Sirdeshmukh, D. (1994). Reducing Competitive ad interference. *JMR, Journal of Marketing Research, 31*(3), 403–411. doi:10.1177/002224379403100308

Vidale, M. L., & Wolfe, H. B. (1957). An Operation Research Study of Sales Response to Advertising. *Operations Research, 5*(3), 370–381. doi:10.1287/opre.5.3.370

Wiggins. (1992). *Information literacy at universities: Challenges and solutions.* Academic Press.

Xie, J., Song, M., Sirbu, M., & Wang, Q. (1997). Kalman Filter Estimation of New Product Diffusion Models. *JMR, Journal of Marketing Research, 34*(3), 378–393. doi:10.1177/002224379703400307

Yli-Olli, P., & Virtanen, I. (1992). Some empirical tests of the arbitrage pricing theory using transformation analysis. *Empirical Economics, 17*(4), 507–522. doi:10.1007/BF01205393

ENDNOTES

[1]   DSGE model describes the behavior of the economy by analyzing the interaction of many decisions. The decisions considered in most DSGE models correspond to some of the main quantities studied in macroeconomics, such as consumption, saving, investment, and labor supply and labor demand. DSGE models are dynamic in nature which study how the economy evolves over time. They are also stochastic, taking into account the fact that the economy is affected by random shocks such as technological change, fluctuations in the price of oil, or errors in macroeconomic policy-making.

[2]   The Kalman filter is a set of mathematical equations that provides an efficient computational (recursive) means to estimate the state of a process. It minimizes the mean of the squared error. The filter supports estimations of past, present, and even future states, and it can do so even when the precise nature of the modeled system is unknown.

[3]   Econometric package STATA has been used to run VARX on times series data on sales and advertisement expenditure.

[4]   Econometric package STATA has been used to run dummy variable regression on panel data on average daily output per worker.

Chapter 11
A Review on Critical Success Factors for Big Data Projects

Naciye Güliz Uğur
Sakarya University, Turkey

Aykut Hamit Turan
Sakarya University, Turkey

ABSTRACT

For an organization every year, a large amount of information is generated regarding its employees, customers, business partners, suppliers, etc. Volume, which is one of the attributes of big data, is aptly named because of the vast number of data sources and the size of data generated by these sources. Big data solutions should not only focus on the technological aspects, but also on the challenges that may occur during the project lifecycle. The main purpose of this research is to build on the current diverse literature around big data by contributing discussion on factors that influence successful big data projects. The systematic literature review adopted in this study includes relevant research regarding such critical success factors that are validated in previous studies. The study compiled these critical success factors as provided in the literature regarding big data projects. Notable success factors for big data projects were compiled from literature such as case studies, theoretical observations, or experiments.

INTRODUCTION

The explosion of data being captured and stored in information systems has created a new area of challenges and opportunities for information technology (IT) professionals. While substantial efforts have been made towards algorithms and technologies that are used to perform these analytics, comparatively, there has been limited empirical research on Critical Success Factors (CSFs) that relate to Big Data projects.

Critical Success Factors (CSFs) are the few key areas where "things must go right" for "the business to flourish and for the manager's goals to be attained" (Bullen and Rockart, 1981, p. 7). Also, they are common means of assessing projects (Nixon, Harrington and Parker, 2012). Various challenges of hu-

DOI: 10.4018/978-1-7998-6673-2.ch011

man and organizational components of a project can be approached and tackled by understanding the related CSFs (Fortune and White, 2006).

The study of CSF for project management began in the 1960s, several lists of factors have been published where some researches have focused on specific problem domains and types of activity, and others have suggested CSFs, which can apply to all types of projects (Fortune and White, 2006). Some of the most studied CSFs are defined and examined in the next sections.

This conceptual chapter identifies the key areas –Critical Success Factors– essential for achieving project success in Big Data projects. A review of the literature indicated a gap exists in the project management literature and the business literature about a comprehensive factor list to support predicting project performance (Cooke-Davies, 2002; Hyväri, 2006).

The lack of critical success factor sources can doom an IS project to an absolute failure. This research promises to help organizations identify factors that impact success – as perceived by practitioners and professionals – on Big Data projects."

The objectives of this chapter are as follows:

- to build on the current diverse literature around Big Data
- to provide insight into the CSFs of Big Data projects
- to present a joint agreement for CSFs
- to generate solutions and recommendations for success

The"research objectives are based on the argument establishing Big Data be used as a tool for the organization to develop and create efficiencies enterprise-wide.

A comprehensive review of the literature is conducted to depict CSFs. The literature review includes relevant research regarding such critical success factors that are validated in previous studies. Several different case studies and theoretical discussions enlist success factors regarding Big Data projects. The study compiled these critical success factors as provided in the literature regarding Big Data projects. Significant success factors for Big Data projects were compiled from literature such as case studies, theoretical observations, or experiments. The chapter identifies the current gaps, definitions, and existing variables from the literature regarding Big Data projects and CSFs.

Different challenges are encountered at an organizational level when implementing Big Data projects (Saltz, 2015). To deploy and exploit Big Data in an optimal manner, the organization must pay more efforts in managing these projects more efficiently. The literature review uncovered several research efforts on project success and performance.

Given the importance of data and information analysis for the success and survival of organizations, big data management and implementation projects present a critical issue for all companies and organizations today. The CSFs introduced and discussed in this study would provide useful guidelines for managers to carry out Big Data projects in their institutions."

BACKGROUND

A"literature review on critical success factor theories led to varying conclusions by different researchers on the importance and the inclusion of factors (Anderson et al., 2006; Baladi, 2007; Delisle, 2001; Hass, 2006; Nasr, 2004; Pinto, 1986; Shao, 2006; Westlund, 2007; Felix et al., 2018; Tokuç, Uran and

Tekin, 2019; Narayan and Tan, 2019). The theories include the dynamic importance of factors theory, critical success indicators theory, integrated project planning, control system theory, competent project manager theory, communication theory, and other theories. Professionals frequently use the principles of these theories to affect project performance.

The dynamic importance of factors theory was used as the foundation for the current study. The literature review yielded conflicting evidence on conclusion validity. The discussion included validity concerns, and concerns that led to excluding theories from the study found.

The concept of success factors was first introduced by Daniel, who discussed it concerning the information management crisis that was being brought about because of rapid organizational change (as cited in Fortune and White, 2006). In 1979, Rockart mentioned the concept of Critical Success Factors in the Harvard Business Review. They are termed as the crucial areas where relevant results are necessary to achieve project success. Since these areas are of critical importance, the project manager should have the necessary knowledge to determine if progress is steady in the respective areas (Bullen and Rockart, 1981).

The study on the CSF approach was established and popularized by several authors; the most relevant research work was done by Rockart (Bullen and Rockart, 1981). In his seminal paper on the topic, Rockart defined the term critical success"factors as "the limited number of areas in which results, if they are satisfactory, will ensure successful competitive performance for the organization" (Bullen and Rockart, 1981). He also emphasized that these are the areas of activity in a business where constant and careful attention from management is necessary to ensure organizational goals (Bullen and Rockart, 1981). Pinto and Slevin have defined CSFs as "factors which, if addressed, significantly improve project implementation chances" (Pinto and Slevin, 1987).

Pinto"(1986) began to contribute a clearer understanding of project lifecycle dynamics on critical success factors. Before Pinto's research, critical success factors were primarily concepts without empirical data to support the concept within informal implementation processes. In the 1980s, the disagreement increased among researchers about single factor importance throughout the project life cycle.

Pinto (1986) used a survey mailed to full-time project managers and then performed data analysis related to critical success factor associations with project success at four milestones in the project life cycle. Pinto sought to establish that critical success factors are not equally important throughout the project. Pinto concluded with a critical success factor list showing a significant relationship to project success. Pinto included beta weighting to evidence the change in single factor importance during the life cycle. In the current research study, Pinto's conclusions were used as foundational work to expand on the existing literature.

Delisle (2001) used exploratory mixed-method research involving three surveys to observe relationships among project success with communication. Delisle focused the sample on virtual teams and establishing critical success indicators. Delisle's research conflicted with previous established critical success factors about traditional project teams, such as project team experience, ability to troubleshoot, skills related to technology, project team culture, and tendency to take the risk. Compared to the established literature, the difference in the research results might be due to Delisle's virtual teams.

Delisle (2001) faced challenges with standard terminology, the inability to establish a foundational project management theory, and the issues resulting from a sample new to the online data collection method. The respondents in Delisle's study had more experience with traditional projects than virtual projects. Delisle observed critical differences between virtual teams and traditional teams. Delisle noted differences in the communication media type used and specific task leadership based on a member's expertise rather than leadership based on formal project roles.

Nasr (2004) sought to improve the existing project management systems by extending existing functionalities with integrated project planning and control systems to improve efficiencies and establish a consistent process for measuring project performance. Nasr noted standard scheduling practices with control techniques were beneficial management functions to project teams. Nasr observed limitations or deficiencies in standard practices that limited the benefits.

Nasr (2004) developed a test case study as a simulation environment to measure performance with the integrated project planning and control system and measure performance without the system. Nasr found the integrated project planning and control system benefits were more noteworthy for less experienced project managers. Nasr failed to prove the integrated project planning and control system provided any additional benefits over existing project management systems for more experienced professionals. Nasr did not prove that existing project management systems are deficient or lacking functionality compared to the integrated project planning and control system.

After conducting a project management literature review, Shao (2006) concluded three elements are critical factors in determining project success: (a) a project manager with competency in project management skills, (b) a project definition that represents the project objectives, and (c) a correctly organized project. Shao examined selecting an appropriate project manager with a questionnaire founded on recommendations from the Project Management Institute regarding knowledge, performance, and personal competency. Shao (2006) used findings to build a new tool to assist with selecting effective project managers. Shao examined a single critical success factor association to project success; the research was not a comprehensive evaluation of other contributing factors, which raises internal validity concerns.

Anderson et al. (2006) concluded that project communication was a success factor based on principal components analysis performed with questionnaire responses on projects. Anderson et al. focused on a single critical success factor association to project success. Anderson et al. excluded other factors, which led to internal validity concerns. The concern pertains to variables other than the predictor variable that may be responsible for the effect observed in the Anderson et al. study.

Baladi (2007) noted that contributing success factors are communication and leadership in a virtual project management study. Baladi established the conclusions with observations in the questionnaire data with a combination of t-tests, Spearman rank correlation coefficients, and chi-square statistical analysis. External validity concerns exist because Baladi (2007) limited participation in virtual project team members, so bias might exist when generalizing to other project types. Baladi did not answer the current research study questions about the effect on information technology project success.

Westlund (2007) and Wu (2006) studied the project success factors associated with skilled technology resource retention and concluded a critical technical resource loss before a project conclusion increases the probability of project failure. Westlund and Wu established an essential factor in information technology project performance. Westlund and Wu excluded other critical success factors related to information technology project performance. The factor exclusion introduced internal validity concerns about other variables that might be responsible for the effect observed in the study.

Hass (2006) indicated that information technology project success factors fail to integrate lessons learned, fail to establish a core team, fail to create a project charter, fail to engage stakeholders, and failure to schedule a kickoff meeting. Hass presented results relevant to the current research study. Hass did not discuss the research methodology used to reach conclusions, so assessment validity was not supported. Hass' conclusions were not considered as a foundation for future research.

Agirre Perez (2007) noted that a risk model is a crucial success factor for high uncertainty projects, such as those found in research, information technology, or aggressive product development. The Project

Management Institute (2015) published a best practices guide reporting project risk management is an essential factor in project success. Risk management encompasses risk identification, analysis of risk, response planning to a risk event, and monitoring and controlling risk elements (PMI, 2015). Agirre Perez's study applies to the current research study, but a single project management activity study raises internal validity concerns. The concern pertains to other factors being responsible for the effect observed by Agirre Perez.

Pinto (1986) established the dynamic importance of critical success factors during a project life cycle with empirical data. Delisle (2001) established critical success indicators by building research on Pinto's conclusions, but the results did not completely support Pinto's conclusions. The conflicting conclusions might be due to the focus on virtual teams by Delisle. If virtual teams affected Delisle's (2001) results, a future research study is needed to explore the effect of team types on relationships among critical success factors with project performance.

Nasr (2004) examined the potential gaps in existing project management standards but did not demonstrate that existing project management systems are deficient or lack functionality, leading to limited management benefits. Shao (2006) used a literature review to establish three factors to determine project success: (a) project manager, (b) project definition, and (c) project organization. Shao substantiated that project manager selection influenced project success.

Research by Müller and Jugdev (2012) highlighted the evolution of project success from the seminal literature to recent literature, increasing the knowledge base of project success concerning ideas, themes, research methodologies, and the founding theories of the concept of project success. The study concludes that the concept of project success is multi-faceted. Some researchers in project success based their studies on organizational theories, reflecting the multi-faceted and intertwined ideas surrounding this subject. Further, Müller and Jugdev (2012) concluded that project success is a product of the combination of personnel, project, team, and organizational factors. The effective combination of these factors results in the successful completion of the project. Also, project success is achieved through effective teamwork, time, cost, and scope management. Project success is also relative according to the perception measurement matrix. Different methodologies have emerged as the concept of project success evolves. These evolving methodologies involve multiple variables that work well for large, small, medium, and complex project types. Finally, measuring project success methods also evolve as new and robust tools, and validated and reliable instruments are being developed (Müller and Jugdev, 2012).

A study by Sudhakar (2012) categorized the success factors for software development projects and identified the various factors in each of these categories. This categorization is a tremendous achievement in the field of critical success factors that affect software development. Before this, researchers spent more time on other aspects of success factors that influence the success of a software development project: technical, communication, and project management factors. Through an extensive search of the literature, this study used a conceptual model to identify seven success factor themes with 80 success factors sub-divided within these themes, and the first five success factors in each of these seven success factor themes are designated as the critical success factors. The selection of these 80 success factors was based on their importance in the software development discipline and their frequent appearance in critical success factor studies. Each of these success factor themes identifies five factors, which are called critical success factors. The critical success factors include communication, top management support, clear project goal, output reliability, project planning, teamwork, project team coordination, quality control, client acceptance, the accuracy of the output, reduced ambiguity, maximized stability, and realistic expectations, and user involvement. Another major highlight of this second study is categorizing these critical success factors into seven themes: project management, technical, organizational, product, environmental, team, and communication.

In the study by Stankovic et al. (2013), technical factors were less valid than people and process factors. Their study yielded a Cronbach's Alpha value of 0,680, 0,794, and 0,778 for the people, process, and technical factors, respectively. This indicates that people and process factors are more likely to influence software development projects than technical factors. The model adopted by the study could report the success of all projects accurately, and it has a very high degree of operationalizing its variables. Further, it establishes that the people factors mainly involve the customer and the team's capabilities. In contrast, the process factors involve project management and project definition processes, and these variables were evaluated based on the four success criteria of cost, time, scope, and quality.

Ahimbisibwe, Cavana, and Daellenbach (2015) systematically reviewed 148 articles and identified 37 critical success factors, which were classified into three broad categories: (a) organizational, (b) team, and (c) customer factors. Under each category, the critical success factors are arranged according to their frequency of occurrence in the critical success factor literature, particularly within the traditional and agile software development methodologies. This study was carried out in four phases. The phases are a comprehensive review of the literature to identify the critical success factors for software development projects and analyzing the identified critical success factors. The other phases differentiate the critical success factors across the different methodologies and develop a contingency fit model. This model is the first comprehensive contingency fit model in the study of critical success factors, and it distinguishes clearly between the traditional and the agile methodologies. This study's contingency fit model helped develop a model that can determine the degree of that influence the critical success factors have on project success.

The lack of proper solution designs or architecture for Big Data problems is among the prime technical problems. The technology to be used needs to be customized according to the type of analysis that is to be done via the project. Storage of data should be taken care of from the initial stages of the project. Data might be needed to be transformed into another form to make it more structured and make it a better fit for the business requirements. There is also a possibility of information loss during transforming the unstructured data into a more structured format (Gopalakrishnan et al., 2012; Cuzzocrea, Song, and Davis, 2011). While merging the data from different sources, other concerns like security and data privacy need to be considered. Access control mechanisms should be implemented to allow specific data access to specific people depending on their role. Data spillage is a significant concern, especially when cloud-based platforms come into the picture. Storage, retrieval, and processing data on such cloud-based systems have a considerable overhead, especially when security comes into the picture (Gao, Koronios, and Selle, 2015).

The research of Saltz and Shamshurin focuses more on the need of people, processes, and technology context of Big Data projects. The authors put forth six categories for the CSF for Big Data projects. They are listed as follows (Saltz and Shamshurin, 2016): Data (access, security, ownership), governance (culture, management, performance), process (project management and change management), objectives (well-defined goals), teams (structure and skillset), tools (technical aspects).

The importance of change management and the inclusion of procedures and policies for data are also stressed by Wamba et al. (2015). Different authors have proposed various challenges in adopting Big Data technologies. Three categories were identified by Yeoh and Popovic (2016), namely, Organization, Technology, and Process. On the same lines, Evers identified the categories as Organizational, Performance, and Technical (Saltz and Shamshurin, 2015).

Chen et al. identified seven critical success factors without categorizing them separately (Chen et al., 2016). These are the customer-centric focus, pre-project value discovery, strong business need, talent planning technology infrastructure, top management involvement, and vendor contract management.

The literature did not provide any empirical studies or publications tied to CSFs of Big Data projects and illustrated their correlation. There is, however, one conceptual model that looks at Big Data projects. Halaweh and Massry (2015) presented a conceptual research model. The five dimensions from Wamba et al. (2015) are data policies, technology and techniques, organizational change and management, access to data, and industry structure. squarely focus on utilizing the field of Big Data as we explore the relationship with successful Big Data projects."

Figure 1. Conceptual Model of Halaweh and Massry
Source: Halaweh and Massry (2015)

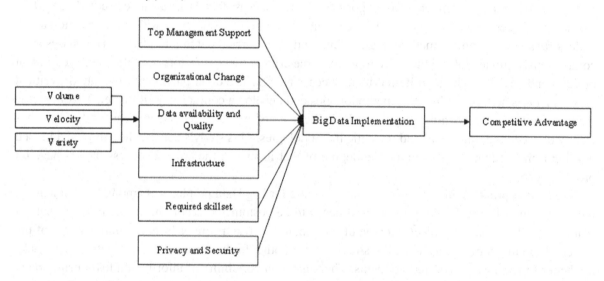

The"model above focuses on the 3 Vs (Volume, Velocity, Variety) for and utilizes challenges, failure and success criteria and obstacles needed for successful implementation of Big Data that exists in the literature.

Felix et al. (2018) presented the concept of Big Data and its benefits. They explored factors identified in the literature as potentially relevant for Big Data adoption and provided a description of the method applied

and the case study. They summarized the propositions regarding the critical success factors for Big Data adoption by virtual retailers in their research.

Tokuç and colleagues (2019) suggested that the management of big data application projects demands an understanding of additional requirements given with the processing of big and as working with multidisciplinary teams. Development teams focus more on the technology and architecture for processing the data, whereas business teams focus more on visualizing meaningful business insights for the customer. Data scientists use data mining, machine learning, and artificial intelligence to generate better insights and make decisions out of raw data. Tokuç et al. (2019) discuss the required skill sets of a project manager to manage such a team in the following sections successfully. Their research considers all of those reasons above; it compiles and discusses the recommended project management approach of the Project Management Institute (PMI) for application to big data projects.Narayan and Tan (2019) explored the potential for big data to be used as a tool to forecast project success. They presented some instances where adopting big data for forecasting in other fields has benefitted in saving resources and discussed the challenges faced in adopting big data and overcoming them.

Organizing the literature on critical success factors involved categorizing findings on causes for low project performance-related factors. The next sections include the literature on several critical factors in the light of CSFs of Big Data projects, provide broad definitions and discussions of the topic and incorporate views of others (literature review) into the discussion to support, refute, or demonstrate your position on the topic.

METHODOLOGY

This chapter adopts the systematic literature review method to gather, filter, and summarize the information and suggest a set of CSFs for Big Data projects. The purpose of the literature review for this research is to examine the previously done research within Big Data projects and project success issues and identify evidence related to the CSF criterion. This will add to Big Data project knowledge and be useful for developing suggestions for other research areas. The focus of this study is on the successful completion of Big Data projects. A deeper understanding of the literature will help define CSFs, Big Data projects, project management, and success. These definitions and concepts will be used throughout the chapter. The materials available through the trusted research engines were utilized, with the narrowed criterion of work created from 2009- 2018, peer-reviewed, and content that contains the full text. The results from these searches had to fall within these six criteria: availability within databases and journals, containing the full article, be peer-reviewed within the journals and contain relevant information about Big Data or CSFs as it pertained to organizational structures, human structures, technology infrastructure, project management, cost and schedule management, and or leadership skills, etc. Search"terms used included: "big data" + project, "big data" + business, "big data" + success, "business intelligence" + project, "business intelligence" + success.

For a comprehensive literature review, this research utilized a custom structure borrowed from Creswell (2009) and Cornell University (2016). The materials reviewed included books and journal articles. The databases used to search for research materials included: Web of Science and Scopus. After the systematic literature review, other databases (Elsevier ScienceDirect, Wiley Online Library, Elsevier ScienceDirect, Wiley Online Library, Sage and Springer, South Western, Oxford, Emerald Insight, IEEE, JSTOR, and Springer) are also included for further details regarding specific issues. The framework for the systematic literature review used in this research employed seven steps 1) Identify the research question(s); 2) Define inclusion and exclusion criteria; 3) Search for studies; 4) Select studies for inclusion based on pre-defined criteria; 5) Extract data from included studies; 6) Evaluate the risk of bias of included studies; 7) Present results and assess the quality of evidence" (Creswell, 2009; Cornell University, 2016).

In the existing literature, Big Data appears ~ 30,000 times across Web of Science core databases. At this juncture, the research utilized only peer-reviewed/scholarly/academic journals that were most commonly used by academics and practitioners alike to acquire information and disseminate new findings and represent the highest research level (Wamba et al., 2015 quoted from Niagi and Wat 2002). That bought the search down to 11,877 articles without any year limitations.

Figure 2. Systematic Literature Review Process

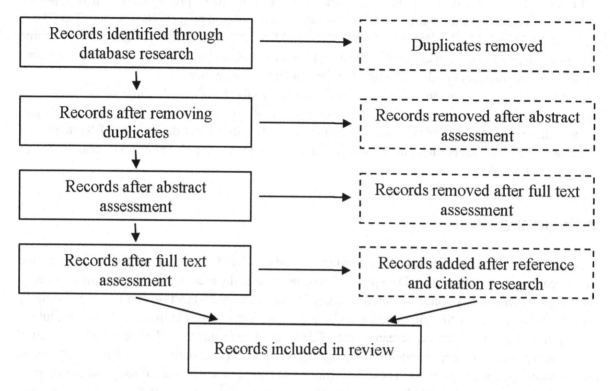

The purpose of this literature review was to address a deeper understanding of the CSFs of Big Data projects, which have come into question (Koskela and Howell, 2002; Mir and Pinnington, 2014). Since the focus was on non-technical articles but still considering the IS (information systems) side of things, the researcher wanted to confine this result with a term that incorporated many Big Data's findings and relevance to the organizations today. The research questions have required an analysis of their topics, their origin through their evolution, and the current practices and research findings. The research utilized various searches using terms such as management, organizations, marketing, analytics, and information technology, to name a few. The five terms that gave the best results and covered an extensive breadth of the Big Data CSF related landscape were Big Data, project, success, business, and business intelligence. Thus, limiting the search using these subject terms dropped the number down to 5445 main research articles spanning between 2009 and 2018. Any further chopping or restriction removed specific articles, and after the full-text assessment, 529 articles are examined as they covered a large surface area regarding Big Data. Ten records are added after reference and citation search, and the systematic literature review is conducted on 539 articles.

The literature consists of various articles on implementations, best practices, case studies, management/organization theories, complementing technologies, big data challenges, big data analytics, and other multiple variations, with each either providing proof (by theory) or identifying challenges regarding Big Data. What was clear was that there was consensus that Big Data was deemed as the future, the real deal, and central in creating big impacts (Halaweh and Massry 2015; Wamba et al., 2015; Wixom et al., 2014; Xu et al. 2015; Chen et al. 2012; Forrester 2012; Church and Dutta 2013, McAfee and Brynjolfsson 2013; Manyika et al. 2013). Furthermore, there was no consensus on the definition of the term, Big

Table 1. Systematic Literature Review Source Statistics

	WoS	Scopus	Records after full-text assessment	Records added after reference and citation search	TOTAL
«big data» + project	736	804	202	5	207
«big data» + business	926	1895	174	0	174
«big data» + success	286	301	83	2	85
«business intelligence» + project	101	146	34	2	36
«business intelligence» + success	122	128	36	1	37
TOTAL	2171	3274	529	10	539

Data (Hartmann et al. 2014; Young 2014; George et al. 2014; Church and Dutta 2013; Manyika 2013; McAfee and Brynjolfsson 2013, Wamba et al., 2015; Halaweh and Massry 2015), evidence of what influences successful Big Data projects.

A systematic review of the literature delineated details allowing a deep understanding of each topic. This provided the groundwork for answering the research questions, concluding, and making future research recommendations.

A significant part of this systematic literature review process is summarized in this chapter, where definitions are reviewed, and literature on factors that can impact successful Big Data projects are examined.

CRITICAL SUCCESS FACTORS

In"the 1970s, the concept of Critical Success Factors was introduced and can be defined as essential elements to successfully execute the project. As discussed in the literature review, many studies throw light on various critical success factors identified and validated for Big Data projects. Ojiako et al. (2008) concluded a universal set of success factors is not possible because contributing factors differ due to size, distinctiveness, industry, perceived complexity versus real complexity, and stakeholder composition. These critical success factors have been categorized so far into generic groups such as People, Process, Technology, etc. A categorization of these critical success factors in Big Data projects perspective is a gap that needs to be bridged. The following CSFs are refined through an in-depth literature survey and can help organizations to identify factors contributing to the success or failure of Big Data projects.

Human Capability

The critical success factor of human capability, according to the literature, refers to appropriate and necessary human resources that will effectively run and manage the project and its available resources (Browning and Ramasesh, 2015; E Silva and Seixas Costa, 2013; Kuen and Zailani, 2012).

Boehm and Turner (2005) stated that the choice of technology and other technical resources is the prerogative of the project manager and, subsequently, the project personnel. Despite the broad approaches available, the project personnel tends to remain within their comfort zones by choosing methodologies they are conversant with rather than choosing the appropriate methodology (Boehm and Turner, 2005). This choice is one significant disadvantage of using unqualified personnel (Howell, Windahl, and Seidel, 2010).

Table 2. Literature on Big Data

Issues related to Big Data	References
IT and Big Data Investments	Snow, 1966; MacMillan and Day, 1987; Solow, 1987; Jacobs, 2009; Chen et al., 2012; Forte, 1994; Williams and Williams, 2007; Lee et al., 2014; Powell and Snellman, 2004; Willcocks and Lester, 1996; Willcocks et al., 1999; Brynjolfsson, 1993; Brynjolfsson and Hitt, 1998; Jones et al., 2012; Dos Santos and Sussman, 2000; Lucas, 1999
Basic Research	Gao et al., 2015; Seddon et al., 2010; Chen et al., 2012; Kumar et al., 2013; Goes, 2014; Agarwal and Dhar, 2014; Bharadwaj et al., 2013; Zott and Amit, 2007; Hoy, 2014; Mayer-Schönberger and Cukier, 2014; Vinod, 2013; Rubinstein, 2013; Beyer and Laney, 2012; Dumbill, 2013; Narayanan et al., 2014
Technical perspective	McAfee et al., 2012; Hu et al., 2014; Zikopoulos and Eaton, 2011; Davenport et al., 2012; Boyd and Crawford; 2012; Katal, Wazid and Goudar, 2013; Bryant, Katz and Lazowska, 2008; Madden, 2012; Gandomi and Haider, 2015
Organizational perspective	Lohr, 2012; Bughin, Chui and Manyika, 2010; Marz and Warren, 2015; Mayer-Schönberger and Cukier, 2013; LaValle et al., 2011; Chen, Mao and Liu, 2014; Siemens and Long, 2011; Michael and Miller, 2013; Villars et al., 2011; Bizer et al., 2012
Analysis methods and algorithms	Lazer et al., 2014; Wu et al., 2014; Scott et al., 2016; Rebentrost, Mohseni and Lloyd, 2014
Decision support	Bughin et al., 2010; Schadt et al., 2010; Cole et al., 2012; Brown et al., 2011; Bughin et al., 2011; LaValle et al., 2011; Meijer, 2011; Sobek et al., 2011; Boyd and Crawford, 2012; Allen et al., 2012; Anderson and Blanke, 2012; Ann Keller et al., 2012; Boja et al., 2012; Beath et al., 2012; McAfee and Brynjolfsson, 2012; Davenport et al., 2012; Demirkan and Delen, 2013; Fisher et al., 2012; Gehrke, 2012; Griffin, 2012; Dansion and Griffin, 2012; Johnson, 2012; Kolker et al., 2012; Lane, 2012; Ohata and Kumar, 2012; Smith et al., 2012; Soares, 2012; Strawn, 2012; Tankard, 2012; Wagner, 2012; White, 2012
Alternative usage and utilization methods for databases	O'Driscoll, Daugelaite and Sleator, 2013; Demchenko et al., 2013; Madden, 2012
Technical deficiencies and problem-solving	Jagadish et al., 2014; Hashem et al., 2015; Kaiser et al., 2013; Katal, Wazid and Goudar, 2013
Organizational value	Lazer et al., 2014; LaValle vd. 2011; Jagadish et al., 2014
Competitive advantage	Chen et al., 2012; Marz and Warren, 2015; Mayer-Schönberger and Cukier, 2013; LaValle et al., 2011; Chen, Mao and Liu, 2014
Performance improving	Brinkmann et al., 2009; Bughin et al., 2010; Schadt et al., 2010; Brown et al., 2011; LaValle et al., 2011; Long and Siemens, 2011; Cole et al., 2012; Sobek et al., 2011; Allen et al., 2012; Anderson and Blanke, 2012; Keller et al., 2012; Beath et al., 2012; Boja et al., 2012; Boyd and Crawford, 2012; Chen et al., 2012; Davenport et al., 2012; Demirkan and Delen, 2013; Fisher et al., 2012; Havens et al., 2012; Huwe, 2012; Wagner, 2012; Johnson, 2012a; Soares, 2012; Kolker et al., 2012; Strawn, 2012; Tankard, 2012; White, 2012; McAfee and Brynjolfsson, 2012
Managing with Big Data	George, Haas and Pentland, 2014; Lohr, 2012; Bughin, Chui and Manyika, 2010
New business models, products, and services	Bughin et al., 2010; Bughin et al., 2011; LaValle et al., 2011; Brown et al., 2011; Long and Siemens, 2011; Ann Keller et al., 2012; Cole et al., 2012; Beath et al., 2012; Boyd and Crawford, 2012; McAfee and Brynjolfsson, 2012; Davenport et al., 2012; Chen et al., 2012; Demirkan and Delen, 2013; Fisher et al., 2012; Gehrke, 2012; Griffin, 2012; Griffin and Danson, 2012; Huwe, 2012; Johnson, 2012; Kolker et al., 2012; Ohata and Kumar, 2012; Soares, 2012; Strawn, 2012; Tankard, 2012; Wagner, 2012
Development of Big Data	Hilbert and Lopez, 2011; Chen, Mao and Liu, 2014; Cukier, 2010; Zikopoulos and Eaton, 2011
Organizational effects	Bharadwaj 2000; Grant 2010; Carr, 2003; Ross et al., 2013; Amit and Schoemaker 1993; Teece, 2014; 2015; Teece et al., 1997; Vera-Baquero et al., 2013; Tonidandel et al., 2015; Kamioka and Tapanainen, 2014; Calvard, 2016; McAfee and Brynjolfsson, 2012; Barney, 1991; Manyika et al., 2011; Knox, 2013; Miller, 2013; George et al., 2014; Davenport, 2014; Mata et al., 1995; Wixom and Watson, 2001; Chae et al., 2014; Chen et al., 2012; Nonaka et al., 2000; House et al., 2002; Dowling, 1993; Lavalle et al., 2011; Grant, 1996; Bhatt and Grover, 2005; Cohen and Levinthal, 1990; Nonaka and Teece, 2001
The potential of Big Data	Wielki, 2013; Linoff and Berry, 2011; Saltz, 2015; Al Nuaimi et al., 2015; Elragal, 2014; Hazen et al., 2014; Simon, 2013; Işık et al., 2013; Dutta and Bose, 2015; Ohlhorst, 2012; Rajpurohit, 2013; Yin and Kaynak; 2015; Franks, 2012; Russom, 2013; Ayankoya et al., 2014
Research by industry	Retail: (Brown et al., 2011; Lee et al., 2013; McAfee and Brynjolfsson, 2012) Healthcare: (Brinkmann et al., 2009; Field et al., 2009; Callebaut, 2012; Chen et al., 2012; Cole et al., 2012) Ecology: (Hochachka et al., 2009) Education: (Long and Siemens, 2011; Soares, 2012) Government: (Sobek et al., 2011; Chen et al., 2012; Mervis, 2012) Manufacturing: (Brown et al., 2011) Service: (Acker et al., 2011; Demirkan and Delen, 2013; Johnson, 2012; Kauffman et al., 2012; Kolker et al., 2012; Kubick, 2012; McAfee and Brynjolfsson, 2012) Technology: (Bradbury, 2011; Reddi et al., 2011; Allen et al., 2012; Chen et al., 2012; Burges and Bruns, 2012; Smith et al., 2012) Miscellaneous: (Jacobs, 2009; Bughin et al., 2010; Schadt et al., 2010; Alexander et al., 2011; Brown et al., 2011; Bughin et al., 2011; Kiron and Shockley, 2011; LaValle et al., 2011; Chen et al., 2012; Cole et al., 2012; Davenport et al., 2012; Griffin, 2012; Dansion and Griffin, 2012; Kauffman et al., 2012; Mervis, 2012; Strawn, 2012)

Organizational Capability

Latonio (2007) executed a phenomenological study design by interviewing 20 project managers from 16 industries. Latonio established project success factors related to leadership influence, management effect, project success criteria consideration, supporting values, communication, and organization leaders' commitment to the project. Ikeda (as cited in Jedd, 2007) reported that project failure is a combination of implementing a project structure without considering the corporate culture and failing to tie organizational strategy with the project priority.

Dinsmore and Cabanis-Brewin (2006) identified inadequate project managers as the primary cause of the project. Dinsmore and Cabanis-Brewin denoted the condition stemmed from an inadequate organizational incentive to transition an individual from a technical expert to a project manager. Dinsmore and Cabanis-Brewin also stated that the insufficient definition of the project manager role leads to a single individual assigned with too much responsibility.

Wysocki (2004) concluded that organizations implementing a project methodology might not benefit from decreased project failure rates if they do not protect the investment. Wysocki found that project teams are encouraged to use the accepted methodology prevalent in an organization, but often the individuals do not fully embrace the change introduced by the methodology or use the methodology tools as intended. Organizational leaders might consider a project methodology implementation an investment and might take measures to protect the investment by ensuring its proper use after implementation to realize higher success rates with projects (Wysocki).

Sidenko (2006) concluded that maintaining technology project success was related to project management maturity models, standard project practices, and project management tools used by personnel in organizations. Ojiako, Johansen, and Greenwood (2008) used a grounded theory study to examine two case studies from major industries and the effect on project success when the project and business objectives did not align. Ojiako et al. concluded a universal success factors checklist is not possible because variables differ due to size, distinctiveness, industry, perceived complexity versus real complexity, and stakeholder composition.

Henry (2004) observed organizational processes in the technology department and the business departments affected project success due to knowledge transferability and project governance alignment. Woodward (2007) advocated project failures are due to (a) inadequate sponsorship at the executive level, (b) unrealistic deadlines from management, (c) incompetent project managers applying wrong project management methodology, (d) insufficient end-user involvement, (e) poor requirement documentation, (f) inadequate change management, (g) insufficient communication, or (h) inadequate cost and schedule estimations.

Connelly and Canestraro (2007) studied information technology projects between governmental agencies. Connelly and Canestraro observed that project failure was related to fundamental organizational issues and behavioral issues. Critical success factors included elements of organizational factors and behaviors factors. Zhao (2007) concluded that organizational behaviors and project management contribute to technology upgrade projects.

Zhao used a mixed-method approach to collect data from 15 project manager interviews and observed the following contributing project success factors: (a) establishing a vision for the organization, (b) establishing a communication plan, (c) minimizing customization, (d) obtaining support from external sources, (e) establishing project management techniques, (f) establishing executive-level support, (g) setting up training, and (h) securing end-user involvement. Zhao collected survey data for use in statistical analysis to establish relationships among contributing factors with project success. Zhao concluded that contributing factors indicated a varying level of importance at different project life cycle points.

Following authors of project performance textbooks, similar results were observed in a public opinion poll administered by the 2007 Computing Technology Industry Association that received more than 1,000 responses (Deliverables, 2007). The survey respondents chose different reasons for the leading cause for project failures: (a) 28% identified poor communication, (b) 18% selected insufficient resource planning, (c) 13.2% selected unrealistic schedules, (d) over 9% choose low project requirements, and (e) over 6% selected insufficient stakeholder buy-in. The remaining responses were undefined project success or closure criteria, unrealistic budgets, insufficient or no risk planning, and an inadequate control process or change process.

Technical Capability

This critical success factor concerns the availability of adequate technology, adequately equipped personnel, and the provision of other technical resources needed to complete the project (Ahimbisibwe et al., 2015; Kuen and Zailani, 2012; Pope-Ruark, 2015). Sauser, Reilly, and Shenhar (2009) and Murad and Cavana (2012) noted that many IT (Information Technology) projects fail due to inadequate technology, ill-equipped personnel, and lack of other technical resources.

Complexity and technical effort are often underestimated in Big Data projects. With the size of the project, the number of project employees and participants, and the number of communication interfaces increase exponentially. Also, there is often tension between the technical procedural requirements (department side) and the technical view (IT side). On the technical effort side, many project teams plan according to best-case scenarios. If reality catches up with the project, high additional costs are incurred, and the duration is extended. With the size of a project, the project environment to be controlled increases with all of its stakeholders and interest groups who try to influence the project.

In technically complex projects, new technologies are often used that are only developed or mature. These innovations are used to take advantage of first-mover benefits. In general, there is nothing wrong with that. The use of new technologies is often the primary trigger for a project. However, new technologies also have their pitfalls." Since they are still untested, there are not the same empirical values as with well-tried technologies. As a result, their use naturally carries a higher risk than traditional solutions. There is often a lack of appropriate know-how (internal and external), as the specialist knowledge must be built up first. In the course of the project, one repeatedly encounters new technical challenges in the detailed work that was not foreseeable. Here, a "new technology" is often seen as a lifeline that seems to solve all problems at once.

If the decisions to use such "rescue anchors" accumulate, a project quickly finds itself where most of the technologies used are new or even have pilot character. This gradually increases the risk of the project failing.

Project Management

Project managers must focus on eliminating distractions from team members (Indelicato, 2007). For example, on a project with constrained resources, a project manager cannot allow resources to become sidetracked by outside distractions (Indelicato, 2007). Parchoma (2007) studied projects to integrate technology into instruction. Parchoma discovered that project performance was affected by adequate time to balance project commitments with other responsibilities. Project managers are responsible for setting limits and disengagement through communication to maintain team members' focus on the team members' area of expertise to achieve the highest project resource efficiencies and effectiveness (Fretty, 2007).

Leach (2005) noted that project success is achieved by strict product scope management through a change request process. Each request is processed upfront and assigned an impact estimate to the budget and an impact on the schedule (Leach). The request is also considered against any additional project risk introduced by the change (Leach). According to Kerzner (2003), the project manager's technical failure and insufficient risk management cause project failures.

Lewis (2007) consistently found that project failure causes were related to the project manager's inadequate project task planning. The planning deficiency led to inevitable rework and wasted time on trivial distractions (Lewis). Lee and Hirshfield (2006) found failures in health-care software implementations stemmed from poor up-front planning fueled by anxious team members, a push to realize a return on investment, and conflicting priorities.

Sauser (2005) concluded that project success relates to practice leadership skills, efficient management skills, and a technical competence project manager. Sauser noted that the project manager must accept responsibility for the project vision, execution, and resulting product. Sauser based conclusions on the observations from case study research.

Kendrick (2003) identified three reasons for project failure: (a) infeasible technical functionality, (b) unrealistic schedule expectations, and (c) inadequate planning by the project manager. Frame (2003) identified project failure as resulting from three primary sources: (a) organizational elements, (b) inadequate requirements, and (c) inadequate planning or control by the project manager. The report published by the U.S. General Accounting Office (1997) after reviewing the U.S. Department of Energy included four significant causes of project failure: (a) unclear product scope or considerable product scope change, (b) incremental project funding, (c) misaligned incentives, and (d) insufficient contractor overseeing.

Peslak, Subramanian, and Clayton (2008) evaluated commercial off-the-shelf implementation projects. Peslak et al. concluded through confirmatory factor analysis, the critical product use factors are preparation, training efforts, and efforts about performance and usefulness. Peslak and Stanton (2007) observed 18 teams using exploratory factor analysis to determine project success factors, including emotions and establishing processes involving the team and related personnel.

Liemi (2004) and Fan (2007) both concluded similarly in separate studies that knowledge management is a crucial success factor to project management. Liemi used a project management survey to observe a positive relationship between project management and knowledge management techniques. Fan established knowledge management technologies, such as data warehousing and data mining, improved the project performance of construction equipment management.

Project Definition

Project Definition enumerates the goals, purpose, and focus of the project. An adequately defined project helps the project team to focus, be on target, be extremely committed, and operate in one accord to achieve project objectives (Kuen and Zailani, 2012). The Project Definition is one critical success factor that the literature has described as very significant for success in every phase of the project lifecycle (Müller and Jugdev, 2012).

The project schedule/plan is also a part of the Project Definition, and it should be planned clearly before the project starts. Project schedule/plan is a comprehensive outlook of the necessary processes, procedures, and all resource requirements, including financial and human resources that will aid in the successful completion of the project (Dezdar and Ainin, 2011; Iamratanakul et al., 2014; Kuen and Zailani, 2012; Moohebat et al., 2011). According to Dezdar and Ainin (2011), the project schedule/plan must detail the project activities, including the appropriate timelines, appropriate human resources, monetary resources, and all other necessary resources that will lead to the successful completion of the project.

Project Methodology

Methods such as machine learning, supervised machine learning, unsupervised machine learning, and deep learning are among the most widespread and currently most essential analysis methods. The method used in a data project depends very much on the question at hand. The latter is the actual focus, which must not be lost sight of here. A project always aims to solve a specific question and not necessarily to do something with big data.

An essential technical solution approach for big data projects is the data repository. This is where data from all possible sources and contexts come together. Cloud solutions can also represent an essential part of big data solutions for various reasons - especially when it comes to data availability speed.

However, an almost confusing situation has arisen in recent years regarding specific tools and technologies. Project methodology employed in Big Data projects may be clustered under two main categories: classic and agile process models and structured IT project management approaches. The waterfall model is examined more closely as an approach belonging to the classic process models and, Scrum is examined as a typical agile process model. Both considerations are carried out against the background of the introduction of a big data management system. Furthermore, characteristic comparison criteria for IT project management are set up, allowing a quantitative investigation through utility value analysis.

The recurring phrases can often be found in the new or further development of software products (Fig. 9). At the beginning of a project, there is always a requirements analysis in which the customer's request is translated into a product specification. Subsequently, as part of the rough design, the product specifications are converted into a model, and the underlying software architecture is defined. The refined design prepares the implementation on a granular level and defines the internal structure of the software. The programming of the previously developed models and architectures begins with the implementation. The goal of the implementation is an executable product that can be tested and merged. Finally, testing and integration ensure that customer specifications are met. In parallel with all phases, continuous quality assurance ensures that each sub-products quality criteria are met. In IT project management, classical process models go through the phases mentioned above to rule from top to bottom.

The sequential, classic procedural models are characterized by a sequence of defined phases. However, the number and sequence of the phases differ depending on the author and procedural model, which is shown, among other things, by the waterfall model. For example, depending on the author and the application, operation, and maintenance are carried out as the last phase after testing and integration, including the IT solution's shutdown. The characteristic of classic or sequential process models is the phase product at the end of each phase, which at the same time represents an approval point and functions as a milestone in the project. The subsequent phase may only be started if the qualifying conditions for the previous phase are met.

Within the group of classic process models, building on the basic process of the waterfall model by Royce from 1970, further process models adapted to the changing requirements. These models include, for example, the V model, which was presented by NASA at the beginning of the 1990s. It has been further developed several times and has been the development standard for the planning and implementing federal IT projects under the name V-Model XT since 2004.

The so-called incremental and iterative process models are an intermediate form of classic and agile process models in the literature. These models aim to eliminate the disadvantages of classic methods and to meet known challenges better. By dividing the IT product into sub-products that can be produced independently and developed in parallel or on top of one another, iterative processes make executable systems available more quickly, and risks can be recognized earlier. Incremental models expand this approach by considering the system development as an evolutionary process, which begins with a prototype and progresses to the end product over several iterations. An example of such a procedural model is the Boehm spiral model from 1988, which gives risk management great importance.

BI and big data applications usually integrate information from many different source systems and a correspondingly large number of interfaces. The best implementation will provide no benefit if the data quality does not deliver what it says on the tin. The applications' performance depends heavily on the volume of data unavailable in development and test environments.

Agile concepts such as DevOps, Test Driven Development, and Scrum provide excellent methodological approaches to meet these challenges successfully. Agile methods have replaced classic project management in software development, and project complexity is why methods such as Scrum are used in data science.

Agile process models are based, following their name, on their agility and flexibility. Agility is the ability to act quickly, flexibly, and situation-related in chaotic and dynamic situations by creating a balance between structuring and flexibility to generate benefits for the customer and oneself. According to this definition, criticism of classic procedural models, such as the restricted flexibility, the lack of customer involvement, or an excessive documentation effort, is remedied by agility. The core of agile process models is numerous feedback processes and a systematic, iterative approach. The goal of agile methods in software development is to obtain executable development results in the shortest possible time in order to shorten the time to market. Also, the high number of feedbacks should enable a better reaction to new or changed product requirements.

Probably the most widely used agile procedure model in IT project management is Scrum. In addition to Scrum, there are numerous other models, such as Extreme programming or Kanban. In addition to the advantages of agile process models presented here, which primarily strive to remedy the shortcomings of classic methods, Padberg and Tichy (2007) show that there are also weaknesses. The limited documentation during the project is beneficial in terms of development speed, but it can be used later, e.g., in software maintenance, problems arise due to knowledge not recorded in writing. The iterative approach also leads to frequent changes in requirements and, thus, numerous restructuring of the program code. Agile process models place high demands on the development team. The employees involved should demonstrate strong technical expertise, personal responsibility, discipline, and safe handling of customers. Padberg and Tichy (2007) also consider using agile process models in large development projects with more than 20 developers involved to be unsuitable, as a high degree of communication and interaction is required. This can only be guaranteed to a limited extent with such dimensions.

Scrum is an agile process model of IT project management, consisting of a small number of very precise rules. Similar to all other agile process models, it is based on the Agile Manifesto. Scrum has three roles: that of the Product Owner, that of the Scrum Master, and the development team. Each role has clearly defined tasks and responsibilities within short development cycles called in Scrum Sprints, creating product increments controlled via a prioritized specification sheet, the so-called Product Backlog.

In Scrum, the product owner is responsible for the economic success of the product. He starts product development with a clear product vision. In line with the product vision, he creates and prioritizes the requirements in the so-called product backlog. All relevant stakeholders are involved in the definition process of the product vision and product backlog at an early stage. Nonetheless, the product owner remains responsible for designing the product requirements.

Scrum is an extremely customer-oriented, agile process model that offers a quick reaction to new or changed customer requirements through frequent iterations. However, through the customer's direct involvement in the development process, requirements also enter the project that would be filtered out at the management level in other process models. The Scrum Master's role has a positive effect, promoting goal and product orientation in the project. Furthermore, the largely independent work of the development team leads to a high degree of intrinsic motivation. The biggest obstacle to using Scrum is the comparatively low predictability of the project costs and the project time frame at the start of the project.

Change Management

Big Data projects require a change process (Hallikainen et al., 2006). It can be viewed from two perspectives: implementing change and adapting change (Garg and Singh, 2006). When a Big Data implementation project is initiated by top management, top management must ensure that their staff will adapt. An environment in which change can be implemented is required for the Big Data implementation (Calvert and Carroll, 2005). If their staff are not aware of the change or do not adopt the change, the implementation may not be expected. In order to make the change effective, it requires change management. Al-Mashari and Zairi (2000) stated that change management facilitated the insertion of newly implemented systems, processes, and structure into the working practice and dealt with resistance. Kemp and Low (2008) indicated that change management was required to prepare users to introduce a new system, reduce resistance towards the system, and influence user attitudes. These objectives ensure the new Big Data project output's acceptance and readiness, allowing the organization to benefit from its use (Esteves and Pastor, 1999).

Kemp and Low (2008) proposed a range of change management activities, such as communication, project championship program, training, users' involvement, and phased implementation. All of them were regarded as critical success factors in other studies. In order not to duplicate, change management was not considered a critical success factor. Nevertheless, change management is still the backbone of the current study because it is believed that Big Data projects require a change process. Sarkis and Sundarraj (2003) indicated that three issues should be addressed for change management: user expectation, user involvement, and user satisfaction.

Communication

Communication is the art of providing a suitable medium for seamless interaction and collaboration among all stakeholders (Fesenko and Minaev, 2014; Kisielnicki, 2011; Sidawi, 2012). Kuen and Zailani (2012) stated that communication is a critical factor that affects the successful completion of an IT project. Effective communication increases knowledge, identifies risks, eliminates or minimizes unproductive activities, reduces errors, and helps create ideas that could lead to the successful completion of the project (Kuen and Zailani, 2012). Communication within the project team is one of the most critical success factors. Browning and Ramasesh (2015) reiterated that collaboration between the project team, the different groups, all stakeholders, and all operations is essential to completing the project. Additionally, effective and appropriate communication between all parts of the system, including personnel, plays a significant role in a project's success.

Besides communicating within the project team, communication with other members of the organization is crucial. Effective communication between the project team and the end-users, particularly during the analysis and design phases, is crucial to successfully producing a project. Effective communication could be achieved through seamless collaboration between the project team and the end-users throughout the Big Data project (Mavetera and Kroeze, 2009). Finally, the effective use of communication tools and techniques is critical to Big Data projects' success. The tools and techniques include media use to inform the project team and all stakeholders of the project's progress, brainstorming meetings, and the use of the pair programming technique (Mavetera and Kroeze, 2009).

It means that information is shared between the project team and communicated to the whole organization the implementation phase's results and goals. The communication effort should be made regularly (Esteves and Pastor, 2000; Sternad and Bobek, 2006). Top-down, bottom-up, and horizontal communications are required in the course of Big Data implementation. It is essential to understand the differences in project team members' perceptions and non-project team members in designing communication mechanisms (Amoako-Gyampah, 2004). Effective communication is a critical element that helps disseminate new information, challenges, or opportunities to all parties involved (Muthusamy et al., 2005). Expectations and goals must be communicated among stakeholders at all levels of the organization. Stakeholders must understand the capabilities and limitations of the Big Data project. Otherwise, the Big Data project may fail to meet stakeholders' expectations (Nah and Delgado, 2006). Zhang et al. (2005) further indicated that an open system culture should be encouraged. People within a closed system would think they would be constrained by the Big Data project, which inevitably led to resistance to the Big Data project.

Communication breakdown is one of the uncertainties in Big Data projects. It is sometimes unavoidable due to languages or technical jargon used. To avoid it, Loh and Koh (2004) suggested that clear instructions and messages should be given all the time. Educational workshops and training can enhance users' knowledge and eliminate or minimize unnecessary communication breakdown.

In short, change management requires user involvement and participation. User involvement and participation require teamwork and effective communication. So teamwork and communication is the first critical success factor identified for the current study.

End-User Acceptance

End-user acceptance, which is the extent to which the client accepts and uses the developed project output (Kuen and Zailani, 2012), is a very vital success factor in IT projects. End-user acceptance is the acceptability and usability of the product by the clients, and this determines if the project is a success or a failure (Kuen and Zailani, 2012; Müller and Jugdev, 2012; Ofori, 2013; Sudhakar, 2012). The literature also reveals that frequent communication and consultation with the end-user to get feedback, particularly about meeting the customers' needs, is essential to successfully implementing the Big Data project. Further, the client must be conversant and agree with the project success criteria from the project's initial stages (Kuen and Zailani, 2012; Pope-Ruark, 2015).

Training

Training is one of the critical success factors in IT projects (Bagchi et al., 2003; Yang and Seddon, 2004). Lack of training and education is the number one IT implementation problem in small and large manufacturing firms (Duplaga and Astani, 2003). In a study about players and activities across the project life cycle, Somers and Nelson (2004) concluded that user training was necessary throughout the implementation cycle. Training is regarded as an important event that must be arranged in consideration of the implementation phases. Calvert and Carroll (2005) pointed out that the timing and scope of training were logically related to the implementation of project phases. In the planning phase, project team members should train on the project output (Clinton and Lummus, 2000; Mäkipää, 2003). Inadequate training will cause many errors and problems in testing the Big Data project; cutting the time allotted to testing and training increase the chance of failure (Markus and Tanis, 2000). End-users training is typically the last activity in the project phase (Markus et al., 2000). Besides the formal training, other mechanisms such as help desk, online help, knowledge management systems, communities of practice, and establishment of power users, must be established (Calvert and Carroll, 2005).

As discussed, training is a necessary event in Big Data implementation, but whether it can lead to success is not determined. Antonacopoulou (2001) indicated that training could not be assumed to produce learning. Training is based on the control and conditioning of individuals' understanding, whereas learning is about broadening and liberating understanding. In training, the trainer can train users on using the Big Data tools with demonstration data of some scenarios. Users must learn how to apply the skill and knowledge to other scenarios not covered in training. If users cannot apply the skill or knowledge to other scenarios, it can say that users complete the training, but the training is not practical because they do not learn what they need to learn. Besides technical and operative knowledge, training should also cause behavior change (Laoledchai, Land, and Low, 2008).

Calvert and Carroll (2005) used the term "change management" to replace "training strategy" because it takes a holistic view of training in a Big Data environment. Change management should ensure that users are learning what they need to learn. Once users can handle the tool themselves, resistance resulting from fear of disruption will be reduced. In the learning processes, users will be familiar with the new tools, new processes, new relationships and structures, resistance resulting from long-standing organizational traditions, and reduced work processes. The effectiveness of training is one of the primary concerns in Big data projects, not training itself.

Top Management Support

Top management support, a critical success factor in all types of investigated projects, essentially relates to the unflinching support of senior management to the success of the project by providing every needed support necessary to complete the project (Elbanna, 2013; Garrett and Neubaum, 2013; Lee, Shiue, and Chen, 2016). Top management support includes but is not limited to providing adequate financial assistance and all other necessary resources for the successful completion of the project (Elbanna, 2013).

Nah et al. (2003) indicated that top management support influenced both commitment to change management and commitment to resources, which were necessary factors for Big Data project success. The implementation project should be identified as a top priority that encourages the entire organization to focus on the project and motivates the project team and users to learn the Big Data tool and truly participate (Wang, Klein and Jiang, 2006). Top management must help project team members move into a high-performance team and then help them move from teamwork to team learning. Teamwork can create synergies and get the problem solved. However, team learning encourages the team members to learn from others, help others learn, and learn about working with each other (Nagendra, 2000).

Top management should also allocate the necessary resources to the Big Data project (Nah et al., 2003). Jafari et al. (2006) found out that allocating necessary resources was the most critical top management duty in a Big Data project. The top management attitude to the Big Data project determines the number of resources allocated (Nah et al., 2003).

Dedication from the executive level is significant during all Big Data implementation and upgrade (Nah et al., 2001; Wenrich and Ahmad, 2009). Without top management support, there is little hope for it. This is especially important in an implementation project (Akkermans and Helden, 2002). Top management must define the Big Data project's objectives to give the project team and users a clear business plan and vision to steer the direction of the project (Loh and Koh, 2004; Francoise et al., 2009). They should also paint a picture of where the organization will portray the anticipated outcomes after the Big Data project (Martin and Huq, 2007).

Although top management support is widely regarded as an essential factor in the literature of Big Data, Nah, et al. (2007) indicated that it acted more like an "enabling" rather than a necessary factor for developing countries. In their study, top management support did not impact the success of projects in developing countries. From the process point of view, top management commitment is a necessary factor that top management must decide to acquire and implement the Big Data project. Without their approval, the project phase will never happen. Nah et al. (2007) also indicated that top management might be necessary to complete a Big Data project but might not directly affect the system's effectiveness. Kamhawi (2007) also found that top management support was not significantly related to both project and business success in regression analysis, but it had a significant relationship with the Big Data success in the correlation analysis. The contrast in results means that although top management support is related to Big Data success, its interaction behavior with the other critical success factors is not significant concerning the success dimension (Kamhawi, 2007).

Based on the literature reviewed, top management is a necessary and essential factor for Big Data projects. However, why does top management have these supportive behaviors? The linking of the Big Data project with enterprise strategy is one of the elements strongly influencing the top management behaviors. Big Data projects are perceived by top management as a means by which an organization can complete its strategic goals, which can be included both tangible and intangible objectives. Intangible strategic goals can be organization development and growth, customer satisfaction, or information availability. Tangible strategic goals may include operating cost reduction or an increase in profitability (Soja, 2008). A Big data tool is a strategic tool to introduce changes to organizations for particular strategic goals, such as standardization, competing against competitors, winning market shares, and sustaining competitive advantages (Kraemmer et al., 2003; Jafari et al., 2006; Baray, Hameed and Badii, 2006; Olugbode et al., 2008; Baray, Hameed and Badii, 2008). From a strategic point of view, a Big Data project's success can refer to the increased value of the business from usage of the Big Data tools (Nah et al., 2007).

Troubleshooting

As a critical success factor, troubleshooting is a general term for troubleshooting, monitoring and feedback, and end-user consultation activities. Troubleshooting mainly concerns the capability to promptly manage uncertainties and inherent issues developing during the project's life cycle (Ahmad et al., 2012; Kuen and Zailani, 2012). Due to unforeseen circumstances, situations may develop, hence the software development team should tackle emerging crises and arising deviation from the initial plans (Kuen and Zailani, 2012). Also, the project team should be versatile in the concept of risk management to troubleshoot effectively should unanticipated incidences arise (Kuen and Zailani, 2012).

The monitoring and feedback is another critical success factor for Big Data projects. This construct allows for prompt and timely intervention in the event of any adverse contingencies that may affect the project's success (Kuen and Zailani, 2012; Shatat, 2015).

Client consultation primarily details active consultation with all stakeholders and incorporates all necessary functions that will aid the software product's usability (Ofori, 2013; Sudhakar, 2013). Also, client consultation allows every stakeholder to provide input, particularly during the project management's initial stages, and be informed of the project's progress (Kuen and Zailani, 2012). Also, stakeholders tend to embrace the project output since they have been involved during its development (Ahmad et al., 2012).

Miscellaneous

In addition to the potential influences of Big Data projects, other variables have been shown to relate to projects' success. Project size is one of these variables. The Standish Group (2010) reported that projects were completed on time, within budget, and with the required functionality only 4% of the time for new application development, 30% of the time for package applications, and 53% of the time for application modernization projects (i.e., software updates). Ajila and Wu (2007) found that project success, defined as completing the project within the planned timeframe, was higher for smaller organizations. For the third component of the iron triangle, quality, small organizations again performed better, with projects averaging 74.2% of their originally-intended features, compared to only 42.0% for projects developed by large organizations (Standish Group, 1995). Work experience has also been showing to predict project success (McHaney, White and Heilman, 2002). For example, Müller and Turner (2007) showed that older project managers with more years of managerial experience were more likely to lead projects that concluded successfully than younger project managers with fewer years of managerial experience. In summary, both years of management experience and project size are critical variables in predicting project success. Years of IT experience have also been shown to predict accuracy in costing and scheduling tasks (Henry et al., 2007).

FUTURE RESEARCH DIRECTIONS

This descriptive study is among the preliminary research efforts toward critical success factors in Big Data projects. Indeed, every Big Data project is unique with the methodology followed. Every project has its unique features. The impact of these critical success factors on every stage of the project lifecycle needs to be justified. The results might include factors that affect differently at different stages. Some factors may not even apply at every stage of project execution. Big Data projects are carried out worldwide. Due to this global nature, it is necessary to gather data about Big Data projects being executed in different countries. The analysis should be carried out if the method of executing these projects differs from country to country or differ from industry to industry. New success factors can be discovered to provide insight into the success of Big Data projects in different markets and cultures. Future studies can also use a qualitative or mixed-method approach. Such an approach can help to understand and carry out research more in-depth into other aspects of Big Data project implementation. Research can include the impact of technology being used on the method of project execution. It is essential to understand if specific technologies or algorithms can change how the Big Data project is being executed. In this case, a newly revised list of critical success factors can be found.

DISCUSSION AND CONCLUSIONS

Project success is a multidimensional variable that can be broadly categorized in terms of efficiency and effectiveness of the project's outcome (Ika, 2009; Ika, Diallo, and Thuillier, 2012). Efficiency describes the project's success in terms of the triple constraints of the Project Management Institute (PMI), namely time, cost, and scope. Effectiveness describes the outcome in terms of achieving project objectives, business objectives, and social and environmental goals (Howsawi, Eager, Bagia, and Niebecker, 2014; Ika et al., 2012; Müller and Jugdev, 2012; Palcic and Buchmeister, 2012; Rolstadas et al., 2014). While there is no universally agreed-upon definition of project success, most do agree that success "is in the eyes of the beholder" (Müller and Jugdev, 2012).

The literature review on project success revealed different conclusions to indicate that researchers and public opinion disagree on leading project success predictors. The current research study's objective was to provide insight into the critical success factors of Big Data projects and Big Data project success.

There are many unanswered questions about big data. These questions range from attempting to define it, asking how it will help decision makers make better decisions, effectively govern the immense volumes of data, and protect customer's privacy. There is an agreement that the sheer volumes of big data will require cutting-edge technology to maintain it and new analytical skills for it to be effectively used.

The various implementations, theories, and proof of successes have been singular (tied to a single instance within the organization), has only dealt with showcasing an area of focus (trying to solve one problem and not organizationally prevalent), and has not been replicable or able to pass on success/learnings to other aspects of the organization.

The need for successful project management is increasing as projects are used to achieve operational goals in various organization types (Hyvari, 2006). Project success might link to national security in some government agencies, such as Jones' (2007) project to implement a passenger tracking system. Leaders of modern organizations using projects to achieve operational goals have a potential opportunity to reduce costs using recommendations from the current research study. Lewis (2007) noted that approximately 30% of development cost is linked to the rework of previously completed tasks.

Woodward (2007) and Ildefonso (2007) both concluded that personnel who follow best practices experience dramatic increases in information technology project success. This study contributes to the literature by summarizing and categorizing factors recognized in best practices.

Hyvari (2006) conducted a literature review and discovered disagreement in the project management literature on what constitutes a successful project within an organization. Shenhar and Wideman (2000) found the same disagreement pertained to defining project success in the business literature. The literature includes material covering a broad concern for project success within organizations and wide disagreement on how to measure project success.

Since the 1960s, researchers have contributed efforts to define a single comprehensive factor set to predict project success but have consistently disagreed on one or more factors (Cooke-Davies, 2002). Pinto and Prescott (1988) indicated that research before 1988 was theory-based without empirical data. Disagreements in the literature on a single factor set might result from a lack of empirical data. The current research study provides empirical data to the body of knowledge of associations between 5 critical success factors and Big Data project success.

Many challenges still exist with Big Data. There is the issue with dealing with heterogeneity, inconsistency and incompleteness, varying scale, timelessness, privacy and data ownership, and visualization and collaboration. (Jagadish et al., 2014)

Big Data research is currently concentrated on enhancing data models and algorithms; however, the best approach to execute projects must also be studied. Complicating the situation is that Big Data projects are exploratory in most cases, and accordingly, the projects lack exact business requirements with subsequent results not easily validated. Moreover, teams performing data analysis and data science work operate in an ad hoc fashion where a trial and error process is used to identify the right tools and accordingly involves a low level of process maturity.

It is also very clear from literature and practitioners that Big Data is here to play a role in our future. For that purpose alone, we must learn, take advantage, and realize its potential to transform entire business processes.

REFERENCES

Agirre Perez, I. (2007). Stochastic project scheduling system: Implications for risk management. *Dissertation Abstracts International*, 68(2).

Ahimbisibwe, A., Cavana, R. Y., & Daellenbach, U. (2015). A contingency fit model of critical success factors for software development projects: A comparison of agile and traditional plan-based methodologies. *Journal of Enterprise Information Management*, 28(1), 7–33. doi:10.1108/JEIM-08-2013-0060

Anderson, E. S., Birchall, D., Jessen, S. A., & Money, A. H. (2006). Exploring project success. *Baltic Journal of Management*, 1(2), 127–147. doi:10.1108/17465260610663854

Baladi, I. W. (2007). An empirical analysis of perceived value of virtual versus traditional project management practice. *Dissertation Abstracts International*, 68(9).

Bullen, C. V., & Rockart, J. F. (1981). *A primer on critical success factors*. Academic Press.

Chen, H. M., Schütz, R., Kazman, R., & Matthes, F. (2016). Amazon in the air: Innovating with big data at Lufthansa. In *System Sciences (HICSS), 2016 49th Hawaii International Conference on* (pp. 5096-5105). IEEE.

Creswell, J. W. (2009). Editorial: Mapping the Field of Mixed Methods Research. *Journal of Mixed Methods Research*, 3(2), 95–108. doi:10.1177/1558689808330883

Cuzzocrea, A., Song, I. Y., & Davis, K. C. (2011). Analytics over large-scale multidimensional data: the big data revolution! In *Proceedings of the ACM 14th international workshop on Data Warehousing and OLAP* (pp. 101-104). ACM. 10.1145/2064676.2064695

Delisle, C. L. G. (2001). Success and communication in virtual project teams. *Dissertation Abstracts International*, *62*(12), 4242.

Félix, B. M., Rodrigues, E. M. T., & Cavalcante, N. W. F. (2018). Critical success factors for Big Data adoption in the virtual retail: Magazine Luiza case study. *Review of Business Management*, *20*(1), 112–126. doi:10.7819/rbgn.v20i1.3627

Fortune, J., & White, D. (2006). Framing of project critical success factors by a systems model. *International Journal of Project Management*, *24*(1), 53–65. doi:10.1016/j.ijproman.2005.07.004

Gao, J., Koronios, A., & Selle, S. (2015). *Towards a process view on critical success factors in big data analytics projects*. Academic Press.

Gopalakrishnan, K., Yusuf, Y. Y., Musa, A., Abubakar, T., & Ambursa, H. M. (2012). Sustainable supply chain management: A case study of British Aerospace (BAe) Systems. *International Journal of Production Economics*, *140*(1), 193–203. doi:10.1016/j.ijpe.2012.01.003

Halaweh, M., & Massry, A. E. (2015). Conceptual model for successful implementation of big data in organizations. *Journal of International Technology and Information Management*, *24*(2), 2.

Hass, K. (2006). *The five deadly sins of project management*. https://www.powermag.com/the-five-deadly-sins-of-project-management/

Müller, R., & Jugdev, K. (2012). Critical success factors in projects: Pinto, Slevin, and Prescott–the elucidation of project success. *International Journal of Managing Projects in Business*, *5*(4), 757–775. doi:10.1108/17538371211269040

Narayan, S., & Tan, H. C. (2019). Adopting Big Data to Forecast Success of Construction Projects: A Review. *Malaysian Construction Research Journal*, 132.

Nasr, E. B. (2004). An integrated project planning and control system approach for measuring project performance. *Dissertation Abstracts International*, *66*(03).

Nixon, P., Harrington, M., & Parker, D. (2012). Leadership performance is significant to project success or failure: A critical analysis. *International Journal of Productivity and Performance Management*, *61*(2), 204–216. doi:10.1108/17410401211194699

Padberg, F., & Tichy, W. (2007). Lean production methods in modern software development. *Business Info*, *49*(3), 162–170.

Pinto, J. K. (1986). *Project implementation: a determination of its critical success factors, moderators and their relative importance across the project life cycle* (Doctoral dissertation). University of Pittsburgh.

Pinto, J. K., & Slevin, D. P. (1987). Critical factors in successful project implementation. *IEEE Transactions on Engineering Management*, *EM-34*(1), 22–27. doi:10.1109/TEM.1987.6498856

PMI. (2015). *Executive engagement: The role of the sponsor*. https://www.pmi.org/business-solutions/white-papers/executive-engagement-sponsor-role

Saltz, J. S., & Shamshurin, I. (2016). Big data team process methodologies: A literature review and the identification of key factors for a project's success. In *Big Data (Big Data), 2016 IEEE International Conference on* (pp. 2872-2879). IEEE. 10.1109/BigData.2016.7840936

Shao, M. G. (2006). Development of project manager selection tool based on project manager competency. *Master's Abstracts International, 45*(2).

Stankovic, D., Nikolic, V., Djordjevic, M., & Cao, D. B. (2013). A survey study of critical success factors in agile software projects in former Yugoslavia IT companies. *Journal of Systems and Software, 86*(6), 1663–1678. doi:10.1016/j.jss.2013.02.027

Sudhakar, G. P. (2012). A model of critical success factors for software projects. *Journal of Enterprise Information Management, 25*(6), 537–558. doi:10.1108/17410391211272829

Tokuç, A. A., Uran, Z. E., & Tekin, A. T. (2019). Management of Big Data Projects: PMI Approach for Success. In *Agile Approaches for Successfully Managing and Executing Projects in the Fourth Industrial Revolution* (pp. 279–293). IGI Global. doi:10.4018/978-1-5225-7865-9.ch015

Wamba, S., Akter, S., Edwards, A., Chopin, G., & Gnanzou, D. (2015). How 'big data' can make big impact: Findings from a systematic review and a longitudinal case study. *International Journal of Production Economics, 165*, 234–246. Advance online publication. doi:10.1016/j.ijpe.2014.12.031

Westlund, S. G. (2007). Retaining talent: Assessing relationships among project leadership styles, software developer job satisfaction, and turnover intentions. *Dissertation Abstracts International, 68*(11).

Wu, W. W. (2006). IT personnel sourcing decisions in IT projects. *Dissertation Abstracts International, 67*(1).

Yeoh, W., & Popovič, A. (2016). Extending the understanding of critical success factors for implementing business intelligence systems. *Journal of the Association for Information Science and Technology, 67*(1), 134–147. doi:10.1002/asi.23366

ADDITIONAL READING

Fortune, J., & White, D. (2006). Framing of project critical success factors by a systems model. *International Journal of Project Management, 24*(1), 53–65. doi:10.1016/j.ijproman.2005.07.004

Gao, J., Koronios, A., & Selle, S. (2015). Towards a process view on critical success factors in big data analytics projects.

Halaweh, M., & Massry, A. E. (2015). Conceptual model for successful implementation of big data in organizations. *Journal of International Technology and Information Management, 24*(2), 2.

Pinto, J. K. (1986). *Project implementation: a determination of its critical success factors, moderators and their relative importance across the project life cycle* (Doctoral dissertation). University of Pittsburgh.

Pinto, J. K., & Slevin, D. P. (1987). Critical factors in successful project implementation. *IEEE Transactions on Engineering Management*, *EM-34*(1), 22–27. doi:10.1109/TEM.1987.6498856

Saltz, J. S., & Shamshurin, I. (2016). Big data team process methodologies: A literature review and the identification of key factors for a project's success. In *Big Data (Big Data), 2016 IEEE International Conference on* (pp. 2872-2879). IEEE. 10.1109/BigData.2016.7840936

Sudhakar, G. P. (2012). A model of critical success factors for software projects. *Journal of Enterprise Information Management*, *25*(6), 537–558. doi:10.1108/17410391211272829

Wamba, S., Akter, S., Edwards, A., Chopin, G., & Gnanzou, D. (2015). How 'big data' can make big impact: Findings from a systematic review and a longitudinal case study. *International Journal of Production Economics*, *165*, 234–246. Advance online publication. doi:10.1016/j.ijpe.2014.12.031

Chapter 12
Blockchain–Based Data Market (BCBDM) Framework for Security and Privacy:
An Analysis

Shailesh Pancham Khapre
Amity University, Noida, India

Chandramohan Dhasarathan
iD https://orcid.org/0000-0002-5279-950X
Madanapalle Institute of Technology and Science, India

Puviyarasi T.
iD https://orcid.org/0000-0003-3668-3264
Madanapalle Institute of Technology and Science, India

Sam Goundar
iD https://orcid.org/0000-0001-6465-1097
British University Vietnam, Vietnam

ABSTRACT

In the internet era, incalculable data is generated every day. In the process of data sharing, complex issues such as data privacy and ownership are emerging. Blockchain is a decentralized distributed data storage technology. The introduction of blockchain can eliminate the disadvantages of the centralized data market, but at the same time, distributed data markets have created security and privacy issues. It summarizes the industry status and research progress of the domestic and foreign big data trading markets and refines the nature of the blockchain-based big data sharing and circulation platform. Based on these properties, a blockchain-based data market (BCBDM) framework is proposed, and the security and privacy issues as well as corresponding solutions in this framework are analyzed and discussed. Based on this framework, a data market testing system was implemented, and the feasibility and security of the framework were confirmed.

DOI: 10.4018/978-1-7998-6673-2.ch012

INTRODUCTION

The amount of data in today's world is increasing rapidly. Since the establishment of Facebook, it has collected more than 300 PB (petabytes) of personal data, and the scale of this is still expanding. Balazinska et al., Researcher from IBM have suggested that 90% of the data in the world today has been generated in the past two years, and with the emergence of new equipment and technologies, data growth will accelerate further. In the era of big data, data is continuously collected and analyzed, leading to technological innovation and economic growth. Companies and organizations use the data they collect to provide personalized user services, optimize company decision-making processes, and predict future trends. People are concerned about the security of personal data and process of extensive data used (Pang et al., 2017), worrying about whether Internet companies that provide services and collect data will protect users' data privacy, and do people have little control over the data they generate and how they use it (Balazinska et al., 2011). In recent years, many incidents related to violations of user data privacy have been reported. The most famous example is that of Facebook's 50 million user data been leaked, and user privacy has been greatly violated.

To ensure the normal circulation, use of data, and maximize the value of big data, in recent years, many new organizations have emerged regarding personal data sharing and transactions. In addition to the traditional method of data circulation (that is, the widespread data exchange service between companies and users), a big data sharing transaction market has emerged to facilitate data transactions by matching data needs with data sources (Zyskind et al., 2015). These data markets are already of considerable size. These data markets are valued at tens of billions of dollars and continue to grow (Zyskind et al., 2015). In the data market, data holders display their data information to attract potential data consumers; data consumers search and select the data sets they need, and obtain data usage rights by paying a certain fee; the data market gains revenue by facilitating data transactions. However, as the scale of data sharing transactions and the value of data increase, it is expected that fraud and leakage in the process of sharing transactions will gradually increase. The general architecture of a centralized data market is shown in Figure 1. In this architecture, the market platform operated by a centralized company or organization plays a vital role in the system.

The parties involved in the data-market, data buyers and market platforms, can obtain higher profits through collusive fraud, arbitrage purchase strategies and so on. In addition, according to (Zheng et al., 2018), the centralized data transaction model lacks effective information communication channels between data buyers and data sellers, resulting in inefficient data transactions (Goldfeder et al., 2017). Finally, the data market platform has more information advantages, i.e., the market platform knows the data content, but the data buyer cannot know the data content before buying the data, so the market platform can illegally obtain profits by constructing information barriers and controlling information disclosure. The centralized data market as highlighter by (Wang & Krishnamachari, 2019) has some inevitable problems such as data security, data privacy protection and data circulation performance bottlenecks. First of all, the intermediary of data transactions (usually the market platform) must be safe and reliable. The market platform needs to have credibility to ensure that it will not illegally use the data in the transaction and leak the privacy of the data holder (Dziembowski et al., 2018). However, the market platform does have such a motive, and even if it uses or sells data illegally, it is generally difficult to pursue this illegal activity. At the same time, the centralized data market can easily become the target of attackers. The user's sensitive information (such as location, chat history, etc.) is stored in a centralized database, and there is a risk of privacy leakage and data loss. Most existing data markets run on centralized servers, and such systems have a single point of failure and a single point of performance bottleneck. Researches designed a centralized system (Missier et al., 2017) have shown that the existing data market will also control the search between buyers and sellers, resulting in inefficient market operation.

Figure 1. Centralized data market architecture

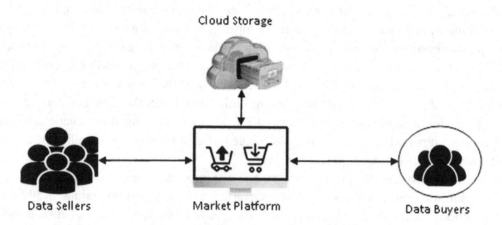

In order to avoid the disadvantages of the centralized data market as depicted in Figure.1, a decentralized data market was proposed. The decentralized data market architecture can circumvent the requirement of relying on trusted intermediaries to intervene in data transactions, get rid of single-point failures and single-point performance bottlenecks, and improve transparency and credibility. However, according to (Cao et al., 2016), due to the lack of centralized management in the decentralized data market, its system design and security assurance will be more difficult than the centralized data market. For example, the problem of "double payment" has always been the difficulty of distributed systems. In recent years, blockchain technology has matured, and the decentralized architecture of blockchain can be used as noted by (Subramanian, 2017) in regards to the underlying architecture of the data market to provide good support. Blockchain is a decentralized distributed data storage technology. The introduction of the blockchain layer according to (Mun et al., 2010) in the data market system will enable individual users to directly conclude transactions with data demanders without relying on any third party. This allows, as stated by (Ming Li et al., 2019) users to maintain ownership of the data and ensure the transparency of the transaction process.

MARKET AND RELATED RESEARCH

Research on Existing Data Trading Market

As data has the function of optimizing decision-making and providing services, various organizations and institutions have begun to pay attention to the circulation and transaction of data. For example, Datashift, Gnip, NTT Data and other companies resell data from social networks such as Twitter, Xignite sells data from the financial industry, Factual is concerned about the transaction of geographic data.

Simultaneously, Big-data sharing trading markets have also emerged to facilitate data trading by matching data needs with data sources, such as Infochimps, AWS Data exchange, Qlik Datamarket, Here, etc. Datacoup is a centralized data market platform that allows users to sell various types of personal data (including financial data and social account data), and its client application allows users to import data from third-party applications (such as Facebook and Twitter). Since Datacoup collects raw data from users, users must completely trust Datacoup in data storage and data management. Similar to Datacoup, People.io is a centralized platform whose biggest feature is that it does not sell personal data directly to other organizations. It uses machine learning algorithms to analyze the user's personal data and then push personalized ads to the user. Although users will not be directly rewarded for providing their personal data, they can earn revenue by receiving personalized advertisements.

The development of the domestic data market is not yet mature, and a complete industrial chain of data circulation and transactions has not yet been formed. For example, there are big data sharing platforms dominated by Internet companies, and most of their data comes from the data collected by their application software, such as Alibaba Cloud. There are also data sharing and transaction platforms such as Data Hall, Sudoku, etc. These platforms collect data from third parties in various ways to realize online transactions of big data resources. In addition, there are government-led big data trading centres, which are mostly government/state-owned enterprises or joint ventures between state-owned enterprises and private enterprises. However, these data trading centres are generally closed, and their specific data market architecture technology is still relatively unknown.

In recent years, the distributed data trading market based on blockchain has attracted great attention from the industry. IOTA is an encrypted "currency" designed specifically for the Internet of Things (IoT), and has used blockchain technology to build a transaction market for IoT data. Similar companies include DataBrokerDAO, Datum, Datapace and Wibson. Some of these companies directly sell their collected data sets, and some collect personal data from the public and sell them to individual users. There are also some examples of using blockchain technology to build data markets. For example, the Shanghai Data Exchange Center uses the alliance chain to store transaction-related information in blockchain nodes to ensure that data transactions are safe, efficient, and credible. Existing blockchain data markets only guarantee certain elements of data market construction, and do not fully consider the goals that should be achieved in constructing a data trading market: decentralization, fairness, privacy, effectiveness, and economic nature. Section 3, will discuss these properties in detail.

Related Research Work

There is also a lot of work in the research community involving blockchain, data markets and related issues. (Wang et al., 2019) discussed the significance of the emerging digital data market and listed research opportunities in this direction. The blockchain has been used to protect the privacy of personal data (Gupta et al., 2019), transforming the blockchain into an automatic access control manager that does not rely on trusted third parties, to clarify the ownership of data and ensure that users control their data, but this work only discusses the storage and sharing of data. In their paper, (Ramachandran et al., 2018) discussed the use of blockchain to share personal health data systems, enabling users to safely control and share their personal health data in a manner consistent with general data protection regulations. Their work focuses on data collection and storage, putting more emphasis on a method to control data quality. To study the issues of fairness, security and privacy in the process of using blockchain (Liu et al., 2019 & Zhou et al., 2018) investigate these issues as concerns to trade physical commodities. The

AdChain Registry as observed by (Wright et al., 2008), is an Ethereum-based advertising publisher's registry that provide recommended publishers for advertisers and a set of recommended data sources for specific data buyers. The main consideration of an effective protocol as put forward by (Sharifi et al., 2014) for fair exchange in smart contracts is to focuses on the realization of fairness of digital goods. A Blockchain-Enabled Decentralized Reliable Smart Industrial Internet of Things (BCIIoT) is designed to meet out Industrial Internet of Things (IIoT) by constructing a Smart Factory (Chandramohan & Shanmugam, et al., 2021).

There are many literature on the use of blockchain to build distributed data markets. The researchers (Christidis & Devetsikiotis, 2016) considered the characteristics of the Internet of Things, constructed a decentralized system, and analyzed its performance. The intention was to construct a market for real-time human perception data. However, these systems often do not consider the appropriate pricing mechanism as noted by (Yuan & Wang, 2016). The market still rely on a credible third party in some form, or just stay on the theoretical analysis, there is no complete system (Chanti et al., 2021). Hybrid authentication technique inevitability is taken into consideration (Chandramohan, et al., 2013b), to preserve user privacy and ensuring end point lock for cloud service digital information. The work on the centralized data market by Scott Stornetta. Focuses on the issue of pricing mechanism and has a more detailed design of the data collection, processing, and auction processes. To provide a personal data vault (Rahalkar & Gujar, 2019) proposes a mechanism that provides for managing data policies, allowing individual users to control access and share data at a fine-grained level. Research communities' targets on intelligence perception system built with blockchain (Schuster et al., 2015). The focus on the characteristics and processing methods of picture data in transactions is conducted by (Satoshi Nakamoto et al., 2019). A structured data with critical features is constructed with a blockchain-based data market and introduces a trusted intermediary in the transaction between buyers and sellers, although this makes transactions between buyers and sellers easier (Baumann et al., 2015), but it will also reduce the security of the system a lot. Although the transaction proposed by Buterin et al. still requires the intervention of a third party, it sets up multiple distributed intermediaries to participate in the transaction during the transaction, which limits the intermediary's monopoly ability. The innovation is that its data transmission and payments are carried out off-chain, which can save the expensive storage space of the blockchain. A design of automated pricing negotiation mechanism for the pricing problem in large and small scale industries could be manageable and improved with the blockchain-based data market. Distributed Data Vending (DDV) is a distributed data transaction framework that sells personal medical records. When a data seller wants to sell his medical records, he must upload his encrypted data to a cloud storage service provider and submit his data information to the blockchain smart contract. DDV Zhou et al. still uses third-party cloud storage services to store data from data sellers. Although data has been encrypted before uploading to cloud storage, data buyers and data sellers must still trust third-party cloud services to achieve data durability and data delivery.

Overview of Blockchain

The concept of blockchain was proposed by (W. Scott Stornetta et al., 1991), described a digital architecture system called "blockchain". In 2008, Satoshi Nakamoto proposed Bitcoin as a new type of "digital currency", and the blockchain technology behind it has also received extensive attention in many research fields.

In the blockchain network, all participants are essentially a group of writers who do not trust each other, and they share a data link without a trusted intermediary. In order to prevent the bifurcation phenomenon from erupting in this distributed environment, the blockchain has designed a consensus protocol. Blockchain nodes can provide computing resources as miners to compete for the power to record transactions in the blockchain, and the winners will receive economic incentives. This is a mechanism for blockchain to reach consensus, called Proof of Work (PoW).

Proof of Work makes it theoretically possible for an attacker to break the blockchain system only if he has mastered more than 50% of the computing power of the entire system. However, the consensus protocol has paid the price of consuming massive amounts of computing power and resources. In recent years, the annual global electricity consumption for Bitcoin "mining" has reached 0.13% of the total annual electricity consumption. Each full node must store all transactions to verify the legitimacy of these transactions on the blockchain. In addition, due to the block size limitation and the time interval for generating new blocks, Bitcoin can only process 7 transactions per second, which cannot meet the requirements of processing millions of transactions in real time.

The concept of Ethereum was proposed by (ButerinV et al., 2015), after being inspired by Bitcoin. Its biggest feature is the increased support for smart contracts. It will run a virtual machine in the user's Ethereum node. The smart contract running in it is written in Solidity. The language can support Turing completeness. In order to meet the needs of running in the virtual machine of the user client, the function of Solidity language is designed to be very weak. Solidity only implements a part of the JavaScript function in a special method, making smart contracts more error-prone in Ethereum.

In addition, all calculations related to status updates performed on the Ethereum network need to consume "natural gas" (gas, in Wei units, which is the smallest unit of Ether), which makes complex calculations on the Ethereum network cost-effective.

Blockchain technology provides a new direction for creating a decentralized data market and reducing the role of intermediaries in intervening between trading parties. Blockchain has some characteristics: First, it is decentralized. In a centralized system, each transaction needs to be verified by a central trusted institution, which inevitably increases the cost and performance bottleneck of the central server; second, its transparency with security, transactions can be quickly verified, and honest miners will not be able to recognize invalid transactions. Once a transaction is included in the blockchain, it is almost impossible to delete or roll back the transaction; The third is anonymity. Each user can use their address to interact with the blockchain. At present, many blockchain systems are committed to making the blockchain a completely anonymous system, such as the Monero coin.

Because of these characteristics, blockchain currently has a wide range of application prospects. Applications in different fields (such as IoT, intelligent transportation systems, naming and storage systems, and health record sharing, etc.) all have implementations based on blockchain technology. The underlying technology of the blockchain, the InterPlanetary File System (IPFS) is a content-addressable peer-to-peer hypermedia distribution protocol, which also has wide application value in a distributed system environment.

DESIGN GOALS OF BLOCKCHAIN DATA MARKET

In data transactions, the blockchain system replaces the status of a centralized data market, and buyers and sellers will directly conduct transactions on the execution of smart contracts in the blockchain. The design of the data market based on the blockchain system mainly considers the following questions.

Decentralization: Due to the disadvantages of the centralized data market, many studies have begun to discuss the establishment of a decentralized data transaction system that allows data holders and data demanders to conduct transactions directly through a secure and trusted distributed system. However, many existing related research and system design still rely on trusted third-party entities in some modules, and these third-party entities have the motivation and ability to benefit by disrupting the buyer-seller transaction. Therefore, for the decentralized data market, we believes that a system should be built that does not rely on any trusted third party and only involves data buyers and sellers. The transaction is directly reached by the buyer and the seller, and various security and privacy requirements are realized by the design of the distributed transaction system.

Fairness: Fairness means that the position of buyers and sellers in the entire transaction should be the same, they will reach a consensus on the transaction data and their prices, and they have the ability to stop the transaction at any time. The most basic fairness should be achieved at the end of the smart contract execution, either the buyer gets valid data, the seller gets the payment, or neither the buyer nor the seller get any revenue, it is necessary to prevent data sellers from providing illegal data, data buyers denying data purchase fees and other unfair situations.

Privacy: Privacy requires the system to protect the user's identity privacy and data privacy. Identity privacy is the anonymity of users in the data market. The anonymity of the Bitcoin blockchain is only a pseudonym, due to increasing and authorized agent to protect all users privacy irrespective of users. There are many blockchain systems dedicated to improving their anonymity. Data privacy means that the data can only be used by the user who purchased the data, and the attacker cannot obtain any additional information about the data from the information stored in the blockchain. In many scenarios, data consumers often purchase the right to use a piece of data. In such a system, data privacy requires that data buyers cannot obtain any additional information about the data after using it.

Effectiveness: For all practical systems that are widely implemented, to be able to implement effectively, it is necessary to ensure the participant's experience, which imposes requirements on the execution efficiency and resource consumption of the system. In the blockchain-based data market, it is necessary to consider whether the execution speed of the blockchain system itself can keep up with the needs of big data transactions. Due to the special mechanism of blockchain smart contracts, smart contracts should be avoided as much as possible for complex calculations.

Economic incentives: A major goal of the data market is to seek benefits for all users participating in the system to encourage them to participate in the big data sharing and trading system. The first is that both buyers and sellers will benefit from the transaction. Data sellers can get as much economic benefits as possible by selling their data usage rights, and data buyers can get high-quality data that meets their needs. At the same time, the transaction fee will inspire other participants to do a good job of maintaining the system platform. In the pricing game, some sellers and buyers may collude to capture the interests of other users. Therefore, while providing economic incentives, the data market also needs to ensure that illegal arbitrage and other illegal strategic actions do not occur.

SYSTEM ARCHITECTURE

The blockchain-based data market system designed in this chapter consists of the following three components: a smart contract in the Ethereum blockchain, a client held by system participants, and a peer-to-peer data transmission network. When a data buyer needs some specific data to calculate a specific task (such as the temperature sensor data near the location to calculate the local outdoor temperature), he will use the data filtering module and notify the smart contract. The entire system locates some qualified data through safe calculation. After the interaction between the data buyer and the data seller, the data pricing module determines the sold data and its price. After the payment is completed, the system runs the buyer's calculation task in a safe manner, and returns the result to the buyer. The transaction is completed. In the process of the transaction, the system needs to ensure the design goals mentioned above, and the modules of the system will be described in detail later.

Data Filtering

Data buyers usually do not need all the data of all users, but care about the specific data of specific users. For example, in a crowd sourcing task, a data buyer wants to know the outdoor temperature of a location, he can put forward a restriction: the location of the sensor provided by the seller needs to be within a certain range, and the data provided must also meet certain timeliness. This process is called data screening. Buyers can organize their data needs into a logical expression or a mathematical function and store it in the blockchain for sellers to query and judge.

The filtering conditions of these data are generally relatively simple, so it is not appropriate to upload the buyer's data filtering needs directly to the blockchain, which obviously exposes the privacy of buyers and sellers. According to the form of data filtering, an attacker can easily deduce the buyer's data needs, thereby obtaining the privacy of the buyer and seller. In the above example, if a location in which the buyer is interested is disclosed, the attacker may infer the range of activity of the buyer, and at the same time, the equipment held by the seller near the location is also exposed. Therefore, in order to protect the privacy of system participants, the target data should be screened out while hiding the data screening conditions. The most intuitive solution is function encryption, that is, the user (buyer) who has the decryption key can obtain the function value of the ciphertext data (data filtering function), but will not obtain any information about the plaintext.

In addition, it is sometimes not intuitive to translate buyers' data screening needs into mathematical and logical expressions. Data transactions sometimes also target some unstructured data, for example, buyers need some pictures of "cats". The buyer may be able to judge whether a piece of data is what he wants, but he cannot quantify these needs through simple and appropriate logic .In order to give a logical expression of buyers' screening needs, some complex data processing algorithms need to be run in the system to get the quality of the data and the degree of fit with the screening needs. Since every potential data needs to be calculated, these algorithms should be simplified as much as possible.

Data Storage

Data storage mechanism is a general term used to describe how to push data and where to store it. Mainstream public blockchain limits the number of transactions and the space blocks, which can be the size of the block (Bitcoin) or block consume "natural" upper limit (Ethernet Square). For the data trading market, it is not feasible to store massive amounts of data directly on the blockchain.

Both Quorum and Corda are inspired by the blockchain platform for the financial field. They propose a model that does not store data publicly on the blockchain. Among them, the data is kept off-chain by the participating third parties (financial institutions), and the consensus function aims to ensure that the interacting parties reach an agreement. This method may be practical for financial institutions, but it violates the design goals of decentralization.

Although it is impractical to store complete data in the blockchain, you can upload a "data summary" that is tied to specific data. Therefore, the generally proposed data market is aimed at non-real-time and fault-tolerant transaction modes. These systems can send data to the data backend in a long time interval. This method requires the assistance of the distributed file storage layer. InterPlanetary File System and Swarm are the two main distributed file storage layers. Both of these technologies are peer-to-peer (P2P) technologies with a distributed file transmission system in which files are addressed by the hash value of their content. When the data is successfully stored in IPFS, the user will receive a hash index, which will allow the user to retrieve the file later. This index will replace the data stored in the smart contract, saving the burden of the entire system. These distributed file systems are also open and transparent, and the data stored in them should be encrypted. At the same time, if all users participating in the system maintain an IPFS or Swarm node, the cost is very high, and some system participants can be used as a distributed file storage service provider to charge a certain fee to users who upload data.

Data Pricing

In the data market, a set of data in the form of the sale price and the design has been an active area of research. This chapter considers the design of the pricing mechanism in a game theory environment. Each data holder has a private valuation of their data, that is, the loss of the privacy of the data holder; the data buyer also has an estimate of the data he will purchase, that is, the value of this data to the buyer. Bidders may choose to dishonestly report their valuation of a piece of data. This will bring trouble to the mechanism design of the transaction. The solution in game theory is to design an incentive-compatible mechanism that allows each bidder to get the highest return when reporting its true valuation. Bidders report that their true valuation can make designing a pricing mechanism much easier.

Bundle pricing for multiple copies of related data is also a common problem in data market transactions. Early research usually simply assumed that for data buyers, the expected value of the bundled data is equal to the sum of the individual values of all data. Later research found that data affect each other, and the value of each piece of data depends on the content of the entire transaction data set. The value of the data set comes from the mutual relationship of the data.

Data as a commodity has some unique properties, which make data pricing complex and the need to consider some additional issues. First, the marginal cost of data is extremely low, or there is no marginal cost at all. Marginal cost refers to the cost of copying a commodity after it is produced. The marginal cost of data is basically zero so that once the data buyer obtains the data seller's data, then he can dispose of and sell the data at will. The second is that the value of data and the amount of data are not necessarily related. For example, for someone who needs some pictures of "cats", a bunch of pictures about "dogs" are almost worthless. The third is the quantification of data value. The value of data is difficult to quantify. It is difficult for data holders to estimate the value of data. At the same time, the valuation of different people is also very different.

In response to the characteristics of these data, the data trading model in the data market has also changed. Traditional data markets directly trade user data, and dishonest buyers can resell data sets that they have purchased without the seller's knowledge, thereby gaining benefits. Many works have found that the vast majority of data consumers only need some statistical results or advanced features behind large amounts of data, such as calculating the average of the data set, or training data for machine learning models, rather than the data itself. Therefore, the data market can collect data from data holders and then serve the computing tasks in the hands of data consumers. The buyer provides a specific task whose input is the one-time use right of the multiple pieces of data it purchases, and the output is the result the buyer wants. In this way, the data itself is isolated from the data consumer.

In the above design, the evaluation of the value of data actually becomes the evaluation of the accuracy of the buyer's calculation task or the value of the calculation result to the buyer's value. Although the value of the data itself is difficult to quantify, the improvement in task results is easy to quantify. Because buyers often need data from multiple sellers, it is necessary to distinguish the individual value of each piece of data in the transaction. To calculate the value of data, (Goldfeder & Bonneau et al., 2017), Shapley value can be used to calculate the contribution of a single piece of data. In game theory, calculating the Shapley value is a solution to distribute the benefits and costs fairly to multiple participants in the cooperation. The computational complexity of the Shapley value increases exponentially with the increase in the amount of data, so in practical use, approximate algorithms are often used.

Safe Computing

Blockchain is an open and transparent, decentralized data storage technology. All information entering the blockchain system is public, and the execution of all transactions or scripts is transparent. At the same time, the computing power of blockchain smart contracts is very weak. Due to the block size and limitations, the calculations that can be performed by calling a smart contract are few, but the cost is high. Therefore, no matter whether the task issued by the buyer is directly run in the smart contract (the smart contract can hardly bear such a burden), or delegated to an untrusted individual on the blockchain, it is still unsafe. Similarly, the data screening process and data pricing process also have such problems. Bitcoin, Ethereum and other blockchain public chain nodes have mutual distrust and are completely open and transparent, which has caused new problems in privacy protection.

The goal of this chapter is that in the entire data market system and the transaction process within the market system, the data market does not disclose any additional information about users and their data. There are many ways to perform calculations in the system safely and correctly, while protecting the privacy of all parties. The role of secure computing is to complete various computing tasks while protecting features such as privacy and fairness. Research in different fields can achieve goals in different degrees and angles.

Cryptography is the most intuitive way to achieve secure computing. Secure Multi-Party Computation-MPC (Missier & Bajoudah et al., 2017), is a subfield of cryptography and a direct solution to the problem of secure computing. The goal of MPC is to create a joint calculation method for all parties, while protecting the privacy of these inputs. Unlike traditional encryption methods, cryptography technology ensures the security and accuracy of communication or storage, and this mode of cryptography focuses on protecting the privacy between participants. MPC can now be seen as a practical solution to various real-world problems (especially those that only require simple linear shared secrets), such as distributed voting, private bidding and auctions, shared signature or decryption functions, private information retrieval, etc. Many simple tasks of buyers can be easily performed through MPC. However, the MPC method cannot be used for deep learning tasks. The core of the mainstream MPC framework uses 2 encryption technologies: encryption circuit and inadvertent transmission. MPC converts the buyer's task function into a garbled circuit, which is then sent out inadvertently. In complex and heavy calculation tasks, converting the deep neural network into a garbled circuit will inevitably increase the amount of calculation and lose certain accuracy. At the same time, in MPC, deep learning may lead to unacceptable communication complexity. In addition, homomorphic encryption and zero-knowledge proofs can also be used for simple tasks.

Another method for implementing secure computing is to use trusted hardware, such as a Trusted Execution Environment (TEE). TEE is a general concept, a safe area of the main processor, which guarantees that the codes and data loaded in it are protected in terms of confidentiality and integrity. Assuming that some users have some TEE hardware, these users are regarded as safe users. The seller will send their data to the secure user's TEE device, the buyer's calculation task will be calculated in the TEE, and the result will be returned to the buyer in a safe manner. Only trusted applications running in TEE can access all functions of the device's main processor, peripherals, and memory. Hardware isolation protects data and computing content from user-installed applications running on the main operating system. Typical hardware technologies that support TEE implementation are the Advanced Risc Machines (ARM) Trust Zone and Intel SGX Software Guard eXtensions. SGX is an extension of the Intel architecture and can protect the execution of application programs at the hardware level. For example, SGX can be used to protect buyer data in a cloud computing environment. Examples include VC3 and Haven. The core of SGX technology is to isolate a special area (called "enclave") in the memory, and the designated program can create a "safe area" in this area, and store the key code and data in the "safe area". Only the CPU or the program itself can access the code and data in the "enclave". These existing hardware technologies are claimed to have vulnerabilities. And some open source projects and large companies are also working to make TEE stronger.

Joint learning is a new (Aledhari & Razzak et al., 2020), collaborative machine learning method proposed by Google that does not require centralized training data. Its workflow is: the data seller downloads the current model from the cloud provided by the buyer, improves the model by learning from the seller's data, and then aggregates the changes into a small update. This update of the model is sent to the cloud using encrypted communication, and the updated model in the cloud is immediately aggregated with the updates of other users to improve the shared model. Therefore, all training data is only saved on the seller's device, and there is no separate update stored in the cloud. Joint learning is usually aimed at the situation where a user has multiple data or a data set, and is not applicable to a situation where a single seller only provides a small amount of data. If the seller provides only one piece of data to participate in the training, the malicious buyer may be able to reversely calculate the seller's real data from the model update, and the data training process requires frequent communication, which is very inefficient.

BCBDM SYSTEM IMPLEMENTATION AND VERIFICATION

According to the data market framework designed in Section 4, we implement a data market system based on the Ethereum private chain, including system participants holding desktop application clients, smart contracts in the Ethereum network, and data transmission networks. The desktop client is written in JavaScript, the Ethereum smart contract is written in Solidity, and the data transmission directly uses

Figure 2. BCBDM - System architecture and interaction between various components

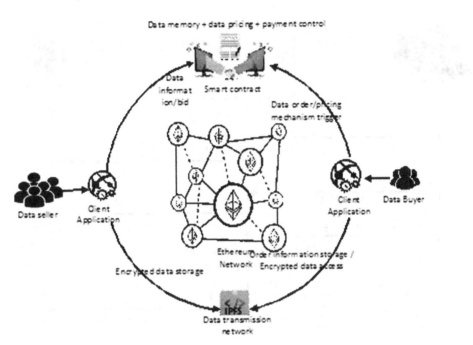

the IPFS JS interface. The system architecture designed and the interaction between various components are shown in Figure 2.

System Implementation Framework

This chapter has implemented a simplified version of the expected system to facilitate the verification and analysis of the correctness and feasibility of the system. It is a simplified system to a buyer and multiple potential sellers to conduct transactions, a buyer only needs one piece of data.

The pricing mechanism uses the second price auction, that is, the data of the transaction adopts the data of the lowest bid by the seller, and the data is paid at the price of the second lowest bid. The buyer's computing task is set to a simple form, and homomorphic encryption or secure multi-party computing can be used to ensure secure computing. We realized two kinds of specific data form transactions in the system, unstructured picture data and structured GPS travel data.

The transaction process of the data market is shown in Figure 3. The data seller adds a new piece of data information in the smart contract, the data buyer adds an order containing the data requirements, and the seller gives a quote after matching the legal data according to the conditions in the order. The system will run the pricing mechanism and calculate the winning data. This data will be used to calculate the buyer's tasks in a secure manner and deliver the data. In the system, the user can perform the following operations.

Register an account. To buy and sell data in the data market, users must first register an Ethereum account, and the client also includes a simple Ethereum account management function. At the same time, the user also needs to register an account in a smart contract hereinafter referred to as Bigdata Data

Figure 3. BCBDM Data market transaction process

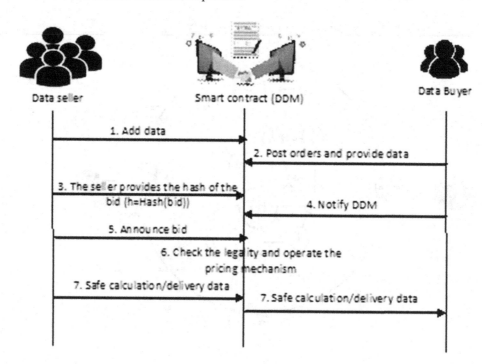

Market (DDM). For example, the user can register an account of a sensor device in the smart contract, which needs to disclose information such as the type and model of the sensor device.

Add data. After generating some data that he wants to sell, the data holder can upload the data to IPFS encrypted, and register this data in the smart contract account, it contains the storage address of the data, the hash value of the data and the registration time. In the BCBDM system design, data buyers are encouraged to set data registration time requirements when adding data orders to purchase data, only data holders who meet the data registration time requirements are eligible to bid for the order to improve the timeliness and reliability of the data.

Release orders. If the data buyer wants to purchase the right to use specific data in the market, then he will add an order in DDM, the order contains the buyer's demand for data (including data type, data selection function, data price limit, data quantity limitation, etc.) and the calculation task of buyers using data.

The data seller provides the hash value of its bid. The data seller selects one or more data that meets the needs of the data buyer, and sets a package price. Due to the completely open and transparent nature of the blockchain, bidding directly in DDM will lead to arbitrage, and sellers of the post-quote can see the bids of other sellers and obtain higher profits by controlling their own bids. We have set a time window in the system, and the seller needs to submit the hash value of his bid within the window, which is equivalent to realizing a sealed auction. At the same time, such a design helps to achieve fairness.

The data buyer informs DDM to obtain the real bid of the market data seller. The data buyer informs DDM to stop accepting users to participate in the transaction and to start accepting users who have already participated in the transaction to disclose their bids. Smart contracts cannot actively execute orders, and need to be triggered by blockchain users. At the same time, data buyers can blacklist some sellers and refuse their bids.

Data sellers publish real bids. The data seller publishes its bid, which needs to match the previous hash value. If the data seller does not announce the real bid within the specified time, indicating that the seller is regrets, the system will reduce the reputation value of the seller as a punishment, and the reputation value of the seller who successfully trades the data will increase. Users with too low reputation value will not be able to participate in the transaction, and the reputation value system can suppress cheating by system participants.

Pricing mechanism, use the classic (Clarke & Groves et al., 2017), Vickrey–Clarke–Groves (VCG) auction mechanism for data selection and price determination. The VCG auction mechanism guarantees authenticity, so each bidder has an incentive to make a real valuation of his personal data.

Safe calculation/delivery data. The system uses homomorphic encryption to calculate the buyer's calculation tasks, and then hands the encrypted result to the data buyer to complete the order. Since secure computing is still at an immature stage, the computational complexity of homomorphic encryption is very high. We have only tested the calculation task of using the additive homomorphic algorithm to calculate buyers. In the future, we will support the other methods according to the secure computing method in Section 4. Data buyers and sellers can also directly trade data, using a hybrid encryption method to encrypt the symmetric key of the data with the public key provided by the buyer. This method can achieve non-communication data transmission in an open and transparent environment.

System Analysis and Verification

We discusse the advantages of the demo system achieved from the design goals of building a blockchain based data market, including fairness, privacy and effectiveness, and also consider the scalability of the system. We found that the system has basically achieved the design goals defined by the blockchain data market, the entire system runs smoothly, the usability is high, and the security and privacy are well guaranteed.

Fairness

Before the transaction result is reached, that is, before the pricing mechanism starts, both parties to the transaction can terminate the transaction. Although this may lead to a reduction in the reputation value of the participants, in the case of "regret" infrequently occurring, the transaction can be terminated at any time. At the same time, after the implementation of the pricing mechanism, due to the characteristics of blockchain and secure computing, neither party to the transaction can prevent the transaction from proceeding. Ethereum transfer and buyer task calculation will be executed, which ensures the non-repudiation of data transactions and guarantees fair transactions.

Privacy

We protect the identity privacy and data privacy of system participants in the system. Identity privacy is achieved based on the anonymous capabilities of the blockchain, while data privacy is fully protected. Data encryption, data selection mechanisms, and security calculations prevent attackers from obtaining any additional information about the data from the execution of transactions. However, the system implemented did not consider exposing the privacy of the seller's pricing of their data. In future work, the privacy of bidding will be considered.

Effectiveness

The operational efficiency of the blockchain has always been criticized. It takes more than ten minutes for a transaction in Bitcoin to be written into the blockchain and the time that this transaction was finally confirmed on the Internet even exceeded one hour. Calculating the data selection function in the client, calculating the buyer's tasks and processing the pictures in a secure manner are relatively time-consuming, which will reduce the user's experience satisfaction with the application. The random click test of the application found that from the perspective of the client user, the average response time of a button is about 4 s, this shows that the current design of the system is not yet able to achieve real-time performance, but it can guarantee the basic use requirements. The system proposed is directly based on Ethereum. To improve the availability of the data market system, a more efficient and lightweight blockchain system can be used.

Table 1. Gas consumption for various operations in the system

Operation	Gas consumption/Wei
Register an account in a smart contract	110 726
Saving money in smart contracts	27 638
Withdrawing money from smart contracts	35 753
Add an image data order	2 228 844
Add an itinerary data order	715 103
Submit bid to order	29 145
Transfer to other accounts	21 000
Add a trip picture data	193 852
Computational pricing mechanism	459 230
Average	424 587

Deploying contracts or any type of transaction in the Ethereum blockchain will incur transaction fees. In the Ethereum blockchain, gas is used to estimate costs. Usually, the mining union in the system determines the price for running some instructions, and the initiator of a transaction (such as a data buyer is adding an order to the blockchain and a data seller submitting a bid to the blockchain) needs to specify the maximum gas consumption. Because miners like to deal with transactions that provide high incentives, transactions with lower gas prices can take a long time. However, because the value of personal data is very low, complex calculations in smart contracts will cause the profits of buyers and sellers to decrease linearly. The system proposed guarantees the interests of system participants by reducing the amount of calculation of smart contracts.

Through several tests, we got the average value of gas consumption for various operations in the system (see Table 1). Based on the current price of Ethereum on the Ethereum public chain (each Ethereum price is about US$250), the average consumption of each operation is 424587×10^{10} USD, even if a data buyer needs tens of thousands of data, he needs very little to participate in the system.

Table 2. Gas consumption under different array lengths

Array length/dimension	Gas consumption/Wei
50	1466256
100	2228844
125	2542012
150	2885446
175	3243954
200	3632920
225	3991512

There may be a lot of transaction-related information stored in the smart contract. Although the smart contract of Ethereum supports multiple complex data types, the slightly complicated structure in practice will cause the request to be invalid. For example, because the length of the array to be uploaded is very long, and each item is also a very complicated decimal, the 1,024-dimensional array cannot be successfully uploaded to the smart contract at all. Ethereum also has a block gas limit, which is set to 8,000,000 Wei by default, so in fact it is not possible to upload data with too high dimensions (see Table 2). Due to Ethereum's restrictions on the amount of gas in the block, Ethereum is set to a maximum of 8,000,000 Wei by default. If an operation consumes more gas than this value, the operation will be rolled back. Therefore, there is a possibility that the order will be returned in the DDM. The system proposed stores complex data structures (such as data selection functions) in IPFS, and then puts its address in the order and stores it in DDM.

Since data pricing is performed on the Ethereum blockchain through smart contracts, its computational cost cannot be ignored. In order to evaluate the data pricing cost of the system, the gas consumption based on the VCG auction-based data pricing was used to test a large number of sellers' bids. Figure 4 shows the relationship between the gas consumption of VCG data pricing and the number of bids received for data orders. Although the implementation of the data pricing algorithm can be further optimized, when

Figure 4. The relationship between gas consumption of data pricing and the number of bids received by the order

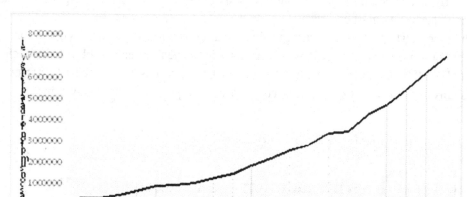

a large number of data sellers bid for the same data order, the data pricing cost will be very high. If the data market based on the Ethereum blockchain is to be realized, the high cost of data pricing will become a major obstacle to the application of the system.

Decentralization and Scalability

Scalability, decentralization and security are the three difficulties aspects which is need to be referred for the inevitable contradictions of the blockchain system. The system is a completely decentralized system and does not depend on any trusted third parties, so scalability and security will be challenged more. In order to ensure security, the system proposed sacrifices scalability, if a support for different data forms, data selling methods and pricing mechanisms is required, then smart contracts need to be rewritten, and compatibility will also have problems, which can be taken into consideration in the construction of the actual data market. In the future deployment of the data market, we will further discuss the trade-offs between scalability, decentralization, and security.

CONCLUSION

Data is an important asset in a data-driven economy, and it has driven the rise of new data trading industries. The data market is an important form of data assetization today. The distributed data market has the privacy protection capabilities and transaction security guarantees that the centralized data market does not have, and has huge market prospects and research prospects. In this chapter, we discuss the characteristics that the future data market should meet, analyze the challenges in the distributed data market based on blockchain, propose preliminary solutions, and discuss the possible future development directions of these technologies. The construction of the actual data market provides reference opinions. Both the data market and the blockchain technology are in the stage of rapid technological development, and researchers need to conduct more in-depth exploration and research based on these issues.

REFERENCES

Balazinska, M., Howe, B., & Suciu, D. (2011). Data markets in the cloud. *Proceedings of the VLDB Endowment International Conference on Very Large Data Bases, 4*(12), 1482–1485. doi:10.14778/3402755.3402801

Baumann, A., Peinado, M., & Hunt, G. (2015). Shielding applications from an untrusted cloud with haven. *ACM Transactions on Computer Systems, 33*(3), 1–26. doi:10.1145/2799647

Cao, T., Pham, T., Vu, Q., Truong, H., Le, D., & Dustdar, S. (2016). Marsa. *ACM Transactions on Internet Technology, 16*(3), 1–21. doi:10.1145/2883611

Chandramohan, Shanmugam, Shailesh, Khapre, Shukla, & Achyut. (2021). Blockchain-Enabled Decentralized Reliable Smart Industrial Internet of Things (BCIIoT). *Innovation in the Industrial Internet of Things (IIoT) and Smart Factory*, 192-204. doi:10.4018/978-1-7998-3375-8.ch013

Chandramohan, D., Vengattaraman, T., Rajaguru, D., Baskaran, R., & Dhavachelvan, P. (2013b). Hybrid Authentication Technique to Preserve User Privacy and Protection as an End Point Lock for the Cloud Service Digital Information. In *International Conference on Green High Performance Computing* (pp. 1-4). Nagercoil, Tamilnadu: IEEE. 10.1109/ICGHPC.2013.6533904

Chanti S., Anwar, T., Chithralekha T., & Uma, V. (2021). Global naming and storage system using blockchain. *Research Anthology on Combating Denial-of-Service Attacks*, 265-281. doi:10.4018/978-1-7998-5348-0.ch014

Christidis, K., & Devetsikiotis, M. (2016). Blockchains and smart contracts for the Internet of things. *IEEE Access: Practical Innovations, Open Solutions, 4*, 2292–2303. doi:10.1109/ACCESS.2016.2566339

Dziembowski, S., Eckey, L., & Faust, S. (2018). FairSwap. *Proceedings of the 2018 ACM SIGSAC Conference on Computer and Communications Security*. 10.1145/3243734.3243857

Goldfeder, S., Bonneau, J., Gennaro, R., & Narayanan, A. (2017). Escrow protocols for cryptocurrencies: How to buy physical goods using bitcoin. *Financial Cryptography and Data Security*, 321-339. doi:10.1007/978-3-319-70972-7_18

Gupta, P., Kanhere, S., & Jurdak, R. (2019). A Decentralized IoT Data Marketplace. *Networking and Internet Architecture, 6*(7), 1-6. arXiv:1906.01799

Li, M., Weng, J., Yang, A., Lu, W., Zhang, Y., Hou, L., Liu, J.-N., Xiang, Y., & De Robert, H. (2019). CrowdBC: A Blockchain-Based Decentralized Framework for Crowdsourcing. *IEEE Transactions on Parallel and Distributed Systems, 30*(6), 1251–1266. doi:10.1109/TPDS.2018.2881735

Liu, K., Qiu, X., Chen, W., Chen, X., & Zheng, Z. (2019). Optimal pricing mechanism for data market in blockchain-enhanced Internet of things. *IEEE Internet of Things Journal, 6*(6), 9748–9761. doi:10.1109/JIOT.2019.2931370

Missier, P., Bajoudah, S., Capossele, A., Gaglione, A., & Nati, M. (2017). Mind my value. *Proceedings of the Seventh International Conference on the Internet of Things*. 10.1145/3131542.3131564

Mun, M., Hao, S., Mishra, N., Shilton, K., Burke, J., Estrin, D., Hansen, M., & Govindan, R. (2010). Personal data vaults. *Proceedings of the 6th International Conference on - Co-NEXT '10*. 10.1145/1921168.1921191

Pang, J. Z., Fu, H., Lee, W. I., & Wierman, A. (2017). The efficiency of open access in platforms for networked cournot markets. *IEEE INFOCOM 2017 - IEEE Conference on Computer Communications*. doi:10.1109/infocom.2017.8057125

Rahalkar, C., & Gujar, D. (2019). Content addressed P2P file system for the web with blockchain-based meta-data integrity. *2019 International Conference on Advances in Computing, Communication and Control (ICAC3)*. doi:10.1109/icac347590.2019.9036792

Ramachandran, G. S., Radhakrishnan, R., & Krishnamachari, B. (2018). Towards a decentralized data marketplace for smart cities. *2018 IEEE International Smart Cities Conference (ISC2)*. doi:10.1109/isc2.2018.8656952

Schuster, F., Costa, M., Fournet, C., Gkantsidis, C., Peinado, M., Mainar-Ruiz, G., & Russinovich, M. (2015). VC3: Trustworthy data analytics in the cloud using SGX. *2015 IEEE Symposium on Security and Privacy*. doi:10.1109p.2015.10

Sharifi, L., Freitag, F., & Veiga, L. (2014). Combing smart grid with community clouds: Next generation integrated service platform. *2014 IEEE International Conference on Smart Grid Communications (SmartGridComm)*. doi:10.1109martgridcomm.2014.7007685

Subramanian, H. (2017). Decentralized blockchain-based electronic marketplaces. *Communications of the ACM*, *61*(1), 78–84. https://doi.org/10.1145/3158333

Wang, Y. L., & Krishnamachari, B. (2019). Enhancing engagement in token-curated registries via an inflationary mechanism. *2019 IEEE International Conference on Blockchain and Cryptocurrency (ICBC)*. doi:10.1109/bloc.2019.8751443

Wang, Z., Yang, L., Wang, Q., Liu, D., Xu, Z., & Liu, S. (2019). ArtChain: Blockchain-enabled platform for art marketplace. *2019 IEEE International Conference on Blockchain (Blockchain)*. doi:10.1109/blockchain.2019.00068

Wright, C. S. (2008). *Bitcoin: A peer-to-peer electronic cash system*. SSRN Electronic Journal. doi:10.2139srn.3440802

Yuan, Y., & Wang, F. (2016). Towards blockchain-based intelligent transportation systems. *2016 IEEE 19th International Conference on Intelligent Transportation Systems (ITSC)*. doi:10.1109/itsc.2016.7795984

Zheng, X., Mukkamala, R. R., Vatrapu, R., & Ordieres-Mere, J. (2018). Blockchain-based personal health data sharing system using cloud storage. *2018 IEEE 20th International Conference on e-Health Networking, Applications and Services (Healthcom)*. doi:10.1109/healthcom.2018.8531125

Zhou, J., Tang, F., Zhu, H., Nan, N., & Zhou, Z. (2018). Distributed data vending on blockchain. 2018 IEEE International Conference on Internet of Things (iThings) and IEEE Green Computing and Communications (GreenCom) and IEEE Cyber, Physical and Social Computing (CPSCom) and IEEE Smart Data (SmartData). doi:10.1109/cybermatics_2018.2018.00201

Zyskind, G., Nathan, O., & Pentland, A. (2015). Decentralizing privacy: Using blockchain to protect personal data. *2015 IEEE Security and Privacy Workshops.* doi:10.1109pw.2015.27

Chapter 13
A Study on Self–Regulating Traffic Light Control Using RFID and Machine Learning Algorithm

Dhivya P.

Bannari Amman Institute of Technology, India

ABSTRACT

Traffic control light frameworks are generally used to control and screen the stream of cars through the intersection of numerous streets. As the quantity of street clients always increments and assets gave are constrained, savvy activity flag controller is an exceptionally real prerequisite. One disadvantage of customary methodologies for movement administration is that they don't consider the distinctive valuations of holding up time lessening of the drivers. This chapter proposed another component for versatile activity control utilizing machine learning. In the proposed framework, the authors are utilizing picture sensor in the LED publication which catches the pictures of streets in every one of the bearings and returns the number of head checks of the vehicles to a machine learning calculation. The machine learning calculation is intended to take in the rush hour gridlock thickness without anyone else with first caught picture and consider reference. In this manner, the proposed activity control framework will be an exceptional technique for self-learning and security improving.

INTRODUCTION

Street Traffic control is a testing work and thought to be a perilous occupation because of the high danger of passing vehicles. Security gear is most extreme imperative. Weariness is a major issue, as worn out Controllers' may neglect to watch their activity, or may coincidentally turn their "Stop bats" to the "Moderate" position. Numerous drivers are irritated by the disturbance to their course, and some are adequately reserved and don't give careful consideration to the street, frequently from utilizing their cell phones, or in light of the fact that coming back from night move work.

DOI: 10.4018/978-1-7998-6673-2.ch013

The requirement for productive movement administration is winding up increasingly vital. The requirement for a protected living condition, enhanced movement stream and answers for stopping issues is expanding, just like the need to deal with all robotized activity objects from one focal framework. The framework gives us the correct information and data to empower ideal activity administration.

Activity signals are indispensable to helping vehicles and walkers securely travel. They increment the proficiency and request of movement to diminish the quantity of mischance. They give clear rules in regards to when autos or people on foot can enter a crossing point or when they should stop and pause. Notwithstanding their numerous advantages, movement signals accompany drawbacks. These incorporate an expansion in mischance, delays and forceful driving.

The present arrangement of movement light have been gives a settled activity control design, which settings depend on earlier activity checks yet might be physically changed. It is the most widely recognized type of flag control for the time being a days and result in unseemly conduct in rush hour gridlock which varies from that which the arrangement was based, for example, the utilization of pointless stages when the movement is light.

The roads turned parking lots are the basic issue in the vast majority of the city on the planet. The one of the fundamental driver of this issue is mishap (Melo et al., 2006). To discover the best approach to augment the movement stream easily can diminish the quantities of the mishap and can lessen the general population time in street. The administration has done a couple of tenets to beat this issue. Alongside take the discipline to all the activity guilty parties, the movement lights have been made at the area that high hazard in mischance.

One downside of conventional methodologies for activity administration is that they don't consider the diverse valuations of holding up time decrease of the drivers (Rafael et al, 1992). These valuations can contrast from driver to driver, e.g., drivers who are late for their prospective employee meet-up have a higher valuation of decreased holding up time than people driving home from work routinely. This likewise applies to trucks with dire load.

To conquer this issue, we propose another system for versatile activity control utilizing machine learning procedure. In the proposed framework we will apply the picture preparing procedure to catch the pictures of the paths and utilize Machine Learning Algorithm for consequently learn and control the signs there by modifying the holding up time and diminish the blockage in streets. Also, to screen the Vehicle robbery, Illegal stopping and crisis vehicles can be recognized and essential moves can be made by utilizing RFID in vehicles.

BACKGROUND

Smart Traffic Light Control System

In this paper the creator expresses the significance of Traffic light control frameworks and examines around couple of issues that happens in the convergence of streets. To beat the issues, the creator proposes a framework in light of PIC microcontroller that assesses the activity thickness utilizing IR sensors and achieves dynamic planning openings with various levels. Also, a convenient controller gadget is intended to take care of the issue of crisis vehicles stuck in the packed streets (Salama, 2010).

Design of Intelligent Traffic Light Controller Using Embedded System

The disadvantages of Present Traffic Light Controllers (TLC) which depend on microcontroller and chip is talked about. It has been expressed that TLC have constraints in view of its pre-characterized equipment, which capacities as per the program that does not have the adaptability of alteration on continuous premise. Because of the settled time interims of green, orange and red flags the holding up time is progressively and auto utilizes more fuel. To make activity light controlling more proficient, development of new strategy called as "Shrewd movement light controller" is misused. This makes the utilization of Sensor Networks alongside Embedded Technology. The timings of Red, Green lights at each intersection of street will be cleverly chosen in view of the aggregate activity on every single neighboring street. Along these lines, advancement of movement light exchanging expands street limit and activity stream, and can avert movement blockages. GSM PDA interface is likewise accommodated clients the individuals who wish to get the most recent position of movement on congested streets. The different execution assessment criteria are normal holding up time, normal separation gone by vehicles, exchanging recurrence of green light at an intersection, proficient crisis mode task and agreeable activity of SMS utilizing GSM Mobile. The execution of the Intelligent Traffic Light Controller was contrasted and the Fixed Mode Traffic Light Controller. It is watched that the proposed Intelligent Traffic Light Controller is more effective than the regular controller in regard of less holding up time, more separation gone by normal vehicles and productive task amid crisis mode and GSM interface. Besides, it has been expressed that the planned framework has straightforward engineering, quick reaction time, ease of use and degree for encourage extension (Salama, 2010).

Design of Intelligent Traffic Light Control System Based on Traffic Flow

The article advances a plan of smart activity control framework in view of movement stream, and proposes the crossing point video picture handling and movement stream identification calculation. Use of DSP innovation, plan the framework equipment, compose the relating programming, and understand the wise control of movement light at the crossing point as per activity stream, enhancing the convergence vehicle limit of section (Jadhav et al, 2016).

Intelligent Traffic Light Control

The proposed thought of setting a movement light in this paper is as per the following. Assume there are various autos with their goal address remaining before an intersection. All autos impart to the activity light their particular place in the line and their goal address. Presently the movement light needs to choose which alternative (ie, which paths are to be put on green) is ideal to limit the long haul normal holding up time until the point that all autos have touched base at their goal address. The learning movement light controllers take care of this issue by evaluating to what extent it would take for an auto to touch base at its goal address (for which the auto may need to pass a wide range of activity lights) when right now the light would be put on green, and to what extent it would take if the light would be put on red. The distinction between the sitting tight time for red and the sitting tight time for green is the pick up for the auto. Presently the activity light controllers set the lights in such an approach to boost the normal pick up of all autos remaining before the intersection. To assess the holding up times, the creator utilizes 'fortification realizing' which monitors the holding up times of individual autos and utilizations a shrewd method to process the long haul normal holding up times utilizing dynamic programming calculation (Melo et al, 2006).

Intelligent Traffic Signal Control System

An Adaptive activity flag control framework introduces a wise movement flag control framework utilizing picture handling system. With the assistance of specific calculation, morphology and picture expected to dodge movement blockage. In this system, the vehicles are identified, perceived and thickness is aligned for controlling movement thickness. This is the most dependable and forthcoming innovation in the street travel framework (Salvi et al, n.d.).

Density Based Traffic Signal System

The proposed framework utilizing a microcontroller of 8051 family appropriately interfaced with sensors, changes the intersection timing consequently to oblige development of vehicles easily maintaining a strategic distance from pointless holding up time at the intersection. The sensors utilized as a part of this task are IR and photodiodes are in observable pathway setup over the heaps to identify the thickness at the activity flag. The thickness of the vehicles is estimated in three zones i.e., low, medium, high in view of which timings are allocated likewise. Advance the venture can be upgraded by synchronizing all the movement intersections in the city by setting up a system among them. The system can be wired or remote. This synchronization will significantly help in lessening movement clog (8. VismayPandit et al, 2014).

Automatic Traffic Signal Controller for Roads by Exploiting Fuzzy Logic

In this paper the creator demonstrates the significance of insightful activity flag controller as the quantity of street clients always increments and assets gave constrained. Therefore the need emerges for mimicking and advancing movement control calculations to more readily suit this expanding request. Be that as it may, a few restrictions to the use of astute activity control exist. Evading car influxes for instance is helpful to both condition and economy like a diminishing in every one of postponement, number of stops, fuel utilization, toxin outflows, and so forth. yet enhanced movement stream may likewise prompt an expansion sought after Optimization of activity light exchanging expands street limit and movement stream, and can anticipate activity blockages. The fluffy controllers will routinely inquiry the movement conditions so as to choose whether to expand or end a present stage. The work demonstrates that supplanting the regular movement control framework by fluffy based activity control framework can impressively diminish movement clog delay (Kirushnacumar et al, 2016).

Adaptive Traffic Signal Control

Profound Reinforcement Learning Algorithm with Experience Replay and Target Network: Adaptive movement flag control, which modifies activity flag timing as per ongoing movement, has been appeared to be a compelling technique to decrease activity blockage. Accessible takes a shot at versatile activity flag control settle on responsive movement flag control choices in light of human-created highlights (e.g. vehicle line length). Be that as it may, human-made highlights are deliberations of crude activity information (e.g. position and speed of vehicles), which disregard some helpful movement data and prompt imperfect activity flag controls. In this paper, a profound fortification learning calculation is recommended that consequently removes every single valuable element (machine-made highlights) from crude ongoing activity information and takes in the ideal approach for versatile movement flag control. To enhance calculation steadiness, encounter replay and target organize systems have been adjusted. Recreation results demonstrate that this calculation decreases vehicle delay by up to 47% and 86% when contrasted with another two prominent activity flag control calculations, longest line first calculation and settled time control calculation, separately (Chavan, 2009).

Traffic Control Using Machine Learning

This work includes in putting a RFID tag in every single vehicle; this sends an extraordinary number and this novel number is connected to the vehicle subtle elements, protection points of interest and driving permit; and when so ever the vehicle approaches the movement flag, the RFID tag sends the one of a kind number to the beneficiary lastly the measure of exceptional numbers we get gives the quantity of vehicles out and about. With this number we are estimating the activity thickness and decide the sitting tight time for the movement flag. The unlawful stopping of the vehicles close to the flag can be found if a similar extraordinary number from RFID tag is acquired for in excess of three rounds of cycles. On the off chance that such a situation happens, at that point that vehicle must be stationary and it is educated to the closest activity police. On the off chance that there is any crisis vehicle crossing the activity flag it can be identified with its one of a kind number and enabled at that point to go through the flag immediately. Vehicle robbery can likewise be diminished since the special number is connected with the vehicle information. The quantity of vehicles can be thought about in any two paths in light of the fact that the time at which the path is red isn't one of a kind for any two paths. So the creator utilized machine learning with straight recursion procedure with a reasonable calculation (Zhao et al, 2012).

MAIN FOCUS OF THE CHAPTER

In the proposed framework we are setting a picture sensor in the LED notice which catches the pictures of streets in every one of the bearings at the same time. The pictures will be prepared and the quantity of head checks of the vehicles will be sent to a machine learning calculation. Thus a RFID tag can be put in every last vehicle which sends a one of a kind number connected to the vehicle points of interest, protection subtle elements and driving permit; and when so ever the vehicle approaches the activity flag, the RFID tag sends the extraordinary number to the beneficiary which distinguishes the quantity of vehicles in every path. The figure1 explains the working of taffic light system using RFID and machine learning algorithm.

The head check from picture sensors and no of vehicles tally from RF Reader will be coordinated and the tally will be sent to machine learning Algorithm. The machine learning calculation is intended to take in the rush hour gridlock thickness independent from anyone else with first caught pictures as reference. The holding up time of the movement flag will be balanced naturally as indicated by the activity thickness in the separate paths in this way diminishing the movement blockage. Likewise. The unlawful stopping of the vehicles close to the flag can be found if a similar interesting number from RFID tag is acquired for in excess of three rounds of cycles. On the off chance that such a situation happens, at that point that vehicle must be stationary and it is educated to the closest activity police. On the off chance that there is any crisis vehicle crossing the movement flag it can be identified with its one of a kind number and enabled at that point to go through the flag immediately. We can likewise diminish vehicle robbery since the interesting number is connected with the vehicle information. Along these lines the proposed activity control framework will be a one of a kind strategy for self-learning and security upgrading.

FUTURE RESEARCH DIRECTIONS

The future of this work is the implementation of self regulating smart traffic system using RFID and machine learning algorithm.

CONCLUSION

Despite the fact that there are numerous developments emerging everyday for controlling the activity motion for giving smooth travel less blockage out and about, numerous calculations neglect to consider the distinctive valuations of holding up time diminishment of the drivers. To defeat this issue, another instrument for versatile activity control utilizing machine learning system is proposed in this paper. The proposed method guarantees to offer need to crisis vehicles, recognizes the illicitly stopped vehicles and controls the movement stream by estimating the activity thickness in every one of the paths. Since the two pictures and RFID information is utilized together to discover the activity thickness the uncertainty in deciding the quantity of vehicles will be lessened all things considered.

REFERENCES

Jadhav, Kelkar, Patil, & Thorat. (2016). Smart Traffic Control System Using Image Processing. *International Research Journal of Engineering and Technology, 3*(3).

Kirushnacumar, A., Arun, M., Kirubanand, A., Mukesh, S., & Sivakumar, A. (2016). Smart Traffic Control System. *International Journal for Research in Applied Science & Engineering Technology, 4*(4).

Melo, J., Naftel, A., Bernardino, A., & Santos-Victor, J. (2006). Detection and classification of highway lanes using vehicle motion trajectories. *IEEE Transactions on Intelligent Transportation Systems, 7*(2), 188–200. doi:10.1109/TITS.2006.874706

Pandit, Doshi, Mehta, Mhatre, & Janardhan. (2014). Smart Traffic Control System Using Image Processing. *International Journal of Emerging Trends & Technology in Computer Science*.

Salama, A. S., Saleh, B. K., & Eassa, M. M. (2010). Intelligent Cross Road Traffic Management System (ICRTMS). *Int.Conf on Computer Technology and Development*, 27-31. 10.1109/ICCTD.2010.5646059

Salvi, G. (n.d.). *An Automated Vehicle Counting System Based on Blob Analysis for Traffic Surveillance.* Department of Economics Studies, University of Naples "Parthenope", Naples, Italy.

Shilpa, S., Chavan, R. S., Deshpande, J. G., & Rana. (2009). Design of Intelligent Traffic Light Controller Using Embedded System. *Emerging Trends in Engineering and Technology (ICETET)*.

Zhao, D., Dai, Y., & Zhang, Z. (2012). Computational intelligence in urban traffic signal control: A survey. *IEEE Transactions on Systems, Man and Cybernetics. Part C, Applications and Reviews*, *42*(4), 485–494. doi:10.1109/TSMCC.2011.2161577

ADDITIONAL READING

Salama, A. S., Saleh, B. K., & Eassa, M. M. (2010), Intelligent Cross Road Traffic Management System (ICRTMS), *2nd International Conference on Computer Technology and Development*, pp27- 31. 10.1109/ICCTD.2010.5646059

Wu, H., & Miao, C. (2010). *Design of intelligent traffic light control system based on traffic flow, Computer and Communication Technologies in Agriculture Engineering*. CCTAE.

Zaidi, A. A., Kulcsr, B., & Wymeersch, H. (2016). Back-pressure traffic signal control with fixed and adaptive routing for urban vehicular networks. *IEEE Transactions on Intelligent Transportation Systems*, *17*(8), 2134–2143. doi:10.1109/TITS.2016.2521424

KEY TERMS AND DEFINITIONS

GSM PDA Interface: A Global System for Mobile Communication uses the interface for communication using Personal Digital Assistant elements.

LED Light: Electric light gives light using Light Emitting Diode.

Machine Learning Algorithm: Machine will think like human to identify the possible outcomes using various algorithms.

RF Reader: Used in Radio Frequency Identification to transmit the data in wireless communication.

RFID Tag: It is used to track the items using smart barcodes.

Smart Traffic System: It uses the advanced technology to control and monitor the traffic.

TLC: Traffic Light Controllers are used to monitor and control the vehicles on the road.

Traffic Light: It uses stop, wait, and go lights to control the traffic on road.

Chapter 14
Application of Machine Learning in Chronic Kidney Disease Risk Prediction Using Electronic Health Records (EHR)

Laxmi Kumari Pathak

Amity University, Ranchi, India

Pooja Jha

Amity University, Ranchi, India

ABSTRACT

Chronic kidney disease (CKD) is a disorder in which the kidneys are weakened and become unable to filter blood. It lowers the human ability to remain healthy. The field of biosciences has progressed and produced vast volumes of knowledge from electronic health records. Heart disorders, anemia, bone diseases, elevated potassium, and calcium are the very prevalent complications that arise from kidney failure. Early identification of CKD can improve the quality of life greatly. To achieve this, various machine learning techniques have been introduced so far that use the data in electronic health record (EHR) to predict CKD. This chapter studies various machine learning algorithms like support vector machine, random forest, probabilistic neural network, Apriori, ZeroR, OneR, naive Bayes, J48, IBk (k-nearest neighbor), ensemble method, etc. and compares their accuracy. The study aims in finding the best-suited technique from different methods of machine learning for the early detection of CKD by which medical professionals can interpret model predictions easily.

DOI: 10.4018/978-1-7998-6673-2.ch014

1. INTRODUCTION

The healthcare system is continuously getting overburdened because of chronic disease. The lifestyles and eating habits in modern cities are affecting the health of people in a harmful way. These living styles increase the risk in people of getting chronic diseases. The patients who show up with the symptoms of any chronic disease require treatment and therapies throughout their live. After the age of sixty, people are more likely to experience kidney and heart problems. When kidney and heart start degrading with age and functioning of the organs do not remain normal for the duration of three months or above, then this situation is chronic kidney and heart disease problem. These are the main causes of deaths worldwide. If they get detected in the early stage then they can be prevented or cured completely.

With aging, hypertension, rise in BP, anemia, disease related to coronary-artery and diabetes become the root causes of kidney and heart diseases. Detecting the kidney problem earlier may result in saving the functions of kidney for the patient's long survival. Early diagnosis can also reduce the treatment cost and can also avoid dialysis and transplants like complicated situations. There are various clinical fields in chronic disease which can be benefited by the approaches of machine learning. This chapter focuses on the predictive analytics that can predict the hospitalization because of the two chronic diseases: heart disease and kidney disease. The first step towards preventing these diseases is the prediction of the disease. By taking the help from prediction, the health systems can target the patients that need the hospitalization most and the available resources can be used more effectively. (*Theodora, 2018*)

By using Electronic Health Records (EHR) of patients, the hospitalization need can be predicted. The EHR contains diagnosis codes (for example, International Classification of Diseases – ICD10); procedural codes (for example, the USA uses Current Procedural Terminology – CPT); laboratory results etc. (*Katherine, 2016*) The EHR data of one year can be observed to predict the hospitalization and also the preventive measures can be taken before hand. Machine learning approaches are suitable for extracting information from vast amount of data of EHR.

Precise review of clinical information facilitates early sickness place, comprehension evaluation and network management with tremendous information creation in biomedical and human resources networks. In any circumstance, where the essence of clinical knowledge is scattered, the test precision is reduced. Different areas often show one of a kind characteristic of some local pathogens, which can undermine the expectation of flare-ups of infections. In this chapter, we smooth out AI (Artificial Intelligence) estimates in illness visit networks for feasible anticipation of unceasing sickness flare-up.

2. BACKGROUND

The Chronic Kidney Disease (CKD) is a situation described by a steady decrease in kidney work in the long run. CKD is otherwise called chronic renal disease.

2.1 The Chronic Kidney Disease

Chronic kidney disease entails diseases, which affect the kidneys by doing the jobs mentioned, and reduce their ability to guard you. In the event that your kidney condition deteriorates, waste will develop in your blood to elevated levels and cause you to feel sick. Abnormal conditions, for example, hypertension, anaemia (decreased blood count), powerless bones, poor stomach related wellbeing and harm to the nerves may happen. Also, the possibility of heart and vein disappointment is brought up by kidney illness. For an extensive stretch of time, these issues can happen gradually. Diabetes, hypertension and different problems can cause constant kidney infection. Therapy and early determination will likewise keep constant kidney sickness from getting deteriorating.

2.2 Symptoms of CKD

Until their kidney failure is advanced, most persons do not have any significant symptoms. However, you may notice:

- Feeling of increasingly drained and have less vitality
- have inconvenience concentrating
- a poor hunger
- inconvenience dozing
- muscle pressing around night time
- feet that have swelling and lower legs
- having swelling around the eyes, mainly found in the initial segment of the day
- dry, irritating skin
- need to urinate even more much of the time, especially around night time.

At any age, any person may get problem of chronic kidney. Any individuals are, however, bound to create kidney disappointment than others. You could be at elevated risk of contracting kidney infection in the event that you:

- have diabetes
- have hypertension
- have hereditary of kidney problem
- are more settled
- part of a general public pack that notice more frequency of diabetes problem or hypertension, for instance, the African American people, Hispanic American people, people from Asia, people from Pacific Islands, and people who are American Indian.

2.3 Main Causes of CKD

Diabetes and hypertension, which are the reasons behind 66 percent of cases, are the two essential drivers of relentless kidney illness. At the point when the glucose is excessively high, diabetes creates, making harm to different internal body organs, that may include the heart and kidney, just like lungs, nerves and eyes. Hypertension, or hypertension, happens as the blood weight is set against the vein increase dividers. Hypertension might be a critical reason for respiratory disappointments, strokes and incessant kidney brokenness if unchecked or deficiently oversaw. Additionally, hypertension can result from persistent kidney disease.

2.4 The Diagnosis Process

To better plan your recovery, your primary care specialist may need to point out your assurance and check your kidney limit. The expert will do the accompanying:

- Calculate the pace of glomerular filtration (GFR) that is one of the most straightforward approaches to know the level of kidney functioning in your body. For knowing your GFR, you don't must have another test. From the creatinine present in your blood, the age you are in, race, sexual direction, and different components, your essential consideration specialist will figure it. Your GFR informs your PCP (Primary Care Physicians) of your kidney disease process and encourages the expert to design your treatment.
- To gain an image of the kidneys and urinary tract, do a test that is ultrasound or CT (Computed Tomography) Scan. This tells your essential consideration specialist if your kidneys are excessively huge or very dainty, paying little mind to on the off chance that you are in a condition for example, having stone or tumor in your kidney, and if your kidneys and urinary tract system have some complications.
- Perform a kidney biopsy to search for a certain type of kidney infection now and then, understand how much kidney injury has arisen, and help prepare recovery. The expert evacuates tiny pieces of kidney tissue to do a biopsy and took a look at them under a magnifying glass.

2.4 Some Facts Related to CKD

- CKD has affected around 37 million of adults in America and a large number of people are at extended peril.
- If detected early, the development of kidney problem to CKD can be prevented.
- Heart sickness is the huge explanation behind death of CKD patients.
- Glomerular filtration rate (GFR) is the most suitable test to check the level of kidney work.
- Hypertension is the main causes behind CKD and CKD can also cause hypertension.
- Persistent proteinuria (protein content found in the urine) infers CKD is accessible.
- High chance get-togethers join the people having diabetes, hypertension and hereditary of kidney malfunctioning.
- African American people, Hispanic people, people from Pacific Islands, American Indian people and seniors are at extended peril.
- Two direct tests can recognize CKD: circulatory strain, urine egg whites and serum creatinine. (www.kidney.org, *2017*)

2.5 Various Stages of CKD

How efficiently the kidneys function is the cause of the five phases of Chronic Kidney Disease (CKD). There may be few signs in the early stages, which is the reason it is important that you approach your PCP for the glomerular filtration rate (GFR) test. This assessment allows specialists to survey how great your kidneys are separating waste from your body and overabundance liquid. The more noteworthy the sum, the better it is for the kidneys.

Stage 1: GFR 90 or higher

This underlying CKD implies that GFR proportions are over 90; however indications of kidney disappointment, for example, protein in the pee, are available. Now, finding out about things you ought to do to guard your kidneys as conceivable is a savvy thought.

Stage 2: GFR 60-89

Stage 2 of kidney sickness depicts brought down kidney working with GFR rates between 60 to 89.

Stage 3: GFR 30-59

The specialist will proceed to track and screen your kidney work just as improve endeavors to control your circulatory strain and other hidden problems as GFR draws nearer to 44.

Stage 4: GFR 15-29

They can start noticing sickness and symptoms of clear jaundice may found as patients arrive at CKD Stage 4. The last condition because of kidney disappointment is stage 4 of CKD. Kidney trade choices for on-going dialysis and possible transplantation are being investigated by doctors.

Stage 5: GFR Less 15

For the rest of the lifespan, people with a GFR under 15 start continuous dialysis techniques or settle on the choice to get clinical consideration without dialysis. Individuals who apply for a kidney relocate proceed with dialysis until it is conceivable to locate a coordinating contributor and mastermind a medical procedure. (www.satellitehealth.com, *2018)*

3. CHRONIC KIDNEY DISEASE: A GLOBAL BURDEN

Although routinely thought to be a comorbidity of diabetes or hypertension, kidney disease has different complex causes. (Levin et. al., 2017) Significantly, such sickness indirectly affects worldwide dismalness and mortality by growing the perils related with at any rate five other critical killers: cardiovascular sicknesses, diabetes, hypertension, infection with Human Immunodeficiency Virus (HIV) and wilderness fever. For example, the Global Burden of Disease (GBD) 2015 assessment assessed that 1.2 million deaths, 19 million Disability-Adjusted Life-Years (DALYs) and 18 million years of life lost from cardiovascular sicknesses were direct attributable to lessened glomerular filtration rates. (Kassebaum et. al., 2016; Wang et. al., 2015)

The GBD 2015 investigation additionally evaluated that, in 2015, 1.2 million people kicked the bucket from kidney dissatisfaction, a development of 32% since 2005 (Wang et. al., 2015). In 2010, a normal 2.3–7.1 million people with end-stage kidney ailment kicked the bucket without admittance to relentless dialysis. (Liyanage et. al., 2015) Moreover, consistently, around 1.7 million people are thought to kick the can from serious kidney injury. (Mehta et. al., 2015) Generally speaking, thusly, an expected 5–10 million individuals bite the dust every year from kidney ailment. Given the constrained epidemiological information, the regular absence of mindfulness and the as often as possible poor access to research facility administrations, such numbers most likely think little of the genuine weight presented by kidney sickness. It is in this way conceivable that, every year, in any event the same numbers of deaths are attributable to kidney affliction as to harmful development, diabetes or respiratory diseases, three of the four basic orders centered by the 2013 movement plan. Also, the evaluated number of DALYs inferable from kidney malady universally expanded from 19 million out of 1990 to 33 million of every 2013. (Murray et. al., 2015) In 2016, the DALYs related with ceaseless kidney sickness, alongside those related with cardiovascular ailment, malignant growths, diabetes and neurological issue, and were found to have expanded essentially somewhere in the range of 1990 and 2015. The GBD 2016 report investigation featured the significant exclusion of spotlight on incessant kidney sickness and recommended that "the SDG plan offers, best case scenario a negligible stage for causing to notice the social insurance and observing needs of constant kidney ailment." (Naghavi et. al., 2017)

Kidney infection is related with a gigantic financial weight. High-salary nations commonly spend more than 2–3% of their yearly social insurance financial plan on the treatment of end-stage kidney illness, despite the fact that those getting such treatment speak to under 0.03% of the absolute populace. In 2010, 2.62 million individuals got dialysis worldwide and the requirement for dialysis was anticipated to twofold by 2030. All inclusive, the all-out expense of the treatment of the milder types of interminable kidney malady gives off an impression of being a lot more noteworthy than the absolute expense of rewarding end-stage kidney contamination. In 2015, in the United States of America, for example, Medicare utilizations on relentless and end-stage kidney infection were more than 64 billion and 34 billion United States dollars, separately. A great part of the use, grimness and mortality recently ascribed to diabetes and hypertension are inferable from kidney disease and its complexities. (Tonelli et. al., 2012) Around the world, significant hazard factors for kidney illness incorporate diarrheal sicknesses, HIV contamination, low birth weight, intestinal sickness and preterm birth, which are all likewise driving worldwide reasons for DALYs. Dangers of kidney malady range the life-course and ecological, disease and way of life etiologies. In case danger factors are perceived early, exceptional kidney injury and unending kidney infirmity can be hindered and, if kidney infection is investigated early, compounding of kidney limit can be moved back or diverted by efficient mediations, a couple of which are on the World Health Organization's (WHO's) claimed best buys list for non-transmittable infection. Such intercessions join prompting for cardiovascular disease, diabetes and hypertension, steady treatment, tobacco control, headway of actual development and the diminishing of salt confirmation through order and food naming. The advantageous conspicuous confirmation and the heads of serious kidney injury and consistent kidney illness address the best method to address the creating overall weight sensibly. (WHO, 2018)

4. MACHINE LEARNING

Machine learning is a division of artificial intelligence that can streamline the computational model-building mechanism for data processing approaches. It helps computers or machines to learn from results, finding the main trends, so that limited to no human involvement can be done to make informed decisions. Machine learning is a use of man-made brainpower (Artificial Intelligence) that allows frameworks the potential to take on and expand a reality automatically without being unambiguously altered. Machine Learning works on developing systems that can understand and use data by themselves. The way to start learning with expected result or having some knowledge, for example models, straightforward interpretation, or directions given, for the sake of looking for data models and later decide on optimal solutions provided by the models offered. The fundamental argument is to allow PCs to adapt efficiently without human mediation or support and adjust operations in the same way.

Machine learning techniques can be categorized as follows:

Figure 1. Shows the various ways of categorizing the techniques of machine learning namely: Supervised Learning, Unsupervised Learning, Semi-supervised Learning, and Reinforcement Learning

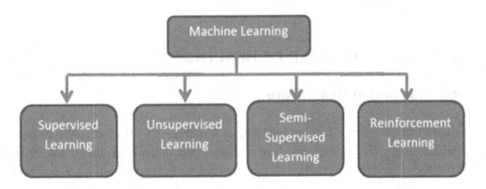

Supervised Learning: In Supervised Learning, we may think about the learning which is guided by an educator in a classroom setup. The dataset that we have helps us as an educator and the main responsibility of it is to train the model or the device. Once our model is trained, it can start giving expected result or choice whenever new data is supplied to it.

The strategies for managed learning work on known assumptions on the named input dataset. Strategies that fall in this classification target building up a connection between the information and yield credits of the labeled dataset. More reliable and accurate model can be built with the help of labeled data, but it is a costly process.

1. **Unsupervised Learning**: In Unsupervised Learning, the model or the device keeps on learning by its own and finds out patterns and structures in the supplied data. These strategies examine the structure of information in the given input that is unlabeled dataset. It assembles planning between the info and yield ascribes, while yield credits are obscure before the investigation.

In Unsupervised Instruction, the inherent difficulty is that the cluster is unable to add labels. It can't say, for instance, that this is a category of apples or oranges, so all apples would be segregated from oranges.

Suppose we presented the model with photographs of apples, oranges, and mangoes. It generates three clusters based on certain trends and relationships and partitions the given dataset into those three clusters. Now, if the model is supplied with new data, it attaches it to one of the three clusters generated. But it is not possible to distinguish which cluster of apples, oranges or mangoes are present.

2.   **Semi-supervised Learning**: During instruction, semi-supervised learning blends a small portion of labeled data and with a huge portion of unlabeled data. Semi-supervised instruction falls between learning without oversight and learning with supervision. The basic idea behind semi-supervised learning is that, similar data will be clustered using an unsupervised learning algorithm and then the existing labeled data can be used to label the rest of the unlabeled data.

3.   **Reinforcement Learning**: It is an agent's capacity to interact with the outside world and find out correct and optimal result. It fits the theory of the process of hit and trial. The agent is credited or punished by giving a point for a right or wrong answer, and the model or device trains itself based on the credit points rewarded for the right answers. And once it is conditioned again, it becomes ready to forecast the new knowledge provided to it.

5. TECHNOLOGIES IN THE FIELD OF HEALTHCARE

5.1. Machine Learning in HealthCare

The social security calculation of Machine Learning is its capacity to process colossal datasets beyond the extent of human ability, and then reliably turn analysis of the information into therapeutic bits of wisdom that instruct doctors in planning and providing treatment, ultimately leading to improved outcomes, lower medical costs, and increased patient satisfaction. As of late, Machine Learning in medicine has stood out as genuinely newsworthy. Machine Learning fits a few processes superior to most individuals. Calculations can offer a rapid benefit for disciplines with reproducible or normalized forms. Similarly, solid up-and-comers are those with large image datasets, such as radiology, cardiology, and pathology. Machine Learning will be ready to see photographs, discern deviations from the standard, and point to regions that require attention, while enhancing the precision of both of these procedures. The family specialist or internist at the bedside will benefit from long distance, Machine Learning. In order to enhance proficiency, unwavering quality, and precision, Machine Learning should provide a target conclusion.

An exclusive stage is utilized to dissect information, and circle it back progressively to doctors to help in clinical dynamic. All the while a specialist sees a patient and enters results, data, and test results into the EMR, there's AI off camera looking at everything about that understanding, and inciting the expert with important information for making an assurance, mentioning a test, or proposing a preventive screening. Long haul, the capacities will venture into all parts of medication as we get progressively useable, better coordinated information. We'll have the option to consolidate greater arrangements of information that can be dissected and contrasted progressively with give a wide range of data to the supplier and patient. When more evidence is available, we have better data to bring to the table patients. Astute computations and AI can give us a prevalent perceptive mortality model that can be utilized by experts to manage patients.

5.2. Big Data in HealthCare: The Electronic Health Record (EHR)

Constant, responsive, oriented records are EHRs that make data available to authorized consumers easily and securely. While an EHR includes patients' psychological and behavioral narratives, an EHR system is structured to perform beyond traditional medical knowledge gathered in an office of supplier and should be informative from a way more comprehensive viewpoint on the consideration of a patient.

The clinical reports from a patient's doctors, nurses, technicians, and other medical professionals are recorded by electronic health records (EHRs). These notes are a treasure chest of unstructured digital knowledge that using natural language processing (NLP) and other techniques will be extremely useful to mine. They offer a far deeper nuance and meaning regarding the medical history, conditions, recovery schedules, test outcomes, and other information of a patient that codes and other reference data will ever be too prevalent in healthcare. A nice report has been released by Health IT Analytics outlining several examples of NLP applied to text notes: The Massachusetts General Hospital used NLP to accurately obtain health information from social factors, and Beacon Health Options uses machine learning and NLP to predict the risk of falling into health system loopholes. EHRs can:

- Store a patient's health related data and medical history, exploring the details, drugs, plans for further treatment, tentative dates for immunization, sensitivities of the patient if any, images of radiology, and results of tests and diagnosis.
- Allow admittance based on instruments that may help the facilitators in decisions making about a patient's mental state
- Automate the work of facilitators and make it easy

The most important highlight of an EHR is the well-being data in a computerized community equipped for delivery to multiple suppliers through more than one social insurance association can be produced and monitored by licensed suppliers. EHRs are designed to provide data to all providers and organizations with human resources, such as testing centers, consultants, forensic imaging departments, drug stores, emergency service areas, schools, and data acquiring offices, therefore they gather data from every professional worried under the watchful eye of a patient.

5.3. Impact of EHR on HealthCare

Our existence has been significantly changed by cutting edge advancement – tablets, PDAs, and devices of Internet access have modified our daily existences and the ways of living. Prescription is an endeavor having very rich data in it. A more noticeable and progressively steady movement of data in a modernized human monitoring system, created by Electronic Health Records that is EHRs, encompasses and utilizes progress and can upgrade the process by which care can be given and reviewed. With EHRs, data is always open for use, whenever and wherever it is needed. With EHRs:

- Patient care can be improved
- Patient Participation can be increased
- Care coordination can be improved
- Patient outcomes and diagnostics can be improved
- Efficiencies can be practiced and cost savings can be achieved

5.4. Technical Challenges in Real-Time Implementation

Human lives are affected by health issues. Health providers gather clinical information about each individual patient during medical treatment, and use expertise from the overall population to conclude how to deal with the patient. Information additionally assumes an essential part in addressing wellbeing challenges, and better information is essential to strengthening medical care. We rely on the electronic health record (EHR), which records the healthcare delivery process and institutional demands, such as the monitoring of the cycle of treatment and income. Although we prefer to concentrate on the hospital context, like most machine learning programs currently concentrate on this information rich climate, we note that clinical information is heterogeneous and arrives in various manners that might be essential to the comprehension of patient wellbeing. (Weber et. al., 2014)

1.   To Understand Causality is Key

Large numbers of the most basic and intriguing medical services difficulties include calculations that can address "imagine a scenario in which?" Questions on what will occur if a methodology is given by a specialist (Schulam, 2017). These problems are beyond the scope of the algorithms of classical machine learning since they need a systematic intervention model.

2.   Dealing with Missing Data

And if all significant variables are present in an EHR dataset, certain observations are likely to be incomplete. Owing to cost and volume, fully full data is always impractical. Learning from imperfect or lacking machine learning data is a daunting challenge and the resulting precision is not assured. (2018, Ding & Li).

3.   Automating Medical Task

To map from a set input space to an output and master the new method, clinicians have to attend rigorous preparation. It is also easy to assess job replacement; success can be assessed against existing expectations. We stress that the algorithm should not be used to replace healthcare workers, but to improve the clinical workflow. As these strategies advance, clinical functions will undoubtedly change, enabling workers to spend more time with patients. (2016 Jha & Topol)

6. LITERATURE REVIEW

There are plenty of experiments that use different methods for early diagnosis to investigate and evaluate chronic diseases.

Dulhare UN and Ayesha M (Dulhare, 2016) used the classifier method of Naive Bayes with attribute selector method of OneR. It can forecast Chronic Kidney Disease by utilizing the UCI digital repository dataset having 25 total attributes. 11 out of 25 attributes were numeric, 13 attributes were nominal, and the last attribute was a class attribute. They were able to increase the detection accuracy by 12.5% and decreased the number of attribute by 80 percent by using OneR.

Gopika M (Gopika, 2017) used a technique of clustering for forecasting CKD accurately and lowered the time involved in diagnosis. The author used fuzzy techniques of k-means, c-means, and k-medoids and able to attain 87 percent accuracy through the fuzzy c-means clustering method for the UCI machine repository dataset.

Charleonnan et al. (Charleonnan, 2016) utilized the algorithm of decision tree, support vector machine (SVM), logistic regression, and k-nearest neighbor (KNN) as CKD predicting classifiers. They used a dataset having two classes, total 400 instances, and a total of 24 attributes. The UCI machine learning repository CKD dataset was used by them. The output shows that the technique of SVM shows comparatively better results by accurately detecting the disease.

Padmanaban KA and Parthiban G. (Padmanaban, 2016) analyze early detection of CKD using the algorithms of machine learning. They applied decision tree and naive Bayes on 600 instances dataset for validating the algorithms. They achieved 91percentt accuracy in CKD forecasting by using the decision tree and reported sensitivity of 95 percent and specificity of 94 percent through the decision tree for forecasting CKD on early stage.

Jing Mei et al. (Mei, 2017) explore the method to develop knowledge-enhanced localized risk models. The model is able to learn from regional Electronic Health Record (EHR) repositories, and also imposing knowledge into the EHR was also possible. They leveraged the Pooled Cohort Equations for developing a localized ASCVD risk prediction model in chronic disease like diabetes. The results show that, by using the PCE algorithm directly on cohort, the AUC was only 0.653, while the knowledge-enhanced localized risk model was able to achieve higher and improved prediction performance with AUC of 0.723.

Zixian Wang et al.(Wang,2018) used machine learning techniques to analyze the datasets from UCI machine learning data warehouse to predict chronic kidney disease (CKD). They used Apriori Association Technique on 400 kidney patients to detect CKD with the help of the testing technique that is 10-fold-cross-validation. They compared the results with various classification algorithms such as ZeroR, OneR, J48, naive Bayes and IBk (the k-nearest-neighbor). The completed and normalized the data that were missing and preprocessed the datasets. They identified the most useful features from the datasets so that the accuracy can be increased and the training time can be reduced to a great extent. The features that they have selected using the Apriori Algorithm gave the results that indicate 99% accuracy in CKD detection. Further, this technique was tested on data samples of four CKD patients.

Theodora S. Brisimi et al.(*Theodora*, 10) focused on the two chronic disease clusters, diabetes and heart disease. They developed data driven methods for predicting the need of hospitalization because of these chronic disease conditions. These predictions were based on the medical history of patients that ware recent and even more distant. These data were described in Electronic Health Records (EHR) of the patients. They formulated the problem of prediction as a problem of binary classification. They used different methods of machine learning such as random forests, sparse logistic regression, and kernelized and sparse Support Vector Machines (SVM). They have given two methods- K-LRT and Joint Clustering and Classification (JCC) for achieving the balance between interpretability and accuracy for the chronic disease prediction. They did the validation of their algorithms on Boston Medical Center's huge datasets.

Min Chen et al. (*Chen, 2017*) found that the growth in big data related to biomedical field and communities of healthcare, the complete and correct healthcare data analysis helps in forecasting the disease in early stage, and providing better patient care and community services. The inherent complexity is that different areas show different characteristics of certain area specific diseases that may lower the accuracy of disease outbreak forecasting. They proposed a unique algorithm that is convolutional neural network based multimodal disease risk prediction (CNN-MDRP), which utilizes the data from hospitals, both structured data and unstructured data. Comparing with different previous prediction techniques, the correctness of the forecasting of their given algorithm attains to 94.8 percent with a convergence pace that more faster than that of the CNN-based uni-modal disease risk prediction (CNN-UDRP) algorithm.

Jena et al. (*Jena, 2015*) used a collection of Filter, Wrapper technique with Bagging and Boosting models with technique of parameter tuning to detect chronic kidney disease. Bagging and Boosting classifiers capabilities were compared and the best ensemble classifier that achieves maximum stability with better accurate results is identified.

All the research done at this point recommends that AI can give significant bits of knowledge into information. Along these lines it can contribute in grouping information into various classes. The outcomes show that AI methods can deliver precise characterization results whenever utilized related to include determination procedures. Along these lines, holding the advantages of order results for AI strategies, this investigation features a lot of the most famous AI procedures in blend with include determination strategy to arrange ordinary patients and patients with kidney and coronary illness.

7. MACHINE LEARNING TECHNIQUES

Machine Learning is a technique of investigating information which computerizes the scientific model-building measure. A structure that can gain from information and perceive significant patterns for better dynamic with practically zero human inclusion is the key concept behind it. In order to have any feedback and optimal outcomes, supervised machine learning algorithms require machine learning abilities. During algorithm preparation, feedback on prediction accuracy is also important. The variables are often calculated and used by a prediction process for study by data scientists. The algorithm applies what it knows and discovers after completion of the training, using an iterative deep learning approach to conclusions.

This chapter studies different supervised techniques of machine learning for forecasting the chronic kidney disease in an early stage. The techniques include Naive Bayes, ZeroR, OneR, IBk, J48, and k-nearest-neighbor for classifying the dataset of CKD detection (*Wang, 2018*). A detailed discussion on these techniques is given as following:

1. **Apriori Association Technique**: The Apriori algorithm is essentially an algorithm for categorization. To create binary knowledge evaluations or find a regression relationship, several algorithms are used. Others are used to forecast initially defined trends and patterns. Apriori is a foundational machine learning algorithm used to organize data into groups. For any data collection process, processing data can be immensely beneficial. It means that new input is analyzed by data consumers and that they can sort out the data they are dealing with.

This machine learning algorithm operates by defining a certain feature of a data set and trying to notice how much that feature shows up in the set. On the part of the individual executing the design and, finally, the machine itself, this concept needs some additional effort. The concept of "frequent" is essentially relative and therefore contextually makes sense. Therefore, by a pre-arranged number decided by either the operator or the algorithm, the concept is applied in the Apriori algorithm. A "frequent" data attribute, known as a support, is one that exists above that pre-arranged number. This approach utilizes a bottom-up method to extract repeated objects in a supplied set of data.

2. **Support Vector Machine Algorithm**: The SVM is a tool for linear and nonlinear both type of classification of data (Aljahdali, 2013). A mapping technique of nonlinear type is utilized to update the particular training details into a larger dimension. It explores the linear optimal separating

hyperplane enclosed by this new dimension, i.e., a "decision boundary" filtering the records of one class from another class. Information from two gatherings will frequently be separated by a hyperplane with a reasonable nonlinear projection to an innately high measurement. The SVM utilizes uphold vectors and edges to find the hyperplane (Cristianini, 2000). Even though the time taken in training of even the quickest SVMs could be inconceivably long, their capacity to display complex nonlinear choice cutoff points is solid and commendable. When compared to other approaches, they are much less resistant to over-fitting. A concise overview of the model that has learned is also provided by SVM initiates. For estimation, along with grouping, SVMs can be used. Extension has been given to them in many fields, including object recognition, handwritten digit recognition, and speaker detection, as well as benchmark time-series prediction studies.

3. **Probabilistic Neural Networks:** Probabilistic Neural Networks (PNN) with a one-pass learning algorithm and strongly parallel structure are more like a Radial Basis Function neural network. In 1990, Donald F. Specht implemented PNN as a memory-based network that offers estimates of categorical factors. The methodology offers a seamless approximation of a target function in a multidimensional space with sparse data (Specht, 1990). Quick learning and simple tuning are the strengths of PNN. Input, pattern (RBF kernel function), summation, and output are four layers of the PNN. A radial base function is used by each neuron of the pattern layer as an activation function.

4. **Random Forest:** The random forest algorithm builds several decision trees to serve as a classification and regression phase ensemble. Using random subsets of the training data sets, a variety of decision trees are created. The greater precision of results is given by a wide set of decision trees. The algorithm's runtime is relatively quick and accommodates missing data as well. The algorithm, not the training data collection, is randomized by Random Forest. The class of decision is the mode of classes created by trees of decision.

5. **ZeroR Technique**: ZeroR is the one of the least complex grouping strategies which depends on the objective and disregards all indicators. ZeroR classifier essentially predicts the greater part classification (class). Despite the fact that there is no consistency power in ZeroR, it is valuable for deciding a pattern execution as a benchmark for other order techniques. This is the least complex characterization strategy filling in as the pattern execution for different classifiers. It disregards all indicators, depending just on track esteems. During the order, it delivers a recurrence table comparing to target esteems to choose the most continuous qualities. ZeroR is the least complex order technique which depends on the objective and disregards all indicators. ZeroR classifier just predicts the larger part classification (class). Despite the fact that there is no consistency power in ZeroR, it is valuable for deciding a standard presentation as a benchmark for other arrangement strategies.

6. **OneR Technique**: OneR, short for One Rule, is an easy and precise, algorithm for classification that produces one rule in each predictor data and then selects the rule as its 'one rule' with the minimum total error. We build a frequency table for each predictor against the target to create a law for a predictor. OneR has been shown to generate rules that are only marginally less precise than state-of-the-art classification algorithms, thus providing rules that are easy to understand for humans. For different predictors in the dataset, this methodology produces "One Rule for One Predictor" to pick the one with the most minimal joined mistake for the indicator.

7. **IBk Technique**: It is a grouping technique that is occurrence based, utilizing k-neighborhood objects that develops yield with mean supreme blunder, disarray grid, and relative total mistake, in

others. This arranges an information set dependent on Euclidean distance that decides the group of an obscure example and is registered utilizing the estimation of k as given below:

$$d(y, z) = \sqrt{\sum_{i=1}^{k} (yi - zi)}.$$

8. **J48 Technique**: It is a choice based on tree method which makes a tree by persistently separating a prescribed dataset into more modest small sets. The output tree incorporates leaf (ending) hubs and choice hubs. The top hub is known as the root hub and plays the major role in making a significant commitment to expectations. This procedure can solve mathematical problems just as downright information.

Stage 1: The leaf is named with a comparable class if the cases have a place with comparative class.
Stage 2: The conceivable information will be figured for each characteristic and the advantage in the information will be taken from the quality test.
Stage 3: Eventually, in view of the current determination rule, the best quality is chosen.

9. **Naive Bayes Technique**: A Naive Bayes Classifier is an administered machine learning calculation that utilizes the Bayes' Theorem, which expects that highlights are genuinely autonomous. The hypothesis depends on the guileless suspicion that input factors are free of one another, for example it is absolutely impossible to know anything about different factors when given an extra factor. Notwithstanding this suspicion, it has proved that it is a classifier having great outcomes.

Naive Bayes Classifiers depend on the Bayes' Theorem that is based upon restrictive likelihood or in simple words, the probability of an event (A) to occur given that another event (B) has already happened. Basically, this hypothesis allows a theory to be refreshed each time new validation is given. The condition given below explains Bayes' Theorem in terms of likelihood:

$$P(A|B) = \frac{P(B|A)P(A)}{P(B)}.$$

Description of each of the above terms:

*   "P" is the symbol to denote probability.
*   P(A | B) = The probability of event A (hypothesis) occurring given that B (evidence) has occurred.
*   P(B | A) = The probability of the event B (evidence) occurring given that A (hypothesis) has occurred.
*   P(A) = The probability of event B (hypothesis) occurring.
*   P(B) = The probability of event A (evidence) occurring.

10. **Ensemble Method:** The Ensemble approach (Dietterich, 1998) is a technique to improve the precision of the indicator or classifier. To increase efficiency, the Ensemble approach utilizes a mixture

of models to construct an optimized composite model. In order to come up with a "strong learner," the key concept in the ensemble strategy is to create groups of many "weak learners." Bagging and boosting are two traditional strategies for building ensembles. Boosting as well as bagging can also be used for prediction and sorting (Han et. al., 2011).

8. STUDY OF THE RELATED WORK

The key purpose of the study provided in this chapter is to explore different techniques of machine learning for successful detection of CKD in terms of detection precision in coexistence with techniques of feature selection. This research uses classification algorithms with different techniques provided by various tools to suggest different prediction models and compare them to correctly categorized instances. For early CKD diagnosis, the established classification technique may provide expected values.

8.1. The Framework

The system that has been studied for creating forecast Machine Learning models and their correlation are portrayed in Fig. 2. The fundamental goal of the current exploration is to give a Machine Learning strategy to anticipate CKD utilizing affiliated and grouping calculations. The studied procedure produces order affiliation rules to decide strategies with a high level of effectively grouped occasions, and recognized classifiers may empower forecasting of CKD in early stage. A general assessment of the discussed methodology is given by utilizing other forefront procedures. Fig. 2 briefly describes the different stages:

1. **Selecting the Dataset**: The dataset is chosen to foresee CKD for information investigation and compelling information. Enough information is needed to actualize a Machine Learning procedure for a chosen set of data.
2. **Preprocessing and Transformation**: The set of data can be set up in property connection document design. The dataset is changed over into a binomial arrangement to actualize cooperative procedures. Also, missing information, copy information, and pointless areas are evacuated for an information group that is considered to be a standard.
3. **Feature Selection:** The best-suited features for the dataset of CKD can be chosen utilizing any of the instruments. Highlight evaluators and quest strategies are utilized for this reason. The relationship based component choice subset identifier is utilized as the component identifier, and the unquenchable step-by-step pursuit strategy is implemented. The chosen highlights incorporate pulse, red platelets, discharge cell, creatinine present in the serum, hemoglobin, high BP, diabetes mellitus, and pedal edema for optimal outcomes from the dataset of CKD.
4. **Selection of Associative Rules**: The Apriori affiliation calculation can be executed, and 10 best standards are chosen to set up the preparation dataset to actualize distinctive arrangement calculations.
5. **Classification Algorithm Implementation**: The appropriate classifiers are prepared utilizing the dataset chose dependent on affiliation rules including SVM, PNN, Random Forest, k-nearest neighbor, naive-Bayes, ZeroR, OneR, J48 etc.
6. **Performance Evaluation**: Any of the machine learning techniques such as SVM, PNN, Random Forest, k-nearest neighbor, naive-Bayes, ZeroR, OneR, or J48 can be prepared and tried utilizing the

recognized CKD dataset, and the exhibition of every classifier is estimated for effectively grouped occasions of the distinguished dataset.

7. **Disease Prediction System**: The distinguished best classifier assists with shaping a keen CKD forecast framework for the exact expectation of other ongoing infections, for example, coronary illness.

Figure 2.

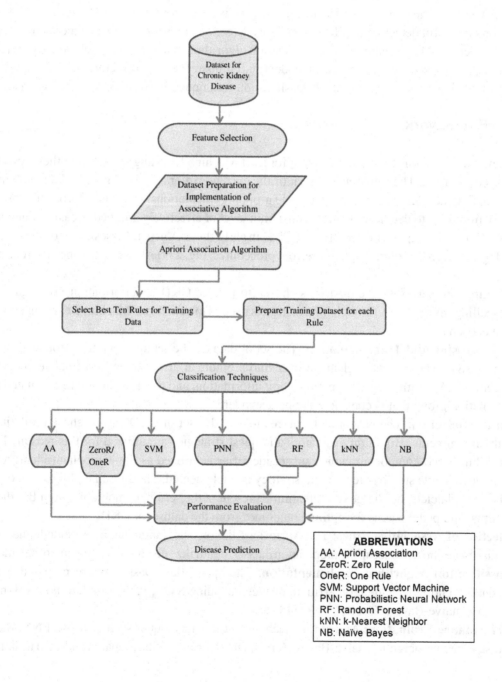

8.2. The Different Attributes

The different attributes and their descriptions are given in the following table:

Table 1. Description of attributes

Attributes	Description
Age	Ranging from [2 -90] (in years)
Blood Pressure	Ranging from [50 - 180] (in mm Hg)
Red Blood Cell	two apparent inputs "normal" or "abnormal"
Pus Cell	two apparent inputs "normal" or "abnormal"
Bacteria	two apparent inputs Bacteria is "present" and "not present"
Serum Creatinine	Numerical value in mgs/dl
Haemoglobin	The numerical value in gms
Hypertension	two apparent inputs "yes" and "no"
Diabetes Mellitus	two apparent inputs "yes" and "no"
Coronary Artery Disease	two apparent inputs "yes" and "no"
Appetite	two apparent inputs Appetite is "good" and "poor"
Pedal Edema	two apparent inputs Pedal Edema is "yes" and "no"
Anaemia	two apparent inputs Anaemia is "yes" and "no "
Class	the class inputs "ckd" represent Chronic Kidney Disease and "nonckd" represent Chronic Kidney Disease not present

Table 2. Comparison of Results from Previous Studies

Sl. No.	Author	Year	Techniques	Accuracy (in percentage)
1	Qin et. al.	2020	Logistic-Regression, and Random Forest by using Perceptron	99.83
2	Nagaraju & Varun	2020	Naive-Bayes	91.54
3	Kotturu et. al.	2019	Random Forest	99.3
4	Almasoud & Ward	2019	Gradient Boosting Classifier	99.1
5	Tekale et. al.	2018	Support Vector Machine	96.75
6	Revathy et. al.	2019	Random Forest	99.16
7	Rady et. al.	2019	Probabilistic Neural Networks	96.7
8	Alassaf et. al.	2019	Artificial Neural Network, Support Vector Machine, Naïve Bayes	98
9	Wang et. al.	2018	Apriori Algorithm with ZeroR, OneR, Naive Bayes, J48, and IBk (k-nearest-neighbor).	99
10	Zeynu	2018	Ensemble Classification	99

9. RESULTS AND DISCUSSION

The characterized benchmark dataset with various order methods applied in different instruments and were used to perform a series of experiments using different Machine Learning algorithms by various researchers. For correctly categorized cases, the outcomes are compared. Numerous classifiers with the 10-fold cross-validation testing technique have been applied in the results. Numerous classifiers on the CKD dataset were also compared to obtain the maximum accuracy.

10. CONCLUSION

In order to do the accurate and early prediction of Chronic Kidney Disease, this study investigates the history of CKD as well as distinctive Machine Learning methods, especially classification and association. The findings are compared for correctly defined cases. The findings from different studies note that with the Logistic-Regression and Random Forest technique by utilizing perceptron achieves the best accuracy i.e., 99.83 percent. Hence, we can conclude that applying this technique to the diagnosis of CKD in practical situations would achieve a desirable solution. In future studies, various controlled and unsupervised machine learning approaches and selection strategies can be assessed with extra yield measurements for better Chronic Kidney Disease forecast.

REFERENCES

Al-Hyari, A. Y., Ahmad, M. A., & Majid, A. A. (2014). Diagnosis and classification of chronic renal failure utilising intelligent data mining classifiers. *International Journal of Information Technology and Web Engineering*, *9*(4), 1–12. doi:10.4018/ijitwe.2014100101

Alassaf, R. A., Alsulaim, K. A., Alroomi, N. Y., Alsharif, N. S., Aljubeir, M. F., Olatunji, S. O., Alahmadi, A. Y., Imran, M., Alzahrani, R. A., & Alturayeif, N. S. (2019). Preemptive Diagnosis of Chronic Kidney Disease Using Machine Learning Techniques. *Proceedings of the 2018 13th International Conference on Innovations in Information Technology, IIT 2018, November*, 99–104. 10.1109/INNOVATIONS.2018.8606040

Aljahdali, S., & Hussain, S. N. (2013). Comparative prediction performance with support vector machine and random forest classification techniques. *International Journal of Computers and Applications*, *69*(11).

Almasoud, M., & Ward, T. E. (2019). Detection of chronic kidney disease using machine learning algorithms with least number of predictors. *International Journal of Advanced Computer Science and Applications*, *10*(8), 89–96. doi:10.14569/IJACSA.2019.0100813

Brisimi, Xu, Wang, Dai, Adams, & Paschalidis. (2018). Predicting Chronic Disease Hospitalizations from Electronic Health Records: An Interpretable Classification Approach. *Proc IEEE Inst Electr Electron Eng.*, *106*(4), 690–707. 10.1109/JPROC.2017.2789319

Charleonnan, A., Fufaung, T., Niyomwong, T., Chokchueypattanakit, W., Suwannawach, S., & Ninchawee, N. (2016). Predictive analytics for chronic kidney disease using machine learning techniques. *IEEE International Conference on Management and Innovation Technology (MITicon)*, MIT-80. 10.1109/MITICON.2016.8025242

Chen, Hao, Hwang, Wang, & Wang. (2017). *Disease Prediction by Machine Learning over Big Data from Healthcare Communities*. Academic Press.

Cristianini, N., & Shawe-Taylor, J. (2000). *An introduction to support vector machines and other kernel-based learning methods*. Cambridge University Press. doi:10.1017/CBO9780511801389

Dietterich, T. G. (1998). An experimental comparison of three methods for constructing ensembles of decision trees: Bagging, boosting and randomization. *Machine Learning, 32*, 1–22.

Ding, P., & Li, F. (2018). Causal inference: A missing data perspective. *Statistical Science, 33*(2), 214–237. doi:10.1214/18-STS645

Dulhare, U. N., & Ayesha, M. (2016). Extraction of action rules for chronic kidney disease using Naïve bayes classifier. *IEEE International Conference on Computational Intelligence and Computing Research (ICCIC)*, 1-5. 10.1109/ICCIC.2016.7919649

Gopika, M. (2017). Machine learning Approach of Chronic Kidney Disease Prediction using Clustering Technique. *International Journal of Innovative Research in Science, Engineering and Technology, 6*(7), 14488-14496.

Han, J., Kamber, M., & Pei, J. (2011). *Data Mining: Concepts and Techniques*. Elsevier. https://www.kidney.org/atoz/content/about-chronic-kidney-disease

Jha, S., & Topol, E. J. (2016, December 13). Adapting to artificial intelligence: Radiologists and pathologists as information specialists. *Journal of the American Medical Association, 316*(22), 2353–2354. doi:10.1001/jama.2016.17438 PMID:27898975

Kassebaum, N.J., Arora, M., Barber, R.M., Bhutta, Z.A., Brown, J., & Carter, A. (2015). GBD 2015 DALYs and HALE Collaborators. Global, regional, and national disability-adjusted life-years (DALYs) for 315 diseases and injuries and healthy life expectancy (HALE), 1990-2015: a systematic analysis for the Global Burden of Disease Study 2015. *Lancet, 388*(10053), 1603–58. doi:10.1016/S0140-6736(16)31460-X

Kotturu, P., Sasank, V. V. S., Supriya, G., Manoj, C. S., & Maheshwarredy, M. V. (2019). Prediction of chronic kidney disease using machine learning techniques. *International Journal of Advanced Science and Technology, 28*(16), 1436–1443.

Levin, A., Tonelli, M., Bonventre, J., Coresh, J., Donner, J. A., Fogo, A. B., Fox, C. S., Gansevoort, R. T., Heerspink, H. J. L., Jardine, M., Kasiske, B., Köttgen, A., Kretzler, M., Levey, A. S., Luyckx, V. A., Mehta, R., Moe, O., Obrador, G., Pannu, N., ... Yang, C.-W. (2017, October 21). ISN Global Kidney Health Summit participants. Global kidney health 2017 and beyond: A roadmap for closing gaps in care, research, and policy. *Lancet, 390*(10105), 1888–1917. doi:10.1016/S0140-6736(17)30788-2 PMID:28434650

Liyanage, T., Ninomiya, T., Jha, V., Neal, B., Patrice, H. M., Okpechi, I., Zhao, M., Lv, J., Garg, A. X., Knight, J., Rodgers, A., Gallagher, M., Kotwal, S., Cass, A., & Perkovic, V. (2015, May 16). Worldwide access to treatment for end-stage kidney disease: A systematic review. *Lancet, 385*(9981), 1975–1982. doi:10.1016/S0140-6736(14)61601-9 PMID:25777665

Mehta, R. L., Cerdá, J., Burdmann, E. A., Tonelli, M., García-García, G., Jha, V., Susantitaphong, P., Rocco, M., Vanholder, R., Sever, M. S., Cruz, D., Jaber, B., Lameire, N. H., Lombardi, R., Lewington, A., Feehally, J., Finkelstein, F., Levin, N., Pannu, N., ... Remuzzi, G. (2015, June 27). International Society of Nephrology's 0by25 initiative for acute kidney injury (zero preventable deaths by 2025): A human rights case for nephrology. *Lancet, 385*(9987), 2616–2643. doi:10.1016/S0140-6736(15)60126-X PMID:25777661

Mei, Xia, Li, & Xie. (2017). *Developing Knowledge-enhanced Chronic Disease Risk Prediction Models from Regional EHR Repositories.* Academic Press.

Murray, C. J., Barber, R. M., Foreman, K. J., Abbasoglu Ozgoren, A., Abd-Allah, F., & Abera, S. F. (2015, November 28). GBD 2013 DALYs and HALE Collaborators. Global, regional, and national disability-adjusted life years (DALYs) for 306 diseases and injuries and healthy life expectancy (HALE) for 188 countries, 1990-2013: Quantifying the epidemiological transition. *Lancet, 386*(10009), 2145–2191. doi:10.1016/S0140-6736(15)61340-X PMID:26321261

Nagaraju, C., & Varun, B. (2020). A Generic Real Time Application for CKD Prediction Using Machine Learning. *International Research Journal of Engineering and Technology, 7*(8), 2578-2585

Naghavi, M., Abajobir, A. A., Abbafati, C., Abbas, K. M., Abd-Allah, F., Abera, S. F., Aboyans, V., Adetokunboh, O., Afshin, A., Agrawal, A., Ahmadi, A., Ahmed, M. B., Aichour, A. N., Aichour, M. T. E., Aichour, I., Aiyar, S., Alahdab, F., Al-Aly, Z., Alam, K., ... Murray, C. J. L. (2017, September 16). GBD 2016 Causes of Death Collaborators. Global, regional, and national age-sex specific mortality for 264 causes of death, 1980-2016: A systematic analysis for the Global Burden of Disease Study 2016. *Lancet, 390*(10100), 1151–1210. doi:10.1016/S0140-6736(17)32152-9 PMID:28919116

Niehaus & Clifto. (2016). Machine learning for chronic disease. doi:10.1049/PBHE002E,Chapter

Padmanaban, K. A., & Parthiban, G. (2016). Applying Machine Learning Techniques for Predicting the Risk of Chronic Kidney Disease. *Indian Journal of Science and Technology, 9*(29), 1–5. doi:10.17485/ijst/2016/v9i29/93880

Qin, J., Chen, L., Liu, Y., Liu, C., Feng, C., & Chen, B. (2020). A machine learning methodology for diagnosing chronic kidney disease. *IEEE Access: Practical Innovations, Open Solutions, 8*, 20991–21002. doi:10.1109/ACCESS.2019.2963053

Rady, E. H. A., & Anwar, A. S. (2019). Prediction of kidney disease stages using data mining algorithms. *Informatics in Medicine Unlocked, 15*(March), 100178. doi:10.1016/j.imu.2019.100178

Revathy, S., Bharathi, B., Jeyanthi, P., & Ramesh, M. (2019). Chronic kidney disease prediction using machine learning models. *International Journal of Engineering and Advanced Technology, 9*(1), 6364–6367. doi:10.35940/ijeat.A2213.109119

Schulam, P., & Saria, S. (2017). *Reliable decision support using counterfactual models. Neural Information Processing Systems*. NIPS.

Specht, D. F. (1990). Probabilistic neural networks. *Neural Networks*, *3*(1), 109–118. doi:10.1016/0893-6080(90)90049-Q PMID:18282828

Tekale, S., Shingavi, P., Wandhekar, S., & Chatorikar, A. (2018). Prediction of chronic kidney disease using machine learning algorithms. *International Journal of Advanced Research in Computer and Communication Engineering*, *7*(10), 92–96. doi:10.17148/IJARCCE.2018.71021

Tonelli, M., Muntner, P., Lloyd, A., Manns, B. J., Klarenbach, S., Pannu, N., James, M. T., & Hemmelgarn, B. R.Alberta Kidney Disease Network. (2012, September 1). Risk of coronary events in people with chronic kidney disease compared with those with diabetes: A population-level cohort study. *Lancet*, *380*(9844), 807–814. doi:10.1016/S0140-6736(12)60572-8 PMID:22717317

Wang, H., Naghavi, M., Allen, C., Barber, R.M., Bhutta, Z.A., & Carter, A. (2015). *GBD 2015 Mortality and Causes of Death Collaborators. Global, regional, and national life expectancy, all-cause mortality, and cause-specific mortality for 249 causes of death, 1980-2015: a systematic analysis for the Global Burden of Disease Study 2015*. Academic Press.

Wang, H., Naghavi, M., Allen, C., Barber, R. M., Bhutta, Z. A., Carter, A., Casey, D. C., Charlson, F. J., Chen, A. Z., Coates, M. M., Coggeshall, M., Dandona, L., Dicker, D. J., Erskine, H. E., Ferrari, A. J., Fitzmaurice, C., Foreman, K., Forouzanfar, M. H., Fraser, M. S., ... Murray, C. J. L. (2016, October 8). Global, regional, and national life expectancy, all-cause mortality, and cause-specific mortality for 249 causes of death, 1980–2015: A systematic analysis for the Global Burden of Disease Study 2015. *Lancet*, *388*(10053), 1459–1544. doi:10.1016/S0140-6736(16)31012-1 PMID:27733281

Wang, Z., Won Chung, J., Jiang, X., Cui, Y., Wang, M., & Zheng, A. (2018). Machine Learning-Based Prediction System For Chronic Kidney Disease Using Associative Classification Technique. *International Journal of Engineering & Technology*, *7*(4.36), 1161. doi:10.14419/ijet.v7i4.36.25377

Weber, G. M., Mandl, K. D., & Kohane, I. S. (2014). Finding the missing link for big biomedical data. *Journal of the American Medical Association*, *311*(24), 2479–2480. doi:10.1001/jama.2014.4228 PMID:24854141

Zeynu, S. (2018). *Prediction of Chronic Kidney Disease Using Data Mining Feature Selection and Ensemble Method*. Academic Press.

Chapter 15
Heart Disease Prediction Using Decision Tree and Random Forest Classification Techniques

Nitika Kapoor
Chandigarh University, India

Parminder Singh
Chandigarh Engineering College, Landran, India

ABSTRACT

Data mining is the approach which can extract useful information from the data. The prediction analysis is the approach which can predict future possibilities based on the current information. The authors propose a hybrid classifier to carry out the heart disease prediction. The hybrid classifier is combination of random forest and decision tree classifier. Moreover, the heart disease prediction technique has three steps, which are data pre-processing, feature extraction, and classification. In this research, random forest classifier is applied for the feature extraction and decision tree classifier is applied for the generation of prediction results. However, random forest classifier will extract the information and decision tree will generate final classifier result. The authors show the results of proposed model using the Python platform. Moreover, the results are compared with support vector machine (SVM) and k-nearest neighbour classifier (KNN).

DATA MINING

In archives, libraries and even other appliances, there is a vast volume of data being stored, since personal and private data cannot be stored somewhere else. Therefore, a method in which both data and information (Dey & Rautaray, 2014) can be safely and securely stored is very important to discover and suggest. Users often find it very difficult to collect and use only valuable knowledge from this tremendous data. Data mining is therefore used to solve this case. Data mining is the method of only sorting, selecting

DOI: 10.4018/978-1-7998-6673-2.ch015

and processing data which is valuable and important for that unique moment of time. This helps the user to view their details from anywhere and at any time. (Oyelade, Oladipupo, & Obagbuwa, 2010).

The files and many other areas are stored with a vast volume of appropriate and irrelevant data. It has given attention to the word data mining, which in the decision-making process can be more useful. It is step of gathering meaningful and significant data from vast volume of data that is collected on the internet nearly everywhere.

It consists of steps in a repetitive sequence:

1. Data cleaning: This reduces unnecessary noise and inconsistent information.
2. Data Integration: By this process, different data sources are integrated.
3. Data Selection: By this stage, entirely different data is retrieved from databases. (Rauf, Khusro, Javed, & Saeed, 2012).
4. Data Processing: The transformation of data in which summary or grouping operations are conducted is carried out in a highly suitable fashion.
5. Data mining: Data is collected in many ways, and is considered to be a very significant step.
6. Information Presentation: Here, with the assistance of multiple representation and visualization methods, the data that is mined is resented to the user.

The logical process that was used to search for interesting and specific data from vast volumes of stored data is data mining. To find the patterns that were already used and established, this method is used. As these trends are identified, they are further used to make decisions for the development of markets and enterprises (Desai, 2013).

Figure 1. Data Mining as KDD Process

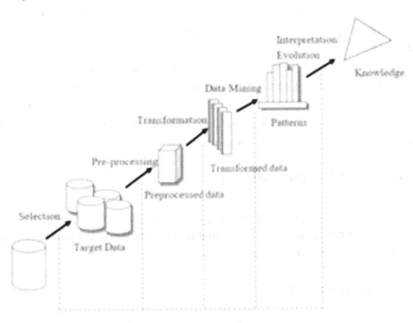

There are 3 phases involved:

- Exploration: In the initial stage, the cleaning and transfer of information is performed in a different fashion. This results in the resolution of the underlying questions associated with the form of data obtained.
- Identification of patterns: As the data is explored, optimized and resolved for a particular reason, a pattern for identification is created. In this, a trend that makes the best forecast is found and chosen.(Taneja, 2013).
- Deployment: To have a desired effect, various patterns are implemented in this phase.

Techniques used in Data Mining

The following are some of the approaches commonly used in data mining:

- **Association:** Association is considered to be the best technique among other data mining techniques. It helps to transfer the same kind of information from one unique image to another. A trend is found here, based upon the partnership. For example, association has been helpful in predicting the existence of diabetes in the body. Through this study, the relationships between different attributes were established.
- **Clustering:** The method in which objects dependent on their similarities are grouped together is known as clustering. Because of its similar features, to perform clustering, an automated method is required. (Agrawal & Nagori). Classes are allocated to objects by clustering in order to describe the mechanism through which objects are assigned to predefined classes. In detecting heart diseases, clustering also succeeds. It groups the risk factors with related types and lists patients who are likely to have heart failure.
- **Classification:** Centered on machine learning, a classic approach is recognized as classification. Each object that is part of the data set is grouped here into pre-specified category and classes of data classification.
- **Prediction:** This approach attempts to establish the relation between the dependent variables and the independent variables. There have been many applications applying prediction to forecast the benefit of the future. Sale is thus regarded in these implementations as an separate variable and benefit as a dependent variable (Sunita, Chandrakanta, & Chinmayee, 2016). This approach uses profit and historical revenue-based data to forecast profit with the aid of a regression fitted curve.

Issues Associated With Data Mining

Data mining is still in its development period, but it is becoming very widespread and successful. It has many problems and difficulties before data mining is used more conventionally, being the matured one or dignified faith. Below, some of the problems are identified.

Security and Social Issues

Security is one of the most critical challenges, since a large amount of material is freely accessible on the internet, which involves the sharing and exploitation of data without permission. During the collection of data, large amount of personal and confidential data is being stored about every individuals or industries. If there is not security measured are employed then all this sensitive data can be misused and illegally used. The new data related to the groups that include several private policies are disclosed here (Gladkykh, Hnot, & Solskyy, 2016). The discovered data is broadcasted here. There is a regular selling of sorting the databases based on the data's value. It is important to hold the important information even when distributing and using the information without control is not possible.

User Interface Issues

The information gathered from data mining is useful as long as it is attractive and unless it is easily understandable to the user. The data can be properly visualized as well as understood by the user whenever it is required. There are various visualization ideas proposed for the effective presentation of data (Nahar, Imam, Tickle, & Chen, 2013). But there is still the research going on to get the good visualization tools for large data sets which are very beneficial to display and manipulate the gathered and mined data.

Mining Methodology Issues

Such issues are very appropriate in data mining techniques. it includes versatility of the mining, diverse availability of the data, domain dimension, detailed analysis, the assessment of the discovered data, the knowledge and metadata can be exploited, the controlled and handled noise present in the data, etc, all leads to the mining methodology issues.

Performance Issues

To performing interpretation and data analysis, several statistical and AI methods can be applied. These methods are not proposed for the very large sized data sets which are being used nowadays and the terabyte size of dataset is very common (Das, Turkoglu, & Sengur, A, 2009). In same manner, sampling can be used for data mining rather than for entire dataset.

Data Source Issues

Several problems among which diversity of data types is one are studied here. As the data is openly available on the internet, so it can be easily accessible to all without the prior permission of anyone. This data can be used illegally and misused in any manner.

Application of Data Mining

In many applications, data mining is used in a manner that valuable details and trends can be found. Organizations are promoting data mining to reduce the job burden of processing vast volumes of data. The method of data mining is considered important because all programs can not be enumerated (Shendurkar & chopde). The popularly recognized data mining applications are as follows:

- **Fraud Detection:** By this approach, an optimal solution for detecting deception in applications is found. Owing to the prevalence of bribery in the processes, vast quantities of money and time are lost. Using the data mining process, the raw data is translated into useful information.
- **Financial Data Analysis:** Because protection in some sectors is the key priority, highly efficient and high-quality systems in the financial and banking industries need to be developed. Some examples are widely used as load repayment estimation and client credit policy analysis for the design and development of data warehouses with the assistance of data mining. This form of research also helps in detecting topics such as money laundering and financial crimes.
- **Telecommunication industry:** Through the development of technology that updates computers and technologies over time, there is a significant rise in the telecommunications sector. There are many facilities provided by this system, including online data transfer, pager, fax and internet messenger. Data mining plays a very crucial role in industrial applications for understanding the requirements of industry. Since QoS is improved, services are better allocated and fraudulent practices are better detected, data mining is provided in the telecommunications industry (Bharti & Mishra, 2015).

Clustering in Data Mining

Data analysis, pattern recognition, market research as well as image processing are some of the widely recognized cluster analysis-based applications. The clustering approach aims to categorize consumer segments and the spending habits to explore the preferences of consumers by advertisers. In addition, the taxonomy of plants and animals may be derived by introducing clustering in the field of biology. (Zurina, 2013).

In different clusters, there are no similar objects in which the objects in one cluster are identical to each other. Thus, to construct the clusters, unsupervised data clustering classification is applied. Cluster analysis is considered to be an effective tool for data processing, close to the (KDD) knowledge of discovery method. Clusters are known as disjoint class sets which are clustered into objects of data. There is a similarity between objects of a similar class, although there is no resemblance between objects of different clusters.

Figure 2. Stages in Clustering

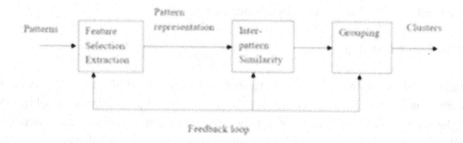

If the pre-defined classes and training courses are not seen as significant considerations for clustering, clustering is recognized to be unsupervisedDecision analysis is defined as the mechanism that distinguishes the area from which the identification of statistical patterns and unsupervised learning vary from each other. This approach is often referred to as discrimination analysis to distinguish objects from a given object category.

There have been several algorithms designed to do clustering (Wu, Zhu, Wu, & Ding, 2013). Some of the essential clustering strategies are described below, based on their characteristics:

1. **Partitioning Methods:** Both data samples with greater similarities must be obtained in such a way that clusters can be formed. This phase is regarded as the foundation of this method. Dissimilar classes are sampled together in distinct clusters and items with correlations are grouped in the same clusters. It is necessary to define the mechanism of each imaginable segment such that in partition-based clustering, global optimality can be achieved.
2. **Hierarchical Methods:** The dataset of given objects have a hierarchical decomposition. This methodology is divided into divisive and agglomerative approaches depending on the kind of decomposition. The separate group is created by agglomerative technique using bottom-up technique in the initial stage. In addition, to create one big cluster, these classes are combined with each other. Initially, all objects are put in one group and then these classes are combined on the basis of the structure required by the client. Initially, in the controversial hierarchical clustering, the objects are collected into one category. In addition, these classes are split into each other in order to create sub-clusters. The operation goes on until the appropriate group structure is reached.
3. **Density based methods:** The distance between objects is seen by most strategies as an important element in the division of objects into clusters. These strategies offer tremendous assistance while the spherical shaped clusters are calculated. In some of the methods, extracting arbitrary formed clusters becomes difficult. The key objective here is to plan the appropriate length of thickness in the area that is constrained. For this approach, a base number of items is at least needed in the field. The strategies are referred to as mode-seeking at the point where the neighborhood mode of the thickness system tests each of the group.
4. **Grid based method:** The space of the objects is quantified into a number of finite cells to design a framework for a grid. The technique used here is regarded as a system based on the grid. In this process, the amount of data objects accessible is not considered a significant consideration and it is executed at higher speeds (Parthiban & Subramanian, 2008).

Heart Diseases Prediction

One of the main reason of deaths nowadays is heart disease. The reasons for heart disease are smoking, alcohol consumption in large amount, pulse rate, and cholesterol. The heart is the operating system of the human body, Which, if not operating correctly, directly impacts the functionality of the other areas of the body. Any of the main variables contributing to heart disease are high cholesterol, high blood pressure and family history poor diet, and much more. Contracting of the blood artery will raise blood pressure, which will again induce rest in the heart. The m,ajor cause of the heart failure is smoke, resulting in about 40 percent of the population dying. That it limits our body's intake of oxygen which stops blood from circulating adequately and tightens the blood vessels. For the data mining outlook, various forms of data mining methods are used. In the KNN algorithm, the causes responsible for inducing heart attacks are defined and represented by k. The classification study is deployed using a decision tree for patients who suffer from heart disease. Through using the naive bay algorithm, the risk of heart attack can be estimated. Last but not least, the neural networks are used at the time of estimation to minimize the errors arising. By using all these approaches, the documents are also listed as regularly (Chadha & Kumar, 2014, Feburary). Each patient's behavior is properly tracked if there is any improvement, and then the patients are advised of the level of risk. Physicians are able to anticipate heart diseases at the very initial level with the aid of all these classifiers.

Classifiers Used in Heart Diseases Prediction

In order to further obtain more precise analysis and forecasts, a data mining methodology where categories are applied to the gathered data is termed as classification. Study of incredibly huge data sets is carried out by classification in a highly efficient way. Decisions are taken depending on the question and behavior is forecast in such a way that an efficient collection of classification rule can created. Using a specific set of attributes in the initial phase of this process, a series of training data sets is generated. The main goal of this classification algorithm is mining.

For the prediction of heart disorders, multiple classifiers are used, such as Neural network, SVM, Naïve bayes, KNN, and decision tree. These classifiers are used and employed so that it is possible to assess the danger of heart disease at its initial phase. This will allow both the doctor and the patient to get the right medication on time (Bahety, 2014). This will aid in the early stages of the detection of diseases. Those classifiers explained briefly as follows:

Classification by Decision Tree Induction

The classification is carried out using the decision tree algorithm in tree form. Here, by dividing the datasets, small subsets are generated. In this process, though, there is a gradual growth of the decision tree. To create the final tree structure, the leaf nodes and decision nodes are deployed. The Decision Node contains two or three branches. In addition, the leaf nodes represent the decision and classification.

Figure 3. Decision Tree

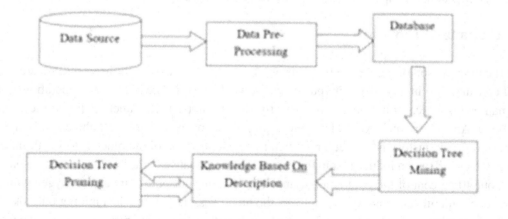

The best indicator is represented by the root node, which is the topmost node. It can accommodate both numerical information and categorical information.

Naive-Bayes Classification Algorithm

The mathematical and supervised learning methods for the representation of this algorithm are used to perform classification. Collecting the different unpredictable situations relevant to the model decides the probability of outputs. This method addresses both predictive and diagnostic issues (Chaurasia & Pal, 2013). In addition, for the resolution of practical learning algorithms, the observed as well as relevant data are combined. The point of view that helps test the algorithms of learning is illustrated here. It assesses the explicit probabilities in the input data and their stable noise.

K-Nearest Neighbor

The classifiers that use training samples to execute leaning is defined as the k-nearest neighbor classifiers. Each independent sample that occurs here describes a point in n-dimensional space. In addition, the total samples of the training are processed in n-dimensional space. The pattern space is recognized by the KNN classifier for k-training samples that are closest to the unknown sample. Based on the Euclidean distance, the concept of closeness is given. Equal weight is allocated by closest neighbor classifiers to each attribute.

Neural Networks

A gradient method is used by the neural network in this, according to the biological nervous system that involves several associated processing constituents such as neurons. This classifier facilitates the operation of the network of learners; the educated networks remove the rules. The neurons grouped in an ordered fashion are used to execute this classifier to solve certain particular problems of prediction. The configuration is changed and the scale is minimized to minimize the chances of mistakes. According to the data available within and outside the network at the time of instruction, the weight is modified so that the error rates are even smaller (Hussain, Durairaj, & Farzana, 2012, March).

Support Vector Machine (SVM)

It is a powerful classifier used to execution of regression, grouping, and general identification of patterns, and is thus called the SVM classifier. Also, in the case of very high input space, without including some prior information, it strongly generalized the output; this classifier is one of the finest classifiers of all and used for binary grouping and multi-class problem solving.

Decision Tree Induction

The classifier used in multiple applications as a classification system is a flowchart like form known as the decision tree. Each node present in the structure defines a test on the attribute value. Every part reflects the result of the exam. The distribution of groups is defined by tree leaves. A predictive model is otherwise known as a decision tree, and is widely used to perform classification. Each interior node in the decision tree checks the value of any input variable against a query for classification (Khobragade & Malik, 2014, April). With the divisions extending from the node, the potential test outcomes are numbered. If the leaf node is reached, the value is returned by intimating the class. The classification of an input instance is done upon initialization from the root node. Dependent on the outcome of the inquiry, sufficient branches are traversed before a leaf node is reached. Thus, using the decision tree, a statistical probability can be calculated. Though there is no awareness of data statistics discovery, the decision classifiers are really easy to build.

LITERATURE REVIEW

Min Chen, et.la (2017) stated a Covolutionary Neural Network-based multimodal disease risk prediction (CNN-MDRP) algorithm. The data was obtained from a hospital which consider data forms that were both organized and unstructured. In this analysis, various machine learning algorithms were updated to make predictions about the chronic disease (Chen, Hao, Hwang, & Wang, April 2017). In this approach, a latent factor model was used to recreate the missing type of data present in the data gathered. In order to assess the efficiency of the proposedo procedure, multiple experiments were considered for a local unceasing condition called brain infarction. Several comparative studies carried out earlier and the proposed method found that none of the previous open approaches were able to accommodate all forms of medical domain data gathered. In addition to the higher convergence rate, the suggested solution showed a prediction accuracy rate of 94.8 percent.

Akhilesh Kumar Yadav, et.al (2013) different computational methods were presented to collect information from vast databases, such as the medical domain, which contained huge data volumes. The actual SGPGI data set was used in this analysis. Many challenges were posed by this data collection (Yadav, Tomar, & Agarwal, July, 2013). Some variables, such as noise presence, large scale and missing values, rendered the classification unproductive. Clustering was used as a replacement due to the many problems encountered by this data collection during data analytics.

Sanjay Chakrabotry, et.al (2014) suggested a standard technique for forecasting weather.To recommend this approach, an incremental K-means clustering algorithm was used (Chakraborty, Nagwani, & Dey, June, 2012). The climate forecast has played a critical role in daily applications. For climate prediction, an additional air pollution database from the state of West Bengal was considered in this report. In general, a classic K means clustering technique was developed using the maximum mean values of the clusters on the important database for air pollution and a climate style track in this analysis. The incremental K-means method was used with the arrival of novel data to organize those data into clusters that had previously identified the form of weather. Therefore, a proposal for forecasting the environment of potential data for the coming period was made in this report. The database used for the forecast was entirely based on the environment of the state of West Bengal.

Chew Li Sa, et.al (2014) suggested a novel method named the System of Student Success Analysis (SPAS). The primary aim of this strategy was to keep track of the progress of pupils from a specific institution (Sa, Hossain, & bin Hossin, Sa, C. L.,2014, November). The architecture and evaluation were conducted on their results reports to forecast the student's success by means of the proposed method. The suggested system used data mining technique findings to produce improved results in student performance forecasting. The grades of the students were used to classify current students by classification, which was a form of data mining.

Qasem A. Al-Radaideh, et.al (2013) stated that the data research forecast for forecasting share earnings played an important part. The previous study could be used to predict the future data analysis (Al-Radaideh, Assaf, & Alnagi, 2013, December). The shareholders used the previous test evidence to predict a better time to purchase or sell shares.

K. Rajalakshmi, et.al (2015) presented a study of the rapidly growing field of medicine (Bansal, Sharma, & Goel, 2017). The vast volume of data was produced on a regular basis in this domain. It was a very difficult task to handle such tremendous data. Therefore, the use of different techniques was essential for proper handling of this data. Subsequently, to obtain useful patterns, information mining was required. The technique of medical data mining achieved optimum results in systems focused on medical line forecasting. Using the K-means equation, various current diseases were analyzed.

Bala Sundar V, et.al (2012) analyzed the datasets of genuine and virtual heart conditions. To forecast the diagnosis of heart defects, these data sets were used (SundarV, Devi, & Saravanan, June,2012). A K-mean clustering technique was used in this analysis to verify prediction accuracy. Clusters is classified into k numbers of clusters using the strategy of clustering. A branch of cluster scrutiny was this method of clustering. With neighboring means, each cluster had its meanings. The entire data was randomly initialized in the primary step. Cluster k was eventually assigned to each cluster. To minimize the distance square of the sum, the proposed method further divided k defined clusters into k fixed numbers. The task above was conducted using the data connecting formula of the cluster centroid and Euclidean distance.

Daljit Kaur, et.al (2013) stated that the technique of clustering has been used to split data containing the same objects. Data with the same objects were placed in a common group, whereas data with different objects were placed in different classes (Kaur & Jyoti, 2013). It was very popular to do clustering using the K-means algorithm. This technique of clustering, however, was very expensive. The consistency of its concluding results was represented by a factor called original centroid selection. The main goal of this was to minimize the challenges of this technique in order to make it more efficient and professional. It evaluated the output of the proposed algorithm. The test results showed that this technique was capable of reducing arithmetical computing hard work and the complexity involved. This technique has preserved lenience in its implementation. The proposed algorithm could solve disabled module problems.

Marjia Sultana, et.al (2016) focused on the issue of predicting heart disease on the basis of multiple input characteristics. Heart diseases has become a chronic illness that has spread worldwide (Sultana, Haider, & Uddin, 2016, September). The prediction of this disease was a difficult challenge, involving proficiency and specialized forecasting knowledge. Data mining techniques were used to retrieve the secret knowledge. In the decision-making process, this strategy was imperative. In this study, a test for the identification of an additional accurate tool for forecasting heart disease was carried out using various data mining techniques. This research used two different data sets, i.e., one for each form of data mining.

M. A. Jabbar, et.al (2016) stated Cardiovascular heart attack is a serious heart disease. Various deaths have occurred worldwide due to this disease (Jabbar & Shirina, Oct, 2016). The method of diagnosis of this disease was complicated as accurate testing was needed all the time. There was, however, the need to invent a method of intelligent decision support. To predict cardiac disease, the invention of this decision support device was important. The use of data mining in the medical context was examined in this report. These procedures presented physicians with a procedure to assess whether or not the patient was facing any heart attack problem. Hidden Naïve Bayes has been described as an improved formof the standard Naïve Bayes technique of data mining. This model was composed of the conditional independence assumption of the standard methodology of data mining. The Secret Naïve Bayes method was used to classify and model heart disease in this research.

Theresa Princy, et.al (2016) presented a study of several classification strategies. These methods estimated each person's level of danger of heart disease on the basis of cholesterol, blood pressure, gender, age, pulse rate, etc. (Theresa Princy & Thomas, 2016). The key purpose of this research was to have a vision by way of data mining methods to detect the extent of threat of heart attack. Various data mining approaches and classification models for professional and successful heart disease diagnosis were examined in this report. The empirical model revealed that various researchers used various instruments and features to detect heart disease. Due to the number of features considered, varying precision has also been demonstrated by different technologies using the ID3 and KNN algorithms, the risk level of heart attack was established. These algorithms have also provided accuracy ratings for a variety of features. The number of features could be limited in the immediate future.

S.Rajathi, et.al (2016) proposed a modern approach with the integration of the Ant Colony optimization method to boost the efficiency of the k-Nearest Neighbor (KNN) algorithm (Rajathi & Radhamani,, 2016). the use of this approach made the prediction of heart disease easy. Heart disease has been a chronic illness that has caused vast numbers of deaths worldwide. Two differing phases were included in the planned solution. The KNN algorithm was used in the preliminary process to identify test results. For the specialized alternatives, the ACO technique was used. The population was initialized by this approach to achieve preferred results. For the presentation of a data set, a condition called Acute Rheumatic Fever (ARF) related to the data package was considered. A fusion of KNN and ACO algorithms was proposed in this report.

Monika Gandhi, et.al (2015) stated that huge data volumes have been stored in the medical industry, but this data has not been used successfully (Gandhi & Singh, 2015). This condition was then defined as rich in details but low in expertise. In order to detect the associations and patterns, the medical records had no effective scrutiny strategies. In these cases, the techniques of data mining have proven very effective. Therefore, to forecast heart disease, vast quantities of data mining techniques have been used. This analysis made use of many details for the extraction of valuable knowledge on various data mining techniques. These methods have been used widely in order to estimate heart disease. Several data mining approaches were investigated in this analysis with the help of medical data suits.

Jagdeep Singh, et.al (2016) proposed a new framework used a cardiac dataset for the prompt prediction of heart disease. Earlier data sets were focused on the techniques of associative grouping, while this data sets were applied to verify numerous data mining methods in the Cleveland heart disease dataset (Sing, Kamra, & Singh, 2016). This Cleveland heart condition was a warehouse for machine learning at Irvine University of California (UCI). Many matrices have been considered to detect heart failure, such as chest pain, blood sugar, blood pressure, age gender, etc.

Ankita Dewan, et.al (2015) presented a study of numerous techniques of classification/prediction. On non-linear datasets, these methods were used. The neural network methodology was determined to demonstrate the best outcomes of all other prediction/classification strategies. (Dewan & Sharma, 2015). The BP algorithm in which modified weighing methods were used was the most suitable Artificial Neural Network classifier. In this process, the backward errors were propagated as well. This methodology has a problem known as local minima. A successful optimization strategy was used in this study to solve his dilemma. The suggested technique increased the level of accuracy and used more forecasting in many applications.

Tülay Karayilan, et.al (2017) proposed a new approach for detecting heart disease. The proposed model has been defined as the perception neural network multilayer. The Cleveland datasets was included in the proposed model. The thirteen medical data thirteen collected as input from Cleveland datasets were used by the neural network system. For the preparation of the proposed method, the back propagation algorithm was used to foresee the occurrence of heart failure in the patient's body. A variety of trials have been conducted in the past three years to estimate heart disease. The findings of these tests ranged at an accuracy rate of approximately 100%. The suggested solution showed a 95% accuracy score.

Sivagowry. S1, et.al (2013) addresses the challenges encountered during the heart disease prediction. The numerous methodologies used to forecast heart disease were also analyzed in this report (Sivagowry, Durairaj, & Persia, 2013). The use of fewer features to forecast heart attack was a key challenge for multiple studies in the data mining method. In data mining to forecast heart disease, the grouping process played a more important role than regression clustering and association law. In some cases, the decision tree classifier demonstrated better efficiency in the classification process, in several other situations, the naïve bayes algorithms and neural network provide better output. Both strategies have their own advantages and disadvantages. With the help of data mining strategies to forecast heart disease, convergence of both algorithms with Fuzzy logic produced optimized results with a reduced number of functions. One other extension used to predict health care data was text mining.

T.John Peter, et.al (2012) presented, the application of pattern recognition and data mining strategies in risk prediction system in the in the medical area of cardiac medicine (Peter & Somasundaram, March 2012). For data modeling and data classification, the data mining method classification procedure was used. One of the big shortcomings of the conventional medicinal grading schemes was the appearance of intrinsic linear mixtures of variables in the input range. Therefore, these questions have not been used to model difficult non-linear interactions in the clinical area. Different classifiers were used in this analysis to deal with this disadvantage.

Ms. Tejaswini, et.al (2017) provided a study performed by the World Health Organization (Mane, 2017, Feburary). This survey for the estimation of heart disease was performed worldwide. More than 12 million causalities have been caused annually by this deadly disorder. Accurate prediction of this disease was, thus, necessary. Big data technique was used for heart disease in this study as this method used the tool to minimize Hadoop Map. To conduct clustering, a customized K-Means algorithm was used, while the classifier of the decision tree was used for the classification process. This indicates the use of the ID3 method in the fusion strategy. Various criteria such as chest pain, age, gender, blood sugar, blood pressure, etc., were considered for timely identification of heart disease.

Sellappan Palaniappan, et.la (2008) present a novel model for the prediction of heart disease. The model developed was referred to as the Intelligent Heart Disease Prediction System (IHDPS). Various data mining methods have been used to develop this model for cardiac disease prediction (Palaniappan & Awang, 2008, March). The test results demonstrated the exceptional capacity of any strategy to understand the purposes of the mining objectives mentioned. The suggested solution addressed certain complex questions such as "; what if"; It was not necessary for the traditional decision support systems to do so. With the help of health reports such as blood pressure, ethnicity, blood sugar and age, etc., the risks of patient developing a heart attack may be expected. Important data such as trends, associations between medical conditions that were related to heart disease were permitted. The suggested solution has been described as an intelligible, adaptive, trustworthy and versatile approach focused on social media.

KanikaPahwa, et.al (2017) in order to select attributes from the dataset, two novel methods called SVM-RFE and gain ratio algorithms were proposed. In the medical sector, there was a large amount of data (Pahwa & Kumar, 2017, October). According to the need, the proper discovery of this knowledge using secret patterns was necessary. It was important to upgrade the data mining techniques in order to make accurate decisions in this field. The attributes implanted in the suggested solution could be used by the random forest and naïve bayes techniques. The success rate of the method suggested should be increased in accordance with the results achieved. Any unique weight was allocated to each function after applying this process.

SarathBabu, et.al (2017) stated that to extract correlations, data mining methods were used and large amounts of data were processed to convert it into useful information. It was the method of retrieving useful data. This experience could later be used for execution. Health data mining played an important role in the medical industry, as it had a high ability to uncover hidden patterns (Babu, Vivek, & Famina, 2017, April). The medical diagnosis was based on these trends. This diagnosis demanded a standardized composition of results. With the aid of health reports such as blood pressure level, ethnicity, age and blood sugar, etc., the chances of patients developing a heart attack may be expected. All achieved characteristics were applied to k-means algorithms, MAFIA algorithms and decision tree classifiers in order to estimate heart disease. To cure heart disease, the data mining methodology was introduced as it provided accurate performance in the study of heart disease. To ensure high standard of services, better diagnosis and management of the patient has been given in this medical in this medical sector.

Sayali Ambekar, et.al (2018) stated that the vast amount of data available in the medical sector has been greatly addressed by the approach to data processing. Despite the outlook, the earlier clinical trials were focused on handling and integrating the large amount of medical evidence. Owing to the rapid data expansion in the biomedical sector and medical industry, accurate scrutiny of clinical data was important for prompt identification of illness and patient care. The partially incomplete healthcare data (Ambekar & Phalnikar, 2018, August) has been analyzed to minimize precision. Data cleaning and assertion were undertaken in this analysis to turn incomplete data into unbiased data and reduce the problem of lost healthcare data. In this study, a dataset was used to estimate heart disease using the Naïve Bayes and KNN algorithm. A novel approach to disease risk forecasting with the help of organized data was suggested as an advancement of this research. A unimodal disease risk forecasting algorithm was proposed in this report. The convolutional neural network was the basis for this algorithm. 65% above the predicted accuracy level was seen in the proposed method. In addition, this scheme offered solutions to questions concerning diseases faced by humans in their life cycle.

Aditi Gavhane, et.al (2018) stated that with the aid of the machine learning algorithms, a novel heart disease prediction framework was suggested. The propose model called MLP offered a prediction result that gave the primary situation of a patient to CAD (Gavhane & Kokkula, 2018, March). Because of modern technological advancement, machine learning algorithms have been built in significant numbers. That's why, because of its expertise and correctness, a machine learning method named Multi Layered Perceptron (MLP) was suggested in this review. Furthermore, this algorithm provided the nearest trusted output on the basis of feedback provided by the customers. More percentages of persons used the proposed system to improve their knowledge of their recent heart disease. Ultimately, this system led to a decrease in people dying due to heart disease. Using latest technology such as machine learning, fuzzy logic, image recognition and many more in the near future, the same forecasting systems can be built for multiple constant or deadly diseases, e.g., Cancer, Diabetes and so on. Furthermore, modern algorithms may be predicted to achieve greater correctness and trustworthiness. Big data technology such as Hadoop can be used to store large data volumes of whole universal clients. In the future, certain technology such as cloud computing can also be used for client data handling or monitoring.

Aakash Chauhan, et.al (2018) stated that one of the biggest factors for small lives was heart disease, in order to achieve specific outcomes in a short period, immense quantities of individuals relied on the medical structure (Chauhan, Jain, & Sharma, 2018, Feburary). The vast amount of data is produced and gathered daily by the medical industry. Using data creativity, the process automation approach has been used to acquire captivating information. A data mining strategy called the Weighted Association Rule was employed to eliminate the manual task. This methodology also supplied support for the direct data collection from electronic reports. This technique decreased the cost of service and also helped save many people's lives. A technique for estimating the risk level of a patient with cardiovascular disease was found in this research. The experimental findings revealed that the most outstanding predictor of heart disease was helped by a large majority of the techniques.

Purushottam, et.al (2015) stated that in the current development in life, cardiovascular disease (CVD) has been indicated as the primary cause of depression and death. proper detection of this disease was important, but it was also a multifaceted task. This task should be carried out incredibly minutely and skillfully. It would be extremely satisfying to have the proper computerization. Normal citizens may not be equally trained as physicians. In the same way, in all sub-specialties, all doctors were not eligible to be fairly skilled. Often, it was not easy to present qualified and expert doctors effortlessly at certain places. An automatic structure in the study of health tests will improve medicinal care and therefore decrease expenses. In this analysis, a novel framework was built to capably evaluate the schemes for predicting the risk level of the patient on the basis of a given fitness parameter.

C. Sowmiya, et.al (2017) state that the heart disease has been identified as one of world's largest problems. Significant numbers of people died from heart disease after the first heart stroke (Sowmiya & Sumitra, 2017, March). Not only was there a heart attack, but there were also other chronic illnesses, including breast cancer, lung cancer, ventricle valve, and so on. For successful identification of the presence of heart disease in thousands of patterns instantly, a structure was required. In this analysis for cardiac disease forecasting, the capacity of nine classification methods was evaluated. To forecast heart disease, the proposed algorithm the Apriori algorithm and the SVM (support vector machine) were used. In order to forecast the incidence heart disease, some medical records containing data on blood pressure, sex, age type of chest pain, fasting blood sugar were used. Patients suffering from heart disease were able to predict the planned solution. In the basis of this predication, there was interest in the discovery and treatment of heart disease in the medical field. It was examined that, relative to other existing approaches, classification-related approaches were highly powerful and achieved greater precision.

R Latha, et.la (2019) proposed a new paradigm for the prediction of heart for using a partly measurable markov decision mechanism (POMDP) (Latha & Vetrivelan, 2019). During the emergency case, the doctor notified the patient using fog computing. The medical transport was dispatched to the site of the patient in emergency condition. The fog computing device called iFogSim provided the doctor with details. A innovative method was Fog computation in the medical domain. In a few days, this method became very popular amongst the study society. Cardiovascular disease, also known as heart disease, has been discussed in significant numbers of trials. The rise in blood thickness has been a key risk factor for heart disease. The incredibly thick blood would not allow the blood to run, causing a blood-flowing barrier. The main risk factors for heart disease is hypertension, overweight, diabetes, higher blood thickness and so on. Using POMDP's states, meanings, attitude, and change of possibility, the patient's fitness was registered. The heart disease forecasting structure called POMDP calculated the law estimate with the aid of situations and time intervals. In order to tabulate returns, the rule calculation was used for different iterations.

Problem Formulation

the study of predications is the method used to forecast possible scenarios dependent on historical evidence. The techniques of predication analysis have three stages: preprocessing, extraction of features and classification. The approaches to predication research are widely divided into methods of unsupervised and supervised leaning. This research paper is linked to supervised leaning for the study of predicting heart disease. The SVM classification methodology for the estimation of heart disease is applied in the previous research paper. It is studied that because of the high execution time and less accuracy for the prediction analysis, the SVM classifier has high complexity.

Objectives

The different aims of this research work are mentioned below: -

1. Hybrid design classifier for the prediction of heart disease in data mining.
2. Implement the new solution and compare it in terms of accuracy, continuity, recall, f-measure, and time of execution with the current method.

Research Methodology

There are different steps in the analysis design of this work and these stages are dataset, pre-processing, extraction of functions and classification.

Figure 4. Research process

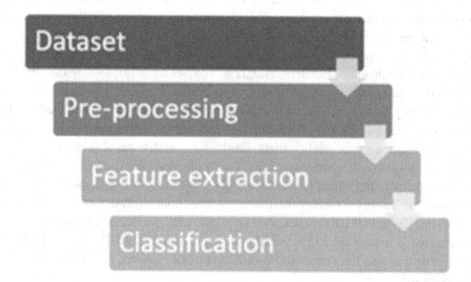

This research work is concerned with the prediction of heart disease. The developed model is based on the integration of the hybrid model with two random forest and decision tree classifiers. For function extraction, the random forest classifier is used and for classification decision tree is used as the basis classifier, the random forest classifier operates and the meta classifier operates as the decision classifier. The suggested method has the following steps: -

1. input datasets and preprocessing: - The datasets will be obtained from the UCI in the first process. To delete incomplete and obsolete values, the dataset is pre-processed. The obtained dataset includes balance data that can be conveniently analyzed for the estimation of heart disease.

2. feature extraction: - For the classification, in the second level, the attributes of the dataset are extracted. The relation between the target set and the attribute set is defined in the feature extraction process. In this step, the random forest classifier method is implemented. The random forest classifier would be the base classifier for the function extraction. The random forest algorithm is an algorithm designed to use a series of decision trees to generate a predictor ensemble that grows in randomly selected data subspaces. Implementing this algorithm is simple and efficient. It produces extremely detailed estimates and can control very large quantities of input variables. At each node, randomly, a small group of input coordinates are picked to divide to create a tree in the array. In addition, to create the tree, it is possible to use the features within the training set which measure the best slip. The CART technique is used to optimize tree size without pruning. The subspace randomization function is associated with bagging to resample the training data set, every time a new individual tree is grown. Collectively, the {r n (x, m, D(n)), m1} randomized base regression trees generate a random forest. Here, the I'd outputs are denoted by _1, _2,.... for a randomized variable. By combining these random trees, the aggregated regression approximation is made.

$$\overline{r_n}\left(X, D_n\right) = E_-\left[r_n\left(X, \tilde{\ }, D_n\right)\right]$$

Here, E_ denotes the expectation of random parameters on X and data set D n. The calculation in the study omits the dependency and one can even write (r n) ?? (X, D n) instead of (r n) ?? (X).

3. Model building and prediction analysis: In the last stage, the input dataset will be split into phases of training and evaluation. More than 50 percent will be the training section and the remainder of the part will be the evaluation set. The data set will be trained using the decision tree classification and the final prediction of the set is generated. The decision is a hierarchical data system that uses a divide and conquer technique to represent the data, called the decision tree. Instead of non-parametric grouping, categorical marks are used for the discussion of the decision trees. Regression may also be done with them. The purpose of decision tree within the classification is to identify the labels for new instances. In the decision tree classifiers, the instances are depicted as attribute vectors. Feature value checks are represented as nodes, marks are denoted as leaves, and there must be one branch available for each feature value at each node. Entropy is used to describe the gain of data in this classifier as a metric. Entropy is defined as the degree of impurity of an arbitrary set of instances. For example, if a list S that contains both negative and positive examples of some target set considered, Entropy is described as:

$$Entropy(S) \equiv -p_{\oplus} \log_2 p_{\oplus} - p_{\ominus} \log_2 p_{\ominus}$$

Figure 5. Proposed methodology

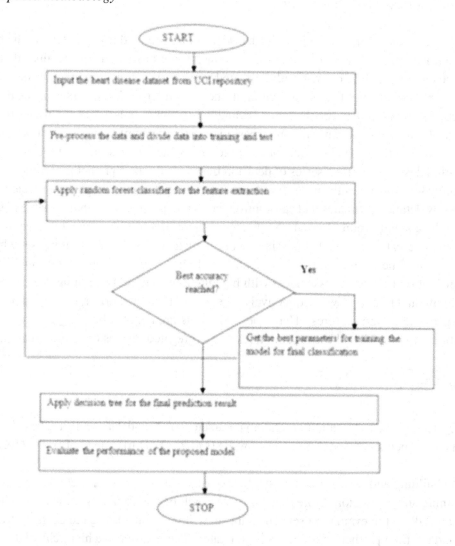

RESULT AND DISCUSSION

The hybrid model is intended for the estimation of heart disease in this study. The mixture of random forests and decision tree classifiers is the hybrid classification paradigm. Data is retrieved from the UCI repository. In terms of precision and execution time, the efficiency of the proposed model is evaluated. For outcome confirmation, the result of the hybrid model is correlated with the KNN and SVM classifiers.

The default anaconda interface is shown as shown in Figure 6, and spider is applied to forecast heart disease using classification methods.

Figure 6. Default interface

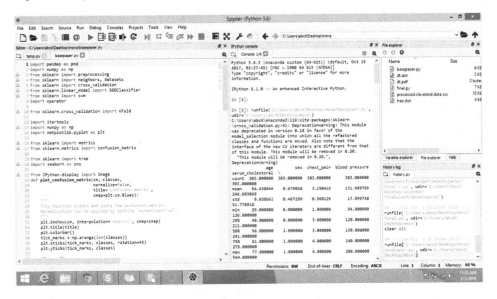

Figure 7. Data description

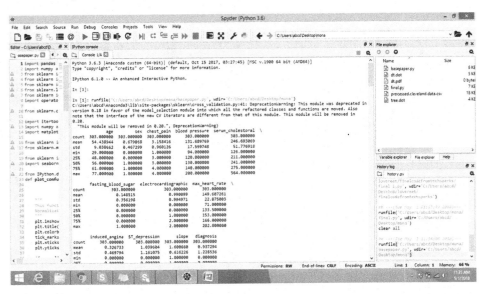

The heart disease dataset is taken from the UCI repository, as seen in figure 7. The data set is defined in this figure, which means value, standard deviation, etc.

AS displayed in the figure 8, The heart disease datasets are derived from the UCI repository. With the SVM classifier, the K-means algorithm is introduced and its consistency is 80%. The K-means basis algorithm is used and the actual relationship between attributes cannot be determined and the precision is lower because of that.

As shown in figure 9, For prediction analysis, the classification technique is implemented to the SVM classifier that can classify the results.

Figure 8. Applying the current approach

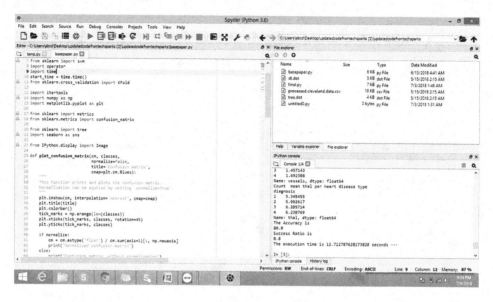

Figure 9. prediction Analysis

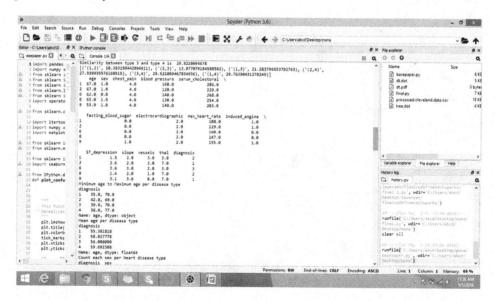

As seen in the figure 10, Data from the UCI repository is taken as the input from which accuracy is expected for prediction. The scatter graph indicates the age vs heart rate of the patients in this figure.

As seen in the figure 11, As the input from which accuracy is required for prediction, the UCI repository data is taken. Age verses electrocardoilogy is seen in this figure scatter diagram.

As displayed in Figure 12, The efficiency comparison compares the efficiency of SVM, KNN and hybrid versions. The hybrid model is tested with an improved accuracy of nearly 92%. The combination is a Random Forest Combination and decision tree classification and techniques.

Figure 10. Plotting of attributes values

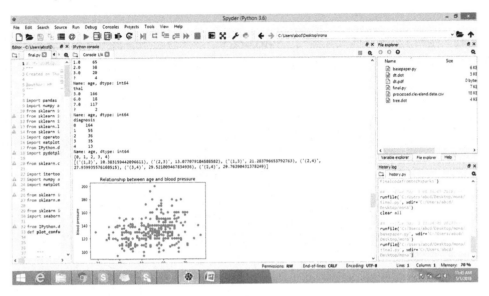

Figure 11. attribute value plotting

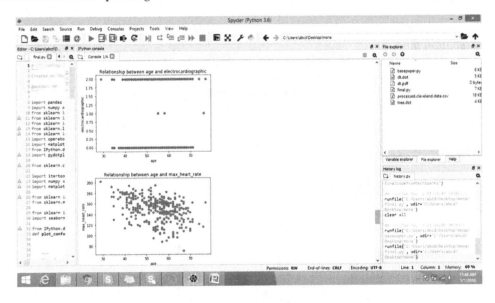

As shown in figure 13, Compared to SVM and KNN, the hybrid classifier's execution time is shorter. In contrast to hybrid classifiers, the KNN and SVM classifiers are complicated since the hybrid classifier has the least time for execution.

As demonstrated in figure 14, The strategy's implied confusion matrix is drawn, which displays the true and predicted value. The x axis shows that the value of the estimate is correct and the y axis shows the prediction value of the specific heart attack.

Figure 12. accuracy comparison

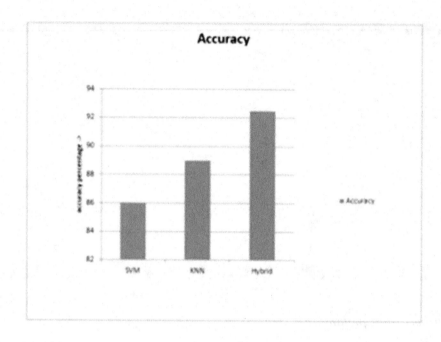

Figure 13. execution time

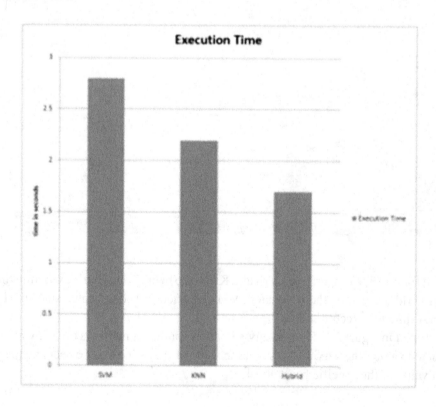

Figure 14. confusion matrix

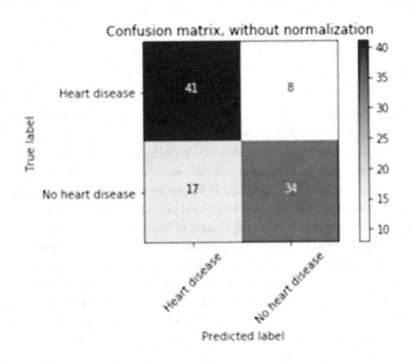

Figure 15. Comparison with precision-recall

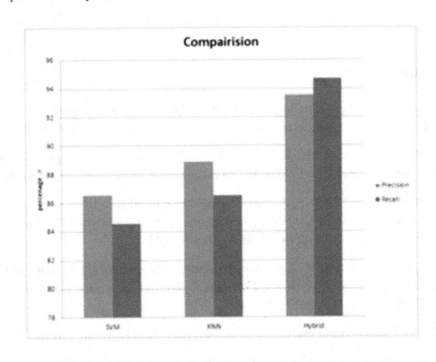

As illustrated in Figure 15, SVM, KNN and hybrid classifiers are compared for consistency and recall values. It is assessed that the hybrid classifier has optimal accuracy-recall values relative to SVM and KNNN.

CONCLUSION

Data mining is called the mechanism by which secret and unknown trends are discovered. Deep learning techniques, datasets infrastructure and predictive evaluation are mixed with one another for the intent of derive hidden trends and associations from huge datasets. With the need for successful knowledge retrieval, the method of data mining is gaining popularity in health insurance. The heart's professional position is the meaning of life. If the functioning of the heart is inappropriate, the other body parts of humans are also disturbed. Owing to multiple variables such as blood pressure, sugar content, etc., the operation of the heart is affected. Owing to many causes, the chance of heart failure may be raised. Today, the bulk of deaths are caused by heart disease. By applying estimation, an effective outcome of diseases can be obtained. The interactions between independent and dependent variables are discovered by prediction, as the name implies. For the discovery and retrieval of secret information relevant to heart disease, it uses a historical database of heart disorders. By addressing complex questions, the heart condition can be diagnosed and thus, the physicians can make intelligent health decisions. In this review, it is concluded that predictive analysis is a method focused on current data that forecasts potential possibilities. The random forest and decision tree combination is the hybrid model designed in this work. In python, the suggested model is introduced and compared to SVM, KNN classifiers, the results are verified. The hybrid classifiers have an average accuracy of up to 92 percent compared to SVM and KNN. The clustering algorithm will in future be extended to the data division with the hybrid classifier process.

REFERENCES

Agrawal, K. C., & Nagori, M. (n.d.). Clusters of ayurvedic medicines using improved k-means algorithm. *International Conference on Advances in Computer Science and Electronics Engineering, 4*(13), 183-195.

Al-Radaideh, Q., Assaf, A. A., & Alnagi, E. (2013, December). Predicting stock prices using data mining techniques. *The International Arab Conference on Information Technology (ACIT'2013)*.

Ambekar, S., & Phalnikar, R. (2018, August). Disease risk prediction by using convolutional neural network. In *Fourth International Conference on Computing Communication Control and Automation (ICCUBEA)* (pp. 1-5). IEEE. 10.1109/ICCUBEA.2018.8697423

Babu, S., Vivek, E., & Famina, K. P. (2017, April). Heart disease diagnosis using data mining technique. In *International conference of Electronics, Communication and Aerospace Technology (ICECA)* (pp. 750-753). IEEE. 10.1109/ICECA.2017.8203643

Bahety, A. (2014). Extension and evaluation of id3–decision tree algorithm. *Entropy (S), 2*(1), 1–8.

Bansal, A., Sharma, M., & Goel, S. (2017). Improved k-mean clustering algorithm for prediction analysis using classification technique in data mining. *International Journal of Computers and Applications, 157*(6).

Bharti, S., & Mishra, A. (2015). Prediction of Future Possible Offender's Network and Role of Offenders. In *Fifth International Conference on Advances in Computing and Communications (ICACC)* (pp. 159-162). IEEE. 10.1109/ICACC.2015.36

Chadha, A., & Kumar, S. (2014, February). An improved K-means clustering algorithm: a step forward for removal of dependency on K. In *International Conference on Reliability Optimization and Information Technology (ICROIT)* (pp. 136-140). IEEE. 10.1109/ICROIT.2014.6798312

Chakraborty, S., Nagwani, N. K., & Dey, L. (2012). *Weather forecasting using incremental K-means clustering.* arXiv preprint arXiv:1406.4756.

Chauhan, A., Jain, A., & Sharma, P. (2018, February). Heart disease prediction using evolutionary rule learning. In *4th International Conference on Computational Intelligence & Communication Technology (CICT)* (pp. 1-4). IEEE.

Chaurasia, V., & Pal, S. (2013). Early prediction of heart diseases using data mining techniques. *Caribbean Journal of Science and Technology, 1,* 208–217.

Chen, M., Hao, Y., Hwang, K., Wang, L., & Wang, L. (2017, April). Disease prediction by machine learning over big data from healthcare communities. *IEEE Access: Practical Innovations, Open Solutions, 5,* 5. doi:10.1109/ACCESS.2017.2694446

Das, R., Turkoglu, I., & Sengur, A. A. (2009). Diagnosis of valvular heart disease through neural networks ensembles. *Computer Methods and Programs in Biomedicine, 93*(2), 185–191. doi:10.1016/j.cmpb.2008.09.005 PMID:18951649

Desai, S. (2013). Intelligent heart disease prediction system using probabilistic neural network. *International Journal on Advanced Computer Theory and Engineering, 2*(3).

Dewan, A., & Sharma, M. (2015). Prediction of Heart Disease Using a Hybrid Technique in Data Mining Classification. *IEEE, 43*(6), 13-24.

Dey, M., & Rautaray, S. S. (2014). Study and analysis of Data Mining algorithms for healthcare decision support system. *International Journal of Computer Science and Information Technologies, 5*(1), 470–477.

Gandhi, M., & Singh, S. N. (2015). Predictions in Heart Disease Using Techniques of Data Mining. *1st International Conference on Futuristic trend in Computational Analysis and Knowledge Management (ABLAZE-2015), 8*(6), 13-48. 10.1109/ABLAZE.2015.7154917

Gavhane, A., & Kokkula, G. (2018, March). Prediction of heart disease using machine learning. In *Second International Conference on Electronics, Communication and Aerospace Technology (ICECA)* (pp. 1275-1278). IEEE.

Gladkykh, T., Hnot, T., & Solskyy, V. (2016). Fuzzy logic inference for unsupervised anomaly detection. In *First International Conference on Data Stream Mining & Processing (DSMP)* (pp. 42-47). IEEE. 10.1109/DSMP.2016.7583504

Hussain, K. Z., Durairaj, M., & Farzana, G. R. (2012, March). Criminal behavior analysis by using data mining techniques. In *International Conference on Advances in Engineering, Science and Management (ICAESM)* (pp. 656-658). IEEE.

Jabbar, A., & Shirina, S. (2016). Heart disease prediction system based on hidden naïve Bayes classifier. *IC4, 4*(11), 23-48.

Kaur, D., & Jyoti, K. (2013). Enhancement in the Performance of K-means Algorithm. *International Journal of Computer Science and Communication Engineering, 2*(1), 29–32.

Khobragade, P. K., & Malik, L. G. (2014, April). Data generation and analysis for digital forensic application using data mining. In *Fourth International Conference on Communication Systems and Network Technologies* (pp. 458-462). IEEE. 10.1109/CSNT.2014.97

Latha, R., & Vetrivelan, P. (2019). Blood Viscosity based Heart Disease Risk Prediction Model in Edge/Fog Computing. In *11th International Conference on Communication Systems & Networks (COMSNETS)* (pp. 833-837). IEEE. 10.1109/COMSNETS.2019.8711358

Mane, T. U. (2017, Feburary). Smart heart disease prediction system using Improved K-means and ID3 on big data. In *International Conference on Data Management, Analytics and Innovation (ICDMAI)* (pp. 239-245). IEEE.

Nahar, J., Imam, T., Tickle, K. S., & Chen, Y. P. (2013). Association rule mining to detect factors which contribute to heart disease in males and females. *Expert Systems with Applications, 40*(4), 1086–1093. doi:10.1016/j.eswa.2012.08.028

Oyelade, O. J., Oladipupo, O. O., & Obagbuwa, I. C. (2010, January). Application of k Means Clustering algorithm for prediction of Students Academic Performance. *International Journal of Computer Science and Information Security, 7*(1), 292–295.

Pahwa, K., & Kumar, R. (2017, October). Prediction of heart disease using hybrid technique for selecting features. In *4th IEEE Uttar Pradesh Section International Conference on Electrical, Computer and Electronics (UPCON)* (pp. 500-504). IEEE. 10.1109/UPCON.2017.8251100

Palaniappan, S., & Awang, R. (2008, March). Intelligent heart disease prediction system using data mining techniques. In *International conference on computer systems and applications* (pp. 108-115). IEEE. 10.1109/AICCSA.2008.4493524

Parthiban, L., & Subramanian, R. (2008). Intelligent heart disease prediction system using CANFIS and genetic algorithm. *International Journal of Biological, Biomedical and Medical Sciences, 3*(3).

Peter, T. J., & Somasundaram, K. (2012). An empirical study on prediction of heart disease using classification data mining techniques. In *IEEE-International conference on advances in engineering, science and management (ICAESM-2012)*, (pp. 514-518). IEEE.

Rajathi, S., & Radhamani, G. (2016). *Prediction and Analysis of Rheumatic Heart Disease using kNN Classification with ACO. IEEE, 4(7)*.

Rauf, A., Khusro, S., Javed, H., & Saeed, M. (2012, January). Enhanced K-Mean Clustering Algorithm to Reduce Number of Iterations and Time Complexity. *Middle East Journal of Scientific Research, 12*(7), 959–963.

Sa, C. L., Hossain, E. D., & bin Hossin, M. (2014, November). Student performance analysis system (SPAS). In *The 5th International Conference on Information and Communication Technology for The Muslim World (ICT4M)* (pp. 1-6). IEEE.

Shendurkar, M. A., & Chopde, R. N. (n.d.). An Ontology based Enhanced Framework for Instant Messages Filtering for Detection of Cyber Crimes. *International Journal on Recent and Innovation Trends in Computing and Communication*, 3(5), 2820–2826.

Sing, J., Kamra, A., & Singh, H. (2016). *Prediction of Heart Diseases Using Associative Classification.* Academic Press.

Sivagowry, S., Durairaj, M., & Persia, A. (2013). An Empirical Study on applying Data Mining Techniques for the Analysis and Prediction of Heart Disease. *IEEE, 4*(1), 13-38.

Sowmiya, C., & Sumitra, P. (2017, March). Analytical study of heart disease diagnosis using classification techniques. In *International Conference on Intelligent Techniques in Control, Optimization and Signal Processing (INCOS)* (pp. 1-5). IEEE.

Sultana, M., Haider, A., & Uddin, M. S. (2016, September). Analysis of data mining techniques for heart disease prediction. In *3rd International Conference on Electrical Engineering and Information Communication Technology (ICEEICT)* (pp. 1-5). IEEE. 10.1109/CEEICT.2016.7873142

Sundar, V. B., Devi, T., & Saravanan, N. (June,2012). Development of a Data Clustering Algorithm for Predicting Heart. *IJCA, 48*(7), 8-13.

Sunita, S., Chandrakanta, B. j., & Chinmayee, R. (2016). A hybrid approach of intrusion detection using ANN and FCM. *European Journal of Advances in Engineering and Technology*, 3(2), 6–14.

Taneja, A. (2013). Heart disease prediction system using data mining techniques. *Oriental. Journal of Computer Science and Technology*, 6(4), 457–466.

Theresa Princy, R., & Thomas, J. (2016). Human Heart Disease Prediction System using DataMining Techniques. *International Conference on Circuit, Power and Computing Technologies, 4(1)*, 23-48.

Wu, X., Zhu, X., Wu, G. Q., & Ding, W. (2013). Data mining with big data. *IEEE Transactions on Knowledge and Data Engineering*, 26(1), 97–107.

Yadav, A. K., Tomar, D., & Agarwal, S. (July, 2013). Clustering of lung cancer data using foggy k-means. In *International Conference on Recent Trends in Information Technology (ICRTIT)* (pp. 13-18). IEEE. 10.1109/ICRTIT.2013.6844173

Zurina, H. (2013). Hybrid of fuzzy clustering neural network over NSL dataset for intrusion detection system. *Journal of Computational Science*, 9(3), 391–403. doi:10.3844/jcssp.2013.391.403

Chapter 16
Predictive Strength of Ensemble Machine Learning Algorithms for the Diagnosis of Large Scale Medical Datasets

Elangovan Ramanujam

iD https://orcid.org/0000-0003-1450-9097

Department of Information Technology, Thiagarajar College of Engineering, Madurai, India

L. Rasikannan

Department of Computer Science and Engineering, Alagappa Chettiar Government College of Engineering, India

S. Viswa

Department of Information Technology, Thiagarajar College of Engineering, Madurai, India

B. Deepan Prashanth

Department of Information Technology, Thiagarajar College of Engineering, Madurai, India

ABSTRACT

Machine learning is not a simple technology but an amazing field having more and more to explore. It has a number of real-time applications such as weather forecast, price prediction, gaming, medicine, fraud detection, etc. Machine learning has an increased usage in today's technological world as data is growing in volumes and machine learning is capable of producing mathematical and statistical models that can analyze complex data and generate accurate results. To analyze the scalable performance of the learning algorithms, this chapter utilizes various medical datasets from the UCI Machine Learning repository ranges from smaller to large datasets. The performance of learning algorithms such as naïve Bayes, decision tree, k-nearest neighbor, and stacking ensemble learning method are compared in different evaluation models using metrics such as accuracy, sensitivity, specificity, precision, and f-measure.

DOI: 10.4018/978-1-7998-6673-2.ch016

INTRODUCTION

Recently, there is advancement in Information and Communication technology that have changed the operations in various domains of life such as intelligent transportation system (Deng et al, 2020), agriculture (Pudumalar et al, 2017), healthcare (Ramanujam et al, 2019), and education systems (Tomei, 2020). However in specific domains of medical applications, still there is a more manual process that has been carried out such as writing lab values, diagnoses, and other notes on the paper. It is very specific that, the health care sector to be concentrated with technology advancement to improve the workflow process and this would improve patient care (Zuckerbraun et al, 2020). As of now the advancements made in the electronic medical records are not remarkable, and the reports generated are also not much better than the traditional process replaced (Juhn and Liu, 2020). In the future, the electronic information provided by the doctor to be totally enhanced by the power of analytics and machine learning algorithms.

These types of advanced analytics may provide better information to the doctors at the point of patient care such as easy access to blood pressure and other vital signs etc. It would be easy to analyze the patients' risk for stroke, coronary artery disease, and kidney failure, etc based on the last 50 pressure readings, lab test results, race, gender, family history, socioeconomic status, and latest clinical trial data. This kind of analysis generates more and advance information to clinicians for taking better decisions about patient diagnosis and treatment options. On the other side, this generates a huge dataset for a single patient for analysis which makes it difficult to analyze. At this point, the value of machine learning in healthcare has the ability to process huge datasets beyond the scope of human capability and reliably converts the data analysis into clinical insights that aid physicians in planning and providing care, ultimately leading to better outcomes, lower costs of care, and increased patient satisfaction (Karthick and Pankajavalli, 2020).

Machine Learning (ML) algorithms are generally categorized into supervised, unsupervised, semi-supervised, and Reinforcement learning (Mitchell, 1999). Currently, ML algorithms provide a significant number of valuable tools for intelligent data analysis, data collection, and data storage. It is widely used for analyzing medical datasets by giving patient records and accurate diagnoses given as input to train a machine learning algorithm (Balachander and Ramanujam, 2017). The resulting classifier can subsequently produce a better outcome to help clinicians to diagnose new patients. In this manner, diagnosis can be accelerated in a more accurate and reliable way. Furthermore, the classifier can also be used to educate student physicians on how to arrive at an accurate diagnosis. In addition, the predictive models' based machine learning algorithms provide the best support for earlier detection of disease detection to the clinicians' knowledge and experience.

The performances of machine learning algorithm depend on the size of the dataset, attributes, and types, the number of class variables, size of training and testing, parameters used, etc (Singh et al, 2016). In addition, the learning algorithms may provide different performances for different datasets. The user can't fix anyone learning algorithms to be more feasible for all kinds of datasets. To analyze the performances of machine learning algorithms, this chapter demonstrates the performances of predictive models in the field of healthcare applications. Various medical datasets are utilized from the UCI machine learning repository for the scalable performance of learning algorithms (Gupta et al, 2016). Further, to overcome the challenges of traditional learning algorithms, this chapter emphasizes developing a Stacking ensemble learning method using traditional learning algorithms for better and dynamic predictions of medical data.

The remainder of the chapter is organized as follows. The following section discusses the machine learning algorithms and their types along with the Stacking ensemble method. Next, the dataset collection and pre-processing of a dataset are presented along with performance evaluation, followed by the experimental results and discussions on a scalable dataset and the performances of learning algorithms. Subsequently, conclusions and suggestions for future research are represented.

MACHINe LEARNING

Machine Learning (Mitchell, 1999) is one of the trending technologies in the field of data engineering which has a number of promising applications in various research domains. Machine learning allows the machines and systems to learn on their own from the given training dataset and predict the future aspects for the test data from the trained model. Learning algorithms finds its applications in a number of days to day aspects such as search engines, e-commerce websites (Rasikannan et al, 2019), social media, cardiovascular disease diagnosis (Padmavathi and Ramanujam, 2015), fetal ECG applications (Ramanujam et al, 2019), etc. The learning algorithms use the data to analyze learns from the dataset and generate a trained model on it using any programming tools. The dataset may be 0-dimensional (Texts), 1- dimensional (Audio signals or time series signals), 2-dimensional (Patterns or Images), 3-dimensional (Video). The learning algorithms are generally categorized into three such as supervised learning, unsupervised learning, and Reinforcement learning.

Supervised Learning

To understand the concept of supervised learning we would look at a simple example. If we want to teach a child to identify a bike and a car, we would show the pictures of both and teach it by explaining the basic features of both. For example, in this case, we would teach the child that a bike has two wheels, small in size, and the car has four wheels and is bigger in size. If we later ask the child the picture of the bike it would identify that it is a bike by recollecting that a bike only has two wheels and would come to the conclusion that it is a bike. Similarly, supervised learning involves input and output where a labeled input is used to generate the output for the test set. The two most widely used approaches in supervised learning are classification and regression.

Classification is used to categorize the data into groups whereas the regression method is used for cases involving real-time data sets. For instance, "what may be the cost of the house?" is a regression problem as it predicts the cost of the house based on certain measurements. Whereas, "cost of the house increases or not" is a classification problem that says 'yes' or 'No'. The classification algorithms use categorical, ordinal, or binary data in other cases, the regression techniques use only the numerical values. The regression technique aims to determine the relationship between a dependent and independent variable using a mathematical function. Some of the classification algorithms are Decision Trees (DT) (Song and Ying, 2015), Naïve Bayes (NB) (Rish, 2001), Support Vector Machines (SVM) (Noble, 2006), k- Nearest Neighbor (k-NN), Neural Network (NN), etc. Linear regression, polynomial regression, CART is some examples of regression techniques. In general, Supervised learning algorithms are used in applications like signal recognition (Ramanujam and Padmavathi, 2016), object recognition, bio informatics, posture recognition (Ramanujam and Padmavathi, 2019), etc.

Unsupervised Learning

Another category of a learning algorithm is unsupervised learning (Barlow, 1989; Ghahramani, 1989). To know the concept, consider an example. If we show the pictures of a dog and cat together without teaching the child then it may get confused and not judge the picture exactly. However, the child may at least group them based on differences and patterns which is exactly an unsupervised learning. This learning clusters or groups the dataset based on the similarity between the groups i.e the inter group has low similarity whereas the intra group has high similarity.

Unlike supervised learning algorithms, the machines are not given with any labeled data for training. Actually, there is no specific training and testing phase in the unsupervised techniques. But during execution, it learns by making out the differences, recognizes patterns, and categorizes into groups. *k*- Means clustering, *k*- Medoids clustering, Balanced Iterative Reducing and Clustering using Hierarchies (BIRCH), Agglomerative Nesting (AGNES), Divisive Analysis (DIANA), etc. Among the listed unsupervised algorithms, clustering is more familiar and used for anomaly detection and sub-module of feature selection technique. Anomaly detection is the task of spotting out the unanticipated items in the dataset. Unsupervised learning algorithm has certain real-time applications as like supervised applications such as Alzheimer disease (Altaf et al, 2018), Pattern Recognition, Object detection, diabetes prediction (Shakeel et al, 2018), etc.

Reinforcement Learning

Reinforcement Learning (RL) has familiar applications in the field of Semi-automated and automated Robots (Kaelbling et al, 1996). RL is an approach where the machines are the agents that learn the environment from the feedback or experiences to find the optimal choice to reach the goal or destination. For instance, Google maps use RL to provide various paths from a source to the destination. Further, it also considers the optimal choice to reach the target in case of traffic or congestion to reach the destination. RL techniques are used mostly in Artificial Intelligence (AI) techniques to train the agents and make decisions in a sequential manner based on the output of past actions.

Ensemble Learning

Machine learning is a wide area and involves huge technology to be explored and, ensemble machine learning is one of the excavations in the huge mine of machine learning. To make the machine learning algorithms more efficient, Ensemble Machine learning is evolved over time. Ensemble learning trains the machine by merging several base models to increase the outcome of learning. Ensemble chooses a meta-learning algorithm that links various learning algorithms into predictive models for decreasing the variance (bagging), biasing (boosting), or increasing the predictions (stacking).

Ensemble learning combines one or more learning algorithms into a single set, in order to make the prediction of test dataset more efficient and accurate in performance. Innumerable algorithms are available but finite numbers only provide a better choice of accuracy and accomplishments. This learning mechanism introduces the usage of better features to predict the results which at times could make even complex tasks easier than the traditional learning algorithms. Thus, in turn, allows better decisions to be made by the machines and are very much helpful in real-world prediction applications where a variety of computational models can give optimal results. Ensemble learning algorithms are categorized into bagging, boosting, and stacking.

Bagging

Bagging is the blended version of the word 'Bootstrap aggregating'. It combines bootstrapping and Aggregation to form an ensemble model voted with equal weight which is mainly used for various predictive applications. Bagging combines multiple models to form a single ensemble trained model using the statistical aspect of train and test data. Further to promote variance, this ensemble model uses a randomly drawn subset of the training model for each ensemble. Random Forest is a familiar algorithm that combines random decision trees with bagging to achieve high classification accuracy.

Boosting

Boosting is an ensemble learning technique that concentrates to decrease the bias of the learner algorithms purposefully designed to merge weak learners to provide strong ensemble learning algorithm. Weak algorithms only match up with the real classification to a smaller extent whereas Strong algorithms have a better tie-in with real classifications. Boosting is of two types Adaboost and Gradient boost. Adaboost algorithms are generally used for classification where the odd man out data points are truncated to provide better performance in classification by increasing their weights. Gradient boosting is applicable for both classification and regression algorithms.

Stacking

Stacking also termed as a stacked generalization approach applicable for both classification and regression techniques. It involves training a learning algorithm to combine the predictions of several other learning algorithms termed as base classifiers. All the base classifiers are trained using the available data and then combined to train a metaclassifier to make a final prediction using all the predictions of base classifiers as inputs. Stacking typically yields better performance than any of the single trained and it provides better results for supervised learning tasks such as regression, classification and distance learning and also for unsupervised learning such as density estimation.

In this chapter, the traditional machine learning algorithms such as k-Nearest Neighbor (k-NN), Naïve Bayes (NB), and Decision Tree (DT) are used for performance analysis. In addition, the Stacking ensemble learning algorithm has been used for performance analysis. In which, the Decision Tree (DT) and Naïve Bayes (NB) are used as base classifiers, and Support Vector Machine (SVM) is used as Metaclassifier. For the performance analysis, the datasets of varying size and classes are used and the details are given in the following section.

Naive Bayes (NB)

Naïve Bayes algorithm (Rish, 2001) is a probabilistic model that follows the concept of Bayes conditional probability theorem. The algorithm works with an assumption on strong independence assumptions between the features. This classifier is highly scalable and requires a number of parameters linear in the number of variables in the learning problem. Naïve Bayes classifier has famous applications in the field of text analytics, document classification, medical diagnosis etc.

Support Vector Machine (SVM)

In machine learning, Support Vector Machines (SVM) also termed Support Vector networks are the supervised learning model that analyzes the data used for both classification and regression (Noble, 2006). This learning model creates the boundary termed as hyperplane which separates the n-dimensional space into several categories so that the data points are organized into correct category. This algorithm uses various points of the given data point that lie on the hyperplane known as the support vectors. SVM has most famous application in the domain of image processing and medical diagnosis.

k- Nearest Neighbor (k-NN)

In machine learning and pattern recognition, the *k*-NN algorithm is a non-parametric method used for both classification and regression. *K*-NN is also referred to be instance-based learning or lazy learners (Laaksonen and oja, 1996). *k*- Nearest Neighbor (Aha et al, 1991) is a supervised machine learning algorithm trained using labeled training data along with target class variable available. More formally the trained model may confidentially predict the output target variables for a set of unlabelled observation. *k*-NN is most widely used machine learning algorithm and it is simple and effective for implementation. The classifier calculated the minimum distance using familiar distance measures such as Euclidean distance, Manhattan distance or Chebyshev distance to calculate the minimum distance between the train and test data in terms of *k*- nearest neighbors. The most common or ranked class among the *k*- nearest neighbors is assigned as the target class variable for unlabelled test data.

Decision Tree (DT)

Decision trees (DT) are non-parametric supervised machine learning approach (Salzberg, 1994; Song and Ying, 2015) used for both classification and regression. This algorithm breaks down a dataset into smaller and smaller subsets using larger Information Gain (reduces the uncertainty towards final decision) which are fitted in a tree structure. Iteratively, this approach breaks the dataset and incrementally develops the growth of the tree with internal nodes and leaf node. The final result of classification can be obtained from the leaf node (target class), and the internal node provides the complex decision rules to obtain the decisions. The root node of a tree corresponds to best predictor node.

DATASET COLLECTION

To analyze the scalable performance of traditional machine learning algorithms and the stacking ensemble learning algorithm various medical datasets are utilized from UCI Machine Learning repository (Dua and Graff, 2019). For the analysis, the datasets are considered with the range of 32 instances to 7200 instances, 6 attributes to 754 attributes and 2 classes to 16 classes. The datasets are categorized into small, medium and large based on the number of instances. Small datasets represents the datasets with no more than 200 instances, medium represents the instances between 201 and 400 and the large represents the dataset with more than 400 instances. In addition, certain datasets have missing values those are replaced using certain mean values of the same attributes as discussed in (Zhang et al, 2003). Mostly all the datasets are freely available and can be used for any research implementation and demonstration. The meta-data of the medical datasets utilized from the UCI repository are shown in Table 1.

Table 1. Meta-data of Medical datasets from UCI Machine Learning repository

S.No	Name of the Dataset	# of Instances	# of Attributes	Missing values	# of classes	Size
1	Arrhythmia	452	279	Yes	16	Large
2	Breast Cancer	286	9	Yes	2	Medium
3	Breast Cancer Wisconsin (Original)	699	10	Yes	2	Large
4	Chronic Kidney Disease	400	25	Yes	2	Medium
5	Dermatology	366	34	Yes	6	Medium
6	Echocardiogram	132	13	Yes	2	Small
7	Heart Disease	294	76	Yes	4	Medium
8	Mammographic Mass	961	6	Yes	2	Large
9	Parkinson's Data Set	197	23	No	2	Small
10	Parkinson's Disease Classification	756	754	No	2	Large
11	Pima Indian Diabetes	768	8	No	2	Large
12	SPECT Heart	267	45	No	2	Medium
13	Thyroid Disease	215	45	No	3	Medium

PERFORMANCE EVALUATION

To analyze the performance of the learning algorithms, the familiar classification metrics such as Accuracy, Sensitivity, Specificity, Precision, Recall, and F-score are used. For better understanding, consider a binary class patient with the specific disease found and not-found as shown in Table 1. Performance metrics involve various terms such as True Positive (TP), True Negative (TN), False Positive (FP), and False Negative (FN).

TP – If a disease is proven present in the patient and the outcome of the diagnostic test also indicates the presence of disease

TN – If a disease is proven not present in the patient and the outcome of the diagnostic test also indicates the absence of disease

FP – If a disease is proven present in the patient and the outcome of the diagnostic test indicates the absence of disease

FN – If a disease is proven not present in the patient and the outcome of the diagnostic test indicates the presence of disease.

Table 2. Terms used for Performance metric calculations

Outcome of Diagnostic test	Disease (Standard Truth)	
	Positive	**Negative**
Positive	True Positive (TP)	False Positive (FP)
Negative	False Negative (FN)	True Negative (TN)

Using the terms, the Performance metrics such as Accuracy, Sensitivity, Specificity, Precision, F-Score are calculated as defined in the equations 1, 2, 3, 4 and 5 respectively.

$$Accuracy = \frac{TP + TN}{TP + FP + FN + TN}. \tag{1}$$

$$Specificity = \frac{TN}{TN + FP}. \tag{2}$$

$$Sensitivity = \frac{TP}{TP + FN}. \tag{3}$$

$$Precision = \frac{TP}{TP + FP}. \tag{4}$$

$$F - score = \frac{2TP}{2TP + FP + FN}. \tag{5}$$

RESULTS AND DISCUSSIONS

For performance analysis, a total of 13 medical datasets are utilized from UCI machine learning repository. These datasets are pre-processed from missing values using certain mean values of the same attributes and classified using the Weka machine learning tool (Srivastava, 2014). The datasets without row header are pre-processed with attribute names as row header and the class variables are transferred to categorical attributes from the numerical representation. In addition, all the learning algorithms are executed using 10-fold cross-validation, 80%-20% training, and testing data and 70%-30% training and testing data for performance comparison and are tabulated with performance metrics such as Accuracy, Sensitivity, Specificity, Precision, F-score. The following section discusses the performances of traditional machine learning and the Stacking ensemble learning method.

Arrhythmia

The aim of this dataset is to classify the cardiac arrhythmia data into 16 groups (Cohen et al, 2005). Class 01 refers to normal ECG signal and the other class from 02 to 15 refers to different arrhythmia classes and class 16 refers to unclassified ones. The performances of traditional machine learning algorithms are shown in Table 3. On comparing the performance for 10-fold cross-validation, the Stacking ensemble learning method shows better performances than other algorithms in Accuracy, Sensitivity, and Specificity. However, in the case of Specificity NB has better performance and in terms of F-Measure, DT has shown nearer value to the stacking method. On comparing the performance of the 80-20 and 70-30 training and testing process, the Stacking ensemble method outperforms all the other algorithms in all aspects.

Table 3. Performance of learning algorithms for Arrhythmia dataset.

Evaluation Models	Classifier	Accuracy (%)	Sensitivity (%)	Specificity (%)	Precision (%)	F-Measure (%)
10 – fold cross validation	k – NN	53.097	53.1	68.6	59.21	43.51
	NB	62.168	62.2	84.2	49.29	46.66
	DT	65.486	65.5	82.8	62.8	64.0
	Stacking	66.371	66.4	78.4	65.66	63.72
80-20	k – NN	53.33	53.3	72.7	57.31	45.6
	NB	73.33	73.33	70.4	52.8	52.24
	DT	68.89	68.9	81.1	68.7	64.5
	Stacking	73.34	73.33	78.2	77.24	73.2
70-30	k – NN	52.94	52.9	69.2	68.33	48.05
	NB	69.85	69.99	69.2	47.89	47.32
	DT	70.58	70.6	81.2	60.22	52.84
	Stacking	74.26	74.3	82.9	78.17	75.77

Breast Cancer

The dataset was recorded at University Medical Centre, Institute of Oncology, Ljubljana, Yugoslavia. This is one of three domains provided by the Oncology institute repeatedly appeared in machine learning literature (Michalski et al, 1986). Breast cancer is a binary dataset that describes the irradiant information about the recurrence and non-recurrence events. Performances of traditional machine algorithms are shown in Table 4. In the cross-validation process, the stacking ensemble learning algorithm provides better performance in Accuracy, Sensitivity, and Precision whereas the NB algorithm has better performance in Specificity and F-Measure. In the case of 80-20% training and testing, the ensemble stacking method completely fails to show better performance, and NB has shown better performance. This is the case when the weak learners fail to produce better results to improve the performance of Meta-classifier. NB has provided better performances in both 80-20 and 70-30 performance evaluations with other algorithms.

Table 4. Performance of learning algorithms for Breast Cancer dataset.

Evaluation Models	Classifier	Accuracy (%)	Sensitivity (%)	Specificity (%)	Precision (%)	F-Measure (%)
10 – fold cross validation	k – NN	72.7	72.7	51.8	70.6	70.8
	NB	72.7	72.7	56.6	71.4	71.8
	DT	71.6	71.7	43.9	68.5	67.5
	Stacking	73.7	73.8	44.8	72.2	69.1
80-20	k – NN	66.6	66.7	21.7	55.1	60.4
	NB	71.9	71.9	42.7	69.2	70.2
	DT	70.1	70.2	32.5	64.4	66.3
	Stacking	64.9	64.9	30.8	61.1	62.8
70-30	k – NN	69.7	69.8	35.1	66.3	67.8
	NB	76.7	76.7	51.1	75.2	75.8
	DT	73.2	73.3	22.2	58.3	64.9
	Stacking	69.7	69.8	35.1	66.3	67.8

Breast Cancer Wisconsin (Original)

This breast cancer database was obtained from the University Of Wisconsin Hospitals, Madison (Wolberg and Mangasarian, 1990). This binary database categorizes the instances to benign or malignant with some missing values in the dataset. Table 5 shows the performance of machine learning algorithms for the Breast cancer Wisconsin dataset. On comparing the performances, the Naïve Bayes and the Stacking ensemble learning method shows the same performance in all the aspects. This is the case, where the other weak classifier (k-NN) doesn't perform well to build the factors for improving the metaclassifier. In this case of implementation, the computational cost will be higher when compared to traditional classifiers than stacking learners.

Chronic Kidney Disease Dataset

The chronic kidney disease dataset has been collected from Apollo hospitals, Madurai for a period of 2 months. This dataset has 24 attributes of information with 11 numeric and 14 nominal data with a binary class label. The performances of machine learning algorithms are shown in Table 6. On comparing the performances, the k-NN outperforms all the other classifiers in all aspects even with stacking ensemble learning classifiers. The k-NN shows a maximum accuracy of 95.24% in 10-fold cross-validation, 93.38% in 80-20% training and testing, and finally 93.39% for 70-30% evaluation models.

Dermatology Dataset

The different diagnosis observations of erythema-to-squamous diseases are collected in the dermatology dataset (Demiroz et al, 1998). This dataset contains clinical observations and histopathological attributes with 12 and 22 features respectively. Table 7 shows the performances of learning algorithms for the dermatology dataset. On comparing the performance of learning algorithms in 10-fold cross-validation, the NB outperforms other algorithms in all aspects with a maximum accuracy of 97.5%, the sensitivity of 97.5%, Specificity of 99.6%, Precision of 97.7% and F-measure of 97.5%. On the 80-20% evaluation model, the NB has very nearer with a difference of 0.02 with the cross-validation model. In the case of a 70-30% evaluation, the NB and DT have shown equal performances in all the aspects. In all the cases, stacking ensemble learning fails to achieve higher performance, mainly due to a lack of training to the weak classifiers. Further, mostly the dataset contains only the nominal attributes which make the traditional classifiers perform better than the stacking ensemble learning.

Table 5. Performance of learning algorithms for Breast Cancer Wisconsin dataset.

Evaluation Models	Classifier	Accuracy (%)	Sensitivity (%)	Specificity (%)	Precision (%)	F-Measure (%)
10 – fold cross validation	k – NN	94.9	95	93.2	95	95
	NB	95.9	96	96.7	96.2	96
	DT	93.9	94	93.5	94.1	94
	Stacking	95.9	96	96.7	96.2	96
80-20	k – NN	95.7	95.7	95	95.7	95.7
	NB	95.7	95.7	95.8	95.8	95.7
	DT	93.5	93.6	93.8	93.7	93.6
	Stacking	95.7	95.7	95.8	95.8	95.7
70-30	k – NN	95.7	95.7	94.8	95.7	95.7
	NB	95.2	95.2	95.1	95.3	95.3
	DT	94.7	94.8	94.3	94.8	94.8
	Stacking	95.2	95.2	95.1	95.3	95.3

Table 6. Performance of learning algorithms for chronic kidney disease dataset.

Evaluation Models	Classifier	Accuracy (%)	Sensitivity (%)	Specificity (%)	Precision (%)	F-Measure (%)
10 – fold cross validation	k – NN	95.24	96.8	91.4	97.16	96.82
	NB	76.32	84.68	53.23	83.33	84.00
	DT	84.39	89.40	69.47	89.72	89.56
	Stacking	84.39	84.4	74.1	84.3	84.4
80-20	k – NN	93.38	92.59	95.35	98.04	95.24
	NB	75.50	79.28	65.00	86.27	82.63
	DT	77.48	79.82	70.27	89.22	84.26
	Stacking	77.48	77.5	64.8	76.7	76.5
70-30	k – NN	93.39	94.64	89.83	96.36	95.50
	NB	74.01	81.93	52.46	82.42	82.18
	DT	73.13	82.10	50.77	80.61	81.35
	Stacking	73.12	73.1	60.7	73.5	73.3

Table 7. Performance of learning algorithms for dermatology disease dataset

Evaluation Models	Classifier	Accuracy (%)	Sensitivity (%)	Specificity (%)	Precision (%)	F-Measure (%)
10 – fold cross validation	k – NN	95.3	95.4	99.2	95.5	95.4
	NB	97.5	97.5	99.6	97.7	97.5
	DT	94.8	94.8	99	95.2	94.9
	Stacking	97.2	97.3	99.5	97.3	97.3
80-20	k – NN	93.1	93.2	98.6	93.8	93.1
	NB	97.3	97.3	99.4	97.5	97.2
	DT	95.8	95.9	98.8	95.9	95.8
	Stacking	94.5	94.5	98.1	94.6	94.4
70-30	k – NN	94.5	94.5	99.1	95.1	94.5
	NB	98.1	98.2	99.6	98.3	98.2
	DT	98.1	98.2	99.6	98.2	98.2
	Stacking	96.3	96.4	99.3	96.7	96.3

Echocardiogram

The dataset provides the observation of survivability of a patient for at least one year after the heart attack (Kan et al, 1986). The survival and still-alive variables are considered for classification as some may be alive and some are not after the case of a heart attack. The dataset contains 132 instances with 13 attributes all numerical. Table 8 shows the performances of learning algorithms for the Echocardiogram dataset. On comparing the performances of all the learning algorithms, DT outperforms all the other learning algorithms in all the aspects and in all evaluation models. This is the case where the dataset contains only the numerical data with the shorter range (uniformly scaled). Due to the usage of Euclidean distance measure, the DT votes the data points in an efficient manner and outperforms the other algorithms.

Heart Disease

The heart disease dataset (Detrano et al, 1989) contains the heart disease diagnosis information from four different hospitals located at different places such as Cleveland Clinic Foundation, Hungarian Institute of Cardiology, Budapest, V.A. Medical Center, Long Beach, CA and University Hospital, Zurich, Switzerland. The dataset contains 76 attributes and all are only numerical data. Out of 76 attributes only 14 are used for the process (Source dataset itself) with 4 class labels. The performances of learning algorithms are shown in Table 9. On comparing the performances of learning algorithms, the stacking ensemble learning outperforms the other algorithms in all aspects. In all evaluation models, the stacking ensemble learning gains better performances, however, the range values are very closer to the Naïve Bayes algorithm. This case clearly shows the k-NN has poor performance in catalyzing the performance of metaclassifier when compared with the NB classifier.

Table 8. Performance of learning algorithms for Echocardiogram dataset

Evaluation Models	Classifier	Accuracy (%)	Sensitivity (%)	Specificity (%)	Precision (%)	F-Measure (%)
10 – fold cross validation	k – NN	90.5	90.5	89	90.7	90.6
	NB	95.9	95.9	94.4	96	96
	DT	97.2	97.3	95.9	97.4	97.3
	Stacking	94.5	94.6	90.9	94.6	94.5
80-20	k – NN	72.2	72.2	67.8	74	70.8
	NB	88.8	88.9	91.1	91.1	88.9
	DT	100	100	100	100	100
	Stacking	94.4	94.4	95.6	95.1	94.5
70-30	k – NN	80.7	80.8	81.1	81.1	80.8
	NB	88.4	88.5	88.9	88.8	88.5
	DT	100	100	100	100	100
	Stacking	92.3	92.3	93.4	93.4	92.3

Table 9. Performance of learning algorithms for Heart disease dataset

Evaluation Models	Classifier	Accuracy (%)	Sensitivity (%)	Specificity (%)	Precision (%)	F-Measure (%)
10 – fold cross validation	k – NN	76.5	76.5	70.7	76.2	76.3
	NB	81.9	82	79.5	82.1	82
	DT	79.5	79.6	72.4	79.3	79.1
	Stacking	82.3	82.3	79.7	82.4	82.3
80-20	k – NN	72.8	72.9	73.4	76	72.2
	NB	81.3	81.4	81.9	84.6	81
	DT	72.8	72.9	73.4	76	72.2
	Stacking	83	83.1	83.5	85.7	82.8
70-30	k – NN	71.5	71.6	66	71.9	70.5
	NB	85.2	85.2	81.1	86.4	84.8
	DT	80.6	80.7	75.6	82.1	79.9
	Stacking	86.3	86.4	81.9	88	85.9

Mammographic Mass

The Mammographic is nowadays mostly used with the screening of breast cancer. This dataset also predicts the severity of benign and malignant of a mammographic mass lesion from BI-RADS attributes and the patient's age (Elter et al, 2007). The dataset has been collected at the Institute of Radiology of the University Erlangen-Nuremberg between 2003 and 2006 with a ground truth of 516 benign and 445 malignant cases. The dataset contains 6 attributes of categorical, ordinal, and nominal data with missing values in all the 6 attributes. Table 10 shows the performances of learning algorithms for the

Mammographic mass dataset. On comparing the performances of all learning algorithms, the DT and the stacking ensemble learning classifier shows equal performance in all aspects and in all evaluation models. In this case, the NB (weak learners) and the SVM (metaclassifier) fails to improve the performance of DT. As a result of stacking ensemble learning method is equal to the performance of the DT classifier.

Table 10. Performance of learning algorithms for Mammographic mass dataset

Evaluation Models	Classifier	Accuracy (%)	Sensitivity (%)	Specificity (%)	Precision (%)	F-Measure (%)
10 – fold cross validation	k – NN	75	75	75.1	75.2	75.1
	NB	78.35	78.4	79.1	79	78.4
	DT	82.1	82.1	81.3	82.2	82
	Stacking	82.1	82.1	81.3	82.2	82
80-20	k – NN	74.4	74.5	74.2	74.7	74.6
	NB	79.16	79.2	80.7	80.4	79.3
	DT	82.81	82.8	83.2	83.2	82.9
	Stacking	82.81	82.8	83.2	83.2	82.9
70-30	k – NN	75	75	75	75.1	75
	NB	77.7	77.8	78.6	78.6	77.8
	DT	82.98	83	81.9	83.2	82.9
	Stacking	82.98	83	81.9	83.2	82.9

Parkinson's Data Set

The Parkinson's dataset was created by Max Little of the University of Oxford, in collaboration with the National Centre for Voice and Speech, Colorado who recorded the speech signals of persons (Little et al, 2007). The recordings contain a range of biomedical voice measurements of 31 people, 23 with Parkinson's disease. The main aim of this dataset is to discriminate the healthy people from those with Parkinson's disease such as 0 –for health person and 1- for disease (binary class variables). Table 11 shows the performance of learning algorithms for Parkinson's dataset. On comparing the performances of learning algorithms the k-NN outperforms all the other learning classifiers in all the aspects and in all evaluation models.

Parkinson's Disease Classification

The Parkinson's Disease Classification (PDC) dataset was collected from 188 patients with PD of which 107 are men and 81 are women with age ranging from 33 to 87 at the Department of Neurology, Istanbul University (Sakaet al, 2019). The dataset was collected using the microphone set at 44.1 kHz and by following the physician examinations. The sustained phonation of the vowel was collected from each subject with three repetitions. On comparing the performances of learning algorithms as shown in Table 12, k-NN outperforms all the other learning algorithms in all the aspects and in all the evaluation models. This is the case as represented earlier; there is a lack of training in the weak classifiers to improve the performance of metaclassifier.

Table 11. Performance of learning algorithms for Parkinson's dataset

Evaluation Models	Classifier	Accuracy (%)	Sensitivity (%)	Specificity (%)	Precision (%)	F-Measure (%)
10 – fold cross validation	k – NN	96.41	96.4	96	96.5	96.4
	NB	69.23	69.2	84.3	83	71.3
	DT	80.51	80.5	65.6	80.2	80.4
	Stacking	80.51	80.5	65.6	80.2	80.4
80-20	k – NN	97.43	97.4	99.4	97.8	97.5
	NB	64.1	64.1	81	83.6	68.2
	DT	89.74	89.7	75.4	89.7	89.7
	Stacking	89.74	89.7	75.4	89.7	89.7
70-30	k – NN	96.55	96.6	98.9	97	96.6
	NB	65.51	65.5	84.2	82.8	67.8
	DT	81.03	81	89.1	87.3	82.3
	Stacking	81.03	81	89.1	87.3	82.3

Table 12. Performance of learning algorithms for Parkinson's disease classification dataset

Evaluation Models	Classifier	Accuracy (%)	Sensitivity (%)	Specificity (%)	Precision (%)	F-Measure (%)
10 – fold cross validation	k – NN	95.23	95.2	91.5	95.2	95.2
	NB	76.32	76.3	62.7	76.7	76.5
	DT	84.39	84.4	74.1	84.3	84.4
	Stacking	84.39	84.4	74.1	84.3	84.4
80-20	k – NN	93.37	93.4	88.3	93.5	93.3
	NB	75.49	75.5	63.8	74.6	74.8
	DT	77.48	77.5	64.8	76.7	76.5
	Stacking	77.48	77.5	64.8	76.7	76.5
70-30	k – NN	93.39	93.4	88.5	93.3	93.3
	NB	74.008	74	60	73.9	73.9
	DT	73.12	73.1	60.7	73.5	73.3
	Stacking	73.12	73.1	60.7	73.5	73.3

Pima Indian Diabetes Dataset

The Pima Indian Diabetes dataset (Karatsiolis and Schizas, 2012) contains the female patient information of at least 21years old from Pima Indian heritage. This dataset is to classify the diabetes case during pregnancies using 8 attributes and 768 instances. Out of 768 instances, 500 are tested negative or non-diabetic and 268 are tested positive. Table 13 shows the performance of the Pima Indian Diabetes dataset. On comparing the performances of learning algorithms, NB outperforms the other algorithm in all aspects however it shares the Accuracy and Sensitivity with Stacking ensemble learning technique. In the case of the 80-20 evaluation model, the DT algorithm performs better than all the other techniques in all aspects. For the 70-30 evaluation model, the stacking ensemble learning model outperforms all the other techniques in all aspects. On comparing these models, each classifier has shown different performances in different models. This clearly evidences that, the learning algorithm plays a major role depending upon the dataset not only with the mathematical foundation of the learning algorithms.

Table 13. Performance of learning algorithms for Pima Indian Diabetes dataset

Evaluation Models	Classifier	Accuracy (%)	Sensitivity (%)	Specificity (%)	Precision (%)	F-Measure (%)
10 – fold cross validation	k – NN	70.1	70.2	62.2	69.6	69.8
	NB	76.3	76.3	69.5	75.9	76
	DT	75.3	75.4	67.4	74.8	74.9
	Stacking	76.3	76.3	68.3	75.8	75.8
80-20	k – NN	74.6	74.7	66.4	74.5	74.6
	NB	77.2	77.3	68.7	76.9	77.1
	DT	78.5	78.6	69.3	78.1	78.2
	Stacking	77.9	77.9	69	77.5	77.7
70-30	k – NN	73.4	73.5	66	73.8	73.6
	NB	76.9	77	68.3	76.7	76.8
	DT	75.2	75.2	62.2	74.3	74.5
	Stacking	77.8	77.8	68.7	77.5	77.6

SPECT Heart

The dataset describes the diagnosing of Cardiac Single Proton Emission Control Tomography (SPECT) images (Kurgan et al, 2001). The dataset contains 267 SPECT image sets categorizing two classes normal and abnormal inferred with the presence of 22 binary feature patterns. Table 14 shows the performances of learning algorithms for the SPECT heart dataset. On comparing the performances, k-NN has outperformed all the other learners in all aspects however shares the performance with DT expect in Specificity. In the case of 80-20, DT and Stacking ensemble learning technique has sharing performance in different aspects and for the evaluation model of 70-30 k-NN outperforms all the other learners.

New Thyroid Dataset

The Thyroid dataset in the UCI Machine learning repository contains a heterogeneous collection of data collected from various hospitals (Quinlan et al, 1987). Among which, this chapter utilizes the new thyroid dataset that contains 215 instances of 5 attributes and 3 classes with no missing values. Table 15 shows the performance of learning algorithms for the thyroid dataset in different evaluations. On comparing the performances, k-NN achieves better performance for 10-fold cross-validation, and NB achieves better performance for the 80-20 evaluation model and in 70-30 evaluations, both NB and stacking have shown better performance.

Table 14. Performance of learning algorithms for SPECT Heart dataset

Evaluation Models	Classifier	Accuracy (%)	Sensitivity (%)	Specificity (%)	Precision (%)	F-Measure (%)
10 – fold cross validation	k – NN	70.41	70.4	67	70.1	70.1
	NB	68.91	68.9	66.8	68.9	68.9
	DT	70.41	70.4	66.5	70.1	70
	Stacking	70.03	70	65.9	69.7	69.6
80-20	k – NN	67.92	67.9	67.1	67.9	67.7
	NB	56.6	56.6	57	57	56.6
	DT	71.69	71.7	70.9	71.8	71.5
	Stacking	71.69	71.7	70	72.9	71
70-30	k – NN	73.75	73.8	71.6	73.6	73.7
	NB	55	55	56.7	57.3	55.3
	DT	73.75	73.8	70.7	73.5	73.5
	Stacking	73.75	73.8	70.7	73.5	73.5

Table 15. Performance of learning algorithms for Thyroid dataset

Evaluation Models	Classifier	Accuracy (%)	Sensitivity (%)	Specificity (%)	Precision (%)	F-Measure (%)
10 – fold cross validation	k – NN	97.2	97.2	96.5	97.2	97.2
	NB	96.7	96.7	93.5	96.8	96.7
	DT	92	92.1	87.7	92.1	92
	Stacking	95.3	95.3	92.3	95.3	95.3
80-20	k – NN	95.3	95.3	98.4	96.1	95.5
	NB	97.6	97.7	96.1	97.8	97.6
	DT	90.6	90.7	91	90.7	90.7
	Stacking	95.3	95.3	92.2	95.7	94.9
70-30	k – NN	90.6	90.6	87.3	91.4	90.1
	NB	96.8	96.9	94	97	96.7
	DT	92.1	92.2	87.7	92.7	91.6
	Stacking	96.8	96.9	94	97	96.7

Discussions

On comparing the performance of learning algorithms for all the medical datasets, each algorithm has its own merits and demerits. Some algorithms may perform best for the smaller dataset, some may perform well for the nominal dataset, ensemble learning algorithm performs best in some cases and in other cases, it fails to achieve better performance as shown in Table 16. The entries in Table 16 are only the best-performing values of all the collated results of medical datasets, ties are not listed. From Table 16 it can be concluded that the performances of a supervised learning algorithm depend on the type may be the categorical, nominal, ordinal, size of the dataset, and the number of target class variables. No learning algorithm can be suggested to be best for any dataset.

CONCLUSION

This chapter emphasizes the importance of Machine learning algorithms in classifying scalable medical datasets. The medical datasets are collected from the UCI machine learning repository of the varying size represented as small, medium, and large datasets. Learning algorithms such as Naïve Bayes, Decision Tree, *k*- Nearest Neighbor algorithm, and Stacking ensemble learning algorithm were implemented to analyze the performances in different evaluation models such as 10-fold cross-validation, 80-20%, 70-30% training and testing data. The performances are measured in different metrics such as Accuracy, Sensitivity, Specificity, Precision, and F- Measure. On comparing the performances, it is concluded that no specific machine learning algorithm is specified to be the best for any dataset. The performance of the algorithm purely depends on the Metadata of the dataset and not only with the mathematical function of the learning algorithm.

Table 16. Collated Performance of learning algorithms for all Medical datasets

10 – fold cross validation	Accuracy	Sensitivity	Specificity	Precision	F-score
k – NN	4	4	5	4	4
NB	1	1	4	2	3
DT	1	1	1	1	2
Stacking	3	3	1	3	1
80 - 20	Accuracy	Sensitivity	Specificity	Precision	F-score
k – NN	3	3	3	3	3
NB	3	3	3	3	3
DT	2	2	3	2	3
Stacking	2	1	2	3	2
70-30	Accuracy	Sensitivity	Specificity	Precision	F-score
k – NN	3	3	4	4	4
NB	1	1	1	1	1
DT	1	1	1	1	1
Stacking	3	3	3	3	3

REFERENCES

Altaf, T., Anwar, S. M., Gul, N., Majeed, M. N., & Majid, M. (2018). Multi-class Alzheimer's disease classification using image and clinical features. *Biomedical Signal Processing and Control, 43*, 64–74. doi:10.1016/j.bspc.2018.02.019

Balachander, J., & Ramanujam, E. (2017). Rule based Medical Content Classification for Secure Remote Health Monitoring. *International Journal of Computers and Applications, 165*(4).

Barlow, H. B. (1989). Unsupervised learning. *Neural Computation, 1*(3), 295–311. doi:10.1162/neco.1989.1.3.295

Cohen, S. B., Ruppin, E., & Dror, G. (2005, July). Feature Selection Based on the Shapley Value. *IJCAI (United States), 5*, 665–670.

Demiroz, G., Govenir, H. A., & Ilter, N. (1998). Learning differential diagnosis of eryhemato-squamous diseases using voting feature intervals. *Artificial Intelligence in Medicine, 13*(3), 147–165. doi:10.1016/S0933-3657(98)00028-1 PMID:9698151

Deng, Y., Zhou, L., Wang, L., Su, M., Zhang, J., Lian, J., & Wei, J. (2020). Radio Environment Map Construction Using Super-Resolution Imaging for Intelligent Transportation Systems. *IEEE Access: Practical Innovations, Open Solutions, 8*, 47272–47281. doi:10.1109/ACCESS.2020.2977855

Detrano, R., Janosi, A., Steinbrunn, W., Pfisterer, M., Schmid, J. J., Sandhu, S., Guppy, K. H., Lee, S., & Froelicher, V. (1989). International application of a new probability algorithm for the diagnosis of coronary artery disease. *The American Journal of Cardiology, 64*(5), 304–310. doi:10.1016/0002-9149(89)90524-9 PMID:2756873

Dua, D., & Graff, C. (2019). *UCI Machine Learning Repository*. University of California, School of Information and Computer Science.

Elter, M., Schulz-Wendtland, R., & Wittenberg, T. (2007). The prediction of breast cancer biopsy outcomes using two CAD approaches that both emphasize an intelligible decision process. *Medical Physics, 34*(11), 4164–4172. doi:10.1118/1.2786864 PMID:18072480

Ghahramani, Z. (2003, February). Unsupervised learning. In *Summer School on Machine Learning* (pp. 72–112). Springer.

Gupta, P., Sharma, A., & Jindal, R. (2016). Scalable machine-learning algorithms for big data analytics: A comprehensive review. *Wiley Interdisciplinary Reviews. Data Mining and Knowledge Discovery, 6*(6), 194–214. doi:10.1002/widm.1194

Juhn, Y., & Liu, H. (2020). Artificial intelligence approaches using natural language processing to advance EHR-based clinical research. *The Journal of Allergy and Clinical Immunology, 145*(2), 463–469. doi:10.1016/j.jaci.2019.12.897 PMID:31883846

Kaelbling, L. P., Littman, M. L., & Moore, A. W. (1996). Reinforcement learning: A survey. *Journal of Artificial Intelligence Research, 4*, 237–285. doi:10.1613/jair.301

Kan, G. E. R. A. R. D., Visser, C. A., Koolen, J. J., & Dunning, A. J. (1986). Short and long term predictive value of admission wall motion score in acute myocardial infarction. A cross sectional echocardiographic study of 345 patients. *Heart (British Cardiac Society)*, *56*(5), 422–427. doi:10.1136/hrt.56.5.422 PMID:3790378

Karatsiolis, S., & Schizas, C. N. (2012, November). Region based Support Vector Machine algorithm for medical diagnosis on Pima Indian Diabetes dataset. In *2012 IEEE 12th International Conference on Bioinformatics & Bioengineering (BIBE)* (pp. 139-144). IEEE. 10.1109/BIBE.2012.6399663

Karthick, G. S., & Pankajavalli, P. B. (2020). Architecting IoT based Healthcare Systems Using Machine Learning Algorithms: Cloud-Oriented Healthcare Model, Streaming Data Analytics Architecture, and Case Study. In *Incorporating the Internet of Things in Healthcare Applications and Wearable Devices* (pp. 40–66). IGI Global. doi:10.4018/978-1-7998-1090-2.ch003

Kurgan, L. A., Cios, K. J., Tadeusiewicz, R., Ogiela, M., & Goodenday, L. S. (2001). Knowledge discovery approach to automated cardiac SPECT diagnosis. *Artificial Intelligence in Medicine*, *23*(2), 149–169. doi:10.1016/S0933-3657(01)00082-3 PMID:11583923

Laaksonen, J., & Oja, E. (1996, June). Classification with learning k-nearest neighbors. In *Proceedings of International Conference on Neural Networks (ICNN'96)* (Vol. 3, pp. 1480-1483). IEEE. 10.1109/ICNN.1996.549118

Little, M. A., McSharry, P. E., Roberts, S. J., Costello, D. A., & Moroz, I. M. (2007). Exploiting nonlinear recurrence and fractal scaling properties for voice disorder detection. *Biomedical Engineering Online*, *6*(1), 23. doi:10.1186/1475-925X-6-23 PMID:17594480

Michalski, R. S., Mozetic, I., Hong, J., & Lavrac, N. (1986). The multi-purpose incremental learning system AQ15 and its testing application to three medical domains. *Proc. AAAI 1986*, 1-041.

Mitchell, T. M. (1999). Machine learning and data mining. *Communications of the ACM*, *42*(11), 30–36. doi:10.1145/319382.319388

Noble, W. S. (2006). What is a support vector machine? *Nature Biotechnology*, *24*(12), 1565–1567. doi:10.1038/nbt1206-1565 PMID:17160063

Padmavathi, S., & Ramanujam, E. (2015). Naïve Bayes classifier for ECG abnormalities using multivariate maximal time series Motif. *Procedia Computer Science*, *47*, 222–228. doi:10.1016/j.procs.2015.03.201

Pudumalar, S., Ramanujam, E., Rajashree, R. H., Kavya, C., Kiruthika, T., & Nisha, J. (2017, January). Crop recommendation system for precision agriculture. In *2016 Eighth International Conference on Advanced Computing (ICoAC)* (pp. 32-36). IEEE. 10.1109/ICoAC.2017.7951740

Quinlan, J. R., Compton, P. J., Horn, K. A., & Lazarus, L. (1987, October). Inductive knowledge acquisition: a case study. In *Proceedings of the Second Australian Conference on Applications of expert systems* (pp. 137-156). Academic Press.

Ramanujam, E., Chandrakumar, T., Nandhana, K., & Laaxmi, N. T. (2019, September). Prediction of Fetal Distress Using Linear and Non-linear Features of CTG Signals. In *International Conference On Computational Vision and Bio Inspired Computing* (pp. 40-47). Springer.

Ramanujam, E., & Padmavathi, S. (2016, February). Double constrained genetic algorithm for ECG signal classification. In *2016 International Conference on Emerging Trends in Engineering, Technology and Science (ICETETS)* (pp. 1-5). IEEE. 10.1109/ICETETS.2016.7603010

Ramanujam, E., & Padmavathi, S. (2019). Genetic time series motif discovery for time series classification. *International Journal of Biomedical Engineering and Technology*, *31*(1), 47–63. doi:10.1504/IJBET.2019.101051

Ramanujam, E., & Padmavathi, S. (2019). A Vision-Based Posture Monitoring System for the Elderly Using Intelligent Fall Detection Technique. In *Guide to Ambient Intelligence in the IoT Environment* (pp. 249–269). Springer. doi:10.1007/978-3-030-04173-1_11

Ramanujam, E., Padmavathi, S., Dharshani, G., & Madhumitta, M. R. R. (2019, December). Evaluation of Feature Extraction and Recognition for Human Activity using Smartphone based Accelerometer data. In *2019 11th International Conference on Advanced Computing (ICoAC)* (pp. 86-89). IEEE.

Rasikannan, L., Alli, P., & Ramanujam, E. (2019, October). Improved Feature Based Sentiment Analysis for Online Customer Reviews. In *International Conference on Innovative Data Communication Technologies and Application* (pp. 148-155). Springer.

Rish, I. (2001, August). An empirical study of the naive Bayes classifier. In *IJCAI 2001 workshop on empirical methods in artificial intelligence* (Vol. 3, No. 22, pp. 41-46). Academic Press.

Sakar, C. O., Serbes, G., Gunduz, A., Tunc, H. C., Nizam, H., Sakar, B. E., Tutuncu, M., Aydin, T., Isenkul, M. E., & Apaydin, H. (2019). A comparative analysis of speech signal processing algorithms for Parkinson's disease classification and the use of the tunable Q-factor wavelet transform. *Applied Soft Computing*, *74*, 255–263. doi:10.1016/j.asoc.2018.10.022

Shakeel, P. M., Baskar, S., Dhulipala, V. S., & Jaber, M. M. (2018). Cloud based framework for diagnosis of diabetes mellitus using K-means clustering. *Health Information Science and Systems*, *6*(1), 16. doi:10.100713755-018-0054-0 PMID:30279986

Singh, A., Thakur, N., & Sharma, A. (2016, March). A review of supervised machine learning algorithms. In *2016 3rd International Conference on Computing for Sustainable Global Development (INDIACom)* (pp. 1310-1315). IEEE.

Song, Y. Y., & Ying, L. U. (2015). Decision tree methods: Applications for classification and prediction. *Shanghai Jingshen Yixue*, *27*(2), 130. PMID:26120265

Srivastava, S. (2014). Weka: A tool for data preprocessing, classification, ensemble, clustering and association rule mining. *International Journal of Computers and Applications*, *88*(10).

Tomei, L. A. (2020). Online Courses and ICT in Education: Emerging Practices and Applications. *Simulation*, 566.

Wolberg, W. H., & Mangasarian, O. L. (1990). Multisurface method of pattern separation for medical diagnosis applied to breast cytology. *Proceedings of the National Academy of Sciences of the United States of America*, *87*(23), 9193–9196. doi:10.1073/pnas.87.23.9193 PMID:2251264

Zhang, S., Zhang, C., & Yang, Q. (2003). Data preparation for data mining. *Applied Artificial Intelligence*, *17*(5-6), 375–381. doi:10.1080/713827180

Zuckerbraun, S., Deutsch, A., Eicheldinger, C., Frasier, A. M., Loft, J. D., & Clift, J. (2020). Risk Adjustment, Mode Adjustment, and Nonresponse Bias Analysis on Quality Measures From a Long-Term Care Hospital Experience of Care Survey. *Archives of Physical Medicine and Rehabilitation*, *101*(5), 841–851. doi:10.1016/j.apmr.2019.11.016 PMID:31904343

Chapter 17
Role of Edge Computing to Leverage IoT–Assisted AAL Ecosystem

Madhana K.
PSG College of Technology, India

Jayashree L. S.
PSG College of Technology, India

ABSTRACT

The medical advancement in recent years is addressing challenges of the dependent people like senior citizens, physically challenged, and cognitively impaired individuals by providing technical aids to promote a healthier society. The radical improvement in the digital world is trying to make their life smoother by creating a smart living environment via ambient assisted living (AAL) rather than hospitalization. In this chapter, an Edge-based AAL-IoT ecosystem is introduced with the prime objective of delivering telehealthcare to elderly and telerehabilitation to disabled individuals. The proposed framework focuses on developing smart home, an intelligent atmosphere for real-time monitoring in regard to meet the needs of independent and isolated individuals. The supporting technologies to leverage the edge computing concept, to enable scalability and reliability are also studied. A case study on proposed architecture for quarantined patient monitoring remotely in the event of epidemic or pandemic diseases is presented.

INTRODUCTION

As claimed by WHO, the old age population above 60 years in the world will double from 12% to 22% shortly. As per 2017 report, the elder population aged above 60 years is 962 Million and is expected to reach more than twofold i.e., 2.1 Billion by 2050 dramatically (World Health Organization, February 5, 2018). For instance, if the elder people experience a better quality of life during their later years, then their value and ability will be more respected. On the other hand, if their dependency on others due to physical or mental health decline increases in these added years, then the impact will be negative.

DOI: 10.4018/978-1-7998-6673-2.ch017

As per the plan developed by WHO on aging and health, it is significant (i) To create awareness on healthy and active aging (ii) To design next-generation pervasive healthcare solutions based on elderly needs and preferences (iii) To provide long-term healthcare monitoring and (iv) To create an elder-friendly environment (World Health Organization, February 5, 2018). In addition to the age-related health risks, the surrounding also plays a major role in declining their risk of developing diseases such as improper intake of food, sleeping disorder, lack of physical activities, lack of simple exercises and so on.

According to the report issued by Market Research Future, it is indicated that the AAL market has produced 13 Billion USD over the period 2017 - 2027 and is estimated to reach 19% by 2027. One of the prime parts of the AAL market namely, the medical assistance system has achieved the highest 22% CAGR (Compound Annual Growth Rate) over the above estimated period (Market Research Future, April 2018). The advancement in the Internet of Things (IoT) technology and smart home technology, a huge growth of the elderly population, and a rapid increase in age-related chronic diseases are the driving factors for the rapid growth of the AAL market. In this regard, the role of healthcare service providers is going to be remarkable in the coming years.

In the present impending IoT era, almost every object or thing can be interrelated with each other in a large number, and it becomes an essential part of every domain of human life. With improved Internet connectivity, the proliferation of IoT enabled devices is expected to reach 75 Billion by the year 2025 (Statistica, 2016). As the booming IoT evolves, it has been adopted not only in many business sectors such as smart agriculture and farming, smart healthcare, automotive, industrial IoT, transportation but also for sophisticated applications like retail stores, luxurious hotels/inns, etc.

Similarly, cloud computing (Emeakaroha et al., 2015; Qabil et al., 2019) enables seamless integration of physical and smart devices by endorsing on-demand delivery of required computation, networking, and storage resources to analyze IoT big data, acquire deep insights and deliver intelligent value-added services to the end-users. Nevertheless, the raw data generated by the IoT devices have to traverse a long way through various intermediate networks to reach the remote cloud data center for further processing and analysis. So, cloud computing becomes unsuitable in meeting the diverse quality requirements such as low latency, limited bandwidth, intermittent connectivity and instant real-time response.

On that account, fog computing or fog networking, the term framed by Cisco (Cisco, 2015), a decentralized computing architecture is introduced to utilize the resources available at the edge of the network. The idea is extending cloud computing to make it idealized for IoT and other mission-critical or industrial applications. Edge computing (Yu et al., 2017) being a subset of Fog computing, has attracted many researchers to come up with real-time solutions. It has brought intelligence near to the end-user. When the data generation source and computation are closer by localizing data processing and storage then it will combat the latency, smoothing real-time interactions by affording instantaneous computing and immediate response.

In other words, the service requests and service consumers are one hop away distant to meet the real-time requirements of emerging services. Thus, edge computing and IoT are the significant elements of AAL, also known as welfare technology, to create a ubiquitous, assisted, and cost-effective architecture for the challenged and elderly people.

In this chapter, an edge-based system architecture for AAL is presented, involving diverse stakeholders, the user's independent atmosphere and the required elements of the edge-IoT ecosystem. The method of how the different elements of architecture are integrated to provide care and assistance to the targeted individuals is given. The role of edge computing in IoT assisted AAL systems to achieve benefits such as ultra-low latency, bandwidth, interoperability, throughput, and reliability is explored. An AAL case study that inherits edge computing technology is also described. Furthermore, the enabling technologies to implement and integrate edge computing with IoT based AAL ecosystem are presented.

BACKGROUND

In the last decade, cloud computing has provided a technological revolution and paradigm shift in the field of data transmission and smart living through Information and Communication Technology (ICT). The proliferation of mobile devices and smart things to trillions in number has leveraged the IoT era. The IoT paradigm can interrelate everyday objects such as physical devices, buildings, machines, embedded objects, sensors, actuators, even people or animals. It enables communication among them without human-computer interaction, using which the physical IoT devices can be monitored or controlled remotely to provide Quality of Service (QoS) and Quality of Experience (QoE) to the users.

Cloud Computing

Cloud computing is similar to old networking technology but when integrated with the Internet during the last decade, it has become more appropriate for broader applications. Cloud data center houses physical servers either a single server or a complex network of multiple server racks to hold computing resources to ensure services like backup, networking, data storage and management. It empowers on-demand provisioning of resources such as platform, infrastructure, storage, software, sensors, actuators, sensing, data, database, Ethernet, etc., through the network connection to the required users. Business vendors and software users do not need to possess physical devices and infrastructure to implement a vast program. Rather, the cloud ensures flexibility of allocation and de-allocation of computing resources on-demand basis using virtual infrastructure by maximizing computing power and minimizing the cost required for such resources.

Edge Computing

Edge computing, one of the middleware technologies under the umbrella of fog computing creates a new genre of the ecosystem along with IoT. It shifts cloud computing capabilities to the network edge, thus enhancing the speed of response and minimizing the network latency. The idea is to utilize the computing features of the peripheral devices to pre-process the data and send only relevant data to the cloud, thus reducing bandwidth costs. The computational resources are brought closer to the users where the actual services are consumed. Enabling real-time perception and actions makes it desirable for time-sensitive applications. Having supported the green computing revolution it decreases the network processing and maintenance cost because it reduces the data load and burden of data traversal through the network. Besides, it supports a high degree of mobility of end-users and serves emerging localized smart applications (Ray et al., 2019).

Under the sub-domains of fog computing, the related technologies have been introduced including cloudlets, mobile edge computing, and edge computing. Both fog computing and edge computing move the intelligence to the edge. As shown in Figure 1, the main difference between edge and fog computing is the place where intelligence and computing power are residing. In a fog layer, the intelligence is available at the LAN and the raw data generated from the edge devices are forwarded to the gateway for

Figure 1. Fog Computing and Edge Computing

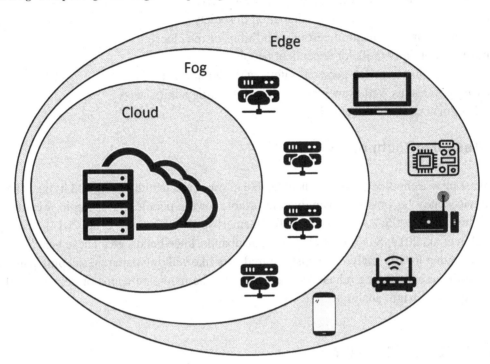

further processing. In an edge layer, the intelligence and the source of data are merely one hop away to mitigate the latency and network backbone bandwidth and to achieve more energy efficiency than the cloud (Bilal et al., 2018).

Edge computing fabric is a heterogeneous environment of edge servers, routers, switches, access points, mobile devices, or any computer-like Single Board devices. Most popular industry leading-edge applications include retail, smart manufacturing, smart city, connected cars, vehicular networks, cognitive computing, augmented and virtual reality, and similar use cases requiring real-time analytics.

Ambient Assisted Living

With the advancement in a connected digital age, AAL attracts multiple fields including academic and industrial research communities and various public sectors. AAL based smart enhanced living place consists of (i) smart objects such as sensors, actuators and smart mobile phones (acting as a gateway for data transmission), interactive set-top boxes, modems, etc., and (ii) physical objects such as TV, lights, fans, stoves, doors, windows, mattress and so on (Haghi et al., 2019).

AAL solutions focus on the following aspects (Foko et al., 2013; Siegel et al., 2014):

- Improve the quality of life of elderly and disabled people by enhancing autonomy and emergency treatment services
- Round-the-clock assessment of an individual
- Reduce the burden on caretakers or relatives
- Improved personal care measures based on individual needs

- Reduce health care costs for the individual and society
- Advanced social interaction and participation in society
- Prevention and management of chronic conditions of the elderly
- Management of daily tasks for dependent people
- Provision of house comfort, personal safety, and edutainment.
- Ensuring physical as well as mental health by inhibiting anxiousness
- Avoid stigmatization of the elderly

Role of Assistive Technology

The role of assistive technology is one such agreeable in smart and healthy aging and living. The medical assistive devices have become increasingly comfortable for the people, for example, wearable fitness monitors (Chou et al., 2005; Zainudin et al., 2017), smartwatches (Ohtsuka et al., 2014), blood glucose monitors (Hou et al., 2019; Siddiqui et al., 2018), armbands, knee bands, etc. These health-monitoring wearables can either locally analyse the unstructured data like walking patterns, sleeping patterns, vital signs, or muscle activity during rehabilitation and notify the medicare teams or connect to the cloud directly for accurate insight analysis.

IOT ASSISTED AAL SYSTEM

Issues, Controversies, Problems

The IoT ecosystem is producing huge volumes of data that leads to a strict dependency on cloud computing platform for data analysis and storage requirements. The data generated by the sensors is forwarded to the remote cloud server where the data is filtered, processed to extract the knowledgeable insights and delivered to the end-users through a standard application interface. It then activates the actuators installed in the sensing environment. In this context, the continuous data requires extensive storage capacity which is provided by cloud computing and machine learning or deep learning models implemented in the cloud accelerate the long-term cognizance analytics.

Over recent years, the frequency of data generated by the IoT devices and sensors is vast to expose as it is, to the network to reach the centralized cloud server for data processing and analytics. For example, a remotely located oil mine produces 10TB of data per well for a single day. Another example is a commercial jet generating 5-10 TB of data per day (Cisco, 2015; Western Digital website, n.d.). When this big data is exposed as raw to get forwarded to the cloud, it not only affects the network performance but also cloud computing inhibits its suitability to serve the above-mentioned use cases.

Meanwhile, real-time and user-centric applications require faster and almost zero-latency response time. For example, across healthcare services, the unstructured data corresponding to the medical conditions of users or ambient data of users' living environments have to reach the distant cloud server. The large real-time medical data if it makes even the smallest delay in service can be a matter of life or demise. In addition, the security of personal and other sensitive data remains questionable when it traverses across multiple networks when stored in a centralized place. The different volumes of data are generated by different models at different rates, will generally be stored, analysed, visualized, and consumed by users of the IoT ecosystem. It consumes a substantial amount of network bandwidth resulting in high latency for real-time services. Moreover, it lacks mainly in three areas: 1) increased response time, 2) heavy load on the backbone network and 3) increased bandwidth costs to forward tons of data. So it makes an adverse effect on IoT tasks and thus becomes unsuitable for latency-sensitive applications such as healthcare. Though the cloud emphasizes a substantial amount of storage, computing, networking resources, services, and applications, there is a need to bring the cloud power much nearer and distributed. Therefore, a distributed network architecture named Fog computing is introduced to make IoT ideal for prominent real-time applications (Ray et al., 2019).

To solve the problems mentioned above, edge computing has been introduced in the recent past. Edge computing technology is a vast growing technology as it gives more opportunities to process data at the network boundary wherever it is most appropriate to do so. For example, in a real-time ECG monitoring system for patients affected with a cardiac problem in telehealthcare, when the measured ECG value enters the risky range of values, the service needs to quickly respond to it as soon as possible. Another example, emergency in a smart manufacturing use case, the service has to react with a low delay so that connected machines have to take measures to avoid any loss of production and safety.

On the other hand, edge computing is not intended to replace cloud computing technology as edge devices do not have much computing power, required battery life for big data processing, and storage capabilities, although the nano-technological components of mobile devices are well evolved. Thus the edge computing is observed as an extension of cloud computing to overcome innumerable problems ranging from communication delay to energy efficiency (Bilal et al., 2018).

However, the distributed nature of the edge paradigm exposes different challenges like ensuring the security of data over scattered devices, maintaining consistency over the data, discovering the service modules in dispersed devices, orchestration of edge devices and services, etc. These issues noted in edge computing grab greater research activities and contributions in the academic as well as industrial fields.

Need for AAL

Due to the expansion in IoT generation, it has evolved as a promising solution for healthcare scenarios which transformed the way healthcare services are provided to the users and other different stakeholders such as patients, relatives, medical practitioners/clinicians, etc. Healthcare becomes one of the increasingly eminent application domains in IoT. In recent years, developing geriatric care solutions for elder people and telemedicine solutions for people affected with neurological disorders or chronic diseases have become a significant element in the healthcare business to improve the quality of life by eradicating the challenges in their daily life.

AAL is one such emerging ecosystem, capable of reinforcing the independence and well-being of older adults, cognitively impaired people, and persons with chronic illness in a safe, secure and relaxed living environment, specifically where they survive or work. AAL provides a domain of wearable and ambient sensors, actuators, personal mobile devices with necessary software applications, computers, and wireless communication standards, aiming as a multi-disciplinary field to afford personal healthcare monitoring and telehealth systems for senior and independent citizens. Thus, AAL is believed to be a counterpart technology to treat the effects of the increasing aged population as a result of a gradual rise in life expectancy rate and decline in birth and mortality rate.

AAL Services

In a smart living context, AAL services, among which some examples are illustrated in Figure 2, can be the solutions for heterogeneous physical challenges experienced by senior citizens or cognitively impaired people. For instance, remainder services are deployed to remind about certain significant activities like intake of medicine, meals, balanced diet, water or health drinks, regular physical exercise, bill payment, etc., to improve physical and mental health and to enable independent living. This service could also be a better way to compensate the neuro-cognitive disabilities like Alzheimer's Disease.

Figure 2. Examples of AAL Services

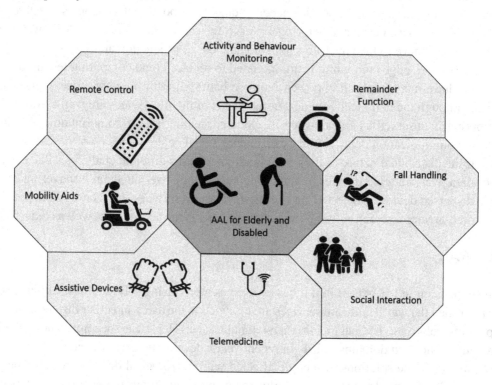

As Shown in Table 1, these set of AAL services are categorized under the independent living, individual healthcare, and social and recreational services (Camarinha-Matos et al., 2015; Labonnote & Høyland, 2015).

Challenges in Elders' Life

To ensure a quality life, elderly people have to be independent for their regular needs and to maintain social and physical interaction with their family members consistently. Their mental health plays a crucial role in promising healthier aging and comfort rather than their physical disabilities. If they are treated lovingly with fulfilled wishes, fun and entertainment they will be healthier and mentally stronger.

Table 1. Categorization of AAL Services

Independent Living Services	Healthcare Services	Social and Recreational Services
• Daily activity Management • Home comfort and safety • Secure Mobility • Indoor Localization	• Remote Patient Monitoring • Behaviour Monitoring • Rehabilitation Services • Fall handling • Sleep Monitoring • Emotion Recognition • Automatic Speech Recognition • Chronic disorder Management • Chronic Disease management • Cognitive Impairment services • Medication and Lifestyle Assistance	• Media Access Services • Home Mood Control services • Entertainment Services • Link with Relatives Services

The circumstances seem different in the case of older people with disorders, in the way they became dependent on caregiving staff or relatives for their daily routines - e.g. feeding, pottery, bathing, dressing, mobility, etc. It is crucial to improve their health status by treating them with the best care services.

Categories of Data

An AAL ecosystem is a collection of myriads of teleservices and thus includes a vast number of sensors deployed in its environment. Sometimes, the sensors' functionality may be redundant in regard to ensure the availability of any such services. Besides, comprehensive parameters are essential in contributing to the health of a person including vital, physiological, and environmental data (Haghi et al., 2019), which are the different types of data. In healthcare, the vital signs of a person include body temperature, heart rate, ECG, pressure, blood oxygen level, and respiratory rate. The physiological data indicate human activities such as walking, sitting, sleeping, and so on. Ambient sensors deployed in the home are involved in obtaining environmental parameters such as humidity, air pressure, temperature, CO_2, CO, NO_2, noise, etc.,

In recent years our smartphones are embedded with multiple sensors to advance personalized services. Such sensors are involved in obtaining AAL user information like their activities, behaviors, and health data in order to improve assistance and user awareness. Like in the existing work, smartphone photography with a high-resolution camera can be useful for early detection of skin-related diseases like melanoma (Vano-Galvan et al., 2015). The embedded accelerometer and gyroscopes in the smartphone with the GPS or any communication interfaces are useful to enhance the users' mobility.

The health-monitoring dedicated wearable devices available in the market sophisticates measuring specific or combined information of the patient namely body temperature, heart rate, blood pressure, oxygen saturation rate, ECG, muscle strength, muscle fatigue status, step count, moving distance, current location, breathing rate, sleep position, calories burnt, sleep tracking, sleep quality, diet, body weight, motion tracking and so on.

IoT-AAL Ecosystem

A general IoT based AAL architecture is illustrated in Figure 3 in which it comprises four layers - IoT layer, Edge Layer, Cloud Layer, and Application layer. Many existing works (Zgheib et al., 2017; Gomes et al., 2015) presented hierarchical IoT-AAL frameworks, in several contexts. An ontology framework (Zgheib et al., 2017) is presented to enable cognitive detection of events with identified changes in smart homes and surroundings using cognitive sensors (virtual sensors). A scalable IoT-based middleware infrastructure for the AAL system is described in (Gomes et al., 2015) for telehealthcare service.

IoT Layer

The first tier, IoT layer comprises of many geographically distributed intelligent devices and sensor nodes - may be in the form of activity sensors (to monitor users' physiological or behavioral activities) deployed in the smart environment or embedded in hand-held devices or medical sensors associated with dedicated wearable devices or ambient sensors, forming wireless sensor networks (WSN).

The raw data obtained by the sensors is heavy, and the generation is based on the behavior of the sensors - continuous, periodic, or event-based forwarding (Gomes et al., 2015). They are forwarded to the edge layer through short-range wireless communication standards such as Bluetooth, Bluetooth Smart (BLE), ZigBee, etc. The sensor nodes form star topology with the gateway device in transmitting the information.

Edge Layer

An edge gateway device is neither a simple sensor collecting analog signal along with sending digital data nor a collection of rack servers, rather it can be any endpoint device with inbuilt processing power and communication capabilities. Mostly, hand-held devices like smartphones, ipads, and tablets are being used as a gateway at the edge layer to transmit the sensor data to the cloud data center. Normally the peripheral devices which can be useful for data collection are any network-enabled processing elements such as notebook computers, laptops, security cameras, drones or low-cost Single Board Computers like Raspberry Pi or small computers like development boards or kits. The software applications installed in edge devices are involved in pre-processing, filtering (unstructured data may contain noise) or aggregating (sensor data may be redundant) the sensor data and forwarded using long-range connectivity standards such as 3G/4G/5G, LoRa, LWPAN, WiFi and so on.

Cloud Layer

This layer is dedicated to executing computing-intensive tasks with an abundant number of resources. The filtered sensor data is sorted out, managed, stored, and analyzed to produce remarkable understandings at the data center. The data center is administered with a deep learning algorithm that enables long-term analytics and storage. The learning model is essential to predict the pattern and behavior of the user data to afford advanced services. The cloud server can also be accessed by authorized individuals - for instance, in healthcare, the doctors are allowed authorized access to patients' medical history. The data delivery and emergency notification can be made to occur manually assigning some parameters such as time interval, priority, etc., by authorized medical professionals.

Application Layer

The users' communication devices like smartphones provide an application interface that delivers procured cognizance from the cloud, both to the service consumers and service producers, expediting personalized services.

Figure 3. AAL-IoT Architecture

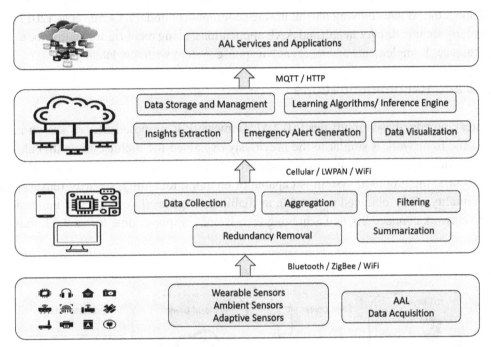

EDGE BASED AAL-IOT FRAMEWORK

With the enhanced growth of IoT devices along with its new business applications, real-time computing and processing power closer to the edge is significant. The edge revolution, a distributed computing topology is transforming massively the way big data is being handled by the server. Consider, a self-driving car is associated with 200+ sensors and capable of generating a 4 TB of data per day (Suhrid Barua, n.d.). Having hundreds, thousands or millions of such devices affects the performance of real-time applications. It results in quality degradation due to latency and increases bandwidth needs.

Nawaz et al. (2016) discussed an embedded vision-based security camera for human monitoring scenarios that employ sensor edge computing to mitigate security and privacy issues in collecting raw video data. Enterprises like NVIDIA introduced an edge platform to bring the power of Artificial Intelligence (AI) to the edge. Nvidia Jetson Nano Developer kit (Sheshadri & Franklin, 2020), one such example edge-based powerful computer, yet as small as credit cards, can run multiple AI algorithms in parallel at the edge. It deploys end-to-end AI-based applications, achieving much higher performance and energy efficiency. Healthcare experts reported that faster and local data processing using the edge paradigm is highly useful to be a life-saving one (CBINSIGHTS, April 28, 2020).

Many works related to the AAL concept blended with edge technology have been studied. Some of the fog computing architecture (Cerina et al., 2017; Nikoloudakis et al., 2016; Vora et al., 2017) for AAL concepts are also examined. A fog-based AAL framework (Vora et al., 2017) for remote patient monitoring applications is proffered in which priority gateway is used for emergency measures if any abnormal situation is found from a regression analysis. It also uses the clustering algorithm in regard to reduce the data to be forwarded to the fog gateway. Another fog-based system architecture for remote patient surveillance applications is proposed (Nikoloudakis et al., 2016) in which ubiquitous alerting service is implemented in a virtual fog layer to locate the activity-challenged individuals. The system notifies the caregivers about the patients moving into an unsafe geographic boundary. Cerina et al. (2017) discussed a multi-level fog architecture for health and AAL applications, using reconfigurable fog nodes to achieve high performance. It implements an emergency response system with low latency.

Solutions and Recommendations

In this context, an edge-based multi-tier IoT-AAL framework is proposed here as shown in Figure 4. The base of the framework is similar to the previously explained IoT architecture with enhanced edge functionalities in order to enable immediate response from the system. Comparing to the IoT based AAL architecture, the proposed system is capable of enabling reliability, security (ensuring integrity and confidentiality of the obtained user data), availability (edge level decision making easily handles intermittent network connection), and achieving zero-latency response time for an AAL individual.

Figure 4. Proposed Edge-based AAL-IoT Architecture

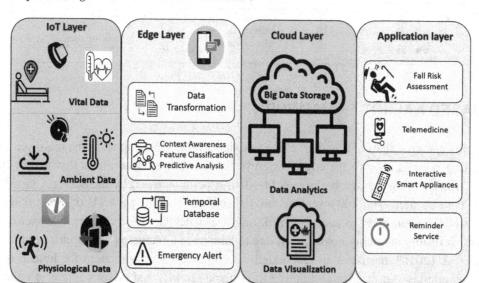

As given in the framework, the mobile edge gateway gathers all data from the IoT layer and involves data transformation operations - aggregation, filter, compression, and fusion. The near-real-time data analytics at the edge requires some extended technologies like machine learning and deep learning model (Bailas et al., 2018) to incorporate the feature of predictive analytics into the edge layer. As the AI technique plays a crucial role in the edge computing paradigm, implementing edge intelligence scenarios in the area of AAL significantly improves the QoE of the user. The added benefit of inculcating AI into the edge is not only enabling various aspects such as data analysis, feature classification, regression analysis, and clustering but also contextual classification of data and achieving reliable end service (Pazienza et al., 2019). Adopting AI techniques to describe intelligent edge architecture is carried out in some researches (Jacome et al., 2019; Keum et al., 2020; Pazienza et al., 2019). One such work is suggested in (Jacome et al., 2019) which deployed predictive analytics at the edge for the IoT-AAL ecosystem suiting healthcare scenarios. An edge intelligent architecture (Pazienza et al., 2019) is introduced to perform the real-time decision-making process in case of complex applications like the AAL concept. Establishing awareness of patients' activities of daily life, an edge-based self-organized device network (Keum et al., 2020) is proposed for real-time user activity monitoring scenarios to determine their physical ability and alert them about their incomplete or forgotten activities.

An AAL environment gathers distinct types of data from different sensors or sensing devices like environmental, medical, and physiological data. It does not mean that all the data is required all the time. Determining the real emergency data among them makes more sense and creates a great impact on life. For example, data from a fire detection sensor is more significant when smoke is detected than the normal range of medical data. Another example, heart rate sensor data is more important when its value falls within an unsafe range for a person with chronic heart disease than other safe ambient parameters. In these similar circumstances, the concept of contextual awareness (Brouwer et al., 2018; Hassan et al., 2019) helps the AAL to predict the real appropriateness for emergency care. An edge-based prediction model for the AAL framework (Hassan et al., 2019) is recommended to identify the emergency medical data with the feature of contextual awareness. An edge-based cascading reasoning framework (Brouwer et al., 2018) is presented for pervasive healthcare to combine the data streams from various medical sensors and create new deep and accurate awareness.

The edge layer is deployed with a temporal database to store processed data and results from predictive analytics for a certain period. The database stores data in JSON format and the query-based language can be used for retrieving data from it. In the event of an emergency alert, the formal stakeholders like medicare teams or caretakers or relatives will be notified with ultra-low latency with an immediate response.

Table 2. Collection of Stakeholders

Formal Stakeholders	Informal Stakeholders
• Hospitals • Medical Centers • Doctors / Medical Professionals • Clinics • Nursing Homes • Rehabilitation Centers • Police • Ambulatory Services • Telemedicine / Telehealthcare Service Providers	• Relatives/ Caretakers • Elder Care /Disabled Home Association • Social Voluntary Groups

AAL Integrated Service Platform

In addition to the AAL market service providers, an AAL ecosystem collaborates with a collection of different formal and informal stakeholders (Camarinha-Matos et al., 2015) as shown in Table 2, in addition to the user in the smart home. In (Camarinha-Matos et al., 2015), a virtual service integrator combines multiple service providers into a single platform to enable the user, a composite set of services.

An edge-based service provisioning AAL platform is employed in (Lopez-de-Ipina et al., 2010), the proposed architecture includes an AAL kit - a collection of software and hardware components and centralized service provisioning and management server. The AAL kit, like a set-top box, can be easily used in the smart home, the required services such as smart TV, emergency or alerts, remote patients' vital signs monitoring and so on can easily be installed or uninstalled whenever required.

The edge-based integrated platform emphasizes service discovery and device discovery using which the devices deployed in the smart home are automatically discovered. It is intended to build a telemedicine solution offering services such as telecare, teletreatment, teleconsultation, home care, and mobility. The dissimilar stakeholders of the AAL system will be given a standard application interface to access the common integrated platform.

ENABLING TECHNOLOGIES FOR EDGE COMPUTING AND AAL

Numerous ground-breaking technologies serve as a solution for blending edge computing and AAL paradigm by achieving even more application performance and instantaneous service response. This section describes some of the enabling technologies such as Mobile Edge Computing (MEC), 5G, virtualization, containers, and Software-Defined Networking (SDN).

MEC

Also known as Multi-access Edge Computing, it is considered another enabler of IoT applications. It brings networking, storage, and computational power to the edge of the radio access network with respect to prohibit long-distance backhauling, thus upgrading network efficiency and service delivery to the consumers. It enables cloud platforms at the network edge and facilitates low latency and high bandwidth access to radio access network resources (Porambage et al., 2018). A MEC-based solution (Pham et al., 2019) is proposed, executing an optimal selection algorithm for service placement and request scheduling placement to improve the total utility (satisfaction) of all the IoT users.

5G

The faster wireless networking technology, 5G, one of the biggest drivers for edge computing increases bandwidth significantly and depletes latency with its distributed nature. Many companies started to deploy this technology as overlapping 5G networks can keep bandwidth-intensive content closer to the edge or even on-premises to meet the ongoing demands for faster and efficient services. The evolution in 5G mobile communications becomes a major key player in AAL healthcare scenarios.

In the 5G spectrum, the expansion of frequency bands inhibits the use of full-duplex channels for data communications. To overcome this, Kaneriya et al. (2019) described an AAL system architecture with a full-duplex communication standard that acquires low delay and more communication accuracy in transmitting patients' vital data. In another work, intelligent peer-to-peer backhaul is procured by establishing a peer port at each mobile station, hence the data streams of IoT devices in a fog environment is allowed to take the optimal route dynamically for the desired speed, delay and cost in alternative radio access networks, providing AAL as a Service (Stainov et al., 2016).

Virtualizations

For intensifying network resource utilization, a virtual sensor network can be formed by connecting logical instances of underlying physical sensor nodes and serve multiple applications rather than a specific service with several numbers of sensors. Khalid et al. (2015) described a middleware architecture integrating and managing resources and communication protocols and standards in smart home and AAL service. Besides, the framework employs a multi-threading concept in order to enable manifold isolated applications to run on dissimilar sensor networks.

Network Function Virtualization (NFV) is a network architecture concept, virtualizing functions of every network element namely load balancing, traffic control, virtual routing, firewall, intrusion detection, and so on. Differing from traditional virtualization, it decouples network functions from the actual physical network hardware elements. NFV based AAL system (Nikoloudakis et al., 2017) is discussed to escalate the user's mobility with the help of assistive technology. Though the patient wearing the dedicated service is allowed to move outside, continuous monitoring is provided and the nearest caretakers will be notified if an emergency is required.

Docker Containers

Docker enables platform-as-a-service by virtualizing operating system (OS) - a set of software packages called containers containing software, system tools and libraries, configuration files to run an application regardless of actual physical infrastructure.

Due to the depletion of computing resources at the network edge, the performance of the application may degrade while executing data-intensive tasks on the endpoint devices because of resource overhead. An AAL healthcare environment contains a spectrum of IoT devices or sensors connected to a single edge gateway and if overhead occurs in the end devices then it will create a great impact on service deployment and meeting the service requirements, increasing the chance of loss of life. An efficient resource management scheme (Ahmeda et al., 2019) is recommended based on Docker container virtualization techniques by mitigating resource overhead and network failures. The virtualization technology helps greatly to enhance the application performance when the learning models are assimilated at the edge (Jacome et al., 2019). Thus it sophisticates service life cycle management and deployment in AAL systems.

In pursuance of maintaining a secured electronic patient record in healthcare service scenarios targeting the AAL domain, a fog computing architecture with blockchain functionality (Cech et al., 2019) is proposed which adopts container virtualization and SDN for dynamic resource management and orchestration. It also ensures secure data processing and retrieval.

Software-Defined Networking

SDN is a network architecture separating the data plane (forwarding behavior) from the control plane (network routing intelligence) and placing the intelligence in a central place called the SDN controller. Contrasting from the traditional networking technology, SDN makes the network programmable and controllable from the centralized controller. Silva et al. (2016) proposed an AAL architecture for managing and distributing context information from smart home to enable context-based processing of raw sensor data and transport the relevant resulting data to the cloud using SDN functionality, upgrading QoS of the presented framework.

CASE STUDY

In this section, a real-life use case study utilizing the AAL concept and its applicability is presented. Considering an AAL patient requiring constant monitoring during the COVID-19 crisis in a quarantined environment, an edge-based model is discussed.

Vital Sign Monitoring During COVID-19 Pandemic

The coronavirus disease 2019 (COVID-19) started as an epidemic, primarily spread within China since December 2019, and is declared as a global pandemic on March 11, 2020, when it started spreading outside china secondarily. It causes 1.6 million deaths and affects more than 75 million people worldwide (World Health Organization, December 22, 2020). As the disease is highly contagious, the spread occurs mostly from person-to-person through respiratory droplets from coughing and sneezing, whilst being in close contact (NPTEL, May 18, 2020). Besides, the patients are reported with acute respiratory distress syndrome and have shown varying degrees of complications, and their severity is diagnosed as mild, severe or critical (Huang et al., 2020; Lescure et al., 2020; Wang et al., 2020). Especially people with comorbidities such as lung disease, heart disease, kidney failure, diabetes, hypertension, etc., have developed severe complications resulting in increased mortality. Hence, the mortality rate of older people with a chronic illness is higher than that of other aged adults.

Due to the high risk of transmissibility of the virus by people with mild illness, the infected or suspected persons should be isolated at hospitals and continuously monitored to know the stage of the illness. This increases the risk of acquiring the symptoms to nursing staff while accomplishing regular monitoring of the patients and possibly to other people or patients who have come in contact with the staff. Furthermore, the travellers have to be quarantined for 14 days as the symptoms may appear 2 - 14 days (estimated incubation period) after exposure to the viral disease for an individual (NPTEL, May 18, 2020).

Among the globally reported cases, around 14% are healthcare people (World Health Organization, September 17, 2020). The physical and mental health of medical professionals is equally important in this pandemic crisis. They are suffering from psychological stress, anxiety, depression and insomnia due to long working hours, fear of direct disease exposure, and being virus transmitters to their family members (Pappaa et al., 2020). Immediate telemedicine technology intervention is essential in managing this crisis in several ways and has become a triage engine during this pandemic period. The people

Table 3. Adopted from NEWS Scoring System (Royal College of Physicians, 2012)

Parameters	0	1	2	3
Body Temperature (degree celsius)	36.1 - 38.0	35.1 - 36 or 38.1 - 39	>= 39.1	<= 35
Heart Rate (per min)	51 - 90	41 - 50 or 91 - 110	111 - 130	<= 40 or >= 131
Blood Pressure (systolic)	111 - 219	101 - 110	91 - 100	<= 90 or >= 220
Respiratory Rate (per min)	12 - 20	9 - 11	21 - 24	<= 8 or >= 25
Blood Oxygen Saturation Rate	>=96	94 - 95	92 - 93	<= 91
Supplemental oxygen	No	No	Yes	Yes
Consciousness	Yes	Yes	Yes	Drowsiness Lethargy
Age	< 65			>=65

with early or mild symptoms and people with travel history can be isolated and quarantined in a smart enhanced living environment enabled with AAL services rather than being at hospitals.

The integrated AAL and telemonitoring technology reduce anxiety and prevent the probability of spreading the infection to the healthcare personnel, by accelerating services such as video consultation with medical care teams, remote monitoring, automatic medication remainders/providers, automatic ventilation control, diet monitoring, sleep monitoring, hygiene monitoring and so on. It paves a way for a massive scale and asynchronous solution to handle such a pandemic crisis. It prevents direct contact between the patient and healthcare teams, thus avoiding the risk of exposure. It enables well in time organized isolation of elderly or infected or suspected individuals. In consequence, telemedicine technology also helps to keep the morbidity level and fatality risk at a minimum.

Some related works (Sandhu et al., 2016; Watson et al., 2020) have been studied in which cloud computing has been exploited in the screening and monitoring of pandemic outbreaks. A cloud computing architecture for smart monitoring of pandemic Influenza A1(H1N1) is presented as a framework in (Sandhu et al., 2016). It calculates an index value to predict the future probability of the person spreading or catching the infection by collecting their medical reports from doctors/clinicians. A notification is sent to the respective caretakers if the patients' condition is at high risk. The remote monitoring service is advantageous in several ways (Watson et al., 2020). It enables the safe delivery of required medical

Table 4. Adopted from NEWS Thresholds and Triggers (Royal College of Physicians, 2012)

Aggregate Score	Risk level	Warning level	Monitoring Frequency	Response	Solution
0	-	-	12 hrs once	Ward based	Monitoring
1 - 4	Mild	Yellow	6 hrs once	Urgent ward based	Monitoring / Intimate doctor
5 - 6	Severe	Orange	1-2 hrs once	Key threshold for urgent	Evaluation and Remote Consultation by Doctor
>= 7	Critical	Red	Continuous	Emergency	On-site Consultation by Doctor

equipment to the patient without direct contact. It ensures the safety of collected data from patients by storing them in a secure database.

The major symptoms of COVID-19 from which one can suspect are fever, cough, and shortness of breath. The other symptoms and associated range of values for the mild, severe, and critical stage are shown in Table 3 and Table 4, adopted from the NEWS (National Early Warning Score) scoring system (Royal College of Physicians, 2012).

The edge-based AAL model for COVID-19 telemonitoring and teleconsultation applications are shown in Figure 5. In this context, having presented the comorbidity status and travel history, the patient is assumed to be isolated in a smart living scenario deployed with vital and medical sensors or equipped with special-purpose wearable devices. It is proven that a healthy diet and personal hygiene are significant to recover soon from the disease by improving the immune system against the virus. The patient should be affirmed to follow the strict infection control protocols established nationwide, being in a safe atmosphere. Hence, the physiological parameters of the patient (diet intake, sleeping habit, hand washing, and other related activities) are also retrieved to ensure the patient is taken good care of as if they were at a hospital-related secure environment.

The edge server with a necessary software application can be useful in gathering vital data from the patient persistently. Then it involves a general pre-processing and filtering of the sensor data. The cloud server distributes the instance of the inference model to the edge device with respect to monitor the disease progression. The edge server can run the distributed instance to predict the risk level of the person and to enable them with suitable clinical responses and solutions. The emergency response will be immediately sent from the edge device to the medical practitioners if the warning level reaches the Orange or Red stage. The healthcare professional can visualize the data stored in the remote cloud for

Figure 5. Edge-based AAL Environment for COVID-19 Isolated Patient Monitoring

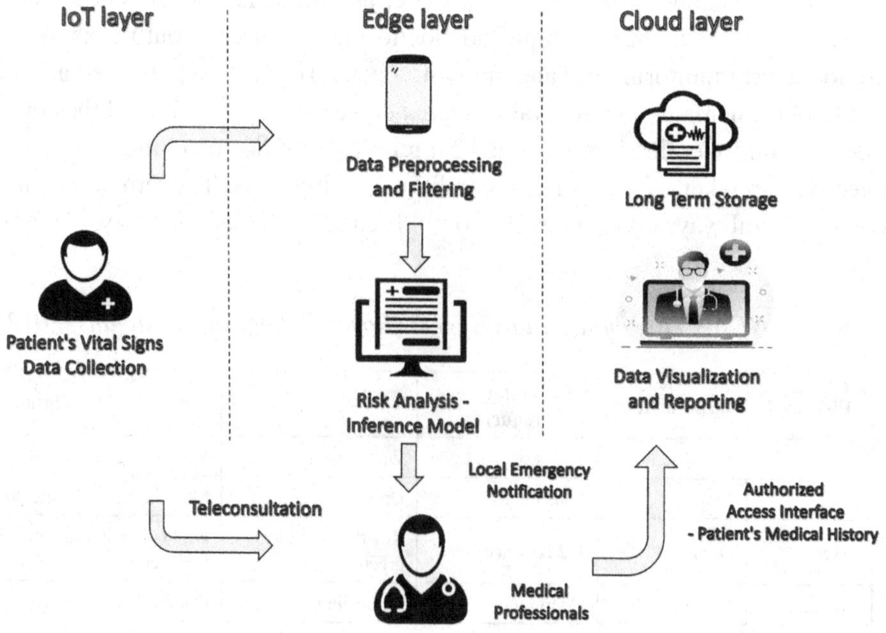

further information via authorized access. Whenever required, the patient and the doctor can have online video consultations about the medication or relevant information.

Instead of the inference analysis occurs at the remote cloud, the edge computing solution can offer low latency and immediate response with the increased number of quarantined persons accessing the same service deployed in a cloud server, supporting scalability for COVID-19 screening.

FUTURE RESEARCH DIRECTIONS

The concept of edge computing crucially relies on edge gateway devices for processing complex tasks and running AI models at the periphery of the users' personalized network. Such devices should support long-range communication standards to leverage their capabilities. The telehealthcare solutions can provide real-time medical recommendations, disease diagnosis or emergency prediction using the power of the edge with regard to control or handle chronic disorders. Furthermore, they are capable of predicting patients' disease patterns and provide customized care services.

Even though telemedicine plays a greater role in AAL business, it is equally important to integrate the AAL platform, healthcare technologies, and formal & informal telehealth stakeholders to enable scalable and sustainable telecare solutions. By including more number of users, practically implemented evidence-based studies and solutions will give direction to future research. However, the elderly or physically impaired person should be self-determined and motivated to use advanced mobile technologies.

CONCLUSION

AAL is an emerging technology providing sustainable telehealthcare solutions to older adults, impaired people, or isolated individuals. The cloud-based AAL system lacks in affording real-time decision making capability to an intelligent environment, especially in healthcare services due to large data communication, processing, and management in the already hectic network. The importance of these issues led to the development of edge-based AAL systems collaborating multiple stakeholders namely medical specialists, remote care centers, caretakers, and so on. The integration of edge computing solutions into these systems helps to improve the QoS of the end-users.

In this chapter, the edge-based IoT framework for AAL scenarios is presented which inculcates AI and deep learning techniques into the endpoint devices. Signifying many edge solutions in the field of AAL, how it accelerates context-based classification and predictive learning from the pattern behaviour in order to enable cloud-like resource infrastructure at one hop away from the end-users is mentioned. In the event of having computational and storage resources at the edge to implement AI algorithms, recent technologies like virtualization, SDN, 5G to strengthen the edge computing capabilities are discussed. Thus, expediting the real-time edge-based health-related emergency response will have the biggest positive impact, improving the health of independently living individuals and the quality of their life in a smart environment.

A case study on remote vital sign monitoring of a COVID-19 patient at his living place itself more comfortable to handle the eerie happening of pandemic crisis. The edge intelligence helps in reacting immediately with the patients' health triggers and providing clinical emergency response.

REFERENCES

Ahmeda, B., Seghira, B., Al-Ostaa, M., & Abdelouahed, G. (2019). Container Based Resource Management for Data Processing on IoT Gateways. In *Proceedings of the 16th International Conference on Mobile Systems and Pervasive Computing*. Elsevier. 10.1016/j.procs.2019.08.034

Bailas, C., Marsden, M., Zhang, D., O'Connor, N. E., & Little, S. (2018). Performance of Video Processing at the Edge for Crowd-Monitoring Applications. In *Proceedings of the 4th World Forum on Internet of Things (WF-IoT)*. IEEE. 10.1109/WF-IoT.2018.8355170

Bilal, K., Khalid, O., Erbad, A., & Khan, S. U. (2018). Potentials, trends, and prospects in edge technologies: Fog, cloudlet, mobile edge, and micro data centers. *Elsevier Computer Networks*, *130*, 94–120. doi:10.1016/j.comnet.2017.10.002

Brouwer, M. D., Ongenae, F., Bonte, P., & Turck, F. D. (2018). Towards a Cascading Reasoning Framework to Support Responsive Ambient-Intelligent Healthcare Interventions. *MDPI Sensors - Wearable and Ambient Sensors for Healthcare and Wellness Applications, 18*(10), 3514.

Camarinha-Matos, L. M., Rosas, J., Oliveira, A. I., & Ferrada, F. (2015). Care services ecosystem for ambient assisted living. *Enterprise Information Systems*, *9*(5-6), 607–633.

CBINSIGHTS. (2020, April 28). *What is Edge Computing?* Retrieved from https://www.cbinsights.com/research/what-is-edge-computing/

Cech, H. L., Grobmann, M., & Krieger, U. R. (2019). A Fog Computing Architecture to Share Sensor Data by Means of Blockchain Functionality. In *Proceedings of International Conference on Fog Computing*. IEEE. 10.1109/ICFC.2019.00013

Cerina, L., Notargiacomo, S., Paccanit, M. G. L., & Santambrogio, M. D. (2017). A Fog-Computing architecture for Preventive Healthcare and Assisted Living in Smart Ambients. In *Proceedings of the 3rd International Forum on Research and Technologies for Society and Industry (RTSI)*. IEEE. 10.1109/RTSI.2017.8065939

Chou, T. C., Chiu, N. F., Liao, F. R., Lu, S. S., Ping, F., Yang, C. R., & Lin, C. W. (2005). A Multi Parameters Wearable Telemetric System for Cardio-Pulmonary Fitness of e-Health. In *Proceedings of the 27th Annual Conference on Engineering in Medicine and Biology*. IEEE. 10.1109/IEMBS.2005.1617233

Cisco. (2015). *Fog Computing and the Internet of Things: Extend the Cloud to Where the Things Are: Whitepaper*. Retrieved from https://www.cisco.com/c/dam/en_us/solutions/trends/iot/docs/computing-overview.pdf

Emeakaroha, V. C., Cafferkey, N., Healy, P., & Morrison, J. P. (2015). A Cloud-Based IoT Data Gathering and Processing Platform. In *Proceedings of the 3rd International Conference on Future Internet of Things and Cloud*. IEEE. 10.1109/FiCloud.2015.53

Foko, T., Dlodlo, N., & Montsi, L. (2013). An Integrated Smart System for Ambient-Assisted Living. *Internet of Things, Smart Spaces, and Next Generation Networking*, *8121*, 128–138. doi:10.1007/978-3-642-40316-3_12

Gomes, B., Muniz, L., Silva, F. J. S., Rios, L. T. E., & Endler, M. (2015). A Comprehensive Cloud-based IoT Software Infrastructure for Ambient Assisted Living. In *Proceedings of International Conference on Cloud Technologies and Applications (CloudTech)*. IEEE. 10.1109/CloudTech.2015.7336998

Haghi, M., Geissler, A., Fleischer, H., Stoll, N., & Thurow, K. (2019). Ubiqsense: A Personal Wearable in Ambient Parameters Monitoring Based on IoT Platform. In *Proceedings of International Conference on Sensing and Instrumentation in IoT Era (ISSI)*. IEEE. 10.1109/ISSI47111.2019.9043713

Hassan, M. K., Desouky, A. I. E., Badawy, M. M., Sarhan, A. M., Elhoseny, M., & Gunasekaran, M. (2019). EoT-driven hybrid ambient assisted living framework with naive Bayes–firefly algorithm. *Springer Neural Computing and Applications*, *31*(5), 1275–1300. doi:10.100700521-018-3533-y

Hou, L., Zhang, H., Wang, J., & Shi, D. (2019). Optimal Blood Glucose Prediction based on Intermittent Data from Wearable Glucose Monitoring Sensors. In *Proceedings of Chinese Control Conference (CCC)*. IEEE. 10.23919/ChiCC.2019.8866572

Huang, C., Wang, Y., Li, X., Ren, L., Zhao, J., Hu, Y., Zhang, L., Fan, G., Xu, J., Gu, X., Cheng, Z., Yu, T., Xia, J., Wei, Y., Wu, W., Xie, X., Yin, W., Li, H., Liu, M., ... Cao, B. (2020). Clinical features of patients infected with 2019 novel coronavirus in Wuhan, China. *Lancet*, *395*(10223), 497–506. doi:10.1016/S0140-6736(20)30183-5 PMID:31986264

Jacome, D. S., Lacalle, I., Palau, C. E., & Esteve, M. (2019). Efficient Deployment of Predictive Analytics in Edge Gateways: Fall Detection Scenario. In *Proceedings of the 5th World Forum on Internet of Things (WF-IoT)*. IEEE.

Kaneriya, S., Vora, J., Tanwar, S., & Tyagi, S. (2019). Standardising the use of Duplex Channels in 5G-WiFi Networking for Ambient Assisted Living. In *Proceedings of International Conference on Communications Workshops*. IEEE. 10.1109/ICCW.2019.8757145

Keum, S. S., Park, Y. J., & Kang, S. J. (2020). Edge Computing-Based Self-Organized Device Network for Awareness Activities of Daily Living in the Home. *MDPI Applied Sciences - Software Approaches to Improve the Performance of IoT Systems*, *10*(7), 2475.

Khalid, Z., Fisal, N., Zubair, S., Ullah, R., Safdar, H., Maqbool, W., & Khalid, U. (2015). Multi-Thread based Middleware for Sensor Network Virtualization. In *Proceedings of the 5th National Symposium on Information Technology: Towards New Smart World (NSITNSW)*. IEEE. 10.1109/NSITNSW.2015.7176421

Labonnote, N., & Høyland, K. (2015). Smart home technologies that support independent living: Challenges and opportunities for the building industry – a systematic mapping study. *Taylor & Francis Intelligent Buildings International*, *9*(1), 40–63. doi:10.1080/17508975.2015.1048767

Lescure, F. X., Bouadma, L., Parisey, D. N. M., Wicky, P. H., Behillil, S., Gaymard, A., Duchamp, M. B., Donati, F., Hingrat, Q. L., Enouf, V., Houhou-Fidouh, N., Valette, M., Mailles, A., Lucet, J. C., Mentre, F., Duval, X., Descamps, D., Malvy, D., Timsit, J. F., ... Yazdanpanah, Y. (2020). Clinical and virological data of the first cases of COVID-19 in Europe: A case series. *THE LANCET Infectious Diseases*, *20*(6), 697–706. doi:10.1016/S1473-3099(20)30200-0 PMID:32224310

Lopez-de-Ipina, D., Blanco, S., Diaz-de-Sarralde, I., & Laiseca, X. (2010). A Platform for a More Widespread Adoption of AAL. *Aging Friendly Technology for Health and Independence, 6159*, 250–253. doi:10.1007/978-3-642-13778-5_35

Market Research Future. (2018, April). *Global Ambient Assisted Living Market Research Report, by System (Entertainment, Communication, Medical Assistance, Transportation), Sensor (Temperature, Occupancy), Service (Installation & Repair) – Forecast till 2027* (ID: MRFR/SEM/0509-CR). Retrieved from https://www.marketresearchfuture.com/reports/ambient-assisted-living-market-1015

Nawaz, T., Rinner, B., & Ferryman, J. (2016). User-centric, embedded vision-based human monitoring: A concept and a healthcare use case. In *Proceedings of the 10th International Conference on Distributed Smart Camera ICDSC '16.* Association for Computing Machinery. 10.1145/2967413.2967422

Nikoloudakis, Y., Markakis, E., Mastorakis, G., Pallis, E., & Skianis, C. (2017). An NFV-Powered Emergency System for Smart Enhanced Living Environment. In *Proceedings of Conference on Network Function Virtualization and Software Defined Networks (NFV-SDN).* IEEE.

Nikoloudakis, Y., Panagiotakis, S., Markakis, E., Pallis, E., Mastorakis, G., Mavromoustakis, C. X., & Dobre, C. (2016). A Fog-Based Emergency System for Smart Enhanced Living Environments. *IEEE Cloud Computing, 3*(6), 54–62. doi:10.1109/MCC.2016.118

NPTEL. (2020, May 18). Live_Covid 19: A Clinician's Perspective. *NPTEL Live Streaming.* https://www.youtube.com/watch?v=8ZUXSXFYEk4&t=4431s

Ohtsuka, S., Usami, T., & Sasaki, N. (2014). A vibration watch using a smart phone for visually impaired people. In *Proceedings of the 3rd Global Conference on Consumer Electronics (GCCE).* IEEE. 10.1109/GCCE.2014.7031094

Pappaa, S., Ntellac, V., Giannakasc, T., Giannakoulisc, V. G., Papoutsic, E., & Katsaounou, P. (2020). Prevalence of depression, anxiety, and insomnia among healthcare workers during the COVID-19 pandemic: A systematic review and meta-analysis. *Elsevier Brain, Behavior, and Immunity, 88*, 901–907. doi:10.1016/j.bbi.2020.05.026 PMID:32437915

Pazienza, A., Mallardi, G., Fasciano, C., & Vitulano, F. (2019). Artificial Intelligence on Edge Computing: a Healthcare Scenario in Ambient Assisted Living. In *Proceedings of the Fifth Italian Workshop on Artificial Intelligence for Ambient Assisted Living (AI*AAL.it 2019), co-located with 18th International Conference of the Italian Association for Artificial Intelligence (AIxIA 2019).* CEUR-WS.

Pham, X. Q., Nguyen, T. D., Nguyen, V. D., & Huh, E. N. (2019). Utility-Centric Service Provisioning in Multi-Access Edge Computing. *MDPI Applied Sciences - Intelligent Centralized and Distributed Secure Edge Computing for Internet of Things Applications, 9*(18), 3776.

Porambage, P., Okwuibe, J., Liyanage, M., Ylianttila, M., & Taleb, T. (2018). Survey on Multi-Access Edge Computing for Internet of Things Realization. *IEEE Communications Surveys and Tutorials, 20*(4), 2961–2991. doi:10.1109/COMST.2018.2849509

Qabil, S., Waheed, U., Awan, S. M., Mansoor, Y., & Khan, M. A. (2019). A Survey on Emerging Integration of Cloud Computing and Internet of Things. In *Proceedings of the International Conference on Information Science and Communication Technology (ICISCT).* IEEE. 10.1109/CISCT.2019.8777438

Ray, P. P., Dash, D., & De, D. (2019). Edge computing for Internet of Things: A survey, e-healthcare case study and future direction. *Elsevier Journal of Network and Computer Applications, 140*, 1–22. doi:10.1016/j.jnca.2019.05.005

Royal College of Physicians. (2012). *National Early Warning Score (NEWS): Standardising the assessment of acute illness severity in the NHS. Report of a working party*. RCP.

Sandhu, R., Gill, H. K., & Sood, S. K. (2016). Smart monitoring and controlling of pandemic influenza A (H1N1) using social network analysis and cloud computing. *Journal of Computational Science, 12*, 11–22. doi:10.1016/j.jocs.2015.11.001 PMID:32362959

Sheshadri, S. H., & Franklin, D. (2020) *Introducing the Ultimate Starter AI Computer, the NVIDIA Jetson Nano 2GB Developer Kit*. NVIDIA Developer. Retrieved from https://developer.nvidia.com/blog/ultimate-starter-ai-computer-jetson-nano-2gb-developer-kit/

Siddiqui, S. A., Zhang, Y., Lloret, J., Song, H., & Obradovic, Z. (2018). Pain-Free Blood Glucose Monitoring Using Wearable Sensors: Recent Advancements and Future Prospects. *IEEE Reviews in Biomedical Engineering, 11*, 21–35. doi:10.1109/RBME.2018.2822301 PMID:29993663

Siegel, C., Hochgatterer, A., & Dorne, T. E. (2014). Contributions of ambient assisted living for health and quality of life in the elderly and care services - a qualitative analysis from the experts' perspective of care service professionals. *BMC Geriatrics, 14*(1), 112. doi:10.1186/1471-2318-14-112 PMID:25326149

Silva, M. P., Nazario, D. C., Dantas, M. A. R., Goncalves, A. L., Pinto, A. R., Manerichi, G., & Vanelli, B. (2016). An eHealth Context Management and Distribution Approach in AAL Environments. In *Proceedings of the 29th International Symposium on Computer-Based Medical Systems (CBMS)*. IEEE. 10.1109/CBMS.2016.15

Stainov, R., Mirchev, M., Goleva, R., Mirtchev, S., Atamian, D., Savov, A., & Draganov, P. (2016). AALaaS Intelligent Backhauls for P2P Communication in 5G Mobile Networks. In *Proceedings of International Black Sea Conference on Communications and Networking (BlackSeaCom)*. IEEE.

Statistica. (2016, November). *Internet of Things (IoT) connected devices installed base worldwide from 2015 to 2025*. Statista Research Department. Retrieved from https://www.statista.com/statistics/471264/iot-number-of-connected-devices-worldwide/

Suhrid Barua. (n.d.). Flood of Data Will Get Generated in Autonomous Cars. *Auto Tech Review*. Retrieved from https://autotechreview.com/features/flood-of-data-will-get-generated-in-autonomous-cars#:~:text=There%20is%20a%20great%20deal,cars%20in%20the%20automotive%20industry.&text=According%20to%20various%20industry%20experts,hour%20of%20driving%20a%20day

Vano-Galvan, S., Paoli, J., Rios-Buceta, L., & Jaen, P. (2015). Skin self- examination using smartphone photography to improve the early diagnosis of melanoma. *Actas Dermo-Sifilograficas, 106*(1), 75–77. PMID:25173155

Vora, J., Tanwar, S., Tyagi, S., Kumar, N., & Rodrigues, J. J. P. C. (2017). FAAL: Fog Computing-based Patient Monitoring System for Ambient Assisted Living. In *Proceedings of the 19th International Conference on e-Health Networking, Applications and Services (Healthcom)*. IEEE. 10.1109/HealthCom.2017.8210825

Wang, D., Hu, B., Hu, C., Zhu, F., Liu, X., Zhang, J., Wang, B., Xiang, H., Cheng, Z., Xiong, Y., Zhao, Y., Li, Y., Wang, X., & Peng, Z. (2020). Clinical characteristics of 138 hospitalized patients with 2019 novel coronavirus-infected pneumonia in Wuhan, China. *JAMA Network, 323*(11), 1061–1069. doi:10.1001/jama.2020.1585 PMID:32031570

Watson, A. R., Wah, R., & Thamman, R. (2020). The Value of Remote Monitoring for the COVID-19 Pandemic. *Telemedicine Journal and e-Health, 26*(9), 1110–1112. Advance online publication. doi:10.1089/tmj.2020.0134 PMID:32384251

Western Digital Website. (n.d.). Retrieved from https://www.westerndigital.com/solutions/oil-gas

World Health Organization. (2018, February 5). *Ageing and Health*. Retrieved from https://www.who.int/news-room/fact-sheets/detail/ageing-and-health

World Health Organization. (2020, September 17). *Keep health workers safe to keep patients safe: WHO*. Retrieved from https://www.who.int/news/item/17-09-2020-keep-health-workers-safe-to-keep-patients-safe-who

World Health Organization. (2020, December 22). *COVID-19 Weekly Epidemiological Update*. Retrieved from https://www.who.int/publications/m/item/weekly-epidemiological-update---22-december-2020

Yu, W., Liang, F., He, X., Hatcher, W. G., Lu, C., Lin, J., & Yang, X. (2017). A Survey on the Edge Computing for the Internet of Things. *IEEE Access: Practical Innovations, Open Solutions, 6*, 6900–6919. doi:10.1109/ACCESS.2017.2778504

Zainudin, M. N. S., Sulaiman, M. N., Mustapha, N., & Perumal, T. (2017). Monitoring daily fitness activity using accelerometer sensor fusion. In *Proceedings of the International Symposium on Consumer Electronics (ISCE)*. IEEE. 10.1109/ISCE.2017.8355540

Zgheib, R., Nicola, A. D., Villani, M. L., Conchon, E., & Bastide, R. (2017). A Flexible Architecture for Cognitive Sensing of Activities in Ambient Assisted Living. In *Proceedings of the 26th International Conference on Enabling Technologies: Infrastructure for Collaborative Enterprises*. IEEE. 10.1109/WETICE.2017.41

ADDITIONAL READING

Aloi, G., Fortino, G., Gravina, R., Pace, P., & Savaglio, C. (2020). E-ALPHA: Edge-based Assisted Living Platform for Home cAre. In *Proceedings of IEEE Conference on Computer Communications Workshops (INFOCOM WKSHPS)*. IEEE INFOCOM 2020. 10.1109/INFOCOMWKSHPS50562.2020.9163018

Ashraf, M. U., Hannan, A., Cheema, S. M., Ali, Z., Jambi, K. M., & Alofi, A. (2020). Detection and Tracking Contagion using IoT-Edge Technologies: Confronting COVID-19 Pandemic. In *Proceedings of International Conference on Electrical, Communication, and Computer Engineering (ICECCE)*. IEEE.

Dilibal, C. (2020). Development of Edge-IoMT Computing Architecture for Smart Healthcare Monitoring Platform. In *Proceedings of 4th International Symposium on Multidisciplinary Studies and Innovative Technologies (ISMSIT)*. IEEE. 10.1109/ISMSIT50672.2020.9254501

Dimitrievski, A., Zdravevski, E., Lameski, P., & Trajkovik, V. (2017). A survey of Ambient Assisted Living systems: challenges and opportunities. In *Proceedings of 12th International Conference on Intelligent Computer Communication and Processing (ICCP)*. IEEE.

Ksentini, A., & Brik, B. (2020). An Edge-Based Social Distancing Detection Service to Mitigate CO-VID-19 Propagation. *IEEE Internet of Things Magazine, 3*(3), 35–39. doi:10.1109/IOTM.0001.2000138

Pazienza, A., Mallardi, G., Fasciano, C., & Vitulano, F. (2019). Artificial Intelligence on Edge Computing: a Healthcare Scenario in Ambient Assisted Living. In Proceedings of Artificial Intelligence for Ambient Assisted Living (Corpus ID: 211567409). Rende (CS), Italy.

Rahman, M. A., Hossain, M. S., Alrajeh, N. A., & Guizani, N. (2020). B5G and Explainable Deep Learning Assisted Healthcare Vertical at the Edge: COVID-19 Perspective. *IEEE Network, 34*(4), 98–105. doi:10.1109/MNET.011.2000353

Stojkoska, B. R., Trivodaliev, K., & Davcev, D. (2017). *Internet of Things Framework for Home Care Systems. Wireless Communications and Mobile Computing*. Hindawi.

KEY TERMS AND DEFINITIONS

Data Aggregation/Filtering: The raw data collected from sensors is unstructured and contains noise. It has to be processed and computed to obtain structured data through a process called data aggregation or filtering.

Data Analytics: The raw data collected by the IoT environment is analyzed in a cloud/edge server to find trends, hidden patterns, and knowledgeable insights.

Edge Intelligence: The devices available at the edge layer have some limited amount of computing resources which can be utilized and incorporated with machine learning or AI algorithms to perform real-time data analytics.

QoS: Measurement of the overall service performance guaranteeing the minimal users' requirements like latency, responsiveness, reliability, throughput, etc., while consuming a service.

Response Time: The time duration between the users requesting the service and the service is actually consumed by them.

Software-Defined Networking: Different from the traditional networking infrastructure, it moves intelligence from the network hardware devices to the centralized place called SDN controller by making all the hardware devices as dummy forwarding devices. The SDN controller where intelligence is available provides global network view and makes network management easier.

Time-Critical Application: The application required real-time or almost zero delayed response is called time-critical or time-sensitive application.

Wireless Sensor Network: It is a self-configured wireless network of sensors or sensing devices to collect physical or environmental data and send the data wirelessly to a central location to get connected to the external world.

Chapter 18
Technologies and Applications of Internet of Things (IoT) in Healthcare

Imran Aslan

(iD) https://orcid.org/0000-0001-5307-4474

Health Management Department, Faculty of Health Sciences, Bingöl University, Turkey

ABSTRACT

Developments in technology have opened new doors for healthcare to improve the treatment methods and prevent illnesses as a proactive method. Internet of things (IoT) technologies have also improved the self-management of care and provided more useful data and decisions to doctors with data analytics. Unnecessary visits, utilizing better quality resources, and improving allocation and planning are main advantages of IoT in healthcare. Moreover, governments and private institutions have become a part of this new state-of-the-art development for decreasing costs and getting more benefits over the management of services. In this chapter, IoT technologies and applications are explained with some examples. Furthermore, deep learning and artificial intelligence (AI) usage in healthcare and their benefits are stated that artificial neural networks (ANN) can monitor, learn, and predict, and the overall health severity for preventing serious health loss can be estimated and prevented.

1. INTRODUCTION

The growing rate of the aging population has brought significant expense on healthcare systems requiring a long-time commitment of medical and human resources. Reliable, effective and smart healthcare service for the elderly and patients with chronic health conditions can be provided with the help of smart technologies. These new technologies can be used in improving physical and mental functions of patients. Real-time monitoring can help in preventing heart failure, management of diabetes, and controlling of asthma through smart medical devices connected to a smartphone application. Blood pressure, oxygen and blood sugar levels, weight etc. data can be collected by Internet of Things (IoT) device and this data can be transferred to authorized folks through connectivity protocols and embedding chips of a smart device.

DOI: 10.4018/978-1-7998-6673-2.ch018

Advancement in the state-of-the-art studies in IoT- based healthcare systems, adopting to the IoT technologies and smart medical service systems can increase the effectiveness in healthcare. Interoperability, machine-to-machine communication, information exchange, and data movement properties can make IoT an effective system in healthcare. Improved medical treatments with less expense can garner the attention of governments. Decreased waiting times, tracking of patients, staff, inventory, enhancing drug management by preventing drug allergies and availability of critical hardware can be accomplished with the help of IoT applications in healthcare. It has been found that there is a 50% reduction in a 30-day readmission rate with the help of remote patient monitoring for patients with heart conditions; making healthcare affordable for people. Furthermore, identification and authentication are used to reduce the possibility of anomalies such as wrong drug usage, dosage, timing or procedure etc. (Nasrullah, 2020).

Wearable monitoring systems such as Google Health provide the user with a complete report of combined health records, health conditions, and possible interactions between drugs and allergies. Some of the smart technologies widely used in the healthcare are as follows:

- MobiHealth: integrates wearable devices with portable devices such as mobile phones and watches
- AlarmNet: provides both the functions of physiological monitoring and location tracking (and)
- Mobile Electro Cardio Graph (ECG): measures ECG for users with a smart mobile phone acting as a base station

Tele-health provides health-related services where a patient can receive professional advice remotely. Stored images, video and audio can be transmitted to another location on an as needed basis. Furthermore, patients and doctors can interact over video conference and remote patient monitoring where diagnosing can be performed with sensed technologies and monitored data. Moreover, doctors for real-time tracking can give notifications about critical parts to patients or family members by mobile apps. Furthermore, remote training can be carried out with that system for patients with chronic illness. In addition, reports can be generated based on patient's diagnosis. Doctors can be contacted in case patients are far away, and online support can be provided to patients until they reach a hospital (Nasrullah, 2020; Yin et al., 2016).

Integration of multiple devices and protocols can be a challenge of IoT in healthcare that there is not a connected device's protocols. Lack of data protocols and standards and ambiguity of data ownership regulation can also be challenges for data security and privacy (Nasrullah, 2020). Varieties of devices have different communication protocols preventing the process of data collection. Handling a tremendous amount of data affecting the quality of decision-making is another extremely difficult situation for doctors as more devices connect internet platforms. Vital healthcare analytics can help quicker decision making with higher precision. Resource-based data accessing method, namely UDA-IoT, has been developed to acquire and process IoT data ubiquitously and has shown great effectiveness in a cloud and mobile computing platform, from which doctors and managers will both benefit (Yin et al., 2016). Hacking of healthcare data is also a problem in the field of cyber-crime that cyber-criminals can use patients' data to write prescriptions and buy medical equipment without patient's consent (Nasrullah, 2020).

This chapter is aimed to provide a systematic review of enabling IoT technologies used in healthcare with some recent literature. Some applications of IoT in healthcare will be explained with their benefits. Furthermore, sensors and fog computing as the main parts of the IoT system will be elaborated upon. IoT systems face various challenges and these challenges will be disclosed and the ways of overcoming these challenges will be discussed.

2. SMART TECHNOLOGIES IN HEALTHCARE

2.1 Internet of Things (IoT)

IoT is defined as "*a dynamic global network infrastructure with self-configuring capabilities based on standard and interoperable communication protocols where physical and virtual "things" have identities, physical attributes, and virtual personalities and use intelligent interfaces, and are seamlessly integrated into the information network*" (Kim & Kim, 2018). Neurology, cardiology, and psychiatry are fields using IoT technologies mostly (Sadoughi, Behmanesh, Sayfouri, 2020) and the economic value of IoT healthcare is estimated to be 2 trillion dollars by 2025 (Kim & Kim, 2018). Hardware, software, connectivity of the network, and any other required electronic/computer are elements of IoT (Singh et al., 2020; Sadoughi, Behmanesh, Sayfouri, 2020). Cloud computing, fog computing, mobile computing, wearable sensors, and big data are new innovative technologies making the life of patients easier and can save lives (Sadoughi, Behmanesh, Sayfouri, 2020). Reduced medical errors and increased patient safety are the main advantages of new technologies (Thibaud et al., 2018).

2.1.1 Internet of Things (IoT) Technologies in Healthcare

IoT characterized with industry 4.0 cloud and fog computing, and big data technologies have improved e-Health named as Healthcare 4.0. Mobiles, smart cards, robots, sensors, and tele-health systems are technologies used in the medical field (Aceto, Persico&Pescape, 2020). Radio Frequency Identification (RFID), Bluetooth, and Wi-Fi can connect object together, allowing them to communicate with each other and with the internet. "*From a hospital-centered model to a hospital-home-balanced*" is created with new technologies and a home-centered model is gaining more popularity (Thibaud et al., 2018). Power consumption, latency, execution time, arbitration time, network bandwidth, vibration, testing accuracy and training accuracy are performance parameters of smart health technologies (Tuli et al., 2020). Patient, physician, medical laboratory, pharmacy, medical insurance scheme, and patient's relatives can come together in IoT platforms. Accurate and timely information, reduction in the spread of contagious diseases, minimizing duplicate laboratory activities and decreasing errors are the main performance measurement criteria in healthcare systems. The costs can be decreased and the quality of services with increased patients treatment and satisfaction can be increased with these new technologies. Furthermore, workflows such as service workflow, treatment workflow and surgical workflow can be optimized (Zeadally & Bello, 2020).

Cloud and IoT based mobile health has been developed to monitor and diagnoses illnesses. Large amounts of data are handled by cloud computing in order to get benefits from data and to use these data for decision making (Kumar et al., 2018). More intelligent and improved prediction capabilities are developed in healthcare to increase the treatment efficiency and decrease increasing health costs. Smart hospitals or healthcare concepts are developed based these new sophisticated technologies. IoT-based healthcare systems are a bridge between sensor infrastructure network and internet in smart hospitals systems as gateways translating between the protocols used in the internet and sensor networks allowing transferring data through internet. IoT-based early warning score health monitoring is applied in healthcare to improve intelligence, energy efficiency, mobility, performance, interoperability, security, and reliability as a cost-efficiency system (Rahmani et al., 2018). Tracking risky patients can be done by remote controlling devices (Azimi et al., 2019). M-healthcare monitoring disease diagnosing framework can predict the severity of a disease. Disease-severity can be handled by alert generation mechanism (Verma, Sood, 2018). Illness experiences can be created from patients and be used for similar patients. Medical expertise by medical professionals is the most important attribute of using IoT healthcare technologies. 24/7 expert support, Smartphone-integrated devices, medical history preferred greater functionality with treatment and the public health insurance system are other critical factors for IoT healthcare service acceptances (Kim & Kim, 2018).

Electronic Health (eHealth), Mobile Health (mHealth) and ambient assisted living systems are used to treat patients at home or at hospital. Body area sensor network, internet-connected gateways, and cloud and big data support are the parts of the general IoT-based health monitoring system created by Rahmani et al., (2018) as shown in Figure 1. Caregivers, family members and authorized parties can control vital signs of patients everywhere. Gateways are hubs between sensors and cloud data center. Various wireless protocols and inter-device communication can be supported by gateways. Local storage, real-time local data processing, and embedded data mining are categorized under a smart e-Health Gateway an intermediary between sensors and cloud storage. Ubiquitous healthcare systems can be employed with the help of smart e-Health Gateways. Individuals, appliances and medicine entities can be managed and monitored by ubiquitous IoT systems. Moreover, android phones were developed to be used as a temporary home gateway, being able to automatically shut down unused devices according to users estimated behavior using local decisions of health states with the help of a hidden markov model (Rahmani et al., 2018). Medical box (iMedBox) and iGate are used as a health gateway and sensors are coupled with RFID link for monitoring the health of users (Khowaja et al., 2018). Facial recognition and language translation were also used in some mobile devices for augmenting human cognition (Rahmani et al., 2018).

Figure 1. Remote health monitoring structure (Rahmani et al., 2018)

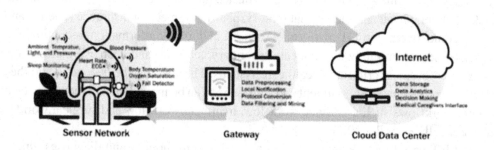

SwissGate application can optimize heating, ventilation, and air conditioning control parameters in the home. Heterogeneous sensor networks with different protocols can interoperate, making them work together by the smart e-health gateway through translating different sensor data. The volume of data and reducing the energy needed for data transmission can be done by data fusion. Operating systems with hardware properties and local database are the main components of the system. Each unit performance is analyzed and the systems benefits are the main attractive purpose of users (Rahmani et al., 2018).

There are four layers (Sensing, Network, Data Processing and Application) of IoT as shown in Figure 2. Sensors, GPS (Global Positioning System), ECG (Electrocardiogram) and EEG (Electroencephalogram) are used to collect information. Smartphones can collect emotions and behavior information by means of mobile applications as explained above. Service-Oriented Architecture (SOA) is applied for supporting more standards such as Extensible Markup Language (XML) and Simple Object Access Protocol (SOAP) for interoperation. CDSS (Clinical Decision Support System) uses processed data for making decisions and giving alerts and reports (Qi et al., 2017).

Figure 2. Layers in IoT (Qi et al., 2017)

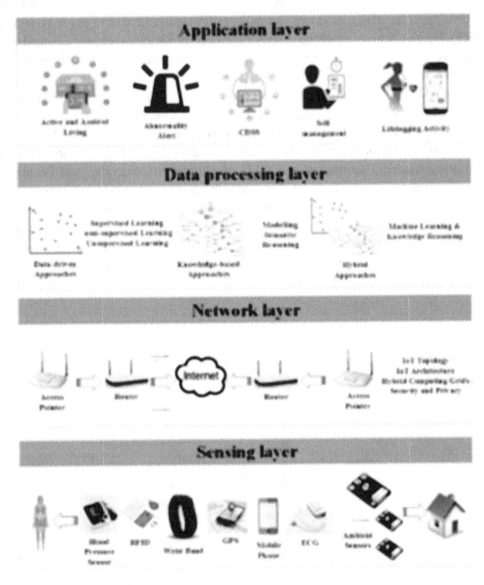

2.2 Sensors

Sensors, services and people can be interconnected through the internet in healthcare. Light and noisy levels, temperature and humidity rates, and air quality can be measured by sensors with the help of RFID and GPS combination. Environment sensors (measuring light conditions, temperature and humidity, noise, and air quality), objects sensors with RFID antennas used for collision detection or fall protection, biometric sensors based on a smart wristband-biometric information, RFID, and GPS are types of sensors used widely (Aslan, 2019; Qi et al., 2018; Khowaja et al., 2018). Bio-signals (e.g., ECG, EEG and EMG) collected data from users' body can be filtered (Rahmani et al., 2018). Accelerometer (Acc), gyroscope (Gyr), heart rate (HR), heart rate variability (HRV), galvanic skin response (GSR), skin temperature (SKT), location sensors, orientation sensor are kinds of wearable sensors. Cosmed calorimeter sensor is used for respiration rate determination. Zephyr sensor a smart chest-worn sensing device is used to determine breath rate, and skin temperature (Bhatia & Sood, 2017). Skin conductance can also detect sodium or potassium concentration in sweet (Qi et al., 2018). This system with sensors as shown in Table 1 can be used for physical fitness, safety and health (Khowaja et al., 2018).

Wearable and implantable medical sensors cannot store data, needing to be stored in another place. Reliability, availability and robustness are the core requirements of remote healthcare monitoring with security and privacy issues (Rahmani et al., 2018). Healthcare IoT, Services, and People (HIoTSP) framework is developed with use of wearable sensor technology. Low-cost and the easiness to use are important parameters for adoption. Energy can be saved in sensors with switching the power-saving mode to increase the quality of the system. Forgetting to recharge the battery can be dangerous for patients. Hence, energy-aware security solution is used in the systems to protect patients. Thermal harvesting from human warmth for Wireless Body Area Network (WBAN) in healthcare applications could be a solution for that purpose. (Dhanvijay & Patil, 2019)

Table 1. Sensor categories, examples and descriptions (Qi et al., 2018)

Sensor category	Sensor subcategories	Sensor examples	Description
On-body sensors	Inertial sensors	Accelerometer	Measures linear acceleration of movement
		Gyroscopes	Measures the angular rotational velocity
		Pressure sensors	Measures object's altitude
		Magnetic field sensors	Measures location for higher spatial resolution
	Location sensors	GPS	Tracks outdoor locations
	Physiological sensors	Blood pressure cuff	Measures human systolic and diastolic blood pressure
		Electrocardiogram (ECG)	Test and records the rhythm and electrical activity of the heart
		Spirometer	Measures respiration, flow rate and lung volume
		Electrooculography (EOG)	Measures eye movement
		Skin temperature sensor	Measure subject temperature on surface of the skin
On-object sensors	Environment sensors	Thermometer	Measures indoor/outdoor temperature
		Hygrometer	Measures indoor/outdoor humidity
		Energy sensors	Measures object's energy usage
	Binary sensors	Window contact	Detects window open/close state
		Door contact	Detects door open/close state
		Light switch	Detects light on/off state
		Remote control switch	Detects remote control on/off state
	Location detectors	Infra-red	Detects human indoor localization
		Active RFID	Detects human indoor localization
	Tags	RFID tags	Detects objects individual interaction with
		NFC tags	Detects objects individual interaction with

Body Area Networks (BANs) are developed by attaching sensors to the human body. Inertial sensors can be used to determine laying, standing, sitting static postures positions. Detecting falling, measuring patient's angular velocity such as bending knees and descending can be done through threshold or value. Near field communication (NFC) can detect object and individual interaction with NFC tag with help of smart phone apps (Qi et al., 2018). Furthermore, stairs behaviors and falling detection can be accomplished by barometric pressure sensors. Magnetic field Sensors can be used for measurement location and detecting a subject's direction. Determining watching TV, preparing a meal or washing clothes activities can be done with the help of on-object sensors such as environment sensors and RFID. In addition, wristband devices are used for recording step counts, distance, and calories burnt (Bhatia & Sood, 2017).

2.3 Fog Computing

Health Fog can integrate diverse frameworks like Fogbus and Aneka (Tuli et al., 2020). Installing the fog computing and IoT can decrease healthcare costs by high speed computing and processing (Mani, Singh and Nimmagadda, 2020). Delays caused by transferring data to the cloud between sensors and cloud computing can be prevented by fog computing (Aladwani, 2019). Reducing energy consumption and the load on data centers by means of improved mobility and quality of services and decreased latency are the main objectives of fog computing. Ubiquitous healthcare not depending on location are the main flexibility of new Fog CoT. Distributing workloads among hosts can be done for balancing workloads and preventing overloading or underutilization by cloud or Fog computing. The nearest cloud server at cloud-tier is applied in this strategy with the help of algorithms (Mahmoud et al., 2018). Aneka helps deployment of distributed applications into clouds as shown in Figure 3 (Tuli et al., 2020).

Figure 3. Health Fog Architecture (Tuli et al., 2020)

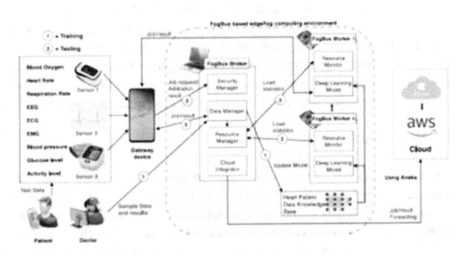

An IoT e-health service estimates the type of heart attack with a mobile application. ECG-based Healthcare (ECGH) system can detect heart abnormalities. ECG, respiration rate, and body temperature data are sent to gateway by wireless communication to take decisions quickly. FogCepCare is used to connect sensors and cloud for optimizing execution time. Resource manager handles job request and task queues of data processing. Deep learning Module trains data sets with a neural network. Ensembling module makes prediction whether a patients has heart disease or not (Tuli et al., 2020).

FogBus can connect different types of IoT sensors. Blockchain, authentication and encryption techniques are used for data security to increase reliability and robustness (Tuli et al., 2020). Security, privacy and data transfer are the main field of fog computing. Redirecting data to different fog servers for preventing data from malicious and unauthorized users, classifying data for minimizing the unnecessary communication, sending data to mHealth and IoT networks efficiently to reduce bandwidth and battery resources, processing large data of sensors to prevent delays by choosing cloudlet or local cloud model are the main usages of health fog (Saheb & Izadi, 2019). Furthermore, edge computing can be used to decrease service latency and ensure security. It is found that the edge system performs better than the cloud system. Many patients' lives can be saved with edge computing through a faster response and better decision-making process. Geographical awareness and lower service latency can save life from possible heart attacks. Open Fog Consortium, Living Edge Lab, ETSI Multi-access Edge Computing (MEC), Cloud Foundry Foundation, EnOcean Alliance, Linaro IoT and Embedded (LITE) Group, Object Management Group, and ULE Alliance are types of IoT edge ecosystem. Cisco Fog Director, Foghorn, Crosser, Swim.ai, Macchina.io, EdgeXFoundry, AWS Greengrass and Edgent are examples of edge software & analytics system (Ray, Dash, De, 2019).

2.4 Deep Learning and Artificial Intelligence (AI)

Wireless and satellite communication channel, machine learning, imaging technology, artificial intelligence and tele-surgical robotics can be used to carry out remote surgery in different regions by supervision of the robots (Zeadally & Bello, 2020). Machine learning is constructed with algorithms in order to make predictions in future. Abnormal behaviors can be predicted with data (Saheb & Izadi, 2019). Transferring data to a centralized database and from a database to cloud data centers can decrease the performance of system. Reducing response time and higher accuracy results can be provided by method of deep learning (Tuli et al., 2020). Detecting tachycardia and stroke can be difficult, requiring experienced doctor observations. However, deep learning can detect heart failures better than doctors; decreasing the need of doctors' requirements. Activity recognition, behavioral pattern discovery, anomaly detection, and decision support are developed with ambient intelligence algorithms in healthcare (Qi et al., 2017).

2.4.1 Artificial Intelligence

AI is defined as '*a field of science and engineering concerned with the computational understanding of what is commonly called intelligent behavior, and with the creation of artefacts that exhibit such behavior*'. AI techniques in medicine, data mining and knowledge discovery, medical expert systems, machine learning-based medical systems and medical signal and image processing techniques are main areas of AI field (Chan et al., 2018). The best possible action in a situation can be taken to maximize the performance with the help of AI (Vetrò et al, 2019). Tasks can be performed without receiving instructions from people by AI. Intelligent algorithms and decision-making models are used to respond to people's requirements. Treatment or diagnosis decisions can be taken with AI and data analytics systems in the IoT ecosystem that doctors' and laboratory test charge can be decreased. Medication alerts can be given to the patients and sent to the patient's physicians and other clinical professionals (Zeadally&Bello, 2020). Data interpretation in intensive care can learn from experience (Qi et al., 2018; Ramesh et al., 2004). Reducing redundant or marginal data from big data can be done via assessing critical data and training algorithms can be developed by using synthetic data (Mantelero, 2019).

Medical imaging detecting conditions such as pneumonia, breast and skin cancers, and eye diseases; echocardiography detecting patterns of heart beats and diagnose coronary heart disease; screening for neurological conditions monitoring symptoms of neurological conditions and surgery knots to close wounds are uses of clinical AI (Nuffield Council,2018). Artificial Neural Network (ANN) used for clinical diagnosis, image analysis in radiology and histopathology (Qi et al., 2018; Ramesh et al., 2004). Abdominal pain and appendicitis, glaucoma, and back pain recognition are diagnostic applications of ANNs. Genetic algorithms are used for predicting ill patients having lung cancer, melanoma etc. (Ramesh et al., 2004). Physical fitness, lower mental stress and anxiety levels are the main aims of healthcare management. Overweight, obesity, type-2 diabetes mellitus, and cardiovascular disease are major problems and these problems can be decreased by effective healthcare management. Physical exercise can prevent these illnesses daily. Room temperature, humidity, meals, and physical distress can also affect human health. The overall health severity can be determined from models in order preventing serious health loss. Bayesian belief networks and ANN can be to make estimations based on physiological, current situation and environmental data by detecting an illness in its early stages (Bhatia &Sood, 2017).

3 APPLICATIONS OF IOT IN HEALTHCARE

Assisted living by smart technologies, tele-medicine, monitoring physiological and pathological signals, self-management for preventing illnesses, medication intake monitoring, personalized healthcare and cloud-based health information systems are the main applications of Healthcare 4.0 (Aceto, Persico & Pescape, 2020). Hearables for people suffering hearing loss interact with the world, ingestible sensors for monitoring the medication in body and warning in case of any irregularities as for a diabetic patient, moodables used for improving mood, computer vision technology with artificial intelligence for visually impaired people and healthcare charting capturing the patient's data used for reducing doctors manual works are major applications of IoT in healthcare (Nasrullah, 2020). A Bluetooth-enabled weight scale and blood pressure cuff together with a symptom-tracking application for cancer treatment, smart continuous glucose monitoring for monitoring blood glucose levels for several days, closed-loop (automated) insulin delivery for automating insulin delivery, connected inhalers helping people with asthma and chronic obstructive pulmonary disease, ingestible sensors monitoring adherence medicine taking, connected contact lenses measuring tear glucose and providing an early warning system for diabetics, the Apple watch app that monitors depression and is a platform for measuring cognitive health for monitoring and assessing patients with major depressive disorder based on mood and cognition, coagulation testing allowing patients to check how quickly their blood clots, Apple's Research Kit monitoring Parkinson's disease and symptoms and Asthma Monitor a wearable smart asthma monitor to detect the symptoms of an asthma attack are major examples of the IoT in healthcare (Econsultancy, 2019). The Ontology decision making process was developed for doctors in emergency cases to develop a treatment method and to decrease death rates by getting information from ontology database in heterogeneous hospital information systems. Real-time information of the patient is collected in the database and then, the collected information is analyzed by experts to conclude the disease whether a patient needs a normal treatment or special treatment. Medicines and dosage are determined by an emergency decision support system (Abinaya, Kumar, Swathika, 2015). A withings device before known as Nokia Health estimates the percentage of fat, the muscle mass, and index of body mass of a user and an activity tracker can be worn on the wrist and life-threatening cases can be prevented with the help of on-time alerts (Nasrullah, 2020). Predicting emergency situations can be carried out by data analyzing as fall detection for elderly people. Remote healthcare centers can reach data and data results via internet (Rahmani et al., 2018).

IoT based m-IoT healthcare services and applications:

IoT healthcare by smart phones: It can be used for managing cancer, diabetes, mental health, fitness controlling for diet, nutrition, weight loss etc. Medisafe is an application used for these purposes that it includes list of pills, intake details, and dosages. Appointments through video conferencing can be done through Telehealth Chiron app with a doctor. The heart rate tracking can offer some sporting activities. The inpatient care mobile app is used for communication, literacy and entertainment with the families and friends (Dhanvijay&Patil, 2019).

Adverse Drug Reaction: A Drug can be identified through the barcode/NFC device. IMed pack uses RFID to prevent any drug reaction.

Community Healthcare: Community Healthcare information monitors municipal hospital, residential area, or rural community.

Children Health Information: It monitors children's health and their behavioral, emotional or mental health problems. Moreover, it can be used for educating, empowering, and amusing the children. Good nutritional and normal life habits with their teachers and parents are encouraged to be developed.

Glucose level sensing: It is used for elderly and diabetic patients and somatic data of blood glucose are collected with IoT networks.

Electrocardiogram monitoring: It drives maximum information about the cardiac system.

Blood pressure monitoring: It uses blood pressure KIT and the mobile phone and consists of the apparatus of the body and the communication module.

Body temperature monitoring: Infrared detection and RFID module can be used to monitor body temperature and send data to IoT.

Oxygen saturation monitoring: wearable pulse oximetry method based on the Bluetooth system is used to measure oxygen saturation.

Rehabilitation system: Effective remote consultations can be managed by patients having physical disabilities by means of providing real-time information applications.

Medication management based on IoT: An intelligent packaging method for medicine boxes is developed to increase public health and decrease costs.

IoT wheelchair management: Different sensors are used to monitor disabled people. Data about the person's and user's environments can be collected in order to assess their health.

Imminent healthcare solutions: They are used for skin infection, peak expiratory flow, abnormal cellular growth, hemoglobin detection, cancer treatment, eye disorder, and remote surgery.

3.1 Vital Body Signs Measuring

Sensors and actuators can help to get blood pressure and electrocardiogram information (Islam & Shin, 2020). OpenAPS application an open artificial pancreas system helps diabetes patients by providing continuous glucose monitoring (CGM). Glucose data are sent to the smart transmitter and then smart phone. Moreover, health treatment adherence can be followed with that system by patients, families and physicians (Zakaria et al., 2019). UCI Repository dataset and the medical sensors are used to predict diabetes based on Fuzzy rule; neural classifier algorithm through IoT devices attached human body. A sub-module is developed by applying fuzzy rules to predict the illnesses (Kumar et al., 2018).

Bio-IoT and Nano- IoT (IoNT) are emerging concepts in healthcare. MicaZ wireless modules connected to pulse oximeter sensors is available; using WSN components. A warning message can be sent to healthcare staffs that there is an emergency related to patient heart rate or the oxygen levels (Akka, Sokullu, Çetin, 2020). Narrowband Internet of Things (NB-IoT) is a device with long battery life and low cost in WBAN to monitor the health situation (blood pressure and heart rate) that a pregnant woman parameters as blood pressure and heart rate can be measured with the sensors (Malik et al., 2018). Moreover, Photoplethysmography (PPG) optical technique synchronous blood volumetric changes in the microvascular bed of tissues related to the oscillation of heart beat and respiration is a low cost and effective technique to monitor the health of patients by exposing light to the skin surface through pulse-oximeter and measuring light absorption. This technique is used in different wearable and mobile applications such as pulse oximeter, smart rings, and smartwatches. However, poor signals in that technique can cause inaccurate vital signs extraction and erroneous decision making (Naeini et al., 2019). Furthermore, a check-up time for a patient having chronic heart disease can be determined based on daily activity detection. Sleep pattern, blood oxygen saturation, heart rate or glucose level can be followed by patients and a conclusion can be drawn from these data (Zeadally&Bello, 2020).

3.2 Retinal Images Analyzing

Retinal images captured using smartphone fundoscopy is a new IoT healthcare application, in which Super-Resolution algorithm is used for improving the quality of images. It is found that 53.5% of rural population have not got any eye examination in developing countries due to the lack of affordability and awareness and 29.1% of the tested population was found having vision disorders. Teleophthalmology can help rural people to have an eye examination without needing to travel. Fundus ophthalmoscopy (fundoscopy) is an important part of ophthalmology providing photo documentation for diagnosing which also shares information with physicians and patients. A new developed smartphone fundoscopy known as smartphone ophthalmological application enabled by iPhone can be used in rural areas, which is cost-effective and easy to use. Retinal image super-resolution IoT healthcare architecture is composed of retinal image capturing through pan optic ophthalmoscope that images are sent to cloud backbone. The cloud backbone is responsible for transmissions and receiving images, selection of ophthalmologist (automatic physician selection technique), classifications and prescriptions. Retinal image super-resolution generating high image resolution with super-resolution algorithms, eye disorder classification of incoming retinal images as a group of disease classification, selection of ophthalmologist based on disease classification, diagnosis by ophthalmologist through looking at retinal images and classification and a prescription generation to patients are the steps of the system as shown in Figure 4 (Jebadurai& Peter, 2018).

3.3 Remote Medical Application

Many beds are empty at private healthcare organizations, which decrease the efficiency. Providing knowledge of healthcare and medicines, asking for advice from doctors, booking the medical appoint-

Figure 4. Teleophthalmology System (Jebadurai&Peter, 2018)

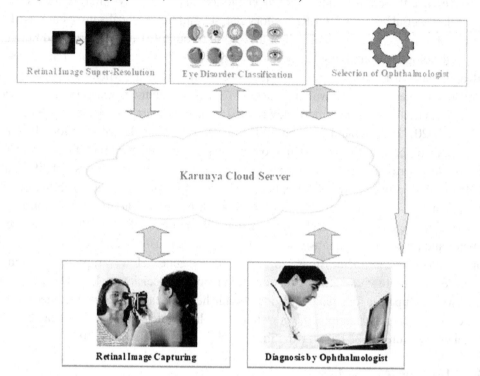

ment with doctors, reminding the personal health check or their relatives, and connecting the network among patients, doctors and clinics are the properties of remote medical models such as uDoctor, eDoctor, Wellcare, Bacsi247. Providing accurate and timely prognostic information, predicting disease outbreaks, and raising health awareness are parameters used to measure reliability of information. 24/7 health monitor can be done for cardiovascular disease, diabetes, high blood pressure through wristwatch automatically measuring body signs. If there is a sudden increase in blood pressure, family members or doctors can be alerted (Tuan, Thanh, Tuan, 2019).

Remote medical application (UDr) is an application developed to connect different stakeholders and to manage the whole system so that nearby doctors and clinics can be chosen based on rating of patients. Online chat box, or phone calls can be used by doctors and patients for communication. Shorter doctor's examination and counseling are the advantages of that system for doctors and patients resulting in saving time and decreasing expenses. In time, increased trust can be created between patients and doctors. Drug delivery services are another time saving application for patients (Tuan, Thanh, Tuan, 2019). In addition, automated prescription, medication delivery and auto-diagnosis can be categorized under remote hospital-level treatments and services. Advanced delivery of prescription medication called Zipline including blood and vaccines delivery can be made in that system (Zeadally&Bello, 2020).

3.4 Physical Activity Recognition and Monitoring (PARM)

From cure to prevention strategy can be realized within Healthcare 4.0 by self-management and monitoring (Aceto, Persico&Pescape, 2020). GPS localization and Bluetooth can be inserted into sensors such as fitness band or mobile phone (Qi et al., 2018). PARM is an important field for smart healthcare. Controlling environments and defining subjects for recognition can be done by sensors and learning algorithms. Physical inactivity can result in many chronic diseases such as diabetes, obesity etc. Physical activities can be monitored to increase the activities of old people (Qi et al., 2018). Intelligent services can store and give feedback. Modifiable risk factors can be detected with algorithms and diabetes and obesity can be prevented through education and good nutritional habits. Moreover, not taking medicines is a problem among chronically ill people and monitoring medication can be effective with disease management by sensor networks, RFID and several mobile apps having reminder scheduling and medication intake (Aceto, Persico&Pescape, 2020).

3.5 ZigBee and Ultrasound Technology

ZigBee and Ultrasound technology are used for disabled people to monitor their health with alarms and smart navigations (Bhatia & Sood, 2017).

3.6 Covid-19

Monitoring COVID-19 patients can be done with IoT technologies as a cost-effective solution. Infected persons are taken into quarantine for monitoring and blood pressure, heart beat and glucose level are to be measured and controlled regularly. It is stated by Singh et al., (2020) that reduced mistakes, cheaper treatment, improved diagnoses, better control and treatment can be done during Covid-19 with these technologies. Effective tracing of the patients can help in obeying rules during quarantine period. Smartphone-based application can inform patients about symptoms, and recovery. ArogyaSetu smartphone application in India was developed to serve these purposes. Real-time warnings system was developed in Taiwan with scanning of QR code, connected reporting of transport history to identify people having contact with infected people. Upcoming situations can be estimated with coming data and models can be developed for precautions. Tracking health conditions of older people is the most beneficiary side of that technology and this group is the most risky group with high death rates. Tracking real-time location

Table 2. Major applications of IoT for COVID-19 pandemic. (Singh et al., 2020)

SNo	Applications	Description
1	Internet-connected hospital	The implementation of IoT to support pandemic like COVID-19 needs a complete integrated network within hospital premises
2	Inform the concerned medical staff during any emergency	This integrated network will allow the patients and the staffs to respond more quickly and effectively whenever needed
3	Transparent COVID-19 treatment	The patients can avail the benefits offered without any partiality and favours
4	Automated treatment process	The selection of treatment methods become productive and helps the appropriate handling of the cases
5	Telehealth consultation	This especially makes the treatment available for the needy ones in the remote locations via employing the well-connected teleservices
6	Wireless healthcare network to identify COVID-19 patient	Various authentic applications can be installed into smartphones, which can make the identification procedure smoother and more fruitful
7	Smart tracing of infected patients	The impactful tracing of patients ultimately strengthened the service providers to handle the cases more smartly
8	Real-time information during the spread of this infection	As the devices, locations, channels, etc. are well informed and connected, the on-time information sharing can be done, and cases can be handled accurately
9	Rapid COVID-19 screening	As the case arrived/found at first instance, the proper diagnosis will be attempted through smart connected treatment devices. This ultimately makes the overall screening process more superior
10	Identify innovative solution	The overall quality of supervision is the utmost goal. It can be achieved by making innovations successful to the ground level.
11	Connect all medical tools and devices through the internet	During COVID-19 treatment, IoT connected all medical tools and devices through internet which convey the real-time information during treatment
12	Accurate forecasting of virus	Based on the data report available, the use of some statistical method can also help to predict the situation in the coming times. It will also help to plan the government, doctors, academicians, etc. to plan for a better working environment.

of medical equipment, following smooth treatment process, helping healthcare insurance companies to prevent fraud claims and to provide transparency and helping decision-making are major benefits of these systems as shown in Table 2 (Singh et al., 2020).

3.7 IoT Technologies Use in Dentistry

Creating a smart dental health can be another application of IoT for consultation, pre-examination and evaluation. Tracking the eating habits of the patient and the proper way of eating for the safety of implantable teeth are the possible benefits of this application. A smart tooth brush can be developed by means of pressure sensors, location tracking and timers through scanning teeth. Detecting the abnormalities and diabetes can be done with smart sensors. Furthermore, predictions can be made for upcoming dental diseases and mouth cavity, food intake and analyzing all activities can be determined by smart teeth application (Halee, Javaid, Khan, 2020).

3.8 Mood State Recognition and Measuring Pain

Employees' physiological conditions can be improved with wearable devices. Psychosocial risks are related to chronic diseases for elderly people can be detected to improve their life conditions (Aslan & Aslan, 2019). Objects can be identified and information can be gathered by accelerator, gyroscope or barometric the physiological situation. Signal data from the sensing layer are transferred to be analyzed in network layer by wired, wireless sensor or actuator networks. Data are classified and analyzed in analysis layer and results are sent to mobile or Personal Digital Assistance (PDA) in application layer (Qi et al., 2018). Facial gesture recognition software and voice analytics can be used to determine the mood of patients for mental health disorders. Smart watches and glasses are types of wearable devices that they can use sound recognition. As a patients' emotional state is determined, intervention may be required (Zeadally&Bello, 2020). Internet-based Cognitive Behavioral Therapy (iCBT) is used for the therapy of depression supported with smart phones as a way of decreasing stigma. Detecting risk of relapse in mental health can be beneficial to prevent further risks (Aslan, 2019).

Personal digital assistants (PDA) and smartphones can be used for pain assessment as a kind of self-management. Facial expressions can be used as a kind of pain indicator. Knowledge-based systems are used to assess pain. An IPhone-based pain diary app known as pain squad has been developed for the assessment of cancer patients' pain. Physiological or behavioral monitoring can be assessed and a score can be given for the pain. These data can be transmitted to cloud as a suitable alternative for pain assessment of patients with limited cognitive and communication abilities, minimizing diagnostic errors by customization of pain management and including relatives in patient care by providing those real-time data remotely (Prada, 2020).

3.9 Occupational Health and Safety

Personal health monitoring systems can help firms to reduce absenteeism, loss of productivity and decrease costs with fitness trackers to improve self-consciousness. Alerts, recommendations and reminders such as taking a break can be done by smartphones. Body-sensors, mixed reality glasses, smart watches, helmets, handsets and location trackers are used in work environments to increase the safety and health of workers. Toxins and high temperature alerts, emergency stops of heavy machinery and anti-ergonomic body- movements' alerts can be created with the help of IoT. Detecting falls earlier reducing response time in work accidents is another major benefit of wearable technologies (Aslan & Aslan, 2019).

Radio Frequency Identification (RFID) can prevent workers from having accidents such as collisions and falls with the proximity warning system as collision detection can be established in a working environment. Unauthorized access to the site and equipment use can be provided with alert systems. Furthermore, RFID, Ultra-Wideband (UWB) nodes and Global Positioning System (GPS) can detect moving objects in the workspace. Smart Personal Protective Equipment interacting with motion of smart containers and smart cranes can give information about dangerous situation like *"walking by accident under a container"* (Aslan, 2019).

3.10 Cancer Treatment

Clinical diagnoses and suggested treatments are the main focusing area of medical artificial intelligence. Improved decision making processes can be carried out in each phase for diagnoses and subsequent treatments by AI (Chan et al., 2018). Risk of developing cancer, risk of disease recurrence or risk of treatment complications, predicting prognosis, radiation treatment planning etc. are common applications of machine learning in healthcare. Predicting pneumonectomy complications after surgical resection of lung cancer was a successful application of AI. Another application of AI was predicting the risk of reoccurrence of breast cancer surgical resection. Identifying breast cancer lymph node metastases was another successful application of a Google trained neural network. Stage of cancers can be determined by AI more accurately to determine the types of treatment. AlexNet and GoogLeNet artificial neural networks were used for differentiating *"tuberculosis"* chest x-rays from *"healthy"* ones with high accuracy of machine learning. (Alimohamed, 2017). An Intra-Tumor Classification network to label tumor regions was done with neural Networks called Convolutional Neural Network (CNN). Deep Belief Network and Dempster–Shafer (DBN-DS-) were used in the pathologic prediction of prostate cancer with 81.4% accuracy (Chan et al., 2018).

Breastcancer.org forum data was analyzed by AI to find common discussed themes. Emotional support and exchange of personal stories were the most common topics of that forum (Khan, Bebb, Alimohamed, 2017).

4 CHALLENGES OF IOT

Scalability ability of a device to adapt the changes in the environment and meeting the changing needs in the future, non-obtrusive wearable sensing (being uncomfortable for permanent monitoring), trustful mobile health platform, IoT healthcare security, low power in IoT healthcare device, network architecture for authentication and authorization for the users, cost analysis of the IoT healthcare system, intelligent data processing and analytic and opacity of analytics, changing individual human behavior in healthcare, quality of services and continuous monitoring for healthcare purposes are major challenges of the IoT healthcare system (Aceto, Persico&Pescape, 2020; Dhanvijay&Patil, 2019 ;Qi et al., 2017).

Inconsistent and incomplete data can lead to failures and wrong data estimation. Vital signs can be misused due to activities and surrounding environment. Data analytic techniques such as machine learning are applied at cloud server. Disunited sensors from the body, losing connection and running out of battery can lead to missing data. Forgetting to use wearable sensor(s) can be another problem of missing data. Furthermore, missing data can generate biased estimates leading to high error rates in health applications. Personalized models named as a personalized pooling are used for implying missing values. The Last observation carried forward imputation, regression imputation, hot-deck imputation, cold-deck imputation and K-Nearest-Neighbor imputation are methods to estimate missing data. Moreover, Artificial Neural Networks, Support Vector Machine and generic algorithms can be used to evaluate missing data (Azimi et al., 2019).

4.1 Security and Privacy

Relying on machines and computers is another uncertainty in the healthcare field (Kim & Kim, 2018). IoT architecture is composed of sensor layer (sensors or RFID tag) collecting information, middleware layer (processing layer dealing deals with the information of sensor layer and transport layer deploying technologies like Bluetooth and Wi-Fi) providing network support and protocols and application layer carrying out application specific functionalities and dealing with security and privacy. The leakage of important information at the network gateway, malicious codes and information over the network, denial of service attacks and replay attack are major type's attacks in these layers (Tewari&Gupta, 2020). Risk of malicious attacks through internet networks is a threat for the privacy. Healthcare systems using IoT can be protected with chaos-based cryptographic applications for securing patients privacy (El-Latif et al., 2020). Secure cryptographic key generation, authentication and authorization of each healthcare IoT component and robust and secure end-to-end communication between sensor nodes and health caregivers were found three main security system of healthcare IoT. Limited memory, processing power, and communication bandwidth are to be considered while designing the security system (Moosavi et al., 2018).

A safe and trustworthy healthcare service was the most important factor requested from potential users than greater functionality. Sensing, displaying, and communicating are properties of devices used in IoT healthcare services. Minimization of human intervention is much preferred by patients and more sophisticated IoT healthcare services can improve the trust of users depending on the quality of data (Kim & Kim, 2018). Reliable data mining, qualified services, and enhanced user privacy and security can increase the trust of users. Distrust and discomfort can be an effective factor for not using new healthcare Technologies. Lack of trust in a system can be the main barrier for adoption of Technologies. (Aqeel-ur-Rehman et al., 2016; Kim & Kim, 2018; Nord, Koohang, Paliszkiewicz, 2019). Personal medical data sharing is an important part of data management in health sector that *"not shared," "shared only within a private service,"* and *"shared with public healthcare,"* options are to be provided to decrease the risks (Kim & Kim, 2018). If security needs of IoT technologies are met, the threats can be prevented as shown in Table 3 for securing data communication, providing confidentiality and integrity of communication. Identification per device; original or some malicious node is a part of security in the IoT system. Device heterogeneity is another challenge in hundreds different types of devices with security issues and requirements. Moreover, Communication between different types of devices is another issue, making difficulties in integration, privacy and identification. Intelligent Transport System (ITS) can be used to overcome this problem (Aqeel-ur-Rehman et al., 2016).

Remotely using IoT sensors can have the problem of connectivity and security issues. Satellite communication for remote areas can be helpful in collecting data. Unmanned aerial vehicles (UAVs) can be used for public safety and they can help for low-power communication, network availability and remote data acquisition to collect data from body sensors and to transmit the health data to a server. In addition, a blockchain system known as BHEALTH can be used to transmit data in a secure way while collect-

Table 3. Core Security threats in IoT Technologies (Aqeel-ur-Rehman et al., 2016)

	Threats	Key Components	Security Need
RFID	DoS Attacks	RFID Tags and Reader Communications	Encryption
	Eavesdropping	User Private Data	Encryption
	Skimming	User Private Data	Blocking Tags
	Relay Attack	Authentication Result	Synchronization
	Side Channel Attack	User Private Data	Authentication
	Hardware Destruction	Tags	Protective Electronic Component
NFC	Phishing Attack Interfaces	Application Processor	Authentication
	User Tracking	User Privacy	Random UIDs
	Relay Attacks	Tag / Reader	Synchronization
	Data Forging Attack	User Data	SSL Communication
WSN	Wormhole	Multi-hop Wireless Network	Time limit on Packets Delivery
	Neighbor Discovery	Network Discovery Protocol	Authentication Supported Protocol
	Spoofing	Wireless Network Packet	Authentication
	Ping Flood, ICMP Flood, Syn Flood	Network Nodes	Use of IDS

ing data from body sensors by UAV to a server. However, sending invalid data and harm to the system can be problems with malicious data for getting the access into the system. Unauthorized access can be prevented in that system by a digital signature algorithm (Islam & Shin, 2020).

4.1.1 IoT Security Risk Management

Authentication process, blood transfusion medicine, medication safety and patient tracking can be done by RFID. Medical assets tracking, patients' location identification, newborns identification, medical treatments tracking, procedure management, surgical process management and validation of staff are other usages of RFID (Zakaria et al., 2019). Incorporating security at the design phase, advance security, making proven security practices, giving priority to security measures and improving transparency in IoT are ways of overcoming security challenges in IoT. It is important that all devices can withstand any attacks in a heterogeneous environment (Nord, Koohang, Paliszkiewicz, 2019).

Control Objectives for Information and related technology (COBIT 5) was developed as the risk management model for healthcare IoT, creating a safe system for machine tools using IoT devices. COBIT IoT Risk Management risk categories data and application and user change management, law management, infrastructure management, operation management, portfolio management, 3rd party suppliers and vendor, and market management are other parts of that system. Each department authority monitors heart rate machine, x-ray and scanner machines, leading to many risks. With help of that system, everything can be centrally controlled. Reducing cost, time and number of tasks are main benefits of that system. Having clear roles, decreasing interruptions, controlling functions and supporting business mission are other advantages of that system (Zakaria et al., 2019).

Using various technologies and protocols, a large number of devices with a lack of authentication, and using social engineering techniques for obtaining sensitive information from the network are threats to the system (Tewari&Gupta, 2020). As the number of connected devices increases, the privacy of IoT becomes a problem. Hence, there is a stronger need of security requirement at application layer such as application verification, secure APIs, and data analytics. Authentication, limited access, threat hunting and encryption are other security measures. Traffic monitoring, abnormality detection, and traffic shaping are security requirements at network layer (Pajouh et al., 2019). Preventing any illegal access with effective authentication, user privacy for each communication, preventing data loss due to large amount of data, and preventing some vulnerability are required at application layer. Present security solutions developed by Pajouh et al., (2019) are shown in Table 4 (Tewari&Gupta, 2020).

Transport layer security increasing confidentiality and integrity of data, encryption for data integrity throughout transporting of data, virtual private network accessing from outside formed by a close group of partners and onion outing encrypting and merging internet traffic from various sources are ways of improving privacy according to Aqeel-ur-Rehman et al.,(2016).

4.2 Artificial Intelligence (AI) Challenges

AI can lead to the need of less skilled staff and autonomy and hence the authority of healthcare professionals can be decreased. Revealing information about patients' health can be the malicious use of AI without their knowledge. Errors can be done while using AI, creating reliability and safety issue in that field. Social isolation of patients replacing staff can also be a problem for patients (Nuffield Council, 2018).

Table 4. The presented security solutions for the network layer of IoT environment (Pajouh et al., 2019)

Challenge	Affected layer(s)	Solution
Replay Attack	Network layer	define timestamp and authentication parameter for packets verification, define checksum by hash value
Insecure nearest node discovery	Network layer	Authentication by encrypted (ECC) based signatures
Buffer Overflow attack	Network layer	installing threat hunting modules like IDS
RPL routing attack	Network layer	authentication via lightweight encryption system, and monitoring connected devices
Sinkhole and Wormhole attacks	Network layer	verification using hash systems, trust level management, device communication analysis, anomaly detection via IDS, using encrypted key management, signal strength monitoring
Sybil attacks	Network layer	Graph analysis, user interaction analysis, Applying access control list
Authentication and secure communication	Network layer	light weight ticket granting system, applying symmetric and asymmetric encryption system for encrypting packet payload dispatch type values with, collecting logs
end-to-end security	Network layer	installing IPSec, applying advance encryption system for authentication and authorization
Session Hijacking	Network layer	using secret key for long-time session, light-weight encryption system

Machine biases *"Machines and humans have different capabilities, and, equally importantly, make different mistakes based on fundamentally divergent decision-making architectures"* are hidden biases requiring accurate testing of the training phase (Mantelero, 2019). Disproportionate datasets generated by a biased sample as from third parties or digital technologies can also lead to different decisions. Gender, ethnicity, disability, and age data bias embedded in the algorithms themselves can cause unfair results (Nuffield Council, 2018). Biases can be in designing, developing, and maintaining AI systems stages (Mantelero, 2019). There are also biased algorithms created by designers as COMPAS algorithmic tool - Correctional Offender Management Profiling for Alternative Sanctions showing black defendants at higher risk and Google AdSense creating results based on racial association or financial institutions. Hence ethical coders are necessary for AI programming to prevent misuses and discriminatory decisions. Biased datasets *"potential hidden data biases and the risk of discrimination or negative impact on the rights and fundamental freedoms of data subjects, in both the collection and analysis stages"* are tried to be hindered by Council of Europe Guidelines on big data (Mantelero, 2019; Vetrò et al., 2019). Furthermore, groups affected by AI applications can detect bias and h can help the removal of biases through participatory forms of risk assessment (Mantelero, 2019).

4.3 IoT Ethics Challenges and Legal Issues

Ethics of emerging Technologies are developed to prepare legal requirements. Informed consent and privacy are main concerns of ethics in healthcare depending on shared data in IoT Technologies that medical ethics literature are to be redefined on internet ethics and robotics. Informational security, physical safety and trust in decision making are other major ethical issues needing legal definitions. What will happen, in a case of a wrong diagnose is developed by IoT Technologies and who will be responsible are key issues needing legal roots (Allhoff, Henschke, 2018).

An international legal body is necessary for accountability of IoT legal issues to secure privacy of information, access to information and integrity of the information to prevent challenges and ethical issues so that the standards and laws are expected to be developed in order to overcome privacy, property rights, life risk and incorrect management issues. For example, limiting the use of the collected data by third parties can be clarified (Bakr & Azer, 2017).

5. CONCLUSION

Fog computing and edge system performing better than cloud system can save lives of many patients by a faster response that geographical awareness and lower service latency can help in handling heart attacks. IoT technologies have more applications in healthcare systems and the importance that technologies have been seen during the Covid-19 outbreak that reaching information on time and remote accessibility can save lives. Furthermore, artificial intelligence decision support systems can create awareness and give alerts to people in order to stay away from infected people and places.

RFID, Ultra-Wideband (UWB) nodes and Global Positioning System (GPS) can detect moving objects in the workspace that many accidents can be prevented and the health of workers can be improved with these smart devices. Smart personal protective equipment interacting with motion of smart containers can help central server to define the place of worker and follow workers during the working day. Risk of developing cancer, risk of disease recurrence, predicting prognosis, radiation treatment planning etc. are common applications of machine learning in healthcare that occupational diseases can be prevented through IoT technologies by controlling critical body signs regularly and getting remote health counseling.

AI in medicine can lead to many benefits, but also carries some risks. For the safety of using AI, it is necessary to achieve such a state in which each diagnosis created by AI will be consistent with the actual state of the patient. For AI to be used on a large scale, it is necessary to test it thoroughly. If AI is well tested, it can be a great supporter of doctors. The treatment and diagnosis of diseases will therefore be much more efficient in shorter time and with higher precision. It will also be possible to support the treatment with that technology in monitoring and following the patient. There are still ongoing activities aiming at introducing effective solutions to medicine for making people's life easier and improving health treatment.

REFERENCES

Abinaya, V. K., Kumar, V., & Swathika. (2015). Ontology based Public Healthcare System in Internet of Things(IoT). *Procedia Computer Science*, *50*, 99–102. doi:10.1016/j.procs.2015.04.067

Aceto, G., Persico, V., & Pescape, A. (2020). Industry 4.0 and Health: Internet of Things, Big Data, and Cloud Computing for Healthcare 4.0. *Journal of Industrial Information Integration*, *18*, 100129. Advance online publication. doi:10.1016/j.jii.2020.100129

Akka, M. A., Sokullu, R., & Çetin, H. E. (2020). Healthcare and patient monitoring using IoT. *Internet of Things*, *11*, 100173. Advance online publication. doi:10.1016/j.iot.2020.100173

Aladwani, T. (2019). Scheduling IoT Healthcare Tasks in Fog Computing Based on their Importance. *Procedia Computer Science, 163*, 560–569. doi:10.1016/j.procs.2019.12.138

Allhoff, F., & Henschke, A. (2018). The Internet of Things: Foundational ethical issues. *Internet of Things, 1–2*, 55–66. doi:10.1016/j.iot.2018.08.005

Argüello Prada, E.J.A. (2020). The Internet of Things (IoT) in pain assessment and management: An overview. *Informatics in Medicine Unlocked, 18*. https://doi.org/10.1016/j.imu.2020.100298

Aslan, I. (2019). The Role of Industry 4.0 in Occupational Health and Safety. *International European Congress on Social Sciences-IV*, 334-345.

Aslan, I., & Aslan, H. (2019). Industry 4.0: The Role Of Industry 4.0 In Agri-Food, Process Safety &Environmental Protection. In Industry 4.0: Industry 4.0 Concept And Common Technologies & Systems. Lap Lambert Academic Publishing.

Azimi, I., Pahikkala, T., Rahmani, A. M., Niela-Vilén, H., Axelin, A., & Liljeberg, P. (2019). Missing data resilient decision-making for healthcare IoT through personalization: A case study on maternal health. *Future Generation Computer Systems, 96*, 297–308. doi:10.1016/j.future.2019.02.015

Bakr, A. A., & Azer, M. A. (2017) IoT ethics challenges and legal issues. *12th International Conference on Computer Engineering and Systems (ICCES)*, Cairo, Egypt. 10.1109/ICCES.2017.8275309

Bhatia, M., & Sood, S. K. (2017). A comprehensive health assessment framework to facilitate IoT-assisted smart workouts: A predictive healthcare perspective. *Computers in Industry, 92–93*, 50–66. doi:10.1016/j.compind.2017.06.009

Chan, Y.-K., Chen, Y.-F., Pham, T., Chang, W., & Hsieh, M.-Y. (2018). Artificial Intelligence in Medical Applications, *Journal of Healthcare Engineering*. doi:10.1155/2018/4827875 PMID:30123442

Dhanvijay, M. M., & Patil, S. C. (2019). Internet of Things: A survey of enabling technologies in healthcare and its applications. *Computer Networks, 15*, 113–131. doi:10.1016/j.comnet.2019.03.006

Econsultancy. (2019). *10 examples of the Internet of Things in healthcare.* https://econsultancy.com/internet-of-things-healthcare/

El-Latif, A. A., Abd-El-Atty, B., Abou-Nassar, E., & Venegas-Andraca, S. E. (2020). Controlled alternate quantum walks based privacy preserving healthcare images in Internet of Things. *Optics & Laser Technology, 124*, 105942. Advance online publication. doi:10.1016/j.optlastec.2019.105942

Halee, A., Javaid, M., & Khan, I. H. (2020). Internet of things (IoT) applications in dentistry. *Current Medicine Research and Practice, 10*(2), 80–81. doi:10.1016/j.cmrp.2020.03.005

Islam, A., & Shin, S. Y. (2020). A blockchain-based secure healthcare scheme with the assistance of unmanned aerial vehicle in Internet of Things. *Computers & Electrical Engineering, 84*, 106627. Advance online publication. doi:10.1016/j.compeleceng.2020.106627

Jebadurai, J., & Peter, J. D. (2018). Super-resolution of retinal images using multi-kernel SVR for IoT healthcare applications. *Future Generation Computer Systems, 83*, 338–346. doi:10.1016/j.future.2018.01.058

Khan, O. F., Bebb, G., & Alimohamed, N. A. (2017). What oncologists need to know about its potential and its limitations. *Artificial Intelligence in Medicine, 16*(4).

Khowaja, S. A., Prabono, A. G., Setiawan, F., Yahya, B. N., & Lee, S.-L. (2018). Contextual activity based Healthcare Internet of Things, Services, and People (HIoTSP): An architectural framework for healthcare monitoring using wearable sensors. *Computer Networks, 145*, 190–206. doi:10.1016/j.comnet.2018.09.003

Kim, S., & Kim, S. (2018). User preference for an IoT healthcare application for lifestyle disease management. *Telecommunications Policy, 42*(4), 304–314. doi:10.1016/j.telpol.2017.03.006

Kumar, P. M., Lokesh, S., Varatharajan, R., Babu, G. C., & Parthasarathy, P. (2018). Cloud and IoT based disease prediction and diagnosis system for healthcare using Fuzzy neural classifier. *Future Generation Computer Systems, 86*, 527–534. doi:10.1016/j.future.2018.04.036

Mahmoud, M. M. E., Rodrigues, J. J. P. C., Kashif Saleem, K., Al-Muhtadi, J., Kumar, N., & Korotaev, V. (2018). Towards energy-aware fog-enabled cloud of things for healthcare. *Computers & Electrical Engineering, 67*, 58–69. doi:10.1016/j.compeleceng.2018.02.047

Malik, H., Alam, M. M., Moullec, Y. L., & Kuusik, A. (2018). NarrowBand-IoT Performance Analysis for Healthcare Applications. *Procedia Computer Science, 130*, 1077–1083. doi:10.1016/j.procs.2018.04.156

Mani, N., Singh, A., & Nimmagadda, S. L. (2020). An IoT Guided Healthcare Monitoring System for Managing Real- Time Notifications by Fog Computing Services. *Procedia Computer Science, 167*, 850–859. doi:10.1016/j.procs.2020.03.424

Mantelero, A. (2019). *Artificial Intelligence and Data Protection: Challenges and Possible Remedies.* EU Directorate General of Human Rights and Rule of Law.

Moosavi, S. R., Nigussie, E., Levorato, M., Virtanen, S., & Isoaho, J. (2018). Performance Analysis of End-to-End Security Schemes in Healthcare IoT. *Procedia Computer Science, 130*, 432–439. doi:10.1016/j.procs.2018.04.064

Naeini, E. K., Iman Azimi, I., Rahmani, A. M., Liljeberg, P., & Dutt, N. (2019). A Real-time PPG Quality Assessment Approach for Healthcare Internet-of-Things. *Procedia Computer Science, 151*, 551–558. doi:10.1016/j.procs.2019.04.074

Nasrullah, P. (2020). *Internet of things in healthcare: applications, benefits, and challenges.* https://www.peerbits.com/blog/internet-of-things-healthcare-applications-benefits-and-challenges.html

Nord, J. H., Koohang, A., & Paliszkiewicz, J. (2019). The Internet of Things: Review and theoretical framework. *Expert Systems with Applications, 133*, 97–108. doi:10.1016/j.eswa.2019.05.014

Nuffield Council on Bioethics. (2018). *Artificial intelligence (AI) in healthcare and research.* Bioethics briefing note, Nuffield Council on Bioethics.

Pajouh, H. H., Dehghantanha, A., & Parizi, R. M. (2019). A survey on internet of things security: Requirements, challenges, and solutions. *Internet of Things.* doi:10.1016/j.iot.2019.100129

Qi, J., Yang, P., Min, G., Amft, O., Dong, F., & Xu, L. (2017). Advanced internet of things for personalised healthcare systems: A survey. *Pervasive and Mobile Computing*, *41*, 132–149. https://dx.doi.org/10.1016/j.pmcj.2017.06.018

Rahmani, A. M., Gia, T. N., Negash, B., Anzanpour, A., Azimi, I., Jiang, M., & Liljeberg, P. (2018). Exploiting smart e-Health gateways at the edge of healthcare Internet-of-Things: A fog computing approach. *Future Generation Computer Systems*, *78*, 641–658.

Ramesh, A. N., Kambhampati, C., Monson, J. R. T., & Drew, P. J. (2004). Artificial intelligence. *Annals of the Royal College of Surgeons of England*, *86*, 334–338. doi:10.1308/147870804290

Ray, P. P., Dash, D., & De, D. (2019). Edge computing for Internet of Things: A survey, e-healthcare case study and future direction. *Journal of Network and Computer Applications*, *140*, 1–22. https://doi.org/10.1016/j.jnca.2019.05.005

Rehman, A., Rehman, S., Khan, I.U., Moiz, M., & Hasan, S. (2016). Security and Privacy Issues in IoT. *International Journal of Communication Networks and Information Security*. https://www.researchgate.net/publication/313574376_Security_and_privacy_issues_in_IoT

Sadoughi, F., Behmanesh, A., & Sayfouri, N. (2020). Internet of things in medicine: A systematic mapping study. *Journal of Biomedical Informatics,* 103. doi:10.1016/j.jbi.2020.103383

Saheb, T., & Izadi, L. (2019). Paradigm of IoT big data analytics in the healthcare industry: A review of scientific literature and mapping of research trends. *Telematics and Informatics*, *41*, 70–85. https://doi.org/10.1016/j.tele.2019.03.005

Singh, R. P., Javaid, M., Haleem, A., & Suman, R. (2020). Internet of things (IoT) applications to fight against COVID-19pandemic. *Diabetes & Metabolic Syndrome*, *14*, 521–524.https://doi.org/10.1016/j.dsx.2020.04.041

Tewari, A., & Gupta, B. B. (2020). Security, privacy and trust of different layers in Internet-of-Things (IoTs) framework. *Future Generation Computer Systems*, *108*, 909–920.

Thibaud, M., Chi, H., Zhou, W., & Piramuthu, S. (2018). Internet of Things (IoT) in high-risk Environment, Health and Safety (EHS) industries: A comprehensive review. *Decision Support Systems*, *108*, 79–95. https://doi.org/10.1016/j.dss.2018.02.005

Tuan, M. N. D., Thanh, N. N., & Tuan, L. L. (2019). Applying a mindfulness-based reliability strategy to the Internet of Things inhealthcare – A business model in the Vietnamese market. *Technological Forecasting and Social Change*, *140*, 54–68.

Tuli, S., Basumatary, N., Gill, S. S., Kahani, M., Arya, R. C., Wander, G. S., & Buyya, R. (2020). HealthFog: An ensemble deep learning based Smart Healthcare System for Automatic Diagnosis of Heart Diseases in integrated IoT and fog computing environments. *Future Generation Computer Systems*, *104*, 187–200.

Verma, P., Sandeep, K., & Sood, S. K. (2017). Cloud-centric IoT based disease diagnosis healthcare framework. *Journal of Parallel and Distributed Computing*, *116*, 27–38. https://doi.org/10.1016/j.jpdc.2017.11.018

Vetrò, A., Santangelo, A., Beretta, E., & Martin, J. C. D. (2019). AI: From rational agents to socially responsible agents. *Digital Policy. Regulation & Governance*, ●●●, 291–304.

Yin, Y., Zeng, Y., Chen, X., & Fan, Y. (2016). The internet of things in healthcare: An overview. *Journal of Industrial Information Integration, 1*, 3–13.

Zakaria, H., Bakar, N. A., Hassan, N. H., & Yaacob, S. (2019). IoT Security Risk Management Model for Secured Practice in Healthcare Environment. *Procedia Computer Science, 161*, 1241–1248.

Zeadally, S., & Bello, O. (in press). Harnessing the power of Internet of Things based connectivity to improve healthcare. *Internet of Things*. 0 074 doi:10.1016/j.iot.2019.10

Compilation of References

Abelló, A., Darmont, J., Etcheverry, L., Golfarelli, M., Mazón, J. N., Naumann, F., Pedersen, T. B., Rizzi, S., Trujillo, J., Vassiliadis, P., & Vossen, G. (2013). Fusion cubes: Towards self-service business intelligence. *International Journal of Data Warehousing and Mining, 9*(2), 66–88. doi:10.4018/jdwm.2013040104

Abinaya, V. K., Kumar, V., & Swathika. (2015). Ontology based Public Healthcare System in Internet of Things(IoT). *Procedia Computer Science, 50,* 99–102. doi:10.1016/j.procs.2015.04.067

Abiyev, R. H., Ma'aitah, M., & Sonyel, B. (2017, December). Fuzzy Logic Traffic Lights Control (FLTLC). In *Proceedings of the 2017 9th International Conference on Education Technology and Computers* (pp. 233-238). Academic Press.

Aceto, G., Persico, V., & Pescape, A. (2020). Industry 4.0 and Health: Internet of Things, Big Data, and Cloud Computing for Healthcare 4.0. *Journal of Industrial Information Integration, 18,* 100129. Advance online publication. doi:10.1016/j.jii.2020.100129

Acharjya, D.P., & Ahmed, K.P. (2016). A Survey on Big Data Analytics: Challenges, Open Research Issues and Tools. *International Journal of Advanced Computer Science and Applications, 7*(2).

Adjei, E., Otoo D., Gyamfi, K. (2018). Towards a Big Data Architectural Framework for Healthcare in Ghana. *Communications on Applied Electronics (CAE), 7*(12).

Aggarwal, C. C. (2018). Neural networks and deep learning. Springer.

Agirre Perez, I. (2007). Stochastic project scheduling system: Implications for risk management. *Dissertation Abstracts International, 68*(2).

Agrawal, D., Das, S., & Abbadi, A.E. (2011). *Big Data and Cloud Computing: Current State and Future Opportunities.* EDBT.

Agrawal, K. C., & Nagori, M. (n.d.). Clusters of ayurvedic medicines using improved k-means algorithm. *International Conference on Advances in Computer Science and Electronics Engineering, 4*(13), 183-195.

Ahimbisibwe, A., Cavana, R. Y., & Daellenbach, U. (2015). A contingency fit model of critical success factors for software development projects: A comparison of agile and traditional plan-based methodologies. *Journal of Enterprise Information Management, 28*(1), 7–33. doi:10.1108/JEIM-08-2013-0060

Ahmeda, B., Seghira, B., Al-Ostaa, M., & Abdelouahed, G. (2019). Container Based Resource Management for Data Processing on IoT Gateways. In *Proceedings of the 16th International Conference on Mobile Systems and Pervasive Computing.* Elsevier. 10.1016/j.procs.2019.08.034

Ahmed, N., De, D., & Hussain, I. (2018). Internet of Things (IoT) for smart precision agriculture and farming in rural areas. *IEEE Internet of Things Journal, 5*(6), 4890–4899. doi:10.1109/JIOT.2018.2879579

Akigray, V. (1989). Conditional Heteroscedasity in Time tock of Stock Returns: Evidence and Forecasting. *The Journal of Business*, *62*(1), 55–80. doi:10.1086/296451

Akka, M. A., Sokullu, R., & Çetin, H. E. (2020). Healthcare and patient monitoring using IoT. *Internet of Things*, *11*, 100173. Advance online publication. doi:10.1016/j.iot.2020.100173

Aladwani, T. (2019). Scheduling IoT Healthcare Tasks in Fog Computing Based on their Importance. *Procedia Computer Science*, *163*, 560–569. doi:10.1016/j.procs.2019.12.138

Alassaf, R. A., Alsulaim, K. A., Alroomi, N. Y., Alsharif, N. S., Aljubeir, M. F., Olatunji, S. O., Alahmadi, A. Y., Imran, M., Alzahrani, R. A., & Alturayeif, N. S. (2019). Preemptive Diagnosis of Chronic Kidney Disease Using Machine Learning Techniques. *Proceedings of the 2018 13th International Conference on Innovations in Information Technology, IIT 2018, November*, 99–104. 10.1109/INNOVATIONS.2018.8606040

Alfazi, Abdullah, Sheng, Quan, Babar, Ali, Ruan, Wenjie, & Qin. (2017). Toward Unified Cloud Service Discovery for Enhanced Service Identification. *The 6th Australasian Symposium on Service Research and Innovation (ASSRI'17)*.

Alford, A. W., & Boatsman, J. R. (1995). Predicting Long-Term Stock Return Volatility: Implications for Accounting and Valuation of Equity Derivatives. *Acc. Rev.*, *70*(4), 599–618.

Al-Hyari, A. Y., Ahmad, M. A., & Majid, A. A. (2014). Diagnosis and classification of chronic renal failure utilising intelligent data mining classifiers. *International Journal of Information Technology and Web Engineering*, *9*(4), 1–12. doi:10.4018/ijitwe.2014100101

Aljahdali, S., & Hussain, S. N. (2013). Comparative prediction performance with support vector machine and random forest classification techniques. *International Journal of Computers and Applications*, *69*(11).

Allhoff, F., & Henschke, A. (2018). The Internet of Things: Foundational ethical issues. *Internet of Things*, *1–2*, 55–66. doi:10.1016/j.iot.2018.08.005

Almasoud, M., & Ward, T. E. (2019). Detection of chronic kidney disease using machine learning algorithms with least number of predictors. *International Journal of Advanced Computer Science and Applications*, *10*(8), 89–96. doi:10.14569/IJACSA.2019.0100813

Al-Radaideh, Q., Assaf, A. A., & Alnagi, E. (2013, December). Predicting stock prices using data mining techniques. *The International Arab Conference on Information Technology (ACIT'2013)*.

Al-Salmi, J., & Al-Foori, A., YasirAl-Jahwari, A., Hajamohideen, F. (2019). Smart emergency — A contextual framework for cognitive understanding of IoT devices using big data analytics. *2nd Smart Cities Symposium (SCS 2019)*, 1-4. 10.1049/cp.2019.0233

Alsghaier, H. M. A. (2017). The Importance of Big Data Analytics in Business: A Case Study. *American Journal of Software Engineering and Applications*, 111-115.

Altaf, T., Anwar, S. M., Gul, N., Majeed, M. N., & Majid, M. (2018). Multi-class Alzheimer's disease classification using image and clinical features. *Biomedical Signal Processing and Control*, *43*, 64–74. doi:10.1016/j.bspc.2018.02.019

Altieri, M. A., & Koohafkan, P. (2008). Enduring farms: climate change, smallholders and traditional farming communities (Vol. 6). Penang: Third World Network (TWN).

Ambekar, S., & Phalnikar, R. (2018, August). Disease risk prediction by using convolutional neural network. In *Fourth International Conference on Computing Communication Control and Automation (ICCUBEA)* (pp. 1-5). IEEE. 10.1109/ICCUBEA.2018.8697423

Analytics CloudS. A. P. (2017). Retrieved from SAP: https://www.sap.com/products/cloud- analytics.html

Ananthanarayanan, G., & Menache, I. (2016). Big data analytics systems. In S. Cui, A. Hero III, Z. Luo, & J. Moura (Eds.), *Big Data over Networks* (pp. 137–160). Cambridge University Press. doi:10.1017/CBO9781316162750.006

Anderson, E. S., Birchall, D., Jessen, S. A., & Money, A. H. (2006). Exploring project success. *Baltic Journal of Management, 1*(2), 127–147. doi:10.1108/17465260610663854

Apache Hadoop. (2018a, October 21). Retrieved from Wikipedia: https://en.wikipedia.org/wiki/Apache_Hadoop

Apache Spark. (2018b, October 23). Retrieved from Wikipedia: https://en.wikipedia.org/wiki/Apache_Spark

Archenaa, J., & Mary Anita, E. (2018). A Survey of Big Data Analytics in Healthcare and Government. *Procedia Computer Science, (50)*, 408–413.

Argüello Prada, E.J.A. (2020). The Internet of Things (IoT) in pain assessment and management: An overview. *Informatics in Medicine Unlocked, 18*. https://doi.org/10.1016/j.imu.2020.100298

Ashifuddin Mondal, M., & Rehena, Z. (2019, May). Intelligent Traffic Congestion Classification System using Artificial Neural Network. In *Companion Proceedings of the 2019 World Wide Web Conference* (pp. 110-116). Academic Press.

Aslan, I., & Aslan, H. (2019). Industry 4.0: The Role Of Industry 4.0 In Agri-Food, Process Safety &Environmental Protection. In Industry 4.0: Industry 4.0 Concept And Common Technologies & Systems. Lap Lambert Academic Publishing.

Aslan, I. (2019). The Role of Industry 4.0 in Occupational Health and Safety. *International European Congress on Social Sciences-IV*, 334-345.

Assuncao, M., Calheiros, R., Bianchi, S., Netto, M., & Buyya, R. (2015). Big Data computing and clouds: Trends and future directions. *Journal of Parallel and Distributed Computing, 79-80*, 3–15. doi:10.1016/j.jpdc.2014.08.003

Ateniese, G., Burns, R., Curtmola, R., Herring, J., Kissner, L., Peterson, Z., & Song, D. (2007). *Provable data possession at untrusted stores*. Cryptology ePrint Archive, Report 2007/202. https://eprint.iacr.org/

Azimi, I., Pahikkala, T., Rahmani, A. M., Niela-Vilén, H., Axelin, A., & Liljeberg, P. (2019). Missing data resilient decision-making for healthcare IoT through personalization: A case study on maternal health. *Future Generation Computer Systems, 96*, 297–308. doi:10.1016/j.future.2019.02.015

Babu, S., Vivek, E., & Famina, K. P. (2017, April). Heart disease diagnosis using data mining technique. In *International conference of Electronics, Communication and Aerospace Technology (ICECA)* (pp. 750-753). IEEE. 10.1109/ICECA.2017.8203643

Bacco, M., Berton, A., Ferro, E., Gennaro, C., Gotta, A., Matteoli, S., & Zanella, A. (2018, May). Smart farming: Opportunities, challenges and technology enablers. In *2018 IoT Vertical and Topical Summit on Agriculture-Tuscany (IOT Tuscany)* (pp. 1-6). IEEE.

Bagavathi, C., & Saraniya, O. (2019). Evolutionary Mapping Techniques for Systolic Computing System. In Deep Learning and Parallel Computing Environment for Bioengineering Systems (pp. 207-223). Academic Press.

Bagiwa, L. I. (2017). Big Data: Concepts, Approaches and Challenges. *International Journal of Computer Networks and Communications Security*, 181-187.

Bahety, A. (2014). Extension and evaluation of id3–decision tree algorithm. *Entropy (S), 2*(1), 1–8.

Bailas, C., Marsden, M., Zhang, D., O'Connor, N. E., & Little, S. (2018). Performance of Video Processing at the Edge for Crowd-Monitoring Applications. In *Proceedings of the 4th World Forum on Internet of Things (WF-IoT)*. IEEE. 10.1109/WF-IoT.2018.8355170

Bains, J. K. (2016). Big Data Analytics in Healthcare- Its Benefits, Phases and Challenges. *International Journal of Advanced Research in Computer Science and Software Engineering, 6*(4), 430–435.

Bakr, A. A., & Azer, M. A. (2017) IoT ethics challenges and legal issues. *12th International Conference on Computer Engineering and Systems (ICCES)*, Cairo, Egypt. 10.1109/ICCES.2017.8275309

Bakshi, G., Cao, C., & Chen, Z. (1997). Empirical performance of alternative option pricing models. *The Journal of Finance, 52*(5), 2003–2204. doi:10.1111/j.1540-6261.1997.tb02749.x

Bakshi, K. (2012, March). *Considerations for big data: Architecture and approach. In 2012 IEEE aerospace conference*. IEEE.

Balachander, J., & Ramanujam, E. (2017). Rule based Medical Content Classification for Secure Remote Health Monitoring. *International Journal of Computers and Applications, 165*(4).

Balachandran, B., & Prasad, S. (2017). Challenges and Benefits of Deploying Big Data Analytics in the Cloud for Business Intelligence International Conference on Knowledge Based and Intelligent Information and Engineering Systems. *Procedia Computer Science, 112*, 1112–1122. doi:10.1016/j.procs.2017.08.138

Baladi, I. W. (2007). An empirical analysis of perceived value of virtual versus traditional project management practice. *Dissertation Abstracts International, 68*(9).

Balazinska, M., Howe, B., & Suciu, D. (2011). Data markets in the cloud. *Proceedings of the VLDB Endowment International Conference on Very Large Data Bases, 4*(12), 1482–1485. doi:10.14778/3402755.3402801

Banker, R. D., & Khosla, I. S. (1995). Economics of operations management: A research perspective. *Journal of Operations Management, 12*(3-4), 423–435. doi:10.1016/0272-6963(95)00022-K

Bano, S. (2015). Big Data: An emerging technology towards scalable system. *International Journal of Innovative and Emerging Research in Engineering, 2*(3), 2015.

Bansal, A., Sharma, M., & Goel, S. (2017). Improved k-mean clustering algorithm for prediction analysis using classification technique in data mining. *International Journal of Computers and Applications, 157*(6).

Barlow, H. B. (1989). Unsupervised learning. *Neural Computation, 1*(3), 295–311. doi:10.1162/neco.1989.1.3.295

Barreto, L., & Amaral, A. (2018, September). Smart farming: Cyber security challenges. In *2018 International Conference on Intelligent Systems (IS)* (pp. 870-876). IEEE. 10.1109/IS.2018.8710531

Bartel, A. P. (2004). Human Resource Management and Organizational Performance: Evidence from Retail Banking. *Industrial & Labor Relations Review, 57*(2), 181–203. doi:10.1177/001979390405700202

Bass, F. M. (1969). A new product growth model for consumer durables. *Management Science, 15*(5), 215–227. doi:10.1287/mnsc.15.5.215

Basuthkar, V. (2016). A Survey of Cost-Effective Big Data in Healthcare Applications. *International Journal of Computers and Applications*.

Bates, D. (2000). Post-87 crash fears in S&P 500 futures options. *Journal of Econometrics, 94*(1-2), 181–238. doi:10.1016/S0304-4076(99)00021-4

Baumann, A., Peinado, M., & Hunt, G. (2015). Shielding applications from an untrusted cloud with haven. *ACM Transactions on Computer Systems*, *33*(3), 1–26. doi:10.1145/2799647

Bendre, M. R., & Thool, V. R. (2016). Analytics, challenges and applications in big data environment: A survey. *Journal of Management Analytics*, *3*(3), 206–239. doi:10.1080/23270012.2016.1186578

Berke, L. (n.d.). *Lindsey Berke*. Retrieved December 11, 2020, from https://www.dimins.com/blog/2020/03/02/big-data-healthcare

Berkowitz, E. N., Kerin, R. A., Hartley, S. W., & Rudelius, W. (1997). *Marketing* (5th ed.). McGraw-Hill/Irwin.

Bertsimas, D., & Kallus, N. (2014). *From predictive to prescriptive analytics*. arXiv preprint arXiv:1402.5481.

Bhardwaj, A., Al-Turjman, F., Kumar, M., Stephan, T., & Mostarda, L. (2020). Capturing-the-Invisible (CTI): A Novel Approach for Behavior-based Attacks Recognition in Industrial Control Systems. *IEEE Access: Practical Innovations, Open Solutions*, *8*(1), 104956–104966. doi:10.1109/ACCESS.2020.2998983

Bharti, S., & Mishra, A. (2015). Prediction of Future Possible Offender's Network and Role of Offenders. In *Fifth International Conference on Advances in Computing and Communications (ICACC)* (pp. 159-162). IEEE. 10.1109/ICACC.2015.36

Bhatia, M., & Sood, S. K. (2017). A comprehensive health assessment framework to facilitate IoT-assisted smart workouts: A predictive healthcare perspective. *Computers in Industry*, *92–93*, 50–66. doi:10.1016/j.compind.2017.06.009

Bhatnagar, R. (2018, February). Machine Learning and Big Data processing: a technological perspective and review. In *International Conference on Advanced Machine Learning Technologies and Applications* (pp. 468-478). Springer. 10.1007/978-3-319-74690-6_46

Bhattacharjee, A., Barve, Y., Khare, S., Bao, S., Kang, Z., Gokhale, A., & Damiano, T. (2019). STRATUM: A BigData-as-a-Service for Lifecycle Management of IoT Analytics Applications. *IEEE International Conference on Big Data (Big Data)*, 1607-1612. 10.1109/BigData47090.2019.9006518

Big Data Analytics Advanced Analytics in Oracle Database. (2013). *An Oracle White Paper*, 1- 12.

Big Data Timeline-Series of Big Data Evolution. (2015, Aug 26). Retrieved from DeZyre: https://www.dezyre.com/article/big-data-timeline-series-of-big-data-evolution/160

Bigdata. (2020, June 26). *Which Are The Real Benefits of Big Data?* Retrieved August 11, 2020, from https://bigdata-analyticsnews.com/real-benefits-of-big-data/

Bilal, K., Khalid, O., Erbad, A., & Khan, S. U. (2018). Potentials, trends, and prospects in edge technologies: Fog, cloudlet, mobile edge, and micro data centers. *Elsevier Computer Networks*, *130*, 94–120. doi:10.1016/j.comnet.2017.10.002

Binder, K., Krauss, S., & Bruckmaier, G. (2015). Effects of visualizing statistical information – an empirical study on tree diagrams and 2 × 2 tables. *Frontiers in Psychology*, *6*(August), 1–9. doi:10.3389/fpsyg.2015.01186 PMID:26379569

Birst Inc. (n.d.). http://www.birst.com

Black, F., Jensen, M., & Scholes, M. (1972). The Capital-Asset Pricing Model: Some empirical tests. In Studies in the Theory of Capital Markets. Praeger Publishers Inc.

Black, F., Jensen, M., & Scholes, M. S. (1972). The Capital Asset Pricing Model: Some Empirical Findings. In M. Jensen (Ed.), *Studies in the Theory of Capital Markets* (pp. 79–124). Praeger Publishers.

Bloom, N., Eifert, B., Mahajan, A., McKenzie, D., & Roberts, J. (2013). Does management matter? Evidence from India. *The Quarterly Journal of Economics*, *128*(1), 1–51. doi:10.1093/qje/qjs044

Bonissone, P. P., Chen, Y. T., Goebel, K., & Khedkar, P. S. (1999). Hybrid soft computing systems: Industrial and commercial applications. *Proceedings of the IEEE*, *87*(9), 1641–1667. doi:10.1109/5.784245

Boswijk, H., & Franses, P. (2005). On the econometrics of the bass diffusion model. *Journal of Business & Economic Statistics*, *23*(3), 255–268. doi:10.1198/073500104000000604

Brisimi, Xu, Wang, Dai, Adams, & Paschalidis. (2018). Predicting Chronic Disease Hospitalizations from Electronic Health Records: An Interpretable Classification Approach. *Proc IEEE Inst Electr Electron Eng.*, *106*(4), 690–707. 10.1109/JPROC.2017.2789319

Brouwer, M. D., Ongenae, F., Bonte, P., & Turck, F. D. (2018). Towards a Cascading Reasoning Framework to Support Responsive Ambient-Intelligent Healthcare Interventions. *MDPI Sensors - Wearable and Ambient Sensors for Healthcare and Wellness Applications*, *18*(10), 3514.

Bullen, C. V., & Rockart, J. F. (1981). *A primer on critical success factors*. Academic Press.

Bura, D., & Choudhary, A. (2020). A novel change impact model for enhancing project management. *International Journal of Project Organisation and Management*, *12*(2), 119–132.

Bura, D., & Choudhary, A. (2020). Enhancing Information Retrieval System Using Change-Prone Classes. In *Critical Approaches to Information Retrieval Research* (pp. 40–68). IGI Global.

Bura, D., Choudhary, A., & Singh, R. K. (2017). A Novel UML Based Approach for Early Detection of Change Prone Classes. *International Journal of Open Source Software and Processes*, *8*(3), 1–23.

Bura, D., Singh, M., & Nandal, P. (2018). Analysis and Development of Load Balancing Algorithms in Cloud Computing. *International Journal of Information Technology and Web Engineering*, *13*(3), 35–53.

Cabral, S., & Lazzarini, S. G. (2015). The "guarding the guardians" problem: An analysis of the organizational performance of an internal affairs division. *Journal of Public Administration: Research and Theory*, *25*(3), 797–829. doi:10.1093/jopart/muu001

Camarinha-Matos, L. M., Rosas, J., Oliveira, A. I., & Ferrada, F. (2015). Care services ecosystem for ambient assisted living. *Enterprise Information Systems*, *9*(5-6), 607–633.

Cao, C. Q., & Tsay, R. S. (1992). Nonlinear time-series analysis of stock volatilities. *Journal of Applied Econometrics*, *7*(S1), S165–S185. doi:10.1002/jae.3950070512

Cao, T., Pham, T., Vu, Q., Truong, H., Le, D., & Dustdar, S. (2016). Marsa. *ACM Transactions on Internet Technology*, *16*(3), 1–21. doi:10.1145/2883611

Cappelli, P., & Neumark, D. (2001). Do "High-Performance" Work Practices Improve Establishment-Level Outcomes? *Industrial & Labor Relations Review*, *54*(4), 737–775.

CBINSIGHTS. (2020, April 28). *What is Edge Computing?* Retrieved from https://www.cbinsights.com/research/what-is-edge-computing/

Cech, H. L., Grobmann, M., & Krieger, U. R. (2019). A Fog Computing Architecture to Share Sensor Data by Means of Blockchain Functionality. In *Proceedings of International Conference on Fog Computing*. IEEE. 10.1109/ICFC.2019.00013

Cerina, L., Notargiacomo, S., Paccanit, M. G. L., & Santambrogio, M. D. (2017). A Fog-Computing architecture for Preventive Healthcare and Assisted Living in Smart Ambients. In *Proceedings of the 3rd International Forum on Research and Technologies for Society and Industry (RTSI)*. IEEE. 10.1109/RTSI.2017.8065939

Chadha, A., & Kumar, S. (2014, February). An improved K-means clustering algorithm: a step forward for removal of dependency on K. In *International Conference on Reliability Optimization and Information Technology (ICROIT)* (pp. 136-140). IEEE. 10.1109/ICROIT.2014.6798312

Chakraborty, S., Nagwani, N. K., & Dey, L. (2012). *Weather forecasting using incremental K-means clustering*. arXiv preprint arXiv:1406.4756.

Chandramohan, Shanmugam, Shailesh, Khapre, Shukla, & Achyut. (2021). Blockchain-Enabled Decentralized Reliable Smart Industrial Internet of Things (BCIIoT). *Innovation in the Industrial Internet of Things (IIoT) and Smart Factory*, 192-204. doi:10.4018/978-1-7998-3375-8.ch013

Chandramohan, D., Vengattaraman, T., Rajaguru, D., Baskaran, R., & Dhavachelvan, P. (2013b). Hybrid Authentication Technique to Preserve User Privacy and Protection as an End Point Lock for the Cloud Service Digital Information. In *International Conference on Green High Performance Computing* (pp. 1-4). Nagercoil, Tamilnadu: IEEE. 10.1109/ICGHPC.2013.6533904

Chandrashekar, R., Kala, M., & Mane, D. (2015). *Integration of Big Data in Cloud computing environments for enhanced data processing capabilities. International Journal of Engineering Research and General Science.*

Chandy, R. K., Tellis, G. J., MacInnis, D. J., & Thaivanich, P. (2001). What to say when: Advertising appeals in evolving markets. *JMR, Journal of Marketing Research*, *38*(4), 399–414. doi:10.1509/jmkr.38.4.399.18908

Chanti S., Anwar, T., Chithralekha T., & Uma, V. (2021). Global naming and storage system using blockchain. *Research Anthology on Combating Denial-of-Service Attacks*, 265-281. doi:10.4018/978-1-7998-5348-0.ch014

Chan, Y.-K., Chen, Y.-F., Pham, T., Chang, W., & Hsieh, M.-Y. (2018). Artificial Intelligence in Medical Applications, *Journal of Healthcare Engineering*. doi:10.1155/2018/4827875 PMID:30123442

Charleonnan, A., Fufaung, T., Niyomwong, T., Chokchueypattanakit, W., Suwannawach, S., & Ninchawee, N. (2016). Predictive analytics for chronic kidney disease using machine learning techniques. *IEEE International Conference on Management and Innovation Technology (MITicon)*, MIT-80. 10.1109/MITICON.2016.8025242

Chauhan, A., Jain, A., & Sharma, P. (2018, February). Heart disease prediction using evolutionary rule learning. In *4th International Conference on Computational Intelligence & Communication Technology (CICT)* (pp. 1-4). IEEE.

Chaurasia, V., & Pal, S. (2013). Early prediction of heart diseases using data mining techniques. *Caribbean Journal of Science and Technology*, *1*, 208–217.

Chawla, I., & Singh, S. K. (2017). A fuzzy-based approach for bug report categorisation. *International Journal of Intelligent Systems Technologies and Applications*, *16*(4), 319–341.

Chen, C., Härdle, W., Unwin, A., & Friendly, M. (2008). *A Brief History of Data Visualization*. doi:10.1007/978-3-540-33037-0_2

Chen, H. M., Schütz, R., Kazman, R., & Matthes, F. (2016). Amazon in the air: Innovating with big data at Lufthansa. In *System Sciences (HICSS), 2016 49th Hawaii International Conference on* (pp. 5096-5105). IEEE.

Chen, Hao, Hwang, Wang, & Wang. (2017). *Disease Prediction by Machine Learning over Big Data from Healthcare Communities*. Academic Press.

Chen, H., Frank, M., & Wu, O. (2005). What Actually Happened to the Inventories of American Companies between 1981 and 2000? *Management Science*, *51*(7), 1015–1031. doi:10.1287/mnsc.1050.0368

Chen, H., Frank, M., & Wu, O. (2007). US Retail and Wholesale Inventory Performance from 1981 to 2004. *Manufacturing & Service Operations Management*, *9*(4), 430–456. doi:10.1287/msom.1060.0129

Chen, M., Hao, Y., Hwang, K., Wang, L., & Wang, L. (2017, April). Disease prediction by machine learning over big data from healthcare communities. *IEEE Access: Practical Innovations, Open Solutions*, *5*, 5. doi:10.1109/ACCESS.2017.2694446

Chen, N.-F. (1983). Some Empirical Tests of the Theory of Arbitrage Pricing. *The Journal of Finance*, *38*(5), 1393–1414. doi:10.1111/j.1540-6261.1983.tb03831.x

Chen, N., Roll, R., & Ross, S. A. (1986). Economic Forces and the Stock Market. *The Journal of Business*, *59*(3), 383–403. doi:10.1086/296344

Chen, Y., Wei, Z., & Huang, X. (2018, October). Incorporating corporation relationship via graph convolutional neural networks for stock price prediction. *Proceedings of the 27th ACM International Conference on Information and Knowledge Management*, 1655-1658.

Chernov, M., Gallant, A. R., Ghysels, E., & Tauchen, G. (2003). Alternative models for stock price dynamics. *Journal of Econometrics*, *116*(1-2), 225–257. doi:10.1016/S0304-4076(03)00108-8

Chernov, M., & Ghysels, E. (2000). A study towards a unified approach to the joint estimation of objective and risk neutral measures for the purpose of option valuation. *Journal of Financial Economics*, *56*(3), 407–458. doi:10.1016/S0304-405X(00)00046-5

Chong, D., & Shi, H. (2015). Big data analytics: A literature review. *Journal of Management Analytics*, *2*(3), 175–201. doi:10.1080/23270012.2015.1082449

Chou, T. C., Chiu, N. F., Liao, F. R., Lu, S. S., Ping, F., Yang, C. R., & Lin, C. W. (2005). A Multi Parameters Wearable Telemetric System for Cardio-Pulmonary Fitness of e-Health. In *Proceedings of the 27th Annual Conference on Engineering in Medicine and Biology*. IEEE. 10.1109/IEMBS.2005.1617233

Chowdhury, A. R. (1994). Advertising Expenditures and the Macro-Economy: Some New Evidence. *International Journal of Advertising*, *13*(1), 1–14. doi:10.1080/02650487.1994.11104557

Chow, G. C. (1960). Tests of Equality between Sets of Coe¢ cients in Two Linear Regressions. *Econometrica*, *28*(3), 591–605. doi:10.2307/1910133

Christidis, K., & Devetsikiotis, M. (2016). Blockchains and smart contracts for the Internet of things. *IEEE Access: Practical Innovations, Open Solutions*, *4*, 2292–2303. doi:10.1109/ACCESS.2016.2566339

Cianchetti, M., Laschi, C., Menciassi, A., & Dario, P. (2018). Biomedical applications of soft robotics. *Nature Reviews. Materials*, *3*(6), 143–153. doi:10.103841578-018-0022-y

Cisco. (2015). *Fog Computing and the Internet of Things: Extend the Cloud to Where the Things Are: Whitepaper*. Retrieved from https://www.cisco.com/c/dam/en_us/solutions/trends/iot/docs/computing-overview.pdf

Cohen, J., Dolan, B., Dunlap, M., Hellerstein, J. M., & Welton, C. (2009). MAD skills: New analysis practices for big data. *Proceedings of the VLDB Endowment International Conference on Very Large Data Bases*, *2*(2), 1481–1492.

Cohen, S. B., Ruppin, E., & Dror, G. (2005, July). Feature Selection Based on the Shapley Value. *IJCAI (United States)*, *5*, 665–670.

Cox, M., & Ellsworth, D. (1997, August). Managing Big Data for scientific visualization. In ACM siggraph (Vol. 97, pp. 21-38). ACM.

Creswell, J. W. (2009). Editorial: Mapping the Field of Mixed Methods Research. *Journal of Mixed Methods Research*, *3*(2), 95–108. doi:10.1177/1558689808330883

Cristianini, N., & Shawe-Taylor, J. (2000). *An introduction to support vector machines and other kernel-based learning methods*. Cambridge University Press. doi:10.1017/CBO9780511801389

Cuzzocrea, A., Song, I. Y., & Davis, K. C. (2011). Analytics over large-scale multidimensional data: the big data revolution! In *Proceedings of the ACM 14th international workshop on Data Warehousing and OLAP* (pp. 101-104). ACM. 10.1145/2064676.2064695

Dahl, Ø., & Starren, A. (2019). *The future role of big data and machine learning for health and safety inspection efficiency*. EU-OSHA.

Das. (2018). Big Data Analytics for Medical Applications. *International Journal of Modern Education and Computer Science*.

Das, H., Naik, B., & Behera, H. S. (2020). A Hybrid Neuro-Fuzzy and Feature Reduction Model for Classification. *Advances in Fuzzy Systems*, *2020*, 2020. doi:10.1155/2020/4152049

Das, R., Turkoglu, I., & Sengur, A. A. (2009). Diagnosis of valvular heart disease through neural networks ensembles. *Computer Methods and Programs in Biomedicine*, *93*(2), 185–191. doi:10.1016/j.cmpb.2008.09.005 PMID:18951649

Das, T. K., & Kumar, P. M. (2013). Big data analytics: A framework for unstructured data analysis. *International Journal of Engineering Science and Technology*, *5*(1), 153.

Davis, F. D. (1989). Perceived usefulness, perceived ease of use, and user acceptance of information technology. *Management Information Systems Quarterly*, *13*(3), 319–340. doi:10.2307/249008

De Berg, M., Bose, P., Cheong, O., & Morin, P. (2004). On simplifying dot maps. *Computational Geometry*, *27*(1), 43–62. doi:10.1016/j.comgeo.2003.07.005

Deb, K. (2001). *Multi-objective optimization using evolutionary algorithms* (Vol. 16). John Wiley & Sons.

Dekimpe & Hanssens. (1995b). Empirical Generalizations about Market Evolution and Stationarity. *Marketing Science*, *14*(3,2), G109-G121.

Dekimpe, M. G., & Hanssens, D. M. (1995a). The Persistence of Marketing Effects on Sales. *Marketing Science*, *14*(1), 1–21. doi:10.1287/mksc.14.1.1

Dekimpe, M. G., & Hanssens, D. M. (1999). Sustained Spending and Persistent Response: A New Look at Long-Term Marketing Profitability. *JMR, Journal of Marketing Research*, *36*(4), 397–412. doi:10.1177/002224379903600401

Dekimpe, M. G., & Hanssens, D. M. (2000). Time-series Models in Marketing: Past, Present and Future. *International Journal of Research in Marketing*, *17*(2-3), 183–193. doi:10.1016/S0167-8116(00)00014-8

Delisle, C. L. G. (2001). Success and communication in virtual project teams. *Dissertation Abstracts International*, *62*(12), 4242.

Demiroz, G., Govenir, H. A., & Ilter, N. (1998). Learning differential diagnosis of eryhemato-squamous diseases using voting feature intervals. *Artificial Intelligence in Medicine*, *13*(3), 147–165. doi:10.1016/S0933-3657(98)00028-1 PMID:9698151

Deng, Y., Zhou, L., Wang, L., Su, M., Zhang, J., Lian, J., & Wei, J. (2020). Radio Environment Map Construction Using Super-Resolution Imaging for Intelligent Transportation Systems. *IEEE Access: Practical Innovations, Open Solutions, 8,* 47272–47281. doi:10.1109/ACCESS.2020.2977855

Desai, S. (2013). Intelligent heart disease prediction system using probabilistic neural network. *International Journal on Advanced Computer Theory and Engineering, 2*(3).

Detrano, R., Janosi, A., Steinbrunn, W., Pfisterer, M., Schmid, J. J., Sandhu, S., Guppy, K. H., Lee, S., & Froelicher, V. (1989). International application of a new probability algorithm for the diagnosis of coronary artery disease. *The American Journal of Cardiology, 64*(5), 304–310. doi:10.1016/0002-9149(89)90524-9 PMID:2756873

Dewan, A., & Sharma, M. (2015). Prediction of Heart Disease Using a Hybrid Technique in Data Mining Classification. *IEEE, 43*(6), 13-24.

Dey, M., & Rautaray, S. S. (2014). Study and analysis of Data Mining algorithms for healthcare decision support system. *International Journal of Computer Science and Information Technologies, 5*(1), 470–477.

Dhanvijay, M. M., & Patil, S. C. (2019). Internet of Things: A survey of enabling technologies in healthcare and its applications. *Computer Networks, 15,* 113–131. doi:10.1016/j.comnet.2019.03.006

Diebold, F. X. (2012). On the Origin (s) and Development of the Term. *Big Data.*

Dietterich, T. G. (1998). An experimental comparison of three methods for constructing ensembles of decision trees: Bagging, boosting and randomization. *Machine Learning, 32,* 1–22.

Difference between Google Analytics and Google Webmaster Tools. (2018). Retrieved October 25, 2018, from Career Bless: https://www.careerbless.com/web/website/general/topic1.php

Ding, P., & Li, F. (2018). Causal inference: A missing data perspective. *Statistical Science, 33*(2), 214–237. doi:10.1214/18-STS645

Dua, D., & Graff, C. (2019). *UCI Machine Learning Repository.* University of California, School of Information and Computer Science.

Dulhare, U. N., & Ayesha, M. (2016). Extraction of action rules for chronic kidney disease using Naïve bayes classifier. *IEEE International Conference on Computational Intelligence and Computing Research (ICCIC),* 1-5. 10.1109/ICCIC.2016.7919649

Dziembowski, S., Eckey, L., & Faust, S. (2018). FairSwap. *Proceedings of the 2018 ACM SIGSAC Conference on Computer and Communications Security.* 10.1145/3243734.3243857

Econsultancy. (2019). *10 examples of the Internet of Things in healthcare.* https://econsultancy.com/internet-of-things-healthcare/

Eichler, M. (2007). Granger causality and path diagrams for multivariate time series. *Journal of Econometrics, 137*(2), 334–353. doi:10.1016/j.jeconom.2005.06.032

Ekeledo, I., & Sivakumar, K. (2004). International market entry mode strategies of manufacturing firms and service firms: A resource-based perspective. *International Marketing Review, 21*(1), 68–101. doi:10.1108/02651330410522943

Elazhary. (2014). *Cloud Computing for Big Data MAGNT Research Report.* Academic Press.

Elijah, O., Rahman, T. A., Orikumhi, I., Leow, C. Y., & Hindia, M. N. (2018). An overview of Internet of Things (IoT) and data analytics in agriculture: Benefits and challenges. *IEEE Internet of Things Journal, 5*(5), 3758–3773. doi:10.1109/JIOT.2018.2844296

El-Latif, A. A., Abd-El-Atty, B., Abou-Nassar, E., & Venegas-Andraca, S. E. (2020). Controlled alternate quantum walks based privacy preserving healthcare images in Internet of Things. *Optics & Laser Technology*, *124*, 105942. Advance online publication. doi:10.1016/j.optlastec.2019.105942

Elleuch, W., Wali, A., & Alimi, A. M. (2016, December). Intelligent Traffic Congestion Prediction System Based on ANN and Decision Tree Using Big GPS Traces. In *International Conference on Intelligent Systems Design and Applications* (pp. 478-487). Springer.

Elter, M., Schulz-Wendtland, R., & Wittenberg, T. (2007). The prediction of breast cancer biopsy outcomes using two CAD approaches that both emphasize an intelligible decision process. *Medical Physics*, *34*(11), 4164–4172. doi:10.1118/1.2786864 PMID:18072480

Emeakaroha, V. C., Cafferkey, N., Healy, P., & Morrison, J. P. (2015). A Cloud-Based IoT Data Gathering and Processing Platform. In *Proceedings of the 3rd International Conference on Future Internet of Things and Cloud*. IEEE. 10.1109/FiCloud.2015.53

Engle, R. (1982). Autoregressive Conditional Hetersokedasticity with Estimates of the Vari-ance of United Kingdom In.ation. *Econometrica*, *50*(4), 987–2008. doi:10.2307/1912773

Eraker, B., Johannes, M. S., & Polson, N. G. (2003). The impact of jumps in returns and volatility. *The Journal of Finance*, *53*(3), 1269–1300. doi:10.1111/1540-6261.00566

Erturk, E., & Sezer, E. A. (2015). A comparison of some soft computing methods for software fault prediction. *Expert Systems with Applications*, *42*(4), 1872–1879.

Fadlullah, Z. M., Tang, F., Mao, B., Kato, N., Akashi, O., Inoue, T., & Mizutani, K. (2017). State-of-the-art deep learning: Evolving machine intelligence toward tomorrow's intelligent network traffic control systems. *IEEE Communications Surveys and Tutorials*, *19*(4), 2432–2455.

Fama, E. F., & French, K. R. (1993). Common Risk Factors in the Returns on Stocks and Bonds. *Journal of Financial Economics*, *33*(1), 3–56. doi:10.1016/0304-405X(93)90023-5

Fama, E. F., & French, K. R. (2004). The CAPM: Theory and Evidence. *The Journal of Economic Perspectives*, *18*, 25–46. doi:10.1257/0895330042162430

Fama, E. F., & MacBeth, J. D. (1973). Risk, Return, and Equilibrium: Empirical Tests. *Journal of Political Economy*, *81*(3), 607–636. doi:10.1086/260061

Farah, B. (2017). Profitability and Big Data. *Journal of Management Policy and Practice*, 47-52.

Farley, J. U., Hayes, A. F., & Kopalle, P. (2004). Choosing and upgrading financial services dealers in the US and UK. *International Journal of Research in Marketing*, *21*(4), 359–375. doi:10.1016/j.ijresmar.2004.08.001

Farooq, M. S., Riaz, S., Abid, A., Abid, K., & Naeem, M. A. (2019). A Survey on the Role of IoT in Agriculture for the Implementation of Smart Farming. *IEEE Access: Practical Innovations, Open Solutions*, *7*, 156237–156271. doi:10.1109/ACCESS.2019.2949703

Faust & Jonathan. (2013), Forecasting Inflation. In *Handbook of Economic Forecasting*. New York: Elsevier.

Félix, B. M., Rodrigues, E. M. T., & Cavalcante, N. W. F. (2018). Critical success factors for Big Data adoption in the virtual retail: Magazine Luiza case study. *Review of Business Management*, *20*(1), 112–126. doi:10.7819/rbgn.v20i1.3627

Ferraris, A., Mazzoleni, A., Devalle, A., & Couturier, J. (2019). Big data analytics capabilities and knowledge management: Impact on firm performance. *Management Decision*, *57*(8), 1923–1936. doi:10.1108/MD-07-2018-0825

Fisher, I. (1933). Report of the Meeting. *Econometrica, 1*, 92–93.

Foko, T., Dlodlo, N., & Montsi, L. (2013). An Integrated Smart System for Ambient-Assisted Living. *Internet of Things, Smart Spaces, and Next Generation Networking, 8121*, 128–138. doi:10.1007/978-3-642-40316-3_12

Fortune, J., & White, D. (2006). Framing of project critical success factors by a systems model. *International Journal of Project Management, 24*(1), 53–65. doi:10.1016/j.ijproman.2005.07.004

Furht, B., & Villanustre, F. (2016). Introduction to Big Data. In *Big Data technologies and applications* (pp. 3–11). Springer. doi:10.1007/978-3-319-44550-2_1

Gandhi, M., & Singh, S. N. (2015). Predictions in Heart Disease Using Techniques of Data Mining. *1st International Conference on Futuristic trend in Computational Analysis and Knowledge Management (ABLAZE-2015), 8*(6), 13-48. 10.1109/ABLAZE.2015.7154917

Gandomi, A. M. H., & Haider, M. (2015). Beyond the hype: Big Data concepts, methods, and analytics. *International Journal of Information Management, 35*(2), 137–144. doi:10.1016/j.ijinfomgt.2014.10.007

Gao, J., Koronios, A., & Selle, S. (2015). *Towards a process view on critical success factors in big data analytics projects*. Academic Press.

Gaur, V., Fisher, M., & Raman, A. (1999). *What Explains Superior Retail Performance?* NYU Working Paper No. OM-2005-03.

Gaur, V., Fisher, M., & Raman, A. (2005). An Econometric Analysis of Inventory Turnover Performance in Retail Services. *Management Science, 51*(2), 181–194. doi:10.1287/mnsc.1040.0298

Gaur, V., & Kesavan, S. (2006). The Effects of Firm Size and Sales Growth Rate on Inventory Turnover Performance in the U.S. Retail Sector. In N. Agrawal & S. Smith (Eds.), *Retail Supply Chain Management*. Kluwer Publishers.

Gautam, K., Puri, V., Tromp, J. G., Nguyen, N. G., & Van Le, C. (2020). Internet of Things (IoT) and Deep Neural Network-Based Intelligent and Conceptual Model for Smart City. In *Frontiers in Intelligent Computing: Theory and Applications* (pp. 287–300). Springer.

Gavhane, A., & Kokkula, G. (2018, March). Prediction of heart disease using machine learning. In *Second International Conference on Electronics, Communication and Aerospace Technology (ICECA)* (pp. 1275-1278). IEEE.

Geczy, P., Izumi, N., & Hasida, K. (2012). Cloudsourcing: Managing cloud adoption. *Global Journal of Business Research, 6*(2), 57–70.

Ge, M., Bangui, H., & Buhnova, B. (2018). Big data for internet of things: A survey. *Future Generation Computer Systems, 87*, 601–614. doi:10.1016/j.future.2018.04.053

Ghahramani, Z. (2003, February). Unsupervised learning. In *Summer School on Machine Learning* (pp. 72–112). Springer.

Ghaiwat, S. N., & Arora, P. (2014). Detection and classification of plant leaf diseases using image processing techniques: A review. *International Journal of Recent Advances in Engineering & Technology, 2*(3), 1–7.

Ghemawat, S., Gobioff, H., & Leung, S.-T. (2003). The Google File System. In *Proceedings of the 9th ACM Symposium on Operating Systems Principles (SOSP 2003)*. ACM.

Gholami, A., & Laure, E. (2016). Big data security and privacy issues in the cloud. *International Journal of Network Security & Its Applications, 8*(1).

Gill, S. S., Chana, I., & Buyya, R. (2017). IoT based agriculture as a cloud and big data service: The beginning of digital India. *Journal of Organizational and End User Computing*, 29(4), 1–23. doi:10.4018/JOEUC.2017100101

Gladkykh, T., Hnot, T., & Solskyy, V. (2016). Fuzzy logic inference for unsupervised anomaly detection. In *First International Conference on Data Stream Mining & Processing (DSMP)* (pp. 42-47). IEEE. 10.1109/DSMP.2016.7583504

Godara, D., Choudhary, A., & Singh, R. K. (2018). Predicting Change Prone Classes in Open Source Software. *International Journal of Information Retrieval Research*, 8(4), 1–23.

Godara, D., & Singh, R. (2014). A new hybrid model for predicting change prone class in object oriented software. *International Journal of Computer Science and Telecommunications*, 5(7), 1–6.

Godara, D., & Singh, R. K. (2014). A review of studies on change proneness prediction in object oriented software. *International Journal of Computers and Applications*, 105(3).

Godara, D., & Singh, R. K. (2015). Enhancing Frequency Based Change Proneness Prediction Method Using Artificial Bee Colony Algorithm. In *Advances in Intelligent Informatics* (pp. 535–543). Springer.

Godara, D., & Singh, R. K. (2017). Exploring the relationships between design measures and change proneness in object-oriented systems. International Journal of Software Engineering. *Technology and Applications*, 2(1), 64–80.

Goldfeder, S., Bonneau, J., Gennaro, R., & Narayanan, A. (2017). Escrow protocols for cryptocurrencies: How to buy physical goods using bitcoin. *Financial Cryptography and Data Security*, 321-339. doi:10.1007/978-3-319-70972-7_18

Gomes, B., Muniz, L., Silva, F. J. S., Rios, L. T. E., & Endler, M. (2015). A Comprehensive Cloud-based IoT Software Infrastructure for Ambient Assisted Living. In *Proceedings of International Conference on Cloud Technologies and Applications (CloudTech)*. IEEE. 10.1109/CloudTech.2015.7336998

Google Analytics. (2018, October 21). Retrieved from Wikipedia: https://en.wikipedia.org/wiki/Google_Analytics

Gopalakrishnan, K., Yusuf, Y. Y., Musa, A., Abubakar, T., & Ambursa, H. M. (2012). Sustainable supply chain management: A case study of British Aerospace (BAe) Systems. *International Journal of Production Economics*, 140(1), 193–203. doi:10.1016/j.ijpe.2012.01.003

Gopika, M. (2017). Machine learning Approach of Chronic Kidney Disease Prediction using Clustering Technique. *International Journal of Innovative Research in Science, Engineering and Technology*, 6(7), 14488-14496.

Green, T. C., & Figlewski, S. (1999). Market risk and model risk for a financial institution writing options. *The Journal of Finance*, 54(4), 1465–1499. doi:10.1111/0022-1082.00152

Grogan, A. (2012). Smart farming. *Engineering & Technology*, 7(6), 38–40. doi:10.1049/et.2012.0601

Grublješič, T., & Jaklič, J. (2015). Conceptualization of the business intelligence extended use model. *Journal of Computer Information Systems*, 55(3), 72–82. doi:10.1080/08874417.2015.11645774

Guest, D., Michie, J., Conway, N., & Sheehan, M. (2003). Human Resource Management and Corporate Performance in UK. *British Journal of Industrial Relations*, 41(2), 291–314. doi:10.1111/1467-8543.00273

Gupta, B. B., Agrawal, D. P., Yamaguchi, S., & Sheng, M. (2020). *Soft computing techniques for big data and cloud computing*. Academic Press.

Gupta, P., Kanhere, S., & Jurdak, R. (2019). A Decentralized IoT Data Marketplace. *Networking and Internet Architecture*, 6(7), 1-6. arXiv:1906.01799

Gupta, R., Gupta, H., & Mohania, M. (2012). Cloud Computing and Big Data Analytics: What Is New from Databases Perspective? *LNCS, 7678*, 42–61.

Gupta, P., Sharma, A., & Jindal, R. (2016). Scalable machine-learning algorithms for big data analytics: A comprehensive review. *Wiley Interdisciplinary Reviews. Data Mining and Knowledge Discovery, 6*(6), 194–214. doi:10.1002/widm.1194

Gürcan, F., & Berigel, M. (2018, October). Real-Time Processing of Big Data Streams: Lifecycle, Tools, Tasks, and Challenges. In *2018 2nd International Symposium on Multidisciplinary Studies and Innovative Technologies (ISMSIT)* (pp. 1-6). IEEE.

Hadi, H.J., Shnain, A.H., Hadishaheed, S., & Ahmad, A.H. (2015). Big Data and Five V'S Characteristics. *International Journal of Advances in Electronics and Computer Science, 2*(1).

Haghi, M., Geissler, A., Fleischer, H., Stoll, N., & Thurow, K. (2019). Ubiqsense: A Personal Wearable in Ambient Parameters Monitoring Based on IoT Platform. In *Proceedings of International Conference on Sensing and Instrumentation in IoT Era (ISSI)*. IEEE. 10.1109/ISSI47111.2019.9043713

Halaweh, M., & Massry, A. E. (2015). Conceptual model for successful implementation of big data in organizations. *Journal of International Technology and Information Management, 24*(2), 2.

Halee, A., Javaid, M., & Khan, I. H. (2020). Internet of things (IoT) applications in dentistry. *Current Medicine Research and Practice, 10*(2), 80–81. doi:10.1016/j.cmrp.2020.03.005

Hamilton, B., Nickerson, J., & Owan, H. (2003). Team Incentives and Worker Heterogeneity: An Empirical Analysis of the Impact of Teams on Productivity and Participation. *Journal of Political Economy, 111*(3), 465–497. doi:10.1086/374182

Hamilton, J. D. (1994). *Time Series Analysis*. Princeton University Press. doi:10.1515/9780691218632

Han, J., Kamber, M., & Pei, J. (2011). *Data Mining: Concepts and Techniques*. Elsevier. https://www.kidney.org/atoz/content/about-chronic-kidney-disease

Hansen, B. E. (2001). The New Econometrics of Structural Change: Dating Breaks in U.S. Labor Productivity. *The Journal of Economic Perspectives, 15*(4), 117–128. doi:10.1257/jep.15.4.117

Hansen, G. D. (1985). Indivisible Labor and The Business Cycle. *Journal of Monetary Economics, 16*(3), 309–327. doi:10.1016/0304-3932(85)90039-X

Haroz, S., Kosara, R., & Franconeri, S. L. (2016). The Connected Scatterplot for Presenting Paired Time Series. *IEEE Transactions on Visualization and Computer Graphics, 22*(9), 2174–2186. doi:10.1109/TVCG.2015.2502587 PMID:26600062

Hashem, I. A. T., Yaqoob, I., Anuar, N. B., Mokhtar, S., Gani, A., & Ullah Khan, S. (2015). The rise of "big data" on cloud computing: Review and open research issues. *Information Systems, 47*, 98–115. doi:10.1016/j.is.2014.07.006

Hass, K. (2006). *The five deadly sins of project management*. https://www.powermag.com/the-five-deadly-sins-of-project-management/

Hassan, M. K., Desouky, A. I. E., Badawy, M. M., Sarhan, A. M., Elhoseny, M., & Gunasekaran, M. (2019). EoT-driven hybrid ambient assisted living framework with naive Bayes–firefly algorithm. *Springer Neural Computing and Applications, 31*(5), 1275–1300. doi:10.100700521-018-3533-y

Haykin, S. (2010). *Neural Networks and Learning Machines, 3/E*. Pearson Education India.

Heatmap. (2018). Retrieved from Optimizely: https://www.optimizely.com/optimization- glossary/heatmap/

Heide, J. B. (2003). Plural governance in industrial purchasing. *Journal of Marketing*, *67*(4), 18–29. doi:10.1509/jmkg.67.4.18.18689

Hendricks, K., & Singhal, V. (2005). Association Between Supply Chain Glitches and Operating Performance. *Management Science*, *51*(5), 695–711. doi:10.1287/mnsc.1040.0353

Hermawanto, D. (2013). *Genetic algorithm for solving simple mathematical equality problem*. arXiv preprint arXiv:1308.4675.

Herodotou, H. (2011). *Hadoop performance models*. arXiv preprint arXiv:1106.0940.

Hoffman, M., & Burks, S. V. (2017). *Training contracts, employee turnover, and the returns from firm-sponsored general training* (NBER Working Paper series No. 23247).

Hoque, A., & Lohse, G. L. (1999). An information search cost perspective for designing interfaces for electronic commerce. *JMR, Journal of Marketing Research*, *36*(3), 387–395. doi:10.1177/002224379903600307

Hori, M., Kawashima, E., & Yamazaki, T. (2010). Application of cloud computing to agriculture and prospects in other fields. *Fujitsu Scientific and Technical Journal*, *46*(4), 446–454.

Hou, L., Zhang, H., Wang, J., & Shi, D. (2019). Optimal Blood Glucose Prediction based on Intermittent Data from Wearable Glucose Monitoring Sensors. In *Proceedings of Chinese Control Conference (CCC)*. IEEE. 10.23919/ChiCC.2019.8866572

Huang, C., Wang, Y., Li, X., Ren, L., Zhao, J., Hu, Y., Zhang, L., Fan, G., Xu, J., Gu, X., Cheng, Z., Yu, T., Xia, J., Wei, Y., Wu, W., Xie, X., Yin, W., Li, H., Liu, M., ... Cao, B. (2020). Clinical features of patients infected with 2019 novel coronavirus in Wuhan, China. *Lancet*, *395*(10223), 497–506. doi:10.1016/S0140-6736(20)30183-5 PMID:31986264

Huang, Y., Chen, Z. X., Tao, Y. U., Huang, X. Z., & Gu, X. F. (2018). Agricultural remote sensing big data: Management and applications. *Journal of Integrative Agriculture*, *17*(9), 1915–1931.

Hu, H., Wen, Y., Chua, T. S., & Li, X. (2014). Toward scalable systems for big data analytics: A technology tutorial. *IEEE Access: Practical Innovations, Open Solutions*, *2*, 652–687. doi:10.1109/ACCESS.2014.2332453

Huselid, M. A., & Becker, B. E. (1997). *The impact of high performance work systems, implementation effectiveness, and alignment with strategy on shareholder wealth. Academy of Management Best Papers Proceedings*. doi:10.5465/ambpp.1997.4981101

Huselid, M., & Becker, B. (1996). High Performance Work Systems and Firm Performance: Cross-Sectional Versus Panel Estimates. *Industrial Relations*, 635–672.

Hussain, K. Z., Durairaj, M., & Farzana, G. R. (2012, March). Criminal behavior analysis by using data mining techniques. In *International Conference on Advances in Engineering, Science and Management (ICAESM)* (pp. 656-658). IEEE.

HussainT.SangaA.MongiaS. (2019). Big Data Hadoop Tools and Technologies: A Review. Available at SSRN 3462554. doi:10.2139srn.3462554

Ichniowski, C., Levine, D. I., Olson, C., & Strauss, G. (1996). What Works at Work: Overview and Assessment. *Industrial & Labor Relations Review*, *35*, 299–334.

Ichniowski, C., & Shaw, K. (forthcoming). Insider Econometrics: A Roadmap to Estimating Empirical Models of Organizational Performance. In R. Gibbons & J. Roberts (Eds.), *The Handbook of Organizational Economics*. Princeton University Press.

Ichniowski, C., Shaw, K., & Prennushi, G. (1997). The Effects of Human Resource Management Practices on Productivity: A Study of Steel Finishing Lines. *The American Economic Review, 87*, 291–313.

Iqbal, R., Doctor, F., More, B., Mahmud, S., & Yousuf, U. (2020). Big Data analytics and Computational Intelligence for Cyber–Physical Systems: Recent trends and state of the art applications. *Future Generation Computer Systems, 105*, 766–778. doi:10.1016/j.future.2017.10.021

Islam, A., & Shin, S. Y. (2020). A blockchain-based secure healthcare scheme with the assistance of unmanned aerial vehicle in Internet of Things. *Computers & Electrical Engineering, 84*, 106627. Advance online publication. doi:10.1016/j.compeleceng.2020.106627

Islam, M., & Reza, M. (2019). The Rise of Big Data and Cloud Computing. *Internet of Things and Cloud Computing., 7*(2), 45–53. doi:10.11648/j.iotcc.20190702.12

Jabbar, A., & Shirina, S. (2016). Heart disease prediction system based on hidden naïve Bayes classifier. *IC4, 4*(11), 23-48.

Jacome, D. S., Lacalle, I., Palau, C. E., & Esteve, M. (2019). Efficient Deployment of Predictive Analytics in Edge Gateways: Fall Detection Scenario. In *Proceedings of the 5th World Forum on Internet of Things (WF-IoT)*. IEEE.

Jadhav, Kelkar, Patil, & Thorat. (2016). Smart Traffic Control System Using Image Processing. *International Research Journal of Engineering and Technology, 3*(3).

Jaiswal, A., Dwivedi, V., & Yadav, O. (2020). Big Data and its Analyzing Tools: A Perspective. *6th International Conference on Advanced Computing and Communication Systems (ICACCS)*, 560-565, 10.1109/ICACCS48705.2020.9074222

Javaid, N., Sher, A., Nasir, H., & Guizani, N. (2018). Intelligence in IoT-based 5G networks: Opportunities and challenges. *IEEE Communications Magazine, 56*(10), 94–100. doi:10.1109/MCOM.2018.1800036

Jayaraman, P. P., Yavari, A., Georgakopoulos, D., Morshed, A., & Zaslavsky, A. (2016). Internet of things platform for smart farming: Experiences and lessons learnt. *Sensors (Basel), 16*(11), 1884. doi:10.339016111884 PMID:27834862

Jayashree, K., & Abirami, R. (2018). Big Data Technologies and Management Innovative in Applications of Knowledge Discovery and Information Resources Management. IGI Global Publisher.

Jayashree, K., Abirami, R., & Babu, R. (2018). A Collaborative Approach of IoT, Big Data, and Smart City in Big Data analytics for Smart and Connected Cities. IGI Global Publisher.

Jebadurai, J., & Peter, J. D. (2018). Super-resolution of retinal images using multi-kernel SVR for IoT healthcare applications. *Future Generation Computer Systems, 83*, 338–346. doi:10.1016/j.future.2018.01.058

Jensen, D., Konkel, K., Mohindra, A., Naccarati, F., & Sam, E. (2012). *Business Analytics in the Cloud*. White paper IBW03004-USEN-00, IBM.

Jeong, Y. S., Hassan, H., & Sangaiah, A. K. (2019). Machine learning on big data for future computing. *The Journal of Supercomputing, 75*(6), 2925–2929. doi:10.100711227-019-02872-z

Jesi, G., Gori, E., Micocci, S., & Mazzini, G. (2019). Building Lepida ScpA BigData Infrastructure. *Big Data, Knowledge and Control Systems Engineering (BdKCSE)*, 1-9, . doi:10.1109/BdKCSE48644.2019.9010604

Jha, S., & Topol, E. J. (2016, December 13). Adapting to artificial intelligence: Radiologists and pathologists as information specialists. *Journal of the American Medical Association, 316*(22), 2353–2354. doi:10.1001/jama.2016.17438 PMID:27898975

Jin, J., Ma, X., Koskinen, K., Rychlik, M., & Kosonen, I. (2016). Evaluation of fuzzy intelligent traffic signal control (FITS) system using traffic simulation. In *Transportation Research Board 95th Annual Meeting, Finland* (p. 11). Academic Press.

John, B. (1990). Benefit segmentation for fund raisers. *Journal of the Academy of Marketing Science, 18*(1), 77–86. doi:10.1007/BF02729764

Juels, A., Burton, J., & Kaliski, S. (2007). Pors: Proofs of retrievability for large files. *Proc. of CCS'07*, 584–597.

Juhn, Y., & Liu, H. (2020). Artificial intelligence approaches using natural language processing to advance EHR-based clinical research. *The Journal of Allergy and Clinical Immunology, 145*(2), 463–469. doi:10.1016/j.jaci.2019.12.897 PMID:31883846

Kaelbling, L. P., Littman, M. L., & Moore, A. W. (1996). Reinforcement learning: A survey. *Journal of Artificial Intelligence Research, 4*, 237–285. doi:10.1613/jair.301

Kaisler, S., Armour, F., Espinosa, J. A., & Money, W. (2013, January). Big data: Issues and challenges moving forward. In *2013 46th Hawaii International Conference on System Sciences* (pp. 995-1004). IEEE.

Kamilaris, A., Kartakoullis, A., & Prenafeta-Boldú, F. X. (2017). A review on the practice of big data analysis in agriculture. *Computers and Electronics in Agriculture, 143*, 23–37. doi:10.1016/j.compag.2017.09.037

Kaneriya, S., Vora, J., Tanwar, S., & Tyagi, S. (2019). Standardising the use of Duplex Channels in 5G-WiFi Networking for Ambient Assisted Living. In *Proceedings of International Conference on Communications Workshops*. IEEE. 10.1109/ICCW.2019.8757145

Kan, G. E. R. A. R. D., Visser, C. A., Koolen, J. J., & Dunning, A. J. (1986). Short and long term predictive value of admission wall motion score in acute myocardial infarction. A cross sectional echocardiographic study of 345 patients. *Heart (British Cardiac Society), 56*(5), 422–427. doi:10.1136/hrt.56.5.422 PMID:3790378

Kapoor, A. (2018, June 9). *Real world applications of big data in healthcare.* Retrieved June 22, 2020, from https://medium.com/the-research-nest/real-world-applications-of-big-data-in-healthcare-5c84696fd3d4

Karatsiolis, S., & Schizas, C. N. (2012, November). Region based Support Vector Machine algorithm for medical diagnosis on Pima Indian Diabetes dataset. In *2012 IEEE 12th International Conference on Bioinformatics & Bioengineering (BIBE)* (pp. 139-144). IEEE. 10.1109/BIBE.2012.6399663

Karthick, G. S., & Pankajavalli, P. B. (2020). Architecting IoT based Healthcare Systems Using Machine Learning Algorithms: Cloud-Oriented Healthcare Model, Streaming Data Analytics Architecture, and Case Study. In *Incorporating the Internet of Things in Healthcare Applications and Wearable Devices* (pp. 40–66). IGI Global. doi:10.4018/978-1-7998-1090-2.ch003

Kassebaum, N.J., Arora, M., Barber, R.M., Bhutta, Z.A., Brown, J., & Carter, A. (2015). GBD 2015 DALYs and HALE Collaborators. Global, regional, and national disability-adjusted life-years (DALYs) for 315 diseases and injuries and healthy life expectancy (HALE), 1990-2015: a systematic analysis for the Global Burden of Disease Study 2015. *Lancet, 388*(10053), 1603–58. doi:10.1016/S0140-6736(16)31460-X

Kaur, D., & Jyoti, K. (2013). Enhancement in the Performance of K-means Algorithm. *International Journal of Computer Science and Communication Engineering, 2*(1), 29–32.

Kawaji, S. (2002). Hybrid soft computing approaches to identification of nonlinear systems. *IFAC Proceedings Volumes, 35*(1), 187-192.

Keller, R., Eckert, C. M., & Clarkson, P. J. (2006). Matrices or node-link diagrams: Which visual representation is better for visualising connectivity models? *Information Visualization, 5*(1), 62–76. doi:10.1057/palgrave.ivs.9500116

Kent, J. (2020, September 14). *How Big Data Analytics Models can impact Healthcare Decision-Making.* Retrieved September 20, 2020, from https://healthitanalytics.com/news/how-big-data-analytics-models-can-impact-healthcare-decision-making

Keum, S. S., Park, Y. J., & Kang, S. J. (2020). Edge Computing-Based Self-Organized Device Network for Awareness Activities of Daily Living in the Home. *MDPI Applied Sciences - Software Approaches to Improve the Performance of IoT Systems, 10*(7), 2475.

Khalid, Z., Fisal, N., Zubair, S., Ullah, R., Safdar, H., Maqbool, W., & Khalid, U. (2015). Multi-Thread based Middleware for Sensor Network Virtualization. In *Proceedings of the 5th National Symposium on Information Technology: Towards New Smart World (NSITNSW).* IEEE. 10.1109/NSITNSW.2015.7176421

Khan, I., Naqvi, S. K., Alam, M., & Rizvi, S. N. A. (2015). Data model for Big Data in cloud environment. *Computing for Sustainable Global Development (INDIACom), 2nd International Conference,* 582 – 585.

Khan, M. A., Fahim Uddin, M., & Gupta, N. (2014). Seven V's of Big Data. *Proceedings of 2014 Zone 1 Conference of the American Society for Engineering Education (ASEE Zone 1),* 3-5.

Khan, R., Khan, S. U., Zaheer, R., & Khan, S. (2012, December). Future internet: the internet of things architecture, possible applications and key challenges. In *2012 10th international conference on frontiers of information technology* (pp. 257-260). IEEE. 10.1109/FIT.2012.53

Khan, O. F., Bebb, G., & Alimohamed, N. A. (2017). What oncologists need to know about its potential and its limitations. *Artificial Intelligence in Medicine, 16*(4).

Khan, Z., Anjum, A., Soomro, K., & Tahir, M. A. (2015). Towards cloud based big data analytics for smart future cities. *Journal of Cloud Computing, 4*(1), 1–11.

Khobragade, P. K., & Malik, L. G. (2014, April). Data generation and analysis for digital forensic application using data mining. In *Fourth International Conference on Communication Systems and Network Technologies* (pp. 458-462). IEEE. 10.1109/CSNT.2014.97

Khowaja, S. A., Prabono, A. G., Setiawan, F., Yahya, B. N., & Lee, S.-L. (2018). Contextual activity based Healthcare Internet of Things, Services, and People (HIoTSP): An architectural framework for healthcare monitoring using wearable sensors. *Computer Networks, 145,* 190–206. doi:10.1016/j.comnet.2018.09.003

Kim, G. H., Trimi, S., & Chung, J. H. (2014). Big-data applications in the government sector. *Communications of the ACM, 57*(3), 78–85.

Kim, S., & Kim, S. (2018). User preference for an IoT healthcare application for lifestyle disease management. *Telecommunications Policy, 42*(4), 304–314. doi:10.1016/j.telpol.2017.03.006

Kiran, J. S., Sravanthi, M., Preethi, K., & Anusha, M. (2015). Recent Issues and Challenges on Big Data in Cloud Computing. IJCST, 6(2).

Kirk, A. (2016). *Data visualisation: a handbook for data driven design.* Academic Press.

Kirushnacumar, A., Arun, M., Kirubanand, A., Mukesh, S., & Sivakumar, A. (2016). Smart Traffic Control System. *International Journal for Research in Applied Science & Engineering Technology, 4*(4).

Kitchin, R. (2014). The data revolution: Big data, open data, data infrastructures and their consequences. *Sage (Atlanta, Ga.).* Advance online publication. doi:10.4135/9781473909472

Knaflic, C. N. (2015). *Storytelling with data: A data visualization guide for business professionals.* Academic Press.

Kothari, S. P. (2001). Capital Markets Research in Accounting. *Journal of Accounting and Economics, 31*(1-3), 105–231. doi:10.1016/S0165-4101(01)00030-1

Kotler, P. (2000). *Marketing Management*. Prentice-Hall.

Kotturu, P., Sasank, V. V. S., Supriya, G., Manoj, C. S., & Maheshwarredy, M. V. (2019). Prediction of chronic kidney disease using machine learning techniques. *International Journal of Advanced Science and Technology, 28*(16), 1436–1443.

Kumar & Goudar. (2012). Cloud Computing – Research Issues, Challenges, Architecture. *Platforms and Applications: A Survey International Journal of Future Computer and Communication, 1*(4), 356-360.

Kumar, M., Punia, S., Thompson, S., Gopal, D., & Patan, R. (2020). Performance Analysis of Machine Learning Algorithms for Big Data Classification. *International Journal of E-Health and Medical Communications, 12*(4).

Kumar, P. M., Lokesh, S., Varatharajan, R., Babu, G. C., & Parthasarathy, P. (2018). Cloud and IoT based disease prediction and diagnosis system for healthcare using Fuzzy neural classifier. *Future Generation Computer Systems, 86*, 527–534. doi:10.1016/j.future.2018.04.036

Kune, R., Konugurthi, P. K., Agarwal, A., Chillarige, R. R., & Buyya, R. (2016). The anatomy of big data computing Journal of Software. *Practice and Experience, 46*(1), 79–105. doi:10.1002pe.2374

Kurgan, L. A., Cios, K. J., Tadeusiewicz, R., Ogiela, M., & Goodenday, L. S. (2001). Knowledge discovery approach to automated cardiac SPECT diagnosis. *Artificial Intelligence in Medicine, 23*(2), 149–169. doi:10.1016/S0933-3657(01)00082-3 PMID:11583923

Kydland, F., & Prescott, E. (1982). Time to build and aggregate Fluctuations. *Econometrica, 50*(6), 173–208. doi:10.2307/1913386

L'heureux, A., Grolinger, K., Elyamany, H. F., & Capretz, M. A. (2017). Machine learning with big data: Challenges and approaches. *IEEE Access: Practical Innovations, Open Solutions, 5*, 7776–7797. doi:10.1109/ACCESS.2017.2696365

Laaksonen, J., & Oja, E. (1996, June). Classification with learning k-nearest neighbors. In *Proceedings of International Conference on Neural Networks (ICNN'96)* (Vol. 3, pp. 1480-1483). IEEE. 10.1109/ICNN.1996.549118

Labonnote, N., & Høyland, K. (2015). Smart home technologies that support independent living: Challenges and opportunities for the building industry – a systematic mapping study. *Taylor & Francis Intelligent Buildings International, 9*(1), 40–63. doi:10.1080/17508975.2015.1048767

Lai, R. (2005). *Inventory and the Stock Market*. Working paper, Harvard University.

Lai, R. (2006a). *The Geography of Retail Inventory*. Working paper, Harvard University.

Lai, R. (2006b). *Does public infrastructure reduce private inventory?* Working paper, Harvard University.

Lakonishok, J., & Shapiro, A. C. (1986). Systematic risk, total risk and size as determinants of stock market returns. *Journal of Banking & Finance, 10*(1), 115–132. doi:10.1016/0378-4266(86)90023-3

Lal, R., & Padmanabhan, V. (1995). Competitive Response and Equilibria. *Marketing Science, 14*(3), G101–G108. doi:10.1287/mksc.14.3.G101

Lam, C. (2010). *Hadoop in action*. Manning Publications Co.

Laney, D. (2012). *The importance of 'Big Data': A Definition*. Gartner.

Latha, R., & Vetrivelan, P. (2019). Blood Viscosity based Heart Disease Risk Prediction Model in Edge/Fog Computing. In *11th International Conference on Communication Systems & Networks (COMSNETS)* (pp. 833-837). IEEE. 10.1109/COMSNETS.2019.8711358

LaValle, S., Lesser, E., Shockley, R., Hopkins, M. S., & Kruschwitz, N. (2011). Big data, analytics and the path from insights to value. *MIT Sloan Management Review*, *52*(2), 21–32.

Lazear, E. P. (2000). Performance Pay and Productivity. *The American Economic Review*, *5*(5), 1346–1361. doi:10.1257/aer.90.5.1346

Lee, A. Y. (2002). Effects of implicit memory on memory-based versus stimulus-based brand choice. *JMR, Journal of Marketing Research*, *39*(4), 440–455. doi:10.1509/jmkr.39.4.440.19119

Lee, G., Chun, B.-G., & Katz, R. H. (2011). Heterogeneity-Aware Resource Allocation and Scheduling in the Cloud. In *Proceedings of the 3rd USENIX conference on Hot topics in Cloud computing (HotCloud 2011)*. USENIX Association.

Lescure, F. X., Bouadma, L., Parisey, D. N. M., Wicky, P. H., Behillil, S., Gaymard, A., Duchamp, M. B., Donati, F., Hingrat, Q. L., Enouf, V., Houhou-Fidouh, N., Valette, M., Mailles, A., Lucet, J. C., Mentre, F., Duval, X., Descamps, D., Malvy, D., Timsit, J. F., ... Yazdanpanah, Y. (2020). Clinical and virological data of the first cases of COVID-19 in Europe: A case series. *THE LANCET Infectious Diseases*, *20*(6), 697–706. doi:10.1016/S1473-3099(20)30200-0 PMID:32224310

Levin, A., Tonelli, M., Bonventre, J., Coresh, J., Donner, J. A., Fogo, A. B., Fox, C. S., Gansevoort, R. T., Heerspink, H. J. L., Jardine, M., Kasiske, B., Köttgen, A., Kretzler, M., Levey, A. S., Luyckx, V. A., Mehta, R., Moe, O., Obrador, G., Pannu, N., ... Yang, C.-W. (2017, October 21). ISN Global Kidney Health Summit participants. Global kidney health 2017 and beyond: A roadmap for closing gaps in care, research, and policy. *Lancet*, *390*(10105), 1888–1917. doi:10.1016/S0140-6736(17)30788-2 PMID:28434650

Lieberman, M. B., & Demeester, L. (1999). Inventory Reduction and Productivity Growth: Linkages in the Japanese Automotive Industry. *Management Science*, *45*(4), 466–476. doi:10.1287/mnsc.45.4.466

Lieberman, M. B., Helper, S., & Demeester, L. (1999). The Empirical Determinants of Inventory Levels in High-Volume Manufacturing. *Production and Operations Management*, *8*(1), 44–55. doi:10.1111/j.1937-5956.1999.tb00060.x

Li, M., Weng, J., Yang, A., Lu, W., Zhang, Y., Hou, L., Liu, J.-N., Xiang, Y., & De Robert, H. (2019). CrowdBC: A Blockchain-Based Decentralized Framework for Crowdsourcing. *IEEE Transactions on Parallel and Distributed Systems*, *30*(6), 1251–1266. doi:10.1109/TPDS.2018.2881735

Lintner, J. (1965). The Valuation of Risky Assets and the Selection of Risky Investments in Stock Portfolios and Capital Budgets. *The Review of Economics and Statistics*, *47*(1), 13–37. doi:10.2307/1924119

Little, M. A., McSharry, P. E., Roberts, S. J., Costello, D. A., & Moroz, I. M. (2007). Exploiting nonlinear recurrence and fractal scaling properties for voice disorder detection. *Biomedical Engineering Online*, *6*(1), 23. doi:10.1186/1475-925X-6-23 PMID:17594480

Liu, C., Ranjan, R., Zhang, X., Yang, C., Georgakopoulos, D., & Chen, J. (2013, December). Public auditing for big data storage in cloud computing--a survey. In *2013 IEEE 16th International Conference on Computational Science and Engineering* (pp. 1128-1135). IEEE.

Liu, K., Qiu, X., Chen, W., Chen, X., & Zheng, Z. (2019). Optimal pricing mechanism for data market in blockchain-enhanced Internet of things. *IEEE Internet of Things Journal*, *6*(6), 9748–9761. doi:10.1109/JIOT.2019.2931370

Liyanage, T., Ninomiya, T., Jha, V., Neal, B., Patrice, H. M., Okpechi, I., Zhao, M., Lv, J., Garg, A. X., Knight, J., Rodgers, A., Gallagher, M., Kotwal, S., Cass, A., & Perkovic, V. (2015, May 16). Worldwide access to treatment for end-stage kidney disease: A systematic review. *Lancet, 385*(9981), 1975–1982. doi:10.1016/S0140-6736(14)61601-9 PMID:25777665

Lopez-de-Ipina, D., Blanco, S., Diaz-de-Sarralde, I., & Laiseca, X. (2010). A Platform for a More Widespread Adoption of AAL. *Aging Friendly Technology for Health and Independence, 6159*, 250–253. doi:10.1007/978-3-642-13778-5_35

Louis, E. (1995). *Contemporary Marketing*. Dryden Press.

Lu, C. W., Hsieh, C. M., Chang, C. H., & Yang, C. T. (2013, July). An improvement to data service in cloud computing with content sensitive transaction analysis and adaptation. In *2013 IEEE 37th Annual Computer Software and Applications Conference Workshops* (pp. 463-468). IEEE.

Made Easy, D. N. S. (2017, December 13). Retrieved from Ultimate Guide to DNS Analytics: https://social.dnsmadeeasy.com/blog/ultimate-guide-dns-analytics/

Mahmoud, M. M. E., Rodrigues, J. J. P. C., Kashif Saleem, K., Al-Muhtadi, J., Kumar, N., & Korotaev, V. (2018). Towards energy-aware fog-enabled cloud of things for healthcare. *Computers & Electrical Engineering, 67*, 58–69. doi:10.1016/j.compeleceng.2018.02.047

Malik, H., Alam, M. M., Moullec, Y. L., & Kuusik, A. (2018). NarrowBand-IoT Performance Analysis for Healthcare Applications. *Procedia Computer Science, 130*, 1077–1083. doi:10.1016/j.procs.2018.04.156

Mane, T. U. (2017, Feburary). Smart heart disease prediction system using Improved K-means and ID3 on big data. In *International Conference on Data Management, Analytics and Innovation (ICDMAI)* (pp. 239-245). IEEE.

Mani, N., Singh, A., & Nimmagadda, S. L. (2020). An IoT Guided Healthcare Monitoring System for Managing Real- Time Notifications by Fog Computing Services. *Procedia Computer Science, 167*, 850–859. doi:10.1016/j.procs.2020.03.424

Manogaran, G., Thota, C., & Kumar, M. V. (2016). MetaCloudDataStorage Architecture for Big Data Security in Cloud Computing. *Procedia Computer Science, 87*, 128–133. doi:10.1016/j.procs.2016.05.138

Mantelero, A. (2019). *Artificial Intelligence and Data Protection: Challenges and Possible Remedies*. EU Directorate General of Human Rights and Rule of Law.

Market Research Future. (2018, April). *Global Ambient Assisted Living Market Research Report, by System (Entertainment, Communication, Medical Assistance, Transportation), Sensor (Temperature, Occupancy), Service (Installation & Repair) – Forecast till 2027* (ID: MRFR/SEM/0509-CR). Retrieved from https://www.marketresearchfuture.com/reports/ambient-assisted-living-market-1015

Martikainen, T., & Ankelo, T. (1991). On the instability of financial patterns of failed firms and the predictability of corporate failure. *Economics Letters, 35*(2), 209–214. doi:10.1016/0165-1765(91)90171-G

Mayer, V. V., & Cukier, K. (2013). *Big Data: A Revolution That Will Transform How We Live, Work and Think*. John Murray Press.

McAfee, A., Brynjolfsson, E., Davenport, T. H., Patil, D. J., & Barton, D. (2012). Big data: The management revolution. *Harvard Business Review, 90*(10), 60–68. PMID:23074865

Mehra, N., Aggarwal, S., Shokeen, A., & Bura, D. (2018). Analyzing Cloud Computing Security Issues and Challenges. In *Progress in Computing, Analytics and Networking* (pp. 193–202). Springer.

Mehta, N., & Panditb, A. (2018). Concurrence of big data analytics and healthcare: A systematic review. *International Journal of Medical Informatics*.

Mehta, R. L., Cerdá, J., Burdmann, E. A., Tonelli, M., García-García, G., Jha, V., Susantitaphong, P., Rocco, M., Vanholder, R., Sever, M. S., Cruz, D., Jaber, B., Lameire, N. H., Lombardi, R., Lewington, A., Feehally, J., Finkelstein, F., Levin, N., Pannu, N., ... Remuzzi, G. (2015, June 27). International Society of Nephrology's 0by25 initiative for acute kidney injury (zero preventable deaths by 2025): A human rights case for nephrology. *Lancet, 385*(9987), 2616–2643. doi:10.1016/S0140-6736(15)60126-X PMID:25777661

Mei, Xia, Li, & Xie. (2017). *Developing Knowledge-enhanced Chronic Disease Risk Prediction Models from Regional EHR Repositories*. Academic Press.

Meier, A., Schindler, G., & Werro, N. (2008). Fuzzy classification on relational databases. In *Handbook of research on fuzzy information processing in databases* (pp. 586–614). IGI Global.

Melo, J., Naftel, A., Bernardino, A., & Santos-Victor, J. (2006). Detection and classification of highway lanes using vehicle motion trajectories. *IEEE Transactions on Intelligent Transportation Systems, 7*(2), 188–200. doi:10.1109/TITS.2006.874706

Michalski, R. S., Mozetic, I., Hong, J., & Lavrac, N. (1986). The multi-purpose incremental learning system AQ15 and its testing application to three medical domains. *Proc. AAAI 1986*, 1-041.

Microsoft, S. Q. L. Server. (2018, October 18). Retrieved from Wikipedia: https://en.wikipedia.org/wiki/Microsoft_SQL_Server

Miner, A. S. (2002). Efficient solution of GSPNs using canonical matrix diagrams. *Proceedings 9th International Workshop on Petri Nets and Performance Models*, 101–110. 10.1109/PNPM.2001.953360

Missier, P., Bajoudah, S., Capossele, A., Gaglione, A., & Nati, M. (2017). Mind my value. *Proceedings of the Seventh International Conference on the Internet of Things*. 10.1145/3131542.3131564

Mitchell, T. M. (1999). Machine learning and data mining. *Communications of the ACM, 42*(11), 30–36. doi:10.1145/319382.319388

Mohammadi, M., Al-Fuqaha, A., Sorour, S., & Guizani, M. (2018). Deep learning for IoT big data and streaming analytics: A survey. *IEEE Communications Surveys and Tutorials, 20*(4), 2923–2960. doi:10.1109/COMST.2018.2844341

Moka, J. A. (2017). *Big Data Analysis*. Retrieved from Data Science Central: https://www.datasciencecentral.com/profiles/blogs/big-data-analysis

MongoD. B. (2018, October 18). Retrieved from Wikipedia: https://en.wikipedia.org/wiki/MongoDB

Moosavi, S. R., Nigussie, E., Levorato, M., Virtanen, S., & Isoaho, J. (2018). Performance Analysis of End-to-End Security Schemes in Healthcare IoT. *Procedia Computer Science, 130*, 432–439. doi:10.1016/j.procs.2018.04.064

Moro, S., Cortez, P., & Rita, P. (2014). A data-driven approach to predict the success of bank telemarketing. *Decision Support Systems, 62*, 22–31.

Müller, R., & Jugdev, K. (2012). Critical success factors in projects: Pinto, Slevin, and Prescott–the elucidation of project success. *International Journal of Managing Projects in Business, 5*(4), 757–775. doi:10.1108/17538371211269040

Mun, M., Hao, S., Mishra, N., Shilton, K., Burke, J., Estrin, D., Hansen, M., & Govindan, R. (2010). Personal data vaults. *Proceedings of the 6th International Conference on - Co-NEXT '10*. 10.1145/1921168.1921191

Murray, S. (2017). Interactive Data Visualization for the Web. O'Reilly, Canada. doi:10.1017/CBO9781107415324.004

Murray, C. J., Barber, R. M., Foreman, K. J., Abbasoglu Ozgoren, A., Abd-Allah, F., & Abera, S. F. (2015, November 28). GBD 2013 DALYs and HALE Collaborators. Global, regional, and national disability-adjusted life years (DALYs) for 306 diseases and injuries and healthy life expectancy (HALE) for 188 countries, 1990-2013: Quantifying the epidemiological transition. *Lancet*, *386*(10009), 2145–2191. doi:10.1016/S0140-6736(15)61340-X PMID:26321261

Naeini, E. K., Iman Azimi, I., Rahmani, A. M., Liljeberg, P., & Dutt, N. (2019). A Real-time PPG Quality Assessment Approach for Healthcare Internet-of-Things. *Procedia Computer Science*, *151*, 551–558. doi:10.1016/j.procs.2019.04.074

Nagaraju, C., & Varun, B. (2020). A Generic Real Time Application for CKD Prediction Using Machine Learning. *International Research Journal of Engineering and Technology*, *7*(8), 2578-2585

Naghavi, M., Abajobir, A. A., Abbafati, C., Abbas, K. M., Abd-Allah, F., Abera, S. F., Aboyans, V., Adetokunboh, O., Afshin, A., Agrawal, A., Ahmadi, A., Ahmed, M. B., Aichour, A. N., Aichour, M. T. E., Aichour, I., Aiyar, S., Alahdab, F., Al-Aly, Z., Alam, K., ... Murray, C. J. L. (2017, September 16). GBD 2016 Causes of Death Collaborators. Global, regional, and national age-sex specific mortality for 264 causes of death, 1980-2016: A systematic analysis for the Global Burden of Disease Study 2016. *Lancet*, *390*(10100), 1151–1210. doi:10.1016/S0140-6736(17)32152-9 PMID:28919116

Nahar, J., Imam, T., Tickle, K. S., & Chen, Y. P. (2013). Association rule mining to detect factors which contribute to heart disease in males and females. *Expert Systems with Applications*, *40*(4), 1086–1093. doi:10.1016/j.eswa.2012.08.028

Naik, P. A., Mantrala, M. K., & Sawyer, A. (1998). Planning Pulsing Media Schedules in the Presence of Dynamic Advertising Quality. *Marketing Science*, *17*(3), 214–235. doi:10.1287/mksc.17.3.214

Narayan, S., & Tan, H. C. (2019). Adopting Big Data to Forecast Success of Construction Projects: A Review. *Malaysian Construction Research Journal*, 132.

Nasr, E. B. (2004). An integrated project planning and control system approach for measuring project performance. *Dissertation Abstracts International*, *66*(03).

Nasrullah, P. (2020). *Internet of things in healthcare: applications, benefits, and challenges*. https://www.peerbits.com/blog/internet-of-things-healthcare-applications-benefits-and-challenges.html

Nawaz, T., Rinner, B., & Ferryman, J. (2016). User-centric, embedded vision-based human monitoring: A concept and a healthcare use case. In *Proceedings of the 10th International Conference on Distributed Smart Camera ICDSC '16*. Association for Computing Machinery. 10.1145/2967413.2967422

Nawsher, K. I. Y. (2014). Big Data: Survey, Technologies, Opportunities, and Challenges. *TheScientificWorldJournal*, 1–18. PMID:25136682

Neves, Schmerl, Camara, & Bernardino. (2016). Big Data in Cloud Computing: Features and Issues. *Proceedings of the International Conference on Internet of Things and Big Data*, 1, 307-314. 10.5220/0005846303070314

Niehaus & Clifto. (2016). Machine learning for chronic disease. doi:10.1049/PBHE002E,Chapter

Nikoloudakis, Y., Markakis, E., Mastorakis, G., Pallis, E., & Skianis, C. (2017). An NFV-Powered Emergency System for Smart Enhanced Living Environment. In *Proceedings of Conference on Network Function Virtualization and Software Defined Networks (NFV-SDN)*. IEEE.

Nikoloudakis, Y., Panagiotakis, S., Markakis, E., Pallis, E., Mastorakis, G., Mavromoustakis, C. X., & Dobre, C. (2016). A Fog-Based Emergency System for Smart Enhanced Living Environments. *IEEE Cloud Computing*, *3*(6), 54–62. doi:10.1109/MCC.2016.118

Nixon, P., Harrington, M., & Parker, D. (2012). Leadership performance is significant to project success or failure: A critical analysis. *International Journal of Productivity and Performance Management, 61*(2), 204–216. doi:10.1108/17410401211194699

Noble, W. S. (2006). What is a support vector machine? *Nature Biotechnology, 24*(12), 1565–1567. doi:10.1038/nbt1206-1565 PMID:17160063

Nord, J. H., Koohang, A., & Paliszkiewicz, J. (2019). The Internet of Things: Review and theoretical framework. *Expert Systems with Applications, 133*, 97–108. doi:10.1016/j.eswa.2019.05.014

NPTEL. (2020, May 18). Live_Covid 19: A Clinician's Perspective. *NPTEL Live Streaming.* https://www.youtube.com/watch?v=8ZUXSXFYEk4&t=4431s

Nuffield Council on Bioethics. (2018). *Artificial intelligence (AI) in healthcare and research.* Bioethics briefing note, Nuffield Council on Bioethics.

Nusrat, S., & Kobourov, S. (2016). The State of the Art in Cartograms The State of the Art in Cartograms. *Computer Graphics Forum, 35*(3), 1–24. doi:10.1111/cgf.12932

Obloj, T., & Frank, D. H. (2014). Firm-specific human capital, organizational incentives, and agency costs: Evidence from retail banking. *Strategic Management Journal, 35*(9), 1279–1301. doi:10.1002mj.2148

Ohlhorst, F. J. (2012). *Big data analytics: turning big data into big money* (Vol. 65). John Wiley & Sons. doi:10.1002/9781119205005

Ohtsuka, S., Usami, T., & Sasaki, N. (2014). A vibration watch using a smart phone for visually impaired people. In *Proceedings of the 3rd Global Conference on Consumer Electronics (GCCE).* IEEE. 10.1109/GCCE.2014.7031094

Omar, T., Bovard, D., & Tran, H. (2020, April). Smart Cities Traffic Congestion Monitoring and Control System. In *Proceedings of the 2020 ACM Southeast Conference* (pp. 115-121). Academic Press.

Omolaye, P. O., Mom, J. M., & Igwue, G. A. (2017). A Holistic Review of Soft Computing Techniques. *Applied and Computational Mathematics, 6*(2), 93.

Östermark, R. (1989). Predictability of Finnish and Swedish stock returns. *Omega, 17*(3), 223–236. doi:10.1016/0305-0483(89)90028-5

Owais, S. S., & Hussein, N. S. (2016). Extract Five Categories CPIVW from the 9V's Characteristics of the Big Data. *International Journal of Advanced Computer Science & Applications, 1*(7), 254–258.

Oyelade, O. J., Oladipupo, O. O., & Obagbuwa, I. C. (2010, January). Application of k Means Clustering algorithm for prediction of Students Academic Performance. *International Journal of Computer Science and Information Security, 7*(1), 292–295.

Padberg, F., & Tichy, W. (2007). Lean production methods in modern software development. *Business Info, 49*(3), 162–170.

Padmanaban, K. A., & Parthiban, G. (2016). Applying Machine Learning Techniques for Predicting the Risk of Chronic Kidney Disease. *Indian Journal of Science and Technology, 9*(29), 1–5. doi:10.17485/ijst/2016/v9i29/93880

Padmavathi, S., & Ramanujam, E. (2015). Naïve Bayes classifier for ECG abnormalities using multivariate maximal time series Motif. *Procedia Computer Science, 47*, 222–228. doi:10.1016/j.procs.2015.03.201

Pahwa, K., & Kumar, R. (2017, October). Prediction of heart disease using hybrid technique for selecting features. In *4th IEEE Uttar Pradesh Section International Conference on Electrical, Computer and Electronics (UPCON)* (pp. 500-504). IEEE. 10.1109/UPCON.2017.8251100

Pajouh, H. H., Dehghantanha, A., & Parizi, R. M. (2019). A survey on internet of things security: Requirements, challenges, and solutions. *Internet of Things*. doi:10.1016/j.iot.2019.100129

Palaniappan, S., & Awang, R. (2008, March). Intelligent heart disease prediction system using data mining techniques. In *International conference on computer systems and applications* (pp. 108-115). IEEE. 10.1109/AICCSA.2008.4493524

Palanisamy, V., & Thirunavukarasu, R. (2017). *Implications of big data analytics in developing healthcare frameworks – A review*. School of Information Technology and Engineering.

Pandit, Doshi, Mehta, Mhatre, & Janardhan. (2014). Smart Traffic Control System Using Image Processing. *International Journal of Emerging Trends & Technology in Computer Science*.

Pang, J. Z., Fu, H., Lee, W. I., & Wierman, A. (2017). The efficiency of open access in platforms for networked cournot markets. *IEEE INFOCOM 2017 - IEEE Conference on Computer Communications*. doi:10.1109/infocom.2017.8057125

Pappaa, S., Ntellac, V., Giannakasc, T., Giannakoulisc, V. G., Papoutsic, E., & Katsaounou, P. (2020). Prevalence of depression, anxiety, and insomnia among healthcare workers during the COVID-19 pandemic: A systematic review and meta-analysis. *Elsevier Brain, Behavior, and Immunity, 88*, 901–907. doi:10.1016/j.bbi.2020.05.026 PMID:32437915

Parthiban, L., & Subramanian, R. (2008). Intelligent heart disease prediction system using CANFIS and genetic algorithm. *International Journal of Biological, Biomedical and Medical Sciences, 3*(3).

Parwez, M. S., Rawat, D. B., & Garuba, M. (2017). Big data analytics for user-activity analysis and user-anomaly detection in mobile wireless network. *IEEE Transactions on Industrial Informatics, 13*(4), 2058–2065. doi:10.1109/TII.2017.2650206

Patel, S., Patel, A. (2016). A Big Data Revolution in Healthcare sector: Opportunities, Challenges & Technological Advancements. *International Journal of Information Sciences and Techniques, 6*(1).

Patil, V. C., Al-Gaadi, K. A., Biradar, D. P., & Rangaswamy, M. (2012). Internet of things (Iot) and cloud computing for agriculture: An overview. Proceedings of agro-informatics and precision agriculture (AIPA 2012), 292-296.

Pauwels, K. (2004). How Dynamic Consumer Response, Dynamic Competitor Response and Expanded Company Action Shape Long-Term Marketing Effectiveness. *Marketing Science, 23*(4), 596–610. doi:10.1287/mksc.1040.0075

Pazienza, A., Mallardi, G., Fasciano, C., & Vitulano, F. (2019). Artificial Intelligence on Edge Computing: a Healthcare Scenario in Ambient Assisted Living. In *Proceedings of the Fifth Italian Workshop on Artificial Intelligence for Ambient Assisted Living (AI*AAL.it 2019), co-located with 18th International Conference of the Italian Association for Artificial Intelligence (AIxIA 2019)*. CEUR-WS.

Pechmann, C. (1996). Do consumers overgeneralize one-sided comparative price claims, and are more stringent regulations needed? *JMR, Journal of Marketing Research, 33*(2), 150–163. doi:10.1177/002224379603300203

Peter, T. J., & Somasundaram, K. (2012). An empirical study on prediction of heart disease using classification data mining techniques. In *IEEE-International conference on advances in engineering, science and management (ICAESM-2012)*, (pp. 514-518). IEEE.

Pham, X. Q., Nguyen, T. D., Nguyen, V. D., & Huh, E. N. (2019). Utility-Centric Service Provisioning in Multi-Access Edge Computing. *MDPI Applied Sciences - Intelligent Centralized and Distributed Secure Edge Computing for Internet of Things Applications, 9*(18), 3776.

Phipps, J. B. (1971). Dendrogram Topology. *Systematic Biology, 20*(3), 306–308.

Pinto, J. K. (1986). *Project implementation: a determination of its critical success factors, moderators and their relative importance across the project life cycle* (Doctoral dissertation). University of Pittsburgh.

Pinto, J. K., & Slevin, D. P. (1987). Critical factors in successful project implementation. *IEEE Transactions on Engineering Management, EM-34*(1), 22–27. doi:10.1109/TEM.1987.6498856

Pivoto, D., Waquil, P. D., Talamini, E., Finocchio, C. P. S., Dalla Corte, V. F., & de Vargas Mores, G. (2018). Scientific development of smart farming technologies and their application in Brazil. *Information Processing in Agriculture, 5*(1), 21–32. doi:10.1016/j.inpa.2017.12.002

PMI. (2015). *Executive engagement: The role of the sponsor.* https://www.pmi.org/business-solutions/white-papers/executive-engagement-sponsor-role

Porambage, P., Okwuibe, J., Liyanage, M., Ylianttila, M., & Taleb, T. (2018). Survey on Multi-Access Edge Computing for Internet of Things Realization. *IEEE Communications Surveys and Tutorials, 20*(4), 2961–2991. doi:10.1109/COMST.2018.2849509

Praveena, M., & Kameswara, R. (2018). Survey on Big data analytics in Healthcare Domain. *IACSIT International Journal of Engineering and Technology.*

Priyanka, K., & Kulennavar, N. (2014). A Survey on Big Data Analytics in Health Care. *International Journal of Computer Science and Information Technologies, 5*(4), 5865–5868.

Pudumalar, S., Ramanujam, E., Rajashree, R. H., Kavya, C., Kiruthika, T., & Nisha, J. (2017, January). Crop recommendation system for precision agriculture. In *2016 Eighth International Conference on Advanced Computing (ICoAC)* (pp. 32-36). IEEE. 10.1109/ICoAC.2017.7951740

Pujari, J. D., Yakkundimath, R., & Byadgi, A. S. (2015). Image processing based detection of fungal diseases in plants. *Procedia Computer Science, 46*, 1802–1808.

Punia, Kumar, Aggarwal, & Malik. (2020). Object Based Learning Using Multi-Dimensional Games. *Journal of Discrete Mathematical Sciences and Cryptography, 23*(2), 509-524. " doi:10.1080/09720529.2020.1728904

Punia, S. K., Kumar, M., & Sharma, A. (2021). Intelligent Data Analysis with Classical Machine Learning. In *Intelligent Computing and Applications. Advances in Intelligent Systems and Computing*, (vol. 1172). Springer. doi:10.1007/978-981-15-5566-4_71

Punj, G., & Brookes, R. (2002). The influence of pre-decisional constraints on information search and consideration set formation in new automotive purchases. *International Journal of Research in Marketing, 19*(4), 383–400. doi:10.1016/S0167-8116(02)00100-3

Purcell, M.B. (2013). Big data using cloud computing. *Journal of Technology Research,* 1-7.

Putsis, W. P. Jr. (1998). Parameter variation and new product diffusion. *Journal of Forecasting, 17*(3-4), 231–257. doi:10.1002/(SICI)1099-131X(199806/07)17:3/4<231::AID-FOR695>3.0.CO;2-L

Qabil, S., Waheed, U., Awan, S. M., Mansoor, Y., & Khan, M. A. (2019). A Survey on Emerging Integration of Cloud Computing and Internet of Things. In *Proceedings of the International Conference on Information Science and Communication Technology (ICISCT).* IEEE. 10.1109/CISCT.2019.8777438

Qi, J., Yang, P., Min, G., Amft, O., Dong, F., & Xu, L. (2017). Advanced internet of things for personalised healthcare systems: A survey. *Pervasive and Mobile Computing, 41*, 132–149. https://dx.doi.org/10.1016/j.pmcj.2017.06.018

Qin, S. J. (2014). *Process data analytics in the era of big data.* Academic Press.

Qin, J., Chen, L., Liu, Y., Liu, C., Feng, C., & Chen, B. (2020). A machine learning methodology for diagnosing chronic kidney disease. *IEEE Access: Practical Innovations, Open Solutions, 8*, 20991–21002. doi:10.1109/ACCESS.2019.2963053

Qiu, J., Wu, Q., Ding, G., Xu, Y., & Feng, S. (2016). A survey of machine learning for big data processing. *EURASIP Journal on Advances in Signal Processing, 2016*(1), 67. doi:10.118613634-016-0355-x

Qlik. (2018, August 27). Retrieved from Wikipedia: https://en.wikipedia.org/wiki/Qlik

Qolomany, B., Al-Fuqaha, A., Gupta, A., Benhaddou, D., Alwajidi, S., Qadir, J., & Fong, A. C. (2019). Leveraging machine learning and big data for smart buildings: A comprehensive survey. *IEEE Access: Practical Innovations, Open Solutions, 7*, 90316–90356. doi:10.1109/ACCESS.2019.2926642

Quinlan, J. R., Compton, P. J., Horn, K. A., & Lazarus, L. (1987, October). Inductive knowledge acquisition: a case study. In *Proceedings of the Second Australian Conference on Applications of expert systems* (pp. 137-156). Academic Press.

Rady, E. H. A., & Anwar, A. S. (2019). Prediction of kidney disease stages using data mining algorithms. *Informatics in Medicine Unlocked, 15*(March), 100178. doi:10.1016/j.imu.2019.100178

Rahalkar, C., & Gujar, D. (2019). Content addressed P2P file system for the web with blockchain-based meta-data integrity. *2019 International Conference on Advances in Computing, Communication and Control (ICAC3).* doi:10.1109/icac347590.2019.9036792

Rahmani, A. M., Gia, T. N., Negash, B., Anzanpour, A., Azimi, I., Jiang, M., & Liljeberg, P. (2018). Exploiting smart e-Health gateways at the edge of healthcare Internet-of-Things: A fog computing approach. *Future Generation Computer Systems, 78*, 641–658.

Rajab, S., & Sharma, V. (2019). An interpretable neuro-fuzzy approach to stock price forecasting. *Soft Computing, 23*(3), 921–936.

Rajagopalan, S., & Malhotra, A. (2001). Have US Manufacturing Inventories Really Decreased? An Empirical Study. *Manufacturing & Service Operations Management, 3*(1), 14–24. doi:10.1287/msom.3.1.14.9995

Rajathi, S., & Radhamani, G. (2016). *Prediction and Analysis of Rheumatic Heart Disease using kNN Classification with ACO. IEEE, 4(7).*

Ramachandran, G. S., Radhakrishnan, R., & Krishnamachari, B. (2018). Towards a decentralized data marketplace for smart cities. *2018 IEEE International Smart Cities Conference (ISC2).* doi:10.1109/isc2.2018.8656952

Ramanujam, E., Padmavathi, S., Dharshani, G., & Madhumitta, M. R. R. (2019, December). Evaluation of Feature Extraction and Recognition for Human Activity using Smartphone based Accelerometer data. In *2019 11th International Conference on Advanced Computing (ICoAC)* (pp. 86-89). IEEE.

Ramanujam, E., Chandrakumar, T., Nandhana, K., & Laaxmi, N. T. (2019, September). Prediction of Fetal Distress Using Linear and Non-linear Features of CTG Signals. In *International Conference On Computational Vision and Bio Inspired Computing* (pp. 40-47). Springer.

Ramanujam, E., & Padmavathi, S. (2016, February). Double constrained genetic algorithm for ECG signal classification. In *2016 International Conference on Emerging Trends in Engineering, Technology and Science (ICETETS)* (pp. 1-5). IEEE. 10.1109/ICETETS.2016.7603010

Ramanujam, E., & Padmavathi, S. (2019). A Vision-Based Posture Monitoring System for the Elderly Using Intelligent Fall Detection Technique. In *Guide to Ambient Intelligence in the IoT Environment* (pp. 249–269). Springer. doi:10.1007/978-3-030-04173-1_11

Ramanujam, E., & Padmavathi, S. (2019). Genetic time series motif discovery for time series classification. *International Journal of Biomedical Engineering and Technology*, *31*(1), 47–63. doi:10.1504/IJBET.2019.101051

Ramesh, A. N., Kambhampati, C., Monson, J. R. T., & Drew, P. J. (2004). Artificial intelligence. *Annals of the Royal College of Surgeons of England*, *86*, 334–338. doi:10.1308/147870804290

Ramey, V., & West, K. (1999). Inventories. In Handbook of Macroeconomics (Vol. 1). Elsevier Science.

Rao, T. R., Mitra, P., Bhatt, R., & Goswami, A. (2019). The big data system, components, tools, and technologies: A survey. *Knowledge and Information Systems*, *60*(3), 1–81. doi:10.100710115-018-1248-0

RapidMiner. (2018, October 5). Retrieved from Wikipedia: https://en.wikipedia.org/wiki/RapidMiner

Rasikannan, L., Alli, P., & Ramanujam, E. (2019, October). Improved Feature Based Sentiment Analysis for Online Customer Reviews. In *International Conference on Innovative Data Communication Technologies and Application* (pp. 148-155). Springer.

Rauf, A., Khusro, S., Javed, H., & Saeed, M. (2012, January). Enhanced K-Mean Clustering Algorithm to Reduce Number of Iterations and Time Complexity. *Middle East Journal of Scientific Research*, *12*(7), 959–963.

Ray, P. P., Dash, D., & De, D. (2019). Edge computing for Internet of Things: A survey, e-healthcare case study and future direction. *Elsevier Journal of Network and Computer Applications*, *140*, 1–22. doi:10.1016/j.jnca.2019.05.005

Ray, P. P., Dash, D., & De, D. (2019). Edge computing for Internet of Things: A survey, e-healthcare case study and future direction. *Journal of Network and Computer Applications*, *140*, 1–22. https://doi.org/10.1016/j.jnca.2019.05.005

Rehman, A., Rehman, S., Khan, I.U., Moiz, M., & Hasan, S. (2016). Security and Privacy Issues in IoT. *International Journal of Communication Networks and Information Security*. https://www.researchgate.net/publication/313574376_Security_and_privacy_issues_in_IoT

Reinganum, M. R. (1981). Misspecification of capital asset pricing: Empirical anomalies based on earnings' yields and market values. *Journal of Financial Economics*, *9*(1), 19–46. doi:10.1016/0304-405X(81)90019-2

Revathy, S., Bharathi, B., Jeyanthi, P., & Ramesh, M. (2019). Chronic kidney disease prediction using machine learning models. *International Journal of Engineering and Advanced Technology*, *9*(1), 6364–6367. doi:10.35940/ijeat.A2213.109119

Reyes-Ortiz, J., Oneto, L., & Anguita, D. (2015). Big Data Analytics in the Cloud: Spark on Hadoop vs MPI/OpenMP on Beowulf. *Procedia Computer Science*, *53*(1), 121–130. doi:10.1016/j.procs.2015.07.286

Rijmenam, M. V. (2018). *A Short History of Big Data*. Retrieved from Dataflow: https://datafloq.com/read/big-data-history/239

Rish, I. (2001, August). An empirical study of the naive Bayes classifier. In IJCAI 2001 workshop on empirical methods in artificial intelligence (Vol. 3, No. 22, pp. 41-46). Academic Press.

Ristevski, B., & Chen, M. (2018). Big Data Analytics in Medicine and Healthcare. *Journal of Integrative Bioinformatics*, *15*(3). Advance online publication. doi:10.1515/jib-2017-0030 PMID:29746254

Roll, R., & Ross, S. (1980). An Empirical Investigation of the Arbitrage Pricing Theory. *The Journal of Finance*, *35*(5), 1073–1103. doi:10.1111/j.1540-6261.1980.tb02197.x

Roski, J., Bo-Linn, G. W., & Andrews, T. A. (2014). Creating value in health care through big data: Opportunities and policy implications. *Health Affairs*, *33*(7), 1115–1122. doi:10.1377/hlthaff.2014.0147 PMID:25006136

Ross, D. (2014, March 18). *Prescriptive Analysis*. Retrieved from duncan3ross: https://duncan3ross.files.wordpress.com/2014/03/gartner2.gif

Ross, S. (1976). The Arbitrage Theory of Capital Asset Pricing. *Journal of Economic Theory*, *13*(3), 341–360. doi:10.1016/0022-0531(76)90046-6

Ross, T. J. (2005). *Fuzzy logic with engineering applications*. John Wiley & Sons.

Ross, T. J., Booker, J. M., & Parkinson, W. J. (Eds.). (2002). *Fuzzy logic and probability applications: bridging the gap*. Society for Industrial and Applied Mathematics. doi:10.1137/1.9780898718447

Roumiantsev, S., & Netessine, S. (2005a). *What Can Be Learned from Classical Inventory Models: a Cross-Industry Empirical Investigation*. Working paper, University of Pennsylvania.

Roumiantsev, S., & Netessine, S. (2005b). *Should Inventory Policy Be Lean or Responsive? Evidence for US Public Companies*. Working paper, University of Pennsylvania.

Royal College of Physicians. (2012). *National Early Warning Score (NEWS): Standardising the assessment of acute illness severity in the NHS. Report of a working party*. RCP.

Russom, P. (2011). Big data analytics. *TDWI Best Practices Report, 19*(4), 1-34.

Sa, C. L., Hossain, E. D., & bin Hossin, M. (2014, November). Student performance analysis system (SPAS). In *The 5th International Conference on Information and Communication Technology for The Muslim World (ICT4M)* (pp. 1-6). IEEE.

Sachin, K., Gunasekaran, A., Goswami, M., & Manda, J. (2019). A systematic perspective on the applications of big data analytics in healthcare management. *International Journal of Healthcare Management, 12*(3).

Sadeghi Bigham, B., Mohades, A., & Ortega, L. (2008). Dynamic polar diagram. *Information Processing Letters, 109*(2), 142–146. doi:10.1016/j.ipl.2008.09.018

Sadoughi, F., Behmanesh, A., & Sayfouri, N. (2020). Internet of things in medicine: A systematic mapping study. *Journal of Biomedical Informatics, 103*. doi:10.1016/j.jbi.2020.103383

Sagiroglu, S., & Sinanc, D. (2013, May). Big data: A review. In *2013 international conference on collaboration technologies and systems (CTS)* (pp. 42-47). IEEE.

Sahalia, Y. A., & Lo, A. W. (1998). Non parametric estimation of state price Densities implicit in Financial asset Prices. *The Journal of Finance, 53*(2), 499–547. doi:10.1111/0022-1082.215228

Saheb, T., & Izadi, L. (2019). Paradigm of IoT big data analytics in the healthcare industry: A review of scientific literature and mapping of research trends. *Telematics and Informatics, 41*, 70–85. https://doi.org/10.1016/j.tele.2019.03.005

Sakar, C. O., Serbes, G., Gunduz, A., Tunc, H. C., Nizam, H., Sakar, B. E., Tutuncu, M., Aydin, T., Isenkul, M. E., & Apaydin, H. (2019). A comparative analysis of speech signal processing algorithms for Parkinson's disease classification and the use of the tunable Q-factor wavelet transform. *Applied Soft Computing, 74*, 255–263. doi:10.1016/j.asoc.2018.10.022

Salama, A. S., Saleh, B. K., & Eassa, M. M. (2010). Intelligent Cross Road Traffic Management System (ICRTMS). *Int. Conf on Computer Technology and Development*, 27-31. 10.1109/ICCTD.2010.5646059

Saltz, J. S., & Shamshurin, I. (2016). Big data team process methodologies: A literature review and the identification of key factors for a project's success. In *Big Data (Big Data), 2016 IEEE International Conference on* (pp. 2872-2879). IEEE. 10.1109/BigData.2016.7840936

Salvi, G. (n.d.). *An Automated Vehicle Counting System Based on Blob Analysis for Traffic Surveillance*. Department of Economics Studies, University of Naples "Parthenope", Naples, Italy.

Sanchez, E., Shibata, T., & Zadeh, L. A. (1997). *Genetic algorithms and fuzzy logic systems: Soft computing perspectives* (Vol. 7). World Scientific. doi:10.1142/2896

Sandhu, R., Gill, H. K., & Sood, S. K. (2016). Smart monitoring and controlling of pandemic influenza A (H1N1) using social network analysis and cloud computing. *Journal of Computational Science, 12*, 11–22. doi:10.1016/j.jocs.2015.11.001 PMID:32362959

Santana, E. F. Z., Chaves, A. P., Gerosa, M. A., Kon, F., & Milojicic, D. S. (2017). Software platforms for smart cities: Concepts, requirements, challenges, and a unified reference architecture. *ACM Computing Surveys (Csur), 50*(6), 1–37.

SAP Crystal Reports Software. (2018). Retrieved from Software Advice: https://www.softwareadvice.com/bi/sapcrystalreports-profile/

Sarwar, M., Hanif, K., Talib, R., Mobeen, A., & Aslam, M. (2017). A Survey of Big Data Analytics in Healthcare. *International Journal of Advanced Computer Science and Applications*.

Schneider, B., Hanges, P. J., Smith, D. B., & Salvaggio, A. N. (2003). Which Comes First: Employee Attitudes or Organizational Financial and Market Performance? *The Journal of Applied Psychology, 88*(5), 836–851. doi:10.1037/0021-9010.88.5.836 PMID:14516248

Schulam, P., & Saria, S. (2017). *Reliable decision support using counterfactual models. Neural Information Processing Systems*. NIPS.

Schuster, F., Costa, M., Fournet, C., Gkantsidis, C., Peinado, M., Mainar-Ruiz, G., & Russinovich, M. (2015). VC3: Trustworthy data analytics in the cloud using SGX. *2015 IEEE Symposium on Security and Privacy*. doi:10.1109p.2015.10

Sedgwick, P. (2013). Convenience sampling. *BMJ (Clinical Research Ed.), 347*, f6304.

Sen, S. (2015). A survey of intrusion detection systems using evolutionary computation. In *Bio-inspired computation in telecommunications* (pp. 73–94). Morgan Kaufmann.

Shakeel, P. M., Baskar, S., Dhulipala, V. S., & Jaber, M. M. (2018). Cloud based framework for diagnosis of diabetes mellitus using K-means clustering. *Health Information Science and Systems, 6*(1), 16. doi:10.100713755-018-0054-0 PMID:30279986

Shao, M. G. (2006). Development of project manager selection tool based on project manager competency. *Master's Abstracts International, 45*(2).

Shao, L., Schleicher, T., Behrisch, M., Schreck, T., Sipiran, I., & Keim, D. A. (2016). Guiding the exploration of scatter plot data using motif-based interest measures. *Journal of Visual Languages and Computing, 36*, 1–12. doi:10.1016/j.jvlc.2016.07.003

Sharifi, L., Freitag, F., & Veiga, L. (2014). Combing smart grid with community clouds: Next generation integrated service platform. *2014 IEEE International Conference on Smart Grid Communications (SmartGridComm)*. doi:10.1109martgridcomm.2014.7007685

Sharpe, W. (1964). Capital Asset Prices: A Theory of Market Equilibrium under Conditions of Risk. *The Journal of Finance, 19*, 425–442.

Shendurkar, M. A., & Chopde, R. N. (n.d.). An Ontology based Enhanced Framework for Instant Messages Filtering for Detection of Cyber Crimes. *International Journal on Recent and Innovation Trends in Computing and Communication, 3*(5), 2820–2826.

Sheshadri, S. H., & Franklin, D. (2020) *Introducing the Ultimate Starter AI Computer, the NVIDIA Jetson Nano 2GB Developer Kit.* NVIDIA Developer. Retrieved from https://developer.nvidia.com/blog/ultimate-starter-ai-computer-jetson-nano-2gb-developer-kit/

Shete, R., & Agrawal, S. (2016, April). IoT based urban climate monitoring using Raspberry Pi. In *2016 International Conference on Communication and Signal Processing (ICCSP)* (pp. 2008-2012). IEEE. 10.1109/ICCSP.2016.7754526

Shi, C., & Zhuang, X. (2019). A Study Concerning Soft Computing Approaches for Stock Price Forecasting. *Axioms, 8*(4), 116.

Shilpa, S., Chavan, R. S., Deshpande, J. G., & Rana. (2009). Design of Intelligent Traffic Light Controller Using Embedded System. *Emerging Trends in Engineering and Technology (ICETET).*

Siddique, M., DebdulalPanda, S. D., & Mohapatra, S. K. (2017). A Hybrid Forecasting Model For Stock Value Prediction Using Soft Computing. *International Journal of Pure and Applied Mathematics, 117*(19), 357–363.

Siddiqui, S. A., Zhang, Y., Lloret, J., Song, H., & Obradovic, Z. (2018). Pain-Free Blood Glucose Monitoring Using Wearable Sensors: Recent Advancements and Future Prospects. *IEEE Reviews in Biomedical Engineering, 11*, 21–35. doi:10.1109/RBME.2018.2822301 PMID:29993663

Siegel, C., Hochgatterer, A., & Dorne, T. E. (2014). Contributions of ambient assisted living for health and quality of life in the elderly and care services - a qualitative analysis from the experts' perspective of care service professionals. *BMC Geriatrics, 14*(1), 112. doi:10.1186/1471-2318-14-112 PMID:25326149

Silva, M. P., Nazario, D. C., Dantas, M. A. R., Goncalves, A. L., Pinto, A. R., Manerichi, G., & Vanelli, B. (2016). An eHealth Context Management and Distribution Approach in AAL Environments. In *Proceedings of the 29th International Symposium on Computer-Based Medical Systems (CBMS)*. IEEE. 10.1109/CBMS.2016.15

Singh, A., Thakur, N., & Sharma, A. (2016, March). A review of supervised machine learning algorithms. In *2016 3rd International Conference on Computing for Sustainable Global Development (INDIACom)* (pp. 1310-1315). IEEE.

Singhal, V. (2005). *Excess Inventory and Long-Term Stock Performance.* Working paper, Georgia Institute of Technology.

Singh, M., Nandal, P., & Bura, D. (2017, October). Comparative Analysis of Different Load Balancing Algorithm Using Cloud Analyst. In *International Conference on Recent Developments in Science, Engineering and Technology* (pp. 321-329). Springer.

Singh, R. P., Javaid, M., Haleem, A., & Suman, R. (2020). Internet of things (IoT) applications to fight against COVID-19 pandemic. *Diabetes & Metabolic Syndrome, 14*, 521–524. https://doi.org/10.1016/j.dsx.2020.04.041

Singh, V., & Misra, A. K. (2017). Detection of plant leaf diseases using image segmentation and soft computing techniques. *Information Processing in Agriculture, 4*(1), 41–49.

Sing, J., Kamra, A., & Singh, H. (2016). *Prediction of Heart Diseases Using Associative Classification.* Academic Press.

Sivagowry, S., Durairaj, M., & Persia, A. (2013). An Empirical Study on applying Data Mining Techniques for the Analysis and Prediction of Heart Disease. *IEEE, 4*(1), 13-38.

Sivanandam, S. N., & Deepa, S. N. (2007). *Principles of soft computing (with CD).* John Wiley & Sons.

Skourletopoulos, G., Mavromoustakis, C.X., Mastorakis, G., Batalla, J.M., Dobre, C., Panagiotakis, S., & Pallis, E. (2016). Big Data and Cloud Computing: A Survey of the State-of-the-Art and Research Challenges. In Advances in Mobile Cloud Computing and Big Data in the 5G Era. Studies in Big Data (Vol. 22). Springer.

Sloss, A. N., & Gustafson, S. (2020). 2019 Evolutionary algorithms review. *Genetic Programming Theory into Practice, 17*, 307–344.

Smith, A., Hawes, T., & Myers, M. (2014). Interactive Visualization for Hierarchical Topic Models. *Proceedings of the Workshop on Interactive Language Learning, Visualization, and Interfaces*, 71–78. 10.3115/v1/W14-3111

Software, D. (2020). Available: https://medium.com/app-affairs/9-applications-of-machine-learning-from-day-to-day-life-112a47a429d0.

SoftwareS. A. S. (2018, September 14). Retrieved from Wikipedia: https://en.wikipedia.org/wiki/SAS_(software)

Song, Y. Y., & Ying, L. U. (2015). Decision tree methods: Applications for classification and prediction. *Shanghai Jingshen Yixue, 27*(2), 130. PMID:26120265

Sonnati, R. (2017, March 3). Improving Healthcare Using Big Data Analytics. *International Journal of Scientific & Technology Research, 6*(3).

Sowmiya, C., & Sumitra, P. (2017, March). Analytical study of heart disease diagnosis using classification techniques. In *International Conference on Intelligent Techniques in Control, Optimization and Signal Processing (INCOS)* (pp. 1-5). IEEE.

Spangenberg, N., Roth, M., & Franczyk, B. (2015, June). Evaluating new approaches of big data analytics frameworks. In *International Conference on Business Information Systems* (pp. 28-37). Springer. 10.1007/978-3-319-19027-3_3

Specht, D. F. (1990). Probabilistic neural networks. *Neural Networks, 3*(1), 109–118. doi:10.1016/0893-6080(90)90049-Q PMID:18282828

Srivastava, S. (2014). Weka: A tool for data preprocessing, classification, ensemble, clustering and association rule mining. *International Journal of Computers and Applications, 88*(10).

Stainov, R., Mirchev, M., Goleva, R., Mirtchev, S., Atamian, D., Savov, A., & Draganov, P. (2016). AALaaS Intelligent Backhauls for P2P Communication in 5G Mobile Networks. In *Proceedings of International Black Sea Conference on Communications and Networking (BlackSeaCom)*. IEEE.

Stankovic, D., Nikolic, V., Djordjevic, M., & Cao, D. B. (2013). A survey study of critical success factors in agile software projects in former Yugoslavia IT companies. *Journal of Systems and Software, 86*(6), 1663–1678. doi:10.1016/j.jss.2013.02.027

Statistica. (2016, November). *Internet of Things (IoT) connected devices installed base worldwide from 2015 to 2025.* Statista Research Department. Retrieved from https://www.statista.com/statistics/471264/iot-number-of-connected-devices-worldwide/

Stergiou, C. L., Plageras, A. P., Psannis, K. E., & Gupta, B. B. (2020). Secure machine learning scenario from big data in cloud computing via internet of things network. In *Handbook of Computer Networks and Cyber Security* (pp. 525–554). Springer.

Subramanian, H. (2017). Decentralized blockchain-based electronic marketplaces. *Communications of the ACM, 61*(1), 78–84. https://doi.org/10.1145/3158333

Sudhakar, G. P. (2012). A model of critical success factors for software projects. *Journal of Enterprise Information Management, 25*(6), 537–558. doi:10.1108/17410391211272829

Suhrid Barua. (n.d.). Flood of Data Will Get Generated in Autonomous Cars. *Auto Tech Review.* Retrieved from https://autotechreview.com/features/flood-of-data-will-get-generated-in-autonomous-cars#:~:text=There%20is%20a%20great%20deal,cars%20in%20the%20automotive%20industry.&text=According%20to%20various%20industry%20experts,hour%20of%20driving%20a%20day

Sultana, M., Haider, A., & Uddin, M. S. (2016, September). Analysis of data mining techniques for heart disease prediction. In *3rd International Conference on Electrical Engineering and Information Communication Technology (ICEEICT)* (pp. 1-5). IEEE. 10.1109/CEEICT.2016.7873142

Sun, A. Y., & Scanlon, B. R. (2019). How can Big Data and machine learning benefit environment and water management: A survey of methods, applications, and future directions. *Environmental Research Letters, 14*(7), 073001. doi:10.1088/1748-9326/ab1b7d

Sundar, V. B., Devi, T., & Saravanan, N. (June,2012). Development of a Data Clustering Algorithm for Predicting Heart. *IJCA, 48*(7), 8-13.

Sundmaeker, H., Verdouw, C. N., Wolfert, J., & Freire, L. P. (2016). Internet of food and farm 2020. In *Digitising the Industry* (Vol. 49, pp. 129–150). River Publishers.

Sunita, S., Chandrakanta, B. j., & Chinmayee, R. (2016). A hybrid approach of intrusion detection using ANN and FCM. *European Journal of Advances in Engineering and Technology, 3*(2), 6–14.

Suzzie, A., & Apenteng, A. (2014). Big Data: A Tool for Development in Developing Nations. *International Journal of Scientific and Research Publications, 4*(5).

Tableau Software. (2018, September 21). Retrieved from Wikipedia: https://en.wikipedia.org/wiki/Tableau_Software

Tahmasebi, P., & Hezarkhani, A. (2012). A hybrid neural networks-fuzzy logic-genetic algorithm for grade estimation. *Computers & Geosciences, 42*, 18–27.

Talia, D. (2013). Clouds for scalable big data analytics. *Computer, 46*(5), 98–101. doi:10.1109/MC.2013.162

Taneja, A. (2013). Heart disease prediction system using data mining techniques. *Oriental. Journal of Computer Science and Technology, 6*(4), 457–466.

Tang, F., Mao, B., Fadlullah, Z. M., Kato, N., Akashi, O., Inoue, T., & Mizutani, K. (2017). On removing routing protocol from future wireless networks: A real-time deep learning approach for intelligent traffic control. *IEEE Wireless Communications, 25*(1), 154–160.

Taylor, S. J. (1987). Forecasting the volatility of currency exchange rates. *International Journal of Forecasting, 3*(1), 159–170. doi:10.1016/0169-2070(87)90085-9

Technology Acceptance Model. (2018, October 8). Retrieved from Wikipedia: https://en.wikipedia.org/wiki/Technology_acceptance_model

Tekale, S., Shingavi, P., Wandhekar, S., & Chatorikar, A. (2018). Prediction of chronic kidney disease using machine learning algorithms. *International Journal of Advanced Research in Computer and Communication Engineering, 7*(10), 92–96. doi:10.17148/IJARCCE.2018.71021

Tellis, G. J., Chandy, R., & Thaivanich, P. (2000). Which ad works, when, where,and how often? Modeling the effects of direct television advertising. *JMR, Journal of Marketing Research, 37*(1), 32–46. doi:10.1509/jmkr.37.1.32.18716

Tewari, A., & Gupta, B. B. (2020). Security, privacy and trust of different layers in Internet-of-Things (IoTs) framework. *Future Generation Computer Systems, 108*, 909–920.

Theresa Princy, R., & Thomas, J. (2016). Human Heart Disease Prediction System using DataMining Techniques. *International Conference on Circuit, Power and Computing Technologies, 4(1)*, 23–48.

Thibaud, M., Chi, H., Zhou, W., & Piramuthu, S. (2018). Internet of Things (IoT) in high-risk Environment, Health and Safety (EHS) industries: A comprehensive review. *Decision Support Systems, 108*, 79–95. https://doi.org/10.1016/j.dss.2018.02.005

Thi, M. L. (2017). Effects of Pros and Cons of Applying Big Data Analytics to Consumers' Responses in an E-Commerce Context. *Sustainability,* ●●●, 1–19.

Thomas, J., & Zhang, H. (2002). Inventory Changes and Future Returns. *Review of Accounting Studies, 7(2/3)*, 162–187. doi:10.1023/A:1020221918065

Thusoo, A., Shao, Z., Anthony, S., Borthakur, D., Jain, N., Sarma, J. S., Murthy, R., & Liu, H. (2010). Data warehousing and analytics infrastructure at Facebook. In *Proceedings of the 2010 international conference on Management of data*. ACM.

Tokuç, A. A., Uran, Z. E., & Tekin, A. T. (2019). Management of Big Data Projects: PMI Approach for Success. In *Agile Approaches for Successfully Managing and Executing Projects in the Fourth Industrial Revolution* (pp. 279–293). IGI Global. doi:10.4018/978-1-5225-7865-9.ch015

Tomei, L. A. (2020). Online Courses and ICT in Education: Emerging Practices and Applications. *Simulation*, 566.

Tonelli, M., Muntner, P., Lloyd, A., Manns, B. J., Klarenbach, S., Pannu, N., James, M. T., & Hemmelgarn, B. R.Alberta Kidney Disease Network. (2012, September 1). Risk of coronary events in people with chronic kidney disease compared with those with diabetes: A population-level cohort study. *Lancet, 380*(9844), 807–814. doi:10.1016/S0140-6736(12)60572-8 PMID:22717317

Tsai, C. W., Lai, C. F., Chao, H. C., & Vasilakos, A. V. (2015). Big data analytics: A survey. *Journal of Big Data, 2*(1), 1–32. doi:10.118640537-015-0030-3 PMID:26191487

Tuan, M. N. D., Thanh, N. N., & Tuan, L. L. (2019). Applying a mindfulness-based reliability strategy to the Internet of Things inhealthcare – A business model in the Vietnamese market. *Technological Forecasting and Social Change, 140*, 54–68.

Tuli, S., Basumatary, N., Gill, S. S., Kahani, M., Arya, R. C., Wander, G. S., & Buyya, R. (2020). HealthFog: An ensemble deep learning based Smart Healthcare System for Automatic Diagnosis of Heart Diseases in integrated IoT and fog computing environments. *Future Generation Computer Systems, 104*, 187–200.

Tzounis, A., Katsoulas, N., Bartzanas, T., & Kittas, C. (2017). Internet of Things in agriculture, recent advances and future challenges. *Biosystems Engineering, 164*, 31–48. doi:10.1016/j.biosystemseng.2017.09.007

Unnava, H. R., & Sirdeshmukh, D. (1994). Reducing Competitive ad interference. *JMR, Journal of Marketing Research, 31*(3), 403–411. doi:10.1177/002224379403100308

V. (2019, January 10). *5 V's of Big Data*. Retrieved June 5, 2020, from https://www.geeksforgeeks.org/5-vs-of-big-data

Vano-Galvan, S., Paoli, J., Rios-Buceta, L., & Jaen, P. (2015). Skin self- examination using smartphone photography to improve the early diagnosis of melanoma. *Actas Dermo-Sifilograficas, 106*(1), 75–77. PMID:25173155

Venkatesh, H., Perur, D.S., & Jalihal, N. (2015). A Study on Use of Big Data in Cloud Computing Environment. *International Journal of Computer Science and Information Technologies, 6*(3), 2076-2078.

Vera-Baquero, A., Colomo-Palacios, R., & Molloy, O. (2013). Business process analytics using a big data approach. *IT Professional, 15*(6), 29–35. doi:10.1109/MITP.2013.60

Verkoou, K., & Spruit, M. (2013). Mobile business intelligence: Key considerations for implementations projects. *Journal of Computer Information Systems, 54*(1), 23–33. doi:10.1080/08874417.2013.11645668

Verma, P., Sandeep, K., & Sood, S. K. (2017). Cloud-centric IoT based disease diagnosis healthcare framework. *Journal of Parallel and Distributed Computing, 116*, 27–38. https://doi.org/10.1016/j.jpdc.2017.11.018

Vetrò, A., Santangelo, A., Beretta, E., & Martin, J. C. D. (2019). AI: From rational agents to socially responsible agents. *Digital Policy. Regulation & Governance*, ●●●, 291–304.

Vidale, M. L., & Wolfe, H. B. (1957). An Operation Research Study of Sales Response to Advertising. *Operations Research, 5*(3), 370–381. doi:10.1287/opre.5.3.370

Villars, R. L., Olofson, C. W., & Eastwood, M. (2011). Big data: What it is and why you should care. *White Paper, IDC, 14*, 1-14.

Volta, G., Jaeger, E. P., Vazquezmontiel, S., & Hibbs, R. (2000). Introduction to evolutionary computing techniques. In *Proceedings of the electronic Technology Directions to the* (pp. 122-127). Academic Press.

Vora, J., Tanwar, S., Tyagi, S., Kumar, N., & Rodrigues, J. J. P. C. (2017). FAAL: Fog Computing-based Patient Monitoring System for Ambient Assisted Living. In *Proceedings of the 19th International Conference on e-Health Networking, Applications and Services (Healthcom)*. IEEE. 10.1109/HealthCom.2017.8210825

Wadhwani, K., & Wang, Y. (2017). *Big Data Challenges and solutions*. Technical Report.

Wamba, S., Akter, S., Edwards, A., Chopin, G., & Gnanzou, D. (2015). How 'big data' can make big impact: Findings from a systematic review and a longitudinal case study. *International Journal of Production Economics, 165*, 234–246. Advance online publication. doi:10.1016/j.ijpe.2014.12.031

Wang, H., Naghavi, M., Allen, C., Barber, R.M., Bhutta, Z.A., & Carter, A. (2015). *GBD 2015 Mortality and Causes of Death Collaborators. Global, regional, and national life expectancy, all-cause mortality, and cause-specific mortality for 249 causes of death, 1980-2015: a systematic analysis for the Global Burden of Disease Study 2015*. Academic Press.

Wang, Y. L., & Krishnamachari, B. (2019). Enhancing engagement in token-curated registries via an inflationary mechanism. *2019 IEEE International Conference on Blockchain and Cryptocurrency (ICBC)*. doi:10.1109/bloc.2019.8751443

Wang, Z., Won Chung, J., Jiang, X., Cui, Y., Wang, M., & Zheng, A. (2018). Machine Learning-Based Prediction System For Chronic Kidney Disease Using Associative Classification Technique. *International Journal of Engineering & Technology, 7*(4.36), 1161. doi:10.14419/ijet.v7i4.36.25377

Wang, Z., Yang, L., Wang, Q., Liu, D., Xu, Z., & Liu, S. (2019). ArtChain: Blockchain-enabled platform for art marketplace. *2019 IEEE International Conference on Blockchain (Blockchain)*. doi:10.1109/blockchain.2019.00068

Wang, C., Wang, Q., Ren, K., & Lou, W. (2009). Ensuring Data Storage Security in Cloud Computing. *Proc. of IWQoS'09*.

Wang, D., Hu, B., Hu, C., Zhu, F., Liu, X., Zhang, J., Wang, B., Xiang, H., Cheng, Z., Xiong, Y., Zhao, Y., Li, Y., Wang, X., & Peng, Z. (2020). Clinical characteristics of 138 hospitalized patients with 2019 novel coronavirus-infected pneumonia in Wuhan, China. *JAMA Network, 323*(11), 1061–1069. doi:10.1001/jama.2020.1585 PMID:32031570

Wang, H., Naghavi, M., Allen, C., Barber, R. M., Bhutta, Z. A., Carter, A., Casey, D. C., Charlson, F. J., Chen, A. Z., Coates, M. M., Coggeshall, M., Dandona, L., Dicker, D. J., Erskine, H. E., Ferrari, A. J., Fitzmaurice, C., Foreman, K., Forouzanfar, M. H., Fraser, M. S., ... Murray, C. J. L. (2016, October 8). Global, regional, and national life expectancy, all-cause mortality, and cause-specific mortality for 249 causes of death, 1980–2015: A systematic analysis for the Global Burden of Disease Study 2015. *Lancet, 388*(10053), 1459–1544. doi:10.1016/S0140-6736(16)31012-1 PMID:27733281

Wang, Y., Lee, K., & Terry, A. (2018). Big Data Analytics: Understanding its capabilities and potential benefits for healthcare organizations. *Technological Forecasting and Social Change, 126*, 3–13. doi:10.1016/j.techfore.2015.12.019

Ward, M., Grinstein, G., & Keim, D. (2017). Interactive Data Visualization. CRC Press. doi:10.1016/B978-0-12-809715-1.00007-9

Watson, A. R., Wah, R., & Thamman, R. (2020). The Value of Remote Monitoring for the COVID-19 Pandemic. *Telemedicine Journal and e-Health, 26*(9), 1110–1112. Advance online publication. doi:10.1089/tmj.2020.0134 PMID:32384251

Watson, H. J. (2014). Tutorial: Big Data Analytics: Concepts, Technologies, and Applications. *Communications of the Association for Information Systems*, •••, 1247–1268.

Watson, H. J. (2014). Tutorial: Big data analytics: Concepts, technologies, and applications. *Communications of the Association for Information Systems, 34*(1), 65. doi:10.17705/1CAIS.03465

Weber, G. M., Mandl, K. D., & Kohane, I. S. (2014). Finding the missing link for big biomedical data. *Journal of the American Medical Association, 311*(24), 2479–2480. doi:10.1001/jama.2014.4228 PMID:24854141

Western Digital Website. (n.d.). Retrieved from https://www.westerndigital.com/solutions/oil-gas

Westlund, S. G. (2007). Retaining talent: Assessing relationships among project leadership styles, software developer job satisfaction, and turnover intentions. *Dissertation Abstracts International, 68*(11).

What is Big Data? - Definition from Techopedia. (n.d.). Retrieved December 11, 2020, from https://www.techopedia.com/definition/27745/big-data

Why Traditional Marketing Analytics Tools Fail and What to do about it. (2020, November 2). Retrieved July 24, 2020, from https://www.pointillist.com/blog/why-traditional-marketing-analytics-tools-fail

Wiggins. (1992). *Information literacy at universities: Challenges and solutions*. Academic Press.

Wiseman, L., Sanderson, J., Zhang, A., & Jakku, E. (2019). Farmers and their data: An examination of farmers' reluctance to share their data through the lens of the laws impacting smart farming. *NJAS Wageningen Journal of Life Sciences, 90*, 100301. doi:10.1016/j.njas.2019.04.007

Wolberg, W. H., & Mangasarian, O. L. (1990). Multisurface method of pattern separation for medical diagnosis applied to breast cytology. *Proceedings of the National Academy of Sciences of the United States of America, 87*(23), 9193–9196. doi:10.1073/pnas.87.23.9193 PMID:2251264

Wolfert, S., Ge, L., Verdouw, C., & Bogaardt, M. J. (2017). Big data in smart farming–a review. *Agricultural Systems, 153*, 69–80. doi:10.1016/j.agsy.2017.01.023

World Health Organization. (2018, February 5). *Ageing and Health*. Retrieved from https://www.who.int/news-room/fact-sheets/detail/ageing-and-health

World Health Organization. (2020, December 22). *COVID-19 Weekly Epidemiological Update*. Retrieved from https://www.who.int/publications/m/item/weekly-epidemiological-update---22-december-2020

World Health Organization. (2020, September 17). *Keep health workers safe to keep patients safe: WHO.* Retrieved from https://www.who.int/news/item/17-09-2020-keep-health-workers-safe-to-keep-patients-safe-who

Wright, C. S. (2008). *Bitcoin: A peer-to-peer electronic cash system.* SSRN Electronic Journal. doi:10.2139srn.3440802

Wu, W. W. (2006). IT personnel sourcing decisions in IT projects. *Dissertation Abstracts International, 67*(1).

Wu, X., Zhu, X., Wu, G. Q., & Ding, W. (2013). Data mining with big data. *IEEE Transactions on Knowledge and Data Engineering, 26*(1), 97–107.

Xie, J., Song, M., Sirbu, M., & Wang, Q. (1997). Kalman Filter Estimation of New Product Diffusion Models. *JMR, Journal of Marketing Research, 34*(3), 378–393. doi:10.1177/002224379703400307

Yadav, A. K., Tomar, D., & Agarwal, S. (July, 2013). Clustering of lung cancer data using foggy k-means. In *International Conference on Recent Trends in Information Technology (ICRTIT)* (pp. 13-18). IEEE. 10.1109/ICRTIT.2013.6844173

Yeoh, W., & Popovič, A. (2016). Extending the understanding of critical success factors for implementing business intelligence systems. *Journal of the Association for Information Science and Technology, 67*(1), 134–147. doi:10.1002/asi.23366

Yeung, A. W. K. (2018). Data visualization by alluvial diagrams for bibliometric reports, systematic reviews and meta-analyses. *Current Science, 115*(10), 1942–1947. doi:10.18520/cs/v115/i10/1942-1947

Yin, Y., Zeng, Y., Chen, X., & Fan, Y. (2016). The internet of things in healthcare: An overview. *Journal of Industrial Information Integration, 1*, 3–13.

Yli-Olli, P., & Virtanen, I. (1992). Some empirical tests of the arbitrage pricing theory using transformation analysis. *Empirical Economics, 17*(4), 507–522. doi:10.1007/BF01205393

Yuan, Y., & Wang, F. (2016). Towards blockchain-based intelligent transportation systems. *2016 IEEE 19th International Conference on Intelligent Transportation Systems (ITSC).* doi:10.1109/itsc.2016.7795984

Yu, W., Liang, F., He, X., Hatcher, W. G., Lu, C., Lin, J., & Yang, X. (2017). A Survey on the Edge Computing for the Internet of Things. *IEEE Access: Practical Innovations, Open Solutions, 6*, 6900–6919. doi:10.1109/ACCESS.2017.2778504

Zadeh, L. A. (1975). The concept of a linguistic variable and its application to approximate reasoning-III. *Information Sciences, 9*(1), 43–80. doi:10.1016/0020-0255(75)90017-1

Zainudin, M. N. S., Sulaiman, M. N., Mustapha, N., & Perumal, T. (2017). Monitoring daily fitness activity using accelerometer sensor fusion. In *Proceedings of the International Symposium on Consumer Electronics (ISCE).* IEEE. 10.1109/ISCE.2017.8355540

Zakaria, H., Bakar, N. A., Hassan, N. H., & Yaacob, S. (2019). IoT Security Risk Management Model for Secured Practice in Healthcare Environment. *Procedia Computer Science, 161*, 1241–1248.

Zakir, J. T. S. (2015). Big Data Analytics. *Issues in Information Systems,* ●●●, 81–90.

Zamora-Izquierdo, M. A., Santa, J., Martínez, J. A., Martínez, V., & Skarmeta, A. F. (2019). Smart farming IoT platform based on edge and cloud computing. *Biosystems Engineering, 177*, 4–17. doi:10.1016/j.biosystemseng.2018.10.014

Zanoon, N., Al-Haj, N., & Khwaldeh, S. (2017). M Cloud Computing and Big Data is there a Relation between the Two: A Study. *International Journal of Applied Engineering Research, 12*(17), 6970–6982.

Zeadally, S., & Bello, O. (in press). Harnessing the power of Internet of Things based connectivity to improve healthcare. *Internet of Things.* 0 074 doi:10.1016/j.iot.2019.10

Zeynu, S. (2018). *Prediction of Chronic Kidney Disease Using Data Mining Feature Selection and Ensemble Method.* Academic Press.

Zgheib, R., Nicola, A. D., Villani, M. L., Conchon, E., & Bastide, R. (2017). A Flexible Architecture for Cognitive Sensing of Activities in Ambient Assisted Living. In *Proceedings of the 26th International Conference on Enabling Technologies: Infrastructure for Collaborative Enterprises.* IEEE. 10.1109/WETICE.2017.41

Zhang, Z. K., Cho, M. C. Y., Wang, C. W., Hsu, C. W., Chen, C. K., & Shieh, S. (2014, November). IoT security: ongoing challenges and research opportunities. In *2014 IEEE 7th international conference on service-oriented computing and applications* (pp. 230-234). IEEE. 10.1109/SOCA.2014.58

Zhang, S., Zhang, C., & Yang, Q. (2003). Data preparation for data mining. *Applied Artificial Intelligence, 17*(5-6), 375–381. doi:10.1080/713827180

Zhang, X., Zhang, E., Song, B., & Wei, F. (2010). Towards Building an Integrated Information Platform for Eco-city. *Proceedings of the 7th International Conference on e-Business Engineering (ICEBE 2010),* 393–398.

Zhao, D., Dai, Y., & Zhang, Z. (2012). Computational intelligence in urban traffic signal control: A survey. *IEEE Transactions on Systems, Man and Cybernetics. Part C, Applications and Reviews, 42*(4), 485–494. doi:10.1109/TSMCC.2011.2161577

Zheng, J. G. (2017). Data visualization in business intelligence. In Global Business Intelligence (pp. 67–82). doi:10.4324/9781315471136-6

Zheng, X., Mukkamala, R. R., Vatrapu, R., & Ordieres-Mere, J. (2018). Blockchain-based personal health data sharing system using cloud storage. *2018 IEEE 20th International Conference on e-Health Networking, Applications and Services (Healthcom).* doi:10.1109/healthcom.2018.8531125

Zhou, J., Tang, F., Zhu, H., Nan, N., & Zhou, Z. (2018). Distributed data vending on blockchain. 2018 IEEE International Conference on Internet of Things (iThings) and IEEE Green Computing and Communications (GreenCom) and IEEE Cyber, Physical and Social Computing (CPSCom) and IEEE Smart Data (SmartData). doi:10.1109/cybermatics_2018.2018.00201

Zhou, L., Pan, S., Wang, J., & Vasilakos, A. V. (2017). Machine learning on big data: Opportunities and challenges. *Neurocomputing, 237,* 350–361. doi:10.1016/j.neucom.2017.01.026

Zhou, Z. H., Chawla, N. V., Jin, Y., & Williams, G. J. (2014). Big data opportunities and challenges: Discussions from data analytics perspectives [discussion forum]. *IEEE Computational Intelligence Magazine, 9*(4), 62–74. doi:10.1109/MCI.2014.2350953

Zicari, R. V. (2017). Big Data: Challenges and Opportunities. *Big Data Computing,* 103-128.

Zuckerbraun, S., Deutsch, A., Eicheldinger, C., Frasier, A. M., Loft, J. D., & Clift, J. (2020). Risk Adjustment, Mode Adjustment, and Nonresponse Bias Analysis on Quality Measures From a Long-Term Care Hospital Experience of Care Survey. *Archives of Physical Medicine and Rehabilitation, 101*(5), 841–851. doi:10.1016/j.apmr.2019.11.016 PMID:31904343

Zurina, H. (2013). Hybrid of fuzzy clustering neural network over NSL dataset for intrusion detection system. *Journal of Computational Science, 9*(3), 391–403. doi:10.3844/jcssp.2013.391.403

Zyskind, G., Nathan, O., & Pentland, A. (2015). Decentralizing privacy: Using blockchain to protect personal data. *2015 IEEE Security and Privacy Workshops.* doi:10.1109pw.2015.27

About the Contributors

Sam Goundar is an Editor-in-Chief of the International Journal of Blockchains and Cryptocurrencies (IJFC) – Inderscience Publishers, Editor-in-Chief of the International Journal of Fog Computing (IJFC) – IGI Publishers, Section Editor of the Journal of Education and Information Technologies (EAIT) – Springer and Editor-in-Chief (Emeritus) of the International Journal of Cloud Applications and Computing (IJCAC) – IGI Publishers. He is also on the Editorial Review Board of more than 20 high impact factor journals.As a researcher, apart from Blockchains, Cryptocurrencies, Fog Computing, Mobile Cloud Computing and Cloud Computing, Dr. Sam Goundar also researches in Educational Technology, MOOCs, Artificial Intelligence, ICT in Climate Change, ICT Devices in the Classroom, Using Mobile Devices in Education, e-Government, and Disaster Management. He has published on all these topics. He was a Research Fellow with the United Nations University.He is a Senior Lecturer in IS at The University of the South Pacific, Adjunct Lecturer in IS at Victoria University of Wellington and an Affiliate Professor of Information Technology at Pontificia Universidad Catolica Del Peru.

* * *

K. M. S. V. D. Akshar is a Computer Science student at Vellore Institute of Technology. He is technology and management enthusiast. His research interests are self-driving cars, Data Science, RPA and Automation. He is curious about how businesses and companies can integrate technology for greater efficiencies and profits.

Imran Aslan has done his four years healthcare education as Emergency Medical Technician at Batman Health Vocational High School between 1996-2000 years, Batman, Turkey. Furthermore, he finished the Marmara University as Industrial Engineer, FHOOW/Germany as Technical manager master graduate and at Atatürk University as PhD graduate. He has published more than 25 international articles at famous SSCI, ISI, Scopus etc. indexed journals , 3 books and 7 book chapters.

Swaminathan B., Ph.D., is a Professor in computer science and engineering and currently works in Rajalakshmi Engineering College, affiliated to Anna University Chennai. His areas of interest are Cloud Computing, Deep Learning, IOT and Data Analytics. He extensively published papers in multi attribute decision making mechanism for peer selection in collaborative peer-to-peer systems. He has completed his doctorate in Information and Communication Engineering from Anna University, Chennai, Master's degree in the computer science & engineering from Motilal Nerhu Regional Engineering

College, Allahabad, Uthar Pradesh, and Bachelors degree in Electronics and Communication engineering from Bharathidasan University, Tiruchirapalli. He is also a member in Computer Society of India.

Akashdeep Bhardwaj achieved his PhD from University of Petroleum & Energy Studies (UPES), Post Graduate Diploma in Management (PGDM), Engineering graduate in Computer Science. He has worked as Head of Cyber Security Operations and currently is a Professor in a leading university in India. He has over 24 year experience working as an Enterprise Risk and Resilience and Information Security and Technology professional for various global multinationals.

Deepa Bura received her Bachelor of Engineering in Information Technology in 2002 from Vaish College of Engineering affiliated to Maharishi Dayanand University Rohtak, and Master of Technology in Information Technology in 2009 from University School of Information Technology affiliated to Guru Gobind Singh Indraprastha University, Delhi. She completed her Ph.D in 2018 from Uttarakhand Technical University in the field of Software Engineering. She has 17 years of teaching experience. Presently she is working as Assistant Professor in Department of Computer Science and Engineering at Faculty of Engineering and Technology, Manav Rachna International University, Faridabad. Her area of interest includes Data Mining, Software Engineering, Cloud Computing, Soft Computing.

Poonam Chahal received her Bachelor of Engineering in Information Technology in 2005 from Institute of Technology and Management affiliated to Maharishi Dayanand University Rohtak, and Master of Technology in Computer Science and Engineering in 2009 from Career Institute of Technology and Management affiliated to Maharishi Dayanand University, Rohtak. She completed her Ph.D in 2017 from YMCA University of Science and Technology in the field of Semantic Web. She has 14 years of teaching experience. Presently she is working as Associate Professor in Department of Computer Science and Engineering at Faculty of Engineering and Technology, Manav Rachna International Institute of Research and Studies, Faridabad. Her area of interest includes Information Retrieval, Semantic Web, Artificial Intelligence, Natural Language Processing, Soft Computing, Compiler Design. She has published around 20 research papers in reputed national/international journals/conferences.

Indu Chawla has been working as Assistant Professor in the department of Computer science and Information technology at Jaypee Institute of Information Technology, Noida, India. She has more than 19 years of teaching experience. She has guided many graduate and undergraduate students. Her research interests are in the area of Database, data mining, big data and software Engineering.

B. Deepan Prashanth is currently pursuing an undergraduate B Tech degree in the Department of Information Technology Thiagarajar College of Engineering Madurai. His areas of interest are data mining, machine learning, and data analytics.

Chandramohan Dhasarathan is currently Senior Assistant Professor, Department of Computer Science and Engineering, Madanapalle Institute of Technology & Science, Madanapalle, Andhara Pradesh, India. His area of interest includes Distributed Web Service, Web Service (Evaluation) Testbed, Software Metrics, GVANET and Cloud Computing, Opportunistic Computing, Evolutionary Computing, Service Computing, Software Engineering, Multi-Agent, Pervasive & Ubiquitous Computing, Fog & Edge Computing, Underwater Communication, Privacy and Security. Currently he is working on E-

Waste Management, Disaster Management, Bio-Inspired Algorithms and Privacy Preserving Generic Framework for Cloud Data Storage, Optimization approach for minimizing Agro-crops. He is having 9-Years of academic and research expertise and 3-years of industrial experience.

Pooja Jha has done her PhD from BIT Mesra. Currently, she is working as Assistant Professor in AUJ. She is having a work experience of about 14 years. Dr. Pooja has contributed towards scopus and SCI indexed research journals, has attended conferences and also has authored book chapters in reputed Journals. Her areas of research interest are Software Defect Management, Software Reliability, Metrics, Soft Computing, Machine Learning & AI.

Jayashree K. is an Engineer by qualification, having done her Doctorate in the area of Web services Fault Management from Anna University, Chennai and Masters in Embedded System Technologies from Anna University and Bachelors in Computer Science and Engineering from Madras University. She is presently working as Professor in the Department of Computer Science and Engineering at Rajalakshmi Engineering College, affiliated to Anna University Chennai. Her areas of interest include Web services, Cloud Computing, Data Mining and distributed computing. She is a member of ACM, CSI.

Madhana K. received the B.E. degree in computer science and engineering from Mepco Schlenk Engineering College, Sivakasi, Tamilnadu in 2012 and the M.E. degree in computer science and engineering from Sona College of Technology, Salem, Tamilnadu in 2014. She is currently pursuing PhD in PSG College of Technology, Coimbatore under Anna University, Chennai in the area of edge computing. She also has 2.5 years of teaching experience. Her research interests include Edge computing, Software defined networking, Internet-of-things and optimization techniques.

Remya Lathabhavan is a Senior Assistant Professor at Department of Technology Management of VIT University, Vellore, India. Her research interests include Glass Ceiling, Corporate Social Responsibility, Human Resource Management, Data Analytics and Career Progression. She (co)authored many articles and book chapters in peer reviewed journals and books.

Supriya M. S. is working as an assistant professor at Ramaiah University of Applied Sciences, Bangalore. Her research interests include Control Systems, Wireless Communication System, Machine Learning, Embedded System, IoT and Software Engineering. She has published research papers in national journal, international journal, and international conferences.

Karpagam Masilamani is a Masters student in Information Systems at The University of the South Pacific.

Dhivya P. is currently pursuing her Ph.D., in Information and Communication Engineering in the area of Big data analytics from Anna University, Chennai. She was completed M.E., in Computer Science and Engineering from SNS College of Technology, Coimbatore and B.E., in Computer Science and Engineering from SNS College of Engineering, Coimbatore. She is having 9 years of teaching experience in an engineering colleges and currently working as Assistant Professor in the Department of Computer Science and Engineering at Bannari Amman Institute of Technology. She is a Life time Member in International Association of Engineers (IAENG). Her research interest includes Internet of

Things (IoT) and Mobile Ad Hoc Networks. For her credentials he published more than 10 papers in refereed international journals which were indexed in Scopus, UGC journals and Google Scholar, one book publication titled "Computer Organization and Architecture" and 12 papers in national and international conferences. She filed a design patent in the year of 2018. She received Best paper award and best ERP Coordinator Award from the Institution.

Laxmi Kumari Pathak is presently working as an Assistant Professor in Amity Institute of Information Technology, Amity University Jharkhand. She has done M.Tech in Computer Science and Engineering from Maulana Abul Kalam Azad University of Technology (Formerly known as West Bengal University of Technology), West Bengal. She has more than seven years of teaching experience. She has research paper publications in various International/National journals of repute and has attended various FDPs and conferences in her career. Her area of interest includes Artificial Intelligence, Machine Learning, and Image Processing.

Manorama Patnaik is a Ph.D. Research Scholar from the Department of Computer Science and Engineering, Birla Institute of Technolgy, Mesra, Ranchi. She has completed her Master of Computer Application from Berhampur University, Odisha. Her area of Research includes the Internet of Things, wireless network security, Data Science, Machine learning and Body Area sensor network.

Archana Purwar has been working as an Assistant Professor in the Department of Computer Science and Information technology at Jaypee Institute of Information Technology, Noida, India. During her teaching career of more than 14 years, she has taught subjects such as database systems, software engineering, object-oriented programming, computer architecture and organization, data mining, and many more. Her area of interest lies in data mining, information retrieval, and soft computing. She has guided many graduate and undergraduate students.

Elangovan Ramanujam received his M.E. in Computer Science and Engineering with distinction from Anna University, Chennai, India and ranked University 4th. He received his B.E in Computer Science and Engineering from Anna University, Chennai, India. He is currently working as an Assistant professor in the Department of Information Technology, Thiagarajar College of Engineering, Madurai, India. His research interest includes Assistive Technology, Machine Learning, Time Series Mining and Optimization techniques. He has published more papers in refereed Journals and Conferences.

L. Rasikannan received a B.E degree from Thiagarajar College of Engineering, Madurai, Tamilnadu, India, and the M.E. degree from Anna University, Coimbatore Tamilnadu, India. He is currently working as an Assistant Professor at Alagappa Chettiar Government College of Engineering and Technology, Karaikudi. He is pursuing his part-time Ph.D. degree in ICE at Anna University, Chennai. His current research interests include handling Search Engine Issues, information retrieval, machine learning, and Sentiment Analysis.

Meenaxy Roy is pursuing her Bachelor degree in Computer Science and Engineering from Ramaiah University of Applied Sciences. Her current research interests include Internet of Things, Web computing, big data analysis and big data in applications of smart city and smart farming.

Nilesh Kumar Sahu is currently working as a Junior Researcher at National Institute of Technology, Durgapur and he has received his Masters Degree (Computer Science) from Birla Institute of Technology, Mesra (Ranchi), India in 2020 and his Bachelor's degree in Computer Science Engineering from Birla Institute of Technology, Mesra India in 2017. His areas of interest include Machine Learning, Deep Learning, Data Science, Artificial Intelligence, Data Analyst, Mobile and Wireless Sensor Networks and Internet of Things.

Keerthana Sasidaran is studying Computer Science Engineering in Ramaiah University of Applied Sciences and has research interests in the fields Machine Learning, Artificial Intelligence and Software Engineering.

Jhumur Sengupta is currently Assistant Professor in Economics at Dinabandhu Andrews College, Garia, Kolkata, West Bengal, India. Prior to this, she has worked in various reputed organizations as faculty as well as researcher. She completed her M.A (in 2000)and M.Phil (in 2003) in Economics from Jawaharlal Nehru University, New Delhi. She did her PhD (in 2009) in Economics from Calcutta University. Her research interest includes Political Economy & Applied Econometrics. With use of modern econometric techniques, she has published empirical research paper in reputed national as well as international journals.

Meeta Singh is having 20 years of teaching experience. Completed her Ph.D. (Computer Science & Engineering) from Bhagwant University, Ajmer in 2015 and M.Tech (IT) from Guru Gobind Singh Indraprastha University, New Delhi in 2007. Also done M.Sc. (Electronics) from Banasthali Vidyapeeth, Rajsthan in 1999. She is currently working as Associate Professor in Department of Computer Science & Engineering, Faculty of Engineering & Technology ,Manav Rachna International Institute of Research and Studies (Deemed to be University). Dr. Meeta Singh has 26 research papers in Conference/journals to her credit.

Parminder Singh is a young dynamic personality with a proven record of a good academician and researcher having an outstanding academic record. He has been working as Associate Professor in Information Technology Department and has more than Fourteen years of rich experience as an academician and researcher. He has published over 70 Journal and conference papers in the areas of Networking, Wireless Networks, sensor computing and Network security. He holds two patents deriving from his research. He has published three books on his research activities. He completed three projects, including one DST project. He has conducted Webinar Sessions related to Network Programming and Software Defined Networks in association with CISCO, Systems to have academia-industry Interaction. He has won best-paper awards including the IEEE "Best Paper Award" in the Year 2012 and 2014. He received "Young Teacher Award" in International Conference ICIC-2018. He has also received faculty excellence and research awards in the year 2011, 2013, 2015, 2016, 2017, 2018 and 2019 from different organizations for excellence in research, teaching and service.

Itu Snigdh received her Ph.D degree in 2016 in the area of Wireless sensor networks, Department of Electronics and Communication Engineering, B.I.T Mesra.She received her Masters Degree (Software Engineering) from B.I.T Mesra(Ranchi), India in 2002 and her Bachelor's degree in Electrical Engineering from B.I.T Sindri, India in the year 2000. She joined the Department of Computer Science and

Engineering at BIT Mesra in 2003 and is currently working as an Assistant Professor. She has authored and coauthored a number of technical journal articles and conference papers. Her areas of interest include Software Engineering, Database Management Systems, Mobile and Wireless Sensor Networks.

Jayashree Subramanian received PhD degree in computer science from Anna University, Chennai in 2009. She is currently working as a professor in the department of computer science and engineering in PSG College of Technology, Coimbatore. She has 19 years of teaching experience and 12 years of research experience. She is being a principal investigator for two ongoing DST research projects under Ministry of Science and Technology, India in the area of wearable Assistive technology. She published more than 30 papers in International Journals and more than 60 papers in International/National Conferences. She has received many awards for her excellence in academics and research including Innovative Project Potential Award in 2019. Her research interests include Internet-of-things, Machine Learning, Artificial Intelligence, Cognitive Analytics and Assistive Technology.

Puviyarasi T. is Assistant Professor, Dept. of. ECE, Madanapalle Institute of Technology & Science, Madanapalle, AP, India.

Aykut Hamit Turan is Professor in the School of Management Department of Management Information Systems at the University of Sakarya in Sakarya, Turkey. Dr. Turan has done research in the field of Management Information Systems. His research interests include global IT management, health care IT, IT acceptance and adoption, and IT diffusion in SMEs. He has published a number of journal articles in such outlets as the European Journal of Information Systems, Journal of Global Information Technology Management, Information & Management, Journal of Theoretical and Applied Electronic Commerce Research and Communication of ACM.

Naciye Güliz Uğur is currently working as an assistant professor in the Department of Management Information Systems at Sakarya University. Uğur received her Ph.D. in the field of Management Information Systems. She has more than five years of industry experience in management and teaches courses on information systems and system analysis and design. Her research interests include technology acceptance and behavioral aspects of emerging technologies.

S. Viswa is currently pursuing Bachelor's degree in Department of Information Technology, Thiagarajar College of Engineering, Madurai. His areas of interest include Data Mining, Machine Learning, and Data Analytics.

Index

A

Ambient Assisted Living 282, 285, 310

Analytical Tools 1-2, 5, 9, 11-12, 14-15, 85-86, 88, 90-91, 94-95

Apache 22, 38, 42, 44, 48-50, 66-68, 88, 90, 92-95

Apache Hives 49

Applications of Big Data 20

Artificial Intelligence (AI) 61, 110, 263, 291, 307, 314, 324

B

Big Data 1-14, 20-21, 29, 31, 38-44, 49-53, 56-65, 67, 69-75, 77-80, 82, 85-96, 99, 102, 104-106, 108, 110, 112, 122, 160-161, 165-169, 172, 174-182, 186-187, 189, 192, 220, 223, 245-246, 283, 286-287, 291, 309-310, 315, 325

Big Data Analytics 1-2, 4, 6-9, 11-13, 21, 40, 51, 56-57, 59-62, 74, 85-88, 90, 92, 94-96, 106, 168

Big Data Tools 3, 10-11, 64, 67, 85, 88, 91-93, 95, 178-179

Blockchain 186, 188-195, 198-202, 295, 314, 322

business intelligence 2, 4, 14, 23, 94, 131-132, 134, 167-168

business research 137, 144, 149, 153

C

Chronic Kidney Disease 213-214, 216-217, 222-224, 230, 269

Classification Techniques 30, 234

Cloud Computing 38-41, 51-53, 77-82, 88, 92, 104-105, 196, 246, 283-284, 286-287, 297, 309, 313

CSF 161-162, 165, 167-168

D

Data Aggregation 305

data analysis 3, 14, 32, 53, 61, 67, 81, 118, 121, 126, 131, 133-134, 137, 143, 153, 162, 182, 223, 237-238, 243, 261, 286, 293

Data Analytics 1-2, 4, 6-9, 11-13, 21, 40, 51, 56-57, 59-62, 74, 85-88, 90, 92, 94-96, 106, 115-124, 168, 242, 292, 305, 307, 314, 324

Data market 186-200, 202

Data visualization 123, 126-129, 131, 134

data visualization techniques 129

Decentralization 189, 192, 194, 202

Decision Tree 223, 234, 240-242, 245-246, 249-250, 252, 256, 260, 264-265, 277

Descriptive Analytics 120-121

Diagnostic Analytics 120

Disease Prediction 28, 223, 234, 245-246

E

econometrics 137-138, 144, 146, 148-149, 151, 153

Edge Intelligence 293, 299, 305

Edge Server 298, 305

Electronic Health Records 213-214, 221, 223

evolutionary computing 21, 28

F

Farming 30, 99-104, 106-108, 112, 283

F-Measure 260, 268, 270

Fog Computing 247, 283-285, 287, 292, 295, 308-309, 313-314, 326

fuzzy logic 21, 23, 29-31, 34, 209, 245-246

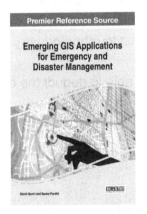
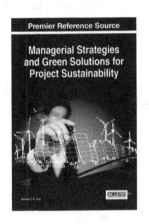

Printed in the United States
by Baker & Taylor Publisher Services